THE EXPENSE OF GLORY

A Life of John Reith

IAN McINTYRE

HarperCollins*Publishers*

HarperCollins*Publishers*
77–85 Fulham Palace Road,
Hammersmith, London W6 8JB

Published by HarperCollins*Publishers* 1993

1 3 5 7 9 8 6 4 2

Copyright © Ian McIntyre 1993

Ian McIntyre asserts the moral right to
be identified as the author of this work

A catalogue record for this book is
available from the British Library

ISBN 0 00 215963 5

Set in Linotron Ehrhardt

Printed and bound in Great Britain by
Hartnolls Limited, Bodmin, Cornwall

Avoid shame, but do not seek glory.
Nothing so expensive as glory.

SYDNEY SMITH,
Lady Holland's Memoir, 1855

Contents

List of Illustrations		xi
Preface		xiii
1	Father of the Man	1
2	Dark Satanic Mills	10
3	Paragon of All Infallibilities	19
4	Rubber Boots and Spurs	31
5	Cuspidors and Iced Water	63
6	Promise Deferred	80
7	Full and By	119
8	Silly Bertie, Mussolini, and the Red Woman	154
9	Full Meridian	182
10	'J. C. W. Reith – late BBC'	214
11	Adrift	244
12	Minister of the Crown	250
13	Business in Great Waters	267
14	Around the World in Fifty-Two Days	278
15	Brave New World	284
16	Anything Legal Considered	300
17	Life Is for Living	335
18	Hills of Home	380
Notes		405
Index		437

List of Illustrations

Frontispiece: John Reith, 1913 *(BBC Written Archives)*

Between pages 96–97

Reith as a child *(BBC Written Archives)*
Reith's parents *(BBC Written Archives)*
Charlie in 1913 *(BBC Written Archives)*
Sussex courtship, 1919:
   Muriel *(BBC Written Archives)*
   Muriel and Reith *(BBC Written Archives)*
   Charlie and Reith *(BBC Written Archives)*
   Charlie and Muriel *(BBC Written Archives)*
Lord Gainford *(BBC Photograph Library)*
Lord Clarendon *(National Portrait Gallery)*
J. H. Whitley *(BBC Photograph Library)*
R. C. Norman *(BBC Photograph Library)*

Between pages 176–177

Reith, December 1926 *(BBC Photograph Library)*
Reith and Ramsay MacDonald *(BBC Written Archives)*
Winston Churchill, 1935 *(BBC Photograph Library)*
Peter Eckersley *(BBC Photograph Library)*
Admiral Carpendale *(BBC Photograph Library)*
R. S. Lambert *(BBC Photograph Library)*
Harman Grisewood *(BBC Photograph Library)*
Early television: Madame Karsavina *(BBC Photograph Library)*
Sound effects at Savoy Hill *(BBC Photograph Library)*
Bridge broadcast from 2LO *(BBC Photograph Library)*

Between pages 272–273

Savoy Hill at night *(BBC Photograph Library)*
Reith locking up at Savoy Hill *(BBC Photograph Library)*
Broadcasting House, 1932 *(BBC Photograph Library)*
Mary Somerville *(BBC Photograph Library)*
Jo Stanley *(BBC Photograph Library)*
'Ariel between Wisdom and Gaiety' *(BBC Photograph Library)*
'This temple of the arts and the muses' *(BBC Photograph Library)*

Between pages 368–369

'May God bless her and all who sail in her' *(BBC Written Archives)*
Dawn Mackay *(BBC Written Archives)*
'Face to Face', 1960 *(BBC Photograph Library)*
Hugh Carleton Greene and Reith, 1961 *(BBC Photograph Library)*
Reith with Irene Maerz (née Wanner), 1966 *(BBC Written Archives)*
Irene in the 1960s *(BBC Written Archives)*
Reith and the President, Sir William MacTaggart, 1967 *(BBC Written Archives)*
'Slipping into vice-regality' *(BBC Written Archives)*

Preface

More than once while writing this book I came close to tears. I did not dream when I began to read John Reith's diaries that I would encounter so much raw pain. Words that Beaverbrook wrote about Earl Haig came to mind: 'With the publication of his Private Papers, he committed suicide 25 years after his death.' (Haig, as it happens, was one of Reith's great heroes.)

'I have kept a diary for more than 20 years,' the BBC's first Director-General told readers of *John O'London's Weekly* in 1930, adding proudly (he had a weakness for Latin tags), 'nulla dies sine linea'. He was exaggerating, but only slightly. There *were* days without a line, but they were few and far between, and he could usually plead *force majeure* – the General Strike of 1926, pressure of work as a wartime minister, serious illness or depression.

By the time he died in 1971, he had written or dictated more than two million words. He also kept scrapbooks (he called them 'enclosure volumes') in which he preserved everything from state papers to old train tickets.

This vast archive is now the property of the BBC and is lodged at their Written Archives Centre at Caversham Park near Reading. It has been the major source for writing this book, and I am deeply grateful to the Corporation for allowing me unfettered access to it.

Lord Reith allowed Asa Briggs to see the relevant volumes of his diaries when Briggs was working on the first two volumes of his *History of Broadcasting in the United Kingdom*. The late Andrew Boyle tried everything he knew over a period of years to gain access to them, but Reith did not yield to his blandishments and the biography which Boyle published a year after Reith's death relied on other sources; it also raced through Reith's post-BBC career (he lived for another 33 years after marching out of Broadcasting House) in little more than 50 pages.

'A man is usually honest in his diary even if he is so nowhere else,' Reith told his *John O'London* readers. 'A written record stands, incredible and even preposterous though some of the later comments read.' Those adjectives describe very precisely a great deal of what Reith committed to paper in his small and disciplined hand. Perhaps – because he constantly re-read it – that is why he could never decide what he wanted to become of this self-absorbed and painful record of his life. At various stages he re-wrote parts of it, contemplated destroying it, solicited advice about it in the personal columns of *The Times*, resolved to sell it. There was even a time when he tried to persuade a young woman he was in love with to take it into her keeping.

A heavily edited version was eventually published in 1975, four years after his death. The selection was made by the late Charles Stuart, student of Christ Church, Oxford and historian of eighteenth-century England. The emphasis is strongly on Reith's public life, and the material is grouped thematically – Reith and broadcasting, Reith and the monarchy, Reith and the Second World War.

My purpose has been rather different. Because much of my own life has been spent in broadcasting my initial interest was naturally in what Reith did at the BBC, but I thought it important to see him in the round – to explore both the public figure and the private man, to consider how they related to each other and to set the extraordinary figure of John Reith in the context of the times in which he lived.

The diaries are mentioned in the footnotes in three different ways. 'Pre-Diary Narrative' refers to the account of his early life which Reith dictated to his secretary at the BBC over a period of three days in the spring of 1929. 'Summarised Diary' refers to the edited version of the first twenty years of the diaries which Reith toiled to produce over a period of several years in the early 1930s. 'Diary' refers to everything from then onwards, although there is a period of six years towards the end of his life for which the entries do not survive in their original form.

I have been greatly helped in writing this life by Reith's children Christopher and Marista, by his son-in-law Murray Leishman and by his nephew Ivor; by Charlie Bowser's surviving son David and by his daugther Hope Readman. I record here my gratitude to them all for the patience and courtesy with which they answered ny questions.

I am also grateful to the dwindling band of those who remember Reith in his BBC days or encountered him on the relatively few occasions when he could be persuaded to return there after the war – Miss Jo Stanley, Miss Janet Adam Smith, Harman Grisewood, John Arkell, John Green and Leonard Miall. I was glad that I was able to visit Andrew Stewart in Glasgow towards the end of his life; Sir Ian Jacob and Maurice Farquharson both died while the book was in the press. I record with particular warmth my indebtedness over many years to Oliver Whitley, for whom, all too briefly, I was once lucky enough to work.

I must thank Mark Jones and his staff at the BBC Sound Library at Broadcasting House for making it possible for me to listen to a number of recordings of Reith's voice. Many of the illustrations for the book came from the BBC's Photograph Library, and I am most grateful to Margaret Kirby, the Library's Manager, and to Nicola Baldwin for guiding me through the riches of their collection.

Over a period of eighteen months or so I was a regular visitor to the BBC Written Archives Centre at Caversham Park. The mark of its first Director-General is stamped more faintly on some parts of the present-day BBC than on others, but its Written Archives Centre constitutes an unmistakably Reithian enclave – well ordered, clear about what it is there to do, devoted to the concept of public service. I am deeply grateful to Jacqueline Kavanagh, the BBC's

Written Archivist, and all her colleagues, and most especially to Gwiniver Jones.
Her knowledge of the Reith material and of the Archives generally is unrivalled,
and she put it at my disposal with unfailing generosity and enthusiasm.

I record my thanks to Sir Michael Checkland, the BBC's former Director-
General; to Michael Stevenson, the Corporation's Secretary, and to John
McCormick who preceded him in that post; and to Glen del Medico and his
colleagues in the BBC Legal Department. (Occasional notes typed in red in
the research transcripts of the Reith diaries say things like, 'Passages from
pages 48 and 94 have been deleted for legal reasons.' These will decline in
number as the years pass – one cannot libel the dead.)

I benefited from the recollections of many people outside the BBC – Mrs
Margaret Cockburn, Mrs Charles Hargreaves and Miss Barbara Hickman were
especially helpful. I had interesting conversations with A. S. Burrows' son
Reggie and with Peter Eckersley's son Myles, who is at work on a life of his
father, and I am grateful to Lord Clarendon for responding to a number of
queries about his grandfather.

Professor R. A. Rankin of Glasgow shed light on Reith's interest late in life
in Sir Arthur Eddington's theories about the cosmical number. Dominic Hibberd and Fraser Steel helped me in a piece of literary detective work, and so
did Dr Tom Hubbard of the Scottish Poetry Library; Mrs Joanna Soden of
the Royal Scottish Academy came to my aid in identifying an illustration. I also
received valuable advice relating to certain sections in Reith's diaries from
David Ellen, formerly of the Metropolitan Police Forensic Science Laboratory.

It would not be possible to make sense of the life of John Reith without
constant reference to the early volumes of Asa Briggs' *History of Broadcasting
in the United Kingdom*. Lord Briggs is not only the BBC's historian but also its
great encyclopaedist, and I am immensely grateful for his readiness on several
occasions to let me lower my bucket into the depths of his knowledge.

Strenuous efforts have been made to trace holders of copyright and I apolo-
gise for inadvertent omissions. I am grateful to those who have allowed me to
quote from the following: *Collected Poems*, W. H. Auden, Faber & Faber; *The
History of Broadcasting in the United Kingdom*, Asa Briggs, OUP; *The Power
Behind the Microphone*, P. P. Eckersley, Jonathan Cape; *Years in a Mirror*, Val
Gielgud, the Bodley Head (reprinted by permission of David Higham Associ-
ates); *One Thing at a Time*, Harman Grisewood, Hutchinson; *Ariel and All
His Quality*, R. S. Lambert, Gollancz; *Collected Poems*, Philip Larkin, Faber
& Faber; *Winston Churchill: The Struggle for Survival, 1940–1965*, Lord
Moran, Constable; *Into the Wind*, J. C. W. Reith, Hodder & Stoughton (re-
printed by permission of the Peters, Fraser and Dunlop Group Ltd); *Wearing
Spurs*, Lord Reith, Hutchinson; *The Reith Diaries*, edited by Charles Stuart,
Collins.

I am grateful to the Librarian of Nuffield College, Oxford for allowing me
to consult the Gainford Papers, to Aileen Hay of the Sun Alliance Group
Personnel Department for letting me read the file on Reith which they inherited
form the Phoenix Assurance Company and to Ruth Edge of the HMV Archives.

The book owes a great deal to the enthusiasm and discernment of my publisher, Stuart Proffitt. I am also grateful to those of his colleagues at HarperCollins who contributed to the success of the project, in particular to Helen Ellis, Rebecca Wilson, Juliet Annan and Caroline Hotblack. The index is the work of Sarah Ereira.

My oldest debt, in all that relates to speech and writing, is to Geoffrey Dixon; as it is now more than fifty years since he first taught me, he may reasonably reflect that I have taken my time to tell him so.

Lastly, I record with love and gratitude that in the writing of this book, as in so much else, I have received no better counsel than that offered by the best of wives.

One

FATHER OF THE MAN

That energy which makes a child hard to manage is the energy which
afterward makes him a manager of life.
HENRY WARD BEECHER, *Proverbs from Plymouth Pulpit*, 1887

They fuck you up, your mum and dad.
They may not mean to, but they do.
They fill you with the faults they had
And add some extra, just for you.
PHILIP LARKIN,
This Be the Verse, 1971

THE SMALL Scottish town of Stonehaven, snug in a bay on the rocky coast
of Kincardineshire, has three claims to fame. The first is its proximity to
Dunnottar Castle, where the Scottish regalia were brought for safe keeping
during the wars of the Commonwealth. The second is that Lewis Grassic
Gibbon, Scotland's most important novelist of the twentieth century, was briefly
a pupil there at the Mackie Academy. The third is that in 1889 it became –
by chance – the birthplace of John Reith.

By chance because the family was there on holiday from Glasgow. The infant
arrived two months prematurely, causing his father, a distinguished minister
of the Free Church of Scotland, to hurry out into the summer twilight in search
of a doctor. A hundred years later, the Stonehaven Heritage Society marked
the spot and the occasion with a small brass plaque:

IN THIS HOUSE WAS BORN ON
JULY 20TH 1889,
JOHN CHARLES WALSHAM REITH,
STATESMAN, ADMINISTRATOR, ENGINEER,
1ST BARON REITH OF STONEHAVEN
AND
1ST DIRECTOR-GENERAL OF THE B.B.C.

Four and five generations earlier, the Reith forebears had been small farmers
in Kincardineshire, working the soil in the same parish as the grandfather of
Robert Burns. John Reith's own grandfather started out as the village wheel-

wright. He became a lawyer and a railway pioneer and for the last twenty-six years of his life he was general manager of the Clyde Navigation Trust. Family photos show him as a rather Balzacian figure – 'Courageous, masterful, inflexible, shrewd, he ruled the river,' Reith wrote admiringly of him in his autobiography.

He also greatly admired his father, although for much of his life he held him in considerable awe. George Reith had been born in Aberdeen in 1842 and educated at the Grammar School and University there. After theological studies at New College, Edinburgh, he had been called, at the early age of twenty-three, to the College Church in the West End of Glasgow as a colleague of the great Dr Robert Buchanan, a veteran of the Disruption of 1843.[1] His ministry there was to last for more than forty years.

John Reith described the College Church proudly in his memoirs as 'one of the wealthiest, most influential, most liberal in Scotland':

> Here were merchant princes, great industrialists, professors, some of the leading theologians of the day. Here also a considerable element of the humbler but equally worthy sort – master-tradesmen and foremen from shipyards and works. It made a deep impression on my childhood mind.[2]

So did his father.

> In magnificence of presence I have not met his equal. His countenance in repose was austere, but his ready smile not just benign – itself a benediction. He was urbane, courteous, cultured; very tall, of great natural dignity, always well dressed.[3]

Reith's mother had been brought up in the Church of England. Adah Mary Weston was the daughter of an affluent stockbroker. She was born in London in the Year of Revolutions. Her earliest recollection was of being taken at the age of three to the Great Exhibition of 1851, and she could also remember the illumination of London after the Crimean War. The family lived in a large house in Westbourne Terrace. There were stables at the rear, and the children were all good riders.

There was also a seaside house at St Leonards-on-Sea, the happy days there 'marred only by the awful bathing woman who immediately ducked us twice whether we would or no'. As she and her sister grew older, there were factory girls to teach to sew; they also taught at a night-school for shoe-black boys at Westminster. She went to lectures by John Ruskin, readings by Dickens, a course by John Morley; she heard Dr Pusey preach, rode in a bus with Carlyle, and attended a concert in the Albert Hall conducted by Richard Wagner.

Adah had met George Reith in the summer of 1868 at Glenfarg, in Perthshire, where a member of his church had a country house. It was not only the good looks of the young Scottish minister which were devastating; so was the indignation which he brought to bear on the moral and social ills of mid-

Victorian society. Within weeks he had proposed marriage, and two months later he travelled to London to give an account of himself to his prospective father-in-law. 'Don't be alarmed at my radicalism,' he wrote to his fiancée, 'it is Scriptural. It is Jesus Christ's.' They were married in July 1870. At about the same time, Weston *père* lost most of his money, partly, it was said in the family, through the dishonesty of a partner, partly as a result of the Franco-Prussian War.

In the ten years following her marriage, Adah Reith bore six children. When, almost a decade later, they were followed by a seventh, she was already forty-one and her husband forty-seven. John was therefore very much the Benjamin of the family. In the summer of 1891, his father was away in Switzerland for some weeks. 'I want to see Non very badly,' he wrote to his wife from Grindelwald. 'Dear wee chap! May the Lord spare him for our comfort in our old age and make him one of His own.'[4]

A number of sepia portraits of the 'dear wee chap' survive. In one of them he is seated sideways on a tasselled chair, his feet resting on a tabouret. The posture is one of stolid assurance. He is got up in a dress and pantaloons, the regulation unisex attire for all small children of the day. His knees are dimpled and the hands and wrists distinctly pudgy. The hair is long and curled. His cheeks are plump, and he has more than one chin. It is the face of a knowing Cupid.

Because of the gap in age between him and his brothers and sisters, his early years were in some ways those of an only child. He was passionately devoted to his mother, and the hour or so he was allowed to spend with her on Sunday afternoons he recollected in later life 'with gratitude and emotion':

> She taught me hymns and psalms and read me stories . . . I remember asking her which was Jesus in a picture showing the welcome of the pilgrims to the Celestial City, and she making a little dot below one of the angels.[5]

Mrs Reith was shy, serious-minded, deeply religious. During the week she was taken up with what her son later described as 'the alien, manifold and exacting duties of the lady of a Scottish manse'. She was also much given to good works beyond the bounds of the parish. A particular interest was the Glasgow Kyrle Society, which sought to improve the lot of working people.

The Society had been founded in memory of the English philanthropist John Kyrle.[6] There was a choir which gave concerts in poor districts and to the inmates of Institutions. The Sanitary Aid branch organised courses of health lectures, and those who attended included the female sanitary inspectors of the city. The Decorative branch aimed to adorn the walls of infirmary wards and mission halls: one year the large room of the Whitevale Prison Gate Mission was painted with pictures illustrating the parables, taken from designs by Millais.

This meant that for much of the time John was left in the charge of his nurse, Maggie Raeside. That, at least, was the formality of the arrangement,

although if his recollection of a spring morning in Glasgow's west-end park
when he was about three is to be trusted, the wretched girl must have felt that
it was really the other way round:

> I was supervising and directing the labours of my nurse when a member of
> my father's church happened along. 'Why don't you pick the pretty daisics
> and buttercups yourself, instead of making Maggie do it for you?' I might
> have said something about devolution of responsibility, but there was a sim-
> pler answer. 'Non', I replied – this being the nearest I could then come to
> my Christian name – 'Non too fat'. In repeating the story, the lady added
> that I had given her an odd look. Quite probably.[7]

There were other nurses, but they were not all as indulgent or accommodating
as Maggie. One of them hit on the idea of dealing with her charge's fits of
temper by holding him upside down by the ankles. Another, who talked to him
in 'an unctuous way' if other members of the family were about, used to get
out of her bed and beat him if he so much as moved in his. The nursery was
a bright room, with two big windows and a balcony, but there was a bogeyman
corner opposite his bed, and his dreams about it remained vivid even when he
was a man.

His father was a remote figure, seen mainly at meal-times and at family
prayers. There were sermons to be written, parishioners to be visited, meetings
to attend. To the normal parish concerns he added responsibility for a mission
district in a poor part of the town. The Boys' Brigade was founded there, and
Dr Reith was its first chaplain.

'Non' was sent for a year to the Park School, an establishment for girls next
door to the manse, and a gentle progression from the order and comfort of
the nursery. He was taught sewing by Miss Sprunt and singing by Miss Waugh.
He was awarded the singing prize, although it occurred to him later that this
may have owed more to Miss Waugh's membership of his father's church than
to any vocal merit on his part.

There was a break in the middle of the morning, and one day he lifted
sixpence from his mother's dressing table and spent threepence of it at the
food bar in the basement. This large sum bought much more than he could
possibly eat, so two or three apple tarts had to be crammed into a pocket, a
messy act of delinquency which did not remain long undetected.

He went to Sunday school, too, and was enrolled, a couple of months before
his seventh birthday, in the Band of Hope. 'Bond of Union', ran the legend
on his membership certificate – 'Abstinence from all Intoxicating Liquors and
Beverages'[8]. Then, in the autumn of 1896, like his four elder brothers before
him, he was entered at Glasgow Academy.

It had been in some respects an indulged and protected childhood, although
once he had emerged from the nursery some of his brothers and sisters clearly
had little time for him. 'You are growing to be a big boy now,' his father wrote
to him in a letter for his ninth birthday, 'and will need to gather sense and

wisdom, patience, and self restraint.' (Dr Reith was in Switzerland again, this time in Saas Fee.) 'Be a good boy,' he added, 'and try to please all the others and make them love you . . .'[9]

That was not easy. His sister Beta, second oldest of the brood, doted on him and had nursed him when he was small, but by the time he was eight she had gone off to train as a nurse in Edinburgh. Jean, closer to him in age, although still eleven years his senior, was the only one of his brothers and sisters still at home during his schooldays, but she got on with nobody. 'Her room was opposite mine, but it was always kept locked. We never spoke to each other.'[10] Jean was intensely jealous of the latecomer's hold on their mother's affections and her temper flared easily.

That left his four brothers. The eldest was Archie, who grieved his father less by his towering rages than by his decision to be ordained in the Church of England. Then came Robert, who had served his time as an engineer in a Clyde shipyard. 'There were some years in which he was getting on fairly well,' Reith wrote later. 'I admired his style of living – hansom cabs, first-class travelling and so forth.'[11] He too, however, had a violent temper, and the relationship was uneasy.

Next in line was Ernest. He was a brilliant boy, and everybody liked him. He had been Dux of the Academy and then served his apprenticeship with a well-known firm of Glasgow accountants. He took an interest in the Boys' Brigade and was Superintendent of the Infant School at the Church Mission. Then, at the age of twenty-one, he became mentally ill. He lived at home for some years, but was eventually committed to an Institution.

The nearest to John in age was Douglas, although even he was almost ten years his senior. He had taken his Master of Arts and Bachelor of Divinity Degrees at Glasgow University and then went off to be a missionary in India. 'He was serious and pious,' wrote Reith, 'but was decent to me, and however little he may have known of the world, tried to help.'[12]

Hardly surprising then that when he picked over the memories of his childhood, the picture he painted was a bleak one, with little family or social life:

> Members of the family shut themselves in their own rooms, my father in his study, my mother writing letters in the dining room or her own bedroom. Being a son of the manse I was made a good deal of, but I had no friends of my own kind in the church, and no real friend at all, although I was longing for one.[13]

A high point of the year was the family summer holiday, and he remembered the weeks that preceded them as periods of intense excitement. His earliest memory was of a house they took at Taynuilt in Argyll, and there were a number of early visits to Arran. In 1897 he was taken for the first time to the Highlands. They stayed at Rothiemurchus Manse, near Aviemore. It was the year of Queen Victoria's jubilee, and he remembered decorating the gates, placing hawthorn branches round her picture. He also remembered swinging on the inner gate in the early morning and wishing he had some friends to play with. 'I think this was the first holiday when I was conscious of an awful loneliness. I wondered whom I would like to have and I thought of Willie Marr in my class at the Academy.'[14]

They were back in the Highlands four years later, near Kincraig in Invernessshire, and he learned to swim in the cold waters of the loch. He got out of his depth one day and thought he was going to drown, but his brother Douglas was at hand and nudged him back in to the shore. The following year saw them in Arran again, this time in the manse at Lochranza. His vacation reading was not exactly frivolous: 'I was 13 during this holiday and read with satisfaction of a Jewish idea that until 13 parents were responsible for the sins of their children, but thereafter the children themselves were.' He became friendly with a boy called Donald Kerr, the grandson of the piermaster: 'He had a sister, Mirita, of whom I imagined myself enamoured. They were obviously not Glasgow Academy class, but I was mightily thankful to know them . . .'[15]

His father was always made much of on these holidays, and his sermons were regarded as something of an occasion. In 1904 he preached in a huge marquee at Aviemore (this because the 'Wee Frees' had taken possession of the local United Free Church).[16] People came to hear him from miles around. There were sheep grazing round the tent, which was pitched on the slope of Craigellachie. From where he sat, the preacher's youngest son could see the whole range of the Cairngorms.

Paradise lasted only for a short season. Back in the grime of Glasgow, life at the Academy, with the reputations of four elder brothers to live up to, was less agreeable. Years later, he recognised glumly that he had not risen to the challenge with any distinction:

> My time at the Academy was most unsatisfactory. I had enough brains to get through all the classes without effort, and so scraped through. I had no inspiration to excel, although strangely enough I felt a kind of intellectual superiority over others . . . I might have done worse had it not been for periodic promptings from my father; but he could not talk the language which I would have understood and to which I am sure I would have responded.[17]

Reith took part in the annual sports with what he described as 'pathetic lack of distinction', although he discovered later that he could run extremely fast and jump quite respectably. (As he was already well on the way to his ultimate height of 6'6" it would have been surprising if he couldn't.) He turned out for rugby, but without ever scoring a try. He burned with ambition to get into the First XV and wear the blue velvet cap with the white tassel: 'The sight of some of the bloods of the first XV with several dates on their caps was almost more than I could stand . . .'

Friendship eluded him, too, and an earlier biographer of Reith's believed that he was something of a bully.[18] He acquired the nickname 'Lord Walsham' and it was not affectionately meant.[19] The only school activity which engaged his whole-hearted interest was extra-curricular. When he was eight, his brother Ernest, a ranker in the Lanarkshire Volunteer Rifles, had taught him rifle exercises with an airgun, and when a Cadet Corps was formed at the Academy in 1901, 'Lord Walsham' was a founder member:

> We were subject to much ridicule; the military spirit must already have been well-developed in me, for I had no figure for the kilt. Parades were out of hours but twice weekly we went to school wearing belt and bayonet below civilian jacket. This suggested that, despite the ordinary schoolboy garb and the form lessons, we were dedicated to some higher potential duty, some vague but critical service.[20]

The Corps did little for his defects of character, which were now pronounced, and when he was fifteen the school put it to his father that his education should be continued elsewhere. He was also, by his own admission, unruly at home – disrespectful to his parents and possessed of a violent temper. His brother Robert suggested that a merchant navy training ship might provide the necessary discipline. A kindlier solution was proposed by his eldest brother, Archie, now vicar of a church in Norfolk. He had heard good reports of Gresham's School at Holt, ten miles from his parish. Reith, having done an examination paper during the summer holidays at Aviemore, was packed off there in the autumn of 1904.

He was the only Presbyterian and the only Scot in the school (in those days many of the boys were the sons of Norfolk farmers) and at first he was acutely miserable. In his second term he ran away – 'a feat never before achieved' – cycling off without leave before breakfast to his brother's vicarage. He was retrieved in the course of the day by his housemaster: 'Archie kicked up such a fuss about the way I had been treated in the school that I was only mildly "sticked" by the Head.'[21]

In later years he formed the view that he had been far too old to be sent to boarding school for the first time and represented his move to Gresham's as a 'violent transplantation':

> The ordered procedure of this establishment was subjected to some strain; it seemed not to have encountered anything quite similar before. I was entirely moral; but otherwise vexatious and difficult.[22]

We have no record of what the headmaster of Gresham's, G. W. S. Howson, thought of his 'entirely moral' new charge. Reith believed that he initially disliked and disapproved of him; as it was Reith's habit 'to question and resist some of his principles of management' that seems entirely probable. On one occasion the Head started a series of Sunday evening concerts, and when he heard that Reith was not attending, he sent for him and asked for an explanation. The true reason was that concerts on a Sunday offended against Reith's deeply felt sabbatarianism, but his courage failed him, and he mumbled that there was no special reason. This was uncharacteristic. His housemaster told him one day that three different form masters had complained of his insubordination.

Gradually, things became more bearable. The Corps, run by an ex-colour sergeant of the Scots Guards, was compulsory. Reith records proudly that he developed an impressive 'word of command'. He became one of the best shots in the school and was promoted sergeant. He went to the public schools camp at Aldershot in 1905 and 1906. In 1906 he was in the team that competed for the Ashburton Shield at Bisley and actually owned to enjoying himself.

He was still lonely, however. They got a lot of time to themselves at Bisley, and he records that he changed into flannels and wandered over the moors wishing he had a friend to walk with – 'always this longing for a real friend'. Back at Holt, it seemed for a time that he had found one:

> I became rather fond of an exceedingly good-looking boy called John Valentine Betts, as much my inferior mentally as he was my superior at games. He was two or three years younger than I, and strange to say, the more fond he grew of me the less fond I grew of him. He was the most popular boy in the house, and it was odd he should have liked me so much. I remember his leaving in my study one night when he came out early from prep. for a bath, a note saying he wished I would go about with him more.[23]

For two terms they had beds next to each other, and would talk quietly to all hours of the night.

During his final year at Gresham's, relations with the headmaster improved, the last two terms passing in what Reith categorised as 'mutual, if measured, esteem'. His rugby improved, and he got into the school XV as full-back. He also made progress academically, winning the school German prize and doing well in Latin prose.

He returned to Glasgow, and the family set off on holiday. Nothing had been decided about what he was to do next, and there is a passage in his memoirs, charged with emotion and reproach, about how little guidance he felt he had been given concerning a career:

> Returned home, as I had left it, a problem. Through the summer holidays of 1906 – a problem. Not my problem; the family's. All set for failure or at best mediocrity. And yet, roaming the Rothiemurchus forest and climbing the Cairngorm mountains, even at seventeen a feeling that I was not meant to be a mediocrity; the beginning of a determination not to be a mediocrity.[24]

It sounds tremendous – the words evoke one of those sequences of growling notes that signal the unleashing of a grand theme in a Beethoven symphony. There is however a small problem. Reith was nowhere near the Rothiemurchus forest or the Cairngorm mountains that summer. It may have been a trick of memory: in the land of the mountain and the flood, one year is much like another. It may have been a deliberate excursion into the realm of tone poetry. Whatever the reason, the prosaic fact of the matter is that in 1906 the family holiday was spent not in the Scottish Highlands but at the small east-coast golfing resort of Carnoustie.[25]

Two

DARK SATANIC MILLS

It is the highest creatures who take the longest to mature, and are
the most helpless during their immaturity.

GEORGE BERNARD SHAW, *Back to Methuselah*, 1921

JOHN REITH'S determination not to be a mediocrity was to be severely tested
over the next few years, because the family's solution to their problem turned
out to be that he should go in for engineering – 'that dreadful dumping ground
for indeterminates', as he was later sourly to describe it. Although he did not
make any great protest at the time, it was a decision that still rankled after a
quarter of a century:

> Even today I feel indignant at the affront to one's intelligence and intellect,
> and at the awful prostitution of intellectual ability which was nothing com-
> pared with what I might have done had I been given more time to develop
> ... I am often worried beyond expression by the upthrusts of intellectual
> emotion and imagination which seem to be born dead, so little opportunity
> have I had or ever will have for developing this side.[1]

Those confused and bitter words were written when he had already been at
the head of the BBC for a number of years and was a nationally known figure.
In 1906 the unformed youth of seventeen felt that he should have been allowed
to stay on at Gresham's for another year, and that if he had he would have
made the grade for Oxford or Cambridge.

It was obtuse of Reith not to consider that there was almost certainly a
financial aspect to the matter – another year at school and three or four years
of university fees would have been quite beyond his father's means. It seems
unlikely that Dr Reith spelt this out. What he said instead was that he believed
in every man learning a trade. One brother said that it would take the nonsense
out of him. Another added that steam was the basis of all power, although it
is possible that he was being sarcastic.

The original plan was that he should embark immediately on an apprenticeship at the Hydepark Works of the North British Locomotive Company – a
place had been offered there, and, 'out of respect to his father', the customary
premium was to be waived – but there was a stay of execution:

> The family doctor intervened; it must have been my mother's doing. I was
> too young and too tall to go straight into works; it would overtax my strength,

he said – and I let him say it. So it was arranged that I should go first to
the Glasgow Technical College for the mechanical engineering course.[2]

So began what he later described as eight years of intellectual and social
frustration. His studies at the Technical College (now the University of Strath-
clyde) lasted until the spring of 1908, and he remembered the time he spent
there as 'something of a nightmare'. Except for mathematics and physics he
had no interest in what he was doing; a good deal of what he was taught in
the pure engineering subjects he could not understand. His fellow students
were mainly from board schools, and interested only in engineering technical-
ities – 'a class of fellow I had not previously met'.

Then he was plunged into the locomotive works:

In the first few weeks in the shops I passed through an acute crisis . . .
There was an attraction in management; an attraction in civil engineering.
But the prospect of five long, weary years in shops, with bits and pieces of
machinery, with the ghastly hours and the squalid circumstances – it was
nauseous and unbearable. I decided to bear it; to go through with it; somehow
go through with it.[3]

It was a punishing routine. Summer and winter mornings alike he got up at
4.45. Half an hour later, he drew the bolt of the manse door and set off,
carrying with him a packet of sandwiches and a small can of soup to be heated
up at dinner-time. Sometimes this careful timetable was subject to minor disruption, and he registered his annoyance in his diary:

There was a burglar scare in the district, so they go behind my arrangements
of using one bolt on the front door, and lock it and use both bolts and then
chain up the inner door also, as if any rational burglar would try to get in
by the front door. This gives me much bother in the mornings, and in the
meantime the windows looking on to the garden are left unsnibbed.[4]

He travelled in a swaying, jolting tramcar and started work at six o'clock. At
8.45 there was a forty-five-minute break and he went for breakfast to what he
called 'a nearby cookshop'. Dinner was from 1 till 2 and then it was back to
work until 5.30. A fifty-six-hour working week was not uncommon in those
early years of the century, but between 1910 and 1912 he also quite often
attended evening classes for three hours in the evening.

One of his brothers had enlarged with some relish on what was likely to
happen to a 'gentleman apprentice' at the hands of his fellows. Reith's height
was to his advantage, but when he turned up at the shops he had also taken
the precaution of practising a ferocious scowl:

An engineer's skip cap at an aggressive angle and a rough cloth muffler
instead of collar framed and enhanced the expression. Colossal bluff; but it

worked. When my position was assured skip cap and muffler were abandoned for more respectable attire. But the expression, seemingly, had congealed.[5]

The tedium and loneliness of those years were relieved by his military interests. When he returned home from school in Norfolk he had joined the Glasgow University company of the 1st Lanarkshire Rifle Volunteers. A year later, Haldane's Officer Training Corps scheme was launched. Reith joined the Glasgow contingent and was one of the first three to be made sergeant. In spite of his long days, he managed to be on parade by seven o'clock three nights a week:

> I took certificate A almost without noticing it, and entered for B. There was something to this; it was supposed to take one to field rank in the regulars without further examinations; military law, army organisation and tactics, and we had to put a battalion of regulars through ceremonial and open-order drill. Seven entered in Glasgow, three passed; and I was enormously proud of the resultant gold star over my sergeant's stripes. It was magnificent; it gave me an opinion of myself; I had achieved something in the world.[6]

He received invitations from three Territorial COs to apply for a commission, but he felt that infantry work would be both less interesting and less exciting than that of other arms. There was another reason, too:

> I mightily desired to wear spurs – just that . . . I used to imagine myself returning unexpectedly from war and going up the aisle of the College Church in Glasgow – but always and essentially to the ring of spurs . . . I know now that I should have joined the regular Navy or army; I had war in my bones.[7]

He was commissioned in the 5th Scottish Rifles in February 1911, but within a year he regretted it. Camping, in which he had delighted at school and in the OTC, now became a penance: 'I could not reconcile myself to the formality of the mess where a second lieutenant was a nonentity.' One day, during a break in manoeuvres, he was sitting with a group of fellow-officers by the roadside when the Brigade Major appeared, leading the Brigadier's horse:

> 'Any of you fellows ride?' he asked. 'Reith can.' 'Splendid,' said he, and asked me to take the mare – a large and forbidding animal – to a rendezvous a mile or more away. I knew enough to measure the stirrup leather; even to mount professionally; and to my much relief the direction taken by the mare was in accordance with requirements. But not for long; there came a cross-roads, fortunately out of sight of my colleagues; the rendezvous was eastwards; northwards three or four miles off lay the camp. The mare went to the camp; I delivered her to the brigadier's groom and retired to my tent to think things out.[8]

His unhappiness as a Territorial officer stemmed partly from the fact that he was still working long hours, but it was also, as he conceded in later years, because he was almost totally lacking in social graces: 'I was not a good mixer nor had I entered into the spirit of the thing; intolerant, reserved and aloof; I suppose I was born that way; anyhow when I was thirteen my father told me that it seemed that I would have to live on a desert island.'[9]

He kept in touch with one or two of the friends he had made at Gresham's, including John Betts. In the winter of 1909 his father accepted a temporary charge at the Scottish Church in San Remo and his parents were in Italy for six months. He was invited to join the Betts family at Babingley Hall near King's Lynn for Christmas. His friend had a sister:

> I was flabbergasted the first night we were there, sitting on a sofa before the fire, John and Gladys and I, John saying to her that I liked having my hair stroked and she immediately proceeding to do it. A night or two later I was sitting alone in a room and she came in to say goodnight, a candle in her hand and looking rather pretty. I pulled her down and kissed her, which she was obviously expecting, and this was the first time I had ever kissed a girl, probably very awkwardly, and anyhow on her cheek. I got fond of her and kissed her about half a dozen times before I went home, but never on the lips.[10]

Although he craved friendship, he did not always respond particularly graciously when it was offered to him. He had kept up over the years with Jack Loudon, whom he had known since they went to the Academy together in 1896, but their interests and outlook were very different; he felt a great regard for him, but no real affection. He also saw a certain amount of a young medical student, three years younger than himself, called George Harley. They had met in the OTC, and quite often went on long walks together. Reith noted in his diary that they seemed to have pretty much the same views about everything. 'I like him very much,' he wrote, but added complainingly that Harley was 'confoundedly reserved'.

Early in 1912 his brother Douglas arrived back in Glasgow after five years in India as a missionary, forced home by ill health. Reith remained untouched by the general excitement that prevailed at the manse and recorded unfraternally in his diary that he was not particularly anxious to see him. He went on to note, somewhat clinically, that Douglas was rather quiet and melancholy and had become very bald; that he was wearing three pairs of drawers and three semets; and that he seemed to be more interested in the cat than in anything or anybody else.[11]

Douglas seems in many ways to have been the most perceptive member of the family and showed a clearer insight than either of their parents into his younger brother's emotional needs. His attempts to meet them were not greatly appreciated. Reith wrote in his diary that he found him 'touchy and opinionative', adding, 'I would prefer to have some pretty girl to keep me company.'

A few years previously, when he was twenty, he had in fact become quite attached to a girl called May MacQueen, a fifteen-year-old member of his father's church.

> She was of course pleased to hear that I, son of the manse, was interested in her, and even in those days I had apparently a reputation of unapproach-ableness and austerity and so on. We often met after evening service, and I walked home by a roundabout route with her. One Saturday there was some kind of a church picnic to Tillietudlem Castle, in a really lovely part of the country with fruit blossom all out. She and I went off by ourselves, and I remember leaning against a fence under a hawthorn tree and telling her I would like to kiss her. She said she would like me to, but it was very awkwardly done.[12]

It is plain from a later diary entry that Dr Reith was quite taken with May: 'Father announced that he would awfully like to have May for a daughter-in-law – a hint which I shall not take.'[13] May does, however, make one more appear-ance in this story. When Reith was in his late seventies and his mind was turning more and more to the past, he appears to have written to a number of the girls he knew when he was young asking them what impression he had made on them. He pasted their replies in his scrapbook, and one of them was from May:

> I was introduced to the good-looking youngest son of the manse and we soon became very good friends. He had a great deal of charm, but could also be very autocratic and thought everyone should think as he did. He had very strong opinions and always thought he was right – as indeed he often was! . . . He spoke often of how he was going to make his mark in the world, although at that time I don't think he himself had any idea how this was to be achieved.[14]

There is another of these strangely poignant testimonials from the sister of a boy he had known at Gresham's. Her name was Dora Hanmer. Reith had stayed with the family in Kent a number of times during the years of his apprenticeship, and had been mildly smitten. She wrote to him from an address in Worcestershire in April 1968. The old lady's punctuation was idiosyncratic, but the eye of memory was sharp and clear:

My dear John,
In the years when you used to visit us just before the first war, this is how I remember you: Very intense, very proud and very sensitive – but determined not to show it (though with me at least you didn't succeed in that). I always recognised that you were in quite a different category from the other lads I knew, and that you had much more drive, more seriousness of purpose – in fact more ambition – I remember you telling me how much you hankered

for responsibility – I thought you would work and work until you achieved something, and also that because of your ideals and enormous integrity it would have to be something far beyond just material success, though that no doubt was important, too – I was right . . .

Of course mother saw all that and probably much more too . . . also she saw with sympathy the difficulties that with your particular qualities, and *without* the leaven of a little light-heartedness, you were bound to encounter in the rather easy-going English world – which must have been so very different from your native atmosphere . . . Your intelligence was always taken for granted – all that you needed was someone to teach you that 'life is real, life is earnest' is not the whole story; and above all to teach you to laugh at yourself – But no one could have called you a prig! just a bit too solemn for your age – that's all . . .

Back in 1909, May MacQueen had been replaced in his affections by a girl called Cissie Murray. Reith was twenty and she was seventeen. She was very pretty and had long golden hair down her back. All through that winter they used to go out together once or twice a week, 'walking round the Park', Reith wrote, 'in the approved housemaid fashion':

I was really quite fond of her, but in addition to never kissing her an even more extraordinary thing was that neither with her nor with any other girl, nor for years afterwards, was there ever any indication of sexual attraction, and as far as I was concerned, she might have been a boy. I did not know the explanation for years afterwards. It was I suppose the strong repression which I had exercised with myself in matters of this sort, all unnatural and probably unfortunate. I was of course as normal as anyone else but was as completely repressed as to be almost unconscious of this side of things.[15]

Three years into his apprenticeship, John Reith started keeping the famous diary which was to absorb such a disproportionate amount of his time and energy over the next sixty years. The cover of the first volume carried a rather high-flown inscription: 'My Diary – being a Chronicle more or less Faithful of the Doings both in Public and Private of J. C. W. Reith, Likewise a Survey of his Thoughts Expressed or Otherwise, and a Record of his Transactions with Others'. One of the first entries, dating from December 1911, describes a visit to his birthplace. He lunched at the Royal Hotel and then climbed Evan Street, 'to find at the very top, overlooking all Stonehaven, a lonely and windswept house, Alexander House, in which I was born'. He was much gratified to discover that an old lady of eighty who lived opposite remembered the occasion and even the name the baby had been given.

Toward the end of his time at Hydepark, the mental condition of his brother Ernest deteriorated and his behaviour became dangerous. One day he had taken it into his head that people should not walk over the coal-hole set in the pavement in front of the manse, and removed the metal cover. When Reith

came home that evening it was to find that two men from the Crichton Institution in Dumfries had come to take him away:

> This evening was a terrible experience. Of course he did not want to go and
> wanted me to help him to keep the men off. I went to see him off at the
> station. I had almost given him a chance of getting off down my fire escape
> earlier in the evening, but I knew that it was my duty to resist natural
> inclinations.[16]

It was not all gloom in the manse, however. One evening he had a gathering
of his old OTC section there. It began quietly enough in the drawing room,
but after supper the party moved upstairs to his room and things began to
warm up:

> Everyone got their hands on some sort of musical instrument. Crichton did
> a clog dance on my drawing board, and altogether the evening was a tremen-
> dous success, the like of which I do not think has been experienced in the
> manse before. Beta had made some delightful marzipan potatoes, of which
> we consumed over a hundred. They left about 11.45, parading at the foot
> of the steps and then marching down the street.[17]

He didn't like to admit it, but as his apprenticeship wore on, he occasionally
found that he was quite enjoying himself: 'I was quite well known in the works,'
he wrote in his Pre-Diary Narrative, 'and I think I was quite well liked. I used
to argue a great deal against socialism, and in fact generally rather asserted
myself, but nobody seemed to mind.' The general manager clearly thought
well of him, and got him shifted round from one department to another – six
months in the template shop, nine months in the iron foundry, six months in
the drawing office. During his stint in the smithy he specially enjoyed heavy
hammering, and became quite expert at it. He recorded that one day he made
a pair of spring tongs, which he presented to his father: 'His gratitude was
tempered by his scruples at receiving what he considered more or less stolen
goods.'[18]

His admiration for his father was boundless, although he still felt keenly the
injustice of having been thrust into 'the most brainless profession imaginable'.
They visited Gresham's together in the summer of 1912 and Dr Reith preached
in the school chapel: 'The sermon was on the lad with the five scones, and it
made a profound sensation, but Father made a sensation enough himself by
his appearance.'[19]

His father was now seventy, and Reith was hugely indignant when he was
passed over for the Moderatorship of the United Free Church: 'It is of course
his own doing, because he is so retiring and takes little part in Church affairs,
but certainly it is to his credit that he never seeks honours for himself, and is
above any sort of intrigue.'[20]

One evening in the early summer of 1913 he came home to find that his father had been run down and badly hurt in the street. A dairyman's horse-drawn van had swung round a corner on the wrong side of the road and had made off without stopping. Reith changed into an old suit, equipped himself with an inch-and-a-half spanner and rushed from the house. He visited the Cranstonhill Police Station, telling a startled inspector that if he found the culprit he would not be answerable for the consequences. He spent the night searching many of the model lodging-houses in the city, but without success.

Maybe as well. I was lying in wait for him at the dairyman's at 5.00 in the morning, but he failed to appear. I do not suggest that I intended to kill him but I would have wrought such summary vengeance on him that there might have been an accident even had the spanner stayed in my pocket. The spanner was only a precaution; it was unlikely that he was stronger than I.[21]

When he wasn't wrestling with Joule's Law or describing methods of finding the focal length of a thin concave lens, he found time to read outside the Technical College syllabus, although without any discernible plan. Diary entries during the last two years of his apprenticeship mention Chesterton's *What's Wrong with the World*, a collection of essays on religion and politics which had been published in 1910, and F. Anstey's *Vice Versa* – 'felt sad at the ending about Dulcie'. He made a start on Macaulay's *History of England* and tackled John Tyndall's controversial Address to the British Association of 1874 on the relation between science and theology. He read *Tom Brown's Schooldays* for the first time, got through Bulwer-Lytton's historical novel *The Last of the Barons*, and sampled some Roman history. 'Reading *In Memoriam* very carefully,' he noted in his diary towards the end of 1912. Later that winter he was busy with Sir William Hamilton's *Lectures on Metaphysics and Logic*.[22] On Easter Day 1913 he recorded that he had started reading *The Egregious Englishman* – 'for the purpose of improving my vocabulary of vituperation, as there was nothing else in it'.[23]

He did extremely well in his night classes at the Technical College, achieving average marks of over ninety per cent in the examinations and gaining first-class certificates, but he was very unsettled as his time at the Works drew to a close: 'I got the idea of going on a railway job in China,' he noted in his diary in February 1913. 'Railways in this country seem hopeless for me.' In April he at last emerged from the chrysalis of his apprenticeship as a Journeyman Locomotive Fitter. At the time he would own to no particular sense of achievement: 'Five blasted years have been spent since I started work in the NBLC,' he wrote in his diary. 'A thousand damns upon them.'

It was an ungracious entry. He left NBLC with a clutch of glowing references. The Chairman wrote that his character was all that could be desired, and the chief managing director that he had made 'the very best use of his time'. Alongside these, he preserved in his scrapbook a mock testimonial in time-honoured style from his foreman which pleased him no less: 'This is to certify that Wee Jock Reith is a very able and willing Loafer. He is very good at doing a job after it is finished. He is also an excellent riser at night.'

John Reith described the memoirs he published after the Second World War as 'a psychological study of an individual with intermittent participation in public affairs'. The book was dedicated to his children, Christopher and Marista. He urged them, in a brooding praescriptum, to read the record in a detached and critical way: 'Determine what was good or bad; worthy or unworthy; well or ill conceived; well or ill conducted; apportion credit and debit. And to the end that they may themselves do better; be of more use in their day; be happier and more content.'

He had relied heavily on the two million and more words of his diary, and he described his criteria of selection:

> To tell the whole truth, exactly what happened, what one man thought or said about another, what oneself thought or said, might be improper or indecent, unkind or hurtful. For value in the story this cannot always be avoided. But the writer will be as much hurt as anyone.

He observed those criteria only patchily. *Into the Wind* runs to well over 500 pages, but he races through the first twenty-four years of his life in the first eight of them. At the end of his time at the Locomotive Works, he represents his situation, as he so often did, with a maritime simile: 'And what now? There I was – like a ship engined, manned, equipped (more or less so), ready to sail . . .' He would have his readers believe that he adopted the conventional Scottish solution and, like some Caledonian Dick Whittington, took the high road to England: 'To London. Same urge as countless others have felt; and without any sound reason.'

His diary makes plain that those two telegraphic sentences in his memoirs convey a good deal less than the whole truth: 'To be in London near C. was what was dominating me perhaps as much as that I had come to the conclusion that I had little future in Glasgow.'[24]

Reith's overriding reason for going to London in February of 1914 was that at the age of twenty-four he was besotted with a seventeen-year-old schoolboy called Charlie Bowser.

Three

PARAGON OF
ALL INFALLIBILITIES

> When it comes will it come without warning
> Just as I'm picking my nose?
> Will it knock on my door in the morning
> Or tread in the bus on my toes?
> Will it come like a change in the weather?
> Will its greeting be courteous or rough?
> Will it alter my life altogether?
> O tell me the truth about love.
>
> W. H. AUDEN, *Twelve Songs* 1938

THE BOWSER family lived just round the corner from the manse, but they were not members of Dr Reith's congregation. Charlie's father, like his father before him, had been Treasurer of the Baptist Union in Scotland; Mr Bowser and his father had also been allied in business as partners in a firm of iron founders and cast-iron pipe manufacturers.

Reith had known Charlie for almost two years. He noted that he had a long conversation with him in the manse garden on 26 May 1912 and that first entry in the diary reads prosaically enough: 'This was the first time I had spoken to him, although I had often seen him about on the streets. Very nice little chap. I like him.'

Charlie (he figures sometimes as C., sometimes as DCB – his first name was David) bobs up again in an entry in September: 'Very good looking and awfully pretty eyes'. He had been passing the manse and had come into the garden because he saw Reith there. He did not come alone, however, and the diarist recorded his annoyance 'because two thick-headed lumpish Connells came in too'.

The lumpish Connells do not make a second appearance, but Charlie is mentioned with increasing frequency. 'DCB round from 7.30 till 10', reads an entry in May 1913. 'I wish to goodness that I did not like that boy so much. I am frightfully fond of him – it is of course quite ridiculous.' His family began to think so too – 'My people do not approve of my liking C. so much' – but he paid little attention and that summer he allowed his infatuation for the boy free rein, writing poetry in his album and having his photograph taken for him at the Romney studio. The poetry was interspersed with a good deal of sermonising prose on the nature of greatness, ambition and strength of will. Many years later, in an old commonplace book, Reith came across an entry he had made in Charlie's album at that time:

> . . . Having become self-reliant you will not be afraid to create precedent, and the opinions and comments of others on your actions will give you no concern. You will find a great deal distasteful in the attitudes and habits of the working class but you will also find much good . . . Never forget that by birth and education and upbringing you are a gentleman with duties and responsibilities therefore incumbent on you, among them to withstand the democratic trend of modern nations and civic politics in order to keep the reins of control in the hands of those most fitted to hold them . . . Spiritual greatness is of course the only thing that finally matters. I shall not presume to say anything on that point except this: cultivate all through an absolute practical faith in God and as an invincible trust preserve the sanctity of the Sabbath Day.[1]

There are also the first signs of the strong proprietary interest Reith was to take in Charlie's career during the ten years of their friendship:

> June 21st. I took him over Hyde Park Works. There was a chance of his going there in the Autumn to serve his time. In the afternoon we had a very enjoyable walk by Baldernock, carving our initials on a tree and later on the seat in the garden. That night I made my debut at their house, being very satisfied with my rig – all brown. I had a long argument with Douglas that night about my being so friendly with C., and the others are huffy about it, too . . .

The idyll was about to be interrupted, however. Reith learned that the Bowser family were moving to London, and in the ensuing months he redoubled his efforts to see as much of his young friend as he could. In late July they went off for the weekend to Comrie, in Perthshire:

> I had been looking forward tremendously to this, and we had a wonderful time together – the first time we had been away overnight. We carved our initials on the seat at the top of the Monument Hill. Of course I was feeling very sad that he was soon to be leaving Glasgow.[2]

They had made a number of visits to the Isle of Arran during the summer, walking from Lamlash to Brodick, visiting Whiting Bay, lying in the sun on the top of a hill and getting 'most frightfully sunburnt'. Arran held powerful memories of childhood holidays for Reith. So did the Highlands, and he deter-

mined that that was where they should spend their last weekend together at
the end of August before the Bowser family's departure.

> C. spent the night with me in the digs, and we went to Aviemore at 4.40
> am, part of the time we spent in the Guard's Van, and I got C. on to the
> engine from Newtonmore. George MacKenzie met us at the station, and we
> spent the day with his people – total expenses 14/- for tickets. It rained most
> of the day, but we walked to Loch-an-Eilan. I saw Dr Martineau's Memorial
> for the first time. Motor drive by Loch Moy, returning in the middle of the
> night, and C. slept with me again.[3]

For the best part of ten years, until they both married, Reith's friendship with
Charlie was the most important thing in his life. To form a definitive view
about the precise nature of the relationship is extraordinarily difficult, because
most of the material that would have shed light upon it – and there was a great
deal – no longer exists. In the years that followed the ending of the friendship,
Reith destroyed most of Charlie's letters – there were many hundreds of them
– and returned the rest. He also, as will be seen, performed extensive surgery
on his diary.

And yet, despite the bitterness of his feelings, he did not feel that he could
totally expunge the story of the friendship from the record: 'I sometimes feel
as if he never had existed. But the diary has too many references to him for
that.' The relationship with Charlie remained a central strand in John Reith's
life until 1922. An account of it has to be pieced together from those references
that remain.

Reith's version of his move to London is misleading not only about his
reasons for going but also about the time-scale. His memoirs suggest that he
stepped on the train the minute he had completed his apprenticeship, but those
few terse sentences in his narrative telescope a sequence of events that was in
fact spread over ten months. Initially, he stayed on in the Drawing Office at
Hydepark, and it is plain from his diary that he was not unhappy to do so.

He did, however, start job-hunting. On 13 September 1913 – Charlie, as it
happened, had left for London that morning and Reith was in a 'dreadful state'
about it – he saw the General Manager of the Glasgow and South Western
Railway and was given to understand that he was to be appointed Assistant
Locomotive Engineer. For someone just out of his apprenticeship it was a
beguiling prospect – he would have charge of sixteen depots and the starting
salary would be £250 a year. He sent off a jubilant telegram to his parents,
who were on holiday in Harrogate, and he preserved in his scrapbook the letter
of congratulation and counsel which came by return from his father. It is plain
that Dr Reith saw his youngest son very clearly:

> It is a responsible thing to be placed over others and tests a man's character
> severely. You have to learn how to be *suaviter in modo* and *fortiter in re*; how
> to avoid being bossy, and yet to make men respect you.

Be always modest and humble; 'before honour is humility'. Be always courteous to inferiors as to superiors. Never brag; never – unless required – drag yourself into conversation. Throw yourself heartily into others' interests, and make people feel that you are as interested in them as in yourself.

And above all things *take counsel with your Saviour*, and make sure that he is with you, approving of every step you take. Remember the prayer of Moses: 'If thy presence go not with us, carry us not up hence . . .'[4]

Several weeks passed without confirmation of the appointment. It then emerged that the General Manager had failed to establish whether his Locomotive Superintendent felt the need of an assistant. It turned out that he didn't. It further transpired that if one were to be foisted upon him – particularly someone aged twenty-three who was totally without practical experience – he would be minded to resign. 'Neither the Chairman nor the General Manager were big enough to put their will across him,' wrote Reith. 'It was a huge disappointment to me.'

He missed Charlie greatly and wrote two long letters to him each week: 'my letters to C. were more like magazine articles – often illustrated at that.' This did not leave a great deal of time for other evening activities, but he still attended prayer meetings at church whenever he could. One week they were required to write an essay on 'the Christian Conception of God' and he noted in his diary in November that in a class of forty he and four others got first class: 'I was annoyed with the other four.' In December 1913, his father was at last elected Moderator of the Church and Reith contrived to sound almost pleased about it:

It was certainly high time. He is in his 72nd year and might never have lived to get it. Others far less worthy of it than he have had it – pushers. He is much too good for Scotland.[5]

Charlie was to be seventeen on 20 December. Reith bought a wristwatch for him and wore it himself to a Territorial Ball. When he got home, at three o'clock in the morning, he sat down to write a letter. The watch, he wrote, was given with all his love and with very best wishes for the future:

You know what I think about you and of the tremendous admiration I have for you. You have made more difference in my life than can be calculated. I pray that we may be friends always and that we may both rise to great positions, or, if that be denied, that at least we may live in Christ and that any change will only strengthen the bond of love between us.[6]

When he had first suggested that Charlie should come to spend Christmas at the manse, Mr and Mrs Bowser had frowned on the idea, but later they relented, and he arrived on the evening of the 26th. 'My excitement was indescribable,' Reith wrote. 'Slept together in spare-room.' The next night, however, he recorded his unhappiness over the amount of time Charlie seemed prepared to give to his various relatives. 'He gave me a lecture about being so stand-offish and reserved.'

On 29 December they caught the ten o'clock train to Comrie, where there was three feet of snow:

All over the place, feeling indescribably happy. Walk after supper also – starlight – then a hot bath together. Monument Hill next day and then Glen Lednock. Ordered a sledge and spent most of next day on it and enjoyed it enormously. A Hogmanay treat in the evening and then long talks till midnight chimed from the church – we on the quiet road below the golf course. So the year ended and 1914 began. We read and prayed together.[7]

The friendship became more and more intense, with what Reith described as 'only a very occasional shadow'. 'C. was frightfully affectionate, but never too much so for me.' They read the Bible a good deal together, and Charlie promised not to smoke again till he was twenty-one. Years later, when Reith was going through these early volumes of his diary, he paused over those few days in Comrie before the first World War:

Of course this was the most exciting holiday I ever had. I suppose it would have been better in some ways if we had never had it, or had had it differently. I became far too much centred on him – far too much. My chief ambition seemed to be to do well for his sake and to hold his admiration and affection. And of course he has become a sort of paragon of all infallibilities.[8]

Charlie returned to London. Reith records that he missed him 'dreadfully', and that he wrote 'most extravagantly' about him in his diary, but the entries do not survive. Thrown back on his own resources, he filled what little leisure he had with reading and with long solitary walks.[9] He notes that he read *Paradise Lost* with his mother and that he plunged 'with immense eagerness' into Morley's *Life of Gladstone*. His interest in politics at that time was more than academic, because he also went to see Gulland, the Liberal Chief Whip for Scotland – 'I was awfully keen to go into Parliament.'[10]

England were to play Ireland at rugby in London on 14 February. He announced that he intended to go to the match but admitted in his diary that this was merely an excuse. He handed in his notice to the NBLC and collected some introductions 'to magnates and near-magnates' in London. 'You'll be back with your tail between your legs,' his father told him.[11] He took the night train, and after a brief visit to a lodging-house took most of his things to the Bowsers' house in Highgate. 'DCB at 7 and of course I was overcome with joy.'

His first call on Monday morning was to the offices of Rendell, Tritton and Palmer, consultants to the Indian government. This produced an offer of 450 rupees a year (about £360) in the locomotive department of an Indian railway, with the prospect of a home inspectorship later. That evening, however, Charlie's father gave him an introduction to E. W. Moir of S. Pearson & Son Ltd – one of the biggest figures in civil engineering contracting, he said, but a hard man. The second bit was certainly right. He asked Reith what sort of pay he was expecting. When Reith said £250 a year, Moir said that Oxford and Cambridge men usually started at twenty shillings a week, but that he would give him thirty shillings to go to the Albert Dock and show what he could do.

He presented himself at the south extension of the Royal Albert Dock at North Woolwich where Pearsons had recently started work on a £2 million contract.[12] The company's agent did not seem particularly pleased to see him, but allowed him to go off in the afternoon to look for digs. He told his mother in his first letter that he would be looking for something north of the river as it was cheaper than the south side. He wrote on paper with the Pearson letter-head. Compulsive correspondent and diarist that he was, he had made an important discovery: 'I was glad to find that they supply all writing books, pencils and such like ad lib. This is a great saving.'[13]

His father wrote kindly to him as soon as he heard he was settled:

> I'm very glad that you have got fixed so soon, and I do hope that you will stick in strenuously, and prove to Mr Moir that you mean business. I have no doubt that you will do so, and approve [sic] yourself a true Scotchman, and one who can stoop to conquer. Never mind your surroundings. The men who make their mark have all had to begin like that. And try to keep on the best terms with your fellow-workers . . .
>
> Be ready and willing for anything. And keep a good conscience, and a courteous tongue, and a pure and humble heart . . .[14]

The stilted opening of Reith's reply shows how closely tied he still felt to the manse and how important his father's approval was to him: 'I should much have preferred writing to tell you all about the job, and asking your permission to take it, but the circumstances were such that I was not able to do this.' He had been 'much relieved' to find a Presbyterian church in North Woolwich and the minister had been most welcoming, urging him to make himself at home in his study whether he was there or not. It could not compare with what he had so recently left behind, however:

> I miss your services most horribly, and shall do always; I am used to so high an order of preaching, that even the best preaching here will rank as mediocre . . . I don't think it is necessary for me to tell you that I shall always go twice to church and shall remember everything which you and Mother have spoken of in days past. I don't think you will have any anxiety about my conduct . . .[15]

There were compensations – 'Dinner with C. at the Piccadilly Pop on Saturday night represented my ideal diversion' – although his uncritical devotion to his young friend does not seem to have been unfailingly reciprocated:

C. wasn't as kind as he might have been always and that always put me in a very bad way. Sometimes I even say he was a cad to me; and this sort of thing is sometimes followed by extravagances about him.[16]

He found lodgings in Forest Gate, in the same house as the chief mechanical engineer at the Dock, a man called Makepeace. Reith quickly decided he was 'a very feeble specimen'. 'He has a good mechanical knowledge, but is absolutely useless at organisation and is afraid of the foremen and other fellows on the staff. I wish I could get him pushed out – I'm absolutely stuck as long as he is here.'[17]

Reith also chronicled for his parents' benefit the ways in which Makepeace fell short of the highest standards in his private life:

His beastly fiancée has arrived for a week's visit to his digs, which doesn't seem exactly the right sort of thing. There's fortunately a second sitting room to which I retire at the very earliest opportunity, but I can hear their idiotic jawing through the wall ... My instinctive dislike was justified as I found that she is not a teetotaller, smokes in public, doesn't go to church, is a rampant suffragette – wishes she were a man, and so on. In about ten words I told her my opinion of such women, but I absolutely refused to discuss the question.

I've asked Charlie to dinner tomorrow evening and shall have dinner in the other sitting room, as I wouldn't let him meet such a beastly woman ...[18]

After a month in the job, his pay was raised to £2 a week. After two months he moved out of his Forest Gate lodgings and found a sitting room and bedroom in Highgate, close to the Bowsers: 'The new digs were only three and a half minutes from C.'s house ... On my way to the station in the mornings I usually woke him up by our whistle.' Charlie went to his rooms several evenings each week, and they usually saw each other on Sundays too, though not as much as Reith wanted. One Saturday he had wanted them to go on the river together, but Charlie had to watch a school cricket match. Nor was Reith best pleased when Charlie announced that he wanted to get to know a couple of girls who attended Highgate Church.[19]

Very unhappy sometimes with C. Even now I can recall it, however ridiculous it seems, but I was obsessed by him. It was always about his people or other acquaintances and my not seeing him enough.[20]

He was very much up and down during those early summer months of 1914. He would dearly have loved to have travelled to Edinburgh to be present at his father's inauguration as Moderator but scrupled to ask for time off so soon after joining the firm, a decision he later regretted. His mind turned constantly to Scotland and to the manse and to the remembered certainties of Sunday services: 'I feel as if I hadn't been in church since I left Glasgow. Other churches are no use. I should like to hear a good psalm such as the second version of the 124th or the second version of the 145th to Duke Street . . .'[21] He was also at this time reading *Annals of the Disruption* – for the second time.[22]

Whitsun fell at the end of June that year – a holiday of which Reith had not previously heard. He took advantage of it to pay a flying visit to Glasgow and was 'tremendously excited' at being home: 'I hate the idea of leaving again, and would not do so if it weren't for C.'[23]

By July, his spirits seem to have lifted. He had joined the London Scottish Rugby Club: 'Fully expect to play fullback for their first next winter,' he announced in his diary. 'I see the chance of an international beyond this.' He had also arranged that he and Charlie would go camping together in North Cornwall in August, and was busy in his methodical way with a list of things to take with them.

He had created a good impression at the Albert Dock. The Pearson agent quickly registered that this young Scot who had been wished on him by his masters was remarkable not solely for his intensity and his immense height, and sensibly increased his area of responsibility. Reith began to think that he might have a future with the company – promotion to sub-agent in a year or two, perhaps, a salary of £1,000 a year or so. Then one day he fell into conversation with the sub-agent on the site, who was called Peppercorn – an appropriate name, as it turned out, because he told Reith that after fifteen years with the company his salary was £250 a year. 'That was that,' wrote Reith. 'My days with Pearsons were numbered, the numbering to be done by me.' He dug out the letters of introduction he had brought from Glasgow, took an afternoon off and had a satisfactory conversation with the managing director of Nobel's.

Then, a few days after his twenty-fifth birthday, an altogether more exhilarating prospect opened before him. He normally wrote his diary in a neat cursive hand, but on 29 July 1914, he felt that something more dramatic was called for: 'WAR. Tremendous excitement. Austria v Serbia. Russia, Germany and France will probably join in, and England also.' He may have been a little vague about who was going to be fighting whom, but he was entirely clear that he intended to be in the thick of it. Reith's martial instincts were, however, tempered by a personal consideration. Camping gear and provisions had already been despatched by rail to Cornwall. 'I am in great fear that my magnificent holiday with my friend is to be spoiled,' he wrote in his diary. 'The Territorials seem to be mobilising.'[24]

The question was, was he still a Territorial? It does not sound a particularly theological question, but Reith already had a highly developed capacity for making complications. After coming to London, he had written to the Adjutant of the 5th Scottish Rifles resigning his commission – he would no longer be able to go to camp or attend drill sessions. His letter, however, had never been acknowledged, so now he wrote to the Adjutant again, telling him he was ready to mobilise 'if the thing was serious', but that otherwise he didn't want to cancel his holiday arrangements.

There was no response to this rather lordly communication, and Reith eventually did what someone with more common sense would have done several days sooner – procured a travel voucher and got on the night train to Glasgow. He assembled his gear and made an appearance in the orderly room in uniform, but there were still several scenes to be played out:

The little Adjutant bristled. I would not be required that day; I would attend at ten o'clock next morning 'wearing my sword'. I was on the point of asking what on earth all the fuss was about, but refrained. If there were to be a row it had better be properly staged.[25]

There were few things Reith liked better than a good row. On this occasion he was denied it and had to settle for the satisfaction of demonstrating to the CO that the Adjutant had sent his mobilisation orders to an incomplete telegraphic address.

His parents were away on holiday and the manse was shut up, but his sister Beta was in Glasgow. She was seventeen years his senior and was now stricken with cerebro-spinal meningitis. They went to their father's church together on Sunday evening, and Reith realised that not all his brothers and sisters were uncaring:

I have discovered a well of devotion of which I must heretofore have been oblivious. I asked for her photograph and she gave me two snaps. She gave me a looking glass, pocket scissors, fruit knife ['still in possession', he noted twenty years later] and a pillow slip.[26]

He called on his friend George Harley, and also saw his sister: 'Connie was looking very pretty as usual; it's a good thing I don't like girls.'[27]

The battalion was told that it was shortly to proceed 'to the war station', and identity discs were issued: 'Lieut. J. C. W. Reith Pres 5th SR'. 'Pres' was short for Presbyterian: 'Something of a shock thus early to be presented with the credentials for burial.' The war station proved initially to be no further away than Falkirk, but after ten days he was sent off with sixty men to Larbert to guard two vulnerable points on the main railway line running south from Perth. Reith helped himself to two of the best sergeants and six of the best corporals and installed himself in some luxury in a farmhouse. On Sunday afternoons, there were local dignitaries to entertain. It was particularly important to be on cordial terms with the Larbert stationmaster:

Our coal ration was insufficient to keep the picquet fires at the required volume during the night, and when we were running short we had only to mention the matter to him. For the rest of the day the passage of trains would be marked by a shower of coal from the engine cab, thrown forth at his instance by friendly drivers.[28]

Charlie came to visit him in his farmhouse. 'My excitement may be imagined,' Reith wrote in his diary. 'He was in uniform!' Excitement soon turned to annoyance, however, because Charlie went off to visit some cousins. Reith thought he was away an inordinate time; it also emerged on his return that he had been 'carrying on a bit with May Fisher'. Reith's response was to sulk, and he went off the next morning without leave to Comrie 'and there visited all the old haunts – where we had cut our names and so on'.[29]

Relations with his NCOs were good. Occasionally – in breach of regulations – he took his meals with them and he frequently spent the night with the picquets, watching day break over the Ochil Hills. One evening, standing at the farm gate, he heard the distant sound of singing, and presently a body of troops came into view:

> Every man in place of his glengarry was wearing a red night-cap and had in his right eye his identity disc attached to a broad red ribbon. There were NCOs in the party, but the man in charge who gave 'Eyes right' and saluted me was a private soldier, the acknowledged 'comic' of the company. As their heads turned smartly, every eye-glass was shot out – a new form of military compliment. The whole affair most irregular and most excellent.[30]

The pleasing irregularity of this first posting lasted only four weeks. News came that they were to be relieved by a body called the National Guard, of which they had not previously heard. Reith paraded his men opposite them and was unimpressed – 'a body of middle-aged civilians in mufti carrying prehistoric rifles and with bayonets projecting from their pockets'.[31] When he took his outfit over to a corner of the field for a few valedictory remarks they cheered him, and he was in no doubt why; he had, he noted in his diary, 'treated them as very few officers would or could – discipline very strict but every sort of privilege'.[32] Then he marched them off the five miles to Falkirk, despondent at the prospect of more humdrum routines.

The next morning, however, an orderly handed him a note from the Adjutant – he was to assume command of Transport. Suddenly 'the sun shone in an unclouded sky':

> The Transport Officer was a somebody; an object of mystification, envy and even respect among his brother officers. He was not, as they, subject to routine parades and orderly duties. He was a power in the land; one with whom it was expedient to be on friendly terms . . . Magnificent – like the gold star.[33]

He took over from a retired Indian Army officer who was never out of jodhpurs and who had presided, in his successor's crisply uncharitable view, over an 'undisciplined rabble'. With men he knew, and with others chosen for their knowledge of horses, Reith soon had things in better shape. He looked on it as his first real job; years later when he had done many others, he remembered the foundry stores-shed at Larbert and recalled the satisfaction with which he had first written his signature over a rubber stamp saying 'Transport Officer, Lieut 5th SR'. 'I had (*horresco referens*) to learn to ride a horse.' That, however, was a small price to pay: 'On appointment I had of course ordered two pairs of riding breeches and leggings, and, with ineffable delight, had procured a gigantic pair of spurs.'[34]

He sat up late over army manuals on equestrianism. The Transport Officer of the 8th SR gave him some discreet practical lessons. Getting into the saddle was what gave him most difficulty, a weakness he concealed by the simple expedient of declining to dismount. His methods of improving the quality of his personnel soon earned him what he described as 'respectful unpopularity' with his fellow-officers. He poached brazenly and discarded without sentiment: with drivers who reported 'there's something wrong with one of the front paws of my horse' he took the view that desperate remedies were required. The fifty or so men of the Transport Section did not know what had hit them. Under the old régime negligent grooming, pilfering and even drunkenness had all been tolerated. They now found themselves under orders 'to clean up and parade for church with the rest of the Battalion'. Before long they were complimented on their turn-out by the Commander-in-Chief, Scotland.

Reith did not find the company of his fellow-officers congenial, and did not always turn up for dinner in the mess. In spare moments he sometimes rode out into the pleasant Stirlingshire countryside with a member of his section. The men were beginning to respond to this strange young officer with the outsize spurs. One night at the end of October they were ordered to Broughty Ferry on the River Tay to relieve a detachment of the Black Watch. The enormous train which steamed out of Larbert station at noon the next day had on board the entire Battalion, complete with horses, stores and wagons. Reith's men had worked well. When they got to Broughty Ferry he marched them into a baker's shop for tea – all forty-nine of them. 'Presumably somebody paid the bill later.'[35]

On Sunday evening he went to St Luke's Church. The Minister and his wife were old friends and they had invited him to supper after the service: 'Kitty, their daughter, was alone in the Manse pew; she signalled to me to come beside her and this I speedily did . . . She was eighteen and very pretty.'[36] He noted in his diary that he wanted to tell her about Charlie, but there was no great occasion; as they sat at table the Transport sergeant appeared with a message – the Battalion was proceeding overseas at once.

Kitty and her parents saw him off the next day. 'Kitty got into the carriage and I kissed her – after politely asking leave.'[37] The horses were restless in the train on the way south. At Berwick they found one aged beast in a collapsed state:

At Newcastle it was dead and we hauled the carcass out on to the platform. 'You can't leave that horse here,' the frenzied officials said; a London express was due at the same platform a few minutes later. What did they expect us to do with a dead horse?[38]

They had six double-horsed vehicles to get from King's Cross to the Army Service Corps depot at Deptford where they were to refit. One of the drivers had gone sick in the night, so Reith took his place, and was very pleased with himself for having negotiated the London traffic in an old-fashioned two-horse dray. Several hours later the party emerged from the depot with twice as many vehicles and three times as many horses. They headed for Waterloo and arrived in style, most of the vehicles taking the last steep slope at a hand-gallop.

Charlie had come to meet him, and they went off to snatch some food in the station restaurant. 'You haven't told me anything about Kitty,' said Charlie:

> 'Kitty,' I said. 'What do you know about her? There's been no time to tell you.' He handed me a telegram which had been sent to me at his home. 'Happy here,' she wired, 'but happier with you.' A very nice message, I thought. But I never saw her again.[39]

Their destination was Southampton. His brother Robert had recently gone there to take up ship survey work. Reith rode to his house and, reining in outside, gave the family whistle. At eight o'clock a telegram was despatched to their parents: 'John is in our bath. His horse rolling in the garden.'

Another telegram reached the manse later the same day: 'France tonight. Much love to Father and Mother. Take care of yourselves.' There had been no time to telephone. On the way to the docks to embark on the SS *Huanchaco* the Transport section of the 5th SR had been too busy 'acquiring' a fine heavy draught horse that had strayed in their direction from some other unit. Reith wrote up his diary and fell asleep on a truss of straw beside his mare.

> The keelies of Glasgow had jeered at us as we marched along Great Western Road. We were only pretending to be real 'sojers'; giving up long hours and summer holidays to it; more fools we. The siren of the *Huanchaco* was the full stop to all that; the consummation and justification.[40]

John Reith was going to war.

Four

RUBBER BOOTS AND SPURS

If I were fierce and bald and short of breath
I'd live with scarlet Majors at the Base,
And speed glum heroes up the line to death.
SIEGFRIED SASSOON, *Base Details*, 1918

What they could do with round here is a good war.
BERTOLT BRECHT,
Mother Courage and her Children, 1941

As THE SUN came up it was plain from the crossing time that they were lying off Le Havre. The big gantry on the dock was unattended. This gave Reith a chance to practise his villainous French on a nearby *fonctionnaire*:

'*Monsieur*,' I said, '*où est l'homme qui fait marcher cette machine?*' He didn't know; perhaps he had gone to his breakfast. Some distance away was another gantry, with a man leaning out of the control cabin high above. '*Louis*,' I called, '*où est votre collègue de cette autre machine?*' He thought he would be back soon. How long? An hour perhaps. '*Mais*,' I said, '*nous désirons arriver à la guerre; nous serons en retard.*' This impressed him; he came to our aid.[1]

By 4.30 their sixty-six horses and twenty-two wagons were ashore. Reith fired off a first volley of mail – a postcard to his mother, a letter to Charlie – which, to his disgust, 'had first to be submitted to Kennedy, the junior major, and which he industriously read before affixing the censor's stamp'.[2]

The next morning they were ordered to the railway station. There were ordinary carriages for the officers and wagons of the 'eight horses, forty men' variety for other ranks. Reith, characteristically, decided to travel in the fodder van. He soon had it fitted out with makeshift sofas and armchairs made from bales of hay and sprawled there with his men: 'The CO probably didn't approve. I was far happier with the NCOs than I would have been with the officers.'[3] When they stopped at stations, peasants handed up tea and coffee and peaches and rolls.

Journey's end was St Omer. They drove nine or ten miles in the dark to the village of Helfault, and once the horses had been fed and watered, Reith was free to call on Mademoiselle Julia Obert, on whom he had been billeted. Many years later, revisiting his old war haunts, he knocked on the door of her farmhouse again and asked, rather superfluously, if she remembered him. *Mais bien sûr.* Not easy to forget 'the officer with the Scotch hat and big spurs'. She also remembered that it had been November and that he had sent home a rose from the farmyard to his mother.[4] Reith had indeed found a rose growing on the farm wall, but what he recorded in his diary was that he sent it to Charlie. He did so by ordinary French post – which meant that it did not have to be scrutinised by Major Kennedy.[5]

On that Saturday night in November 1914 Mademoiselle Julia and her sister offered him coffee, marvelled at his fountain pen, and showed him to a small room filled with two enormous and ancient beds. He had not seen sheets for a week. He knelt to pray, and so did the officer who had been allocated the other bed:

> I wondered what he was saying to the Almighty. For my part I made it clear that I was greatly thrilled and was expecting to enjoy myself. But since I had been landed in such an extraordinary situation without any intent or design of my own, I was expecting Him to see me through. For, looking north-west from the farmyard gate I had seen and heard what I had never seen or heard before – the flash and explosion of distant guns in action.[6]

He woke at seven. The weather was magnificent and it was the Sabbath Day: 'Thought badly of CO for letting the day pass without service or recognition of God of any kind. For all we know it might be the last for some of us.'[7] Some of the men, particularly those without Territorial experience, were jittery; Reith assembled them and gave them a pep-talk.

His threshold of boredom was never high, and he chafed under the enforced inactivity of these early days. Letters from home were initially slow to come. The first to arrive was from Kitty; from Charlie there was only one in the first three weeks. Reith wrote to him constantly. He also wrote at length *about* him – not only in his diary, but also in letters to his parents:

> I wish to goodness he were here with me, and he wishes to be with me. He would make a good officer, even though he is not 18 – in fact compared with some we have he would have been magnificent, in spite of being so young. There are very few boys of his age with half his ability and strength of will. My word Charlie is one in a million – and it would absolutely make all the difference in the world to me to have him here, because I've never in my life been so much in need of a friend as now, and he is my only real friend.[8]

The Battalion soon moved up country. He bade farewell to the Mesdemoiselles Obert, leaving with them as a token of gratitude 'a decrepit horse and sundry bits of gear for which we had no use'. The next day, on the way to Bailleul, they encountered the remnants of the London Scottish, who had reached France six weeks earlier:

> There was an awe about this meeting with the London Scottish; stupidly we were not halted but some of them walked beside us and gave us bits of their story. We were tolerably smart; they were unshaven, weirdly clad and caked in mud. They had already made their name glorious. What would we do?[9]

The next morning was dry and frosty. They passed a customs post at Erquinghem and came into a built-up area – houses, offices and shops, tram-lines. The streets were deserted. They were told the Germans were less than two miles away. They had reached Armentières.

The Transport section was allocated the local lunatic asylum, which stood in six or seven acres. It was a comfortable billet – there was, naturally, a padded cell – and once Reith had seen his horses and men installed he went off in search of lodgings. He and another officer ended up in an imposing mansion – Number 82, rue Sadi Carnot. The owners had fled, leaving the house in the care of their servants, three sisters who slept in the cellar. The bedrooms were spacious and the palatial bathroom well stocked with bath salts. The only drawback was that there was no light or hot water. Gas and electricity were both supplied from Lille, and Lille was in the hands of the Germans.

Before they had been there long, they were waited on by a French priest and an English Roman Catholic chaplain. Might the two officers consider moving to another house in the same street? It was in every way comparable – indeed it enjoyed the advantage of a supply of hot water from the kitchen range. They would be able to sleep in the security of the cellar, they would have the services of the same maids . . . Reith didn't really see the point. He was entirely comfortable where he was. The priests' attempts at inducement gave way to embarrassed explanation. The matter was delicate. It went without saying that no reflection was intended, but the fact was that one of the servant girls was shortly to enter a convent. *Alors, vous comprenez* . . . Reith, who was a considerable innocent, did not, as it happened, begin to understand, but he and his brother officer did agree to move the short distance to No. 78. It was perhaps as well for the two priests that it was several years before Reith grasped what it was they had actually been driving at.

The sector was quiet. There was time to exercise the section in the grounds of the asylum and to make his number with the Veterinary Officer, who found him a bay mare for his own use. They had joined the 19th Brigade, and found themselves alongside four other Battalions, including the 2nd Argyll and Sutherland Highlanders. To Reith's satisfaction, the chaplain to the Argylls conducted a Presbyterian service on Sunday morning: 'I thought of the services in the College Church at home and wished I could be there – but only provided I were back in Armentières by 5 p.m.'[10]

The proviso was because the Quartermaster of the 1st Cameronians had offered to take him up to the ration dump behind the front line. Once there, he asked if he might go into their trench. It was all very snug – two oil lamps, a couple of tables, a bookshelf, a coal fire. The Germans were just eighty yards away. He was warmly received, plied with refreshments, sent on his way with three packets of chocolate. Come again, said the CO. Any time. They could probably arrange to have a German for him to shoot:

> I was glad to feel no fright when crossing the exposed ground. Matter of nerves or temperament or both; no question of being brave or not brave. Some men are lucky, others unlucky, in their make-up . . . Interesting to walk across a turnip field knowing that at any moment one will stop walking for the most conclusive of reasons.[11]

What pleased him most about the evening's outing, however, was that he had chalked up a 'first': 'as the 5th were I believe the first Territorials to get to the front line from Scotland, it appears that I was the first Scottish Territorial to visit the actual trenches . . .'[12]

There were other causes for satisfaction. He discovered that in the Army Service Corps and the other Battalions officers' letters were not read, so he decided that he would become his own censor and stamp his own letters. If Major Kennedy suddenly had less to read, Reith had plans for Charlie to have a good deal more. He discovered that a chaplain called Webb-Peploe was going to London on leave, and persuaded him to carry his diary with him. 'I am near the end of volume 5 anyhow. So Charlie will see all we have been doing.'[13]

One item of incoming mail caused him some perplexity. A parcel arrived from the Hanmers, and inside was a photograph of Dora: 'I was horrified at the thought of being killed with a girl's photograph in my possession.' He sought counsel from one of his NCOs, an ex-shipping clerk called Whitelaw, but Whitelaw didn't see the problem, declaring that he would be happy for such a picture to be found on him – dead or alive. There was only one solution and it was not a particularly gallant one: 'After due deliberation, I burned it.'[14] There were, however, two photographs which he carried with him throughout his time at the front and which remained in his scrapbooks till the day he died – one was of his father, the other of Charlie.

There was nothing in the least furtive about his friendship with Charlie. He wrote to his mother in the middle of December reminding her that it was Charlie's birthday the following weekend, and he sent Mr Bowser a cheque for £3, asking him to buy him a pair of cuff-links. He also raised with the Adjutant and the CO the possibility of getting Charlie into the Battalion. The scheme came to nothing, and there is a confused passage in a letter to his father in which Reith described his mixed feelings:

> Charlie could have received the offer of a commission in the Battalion with a view to joining here almost immediately, but for some unaccountable reason the doctor there . . . said he wasn't fit for the mental and physical strain at

the front. I must say that, on the whole I am glad, because, had he been here, I should have been frightfully anxious about him – but I felt it my duty to give him the chance and he appreciated it at its true worth.[15]

Although he had liberated himself from the constraints of censorship, he was scrupulous about security and never mentioned his whereabouts. He had, however, devised a code, which involved putting dots under certain letters, and by reference to an atlas his parents and Charlie had been able to work out that he was in Armentières.[16] He was a demanding correspondent. 'I am not getting quite so many letters from you as I would like,' he wrote to his mother a week before Christmas. He went on to tell her of an experience he had had the day before when he had gone to get his hair cut:

> In the middle of the proceedings a shell landed on a house on the opposite side of the street. The man didn't wait for a second one, but with a frightened cry of 'Obus' he made headlong for the 'cave' or cellar which nearly all houses here seem to have. I couldn't get the job finished at any price, so just had to walk off with my hair half cut.[17]

This was not the only way in which his appearance was calculated to attract attention. When he had worked at the Albert Dock, he had worn a pair of rubber boots which were fitted with hobnailed leather soles. He now sent for these and had his spurs attached to them in such a way that he could get the boots on and off without removing the spurs. It was an arrangement he described as 'pleasing, if unmilitary', and he went about in them all day long – except on Sunday. He also occasionally sported an outsize umbrella which he bought in Bailleul and which he carried back with him into civilian life.

There was little news at the front, but any amount of rumour. That Lord Roberts had died at St Omer – true. That the Germans were about to pull out so as to have more men available for the eastern front – false. That the Battalion was to be inspected by the King and the Prince of Wales – true. The troops were given new glengarries and marched to a village about three miles back. The pipes were playing 'The Green Hills of Tyrone', and Reith found it all most thrilling. The King was in uniform and was wearing a British warm overcoat. 'He had nothing to say to us,' Reith noted, 'but he looked sympathetic and worried':

> I may have imagined a lot, but the look he gave as we shook hands seemed to convey this: 'I've nothing to say to you. I can't find words to say what I feel. It's awful that you should be lifted from your ordinary job of work and have to undergo such hardship and danger here. And you may be killed – considering the length I've got to look up to you you'll probably catch it in the head. I represent what you're fighting for. In a sense you're doing it for me. Good luck to you and a safe return home.'[18]

Later that month he was in Bailleul to see an army dentist. At lunch in a hotel afterwards, someone pointed out an officer in the 13th Hussars who was sitting at another table. ' "Whatever is *he* doing here, and in khaki?" I could not answer either question; had never seen the man before. I could not know that a quarter of a century later my fate was to rest in his hands. Winston Churchill.'[19]

Reith's skills at foraging were developing all the time, and he was becoming an expert 'liberator' of things that looked as if they might be more useful to him than to their owners. He was also beginning to display a tendency to recklessness. On the exposed side of Houplines he had noticed a huge stack of straw, something the men were badly in need of for sleeping on:

> As it got dusk I took two wagons up under cover of an empty house where a fatigue party were waiting with a sergeant. TW wasn't very keen on driving his wagon on the exposed ground so I went up on the high box myself and had the men walk under shelter of the wagon. I galloped the horses round the stack to get turned. It was fine stuff. As I was standing on the box with the reins in my hand a bullet went by, about a foot from my head it seemed . . .[20]

In mid-December 1914 Armentières was heavily shelled. The Transport section was unscathed – no injury to horses or men, no damage to vehicles. Picking his way past the shell-holes the next day, Reith marvelled at their escape. The words of the 91st Psalm ran in his mind, and an imperfectly remembered text from Hebrews: 'There remaineth, therefore, A Sabbath rest to the people of God.' He made a sombre note in his diary: 'Beginning to feel very deeply the responsibility of the lives of the men under me – at least not the lives but the souls.'[21]

Reith felt that he had done less well than most in the matter of mail from home – the other officers all seemed to have many more female friends. Shortly before Christmas, however, he received eight parcels by the same post. The one from the manse contained a Christmas bun, two boxes of toffee, two of butterscotch, a packet of ginger biscuits and a calendar. From Gresham's there came a mechanical lighter, a letter signed by four masters and six boys and the promise of a tuck box in the New Year. A Miss Miller (he had no idea who she was) sent him two boxes of chocolates. Charlie sent him so many goodies that they had to go in more than one parcel – a tin of biscuits, a tin of cakes, some soap, some Edinburgh rock and a box of chocolates. 'Charlie's parcels quite affected me,' he wrote, 'and I didn't like to throw away the wrappings.'[22]

On 23 December snow fell, and on Christmas Day, preferring the company of his Transport 'staff' to that of his brother officers, Reith entertained them to dinner in the cellar of his billet. The maids dressed up for the occasion. They produced not only white tablecloths and plate but also four enormous silver candelabra, each of which held four candles. There was roast chicken, preserved fruit, chocolate creams and ginger. There were also six bottles of champagne, which one of the corporals had acquired in Bailleul on Christmas Eve. ('I didn't take any of course,' Reith wrote in his diary.)

This festive breach of King's Regulations went on into the small hours. The party broke up only when an orderly arrived with news that the Battalion was to be relieved by the Queen's Westminsters at 6 a.m. As he rode back out of the line Reith discovered that strange stories were circulating. His dinner party had not been a unique act of fraternisation. The day before, out in No Man's Land, German and British troops had celebrated the birth of Christ by playing football against each other.

As the year drew to a close, Reith sank into a fit of depression. It was exactly a year since he and Charlie had been on holiday in Perthshire, and he was missing him very much. Years later, when he was summarising his diary, he wrote, 'How infinitely happier I should have been with no affection like this pulling at me all the time.' Various dinner parties were held, but he received no invitations. He had seen to it that his men in Transport would be able to welcome the New Year in style, but he was in a brooding and jealous frame of mind and in no mood to celebrate:

Largely C. and the memories of Comrie this time last year were responsible. He is to spend the weekend with two of his schoolfellows. I don't like this.[23]

In the first eleven days of the New Year he received only one letter and one postcard from Charlie and that did little to ease his despondency. Then, on 13 January, the clouds lifted: 'Letter from C. at last and a magnificent one. I was tremendously delighted and wrote him at great length. I feel very responsible for him.'[24] His spirits were also raised by the appearance of a new chaplain. His name was Matheson. White-haired and well into his fifties, he was the Minister of the United Free church at Galashiels in the Scottish Border country. 'I think he will do very well,' Reith noted. 'I told him I was enjoying the war except for Croft, and being away from my friend.'[25]

Croft was the Adjutant, and Adjutants do not in general take kindly to headstrong and freebooting junior officers. Quite apart from Reith's stand-offishness in the Mess, it is likely that something had come to the Adjutant's ears of his Transport Officer's free and easy ways with his men – he was, for instance, in the habit of having the NCOs in turn to dine and sleep and take a hot bath in his billet in the rue Sadi Carnot, although he must have known well enough that authority would regard such an arrangement as 'prejudicial to good order and discipline'.

His first brush with Croft was in early January. The CO of the 5th SR had been persuaded that they should give up some large and rather superior sheds which they were using as stables. The Adjutant was away, and so was Reith (he had gone off to have a bath in his old billet) but the minute he returned he shot in to the orderly room and subjected the CO to a brisk interrogation:

'Did you get this from Brigade, sir?' No, it was an officer of the Rifle Brigade who had told him. What rank? A captain he thought. I said it was their

Transport Officer and that I didn't think we ought to move a horse or a man unless Brigade said so. 'Will you leave things to me, sir?' He looked at me and a faint smile came to his eyes. I always felt I might have got on with the colonel. 'Carry on, Reith,' he said.[26]

It was true that Reith's men had been in possession of the sheds only since the previous day; it was also true that their acquisition of them had been entirely irregular. Reith did not feel that need concern the Rifle Brigade captain. He found him sitting on a fence outside and quickly faced him down. Unless he produced written authority from Brigade, he could take his column elsewhere. The captain rode off, threatening 'to get the general', but the general never came. That evening, another officer told the story to the Adjutant:

'Have you heard how John Reith refused to budge when the Rifle Brigade tried to collar his billets?' The little adjutant snorted. 'Aren't you proud of your Transport Officer?' Campbell asked. 'Reith's job is to obey orders,' he snapped. Whose orders, anyhow? Nasty little man.[27]

A week later there was a more serious clash. Reith was once again soaking in a bath in the rue Sadi Carnot when an orderly pushed an envelope under the door. It was from the Adjutant. The CO had been round the Transport quarters and found two horses not groomed. An explanation was required. This put Reith into a great rage, and the account he wrote of the incident years later is highly entertaining – 'I lay back in the bath and sang loudly selections from the more vituperative of the Psalms of David:

O Lord my God, in thee do I
My confidence repose:
Save and deliver me from all
My persecuting foes;
He made a pit, and digg'd it deep,
Another there to take;
But he is fall'n into the ditch
Which he himself did make.[28]

Powerful stuff. A prayer of the virtuous under persecution. David pouring out his heart to Yahweh about Cush, the insufferable Benjaminite. Psalm No. 7 in the Scottish metrical version. Reith, however, in both his autobiographical volumes, was embroidering after the event. His diary entry for 16 January puts a different complexion on the matter: 'Sang 23rd Psalm which put me in better spirits.' There is nothing remotely vituperative about the Psalm of the Good Shepherd. Reith was certainly angry, but he was also hurt and upset. He got out of the bath, established the facts of the matter and wrote a reply to the Adjutant: 'It was a bit of a snorter, but my indignation had abated.'

The 23rd Psalm figured in another diary entry two days later, because Reith discovered that his batman did not know it off by heart. Tudhope was sent off to attend to this chink in his spiritual armour and instructed to come back that night and recite it – in the Scottish metrical version, naturally. In his own religious observance Reith was punctilious. He read his Bible every evening, and night and morning read a small devotional book called *Daily Light* which he had had from his mother when he was small. There is a wistful passage in a letter he wrote to his mother about this time: 'I am very strong in the observance of Sabbath. I would like the old Highland sabbaths to come back again, and perhaps they will.'[29]

He had been anxious about Charlie's health, but letters he had in the middle of January reassured him. They were writing to each other almost every day. Charlie had received the latest instalment of the diary safely, and had sent Reith a fine copy of *In Memoriam*: 'I was delighted with what he had written inside it,' Reith wrote in his diary; in return he sent Charlie a clip of German cartridges.

Reith was walking back from Armentières through a blizzard one Monday morning when a cyclist orderly rode up. He was instructed by the Adjutant to report at once to Brigade HQ. Reith relieved the orderly of his bicycle and bumped away through the snow over the stone setts. He had assumed that anything to do with the Adjutant was bad news, but he was wrong. The Brigade Transport Officer was going on leave, and the General wanted Reith to act in his place. 'This was tremendous,' Reith wrote. 'I wished he would stay on leave and never come back.' Characteristically, although he was only to be in the job for ten days, he began to stir things up:

With the cordial approval of the Staff captain I had pack ponies, carts and wagons of every sort not on duty, and spare horses, taken out for exercising route marches, though some of the Quartermasters did not approve of this sudden activity in their units . . . As Transport Officer to the 19th Brigade I began to think I was of some importance to the war.[30]

On his second day in the job he fell ill, and he observed wryly that being a teetotaller had its disadvantages. The light beer sold in the *estaminets* was quite safe; the drinking water was not. It was a bad bout of dysentery. The castor oil and No. 9 pills which the medical officer gave him had no effect and his condition was aggravated by long hours in the saddle. He soon became very weak, but he was mulishly determined to hang on to his precious Brigade job and would not go on the sick list. Eventually the MO ordered him to bed, but even then, with the connivance of his faithful NCOs, he played a mad game of going to Brigade each day, making sure he was back in bed each evening in time for the doctor's visit.

At night he was consumed with thirst, and dreamed feverish dreams – that he had sent Tudhope upstairs to ask his mother to come down to him; that he was bathing in a beautiful clear river with Charlie.[31] Eventually some new medicine was prescribed and began to have an effect. The padre was already in on his secret, and now Reith owned up to the MO. 'Damnation to you,' he said. 'That accounts for your high temperature every night which puzzled me so much.'[32]

Some nights later, during a local attack, the half-battalion and Transport were ordered out. The infantry companies merely had to get themselves into marching order; Reith's men had horses to harness and pit ponies to saddle with ammunition boxes. By his reckoning it would have been a creditable performance if they had paraded fifteen or twenty minutes after the companies; as it was, they were well ahead of them, and Reith was very pleased with himself. There was a brief lull in the gunfire, and as he moved forward towards the head of the column, he encountered the Adjutant: *'Where the devil have you been, Reith, and why isn't Transport out?'* Reith replied that he had been on parade for the last eight minutes, and when that elicited no response, his temper flared.

> 'You've no right to talk to me like that and accuse me of not being on the job at the right time in the middle of a battle.' With a savage jab of my long spur on the near flank and a push on her neck, I spun the mare round in her own length and shot off down the road in a shower of sparks. Well, that's that, I thought, wheeling into position again, and probably the end of me.[33]

They were stood down at about 10.15. Half an hour later, the Adjutant was shown into Reith's billet and said, 'I've come to apologise to you, Reith: I was in the wrong tonight.' Reith, normally too stiff-necked to offer apologies himself, was equally unschooled in how to receive them. 'I was completely taken aback,' he wrote in his memoirs. 'A man of the world would have said: "Very good of you, sir. Won't you sit down and let's have a talk." I was embarrassed; muttered incoherent thanks; lost control of the situation.'[34] It is plain from Reith's diary entry for the day that the Adjutant pressed home his advantage:

> Then he gave me a jaw about my temper, said I went hunting around for trouble, putting people's backs up, jumping down their throats. I took it all, because it must have been a struggle for him to come round, but he tried to get on his high horse once or twice, and I showed him I wasn't caring what happened, and he said he knew I didn't care.[35]

Early in February he got the chance of six days home leave. Reith, who retained throughout his life a childish pleasure in springing surprises, had originally intended to turn up at the manse unannounced. Just before leaving, however, he saw from the parish magazine which he received regularly from home that his father had a preaching engagement elsewhere that weekend. All thoughts of surprise were abandoned. Instead he sent a telegram announcing his arrival on Sunday morning – and asking his father whether he couldn't change his arrangements and preach at home instead.

He travelled with his brother Douglas, who was serving as a padre in Boulogne. There was a logistical problem – he had acquired a German drum and a German helmet for Charlie, and was doubtful whether he would get them through. There was also a moral dilemma to be resolved. When he left home, his mother had impressed on him the importance of wearing a body belt. No parcel from the manse was complete without one. Reith, finding them a penance to wear, had done so for only one day, but now, not wishing his homecoming to be clouded by deceit, he put one on. The crossing to Folkestone was rough. Reith, normally a good sailor, began to feel queasy:

> I was sure the tight body belt was responsible, so, borrowing an old-fashioned razor from my brother and proceeding to the bow of the ship, I opened up burberry, overcoat, tunic and shirt and slit off the offending, or at any rate suspected, article. I could (and did) tell my mother that I was wearing one when I went on board ship.[36]

The fact that he had burned Dora Hanmer's photograph some weeks earlier had not prevented him sending her a postcard to say that his leave train would pass through her local station at such-and-such a time. There she was on the platform with her sister, and Reith threw out an envelope containing some German shrapnel bullets. As the train approached London, his excitement grew, because he knew that Charlie would be there to meet him:

> Victoria. A great crowd behind the barriers. I got D. and all my gear and his into a taxi. Then I saw C. No word could convey the joyfulness of that meeting. He rushed to me and threw his arms around my neck and kissed me. Douglas said some days later that he was awfully impressed.[37]

The taxi took them to Charlie's house: 'Saw his father and mother and then up to our room.' Later the two friends took the tube to Piccadilly Circus and went to Lyons Corner House: 'Just like old times,' Reith wrote in his diary. 'I couldn't eat half as much as I wanted to, not being used to such repasts.'[38] He also noted disapprovingly 'the crowds of young men who should, one thought, be in uniform.' Charlie saw the brothers off on the midnight train from Euston. When they arrived in Lynedoch Street, Douglas got out of the taxi a little way from the house so that they might each have their separate entrance. 'Picture of my mother in the doorway as I mounted the steps. *Mater dilectissima*.'[39]

'An hour later,' he wrote in *Wearing Spurs*, 'one of childhood's silly (or splendid) fantasies came true – turning up at church from war; and to the ring of spur.' They were a little late and made what he described as 'a most dramatic entry' from the vestry door beside the manse pew. 'I knew everyone would be looking at us, but I didn't look up at all.' He went to church again in the evening. At the conclusion of the service, 'the organist thundered out *The Ride of the Valkyries* for me; it would put me in form for the duties and hazards to which I should have returned by the following Sunday.'[40]

He was at home for three crowded days. He fitted in several visits to the dentist – army biscuits had been hard on his fillings. He also paid innumerable visits to the homes of his NCOs and men – 'I could not regard my leave solely as a personal affair.' Being at home gave him an extraordinary sense of safety and security: 'Mother comes and tucks me up each night. I am beginning to realise that the last three and a half months must have been a bit of a strain.'[41]

Leaving the manse was harrowing: 'Father's face nearly made me cry. He looked so frail and sad and yet so very fine.' (Not that the pain of parting affected Reith's appetite: on the morning of his departure he made a hearty breakfast of fish roe.) Then, by his own choice, he set off alone for Glasgow Central Station. He had with him (he always would have when he travelled) an inordinate amount of gear – the families he had visited had laden him with enough parcels to fill an extra suitcase. His father had given him a volume of Whittier to read on the train and had written on the flyleaf some words from the 91st Psalm – 'He shall cover thee with his feathers.'

It was easier for him than for his parents. He was on his way back to a job that he loved, Adjutant or no Adjutant. And he was – briefly – on his way back to Charlie. The journey to Euston passed quickly. 'Met by C. and of course overjoyed to see him. To our room about 9 and lay in front of a huge fire.'

Charlie had to go to school the next day, but they met at Baker Street at 4.45 and 'wandered about in the old style'. The boat train, which had been due to leave at 7.50 the next morning, was postponed till the evening, so they had an extra day in each other's company. They went to be photographed together in a studio in the Edgware Road. Reith bought Charlie a knife and a pocket book and a jewel case for him to give to his sister – '£2-9-0 in all', he noted in his diary. They also visited Swaine and Adeney's, where Reith bought a riding switch for himself and a leather stick for Charlie. Then back to 'our room' in Highgate, where the detail of their time together had to be recorded:

> C. finished the diary for this day and that part stayed behind. His notes written after I left were very touching. We read the Bible together and had a prayer. He had been wearing my ring all day and he put it back on my hand and kissed it. I said I would never take it off till I saw him again. It was awful at Victoria.[42]

He had returned half expecting to be reprimanded. On mobilisation, officers had been required to grow a moustache. Reith had been rather pleased with his, which he thought of as 'Kaiserish' – quite unlike the stubby toothbrush affairs which seemed to be the norm. Before going on leave he had shaved it off, but the change in his appearance seemed to go unremarked. His men were delighted to see him. All that had happened of note in his absence was that the CO had got the CMG. Reith did not congratulate him. 'He has never seen a trench in daylight,' he wrote in his diary. 'It is sickening.'[43]

He was having trouble with his old mare. She had become difficult in traffic and was turning out, as one of his NCOs put it, to be a proper 'screw'. Reith determined that she must be replaced – but by a really good blood one. With one of his NCOs he rode off to the Division veterinary hospital:

> In a yard a dozen animals were tethered to a rope. They were not evenly spaced though their headropes were fixed at regular intervals; there was a crowding at both ends of the rope and in the centre was the cause of it. A bay mare with black points, 15.3 hands, ears flat back, was swinging round first to one side and then to the other, a flying kick each time. The other animals were giving her all the room they could. Whitelaw and I pulled up. 'That's the sort you want, sir.' Yes; it certainly was.[44]

The beast had come in for a rest. Its owner, a Royal Artillery staff captain, had gone home that day. Ten minutes later, Reith and Whitelaw left with the mare on a halter, bursting with excitement and riding hard in case the officer in charge had second thoughts. Their return to Transport caused a sensation. 'The Adjutant will be after her,' said one of his men. (Croft's own horse had recently gone lame.) Whitelaw said that she was very like a mare called Sailaway which had won the Ayr Gold Cup the previous year, and that became her name. For a time she rated almost as many mentions in Reith's diary as Charlie.

The question of what he would do after the war preoccupied him greatly. He felt that he would very much like to go to Oxford, and wrote a sixteen-page letter to his father on the subject. The text does not survive but, from his account of it in the diary, he does not appear to have marshalled his arguments all that coherently:

> I said I was desperately anxious to make money and was probably on a fair way to doing so. At the same time I didn't think that would be doing full justice to myself because I believe God has given me intellect which is an exceedingly rare and precious gift – quite different from brains. I don't feel that I'm going to get the chance to use my intellect to any real advantage if I stay in the same line as I'm in now. I want to go to Oxford and I'm sure I should take an Honours degree – philosophy and literature, and then politics. It is a matter for serious and earnest prayer.[45]

Dr Reith had his letter within three days and replied by return, cautioning him that Parliamentary life was not the desirable thing he seemed to think it: 'a talk with some of the men already in the House might surprise you.' He went on to contest the claims Reith made for the intellectual life:

> You wish, of course, to make the most of your abilities; but I don't fancy that your intellect can't be developed in Pearson's. The work is a big enterprise, and you will find scope in it for the best brains you have got. And even were it rather monotonous, you can in your leisure hours get through a systematic course of reading. Remember what Carlyle said, (and he ought to know,) *that the best University is a good library* . . . The best thing a university

can do for a fellow is to give him fellowship with other young fellows. You
can get everything else from Books, and the standard authors can be had
for a trifle.[46]

This was not at all the sort of advice Reith wished to hear, particularly as it
ended with a reminder of the Biblical warning that 'before honour is humility'.
He dashed off a lengthy and indignant reply. He *had* spoken with men in the
House. It was not that he saw glamour in the prospect of a political career:
'Ever so many elements will be most revolting – as for instance the necessity
for "keeping in" with one's constituents and voting on some occasions as the
party whip ordains.' He still for all that saw his duty plainly marked.

It is a remarkable letter – the words come tumbling out onto the page in a
sustained cry of frustration and exasperation at what he saw as his father's
inability to understand him:

Can you not tell the difference between brains and intellect? Intellect can
never, *never* be nourished in any engineering concern. Every single element
is prejudicial to its growth. Intellect is for those who study the works of
philosophers and historians and economists, and who read other forms of
literature, for orators, and men who can control vast audiences by a look or
a gesture or a word – that's intellect – not your ill-educated rude mechanics
who argue about the size of a screw – the pettiness of the whole thing is not
only distasteful but utterly revolting to anyone constituted as I am, because
I would a thousand times rather see a sunset than the most wonderful piece
of engineering in the world.[47]

It was Easter. Reith's evangelical efforts had not been directed solely to his
batman. He had also urged his NCOs to read their Bibles. 'Funny business,'
Reith mused. 'They added it to routine duties like cleaning their spurs.'[48] Now
came further cause for satisfaction. The men under him – there were about
fifty-five of them – were all nominally Presbyterians, but only nine were church
members. Reith had worked on them ('delicately', he said), and on the morning
of Good Friday, with a British battery thudding overhead, the chaplain conducted a service of admission for twenty-two of them.

It took place in the tap room of a deserted *estaminet,* and so did Holy
Communion on Easter morning, bottles serving as silver flagons and tumblers
as chalices. Reith wrote that he was profoundly grateful that he had been able
to influence so many. He entered them all in a sort of roll of honour – that
evening in his diary and again, many years later, in *Wearing Spurs*: 'Their names
may be of little interest now, and most of them have gone, but it pleases me
to record them.'[49] He wrote to his father telling him all about it, and also to
Charlie – his forty-second letter to him from the front.[50]

Something else that Reith wrote that weekend had unforeseen and disagreeable consequences. The Army Service Corps farrier-sergeant attached to his
section had never fitted in with Reith's tightly knit *mafia* of NCOs. He now

sent a request to the OC of the Brigade train that the man should be replaced by someone who was both younger and more amenable, and a new farrier-corporal duly arrived. Not for the first time, however, Reith had failed to do things by the book: 'Croft the cad got nasty about Pierce's transfer and I sent him a three word reply. It hadn't occurred to me to consult or report to our orderly room about him as he was an ASC man.'[51]

Reith was in the wrong. He had always dealt with the Service Corps direct in the matter of horses and wagons, but men were different. Sergeant Pierce, although an ASC man, had been on the Battalion's nominal roll. When Reith was summoned to the orderly room by the Adjutant to amplify his unwisely economical reply, he misjudged the situation disastrously. As the CO was not present, he did not think it was a formal occasion and lowered himself into an armchair. 'Don't you realise I'm givin' you a tellin' off?' snapped the Adjutant. 'Stand up, will you?' Reith complied, but the increase of elevation did nothing to improve the performance of his antennae. He conceded later that he should simply have apologised, but that was beyond him:

> I said I would give him no explanation and asked to see the CO. Of course I knew – or might have known – that this was useless – Douglas being a contemptible puppet in his hands. He immediately threatened me with losing the Transport and going back to the Companies. This infuriated me and was certainly damnably unjust. Was it a privilege to be in charge of Transport? I had done my work excellently throughout. Why should I have a threat like that? And what actual power had he to make it? He wasn't CO.[52]

Entirely predictably, he got no change out of the CO, 'who merely stuttered out that I was "returned for duty"'. That day's orders announced his return to A Company, and at 5 p.m. he handed over as Transport Officer to his successor, a Lieutenant Struthers, 'a new officer who came with the draft, and who as far as I had seen was a harmless, rather feeble creature'.[53]

Reith's immediate concern was to prevent Sailaway from falling into the clutches of the Adjutant. Immediately after his interview with the CO he had written a note to the Divisional Veterinary Officer, telling him he intended to apply for a transfer to the Royal Engineers and asking if he would care for the horse until he could claim her. While he waited for an answer (he had no great hopes it would be the one he wanted to hear) he rode out on the mare, taking roads that not even he would normally attempt on horseback in daylight: 'If I had been caught by a sniper,' he wrote melodramatically in *Wearing Spurs*, 'it would have been an easy ending; but everything was quiet.' In fact the vet came up trumps. He accepted Sailaway as a sick horse the next morning and even found an ex-jockey to look after her.

The next morning, with the permission of his successor, he paraded his men to say goodbye. He thanked them for their good work, and one of the sergeants called for three cheers for him. Half of the men were close to tears, and so was Reith. He wished them good luck and walked off leaving them standing stiffly to attention: 'It was all that I could trust myself to say. I supposed that somebody would dismiss them.'[54] His batman, Tudhope, pleaded to be allowed to go with him to the Company: 'I didn't want him to do so on account of the rougher conditions and rougher fellows he would be with. When I told him I didn't want to take him tears came to his eyes, so of course I said I would. It was awfully nice of him.'[55]

The officers of A Company greeted him sympathetically, but their quarters were not at all what he was used to – a single room on the first floor of an *estaminet*. The *estaminet*, moreover, was still open for business ('the kitchen', Reith noted with disgust in his diary, 'is always full of French people'). He found himself sleeping on his valise on the floor with five other officers. He spent a miserable and restless night and dreamt about his horses.[56] His mood was not improved by the discovery that he was to have charge of a platoon; by virtue of his seniority he was second-in-command of the company, and had assumed that this would relieve him of such chores. It took a lot to put Reith off his food, but the next day he ate neither breakfast nor lunch. 'I shall certainly not be very careful of my life in the trenches,' he wrote in his diary, 'and shall volunteer for any dirty work that is going.'[57]

Because it was Sunday there was little to do. Unwisely, but entirely character-istically, he went back to Transport and discovered that they were being shifted out of their superior quarters, his successor having apparently agreed to go without even having seen what they were moving to. 'This would never have happened if I had been there,' he wrote that night – a refrain that was to become tiresomely familiar to many people who encountered John Reith in the course of his long life.[58]

His appeal to Brigade was a fiasco. Reith had given no thought to the tactics of such an occasion. The General was friendly and said all manner of complimentary things, but there it was – his Commanding Officer had taken the view that he must revert to company duties and that was not a decision it would be proper for him to overturn. When asked if there was anything more he wished to say, Reith said practically nothing. Afterwards he was both furious with himself for his feeble performance and baffled by it; perhaps he had been thrown by the General's friendliness; perhaps he should have told him what they all thought about Croft. Many years later he could still not understand why he had 'made such a miserable show'.

The incident is interesting because of the light it sheds on Reith's attitude to authority. For all his arrogance and impatience, there was a strongly conform-ist strand in his make-up. He would not defer to the likes of his Commanding Officer and the Adjutant because he did not respect them; but there were a number of occasions in his life – they were rare – when it was almost as if the recognition of true authority reduced him to something approaching helpless-ness. He had faced his headmaster at Gresham's and been unable to articulate his true reasons for not attending the Sunday concerts. He had stood before his father at the end of his schooldays and had not found arguments to save himself from an engineering apprenticeship. Now he stood stiff-backed before a kindly Brigadier-General and once again the right words did not come. The interview was plainly at an end. The CO and the Adjutant saluted and turned about. Reith hesitated briefly and then did the same. Brigade HQ was about half a mile distant from the quarters of the 5th SR: 'I walked about 3 yards behind Douglas and Croft all the way back to the Battalion billets – vastly to their embarrassment. The dirty little swine.'[59]

After lunch he went to visit Transport in their appalling new quarters, and in a day that had been full of bitterness there came a moment that was sweet to savour. That morning, his successor had had a note from the Adjutant asking for Sailaway to be sent round to his quarters. Lieutenant Struthers had been obliged to reply that the mare was nowhere to be found.

He was plunged immediately into his first spell of trench duty. He decided that if the first day was anything to go by, it was going to be an appallingly dull existence – 'sleeping and eating and standing about, and all more or less in a ditch'. He observed that the nerves of his fellow-subalterns were good, but formed the impression that they expected his to be less so. This called for a demonstration of some sort, and he set about providing one. He was later to describe his performance as both 'artificial and reckless', and it got him into trouble with the Major:

> He asked if it were true that I had walked along the whole line in front of the sapheads. Yes. He said it was needless exposure, and while he was at it the same applied to the way I went about by day with my head exposed. 'Are you wanting to get killed to spite the Adjutant?' 'No,' I replied, 'I'm not *wanting* to get killed. I don't much mind if I do. But I think I would like to kill him first. Am I likely to get the chance?' He looked at me in mingled sorrow and horror. 'I wouldn't put it past you, Reith.'[60]

The post brought news that his father, indignant at the treatment he had received, had written to the Colonel, and the next day he was summoned to the orderly room. 'I have had a letter from Dr Reith about the circumstances of your leaving Transport. You may tell your father that I have received it, but that I cannot answer it.' It was not the wisest thing the unworldly Doctor had ever done, and his unbending son did little to mend matters by the tone of his reply: 'My father is not accustomed to having messages of that sort, sir. I shall not give it.'[61]

He slept as if drugged, struggling on waking to remember where he was. One morning, when he had slept through two hours of particularly heavy shelling, the men thought it best to rouse him. Most unwillingly, Reith stirred himself to face the day, shouting for Tudhope, and word of his imperturbability went the rounds: 'Called for his shaving water, he did, in the middle of a ruddy shelling.'[62] He took no interest in such things as extended order drill, but he treated his platoon with much the same pastoral indulgence as he had shown to his men in Transport. He put them on their honour in the matter of letters home and handed over the censor's stamp to the Sergeant.

He himself wrote endlessly. The two-way stream of letters between himself and Charlie continued unabated, and every detail of the correspondence was meticulously recorded. Shortly after going into the trenches he noted that he had received his forty-second letter from Charlie and written number 56 to him.[63] His eagerness to receive letters did not, however, submerge his native thrift: 'On my suggestion C. often sends his letters without stamps and I never have anything to pay.'[64]

A savage little diary entry for 21 April showed that so far as his feelings for his superiors were concerned, he was still nursing his wrath to keep it warm: 'Our gallant CO (CMG and a mention for distinguished conduct in the field, forsooth) paid his first visit to a trench by daylight. I kept clear of him though I should like to have held him up on the parapet.' Reith knew well enough, for all that, that his attitude to the Colonel and to Croft did not reflect well on him. The following Sunday there was a church service in the old school billet: 'Communion afterwards, for which I naturally did not wait with feelings to others as they are.'[65]

He had heard that the 1st London Field Company of the Royal Engineers had recently arrived in Armentières. On his second spell out of trenches he took tea with his old Transport NCOs, borrowed a bicycle from them, and soon tracked the Sappers down near his old billet in the rue Sadi Carnot. He had not yet applied to be transferred to the RE; the sapper officers were friendly, entertained him to supper and offered him sound advice about how he should proceed. The Commanding Royal Engineer of the Division was equally friendly when he saw him the next day. Reith came clean about his difficulties with the Battalion and emphasised that he did not wish to be sent home to a depot but was eager to be transferred in the field.

Meanwhile he busied himself with work in the trenches. One of his first initiatives had been to go out one night with one of his men and rig up a telephone connection between the A Company officer's dug-out and HQ. When there were digging jobs to be done he took his turn with pick and shovel. The trenches all had names. He was particularly proud of the work they did on Shaftesbury Avenue. It was ten feet deep and wide enough to let three men walk abreast; at the entrance there were six palm trees in tubs.

Early in May there was increased activity on the German side. There were reports that the wire had been cut, and this was taken to presage an attack. Reith went out and lay beyond the sapheads and satisfied himself that at least on their immediate front the wire was intact. There were also rumours that the Germans were contemplating the use of gas, and the wagons brought up supplies of primitive gas masks and quantities of bicarbonate of soda. Reith and some of the other bolder spirits wanted to patrol up to the enemy lines to see what was going on, but the Major said no. 'Wrote C. giving him full instructions as to what to do with all my stuff in case I was killed,' Reith wrote in his diary.[66] The next day there came a parcel from home that gave him particular pleasure. His mother had sent twenty-two khaki-bound New Testaments – one for each of the Transport men who had joined the Church at Easter. Reith wrote their names on the flyleaf, adding 'Easter Sunday 1915 JCWR'.

He fell ill again. He had a temperature of 102° and was ordered to bed. Reith resisted attempts to send him to the Field Ambulance. Tudhope discovered an empty room with a bedstead in it on another floor of the *estaminet*. Reith considered, but only very briefly, offering it to the Major and then moved in. The MO thought there might be an element of the psychosomatic in his illness: 'although I did not see how this could be I thought it a nice idea.'[67] He was allowed up for an evening to go for a further satisfactory interview with the Commanding Royal Engineer of VI Division: 'I thought this an answer to prayer,' he wrote in his diary. He spent time reading the Psalms (which he found helpful), and made a start on the *Manual of Military Engineering* (which he found rather heavy-going).

Towards the end of the month he was off the sick list and back in the trenches, increasingly impatient at hearing nothing further from the Sappers. His company commander, he wrote complainingly, 'has repeatedly declined to let me go out to do some stunt or other'.[68] He managed, for all that, to get out on the wire a good deal:

> One night visiting a saphead post I found the lance-corporal and his companion fast asleep. This was of course a heinous crime though one could not but admire the mentality of men who found saphead duty, with nothing between them and the Germans, so boring that they fell asleep over it. I sat beside them till they woke up.[69]

On Sunday afternoons he was in the habit of going off by himself to be alone with his thoughts. His thoughts about his superiors continued to be profoundly un-Christian, and it is plain from a passage in *Wearing Spurs* that his feud with them had become something of an indulgence:

> If I could convince myself that the Christian and strongest course would be for me to forgive the blasted CO and Adjutant, or anyhow no longer to cherish feelings of such animosity, I might perhaps bring myself to it. But I could not so convince myself; possibly did not want to. Life was dull now and a vendetta of this sort brightened things up a little – even though so one-sided in its results, all the tyrannical power being with them.[70]

In the early evening of 16 June, while Reith was sitting writing in the HQ dug-out, there was very heavy shelling. He counted forty-five shells in as many minutes. The first of them went into the parapet immediately behind the dug-out: 'I was pleased to find that my hand hadn't moved off the word I was writing,' he noted rather smugly in his diary. A little later, they had a visitor:

Croft, the worm, was up about evening stand-to time. He was blowing off about advanced posts and wire and such like and of course he had never been out in front. I hadn't gone out of the dug-out as I normally did when he came in so I said, 'Wouldn't you like to go out in front, Captain Croft?' There was a little pause and much tension in the dug-out before he replied in a very odd but cocky way, 'I should love to.'

Reith led the way along the trench to the entrance of the nearest sap – a shallow trench which extended forward for about twenty-five yards and passed under the main wire. The gap in the parapet was blocked by a *cheval de frise* – a movable entanglement of barbed wire. Reith pointed to it and said to the Adjutant, 'That is one way of getting into the sap. We usually go this way,' and getting up onto the parapet he stood there full height. Captain Croft said he preferred to go 'the proper way' and crawled forward to take a quick look at the saphead, Reith walking foolhardily beside him over the open ground. His diary entry reads like a parody of a soliloquy from a Jacobean revenge tragedy: 'How very amusing and appropriate it would have been if he'd been sniped while out with me. I should have been nicely avenged thus.'[71]

Reith's own letters for this period do not survive, but he clearly banged on endlessly about his superiors when writing to his parents; so much so that his father eventually wrote to him in terms of gentle reproof:

If you will be advised by me you will cease to fulminate where you are against the Colonel and the Adjutant. I don't mind your letting your soul out to me; but it would be wiser, and more gentlemanly in truth, to keep quiet among your colleagues. Let them speak, but be you silent. They really are not worth your powder and shot. If you want to preserve your dignity, say as little as possible ... Do your duty and bear slights.[72]

More than thirty years later, when writing his memoirs, Reith admitted soberly that he had perhaps been luckier than he deserved on that summer night in 1915. He was also prepared to take a more generous view of the Adjutant:

He had behaved entirely properly and sensibly; by the end of the war he had the DSO with three bars.

And he has read this story; says it confirms his view at the time that I suffered from an overweening sense of my own importance; and that I had little idea of team spirit and discipline if it did not suit me. Perhaps he is right.[73]

When he was in his forties, Reith used to grumble about the demands made upon him by public life. There was, he would say, so much he wanted to write about. It is the greatest of pities that he was never able to tear himself away from his interminable communings with himself in his diary and grapple with those larger literary ambitions. He could write with powerful economy. He might be a law unto himself in the matter of punctuation; the urgently tele-graphic style, with its occasional one-word sentences and sparing use of main verbs, was certainly idiosyncratic, but it gave him a secure hold on the reader's attention. He had a sharp eye, a good ear, and a sardonic turn of mind; his two volumes of autobiography are full of vivid and entertaining cameos:

> Among the transport men was a middle-aged individual who pre-war had plied for hire in a hansom cab on the Glasgow streets . . . In token of his extreme thinness he was known as Shadow. One evening I came on him driving his wagon, not from the driver's seat but from the footboard. When there was much sniping this was a natural thing to do. 'Have they been shooting at you, Shadow?' He hauled in his pair, leant over to me, terror in his eyes; a sepulchral whisper: 'No, surr, no' the nicht. But Ah've got a *corrp* in the cairrt ahint me.' A blanket shrouded form lay on the floorboards; he was as far from it as possible.[74]

Reith had now been waiting for his transfer to the Engineers for more than two months. His platoon sergeant managed to allay some of his impatience by finding him a new billet in the house of the village schoolmistress – a sitting room and bedroom, sheets on the bed, vases of carnations and sweet peas from the half-acre garden. These agreeable surroundings prompted an access of sociability in Reith. To their considerable surprise, his brother officers found themselves bidden to lunch. They were offered tomato soup, chicken, ham and tongue mousse, peas, new potatoes, salad, mayonnaise, a chocolate shape, ices, cherries and coffee; as they ate, three pipers played in the garden.

Their host's dress on these occasions was not always entirely orthodox. He had asked his mother to send him some rather lighter khaki shirts for summer wear. And light they turned out to be, in colour as well as in weight – almost yellow, in fact. 'Don't let the Adjutant catch you in that,' said the Major, but Reith found them 'very swagger'. He applied the same term to another garment he was very fond of wearing about the billet and in trenches – a London Scottish rugby foot-ball shirt, dark blue with a red lion rampant. A paragraph appeared in Battalion orders: officers' shirts must be of regulation pattern and colour.

It was high summer: 'Corn ripening where no man might scythe it except in peril of that other scythe.' They were pulled back nine miles to rest. The men had to bivouac in fields and the A Company officers found two bare rooms in a farmhouse. The water carts had not arrived. The other officers had supplies of beer, but Reith went to the pump in the farmyard. *Eau potable? Oui, monsieur.* He drank deeply and filled his water bottle, but in the morning it was plain that he had once more paid the price for that pledge he had made in the Band of Hope all those years before. The water from the pump had been percolated through the dung heap in the farmyard, and the following day Reith was put on a stretcher and taken to a local Field Ambulance.

When he was moved on to the casualty clearing station at Merville the senior

Medical Officer told him he was lucky it was only dysentery: it could have been typhoid. He was sent down-country in a hospital train – putting his spurs on for the journey, naturally. He spent a week at a convalescent hospital near Dieppe, a palatial hotel on the edge of the cliffs. He went to bed at eight each night, made small excursions to buy postcards and chocolate, strode along the beach: 'I sang Psalms loudly, which I hadn't been able to do for months.' He was making a rapid recovery. Blood tests were pronounced satisfactory, and he was told that subject only to a test of 'the stool' he would be shipped home to England: 'I'm tremendously excited at the prospect of surprising first C. in London and then dear old father and mother.'[75]

There was very nearly a hitch. Reith did not know what a stool test was and had to ask. The instructions were very simple – 'don't pull the plug in the morning' – but he forgot about them:

> I did not want to be held up for another week, and I was sure there was nothing wrong. Another officer came along the corridor – a wound case and therefore quite safe. I explained my predicament and asked him not to pull the plug, remaining nearby to see that he did not. In due course I reported that in *cabinet numéro dix* would be found what was required.[76]

From Victoria he took a taxi straight to Charlie's house: 'I was in a tremendous state of expectation. His surprise and his reception of me were wonderful.' They spent the whole of the next day clearing things out in Charlie's room. Then, Reith having put on his uniform at his friend's request, they dined at the Trocadero: 'I thought it was a magnificent dinner, but I was in a frightful stew going down Piccadilly at the crowds of civilians and the officers swanking about. It all irritated me beyond measure.'[77]

Then he went north. His father and mother were away on holiday, staying at a farm in the Highlands, and he followed them there. He had given no warning of his arrival. At the station he climbed into a victoria, and as it turned into the lane that led to the farmhouse he saw them setting off for an evening walk. He remembered the occasion with emotion and sentiment more than thirty years later: 'I wish I could still walk across a field to meet them and see them turn to bid me welcome in a summer Scottish sunset.'[78]

He had been given a month's leave. He lay about in the grass and read a good deal; his mother had given him a copy of a novel called *The Governor of England*, and his life-long admiration for Cromwell was born.[79] Then, on 21 August, Charlie arrived, and his happiness was complete:

> Indescribably fine having C. here. We explored the Shaggie Burn for bathing places and found two. Topping to be chasing around together. Church at 11. In afternoon to Monzie Falls and had a ripping bathe, climbing about naked all over the place. Tea at 5 and then read *Paradise Lost* to mother and C.[80]

He was plunged into gloom by an official communication: no trace could be found in the great maw of the War Office of the papers relating to his transfer – he must renew his application on his return to France. That evening, at family prayers, he took what comfort he could from the words of the 40th Psalm, sung to the tune of 'Stroudwater':

> I waited for the Lord my God, and patiently did bear;
> At length to me he did incline, my voice and cry to hear.

Three days later there was evidence that his line of communication to the Almighty was gratifyingly direct. Word came from France that his transfer to the Sappers had already been posted in Battalion orders – not, it is true, to the Company he wished to go to, but that was a detail that could be attended to on his return to the front. There were still some days of holiday to be enjoyed. They went to Crieff and hired horses. Charlie couldn't ride, but Reith found him an apt pupil. He also planned to take Charlie to Mull for a few days, but his parents seemed so disappointed that he abandoned the idea. Instead they went roaming in the woods together and had another 'magnificent bathe' in the Shaggie Burn. The weather turned to rain, and there was time to finish *The Governor of England*: 'It is a fine story. I wish there were an Oliver Cromwell in England now and that he had the same position.'[81]

The family returned to Glasgow, and Reith found what he called the 'utter war-unawareness' of the city claustrophobic. Determined to do what he could to force the issue of his transfer, he got himself measured up for Royal Engineers uniform (succumbing at the same time to the temptation to buy a pair of big new spurs which clinked). When he appeared in his new rig before a medical board, they were puzzled – they had been expecting to interview an infantry officer. Reith decided to take the problem of his dual military identity to Scottish Command in Edinburgh. The Military Secretary there had been his adjutant in OTC days. Reith explained his anxieties, returned to Glasgow, and for several days threw himself into an activity that seems throughout his life to have had strong therapeutic value for him:

> 'Redding up' in the manse – getting rid of the accumulated rubbish of forty years – not my rubbish, other people's. I have a peculiar talent for this beneficent activity. A lumber room is not an asset; it is a liability and a snare. In the ordinary house, room, cupboard, desk, drawer, how much of the contents could be thrown out and no one ever miss them . . . Getting rid of rubbish is as near godliness as cleanliness; functions of waste paper basket as important as those of closet.[82]

Although, like a good Scot, Reith always watched the pennies, he was a generous man. His army pay was supplemented by what he still received from Pearsons, and he spent open-handedly, both on his family and on Charlie. On a shopping expedition with his mother and Douglas, they chose a fine gramophone for the manse. It was delivered the same evening with twenty-four records, and it gave his father great pleasure. He bought Royal Engineer brooches for his mother and for his sister Beta. He also visited a jeweller's, buying a silver stop-watch and chain and a silver matchbox for Charlie and an ironclad watch for himself. Charlie was very pleased with the watch; Reith presented it to him in the evening 'with a little speech of thanks to him'.[83]

When the long-awaited telegram came, it was addressed to Lieutenant J. C. W. Reith, 5th Scottish Rifles: 'Report as soon as possible to Embarkation Officer, Southampton'. He and Charlie travelled south that evening, Reith wearing his Engineers' uniform. They went to Highgate Presbyterian Church and spent Sunday afternoon together in their room reading the life of St Francis of Assisi. In the evening they went to Ferme Park Chapel: 'harvest services, fine singing, clear moon. Hymns after supper. C. sang, which almost bowled me over. I felt awful.'[84]

The next day they were astir early. As sometimes happened when they were together, Charlie wrote up that morning in the diary, and Reith left the volume with him – it can't have been a particularly lengthy entry, because a taxi had been ordered for seven. They prayed together, and Charlie put Reith's ring on and kissed it. 'It was an awful struggle to keep up in the taxi. Gave him £2. I kissed him on the platform.' He managed to telephone home from Southampton, recording in his orderly way that he spoke for six minutes and fifty-nine seconds at a cost of 4/7d. Then he sent a telegram to Charlie – 'Goodbye wee boy. Take care of yourself. My love. Johnnie.'[85]

He fetched up at the Territorial base at Rouen early on the morning of 22 September. His sleep had been disturbed. When the RTO came into the compartment to waken him, he had no idea where he was: 'I called out "Charlie" and then asked where my father was. It was horrid.' Eyebrows were once again raised at his sapper uniform, and he was logged in as belonging to the 5th SR, although he was able to produce the number of the GHQ order that had sanctioned his transfer. His spurs were greatly admired – no one had ever seen any quite so long – and he had some agreeable talk with the officer next to him, who was a teetotal, non-smoking Wesleyan. He thought less well of a Roman Catholic padre whom he saw downing three or four whiskies in the mess: 'The RC chaplain is a dirty-mouthed beast.'[86]

There were rumours that 'something big' was about to happen, and he was impatient to be up the line. When he was instructed to join the 1/2nd Highland Field Company, a train took him as far as Béthune. There, having established that the unit he was destined for was some five or six miles further on, he jumped into a civilian *fiacre* and instructed the unwilling driver to take him there. They had to thread their way through all manner of guns and transport, and the roads were clogged with troops. The driver liked it less and less, but Reith brandished his riding switch and urged him on: *En avant! Il faut que j'arrive a Noyelles. Il y a grand besoin de moi au champ de bataille.*[87]

This turned out to be something of an exaggeration, because when he finally came upon the 1/2nd Highland they knew nothing about him. There was a heavy bombardment in progress; Reith had seen dead men and dead horses before, but not in numbers like these. He found his new colleagues in a dug-out some twelve feet below ground, and the Major was not especially welcoming. He had been expecting a second lieutenant from Aberdeen; Reith's seniority as first lieutenant, which dated from August 1914, was inconvenient.

Reith decided to go above ground to get the lie of the land and found himself witnessing the early stages of the Battle of Loos. The plan formulated by General Joffre had been to attack on both sides the great salient formed by the German front in France. The British Expeditionary Force had already suffered heavy losses earlier in the year. Sir John French had been unwilling to commit his troops until the following spring, when reinforcements of men and matériel would be available, but he had been overruled and ordered to cooperate with the French. He would succeed in denting the German line, but his general reserve had been kept too far back, and he was unable to press home his advantage. The price paid by the British for the three-week offensive was 60,000 men killed, wounded or missing, a casualty rate three times higher than that of the enemy.

Reith, standing on his parapet with his field glasses on that September evening, got a strictly worm's eye view of the proceedings. There was heavy shelling and a good deal of shrapnel. Nobody was quite sure where the Germans were. About half a mile to his left he saw a Scottish regiment charging over open ground towards a group of houses. Many of the kilted figures went down before the German fire. Reith went back down below to find out what role there was for him in this confusion.

The NCOs of the Field Company were mostly from Aberdeen, and he was quickly on good terms with them and with the other officers. The Major, a lawyer in civilian life, was popular with no one. Reith, never slow to size people up, formed the view that he was a very stupid man and observed that he drank a great deal: 'My *sangfroid* and experience is rather upsetting to him obviously,' he wrote patronisingly in his diary. On 30 September they received the welcome order to move back to Vermelles. The men bivouacked in a field, and the officers found quarters in what remained of some houses. This put them about 1200 yards behind the front line. He discovered to his joy that he was only two and a half miles from where his old Transport section was quartered, and he borrowed a horse and rode over to see them.

The work consisted mainly of strengthening the newly won front line with barbed wire entanglements. One of Reith's first jobs was to go up and wire along that part of the 58th Brigade front that was held by the Wiltshire Regiment. There was a great deal of shelling and sniping, and the infantry were very jittery. Reith was well pleased with what he was able to do, and the Wiltshire officers were extremely grateful to have something between them and the Germans. They were also greatly entertained by the unusual spectacle of an officer of the Royal Engineers striding out towards the enemy lines for the purpose of relieving himself:

While superintending the erection of the barbed wire I was suddenly 'taken short'. I had forgotten to take my usual dose of chlorodine that morning – necessary since my feat with the manure water. Instead of going back to the trench and enquiring if they had a latrine handy, I went about twenty yards further out into No Man's Land. I was not conscious of doing anything foolhardy; as a matter of fact I did not know if the Germans were a hundred or a thousand yards off. But it was general knowledge in the Field Company next day.[88]

There was more wiring the following night, this time for the Cheshire Regiment. On this occasion the thump of the trench mortars told him that they were very close to the enemy lines. He saw an aerial torpedo land close to where he had been the night before, and was told that it had buried a whole platoon. He recorded that he always made a point of walking about on the German side of any working party and that stories were beginning to circulate about his lack of fear.[89] The next day he was out with some men in daylight repairing and strengthening a bridge over the La Bassée canal – 'This was a real RE job of work.' He was beginning to enjoy himself; the Major, impressed by the accounts he was getting of Reith's work on the wire, was becoming quite friendly; he even dropped his opposition to the idea of sending for Sailaway, and an arrangement had been made for a corporal and a man to go and fetch her.

On the morning of 7 October Reith got up about nine and took a leisurely bath. He had the morning off, and was planning to ride over to see his old Transport section. He put on one of his yellow shirts and his best tunic and riding breeches. Over breakfast, the Major said he had it in mind to go up the line and look at some redoubts. Reith volunteered to escort him; there were reports that a mine had exploded, and it was an opportunity to see what work would need to be done that night under cover of darkness. It occurred to him that he should change into old clothes, but he didn't.

The communication trench was crowded. Reith followed his usual rash practice of climbing up onto the open ground and invited his companion to do the same, but the Major preferred to push his way slowly through the outgoing troops; when they were clear of the crush, Reith jumped down again beside him. The front line was in a mess; in some places the parapet had been blown clean away. Reith was impatient to see what damage had been done by the mine. It was just round the next traverse, and he pressed on ahead of the Major.

Suddenly he felt a smack on the cheek and a terrible singing in his ears. It was like getting a cricket ball in the face – that had happened to him once at school. The Germans, however, were not a cricketing nation, and he realised that he had been struck by a bullet. He saw blood pouring down onto his nice new tunic, and that agitated him considerably; then he explored the inside of his mouth with his tongue to make sure that his teeth hadn't been smashed. His next thought was that the bullet was still in his head and that that was the end of him; only then did it occur to him that he was probably still in the sniper's sights and that it would be sensible to lie down.

All this took place in a matter of seconds, but the sequence of thought and action remained clear in his mind. He remembered the Major as being 'in an awful stew'. A sergeant of the Wiltshire Regiment came crawling along the trench and fumbled for Reith's field dressing, but because it was his best tunic he didn't have one. The sergeant used his own, but it did little to staunch the flow of blood from his cheek. Reith asked for paper and the sergeant tore some out of a notebook. Reith got out his fountain pen and scrawled the briefest of notes to his mother. The scrap of paper survives, pasted into one of his scrap-books – the Major enclosed it in a letter to Mrs Reith later that day. The handwriting is very shaky; apart from his mother's name and address he wrote simply, 'I'm all right'.

When he wrote up his diary for this eventful day, he explained that this message to the manse was intended to be understood cryptically:

> I thought I was going to die, and the 'all right' which I wrote referred to my readiness to meet death. It had nothing to do with my physical condition at all. I lay on my back then, looking up into the clear blue sky and thought of heaven and that I should soon have the great mystery solved for me. I was perfectly serene and content. I knew father and mother would join me before so very long.[90]

When Reith worked up his war diary with a view to publication, this particular entry was somewhat embellished.[91] In the event, his parents' cryptographical skills were not put to the test. Reith makes no mention of the fact in either of his biographical volumes, but the note saying 'I'm all right' was not the only one he wrote as he lay in the trench. The other, which said 'Cheer up, dear old boy', was the quicker of the two to reach its destination. The first news that Reith had been wounded reached his parents two days later in a telegram signed 'Charlie'.[92]

John Reith's serenity was short-lived. By the time the stretcher-bearers arrived, he was feeling rather foolish and very angry. The Wiltshire sergeant had estab-lished that he had a second wound in the shoulder. Reith worked out that as he was facing in the direction from which the bullet had come, it could not have hit his shoulder first. It was therefore no longer lodged in his head: 'All this soliloquising about Heaven was premature. I wasn't going to die. I was only badly wounded.'[93] The trench was narrow and Reith was heavy; to the general astonishment, he asked to be put down and walked half a mile of the way to the dressing station with his hand on the shoulder of a man in front. The wound on his face measured five inches by three, and the doctor applied iodine with a swab brush. Reith felt that he must have done an injury to the RAMC sergeant who held his hand.

At the Field Ambulance his wounds were properly dressed and he was told that his war was over. Initially, there was concern for the sight of his left eye; Reith was more concerned about the whereabouts of his kit. A good deal of the cheekbone had been shot away; he quickly established a reputation as a bit of a card by asking whether he would be left with a mark on his face. He was very hungry, but could take only liquid food. He was also very cold, and they gave him three hot-water bottles. Morphia didn't do much for him. He tried to sleep, and for the first and only time in the war found himself in the grip of a nightmare – a German searchlight had picked him out on the wire and there was a machine-gun trained on him.

He was moved to a General Hospital at Wimereux. Reading with one eye was painful, but he got hold of a prayer book and read the collect. He also got his hands on a pad with numbered pages and began to write – to Charlie, to the men in Transport, to his parents. The four pages that he scrawled in purple crayon to his mother survive:

> I am more disgusted than I can say – I was getting on so well and enjoying the work and everything – but I also know that I have had an extraordinarily narrow escape and I am very grateful. You will see later how near a thing it has been – another half-inch would have done it, I think. As it is my eye doesn't seem to be affected at all – nor my teeth, though the cheek bone is broken and my left cheek is chiefly remarkable for the amount that isn't there so to speak.[94]

The crossing to England was smooth. In London he was sent to the Queen Alexandra Military Hospital on Millbank. An elderly nursing sister in the ambulance said she would send a telegram for him to Charlie and refused to accept payment – that, she said, was the least she could do. Charlie turned up to see him at five o'clock, wearing his OTC uniform and carrying a large box of chocolates:

> Couldn't describe my feelings at seeing him again. Poor boy got an awful shock as my wound was being dressed at the time and he saw it all. He said it nearly knocked him over. He was awfully sympathetic. I felt sorry that I should always look such a sight.

His brush with death had made a deeper impression on him than he knew. In later years he always noted the anniversary in his diary, and he preserved in his scrapbook a large-scale map of where it happened, inscribed in red crayon '7.X.15. Where I was nearly killed'. The warren of trenches is carefully drawn out, and each is marked with its name – Old Boots Trench, Ikey Terrace, Cabbage Patch, Old Kent Road, Lovers' Lane. A few days after arriving at Millbank, he saw in a newspaper that George Harley, his friend from the OTC in Glasgow, had been killed on the second day of the Loos offensive within a mile or so of where he himself had been wounded. He remembered their long walks on the Kilpatrick Hills and the Campsie Fells in the days before Charlie came along, their talk almost invariably of war: 'I think Azrael got his lines crossed.'[95]

He was told initially that he would be in hospital for a couple of months, and there was talk of inserting a silver plate in his cheek, but the wound healed extraordinarily quickly. He was examined by an oculist, who confirmed that his sight would be unimpaired but said that for a time he must wear dark glasses in artificial light. His parents were eager to visit him, but he dissuaded them. Charlie was a frequent visitor, and Mr and Mrs Bowser also came, bringing flowers and grapes and a copy of Chaucer's *Canterbury Tales*. Soon he was allowed out, although his bandaged face made him feel very conspicuous. He was not best pleased that Charlie sometimes had a schoolfriend in tow when they met, and there was the occasional tiff: 'I was sick with him. He seems dashed fond of wee Banks.'[96] Charlie's performance in class benefited from his friend's presence, because Reith took to helping him with his homework: 'The essay I did for him at 12.30 the other night has got the only A in the form.'

One morning he had an unexpected visitor. Just before he was wounded, Reith had taken it into his head to write to his old boss W. E. Moir and tell him what he was up to with the Royal Engineers – he was particularly pleased with himself over the repair job to the La Bassée bridge. When a good-looking and smartly dressed woman carrying a bunch of red roses stopped at the foot of his bed, he realised just in time that it was Mrs Moir: 'For a Pearson engineer it was almost like a visit from royalty.'

Mrs Moir mothered him intensely. She took him out for drives and had him to her house; she also told him of a big new project at Gretna on which Pearsons were embarking for the Ministry of Munitions. That did not interest him hugely, but when Moir himself told him that he had been asked by Lloyd George to go to the United States to organise munitions supplies, Reith immediately pricked up his ears. He also conceived the idea that when the war was over there might be some sort of opening at Pearsons for Charlie. He raised the subject with Charlie's mother and sister over tea one afternoon, and subsequently called on Mr Bowser at his office to put it to him.

Reith was discharged from hospital, sent on indefinite leave and told to report for a medical board in three months' time. In mid-November he had an encouraging letter from Moir – 'there is quite a chance of my going to America', he wrote in his diary. Meanwhile, he decided that there was nothing to be lost by looking in on what was going on in Gretna, and he arranged to do so on his way north to visit his parents.

His diary for those weeks of convalescence in October and November of 1915 shows that his feelings for Charlie fluctuated wildly. He was intensely possessive. So long as he could have him all to himself, everything was fine: 'Lunched with C. at Regent's Palace and talked about his going to Pearson's,' says an entry on 30 October. 'Went to the Scala movie and saw *The Birth of a Nation*. Wonderful. Very happy to be spending the night together.' The following week, however, Charlie accepted an invitation to dine at the house of a friend: 'I was sick with him,' Reith wrote. 'I wasn't at all kind to him.'[97]

When the time came for him to set off for Scotland a couple of weeks later, they had made up their differences, and on the evening of his departure they followed their usual practice of reading and praying together. 'Felt most awfully sad at leaving him,' Reith wrote. They took a car to the station more than two hours before the time of the train. Although they had had dinner *en famille* at the Bowsers', Reith felt that 'a little supper' was called for at Euston. They tucked into hors d'oeuvre, asparagus soup, sole, pheasant, peach melba – and cider. For one evening, abstinence was set aside – 'we were quite biffed.'[98]

The Pearson office in Gretna was just by the station. Ernest Pearson, Lord Cowdray's brother, kept him waiting 'an infernal time' and then offered him a temporary job as some sort of mechanical inspector at £350 a year, which was roughly equivalent to his pay as a lieutenant in the Sappers. Reith affected coolness, said he would let them know in a week's time, and continued to Glasgow.

He was concerned about his parents. They both had bad colds and looked tired and old. He went to church in a new black and grey coat he had bought in London: 'I certainly made a sensation,' he noted immodestly in his diary. He was also roped in to be best man at the wedding of a friend called Woods Humphery who was marrying his landlady's daughter: 'These marriages give me palpitations,' Reith wrote. 'How frightful it must be to find oneself married.'[99] He wrote to Ernest Pearson to say he would take the job at Gretna and then, in a state of high excitement, headed for Perthshire; an arrangement had been made for Charlie to stay with his brother Douglas for a time and be tutored for the London matriculation:

> Overjoyed to see him. Poor C. will be frightfully lonely here. Arranged things in our room and then dinner. Along quiet road and over fields to a pond for skating. C. was excellent. He seems good at everything. I was feeling awfully fond of him and so happy to be with him. Music after tea. Fire in our bedroom which we greatly enjoyed after a hot bath.

He started work at Gretna in December. The arrangement was a strictly irregular one, but that was something he felt could be left to Pearsons, the Ministry of Munitions, and the War Office. He found the Dumfriesshire countryside wild and romantic, but felt lost and lonely and began to regret that he had come.

Charlie took time off from his matriculation preparations to come and see him, and as always the language of Reith's diary entries takes on a tone that is descriptive not just of friendship but of infatuation:

> Wire from C. that he was 3 minutes late at Coatbridge. At 1.10 when I was sitting at my desk the phone rang and it was he. He got the 1.20 from Carlisle and I joined him at Gretna Green Station at 1.35. It was tremendous.

He was very pleased to hear that I engaged a sleeper for him by phone. Walked from Cummertree Station by the way I always go. The pony saw us far away and came galloping over. C. gave it some sugar. Topping dinner in the upper sitting room. C. was very pleased with my rooms and all the photos I had of him. He was anxious to see what I looked like in my running kit, so I changed into them [sic] and then back.[100]

In what spare time he had he busied himself looking for jobs for other people. He found one for Bob Wallace as a foreman carpenter; there was a tied cottage, and he would have been able to get married.[101] Reith had also now turned his mind to trying to get Charlie into the Royal Engineers, and he expended considerable time and energy on trying to pull strings to that end so that matters could be settled before Charlie's new term began on 18 January.

Momentarily checked by a new order that there were to be no more RE officers for a time, he turned to a Sapper acquaintance whose father had an engineering business in Glasgow. On 16 January he was hugely pleased with himself at being able to shoot off a telegram to Charlie's father: 'Niven Senior, of Niven and Haddin, civil engineers, will take Charlie and give full experience indoor and outdoor work, with certificate 3 or 6 months, until RE possible.' This grand design appealed less to the Bowsers than it did to its architect. Two days later there was a letter from Charlie to say that he was after all going back to school. 'Can't understand it,' Reith wrote biliously in his diary. 'It's his people, of course. He seems to be seeing a lot of Banks, too.'[102] He sulked briefly. The flow of letters to Highgate was interrupted, but only for a few days; a twelve-page letter from Charlie arrived, enclosing a 'very fine photo' of himself in rugger kit, and the correspondence resumed.

Reith was becoming increasingly restive about America and early in February he decided that a visit to the Ministry of Munitions was called for. The matter was settled in a day. He was to take charge of the inspections of small-arms contracts. He was to have a salary of £500 and an American allowance of half as much again. He was to sail the following week. He kept in his scrapbook the official notification from the Director-General of Munitions: 'Sir, I have to acquaint you that the passage to New York has been ordered for you in the Holland-America Line SS *Rotterdam* which will leave Falmouth on the 21st instant. You are entitled to 40 cubic feet of personal baggage which quantity is conveyed free of charge on the ship.'

He met Charlie later in the day but couldn't bring himself to tell him the news till that evening. They spent the next three days together, but on the evening he left to go north he had to compete for Charlie's attention with a relative who was passing through town: 'They were making a great fuss about him,' Reith noted peevishly. 'C. said, "He's my cousin," as if that necessitated obligations and interest and affection.'[103]

The few days he spent in Glasgow showed him at his best and at his worst. He went one day to visit his brother Robert in his office, and as they emerged together he caught sight of his old CO, Colonel Douglas:

I had time to collect myself. One of the biggest exercises of will I have ever put through. He saw me some way off – smiled broadly and changed his course to speak to me. I just stared at him and gave no recognition at all. The smile faded from his face and blank bewilderment took its place as he changed his course again and passed.[104]

He could, however, be as generous as he could be unforgiving. A few years earlier, out walking with his father, they had passed an acquaintance who was wearing an expensive fur overcoat with an astrakhan collar. Reith had asked his father if he would like a coat like that, and Dr Reith had replied, rather primly, 'Not if the money came as his does.' On his last day at home, Reith had two such coats sent to the manse from Forsyth's, one of the best men's outfitters in town. They were priced at £22-10s.0d. He laid them out and invited his father to choose: 'He looked awfully nice in it and was quite overcome.' He also took his mother to her tailor's to buy a new costume and some furs.

Back in London, Reith presented Charlie with a vest-pocket Kodak camera. They took pictures of each other and went walking in Highgate Woods. Then, to his dismay, he discovered that Charlie was in danger of being called up, which would have dislocated the plan for him to get some engineering experience. Reith shot off to see the Holloway recruiting officer and then pursued the clerk of the local tribunal: 'Islington Town Hall at 4 for the wretched tribunal. I was very thankful I was there to help him through. We just did it with the help of chairman and clerk – two months exemption.'[105]

The parting was painful. They prayed together upstairs after breakfast, and then joined in family worship downstairs: 'Mrs B. prayed very nicely for me. C. read the 91st Psalm. It nearly did for me.' They got to Paddington at ten, walked up and down arm in arm, kissed goodbye.

The *Rotterdam* weighed anchor at 11.50 next morning. Reith discovered that one of his fellow-passengers was von Papen, returning to his Washington Embassy. He explored the six decks with their saloons and writing rooms and was greatly struck with the magnificence of the ship's appointments. He was in low spirits as he watched the English coastline slip away: 'I had no idea what I was going to and it was all a little alarming.' He sent the two inevitable telegrams – to his mother and father and to Charlie: 'Take care of yourself. All my love. Back soon. Au revoir. Johnnie.'

Five

CUSPIDORS AND ICED WATER

O my America! My new-found-land.
JOHN DONNE,
To His Mistress Going to Bed,
c. 1593-8

LIKE MANY another Scotsman before him, John Reith took to the United States like a duck to water. He spent eighteen months there, and thirty years later he would write that they were as happy a time as he had known. If the war had been over before his work there came to an end, he might very well have stayed. 'I had acquired an American outlook,' he wrote, 'adopted much of American practice and procedure; above all tuned-in to American *tempo*. I was too young to move quickly in England.'[1]

He had not hugely enjoyed the voyage. The ship ran into fog, pitched and tossed a good deal, and for much of the time was sheeted in ice. Reith retreated to his cabin and more or less went into hibernation, which also served to blot out his homesickness. Long Island came in sight on 5 March, and he was busy with his camera; several big German liners were laid up, including the *Vaterland* and the *Kaiser Wilhelm*. Moir was at the quay to meet him. He was quickly installed in fine rooms on the fifth floor of the Belmont Hotel for $2.50 a night and was greatly taken with all the gadgets. He also encountered that ubiquitous adjunct of American life, the spittoon. 'My early impressions of America,' he wrote in his diary, 'were largely of cuspidors and iced water.' He travelled on to New Haven, and set off through the snow to find the offices of the Winchester Company.

He had come to see a major in the British Army called Smyth-Piggott, a middle-aged officer who was the deputy chief inspector. Moir had said he should make his number with him before going on to the new Eddystone Works near Philadelphia where he was to be based. Reith, innocent of the ways of Whitehall, had assumed that Moir was in charge of everything relating to the supply of munitions to Britain, but he now discovered that this was far from being the case. The War Office was engaged in hostilities not only with the Kaiser but also with the Ministry of Munitions, and Reith found himself caught in a bureaucratic crossfire. Moir had not only neglected to clear Reith's appointment with Smyth-Piggott's superiors; there was also a colonel in New York whose nose was easily put out of joint, and the entire Army Inspection department in London.

It took almost two months for ruffled feathers to be smoothed and for Reith's position to be regularised. Luckily for him, Smyth-Piggott took a liking to him. He was impressed by Reith's engineering background and eager to hear his tales of life at the front; without his persistent representations to authority, Reith could well have found himself back there.[2] Eventually a general arrived from London to bang heads together and he ruled in Reith's favour. He did so just in time. The benevolent Smyth-Piggott had been laid low with acute appendicitis, and the day after he had been confirmed in his appointment Reith heard that his new friend had died.

On his first visit to Philadelphia he was received with deference and invited to say how he would like the suite of rooms put at his disposal to be furnished: 'My office is gorgeous, as luxurious as any I have seen. Roll-top desk, two or three tables, a private lavatory, a thick carpet and so on.'[3] The Remington Arms Company had started building the factory only ten months previously. It had cost £5 million and had a work force of 13,000. Reith learned that his British Inspection Department would be about 200 strong. The men would be recruited locally and trained by a small team of experts who had already arrived from Enfield. The British government had placed an order for two million rifles. Reith was unperturbed by his ignorance of the manufacture of small arms: 'It would be largely commonsense and self-confidence; there was an ample supply of the latter anyhow.'[4]

He fretted at the slowness of mail from home. Nothing came from Charlie for several weeks, and from the manse there was a letter that worried him because his mother told him they were £200 overdrawn. He soon began to feel more at home, however. He rented a small house in the agreeable suburb of Swarthmore, about ten miles from the centre of the city. 'Love at first sight,' he wrote thirty years later. 'I had never seen any place like it.' The houses stood well back in gardens of an acre or more; he noted approvingly the absence of hedges or walls between them. The broad streets were lined with magnolia trees.

The local community was extremely welcoming; indeed, an invitation extended to him on his very first weekend in Philadelphia had been the cause of some embarrassment. He was introduced at the factory to Sam Vauclain, the multi-millionaire president of the armaments firm Baldwin's, who immediately asked him out to his house: 'Not my idea of spending Sunday and I had been looking forward to going to church in the morning.'[5] The local churches were well attended and well supported. On Easter Sunday he went to the 2nd Presbyterian Church in Philadelphia and the collection amounted to £2000.

Reith's main problem in the factory was to reconcile the perfectionist standards of his specialists from Enfield with the mass-production methods devised by the Remington management. The daily output at Eddystone was much the same as the annual output which the specialists had been accustomed to in peacetime at home, but they were disinclined to lower their standards. Inspection was wide-ranging – of components, of assemblies, and of short- and long-range firing. Two months after Reith's arrival, the inspectors turned down three rifles out of every four, and even then were still regarded as lax by the authorities at home.

The object of the exercise being to produce weapons to kill Germans, quantity was also an important consideration. Shortly after Reith arrived, production stood at fifty rifles a day. By the middle of June the daily loadings into the huge freight cars at the end of the packing shop had risen to 500, and this in spite of an instruction Reith had received from London at the end of May that three substantial modifications of design were required. Reith was asked to establish what all this would cost and how long it would take. He was told a few days later by the Eddystone management that the changes would be made immediately and that there would be no charge; and he was gratified to hear from Vauclain that this had been done as a tribute to him.

Letters from Glasgow had begun to arrive regularly, and by mid-April Reith had already begun to urge his parents to go out and visit him. His first letter from Charlie did not come until 24 April; quite a few had plainly gone adrift, because it was marked number 11. His exemption had been withdrawn and he was joining up as a sapper for six months before going for a commission course. He also needed some money. Reith didn't think this too unsatisfactory, although he felt it was bad luck that he had to begin in the ranks. A conversation with one of his new American acquaintances at about this time planted the idea of getting Charlie out to work with him at Eddystone; there are several references to this in the diary over the next few months, and he discussed it with Vauclain and others and also spoke to Moir, who saw Charlie on one of his visits to London.

Charlie clearly found army life something of a trial. Several years previously Reith had extracted a promise from him that he would not smoke before he was twenty-one. Charlie now wrote saying that he was having such an awful time that he would like to get out of this: would Reith cable his consent?

> Accordingly I sent 'Quite understand. Smoke.' This put the wind up the censor's department properly, and I was asked to explain what it meant . . . Incidentally the censors were most irritating all along, opening my letters in both directions – probably a crowd of silly girls of no intelligence. I cannot understand why I did not make arrangements at the outset to have my letters put through the embassy, or Moir's office.[6]

Reith quickly picked up a good deal about American factory management. One thing he observed was that Remington Arms ran a pretty tight ship:

> On one occasion there was a strike threat. The preparations made by the management were certainly thorough; two sheriffs and twelve deputy-sheriffs on the job; several vans to transport the unruly to the local gaol; even two

or three representatives of the Pennsylvania mounted police, whose effect
on the neighbourhood appeared to be something of the sort one associated
with the Canadian Mounted Police. There was no strike.[7]

Reith himself showed no great inclination to use the velvet glove. On 13 June
he noted that he went down to the 100 yards range and exercised what he
called 'a sudden and strong disciplinary action', sacking two people and telling
them to leave the factory at once. 'I enjoyed doing it, and the factory management were vastly amazed.'

He came into frequent contact with a good many financiers and industrialists,
and he was flattered by the attention they paid him – a visit from Corey, the
boss of United States Steel; a call from Vauclain to say that he would like to
bring John D. Rockefeller Jnr to see him. Vauclain was particularly friendly,
entertaining him at his house, showing him the beauties of the Pennsylvania
countryside: 'A long drive in the afternoon through wonderful country. Vauclain
said that after the war he would take C. and me for a wonderful trip in the
Far West by train in a special saloon.'[8]

His neighbours in Swarthmore made much of him, too, particularly those
who were Presbyterians, but he also made friends among the many Quaker
families in the town. The two communities differed sharply in their attitude to
the war and on the possibility of American involvement, and Reith conceded
that he took a mildly malicious pleasure in shocking Quaker sensibilities:
'Visited Dr and Mrs Battin and made them laugh a great deal at my stories
about the war. I thought this was good for them as they are both great pacifists.'[9]

He became something of a celebrity. 'You may have noticed a man in Philadelphia recently,' wrote a local journalist, 'who towered head and shoulders
above the men beside him and who bore on his left cheek an angry-looking
scar that ran almost from cheekbone to chin . . .' Captain Reith, the writer
went on, was an example of what the great war had done 'as a maker of Men,
with a capital M'. He had been struck not only by Reith's height, but also by
'the impression of grim resoluteness which his steady grey eyes, his iron-cut
chin and his terse speech provide'. There followed an account of Reith's experiences at the front which made him sound like a forerunner of 'Bull-dog'
Drummond: 'There's a pretty little job to be done nightly by the Engineering
Corps which is enough to freeze the blood . . .'[10]

He began to get invitations to speak at dinners. He was thrown in at the
deep end at a banquet given by the St Andrew's Society of Philadelphia.[11]
Someone he had met in the way of business had invited him along, promising
him 'a breath of home', but when he arrived he found he was billed as the
guest of honour. The company was a distinguished one, numbering a hundred
or more. Reith was piped into the hall and had to sing for his supper.

He appears to have done so to some effect, and he described his theme in
a letter to his father a few days later:

I drew three parallels. The attention of a thousand men is centred in keeping in good repair 300 yards of a barbed-wire fence in a turnip field in France. Meanwhile, their former comrades, with pockets swollen with increased pay, bedeck themselves and their womenfolk in all the cheap and vulgar finery in which ignorance delights ... Second, that while Scottish soldiers are massing in a trench preparatory to the charge, their erstwhile associates are crowding to the strike meetings in munitions areas, demanding unholy increases in the already exorbitant wages they get – holding up the blood of their brothers to ransom. Third, that the graves of Scottish soldiers are strewn on the fields of three continents and that the haunting strains of the pipes will never pass from the memory of the peasants who hear in ten thousand wayside graves *The Land o' the Leal* and *The Flowers of the Forest*. Meanwhile, the sound of drunken revelry is rising from ten thousand public houses by the Clyde ...

The white-waistcoated magnates of Philadelphia had not heard anything quite like this before, and their young guest, sensing that they liked what they heard, pulled out the stops even further. 'I couldn't leave it at that,' he told his father, 'so I brought in a wind-up about the men "from Highlands and Lowlands and the stormy islands of the west" – a whole lot of rot about glens and forests and straths – "from a hundred lonely crofts on a hundred distant hills"':

I brought in the names of the famous regiments from Galloway and the Borders, Edinburgh and Midlothian, Royal Scots and the King's Own. From Ross and Inverness the Seaforths, from their own counties the Argyll and Sutherland, from Aberdeen the Camerons and the wonderful Gordons and so on. They liked that. What were they fighting for? The King – the heritage of the past – the covenanting traditions of the land, the glory of Scotland – awful rot of course, but it went well. I gave various stories of things, too – 'And if they die, remember only this of them, that there's some corner of a foreign field that is forever – Scotland.' That was the end. Selah.[12]

The phrase 'over the top' was not to enter the language for another half-century or so. It was a preposterous performance, and the audience loved it. When, after about twenty-five minutes, he finally sat down, there was pandemonium. Somebody rushed to the piano and struck up 'God Save the King'. The secretary of the Society presented him with a bouquet of red roses and maidenhair and with three miniature flags – the Royal Standards of Great Britain and of Scotland and the Stars and Stripes. Guests crowded on to the platform to shake his hand – one of them, a prosperous-looking bank president, told him he was the son of a labourer on the Grant estate and had attended the old Inverdruie Schoolhouse at Rothiemurchus. He also met John Gribbel, who had bought the Robert Burns Glenriddel manuscripts and made a gift of them to the Scottish nation.[13] John Reith had made an important and unsettling discovery: 'I had come on something within myself of the existence of which I had been vaguely and vexatiously aware, but which I had never had opportunity to disclose or develop.'[14]

Such opportunities now crowded in on him. A couple of weeks after his *tour de force* at the St Andrew's Society he was inveigled out to a country club where the Business Science Association of Philadelphia was holding its annual dinner: 'It is an infernal nuisance, and I was terribly tired. However, the reception I got stirred me up, and I spoke for three-quarters of an hour.' This time he had made some notes on the train. He once again found an appreciative audience – the man billed to follow him with an account of a recent tour of the West begged to be excused and everybody stood up and sang *Rule Britannia*.[15]

> Then came what I shall never forget and a thing that makes me feel more kindly towards Americans. I had said something about the anxiety for those not at the Front and mentioned what I would feel like if Charlie were sent out. A man said he was voicing the prayers of them all when he said he hoped I would find 'my dear friend' came through without harm and that when I returned home after the war he would be there to meet me.[16]

His thoughts turned very often to his ageing parents. 'You have quite decided to come here next spring, haven't you?' he wrote in the letter just quoted. 'I can't send you much money as I shall have to save up to buy a motor and a decent little house. I shall fix everything fine.'[17] He did send them £100 a fortnight later, however, and in the middle of July he wrote offering the gift of a communion table for the church to mark the Jubilee of his father's induction. Two days later he was shocked to receive news that his father had undergone an operation. He was told at the time that it was a minor one, but that was not the case. His father was well aware of the risk attending surgery in someone of his age, and wrote a letter to be sent to Reith in the case of his death.[18]

He took it into his head one weekend to go off to see the Niagara Falls and crossed the suspension bridge into Canada. He put up at the Clifton Hotel, and he recorded an encounter his secretary, McCarthy, had with a chambermaid: 'I had sent him to get something from her, but he came back to say that she could not understand English. Thinking that the Quebec influence might be found here I spoke to her in French, and she replied in a broad Glasgow accent.'[19]

He was happiest, however, during quiet evenings and weekends at Swarthmore where he could try his hand at baseball on the green or sit holding court on his porch. He found it easier to make friends with young people in their teens than with those of his own age. There are frequent references in his diary to one boy in particular, who reminded him of Charlie: 'Jimmy Laws came to my billet. He's fourteen and a half and more like an English public schoolboy than anything I've hitherto met.'[20]

Reith took him to the factory and showed him round: 'I let him try rifles on the hundred yard range. I like him very much.' Charlie, however, was not forgotten. As his birthday approached, Reith visited a jeweller's and ordered a signet ring for him, with his crest and an inscription inside – 'Carissimo sodali xx. xii. 16. Benedicat tibi Dominus et custodiat te.'[21] Nearer Christmas, he sent McCarthy to the same shop to get a gold wristwatch for Charlie. On reflection, he decided that this was no good for rough army work, so he bought a silver one instead.

As pressure grew for the United States to enter the war, a reserve company of the National Guard was formed in Swarthmore. A prime mover was Dr Tuttle, the minister of the Presbyterian Church, and there were veterans of the war with Spain in 1905 to act as officers. It was all entirely unofficial. They provided their own uniforms, and Reith provided them with rifles which had been found sub-standard at the factory; he and senior members of his staff also acted as instructors.

Toward the end of 1916, Reith was also active behind the scenes in a political sense. Hard on the heels of a series of military successes, the German government had published a range of peace proposals calculated to appeal to the strong strand of pacifist sentiment in the American public mind and to lessen the likelihood of the United States entering the war. A group of Philadelphia churchmen, concerned to counteract this initiative, drew up a statement which they circulated to religious leaders throughout the country. It was endorsed by sixty-one prominent churchmen from nine denominations, and subsequently sent to each of the 150,000 clergy in the United States.[22]

There were, the statement said, seven vital issues to be settled before there could be a just peace: the ravage of Belgium and the enslavement of her people; the massacre of a million Armenians; the desolation of Serbia and Poland; the sinking of the *Lusitania* and of other merchant ships; the starvation of Jews and Syrians in the Holy Land; the attempt to array Moslems against Christians in a 'Holy War'; the intimidation of small nations and the violation of international agreements.

Although principally directed against efforts at premature peace in Europe, the document was also intended to counter the pacifist propaganda of the Carnegie Church Peace Union.[23] The signatories resented the impression that the churches of America were for peace at any price:

> The just God, who withheld not His own Son from the cross would not look with favour upon a people who put their fear of pain and death, their dread of suffering and loss, their concern for comfort and ease, above the holy claims of righteousness and justice and freedom and mercy and truth. Much as we mourn the bloodshed in Europe, we lament even more that supineness of spirit, that indifference to spiritual values, which would let mere physical safety take precedence of loyalty to truth and duty.[24]

The press was told that the document had been prepared 'by trained lawyers and thinkers of national repute'. Whether Reith had a hand in the drafting is not known – it is certainly similar in tone to some of the speeches he was making at the time, and he was on close terms with a number of the signatories. What we do know is that at the request of one of them, Dr William T. Ellis, he travelled to Washington two days before the document was released to the press to brief the British Ambassador, Sir Cecil Spring Rice, and to ask that the Allies' response to the German peace proposals, which press reports said were expected within forty-eight hours, should be delayed. Reith noted in his diary that Rice received him very kindly and was much impressed with the news he brought: 'he said he would certainly cable to England at once to suggest that the reply to the German proposals be delayed.'[25]

In January of 1917 he was invited to address the Presbyterian Social Union on the subject of 'War and Character', and the text he spoke from survives. He treated his audience first to a colourful evocation of the history of the Presbyterian Church in Scotland ('the most glorious and the most tragic recital of high valour upon earth'). That, however, was merely by way of clearing his throat. His main object was to demolish the case for neutrality, and he plunged in with characteristic directness: 'I happen to be a British Officer, but I imagine that there are those here whose sympathies lie in another direction, and I am not at all embarrassed by having to speak in their presence, because I would rather meet any day of the week a pro-German of the most pronounced variety than a man who professed blatant and aggressive neutrality.' In case anyone hadn't caught his drift, he rammed his message home with a quotation from the Book of Judges: 'Curse ye Meroz, said the angel of the Lord, curse ye bitterly the inhabitants thereof; because they came not to the help of the Lord, to the help of the Lord against the mighty.'

War, he told them, is apt to make evangelists of us all: 'I was brought up in a Christian home if ever man was but I admit with regret that I was never really actively concerned about the eternal welfare of any other man's soul (with one exception) until I found myself at the Front in charge of men.' Then he launched into a sustained rant about the horrors of life at the front:

> If you see one minute a brother officer, laughing gallant at one's side, the next moment an unrecognisable bloody mass in a ditch, you would thank God that you could say in the words of the Shorter Catechism, 'The Souls of Believers are at their death made perfect in holiness and do immediately pass into Glory.' If you have stood by a hundred open graves and seen your comrades laid in that shallow bed – about two feet deep with nothing more than a sandbag over their face, and the fair hair which was once a mother's pride mingling with the clay of a foreign land – you would realise something of the necessary preparedness of war . . .

Reith had judged his audience shrewdly. The deep purple of his prose and the revivalist fervour of his delivery produced a powerful effect on them. His friend Dr Ellis was present, and the next day he wrote to Reith's father:

Our Moderators look upon an address for the Presbyterian Social Union as rather the blue riband night of their term of office ... I heard one of our laymen say last night that Captain Reith's speech made the Moderator's address look like thirty cents – which is American colloquialism that perhaps you will not understand. Captain Reith's message was so overwhelming, and moved his hearers so profoundly, that the only proper thing to do under the circumstances was to sing the 23rd Psalm and then go home.

'He will be burdened with many requests to make addresses in the months to come,' Ellis wrote, and he was indeed bombarded with invitations. He mentioned in a letter to his father that he had turned down some thirty invitations to speak in March and April alone: 'I'm told I could make a great deal of money by speaking and the fees which have been mentioned are £10 or £20, and I think I could get even more.'[26]

He attended the inauguration of a Red Cross drive at Williamsport in up-state Pennsylvania. He spoke to an audience of 5000, and was deeply affected by the sight of thirty Civil War veterans who mustered in their faded blue uniforms and campaign medals and paraded their tattered colours to the fife and drum. What appealed to him even more was that he travelled there in style through the Susquehanna Valley in a special train laid on by the Pennsylvania Railroad.

Another invitation which he did not refuse was to the annual dinner of the Pennsylvania Scotch-Irish Society – 'by far the most brilliant gathering I've yet attended', he noted in his diary: 'railroad and bank presidents, judges of the High Court and suchlike'. One of his fellow-speakers was Herbert Hoover, who had won great celebrity for his work with the Commission for Relief in Belgium, but that did not cramp Reith's style, and he waded into the United States for their reluctance to take up arms. 'Practically every man I have met in this country has made excuses,' he told his listeners:

It is all light and laughter and freedom from care here, and unprecedented prosperity. I do not know how many of you have been in London or Edinburgh or Belfast or Glasgow since the war, but you may know there is very little light there, very little laughter, a very great deal of anxiety, and the pinch of the war is felt by old, by young, by rich and by poor. How often I have heard it here, 'I have made a little fortune in the last two or three years. I have cleared something off the conditions.' There you hear them saying, 'I too have lost my only son.'

Reith did not on this occasion confine himself to haranguing his audience about the war. He also decided that they would benefit from a few home truths about the American work ethic:

You may talk of antiquated methods of red tape, and we admit it, but do not talk about sacrifice. You can teach us how to run an electric power plant and a telephone system so that these conveniences may be taken into the humblest homes. You can teach us factory and railroad organisation, and, my conscience, we need it, but you cannot (I have been here for a year) teach a man in Scotland or Ulster what an honest day's work is, how to do a job of work in such a way as to be proud of it for its own sake. I heard a lot about hustle and I like to hustle. Nothing on earth pleases me better than to hustle, but I am sorry to say with all your hustling, among working men, and possibly among other kinds of men, there goes much individual inefficiency and a superficiality of workmanship.

A British colleague who was present told him afterwards that he wished the floor would open and swallow him. 'Reading the speech today,' Reith wrote years later, 'I cannot think how I had the face to give it, as it was most insulting to the Americans.'

No such thoughts appeared to detain him on that February evening in 1917. There had recently been a meeting in the town of a body called the Fellowship of Reconciliation – 'an association of individuals who fortuitously foregather, much in the same style as the sparrows do, under the sheltering cornices where the rain showers are beating down, there to indulge in much twittering of idle tongues and preening of feathered hypocrisy.' Reith took a contemptuous swipe at an English clergyman and an English MP who had attended it – 'I could give them both first class jobs if I were back where I was this time last year, and that is repairing wire entanglements under machine gun fire.' His listeners loved it and they loved his peroration, even though he used it in effect to turn his fire directly and challengingly on them:

Let us not talk about reconciliation and fellowship as long as there is destruction and desolation in the land, piracy on the high seas and flying murder in the air. If you are going to be in at the death it is time you set about purchasing a horse.

'He gave us hell,' he overheard one of his hosts say, 'but we deserved it.'

His success as a speaker both gratified and unsettled him. It also had the effect of turning his mind back towards politics. In February he visited Washington, and at dinner one night caught sight of Robert Lansing, the American Secretary of State, at a nearby table. 'Seeing big men always makes my inside stir up and I feel very impatient,' he wrote to his father. 'I'm pretty certain that I shall find my chief work in politics – either here or in the old country. I cannot ever be President of the United States as one must be born a citizen. Politics are pretty rotten both here and in England, but good men are therefore all the more needed.'[27]

Whether for politics or business, the idea of establishing himself in America was quite often in his mind: 'I think it's pretty certain that I shall come back here after the war and there are big things to be had,' he wrote to his mother:

When the war is over we can have a very good country house probably near Philadelphia 10 – 12 miles off and you can go off to the Holy Land and India for a trip and Egypt just as soon as ever travelling conditions are restored to normal . . . I'm looking forward with pride and delight more than I can ever tell you to having ten, twenty or thirty years ahead to take care of you and give you the finest time with plenty of peace and quiet and rest and nothing on earth to worry about.[28]

It is clear from his correspondence that Charlie also figured centrally in his post-war plans, and that he discussed his ambitions freely with his influential new friends. He had been made an honorary member of the Union League, and he described to his mother a lunch there with John Gribbel: 'He said I should come right back here after the war with you and papa and Charlie. He is a very fine man and of vast business connections.'[29]

He heard in the middle of March that Charlie had been gazetted to the Royal Engineers and had been posted to the company of his choice, the 3rd/1st Highland, at Kilwinning in Ayrshire. Dr Reith, in one of his letters, had mentioned in passing the subject of one of his recent sermons. 'I should like to have heard you preach on David and Jonathan and their friendship,' Reith wrote in reply. 'Personally I think Charlie and I can make the David and Jonathan business look like 30 cents. I do mean that indeed.'

Reith continued to see a great deal of Jimmy Laws: taking him out to dinner and to the movies, going for long walks – and talking endlessly to him about Charlie. 'He is certainly very fond of me,' says a diary note in March, 'and is very sensitive to any sign of my not liking him.' The boy wanted to call him by his Christian name, but announced that he preferred the second one; for the Laws family, therefore, Reith became 'Charlie' and it was as 'Charlie' that he was introduced to Jimmy's elder sister Jeannette during the Christmas holidays. 'She is the prettiest girl I have seen in this country by a very long way,' he wrote in his diary. 'Is, moreover, clever. She is at Smith College, Massachusetts, second year. She is rather fine, I think.' At the end of March she reappeared in Swarthmore for Easter. By now Reith thought her 'quite a sensation', and for some weeks she makes frequent appearances in the diary.

He showed her over the plant (Jimmy in attendance): 'she was looking awfully pretty and I felt very pleased with myself.' She shot off a rifle in the range and they took tea in Reith's office where George, the janitor, had thoughtfully placed some nice carnations. He had clearly planned the afternoon with his usual attention to detail: 'I gave her a round of ammunition all polished up with her initials on it. Also an ejector with her initials on it and my Government stamp.' In the evening he took her out to dinner – 'she was looking perfectly lovely and there was no one in the room to come near her.' Then to the theatre to see Bernard Shaw's *Getting Married* – 'a somewhat indelicate play, but the acting was exceedingly good and there were some very funny things in it.'

They sat together in church on Easter Day and in the afternoon they went out walking in the snow. He wrote to her, and received a reply by return: 'I was rather frightened of it,' he wrote. 'It was very affectionate. Then I go on to record a magnificent one from C. and that fact that though I may be very fond of Jeannette she does not enter into the picture compared with him.'[30]

This seems to have been rather less than the whole truth. In fact his diary entries at this time indicate a state of considerable emotional confusion. He recorded that he was feeling 'very over-strained' at being away from Charlie for so long, and yet there was a period of several weeks between late March and early May when he stopped writing to him altogether. He called on Jeannette the evening before she went back to college and they sat together by the fire:

> I found she was actually wearing the little ejector thing on a chain round her neck, although she did not want me to know this. She said she was going to wear it always, or else have it in her pocket. She came over and sat very close beside me, but I did not touch her. I do not know whether she expected me to kiss her or not. It was a very nice starry night and a full moon. We walked along the country roads, stopping to talk every now and again, and were in very good form.

She wrote to him frequently, and he did not always know how to reply: 'Wrote a very affectionate letter to Jeannette, which I subsequently tore up and sent one less so.'

One morning he caught sight of Jimmy hurrying towards the station; another of his sisters had developed measles, and he was being sent away to cousins in the country. Reith immediately suggested that he should come and stay with him. The boy moved in, and Reith took him horse-riding and taught him to drive his car. 'In spite of all this friendliness with JL and his sister I never felt it made the slightest difference to my feeling for C.,' he wrote, 'and I'm getting more and more anxious to see him again.' While Jimmy was staying with him he received a 'very pathetic letter' from Charlie about his not having written. He sent off a cable promising that he would in future write every day.

At the factory things were going well. In the twenty-two working days of February they shipped 84,500 rifles. Once the United States entered the war in April 1917, however, Reith realised that it would be only a matter of time before the American government required the plant for its own purposes, and he began to consider other outlets for his energies. One of his Swarthmore friends knew the US Army Chief of Staff, Major-General Hugh Lenox Scott, and an interesting letter which he wrote to him about Reith survives:

> Mr J. C. W. Reith, who is the head of the British Inspection Dept. of the Remington Arms Co., Eddystone, Pa., and one of the most remarkable, if not the most remarkable young Englishman who has come over here to work, is desirous of offering his services to train men in the United States after

his term of service as Inspector of Rifles at the Remington Arms Co. ends. Reith is a thoroughly fine fellow, of splendid physique, 6' 6" in height, was in the trenches for 11 months until his face was finally shattered and he was sent to the United States, to serve his government here.

I don't know anyone living who would have a better influence over our officers' training camps than Reith ... I am satisfied when you know him you will wish to secure his services for the tremendous benefit which it would bring to those who would come under the influence of his training.[31]

Friendly gestures like these greatly appealed to his vanity, as did the not infrequent references to him in the press: 'The newspapers are beginning to put paragraphs about me,' says an April diary entry. 'Uncommonly fine looking, etc.' Just occasionally, the reporting of some of his performances got slightly out of hand: 'Captain Reith was one of the "first hundred thousand" sent by England into the war,' read one account of a speech in Swarthmore. 'He has seen service in the Boer War in which he received a wicked sabre slash on the cheek ... "If I thought that war would make half the man out of me that it made out of Reith, I'd enlist tomorrow," said one of his listeners.'

Early in June he was invited to speak in the chapel at Princeton, and the following week he was given an honorary Master of Science degree at Lafayette University: 'A tried soldier in the present emergency', said the citation: 'An eloquent interpreter to America of the spirit and purposes of the world war'. At the lunch afterwards, a local congressman was unwise enough to predict that America would emerge from the war (which she had entered every bit of four weeks previously) as the dominant world power. 'That put me into form,' Reith wrote. 'I said exactly what I thought about the congressman's remarks; they reminded me of Kaiser Wilhelm. At the end the audience was on its feet cheering and waving table-napkins.'[32]

He was a considerable peacock; his Master's hood, he told his parents, was 'rather pretty – yellow velvet in front and down the sides of the back and dark red and white in the inside of the back'. And he was eager that his exploits should not go unrecorded on the home front:

> The *Glasgow Herald* should put in a paragraph about the degree, giving the quotation [sic]. Please see that this is done – I certainly think it is time people in Glasgow knew what I was doing ... It will seem so extraordinary that I've never got a DSO or promotion or anything unless people know that I've been away. Do please see to this. I am AMICE and AMIMechE, that should go in as well as the bit about the degree ... Do not say it was at my instigation. It is much more on your account and papa's than on my own.

The almost manic attention that he was to pay throughout his life to the ordering of his correspondence is already apparent. At the end of a letter to his mother at about this time he writes, 'Please send this letter to Beta to read, then to G and D and Ernest and have them returned to you. Please be sure to do this.' At the bottom of the page, almost as if he were running a private circulating library, he writes 'To initial when read', and this is followed by a string of family initials – GR, MR, AER, GDR. All but one have obediently complied – and added the date. When he was particularly busy in the office, he quite often dictated his letters home. He kept duplicate copies of these, but also of those that were written by hand. Letters were not the only thing he preserved. Every square inch of one whole page of his scrapbook for 1917 is covered with Pullman and luggage tickets – a vast collage cataloguing every strand in the cat's cradle of rail journeys he made during his eighteen-month stay: Toronto–Buffalo, Atlantic City–Philadelphia, Utica–New York, Cincinnati–Washington . . .

Towards the end of June, Jeannette came home from college for the summer. Reith dined with the family and found her looking very pretty, but he still shied away from her obvious affection for him:

> When I went in she had a rose in her hand which I imagine was meant for me, and I felt rather rotten in not asking her to put it in my coat, but I was frightened. I'm not fond of her enough for that. She and I sat on the verandah after dinner and she wanted me to go for a walk but I got out of that.[33]

Jeannette also now had a rival for his affections. Reith was on friendly terms with another Swarthmore family called Stewart, and they had a daughter called Betty. 'She is ravishingly pretty,' Reith wrote in his diary just before Jeannette's return, 'and I feel quite enamoured of her.' He found her 'most fascinating and upsetting', and decided on his next visit to the Laws that she had 'quite put Jeannette in the shade'. He taught her to drive his car, bought her a gold bracelet for her birthday, took enough photographs of her to fill an entire page in his scrapbook. 'She is really rather like a fairy princess,' he wrote in his diary. Jimmy Laws seems to have been not best pleased to discover that there was a new girl in Reith's life; his sister seems to have had greater reserves of equanimity: 'Jeannette rang up to ask if I would go for a walk which of course I had to do. I told her how much I liked Betty and she did not seem to think it as odd as I had expected.'[34] What she might have found odd was that Reith's fairy princess was only twelve and a half years old.

His emotional life was now beginning to resemble that of Captain Macheath in *The Beggar's Opera*. The plot was further complicated by the introduction of the Russell family. Mr and Mrs Russell had a great deal of money and two daughters: 'Both Helen and Constance seem to be very fond of me. They are both very nice. Constance is the one I like – in fact I like her very much – but it is always the elder one who is told to do things with me.'[35] He continued to see Jeannette Laws, but she must have found their meetings pretty hard going: 'Prayer meeting and then a walk with Jeannette. Whatever she may have thought possible beforehand, she would not think so now, but I was quite kind to her.'

It was perhaps as well that his American idyll was drawing to a close. He was by now responsible at the factory for some thirty experts from Enfield and about 1500 inspectors who had been engaged locally. The day after the Fourth of July holiday he was visited by a Major Woodbury of the US Ordnance who was to take over from him. 'There is a ghastly amount of bungling over the whole thing,' he wrote, 'and no one seems to know what is to happen.'

The crystal ball was equally cloudy about his own future. He told a visiting colonel that he was anxious to return to the front, and he was given a letter of introduction to a senior Engineer. His interest was also quickened when he heard that a man called Atterbury, who was Vice President of the Pennsylvania Railroad, had been asked to go to France as Director General of Railroads for the American expeditionary force, and that the possibility had been mooted of his taking Reith with him.

He plunged into one of his favourite activities:

> Had a tremendous clearance of files and papers generally, piles and piles of stuff. This is quite contrary to the usual government procedure, but I am not going to be party to the absurdity of sending crate upon crate home. Holland said we had better send something home to show that there had been an office.[36]

He showed his usual concern for the interests of those who had worked for him, and set about finding places for them. For his private clerk, McCarthy, he arranged what he described as a 'ripping job' as Secretary of the Committee of Public Safety of the Commonwealth of Pennsylvania. McCarthy wrote a touching letter of gratitude: 'my aged grandmother does not fail each evening to impress upon me the fact that should I ever forget you, I will be a base ingrate.'[37]

A few weeks before leaving for home he celebrated his twenty-eighth birthday: 'A cable from Charlie. I had a wonderful letter from him yesterday, the finest I have ever had, twenty-two pages and an extra one for my birthday.' Although his recent behaviour towards her had been that of a clod-hopper, he also received greetings from Jeannette. 'Friend of Mine', she wrote:

> . . . I think the first thing I hope is that life will come right for you. Your plan regarding Charlie is so unusual that it makes me fear for you a little and hope for you a great deal. In a little book which I keep always on my table is this quotation – 'This above all things to thine own self be true/And it must follow as the night the day/Thou canst not then be false to any man.' I like that. It kept repeating itself last evening when we were talking. Nothing will happen to the boy. I still pray for him and you and Charlie, please believe that I shall not fail you there *or misunderstand. I know we can still be friends. You need never feel again that I assume anything but friendship, pure and simple.* And so in the end life will come right for you.
>
> Tomorrow you will be thinking of Scotland and Charlie and your dear father and mother. Tomorrow – well I shall think of you then *because I am your friend if you wish me to be – without any 'what are your intentions?' or like*

foolishness, because your happiness is my concern – and because what I have given you, I gave in absolute sincerity.

   Believe me then what I have been and shall continue to be – Your sincere friend,
'*Jeannie*'.

Reith probably didn't notice that her quotation from *Hamlet* was slightly adrift. Nor is it certain that he was equipped then or later to appreciate what a strikingly wise letter it was from a girl still in her teens. The underlinings are his and a handwritten note at the top of the page suggests the letter may at some later date have been produced during a jealous altercation of some sort: 'To Charlie – please note particularly this was written 19/7/1917.' At the end of the letter he has written, 'Preserve this – precious evidence!!' He did not say of what: but certainly of a very big heart.[38]

He left the plant on 14 August. He was presented with a gold watch and chain and with a silver card-case. The signet ring which Charlie had bought him for his birthday arrived, and he posted his last letter to him from America, noting that it was the 210th since his arrival eighteen months previously. He also wrote in his diary, 'I wonder what Betty will be like when I see her again?'[39]

His friends had exerted themselves to make the voyage home as comfortable as possible. One of the letters waiting for him in his cabin was from Mrs Bayard Henry: 'Talked with the Manager of the American Steamship Line in Philadelphia as soon as I reached the office today. I told him of your expected sailing and dwelt upon the fact that you needed additional length in your state room.' Another came from John Ellery Tuttle, the Minister at Swarthmore: 'You will please try not to flirt with all the ladies on board and remember that your pastor has the eye of his imagination upon you . . . Come back as soon as possible to the friends and the land that love you as their own.'

He was placed at the Captain's table. On the last night at sea there was a full moon – ideal conditions for a submarine attack – but when he woke on the morning of 2 September they were within three miles of the Irish coast. The embarkation officer at Liverpool furnished him with a rail ticket to Glasgow. He surprised his parents at dinner and piled the table high with all that he had brought from New York – pears and peaches, sugar biscuits, preserved fruits, chocolates, twenty-five pounds of sugar. He had planned to go to Kilwinning and surprise Charlie, but his impatience got the better of him and he telephoned. Charlie came to Glasgow the next day:

   To meet C. at St Enoch's in the wildest excitement. 'The happiest moment of my life', he said when he got to the manse. He looked awfully smart in his sapper kit. I wrote 8 pages in my diary about our reunion. We had a prayer together up in my room – just as in 1913.

He had done remarkable things in the United States, both at the plant and on the public platform. A month after his return he received a handsome public compliment on his work when *The Times* printed a letter from the editor of the *Philadelphia Public Ledger*: 'The speeches of Captain Beith and Captain Reith have caught the public ear and materially assisted in moulding pro-ally senti-ment in the Eastern States.'[40] In some respects – socially if not emotionally – he had returned home more mature. America stayed in his mind as the Land of Cockayne, and the affection with which he remembered it was sometimes tinged with regret:

In reading over the diary pages of this period, newspaper cuttings, letters home, and above all letters then and later from American men and women, I find myself wondering what happened to the youth of twenty-six who made such an impression in Philadelphia thirty years ago; he was surely a lad of promise.[41]

Six

PROMISE DEFERRED

So many worlds, so much to do,
So little done, such things to be.
ALFRED, LORD TENNYSON,
In Memoriam, 1850

REITH'S HOPES of returning to the front were not realised. He spent the
rest of the war in England, and for the first nine months or so after his return
from America he raged at the inability of the authorities to find him work which
he regarded as sufficiently demanding. His frustration would have been a good
deal greater if he had not been able to contrive a succession of joint establishments with Charlie. Charlie had matured. Reith found him 'readier to discuss serious things', and one of the first things they discussed was what they
would do after the war: 'We would like to go together to America and settle
there.'

At the end of September, Reith received orders to report to Kilwinning. 'I
suppose it was to my credit,' he wrote, 'that, in spite of this being C.'s Company,
I was simply furious and most disgusted. I wanted to get straight back to France
– preferably in railroad work.'[1] He had at least the consolation of Charlie's
company: 'C. and I arranged a sitting room with great joy – first room we have
actually shared on a permanent sort of basis . . . All sorts of silly routine duties
were tolerable because we shared them.'

This interlude of domestic felicity proved to be brief; within a couple of
weeks he got orders to report to the Railway Operating Division:

Fearfully sad at leaving C. again for Aldershot. There are 6 pages to this
day in the diary. Our friendship touched high levels of spirituality often. I'm
less inclined to report observations on this score than on other more ordinary
ones; but let there be no mistake about it. We never missed our prayers nor
reading together and especially when we were being parted again did we
come together before God – or tried to.[2]

It seemed for a time that this new posting might get him back to France. He
was promoted substantive captain with seniority of June 1916. But then it was
decided that no more captains were required with railway engineering units

overseas, and he was back where he started. The next move in this game of military snakes and ladders took him to Norwich. 'The situation here is simply ghastly,' he wrote. 'I could hardly contain myself in my longing for C.'[3] He had landed in a notably unmartial sapper unit; the Commanding Royal Engineer was a draper from Aberdeen who enquired of Reith what reinforced concrete was.

He wrote to Charlie every day and they spoke on the telephone each Sunday evening. He cleared out twelve sacks of rubbish from the company office; he also wrote a lengthy memorandum demolishing the Adjutant, who had been foolish enough to request particulars of the service which entitled Captain Reith to wear one red and three blue chevrons.[4] He was constantly on the look-out for work that would extend him, and in March he got wind of a big project in the civil engineering department of the Admiralty. Without saying anything to his superiors, he went up to London to sniff out the possibilities; within weeks he had been offered a transfer, and in the middle of May he reported to the Royal Marine Engineers colonel in charge at Southwick in Sussex.

The plan was to construct a submarine hydro-electric barrage which would stretch across the bed of the Channel to the French coast. Eight colossal floating towers were to be built, 193 feet by 162 feet at the base; there were to be four concrete decks on each rising to a height of 82 feet, with a 92-foot steel structure on top of that. Reith was initially given the job of levelling off for the foundations of one of them. His drive quickly commended him to the Colonel, and he was soon put in charge of the construction of the actual towers. He was plainly in his element:

> I always wore old clothes on the job and no belt. Also I stopped people saluting me on the job. I hated the mixture of 'contract job' and military discipline. By this time I had 1800 men under me and about 20 officers, several of them engineers of considerable experience and I had annexed more and more of the work – rather to the discomfiture of the others. Also I used to steal gangs of men from Boyle and he would spend half the day looking for them.[5]

Two of the men under him were the chief engineer and the sub-agent from his job with Pearsons at the Albert Dock before the war; Reith offered them his apologies, but they said they were entirely happy. So was Reith: he was building Brobdingnag. He was on the go day and night, absorbed by the diversity and complexities of the work – muck-shifting and dredging one day, reinforced concreting or the erection of intricate steel superstructures the next.

At the end of May he was gazetted major – 'a major is "somebody",' he wrote in his diary. Two days later he went to evensong in the tiny village church at Kingston Buci, and was shown into a box pew where there were already other people:

One was a girl in uniform and I liked the look of her. I wondered who and what she was and whether she was a lady. (And she thought I looked interesting and distinguished and that my tunic fitted well and my spurs were very long and that I was very restless . . .)[6]

The girl in the uniform of the Women's Legion clearly drove a good many other things out of his mind – he records that he didn't write to Charlie for a whole week – but it took him more than a fortnight to find an opportunity of speaking to her. She turned out to be the driver of his commanding officer's official car and her name was Muriel Odhams.

At the time he got to know her he was deeply preoccupied about the health of his father. Dr Reith was now seventy-six, and on his return from America Reith had been shocked by his appearance – 'I was so afraid he might not be long with us.' He now decided on an impulse that he must go north and took the night sleeper, preferring as he so often did to arrive unannounced.

Father wasn't at all well and had actually given up all idea of preaching, but he resolved to do so. He was so terribly frail. I shall never forget this Communion service. It was the last time I saw my dear father in the pulpit. The sermon was on Psalm 45 v.1 – 'I speak of the things which I have made concerning the King' – Jesus Christ in his Beauty, Grace and Power. It was simply magnificent. He looked dreadfully haggard and frail and his eyes were uncannily bright. I shall never forget his appearance. It was almost too much for me. When he held the Cups up in his hand his appearance was overwhelming. God help me be worthy of such a father.[7]

When he got back to Sussex he arranged that his parents should come and spend a holiday with him there, and they were at Southwick for July and August. The Colonel offered them the use of his car, which meant that Reith saw more of its driver: 'The motor girl wished me many happy returns,' says a diary note on his birthday. When his parents returned to Glasgow there was less occasion to see her – 'I haven't seen Miss Odhams for exactly a month,' he wrote plaintively.[8] He was seeing something at the time of a brother-officer called Thompson. Thompson was very religious, and the pair of them got on well. One Saturday evening, when he was feeling particularly lonely, Reith invited him up to his 'cabin' and they sat up late in earnest conversation – 'about Charlie, and friendship and the difficulty of reconciling ambition with Christian ideals'.[9] Reith soon discovered that they had something else in common, which was that they both greatly admired Miss Odhams.

In the middle of October, a main cause of his loneliness was removed. Reith had for some time been going through his customary routine of trying to arrange for Charlie to come and work with him. He had already been down on a short course, and now he arrived for good: 'I was overjoyed to have C. here at last and no one is likely to interfere with either of us for the rest of the war.' That entry in his diary is dated 18 October. It is a striking illustration of Reith's self-absorption. It was true that Northcliffe had said a few weeks previously 'None of us will live to see the end of the war', but it was also true that the German government had appealed to President Wilson for the opening of peace negotiations a fortnight previously and that the Armistice was little more than three weeks away. When Reith wrote 'This was one of the most interesting and exciting times in my life', it is clear that the interest and excitement did not derive from events in the greater world. He reacted to the end of hostilities with indifference. 'The war is over,' he noted flatly in his diary on 11 November. 'I let any officer go to London who wanted to. C. went, which made me lonely, but I was glad for him.'

He and Charlie started house-hunting. Early in December, Miss Odhams drove them to look at a bungalow, and they decided to take it. Reith went home for Christmas, but his diary entries did not exactly exude the spirit of the season:

> Robert and his wife here unfortunately – sponging as usual. I learned that Jean had had the electric light put in her bedroom without a word to me. I had arranged for it to go on the first floor only. I mentioned to her that it might have been referred to me. Father was very upset when I told him I had done this. There is a veritable reign of terror in the house. When I came back from a short walk I found Jean having violent hysterics in father's bedroom. He blamed me for it! It is really awful.

He went down to Dumfries and spent a day with his brother Ernest. He also saw something of Cissie Murray; he had written her a letter, 'chiefly about her religious ideas', and she told him she was very grateful. They had tea together, went to the cinema, sat by the river and in the park:

> I asked her if she would like me to kiss her. I knew she wanted me to very much, but I didn't . . . I shall tell Charlie, of course, about all this, everything we've said and done. My diary is very clear in recording that there is nothing in it beyond a stirring up of boyhood memories and friendships; and that I found this very pleasant and that it made me feel young again. We often spoke of C. and I told her all about him.[10]

He travelled back to Southwick, but the conversation on New Year's Eve in which he told Charlie about Cissie took an unexpected turn:

> Last night we had a frightful argument about our getting married – almost quite a row. This is a most momentous entry. I had said I never thought of getting married, being satisfied with my friendship with him. I had rejected several good chances already. He astounded me by saying that he intended to get married. I knew that marriage and our friendship were not compatible.[11]

The disagreement did not interfere with their removal plans. 'Give my best wishes to Prince Charlie,' said a letter from his father, 'and tell him to take good care of his money and of yours. The bungalow will not be cheaper than the camp.'

There was a letter from Cissie, too, which 'struck me all of a heap. It was exceedingly affectionate. C. read it and my reply.' As Reith's diary continued to be common property, Charlie would also have read an entry on 3 January which said, 'Miss Odhams is an awfully fine girl and should make an excellent wife for Thompson'; but a couple of weeks later Reith walked with her a little way up onto the Downs, and that night he wrote, 'I don't know whether it is right or wrong but I surely am very fond of her indeed and she is an awfully nice girl.' He plucked up courage to ask her for a photograph, and she sent round four for him to choose from. 'Two I liked awfully,' he wrote in his diary. 'C. helped me choose, of course.'

In spite of what he had said to Charlie about marriage on New Year's Eve, it is plain that he had sought his father's advice on the matter, and Dr Reith sent him a reply that combined practicality with moral earnestness:

> When 'waiting on God' by prayer that puts the whole matter into his hands, you have the opportunity for yourself of discovering some very essential things.
>
> Does the girl you are attracted to come of a healthy stock, and is she thoroughly healthy herself?
>
> What do brothers and sisters think of the girl? How does she conduct herself at home, to her parents especially, and to her brothers and sisters, if there be any? You can't pay a few visits to her house without finding out by quiet observation whether all she is abroad she is and a great deal more, at home.
>
> One momentous consideration is; will she help me to love and serve my Saviour more than I do? Shall we go hand in hand in the things that are of profoundest import?[12]

Reith now took the bull by the horns and asked his friend Thompson whether he wanted to marry Miss Odhams. If the question was strange, the answer was not less so:

> He is very much in love with her and very keen 'humanly' to marry her, but doesn't feel that she is sufficient of a Christian to be his wife . . . I'm rather amazed. I was ready to say I would keep right clear. Accordingly till he can be sure, he's keeping right out of it altogether and not wanting to mislead her – nor wanting to run the chance of making her pretend to be a greater Christian than she is, in order to get him.[13]

By late January, but not before agonising over the matter at inordinate length, Reith had decided that he might call Miss Odhams Muriel, although he recorded that his feelings towards her were more and more mixed: 'Charlie is the same as ever to me; no one, man or girl, can ever change my devotion to him.'[14] The idea that he and Charlie might go and settle in America still ran in his mind, and he wrote to a number of his friends to explore possibilities. Muriel told him that she had been engaged to someone who had been killed at the front. She also told him that she was concerned about the things of eternal life: Thompson had given her a tract called *Safety, Certainty and Enjoyment*, 'which apparently was to do the business of making her fit for him.' It had, she said, had no effect on her. Reith countered with the suggestion that she should think over the hymn 'How sweet the name of Jesus sounds'. If she took this literally and put it to practical test she would be helped.

Sturdy, placid, uncomplicated Miss Odhams might have been forgiven for thinking that she had strayed into the action of a comedy by Molière. A sub-plot developed in February when it emerged that Charlie, too, was becoming fond of her. One night Reith escorted her to a dance. He spent a good part of the evening arranging for her to dance with other people ('it was ripping to watch her') but contrived to sit out five times with her in a secluded alcove which he had reconnoitred in the afternoon. At one stage he walked out under the stars, looked out over the sea, and prayed for guidance, and as they walked home he told her something of his obligations to his father and mother. 'We said goodnight at 2.10,' he recorded in his diary with matter-of-fact precision:

> She held my hand for ever so long and looked straight in my eyes. I kissed her hand twice and her hair twice. I didn't kiss *her* but there was ample opportunity, especially in the alcove. Charlieboy was waiting up for me, which was wonderful of him. I tried to tell him everything, but he *wouldn't* understand.[15]

The following Sunday Muriel was to have gone for a walk with Reith, but telephoned to say that her mother thought she had better not. This put Reith in a rage, of which Charlie took the main force, but the walk took place after evensong instead, and in the course of it Reith made a declaration of his love:

> I had told her that for years the only people in the world I loved were my father and mother. Then C. came and without making any difference in my love to the old folks I loved him more than all the world. I said that now without lessening that, another love had come. C. was waiting anxiously and I told him everything. He was most awfully pleased and of course this makes the whole thing possible. I was very grateful to God for this happy ending to a trying day. We had a prayer together.[16]

The trials of the day were not, in fact, quite over, because at this point the wretched Thompson showed up ('much to C.'s disgust', Reith noted, but presumably to his, too). They took him out walking for three-quarters of an hour, and Reith made it plain that he no longer regarded him as having any prior claim on Muriel's affections. Thompson, who was either astonishingly meek or extremely thick-skinned, responded by asking if he might go back with them and join in their evening prayers, and neither Reith nor Charlie could think of a way of saying no.

It was by any standard a bizarre courtship. It is impossible to read the story of Reith's wooing of Muriel Odhams without a feeling of bewilderment, and that bewilderment is occasionally jostled by disbelief. The day after they had seen Thompson off, Charlie admitted that he too was very much in love with Muriel. 'I was awfully pleased,' Reith wrote in his diary.

He records that in no part of his original diary were there such lengthy entries as in these two months of February and March 1919. He normally wrote about a page a day, but there were now occasions on which the small, orderly handwriting ran on over as many as six. The febrile quality of the fragments that survive shows that he was in a state of considerable turmoil. It was a period in which he and Charlie were living in an emotional hothouse, their nerves frequently a-jangle. It is not clear that either of them knew what they were about; they appeared for a time to believe that the courtship of Muriel, like everything else in the years of their friendship, was something that they could in some way undertake together.

On the first Saturday in March the three of them wandered for hours over the Downs in the early spring sunshine: 'We were all three ever so happy – just like children again.' The next morning, however, he records that he walked slowly to church repeating to himself a verse from Hebrews – 'Let us therefore come boldly unto the throne of grace, that we may obtain mercy, and find grace to help in time of need.' The following evening the three of them again walked out together, arm in arm up Roman Road: 'At the end,' says an entry in Reith's summarised diary, 'I very stupidly and for no reason on earth asked C. to go off. Immediately I had done it I was awfully sick with myself and wanted him back, but he had gone. Even now, 14/3/31, 12 years later, I can't look back quietly on that action. Three years later to a day he was married and gone for good.'[17]

He took Muriel home and then, full of remorse, went in search of Charlie:

> He told me he really had been jealous of me, which he had never been before and didn't want to be again. Poor Charlieboy certainly was in an awful state about it and I comforted him as best I could. He said he was getting most awfully fond of Muriel – loved her very much, enough almost to fall out with me if ever I was unkind in anything I said to her. We had a very fine talk and understood each other better than ever. Bed at 4.30 as I did a great clearance having made up my mind to get out of here and be with C. somewhere. He went to London next day on leave.[18]

The Odhams family home was an attractive old house in Southwick called The Homestead, and Reith was now a regular visitor there. Although Muriel does not seem to have thought there was anything odd about the relationship, an entry in Reith's diary for 10 March makes it plain that her parents took a different view: 'M's people were silly about her going out with C. and me,' he wrote grumpily. 'Went to her house in the evening and saw her mother for a bit and told her what I felt about things.' His irritation was dispelled by the sight of Muriel, looking 'awfully pretty' in a black velvet dress, and both then and the following evening she was very affectionate:

> She put her arms round my neck and held me ever so close and I said 'Kiss me, darling.' So she put her lips to mine and then away and then back again and we kissed each other. Her lips were trembling and I was shaking all over. It was a long and very thrilling kiss and then we sat still for a bit. Then we did it again – ever so long and close. I said goodbye at the gate and hurried home to C. He saw at once that it had happened and of course I told him all about it; he was awfully pleased. We are more fond of each other than ever. It is, of course, magnificent that he takes it this way, otherwise the whole thing would be impossible for me.[19]

Towards the end of March, Reith went to see the rector of Kingston, whom he now knew quite well: 'I told him how things were and he strongly advised me to get engaged. His knowledge of psychology was limited – or else stupendous.' When, however, Muriel told him the next day that her parents thought there should be 'something definite', he was intensely annoyed: 'T. may get her yet is what I feel this morning,' he noted crossly in his diary. Events later the same day did nothing to decrease his indecision:

> C. saw her with her hair down and was quite overcome. He's very much in love with her. I had a wonderful evening with her. She took her hair down for me. C. was in a very bad way. He came into bed beside me; said he wanted to cry but that it wouldn't come. Next day he said after I'd gone to sleep he had 'sobbed his wee heart out'. I was most awfully sorry for him. It was all on account of his love for M and I don't know if I should get engaged to M loving him so awfully as I do. It's a terrible dilemma.[20]

Although he kept a fair number of his parents' letters, there are few from this period. His own letters to them, however, obviously conveyed something of the confused state he found himself in at the time: 'Mother doesn't seem to understand the position with Muriel,' he noted toward the end of March. 'Charlie is to help me out on this.' Charlie did, in fact, now begin to urge him to become engaged, and on 1 April he visited a shop called Hinderlich's in Hatton Garden and bought an engagement ring. He went round to The Homestead that evening, and found Muriel 'looking gorgeous' in a blue dress, but if she had expected him to slip his new purchase onto her finger, she was disappointed:

> I showed her the ring and she was awfully excited about it; didn't touch it; saw it flashing in the firelight. We had a wee prayer together which was very fine indeed, though I was rather frightened.[21]

Muriel's parents gave continuing signs of restiveness, and now decreed that the Saturday afternoon walks *à trois* should cease; their attitude, Reith wrote, was 'iniquitous'. He and Charlie jointly composed a letter to the manse telling the whole story, but this crossed with a cry of distress from his mother at the prospect of 'losing her boy'. Reith, deeply upset, made his way to the telegraph office at Shoreham: 'Letter explaining everything will reach you morning,' he wired to his father. 'I shall do nothing till you telegraph. Whatever happens your position and mother's remains unaltered always and is my first care. This is understood. Very much love, John.' Their reply said simply 'Love and blessings to you both', which did not satisfy Reith, and he telegraphed a second time. 'We really mean it,' came the answer. 'Heartily happy in your happiness.' It is not altogether certain that this was the response which Mrs Reith's boy wanted: 'I was in a most awful quandary,' he wrote in his diary.

The next day was a Saturday. It was an important day in Reith's life, and the two accounts he has left of it – in his diary and in a letter to his mother – tally very closely. In the afternoon, defying the displeasure of Mr and Mrs Odhams, he and Muriel and Charlie took the train to Bramber. It was a warm day, and they hunted around for primroses. They sat on a stile and Muriel put an arm round each of her escorts. After tea they went into the churchyard; Reith told Muriel of the exchanges with his parents, and repeated that his first care had to be for them: 'She understood perfectly and I know, of course, that she is absolutely the right sort for my dear old people and they would like her tremendously.'

They set off back across the Downs for Southwick:

> In the churchyard C. handed me the ring and wanted me to ask her then to give herself to me, but I couldn't. However on the way back from 7 to 8.30 I prayed about it and thought over it all and then at 8.30 I asked Mu to walk on by herself and took Charlie by himself and asked him, would I do it? He said yes, and was very anxious for me to do it, so I told him to ask Mu to wait for me and I went up to her, with my hat in my hand. I said I wasn't much, but that I did try to be better – a better Christian, too, and that, if she put her life in mine and trusted me, I would do all I could to make her happy. I asked her if she really loved me and was sure enough of me to take this step. She was very much affected though pretty calm outwardly. I stood away a little and watched her. Presently she came up and put her arms round my neck and kissed me ever so wonderfully and said 'Yes, John.'[22]

It was now almost dark. Reith suggested that they should rejoin Charlie and pray together, but Charlie was praying at some distance by himself and did not immediately come when Reith whistled:

> I went up to him and put my arms round his neck and kissed him and broke down and cried. I felt as if I had left him in some way. Nothing can ever

lessen or dim my overwhelming devotion to him and he stands as ever he did with me. Mu knows and understands all this perfectly; it could not be otherwise. He took her in his arms and said, 'Mu, my darling, I'm so glad.' We all stood together close and C. prayed wonderfully for us all. I had asked M if I should put on my ring and she had said yes, and so when we came to C. she was wearing it. Both C. and I kissed it. Then, hand in hand, we all set off down the hill together, though I broke down again before we left. Mu was tremendously happy. We walked arm in arm when we got to the road and we kissed her at the gate ... I was terribly concerned lest C. should think any girl could affect the intense fellowship between us.[23]

The engagement was a lengthy one, although Reith was now in his thirtieth year and Muriel was twenty-six. Mr and Mrs Odhams said that they were very dependent on their daughter and would not wish her to be married for two or three years; Reith, for his part, had no wish to tie the knot until he found himself securely settled in peacetime employment. Muriel quickly won his parents' hearts. 'I know how splendid John is and his great love to you and his Father,' she wrote winningly to Mrs Reith. 'I do hope that my coming in will make no difference, and that if in the future we have a little home of our own, you will always come and share it with us, if you will.'[24]

Reith was not demobilised for another four months. The day after Muriel accepted him, he received a telegram ordering him to report to the Chief Royal Engineer, Salisbury Plain. A large military housing scheme was planned there. He moved into furnished quarters and was quickly on good terms with the General Officer Commanding, the Chief Engineer of the Command, and the CRE. They told him that even if nothing came of the housing scheme they would like to have him as assistant CRE of Salisbury Plain. The War Office, however, had other ideas, and when a regular major was appointed to the vacancy, Reith decided that the time had come to return to civilian life: 'Between September 1917 and August 1919 – twenty-three months – I had done about six months' useful work.'[25]

The summer of 1919 was not a happy time for him. It became apparent as the months passed that his father's life was drawing to a close. Dr Reith's letters became shorter, and the writing increasingly spidery; there were days when he could scarcely raise his head from the pillow. Reith went to see him several times, travelling back each time depressed not only by his father's condition: 'Things are ghastly in the manse,' reads a diary entry in early June. 'Horrid scene at tea as mother fled from Archie's denunciation of Jean.' Their nerves were all clearly badly frayed: he was back in Glasgow in August, and Jean's temper flared one day over the lunch table:

I said she hadn't been to see father for three weeks. She said that was her business, I said it might be mine after his death. She disappeared and then mother wanted me to go and say I'm sorry. Why in heaven's name? All through life I've been badgered to say I was sorry to Jean. Mother was very miserable and just after lunch went up to Jean's room and I heard Jean storming and screaming at her for over an hour. It is *awful*.

It is plain from a chilling diary entry during this visit that Reith lacked the wit to spare his dying father involvement in these painful scenes:

He came near to my view that I can't possibly be expected to recognise Jean, after his and mother's death, as having the slightest claim on me. I was exceedingly glad that father was coming nearer my view on this, as he had usually hitherto seemed to expect me to treat her as if she were my sister.[26]

He applied for the job of Director of Housing in Glasgow, equipping himself with testimonials from a number of people prominent in the life of the city. One was from Mr J. A. Roxburgh, who was an ex-Lord Dean of Guild. It survives in Reith's scrapbook; a handwritten note on the corner of it says, 'I only thought of this loathsome job so that I might be in Glasgow when father was dying', but he was indignant when the position went to a local sanitary inspector. He was also given an introduction to the Governor of the Gas Light and Coke Company, who told him that if he were prepared to spend a few months going through the mill, there would be an opening for him as assistant chief engineer. It was the Glasgow and South Western Railway story of 1913 all over again: 'Milne-Watson had omitted to secure the acquiescence of his chief engineer, and that was that.'[27]

A vacancy came up at the Ministry of Munitions as Assistant Director of Ordnance Supply at a salary of £500–£750. Reith went to be interviewed and announced that £750 was his minimum. One of the officials he saw said he had not expected anyone of his calibre to be thrown up by the Ministry of Labour; he started in at the end of August. 'The department is in a ghastly state,' he noted. 'Trouble to know where to go for my cocoa and two buns at lunchtime.' He also recorded that he was very lonely in the evenings – and that he had begun to consider how he might get Charlie into the Ministry.[28]

The work was concerned with the running down of war contracts. It involved him in dealings with many of the big armaments firms and brought him into contact with the likes of the Director of Artillery and the Master-General of the Ordnance. Although he found things in a considerable mess, he presented his chief after three weeks in the job with his operation orders describing how he proposed to clear it up:

The Financial Secretary said I had saved at least £2 million on 18-pounder contracts alone and had got about eight hundred more complete equipments than were expected. I did a great deal without authority, but knew that everything would stand, as it later did, any amount of investigation.[29]

He was coping less well with the skein of his emotional entanglements. He badly needed a set of operation orders in his private life, but that was beyond him. It is plain from his diary entries that he was no less confused after his engagement than he had been before it:

> Mu and I had the most wonderful time we've ever had . . . She was lying almost right on top of me and I had my hand a wee bit inside her dress. She leaned up to let me put my hand down on her heart and it was wonderful. I said, 'Shall I?' and she said yes. I was awfully bewildered by it all, and I felt it was a great honour somehow. She and C. had some good times, too. When we left I kissed her hand. She would hardly let me go even at 11 o'clock and held me ever so close with her arms round my neck. I was quite unconscious of any 'sexual' attraction or excitement – very odd and significant. C. was quite otherwise with M. C. and I had a magnificent time later.

One Saturday in early May they all three took the train to Steyning and walked up Chanctonbury Ring. The downs were bright with flowers – hyacinths, primroses, cowslips, violets, sweet briar – and they lit a fire and had tea: 'We shall not forget this wonderful walk,' Reith wrote in his diary:

> I confess, I was wanting to talk to C. about things. I love M. very much but C. was my love years before I knew her, and I cannot let him go. He is all the world to me. It is awful; I don't know what to do . . . I had a very wonderful time with M but I don't seem to be so much in love as C.

A few days later Muriel said she found his behaviour towards her neglectful, and her edginess did not diminish when Reith began laying down the law about where her maternal duty would lie – it was, he informed her, the mother's job to teach her children to pray and tell them about Christ. When Muriel told him he would have to attend to that sort of thing, what had begun as conversation suddenly lurched into catechism: 'I asked her what Christ meant to her. "Very little, I'm afraid," she said.' Then she put her head on his shoulder and wept.[30]

Ten days after this he made a will leaving everything to Charlie, and early in June he wrote in his diary:

> I love M. enough I think to make her very happy if only she will be sensible and understand. She seemed to do all this before we got engaged. Why not now? C. comes first and it will be to our happiness if she can be content. Heaven knows what will happen otherwise. I am fearfully worried.[31]

The next day he talked things over with Muriel, and his worries were swept away:

> She made me most tremendously happy by saying she had been thinking things over and had come to the conclusion that she must share me with C.

and be happy in this. This is what I had hoped and prayed for; it is the solution of my wretched anxiety and I am very thankful.

He discovered that Muriel required instruction in more than maternal duty: 'Muriel doesn't know the first thing about sex nor how babies come. This is nice in one way but all wrong in another.' She also vexed him by saying that she didn't at all object to Sunday games if people couldn't play during the week and if they'd been to church once – 'she's quite decided about it.' When he was not taken up with Muriel's backsliding, there were problems of Charlie's to be attended to: 'C. wrote asking guidance in the matter of his love for M. Poor boy, I'm tremendously anxious to prevent his being wounded in any way and I wrote a long reply – 14 sides.'[32]

His birthdays were frequently the occasion for bouts of self-examination. On his thirtieth he did not much like what he saw, and went on about it for almost two pages:

> What a ghastly business I've made of my life so far; so much to ask forgiveness for; such cause for shame and sorrow, and for fear of a neglected and outraged God . . . It may be that I am not to realise any of my ambitions in any degree and that my greatest witness to Him is only to be in the subordination of my will in this respect. If so – well I hope he gives me the grace to be content. As for Charlie, nothing can convey my sense of indebtedness to him, my longing to be of service to him and that we do some great and good work together and share eternal happiness.[33]

He went through the formal process of demobilisation in September and went north. It was plain that his father was drifting into death. The old man imagined that he had been away in Aberdeenshire; he was also convinced that he was to appear in court charged with some offence, and had written letters to three friends asking them to defend him and arrange bail.[34] Dr Reith had not, for all that, entirely lost his grasp of the things of this world; shortly after his return to London, Reith had one of the last letters he was to receive from him: 'You won't run the risk of shoving Charlie in over some man displaced,' Dr Reith wrote. 'That could lead to trouble. Charlie can fend for himself.'[35]

That matter, however, had already been settled: 'Tremendous news on Monday morning,' Reith wrote in his diary. 'C. can come onto my staff at once. I got him on the phone at Euston and he was awfully pleased. He has been getting worried about a job. We are very thankful to God for this.' Before the end of November, although without formal promulgation, he had contrived to work Charlie into the position of second-in-command.

On 9 December he was handed a telegram: 'Father passed away peacefully this morning at three.' He rang for Charlie, and they walked round a quiet part of the building together. He stayed at the office all day, although unable to do any work. At 5.30, he left the Ministry with Charlie and went to the room at the Regent Palace Hotel which he had recently moved into: 'There I broke down. We prayed together and then sat in the dark. I did so long for my dear father to come to me in some form or other to comfort me.' Charlie saw him onto the night train.

His father's death was a devastating blow. 'I'd been persistently trying to keep my mind fixed on the glory of his present state,' he wrote, 'and I hoped this would outweigh my grief and loss, but it wasn't so at all.' His mother was entirely composed, and after lunch she took him to the room where his father's body lay:

> She drew back the little cloth and there was his dear face, so drawn and white and yet so *perfectly* peaceful. His hands were crossed on his breast and they were so thin too. Mother stood smiling down on him – looking so happy and content she was – almost radiant – 50 years comradeship. I put a sprig of white lilac in his hands. I had many silent prayers in this sacred and solemn room today and each day. With my eyes on his face and my hands on his I asked God to help me live pure and straight, and to dedicate myself to Christ, and to be born again – one of the last things he had said to me.[36]

Charlie arrived the next day and took charge of a good many things for him – there were, for instance, between two and three hundred letters and forty or fifty wreaths, and Charlie listed the names of the senders and noted the messages. Bereavement did nothing to draw the sisters and brothers closer together: 'Awful that family quarrels can't be kept in abeyance even at such a time,' Reith wrote. His brother Robert bullied their mother. His brother Archie, the Anglican vicar, who was in Glasgow, had decided that he and his wife would not attend the funeral, but that did not prevent him writing Reith a peremptory note asking him 'to be good enough to submit the suggested funeral arrange-ments to me'.[37] His brother Douglas was away in West Africa, running an ex-German mission.

He got through the funeral 'only by entering tremendously into the service and singing very loudly'. The coffin was borne out to Chopin's *Funeral March*, and the steps of the church were lined by the boys of the 1st Company of the Boys' Brigade; the grave, at his father's wish, was lined with green leaves. Charlie had to return to London before him; Mrs Reith pressed upon him her husband's black overcoat – the one with the fur collar which Reith had bought for him in 1916.

He attended to the valuation ('I looked after the man and kept things down to a minimum'), learned to his satisfaction that his mother wanted to come and live with him, and went south as soon as he could. He did his Christmas shopping – a leather bag for Muriel, the works of Thackeray in seventeen volumes for Charlie – and spent a few days quietly in Sussex with the Odhams. He was no sooner back at the Ministry after the holiday than Archie descended on him. His plans, which included a visit to Kilburn Music Hall, struck Reith as bizarre: 'Apart from the fact that I do not go to Music Halls I think it is rather odd to suggest this so soon after father's death.'

His social life was restricted. When he was in London at weekends, he had started going to the Presbyterian Church in Regent Square, not far from the Foundling Hospital in Coram's Fields. The surroundings were uncongenial and the journey unpleasant, but it was the church in which his parents had been married and he quickly came to feel at home there. Otherwise, he saw few people outside the Ministry. He dined out only rarely. When he did, the evidence is that his conversational style was robust. He recorded that one evening he had met a young artist called Gawsden: 'I made a special effort to extract from him some intelligible explanation of what so-called modern art was getting at in the weird and repugnant things nowadays produced. Much of what he said was twaddle, and he seemed to recognise this himself.'[38]

Some of his weekend visits to The Homestead passed off more agreeably than others. Mrs Odhams, in particular, he found reserved and cold, although from his accounts of some of their conversations it is conceivable that she merely found her prospective son-in-law alarming:

> Some argument about church matters. I was trying to find out if Mrs O would prefer me to be a 'churchman' of the ordinary type, amounting to nothing beyond a perfunctory and spasmodic attendance and possibly not even that, or an enthusiastic and perhaps even aggressive Presbyterian. No answer.[39]

The manse was up for sale. His account of his last two visits to the old family home read like passages from *Cold Comfort Farm*. Douglas, home from Africa with his wife and children, had been choosing some bits and pieces for his new home: 'I was glad to find that the second instalment of stuff for his house was going that day, so I managed to get a good deal of rubbish into the van on the quiet.' There was some minor unpleasantness with Robert, and then a major row with his sister Jean:

> She refused to leave the doors of her rooms unlocked, though I had asked her especially to do so as the man McGuire, who was buying the house, was coming to see over it, and I was anxious to foist off undesirable stuff onto him ... It is sad to think that the manse where my father has lived all these years should pass into the hands of a Roman Catholic panel doctor. The church might I think have seen that it had some more appropriate use.

There was further trouble over the arrangements Jean had made for their mother – the beginning of a sullen tug-of-war with his sister that was to continue until Mrs Reith's death in 1935:

> Jean in hysterics about my wanting to hustle mother away from Glasgow ...
> I offered to take any things up with me to London that mother wished. She

was anxious for me to do this, but Jean made a row about it. I was to take the gramophone, for instance, which I had bought, but Jean went and stormed at mother about it. Mother is completely under her thumb.

Mrs Reith had not been left in a strong financial position. When Reith received the details of his father's estate from his friend Loudon he was shocked; there was an insurance policy that would yield something over £900, investments totalling £700, and a bank balance of about £100. The funeral had cost £66 and estate duty was assessed at £193.[40] Determined to get his mother down to London, he began house-hunting. He saw almost exactly what he wanted – a house about a mile from Mill Hill in North London to let unfurnished; he missed it by half an hour. Then his mother began to hedge about coming to live with him in England; Jean's husband was working abroad, and she felt she must remain with her daughter at least until he returned.

Reith was in the market for a job as well as for a house, although he had no clear idea of what he wanted. Towards the end of 1919 he had spotted an advertisement for a position with a Scottish engineering firm called William Beardmore and Company who wanted a general manager. He got onto a short-list of three, but heard soon after the death of his father that they did not intend to take the matter further: 'The poor boobs at Beardmore think I am too young for that job,' he wrote, 'and they are not going to make any appointment.'[41] He had also looked at a job in India. The salary offered was £2500, and Reith's father, in his last letter to him, had urged him to consider it seriously: 'I rather favour the wedding in India – in the Bombay Cathedral where so many Anglo-Indians have been married,' he wrote.[42] When the firm offer was made, however, he reflected for five days and then turned it down, giving what was to become a characteristically Reithian reason: 'I told Sir George Buchanan that if one Lewis, to whom he has offered the first job at Bombay, declined, I would take it, but that I did not wish to be second.'[43] Lewis did not oblige.

He had not abandoned the idea of politics. In the spring of 1919, trading on his American experience, he had forced himself on the attention of Lord Bryce. They talked about the United States and about Parliament. We do not know what the Liberal elder statesman, former ambassador in Washington and author of the classic work on the American Commonwealth, made of Reith. 'I wasn't impressed with him at all,' Reith wrote in his diary.[44] Nothing came of the encounter. Two months later he answered an advertisement by a Liberal MP called Kenworthy (later Lord Strabolgi) who was looking for a secretary. Kenworthy, he noted, had 'liked my reply out of a thousand. Could have had the job but he isn't enough of a personality for me; his views too radical, salary too low.'[45]

The only thing that could be said with certainty about Reith's own rather unformed political views at this period is that they were not Conservative. In March of 1920 he addressed an extraordinary letter to J. R. Clynes, the Vice-Chairman of the Labour Party.[46] He began with a considerable *non sequi-*

tur: 'I am actually a civil engineer, and the fact of my having just received an offer of an appointment of the most exceptional professional and financial attractiveness in India has made me resolve to lose no further time in writing to you.' Then he plunged straight in:

> The matter is that since boyhood I have been of a mind that I might do the best service (I use the word in its highest significance) by entering politics, though I almost hesitate to write those words so travesty [sic] have they become . . .
>
> My father was a clergyman in Scotland – Moderator of the Church – famous for his impassioned advocacy of righteousness in every department of human activity. Is this what the Labour Party of today stands for, or is it not?

Such ideals, he told Clynes, were only to be realised by an 'unqualified, deliberate, manly and aggressive adoption of the principles adopted by Christ'; the surest foundations for political guidance were to be found 'in some of the tremendously impressive, if somewhat volcanic, utterances of the Old Testament Jehovah'.[47] Clynes took some time to reply, pleading pressure of work, although this could have been a euphemism for bafflement. 'It is', he wrote, 'difficult to advise on the outstanding point of your letter. A more reliable opinion than I can give might be expressed by Mr Arthur Henderson, MP. He has been more in touch with the work of religious bodies in relation to Labour movements . . .'[48]

Then Beardmores came back into the picture. On the day the removal men came to the manse, Reith travelled out to Parkhead to see Sir William Beardmore. His appointment was for three, and throughout his life punctuality was one of a number of virtues which Reith placed next to godliness. He wrote in his diary that he was kept waiting for an hour and a quarter; by the time he came to write his memoirs, it had come down to thirty minutes. Whatever the precise time of day, Sir William's secretary caught up with him halfway between the waiting-room and the exit. He was offered the general managership of the Beardmore works at Coatbridge, asked for a salary of £1200 with a bonus on output, and was invited to go straight out and look the factory over.

He did not immediately accept the offer, although Charlie's father, whose advice he sought, felt it held out better prospects than the Bombay one. He was irritated by a letter from Mrs Odhams asking him to go down to Southwick: 'she wanted to have a little talk before we begin on M's trousseau.' Muriel, now twenty-seven, was becoming worried about the length of their engagement. Mrs Odhams was concerned less with its length than with its soundness. Tongues were wagging. Muriel's brother, observing Muriel and Charlie together at a dance, had formed the view that Charlie was in love with his sister.

It was the Easter weekend, but Reith shied away from going to Southwick and went off instead with Charlie for a few days' holiday in Devon. They took

Reith as a child

Reith's parents

Charlie in 1913: 'This photo was in my pocket all the time at the Front.'

Muriel 16.1.19.

Sussex courtship, 1919:

Above: Muriel and Reith

Left: Muriel – the first picture Reith had of her (which Charlie helped him to choose)

Above: Charlie and Reith

Left: Charlie and Muriel

Above: Lord Gainford, 1926

Above right: Lord Clarendon, 1930

Right: R. C. Norman, 1936

Below: J. H. Whitley, 1931

a room in the boarding-house where his mother and father had stayed in 1914, their window looking over the sea and the Lyne valley. They walked along the steep cliff road to the Valley of the Rocks, savouring the scent of the pine trees; they played with a hard rubber ball and rolled big stones down the cliff; they put away prodigious quantities of pressed beef and ham and rhubarb tart and Devonshire cream and cider. Some acquaintances turned up, and they made a joint expedition. 'We had good fun,' Reith wrote, 'although I would rather that C. and I had been alone.'

5 April was the anniversary of his engagement, and he acknowledged in his diary that 'the present situation is certainly rather extraordinary.' A letter arrived confirming the Beardmore offer, and after much deliberation he decided to accept it. It was the last day of their holiday. The weather was fine. They gathered primroses and sat talking beside the sea at Lynmouth: 'C. did not know what to advise me to do about M. After dinner, a walk along the North Cliff for the last time. We were very grateful for this magnificent holiday together.'[49]

On his return he went to see Muriel. Relations were strained, and they sat on the West Pier at Brighton for two and a half hours trying to resolve their differences. It was raining and it was very cold. Reith remembered the discussion as 'rather bitter at times on her part and perhaps callous on mine' – he told her among other things that he felt he had been hurried into the engagement by her mother:

> I had also said that I would not be likely to act in what was apparently the usual way for a *fiancé*, but that that was no indication whatever of my feelings. I reminded her that she had often said that I was differently constituted from other people ... She said she would not be distrustful again; but it had always come round that she was, and each time more than before.

Muriel asked him whether he wanted to break off the engagement. Reith said that he did not, but that a 'distrustful attitude' on her part would bring that about.

> I asked her what she would feel like if we did break it off, and gathered very clearly that she would feel it most frightfully ... Of course she said a lot about what people were alleged to be saying and thinking, which I always said was so ridiculous. However things seemed to finish off satisfactorily and she to be happy again, and she said she would not be distrustful and so on any more. In the station I said I would like to kiss her, and meant it, but of course she said, 'Oh no, not in the station,' etc.[50]

Having decided to join Beardmores, he set about arranging for Charlie to succeed him at the Ministry; it was quickly agreed that he should do so at a salary of £650.[51] He brought his mother south, and in his last weeks in London took her about a good deal – to Drury Lane to see Pavlova ('I had no interest in this, but she enjoyed it greatly'), to Chelsea to visit Carlyle's house, to Chalfont St Giles to visit Milton's cottage. They went to Oxford: 'I was possessed of a solemnity and an awe and was greatly impressed and affected.' It also unsettled him – 'It all represented a range of experiences which I have missed. I have come to a sense of responsibility and to responsibility *too* early.'

During his mother's visit, they had a long discussion about her will: 'eventually decided that she should have one leaving everything to me and that gradually she would write down instructions regarding details. Nothing will actually come to me, but this would enable me to see that things were done properly.' He also poured out to her his troubles with Muriel and her family, and felt that he got a sympathetic hearing: 'I found that she was of my way of thinking especially about my going to Lynton instead of Southwick.' It is possible that he also discussed his emotional problems outside the family; a brief diary note recording a visit to the Pensions Ministry reads, 'they think I should have psycho-therapeutic treatment', but he did not immediately follow this advice.[52] Then, in the middle of May, he set off for Glasgow:

> Very sad at leaving C. Looking forward to a reunion in two months or so, as I was quite sure I could get him a job with me. Put up at Central Hotel, Glasgow and posted No. 1 to C.[53]

He arrived in Glasgow both depressed and apprehensive. His mood was not improved by a visit from his brother Robert, who tried to touch him for £100, or by the discovery that there was a smallpox scare in the city and that he had to be vaccinated. He was not at all sure he had done the right thing: 'This factory work doesn't really interest me greatly. If I had found a suitable house near London I should have stayed there and found a job.' He was worried each evening by the departure from Central Station of the 9.45 London train, and wished he were on it. He wrote a personal note to his former boss at the Ministry of Munitions asking him to recommend Charlie for an OBE.

At Coatbridge, where the flow of lucrative military contracts had dried up, he did not like what he saw: 'There is no sort of coordination in the factory; oil engines, steam engines, pumps, motor cars, all running quite independently.' The absence of method in the changeover to peacetime production was compounded by a lack of discipline:

> Foremen had not the authority of their North British Locomotive counterparts; some of them did not even wear the traditional and symbolic bowlers. I issued a quick order about this and it was obeyed. One of them seemed embarrassed and rueful. I asked him if he disliked it. 'Eh, surr, ma wife says Ah'm ower saft in the heid fur to wear a gaffer's hard hat.'[54]

He arranged to have an old thirty-horsepower Austin Daimler fitted up for his use, and he plunged into a course of reading on psychology, with special emphasis on industrial efficiency. His grasp of this new discipline was put to an early test when the pattern-makers' shop stewards turned up to see him without an appointment: 'I won't have that again. My first experience of shop stewards. I settled them and their complaint.'[55] Early in July he wrote an official letter to Charlie offering him a job at a starting salary of £500: 'although he is well worth it, there are few fellows of 23 getting such a salary.'[56]

Later in the month, Muriel came north for a short holiday. They visited Dunblane in Perthshire and saw a house called Dunardoch which they very much liked, and when Charlie arrived at the end of July to start work at Beardmores it was in lodgings in Dunblane that he and Reith installed themselves, sharing a bedroom and sitting room. An early caller was the Minister of the United Free Church; this was an embarrassment to Reith, who felt much attracted by the music of Dunblane Cathedral, which belonged to the Church of Scotland. He and Charlie went there on their first Sunday, and sat on after the service listening to the organist: 'I saw that C. had tears in his eyes. He said he was thinking of Mu. I felt very sad about it.'[57]

Reith pressed on with his efforts to improve discipline at the factory. The introduction of a time clock was not popular, but when the men were given the choice between punching in and getting a week's notice they fell into line. Reith ascribed the bad spirit he had detected on his arrival to 'disruptive, communistic activity'. 'I had no particular feelings about Communism,' he wrote in his memoirs, 'but I was determined to secure a good spirit, with or without Communism.'[58] He did this by isolating one not particularly effective convener. 'Saw Aitken the Bolshevist and made him take his hat off in my room,' he noted briskly in his diary on 23 August. The wretched Aitken was totally unfamiliar with the tactics of psychological blitzkrieg and in a matter of weeks passed out through the factory gates for the last time.

There were carrots as well as sticks, however. Lectures and dances were arranged, and there were concerts and football matches. Reith also pursued the interests of his staff in the local community:

> Entertained the Provost and Town Clerk of Coatbridge at the factory with ulterior motives, namely twenty of the new council houses for our staff. I thought they should realise the size of the factory. I also wanted a street renamed. They were much impressed.[59]

In September he went briefly to Sussex, but quickly regretted it. It is plain from his diary that relations had once again become scratchy:

> I've had another affair with Muriel on the same old line. She wonders if I want to break off the engagement. It is perfectly *awful*, and she never will be happy or believing as long as she remains under the yoke of parental domination. She admits being frightfully cold and reserved and even wrote that there are times when she feels she would rather do anything than let me think she cared for me! . . . Her mother of course blames me – one can

see that simply sticking out of her whenever I go to Southwick and even Mr O makes cryptic innuendoes.[60]

The contrast between the drive and assurance that characterised Reith in the workplace and the doubts and uncertainties that assailed him in his private life is striking. By the closing months of 1920, however, for all his hesitations, he was finally edging towards matrimony. He had begun negotiations for the purchase of Dunardoch. He had heard that it had changed hands a year previously for only £750, but the asking price was now £2000. He went to see the vendor and got him to throw in all fixtures and fittings.

Reith had concluded fairly quickly after his arrival at Coatbridge that Sir William Beardmore had little grasp of what went on in the sprawling organisation that bore his name. One of his main complaints was that although he was directly responsible to Sir William, he saw next to nothing of him. There survives in his scrapbook a copy of the report he wrote to the Chairman after he had been in the job for six months. 'Woeful lack of system' – 'past negligence and mistakes' – 'appalling condition of affairs six months ago' – 'gross mishandling': not a document calculated to endear Reith to colleagues in the parent company. He pointed to the increased productivity that had resulted from improved industrial relations and to the progress he had made in devising planning, progress and costing systems. He also entered a robust defence against the continual criticism directed at Coatbridge by the London office and by customers for failure to execute outstanding orders.[61]

Reith's experience of organised labour at Coatbridge had a pronounced effect on his political outlook. There were municipal elections in November, and Labour increased its representation on the Corporation from twenty-four seats to forty-four. 'A rotten business', Reith wrote in his diary. For someone who had written to J. R. Clynes as he did only a few months previously, his political views had clearly evolved with some rapidity. On a specific issue submitted to the test of public opinion at the time, he remained consistent. The elections were accompanied by temperance polls. In Glasgow, only four wards went dry, while nine opted for some restrictions. 'Very few districts in Scotland have gone dry,' Reith noted disapprovingly. 'It is a wretched business.'

Early in the New Year, he went to see Muriel again and things went rather better, although some of the good work done by a large box of chocolates was undone by his informing her that she required a lot of new dresses. Later in the day, he gave her the benefit of his advice on another matter: 'I gave her quite a talk about developing self-reliance, which I feel to be exceedingly important for her. She has been made far too dependent on her mother.'

He returned to Dunblane and to Coatbridge, and on 1 February 1921 he wrote in his diary, 'I got sick of the factory so went to the Motor Show at the Kelvin Hall.' He sounded the same note two days later, and it announced a theme that he was to return to repeatedly throughout his life – 'I'm not really getting enough to do in the Works and feel it is a horrid prostitution of my abilities to be going there every day.'

Reith had now known Charlie for almost nine years. As the time of his marriage approached, he decided that Charlie too must have a bride and that he must play the improbable role of matchmaker. The girl in question made her bow in Reith's diary in the first week of April 1921. Charlie had been to Glasgow the previous day to visit an Irish cousin, and returned to their lodgings in Dunblane late:

> We stayed in bed next morning and I had insisted on his taking the day off anyhow in order that he could go to tea with Mrs Dunn to meet a girl, Maysie Henderson, who lives alone with her mother at Argaty and has £20,000 a year of her own. This was with a view to matrimony . . . C. quite liked the girl so I felt I would have to do more about it . . .[62]

A fortnight later, Charlie and Reith were invited to dine at Argaty:

> Mrs H. and the girl were very kind and cordial. I had never met them before. I found them already calling C. by his first name and he likewise to the girl. This was a surprise, but it showed the rate of progress. They have 1500 acres and we walked all over the place. I've never seen such a mass of daffodils. A good deal of work is being done building cottages etc. From one point there is a magnificent view of the western hills. The girl is not good-looking at all but is very cheery and probably a good sort.[63]

Reith was quickly organising Miss Henderson in the way that he organised Charlie. Visiting Argaty with his friends the Dunns a few evenings later, he discovered that she was going off to Switzerland but had been unable to get a berth on the London sleeper. Reith told her that he would arrange that; he further suggested that Charlie should meet her at Buchanan Street Station in Glasgow, and that the pair of them should entertain her to dinner at the Central Hotel before seeing her onto the train. This struck the company as extremely high-powered: 'Mrs H. jumped at it. Dunn was overcome with what he called my master-stroke, and recounted it with much spirit to Mrs Dunn when we went in there to report.'[64]

By the time Miss Henderson arrived in Glasgow, Reith had devised a number of refinements: 'On my suggestion C. gave her an envelope, stamped and addressed, and some paper for her to write to her mother on. C. wrote to Mrs H. also. This shows the detail of my arrangements.' Miss Henderson was much impressed, and asked Reith to call her by her first name. 'My feelings are very much mixed about his getting the girl,' he wrote in his diary, 'but I'm doing everything I can for him.'[65]

Charlie was soon a regular visitor at Argaty, sometimes with Reith and sometimes without. He laid out £39 on a gun, and one evening in the middle of May he bagged his first rabbit. He was also making his mark at Beardmores, and the question was mooted of his going to China under the joint auspices of Beardmore and Jardine Matheson: 'It is an awful prospect,' Reith noted, 'but a great opportunity for him.' Without Charlie's knowledge, he wrote about it to Maysie Henderson, who was still in Switzerland: 'It seemed to me that if he went nothing more would happen in that direction, but that if she said she did not want him to go they would be engaged in a very short time.'[66] Charlie had become badly run down, and the doctor ordered a week in bed. When Reith went to visit him one evening, there was an envelope at the bedside marked 'Prime Minister': 'I opened it without enthusiasm but was tremendously pleased afterwards. An OBE is a poor thing but it is quite good to get it at his age.'[67]

He was busy with his own affairs as well as with Charlie's. Dunardoch had become his earlier in the month. He visited the burgh surveyor's office with plans for alterations; interviewed a cook ('but she was uncouth'); set aside the best room in the house for his mother's use, furnishing it entirely with her own things. He was in correspondence with the Sliaghan Hotel in Skye over arrangements for the honeymoon and with Muriel about the banns: they were published in Dunblane Cathedral on 12 June, Muriel being described as 'furth of Scotland'.

Charlie went to London to meet 'the Henderson girl' on her return from Switzerland. He also went to Beardmore's London office and turned down the China job. A week later, he became engaged: 'The whole credit for this, if it be a matter of credit,' Reith wrote, 'is with me.' He rehearsed the chronology of the courtship in his diary with an attention to detail approaching the manic. Late on the evening of the engagement, when they were all three at Argaty, Maysie said she would like to speak to him alone, and they sat talking for an hour in the garden:

> She said she would never go on with the thing unless I was in favour of it, as she did not want to come between C. and me ... Of course my real feelings were indescribable, but I would do anything for C., including this. When we got home I began to feel it rather badly, in fact it was dreadful. We talked till about three in the morning.[68]

Reith was not at his best in the three weeks between Charlie's engagement and his own marriage:

> C. spent this afternoon and evening at Argaty, which I thought he would not do as I needed his help so badly at the new house. I felt quite sad at dismantling our room at St Ola, and even already I thought the new one would not see very much of him ... His going off today was the first sign of trouble.[69]

He admitted in a diary entry two days later that he was beginning to feel jealous of Maysie; he felt that she was monopolising Charlie, and noted sourly that they were already talking of getting married in September and buying a house in Dunblane. He went briefly to London, and Muriel and he paid a hurried visit to Whiteley's to choose some bedroom and dining-room furniture.

He also looked at engagement rings for Charlie, taking away three samples to choose from, but he returned to Scotland as glum as he had left it – 'I cannot see how our friendship is to continue with things as they are now shaping.'

His send-off at the factory took place in an atmosphere of carnival. 'Cupid has been exceptionally busy during the past two months,' said *The Beardmore News*, 'when no less than four of our esteemed colleagues were inextricably entangled and joined the happy band of benedicts.' The works were decorated with flags and streamers. When the hooter went at 4.45, the entire work force and office staff assembled beneath the main steps. 'Peters made a speech which any general manager would have been proud to hear from the convenor of shop stewards,' Reith wrote, and that is borne out by the house newspaper's account of it: 'It is only by having gentlemen like Mr Reith to guide and direct the work and take an interest in the welfare of the workers, that we can hope to see the dawn of a brighter day, when the dark industrial clouds have passed away.'

There was a handsome presentation of silver – a dozen fish knives and forks, the same number for fruit, and a pair of toast racks. Reith made a gracious reply, expressing the hope that they would have many years together of 'good trade, good fellowship and good understanding'. Then his car was roped up and hauled to the factory gate, with much cheering and confetti.

The wedding took place in Sussex two days later. His last evening as a bachelor was spent with Charlie: 'After dinner we walked in the gardens on the front and sat on the beach and talked till 11. It was all very trying and I was feeling in an awful state. It was not at all that I did not want to get married, but was so worried about relations with C.' His brother Douglas was to assist in the service; he had, he told Reith, had a struggle with the rector to get him to omit 'the silly parts of the marriage service'. Presbyterianism triumphed, however, and the proceedings began with Douglas reading 'a very much revised version of the Prayer Book *Reasons for Marriage*'. Reith thought that Muriel looked 'exceedingly pretty and sweet'; she wept a little, as brides have been known to do, though Reith could not think why.

He found the reception boring, and was glad to escape upstairs at 3.30 for a short prayer with Charlie and Douglas. They were driven to London, and Charlie and Maysie saw them onto the night sleeper for Scotland: 'I kissed C.'s girl,' Reith noted, 'but our feelings to each other are very different from those of C. and M. His girl knows that he very nearly married M.' Muriel did not have a good night, and woke Reith at two o'clock. She also had an early morning, because Reith was awake again a couple of hours later to point out to her the factory at Coatbridge. The next stage of the journey, which took them up the Highland Line, was more enjoyable, although when the time came to change at Inverness, he was not best pleased to find the train full of holiday-makers from Glasgow. They reached Sligachan in time for dinner and drank in the view of the Cuillin Hills.

It was not a long honeymoon. There was no church nearer than three miles, and they discovered that the service there was in Gaelic. The company at the hotel was congenial, and one evening after dinner they danced some reels, but it is plain from Reith's diary that he quickly became restless:

> At 3 I suddenly resolved to go to Loch Coruisk, 9 miles off. We went over very rough ground, rocks and streams, for about 7 miles and climbed for the last two. It was very tiring and we were going at a good pace. A view from the top of the ridge, with the loch 1000ft below us, was magnificent. M did awfully well and I was very glad indeed that she got through.[70]

He wrote to Charlie every day – had indeed written him a note before the train pulled out of Euston. He had fired off a volley of telegrams during their stop at Inverness and he now followed these up with letters to his mother and to Douglas, who had stayed on at Southwick after the wedding. We do not know in what terms he wrote to his brother, but the gist of it may be surmised from Douglas's lengthy and quite extraordinary reply, which survives:

> . . . Charlie's love to you has been wonderful. But do you know I think you are only at the threshold of one of its most wonderful stages – the stage of renunciation. The best the finest purest and most unselfish love is the love that will relinquish, if and when necessary, all bodily and earthly possession of and contact with the beloved, in obedience to the will and purpose of the Highest Love of all . . .
>
> We read that God SO loved the world that He gave his only begotten Son . . . and gave Him to death. No such gift or sacrifice is called for from you or from any mortal. But yet at this time a real renunciation is called for from you. You are not asked to love Charlie one whit less but you are asked to show your (boundless) love for him in a special way at this time and that way is the practising of a certain amount of renunciation . . .
>
> Your feelings towards Muriel may not be what you think they should – I do not know of course – but for all I have seen and hear of her she seems a splendid girl – a star whose worth's unknown although its height be taken.[71] If *she* loves *you*, as of course she does, she is sent by God into your life for no other purpose than one of infinite goodness and grace and love. Do not therefore even in your thoughts belittle so tremendous and fathomless an event, none other than God's appointing. Be led by the hand however perplexed and doubting at first.[72]

After a week in Skye, Reith began to feel they had been there long enough, a feeling reinforced by a day of rain and a bout of toothache. 'I suppose I have lost the faculty for enjoyment,' he wrote gloomily. Another few days and they headed south: 'I was glad to be going back to work again and even the noise and dirt of Glasgow did not annoy me.'[73] They settled in at Dunardoch. Reith found it necessary to have a talk with Muriel about handling the servants 'as she is rather diffident in this line'; he also showed her how she might keep her household accounts, a lesson she did not welcome.

Muriel told him that everybody at Southwick had been 'dreadfully dis-appointed' with Maysie – 'her dress, loudness and everything' – and thought that she would wear Charlie out. 'I am quite sure that everything is going to be broken off,' Reith wrote:

M. cannot stand his girl, though she has tried hard to. I'm sure it's very largely because there are so many things about her which do not ring true. She is damnably possessive of C. and always appears so unfortunately patron-ising. Of course I am jealous of her but I would not have been so if she had been natural and straightforward with me.[74]

Reith's friend Jack Loudon was also unimpressed, describing her as 'a senti-mental servant girl'. 'How on earth could a chap like Bowser take a girl like that?' he asked, adding unwisely, 'It's damned well up to you to get him out of this mess.'[75]

Reith now started to refer to Maysie in his diary as 'Miss Henderson'; Mrs Henderson had also been entered in his black books, and on the 'Glorious Twelfth' his resentment boiled over:

I had expected to have my first experience of grouse-shooting to-day, but I was neither invited to Argaty, nor do I think I would have cared to go. I was very annoyed about it, however, and it shows how very insincere Mrs Henderson was in all the fine plans and promises she made. According to her I was to share in Argaty with C.[76]

Things were not going well at Coatbridge, either, and in an effort to reduce costs he was obliged to give notice to several members of staff. The work was also ceasing to hold his interest. Within a month of returning from his honey-moon he had decided that he wanted to go back to London, and that if that were not possible, he would much rather be in Glasgow. A brief visit to London lifted his spirits a little, but they sagged again almost at once:

Back to Glasgow. C. met me – or a bit of him did. Before I went to London things had seemed better, but today he said he saw no light at all and that his feelings towards me had undergone a radical change and that practically none were left.[77]

As Muriel was going south to visit her parents, Reith and Charlie drove off for the weekend together, heading north to Aviemore. Reith was in a state of great excitement, but his hopes that things might be patched up between them were disappointed. A week later he went to the Psychological Clinic in Glasgow and arranged to attend weekly. 'I do not think it will do any good,' he wrote. 'I think I know as much about psycho-analysis as the people there.' But he was pleased with a conversation he had with one of the doctors on his next visit:

He said I knew about as much as he did on the psychological side, but he has an interesting theory that the noises in my ear are caused by muscular strain set up by the wound and still continuing owing to the facial nerve being strained.[78]

In spite of their growing differences, he still craved Charlie's company. They went walking over Sheriffmuir together one Sunday afternoon towards the end of October: 'This weekend was like old times as we were getting on excellently. I told him I thought it was a great pity that he would have so much money as he might slacken his efforts to do big things, and he quite saw the point of it.'[79] A few days later he recorded that they had discussed the possibility of going into partnership with someone who was in business in Southwick. These unceasing attempts to shore up his friendship were the source of some distress to a bride of three months: 'M said she could be happy when she was stupid enough to forget about C.,' reads an entry on the same day,[80] but that was something she was allowed little opportunity to do.

20 December was Charlie's twenty-fifth birthday, and Reith presented him with a silver plaque. It had his crest on it and a lengthy Latin inscription. 'Fight the good fight of faith,' it began. 'To my dearest companion, on his twenty fifth birthday, in token of ten years of highly esteemed friendship, in deepest gratitude and admiration.' They gave a dinner party for him and Muriel decorated the house very prettily. Douglas and his wife came, and their neighbours the Dunns, but there was one omission from the guest list:

> We lighted twenty-five little candles in his honour. Music afterwards and everything was most successful. I suppose he was very vexed with me for not asking his girl, but it was the last chance I should have of having him on his birthday alone as I have done for so many years.[81]

Reith's mother was to have joined them for Christmas, but their plans were disrupted because his sister Beta, who had been in poor health for years and had very largely cut herself off from the family, was taken ill. On 26 December, alarmed by a message about her condition, he drove to Glasgow. She was suffering from pneumonia and pleurisy and much of the time was delirious, although there were moments when she recognised 'my own wee Johnnie'. She died on the last day of the year. Reith took two Gloire de Dijon roses from the wall of the house in Dunblane and laid them beside her: 'I prayed that I might be worthy of all the great love that she had had for me and which I have made so little use of. She understands now how difficult it was, and how very perplexed I often was about it all.'[82]

Grief at the death of his sister, uncertainty over his work, anxiety lest he lose Charlie – 1922 did not begin well for Reith. Beta's death brought him briefly closer to Muriel, but his relations with Charlie deteriorated sharply. On 4 January they had attended a lecture given by Jack Loudon in Glasgow and at the Central Hotel afterwards Reith gave Charlie a letter; he had written it on New Year's Day and he was convinced that it would make him very happy:

He didn't say anything for a long time and then launched out in protests at my being fond of him. A miserable evening of it . . . I have absolutely dropped out of everything and his Jezebel is all that matters. He has behaved in an utterly astounding way. It's tragic that his career is being cut short by all this money. He might have done great things.[83]

Charlie gave further cause for offence when he announced a few days later that he had applied for a pew for his future wife and himself at Dunblane Cathedral, and this prompted a further bitter cry of rage:

It hadn't occurred to me that he would carry his exclusion of me as far as this. We had often talked of our all sitting together. I wished I could bring myself to have nothing more to do with him – which is what he most certainly deserves. With all these examples of his cruelty – as I regard it – I still love him. Of course he's not responsible. It's the damned woman and her damned mother.[84]

In spite of these extraordinary tantrums, Charlie appears to have been remarkably patient and accommodating, and when Muriel went off again to see her family he once more agreed to go away with Reith for the weekend. They set off by train to visit their old haunts at Comrie, and were soon installed in what Reith called 'the dear old billet'. There was a lot of snow – more than there had been for forty years, the newspapers said – and they made a snowman. They also climbed the Monument Hill, where they found their names carved in various places, and old memories stirred. But then Charlie announced that he must go to the Post Office to make a telephone call, and the spell was broken:

It really was infuriating – to think he can't leave things off for this one weekend. He had two big photos of her displayed on the mantelpiece. I was very sick about this but said naught. While he spoke to his beloved I went out and hung over the Earn Bridge. The water was black and very swift.[85]

They had, for all that, what Reith regarded as a satisfactory conversation about their going into business together, and they discussed the arrangements for Charlie's wedding: 'I agreed even to usher,' Reith wrote, 'having been very much against doing anything at all, seeing that he preferred his brother to be best man.'[86]

His own marriage, however, after six months, was not going well. Muriel, he noted in his diary, 'writes every day to her mother and gives all private news for her family to read' – a curious complaint for him to make. 'We were not at all happy.'[87] Muriel was sufficiently concerned about him to ask the local doctor to call, and he advised a month's holiday in France. Reith's mind, however, fixed on the question of what could be salvaged of his friendship with Charlie, returned obstinately to the idea of some sort of business partnership. He got nowhere. 'He has become so infernally dogmatic . . . I can't teach him anything these days. He seems to resent any suggestions from me.'[88]

The wedding had been fixed for 2 March, and Reith's diary entries for February are a crescendo of jealousy and rage:

> He showed me his wedding present to Jezebel – a brooch of diamonds and pearls costing £43. Sand to the Sahara. Of course on his wedding he becomes possessed of a separate income of several thousand a year from Jezebel's mother and he is heir after Jezebel to Argaty and all the rest of it.[89]

Very unwillingly, he went with Charlie to their old lodgings and helped him move his things to their new house:

> I didn't want to go into their bedroom but had to. The idiots have only one bed and a very small one at that . . . Felt simply miserable and wished I could clear right out. Am more fond of C. than ever. What a tragedy. I wish to heaven I had the dignity and the courage to tell him finally what I think of his dastardly treatment of me and of his accursed woman, and cut off from all association with him.[90]

There was a presentation for Charlie in the works canteen. Reith was much affected by the speeches, and thought that Charlie spoke very well in reply – 'I had written it out for him last night, and he more or less said it exactly.' He went off and bought a gold matchbox. He presented it to Charlie when they met for dinner that evening, expecting that he would put it on the chain he had given him the year before; he also gave him the gold watch he had bought for himself in the United States:

> I found he wasn't going to take these away with him. Jezebel has given him a silver cigarette case and match box, though he already had a gold one from me. I had also given him a silver matchbox years ago. She is carefully duplicating or has already duplicated almost every gift I gave him. She is sure to give him a gold wrist watch soon. It is abominable. However I was determined not to let any shadow cross this last night.[91]

Reith's anguish about Charlie in those early months of 1922 had been accompanied and no doubt aggravated by mounting frustration and disgust over the state of affairs at Beardmores. The production capacity he had organised there was based on the volume of orders he had been assured would be generated by the London office. The orders did not materialise. Reith felt that in the poor trading conditions of 1921 he had done well to keep the loss for the year down to £49,000, but by January 1922 there was a question mark over the future of the factory. A meeting he attended on the day of Charlie's wedding presentation convinced him that they were, as he put it, 'trying to scapegoat me to save their own dirty faces'. By the time he reached Coatbridge the following morning, the adrenalin was clearly running freely: 'Felt in great form when I got to the factory – dictated my resignation at once and took care to let it be known.'[92]

He was very much on edge on the day of the wedding. The guest list was small, and his duties as usher correspondingly light. He was annoyed that his mother insisted on sitting at the back of the church with Jean; even more annoyed because he thought his sister very badly dressed. He did not like the look of the minister, and found the service 'weird'. The choice of the 90th Psalm, with its emphasis on the brevity of human life, struck him as extraordinary; what some might have thought stranger was that it was sung to a tune that he and Charlie had composed and to which Charlie had given the name 'Argaty'. Mrs Henderson walked up the aisle with the bride on one arm and a friend's baby on the other. Mrs Dunn, Reith's fellow-matchmaker from Dunblane, begged Muriel not to take it as 'a fair sample of a Scotch wedding'; it was, she said, 'the funniest she had seen'. For Reith, the most trying time was when Charlie came down the aisle after the ceremony: 'Worse than when the ring was being put on,' he wrote in his diary, 'but I certainly prayed for his happiness.'[93]

He was desolate without his friend. He and Muriel went off for the weekend to Aberdeen, a town filled with family memories. He went to Nellfield Cemetery and saw the graves of his grandparents and of five other members of the family. They also visited Chanonry Lodge, the residence of the Principal of the University. Sir George Adam Smith and his wife had known his parents. They thought Reith very like his father, both facially and in voice, and Lady Adam Smith wrote to Mrs Reith to say how much they had liked Muriel – 'She is such a typical sweet English girl – with that lovely colouring and fresh look and those beautiful teeth – we were all charmed with her simplicity and naturalness.'[94]

He heard twice from Charlie in the ten days following the wedding, but did not reply: 'I almost prefer not to hear from him as his letters are so different from those of old days,' he wrote. 'Feeling very annoyed with all C.'s people, but of course they are carried away with Jezebel and all her money, and would no doubt like to forget about me altogether.'[95] A week later he took an afternoon off to choose some wallpaper in Glasgow with Muriel. 'She gave me a letter from C. which I read there and which broke off our friendship finally,' says a cryptic diary note. 'The most amazing document I have ever received.'[96]

The terms of this 'most amazing document' are lost to us, but there are clues to it in two letters from Reith's brother Douglas which do survive. Douglas was present at a family dinner party at the Central Hotel in Glasgow on the night Reith received Charlie's letter, and must either have seen it or been given an account of its contents. Two days later he did his best to offer comfort and explanation, beginning with the boldly improbable assertion that things were really much better and brighter than Reith imagined: 'The passionate friendship, sacrifice, adoration, inspiration and love of ten years is a fact, a spiritual reality, which nothing that ever happens in this world or in the world to come can affect or efface.' He then reverted to the theme of renunciation that he had developed in the letter he had sent to Reith on his honeymoon:

> I'm absolutely certain that it is just because God values your nature and your powers of affection so highly as He does, that He cannot afford to leave you and your love to rest on any plane except the very highest. The highest love is that which renounces the bodily presence of the loved one . . .[97]

The following week, Douglas wrote a second letter. He and Reith had obviously spoken further, and this time he was a good deal more direct: 'I have prayed constantly that your and Charlie's friendship might take a different form from what it had up till lately, because I always felt and sometimes told you, that it was not worthy of you in some respects and therefore good neither for you nor for him.' He told Reith that his friends ('of whom I am privileged to be one') had long since concluded that Charlie would one day want to marry, and felt that this would help them both to 'a more desirable form (though not in the least necessarily less passionate) of mutual friendship'.

They are very Victorian, totally pre-Freudian letters. Now that Reith and Charlie were both married, Douglas wrote, the 'operation of natural forces' was in progress. This was neither to be regretted nor dreaded. Its effect would be to purge their friendship, taking from it 'nothing which constitutes the essence of the healthiest, manliest and most unselfish of friendships as between *man and man*':

> In justice to Charlie I must say that I know he had for months been feeling qualms at the exclusiveness of the friendship, and I expect he expressed himself as freely as he felt he could to you on the subject . . . When Charlie came between us I never grudged him, because I believed he was sent by God to fill a niche in your life at a time when I was incapable of it . . . You will yet live to be immense and intense friends. I feel certain your later friendship will have a peculiar quality of understandingness and unselfishness and sacredness about it which it never could have without some trial of this sort. It would in some ways have been better for you if when you first met Charlie you had instead fallen in with a chap about your own age whom you could have loved as intensely. For one so much younger than you as Charlie could not supply that independence of mind and will which is needed for the best kind of friendship. That Charlie is manifesting this now should give you a feeling of satisfaction, for in so doing (though it causes you such pain at the moment) he is sure of fitting himself to be a better friend to you later.[98]

Reith later dismissed his time at Beardmores as an 'industrial interlude'; when he came to write his memoirs, the two years he spent there detained him for little more than a page. 'I had feelings of unalloyed relief at getting away from this terrible place and such an abominable firm,' he wrote in his diary, although he owned to a twinge of regret at leaving 'so many good fellows'. He pasted into his scrapbook a letter from the office-bearers of Speedwell's Own Masonic Brethren expressing regret at his departure and thanking him for the interest he had taken in them.

The break with Charlie was a different matter, and it is plain even from what remains of his original diary that for the next two months he was in a state of suppressed frenzy. Charlie called to see him at Dunardoch one Sunday morning, and stayed for two hours. Reith found him 'quite changed and adamant – really amazing. He is simply not the same individual.'[99] This was followed by an exchange of notes, as frigid as they were unfruitful. Toward the end of April he went off to London to explore the job market; there was still a prospect of something in Bombay, and he discussed the possibility of a £3000 a year opening as General Manager of a railway company on the Amazon.[100]

When he got back to Dunblane, Muriel once again called in the doctor, who repeated his advice to go away. His mother arrived for a visit. She was greatly taken with the house and garden but not at all pleased with the state in which she found her son. The Minister of the Cathedral asked him to read the lessons, and Mrs Reith persuaded him that he should: 'The first was about Elijah fleeing for his life from Jezebel – extraordinary coincidence.'[101]

His state of mind was not improved by exposure to small-town gossip. Their neighbour Mrs Dunn came to tea and reported that the Bowsers were entirely self-centred and talked of nothing but themselves; 'also that C. is all taken up with silk socks, etc.' Mrs Reith senior pronounced Charlie's behaviour to be 'damnable'. It is not clear what she hoped to achieve, but she was sufficiently incensed to march round to his house one evening. In the course of an interview that lasted for an hour and a half she told him that he might well be responsible 'for wrecking two lives and a new home'. Charlie said he didn't care, and there is a preposterous sentence in Reith's diary for that day which shows how close he was to being unhinged: 'My beloved friend of nearly ten years fell sick of a grievous poisoning on 26/6/21 and died 3/3/22' – the dates of Charlie's engagement and marriage.

Reith still refused to go abroad, but at the end of May Muriel succeeded in getting him as far as the Channel Islands. The countryside reminded him of France and the war. He indulged his passion for bathing and lying in the sun, but he was disappointed by the size of the place and put out by the 'awful crowds'. His mother wrote, gently but firmly urging him to 'commit DCB and the whole business to God, not forgetting your own mistakes in it'. She also reminded him of a favourite text of his father's from the Epistle to the Philippians – 'This one thing I do, forgetting those things which are behind, and reaching forth unto those things which are before', but those were words to which John Reith would remain deaf until the day he died.[102]

He had been invited to address the Sociological Society at his old school, and when he travelled to Holt in June he made an insertion to his prepared text:

> A great deal might be said on the subject of friendship . . . I would recommend one real friend rather than a dozen lesser ones. It may be the divinest thing in your life. Few attain it. Take care, however, that the loss of it, for any reason, will not destroy your mental equilibrium. I speak from experience.[103]

In London, the search for work was conducted from the Cavendish Club in Piccadilly, which he had joined a couple of years earlier, and there is further evidence of his state of mind in something he committed to paper there one day in that summer of 1922. 'I believe in God Almighty,' he wrote, 'and at this time when I am living in great anxiousness – overshadowed with the sorrow of a ruptured friendship and in much concern as to my future work – I take comfort in repeating this stupendous assertion as a talisman to exorcise the demons of doubt, depression and even despair.' Then, this quintessentially Reithian cry:

> *Here I am now conscious of abilities which almost overwhelm me*, and yet nothing to do. I am dreadfully perplexed as to where my future work is to lie, for I would use my powers of organisation in some high place and yet I am eager to pass on the fire of inspiration from pulpit or pew or printed page which burns within me. I suffer now no doubt for many sins of the past; may I be led nearer to Christ and kept there in future.[104]

This petition was not immediately heeded. What he was led to in the first instance was what the editor of his Diaries has described as 'a tepid and superficial flirtation' with a local tennis partner in Dunblane.[105] He had travelled north in the middle of June. In church on his first Sunday at home he sat at the back, but the sight of Charlie and the singing of the 23rd Psalm were too much for him, and he walked out. He could not avoid seeing the large car which Maysie had bought for Charlie, and Charlie also figured constantly in his dreams (which prompted him to start reading Freud).

On the eve of his thirty-third birthday he went and stood at midnight at the gate of Charlie's house. 'Awful longing for C.,' reads a diary entry shortly afterwards. 'Such stirrings of ability, too, and the desire to do something great in the world. It is dreadfully trying to be without work, but that is nothing to the other sorrow. Muriel can't or won't help now.'[106] It is plain that he was close to mental breakdown.

He played a certain amount of tennis, and in the middle of August he did so in a party that included a young woman called Norah Whitehead: 'I had heard a lot about her – very fast and so on – just the type I detest normally,' he wrote. 'She was awfully amusing and clever but awfully loud.'[107] Loud or no, Miss Whitehead figured prominently in his diary over the next few weeks, variously described as 'an extraordinary creature' and 'really very attractive'. She lived with her mother in a big house opposite Dunardoch, and at the end of the month they gave a party, to which Muriel, who was not blind, went with reluctance. There were games and there was dancing, Reith partnering Miss Whitehead in a reel:

> Then she and I went into the garden and I had my first experience of kissing a girl on the lips with anything more in it . . . This short affair with that girl is very regrettable and naturally I am ashamed of it. I record it nevertheless for various reasons. It would never have happened if I hadn't been in such an appallingly unsettled state myself and if I hadn't been in a bad way with Muriel also. We seemed so far apart, and of course it was simply rotten for her that I should be so centred in C.[108]

Mrs Bowser senior had also now entered the lists by writing a letter which Reith described as 'abominable' but which might have made a wiser man thoughtful:

> She wrote in a smug self-righteous way – thanked me for what I had done for C. and then said she hadn't cared for our friendship much because it had caused dissension in their family; said C. sometimes had a fearful time because I was so tyrannical and overbearing. Muriel wrote her a perfect stinker back which she deserved.[109]

Reith picked up from his friend Mrs Dunn that there was a certain amount of gossip about him and Miss Whitehead, but this did not prevent him from accepting an invitation to 'visit her studio' where she showed him her drawings. A few days later, while they were out walking together, she attempted to improve his education in another direction: 'She was sarcastic about my not knowing how to kiss a girl, as she put it, and endeavoured to show me how it should be done.'[110] None of this did much for his relations with Muriel, but he noted that it affected him in another way: 'I've had practically no thought of C. since NW came on the scene, but perhaps the cure is worse than the disease.'[111]

Slowly, he began to pull himself together, and by the time he set off again for London in October he was feeling rather ashamed of himself: 'I had an awfully good farewell with Muriel,' he wrote. 'I was loving her very much and felt awfully sorry for her. I asked her to pray for me. I felt I had gone far from my old principles and far from God. I asked forgiveness and to be brought back.' When he went to Regent Square Church on his first Sunday morning in London he found that it was Communion and hesitated at the door for a little, but eventually he went forward: 'I felt it was rather a crisis. The sermon and the whole service was awfully fine and I felt very sorry for the past and much more settled for the future.'

He went to Regent Square again in the evening, and the Minister preached from the twenty-second book of Ezekiel, in which the prophet inveighs against the guilt of Jerusalem: *And I sought for a man among them, that should make up the hedge, and stand in the gap before me for the land, that I should not destroy it: but I found none.* Perhaps, the Minister said, there was someone in the church that very night who would save the country from heathendom, immorality and love of money . . . Reith returned to the Cavendish and his diary:

I had the sense for perhaps the first time that the blood of Christ can avail for me. I felt I must seek a complete submission to my present grievous state – even though it continued long yet. I still believe there is some high work for me in the world but that it won't come till I have reconciled myself absolutely to God's way of working.

He settled himself with his typewriter in a little-used room at the back of the club and redoubled his efforts to find work. One of the boys in his audience at Gresham's in June had been the son of a solicitor called Sir William Bull, who was the Conservative MP for Hammersmith. Reith had written to Bull before leaving Dunblane; he now went to see him and came away feeling much encouraged: 'I do think there is some chance for me in a political line at last.' The following week there was a letter from Bull offering him the secretaryship to the London Unionist group of MPs, who met fortnightly while the House of Commons was sitting; it was a modest enough position, but could lead to other things.

The next morning, Reith's eye was caught by an advertisement in the public appointments section of *The Morning Post*: 'The British Broadcasting Company (in formation). Applications are invited for the following officers: General Manager, Director of Programmes, Chief Engineer, Secretary. Only applicants having first class qualifications need apply. Applications to be addressed to Sir William Noble, Chairman of the Broadcasting Committee . . .' As Reith had no idea what broadcasting was, he had no means of knowing into which class his qualifications fell, but that did not inhibit him. The grand manner was clearly called for; he even managed to press his brief holiday in Jersey into service. 'Since relinquishing my last post,' he wrote, 'I have been abroad, but came to town last week to make enquiries and arrangements for future work. You will observe that I am an engineer by training, but that I have had wide commercial experience . . .'

He posted his application for the general managership in the club letter-box. Only then did it occur to him that it would have been prudent to look up Sir William Noble in *Who's Who*. Having done so, and persuaded a club servant to bend the rules by retrieving his letter, he inserted another point-stretching sentence before the one about having been abroad: 'I am an Aberdonian, and it is probable that you knew my family . . .'

Reith heard nothing more about The British Broadcasting Company for the best part of two months, but he was very far from idle. He had, he wrote in his memoirs, 'gotten involved in an odd political set-up'.

The National Coalition led by Lloyd George had been steadily drifting towards the rocks. Since the end of the war, Labour had won fourteen by-elections, and there were Conservatives who felt that the Welsh Wizard would inflict as much damage on their party as he had inflicted on his own. There were rumblings over the government's policy in Ireland, and it looked for a time in the autumn of 1922 as if the Prime Minister's enthusiasm for the Greeks would shatter the fragile peace with the new Turkey of Kemal Atatürk that had been established by the Treaty of Sèvres two years previously.

An unsigned letter in *The Times* on 7 October declared that 'we cannot act alone as the policeman of the world.' It quickly became known that the writer was the former Tory leader Bonar Law. Lloyd George, with hawkish support from the likes of Churchill and Birkenhead, misread the public mood and got cabinet agreement to an immediate general election on a Coalition ticket. Austen Chamberlain, Law's successor as the Leader of the Conservatives, undertook to scotch resistance within his own party, and called a meeting of MPs at the Carlton Club for 19 October. He failed to carry the day. His authority was challenged by both Baldwin and Bonar Law, and a resolution that the Conservatives should fight the election as an independent party was carried by 187 votes to 87.[112] Lloyd George resigned before the afternoon was out and never held office again.

It is not clear how firm a grasp Reith had of the complexities of the political situation as the election campaign got under way, or indeed where his sympathies lay. 'The Independent Liberal Manifesto is really very good,' he noted in his diary on 23 October, but on the same day, having already written to volunteer his services to the Tory Chief Whip, he was interviewed by an official at the Unionist Central Office. He also wrote to W. C. Bridgeman, who had become Home Secretary in Bonar Law's caretaker administration. Then Sir William Bull telephoned to ask if he would lend him a hand. Bull was a Chamberlainite, and Reith therefore found himself supporting the efforts of those Conservatives who wished to maintain the coalition with the Liberals.

Bull, unconcerned that Reith was no Tory, initially harnessed his energies in the constituency – one of his first chores was to draft Bull's election address.[113] Quite soon, however, he found himself caught up more generally in the campaigning efforts of those Conservatives who were running on a Lloyd George ticket. Years later, Reith said that he did not much like the position he had drifted into but that he had nothing else to do,[114] but the evidence of his diary is that he enjoyed it immensely. He met a number of well-known politicians. Early in the campaign Bull took him to see Lord Birkenhead: 'The house was full of books and beautiful pictures. He was wearing a tweed suit and red and white tie and kept pacing up and down the room.'[115] Bull also sent him to Birmingham to get some guidance on policy from Austen Chamberlain, who received him in his sitting room in his dressing gown:

I liked him and he was very civil to me. I put various questions to him and got it definitely that he did not want to create embarrassment or dissension in the party . . . He thinks it is most unfortunate that in these days moderate-minded men should not be united in the face of the Labour menace.[116]

Most thrilling of all, he was introduced to Lloyd George, who quizzed him about Chamberlain's views and criticised Bonar Law's lack of policy. 'He was very polite and most interested,' Reith wrote in his diary. 'He said several times that I ought to be in Parliament and said he remembered my father's name.'[117]

Reith also learned something of how the wheels of the political machine were greased. When Muriel came down to visit him he took her out for a meal to a Lyons Corner House and enjoyed her astonishment when he produced an open cheque for £3000 which he had been given by Bull. Bull told him that there was plenty more where that came from, and by the end of the campaign, Reith had distributed considerable sums, often in cash:

I rarely knew the purpose. £15,000 passed through my hands, and Bull was vastly worried by what he called my 'meticulous bookkeeping'. I was mighty careful to keep a record of every transaction; it seemed that he would have preferred to have had no records kept at all.[118]

It was money ill spent. When the results were declared on 16 November, Bonar Law had a majority of 77 over the other parties combined. The National Liberals were destroyed. Lloyd George held on to Caernarvon, but Churchill was defeated at Dundee by a Prohibitionist; having undergone an operation just before polling day, he now, as he put it, found himself 'without office, without a seat and without an appendix'.

Reith was in a happier state. On 7 December he had a letter from Sir William Noble inviting him to an interview, and he presented himself at Magnet House in Kingsway six days later. Noble greeted him 'with the cordiality of an old friend'. The previous night, Reith had 'put all before God', but that was the limit of his preparation:

They didn't ask me many questions and some they did I didn't know the meaning of. The fact is I hadn't the remotest idea as to what broadcasting was. I hadn't troubled to find out. If I had tried I should probably have found difficulty in discovering anyone who knew.[119]

Noble offered him the job the next day and told him there had been six on the shortlist – nothing is known for certain of the other five.[120] Reith had asked for £2000 a year, but settled for £1750. 'I am profoundly thankful to God in this matter,' he wrote in his diary. He did not hang about. When he wrote to Noble six days later formally accepting the position, he told him that he had already spent some time each day with members of the new staff.

He was so relaxed that he trusted himself to write a letter to Charlie for his birthday – 'I wish you the best birthday you have ever had and am sure it will be so. I also wish you every possible happiness at Christmas and the New Year. As always, John.' There was a cold little reply by return – 'Please accept my thanks for your letter, the wishes therein expressed are most heartily reciprocated. Yours sincerely, D. C. Bowser.' 'Smug little cad', Reith wrote in his diary. 'Of course,' he added, 'he could have been Assistant General Manager of this new concern.'

He went home to Dunblane for Christmas in great good spirits; eager as always to surprise, he scared Muriel half out of her wits by trying the back door before ringing the bell at the front. When he had written to his mother to tell her about his appointment he had said that the only fly in the ointment was leaving Dunardoch. 'But I don't consider I am leaving it at all,' he added, 'as you will live there in much comfort and I shall be there quite a lot.' When the time came to travel south again after the Christmas break, it was the parting from his mother which he felt most keenly:

> I told her that I wanted her to live to see me a knight anyhow. I feel if this job succeeds and I am given grace to succeed in it, I might not be so far off this. I do want a title for dear mother's sake and Muriel's.[121]

At nine o'clock on the morning of 30 December, he turned up at the offices of the General Electric Company in Kingsway. It was a Saturday. He was told that 'the new company' was not expected till Monday morning, but he was taken up in the lift to the second floor:

> A room about thirty foot by fifteen, furnished with three long tables and some chairs. A door at one end invited examination; a tiny compartment six foot square; here a table and a chair; also a telephone. 'This,' I thought, 'is the general manager's office'; the door swung to behind me. I wedged it open; sat down; surveyed the emptiness of the outer office. Though various papers had accumulated in the past fortnight, I had read them all before; no point in pretending to be busy with no one to see.[122]

Half an hour later, a man in a silk hat appeared. He carried two attaché cases and a number of legal books. It was Major Anderson, the Secretary: 'I hadn't seen him before. It was an awful shock. I saw at once that he would never do.'[123] The new General Manager had made his second managerial decision.

The first had already been conveyed to another of his new colleagues, the director of programmes, A. S. Burrows, and Reith recorded it in his diary on the last day of the year: 'I had told Burrows – my first order to him – that we would observe Sundays and that we should ask Dr Fleming of Pont Street to give a short religious address tonight.' Reith had not previously met Fleming, minister to London's most fashionable Scots Presbyterian congregation. He did so that night on the top floor of Marconi House, in the Strand, where the London Station was then housed – one small room for office and studio, another for transmitter.

The British Broadcasting Company was in business. It had a staff of four.

Seven

FULL AND BY

If you wish to obtain a great name or to found an establishment, be completely mad; but be sure that your madness corresponds with the turn and temper of your age.

VOLTAIRE, 'IGNATIUS LOYOLA', *Philosophical Dictionary*, 1764

JOHN REITH had a great love of the sea and a considerable fondness for nautical metaphor; he quite often talked about 'squaring yards' with somebody, for instance, or about 'booming them off'. There is also a tang of salt spray to the titles of the three parts into which he divided his memoirs. He raced through the first thirty-three years of his life in less than eighty pages; that section is called 'Fitting Out'. For the later part of his career, when things went less well, he hit on 'Shipping it Green'. The middle section of the book, which describes the fifteen and a half years he spent at the BBC, he called 'Full and By', words that suggest the exhilarating surge of some great clipper sailing close-hauled to the wind.

That was certainly the way it was in those earliest pioneering days. Reith assumed that the Chairman of the new company and his fellow-directors might spend quite a lot of time looking over his shoulder, but Sir William Noble quickly disabused him: 'Oh, no,' he said, 'we're leaving it all to you. You'll be reporting at our monthly meetings and we'll see how you're getting on.' That suited Reith down to the ground. Nothing ever pleased him more than to be given sole command and presented with a blank sheet of paper.

He was so busy in the first days of 1923 that he fell three weeks behind with his diary, normally a daily routine akin to religious observance:

Immediately involved in an almost overwhelming intensity and complexity of activity; confronted with problems of which I had no experience. Copyright and performing rights; Marconi patents; associations of concert artists, authors, playwrights, composers, music publishers, theatre managers, wireless manufacturers.[1]

There was also a good deal of history to be absorbed. The first primitive attempts at broadcasting speech and music took place in the United States in 1906. By 1920 station KDKA, owned by Westinghouse, was operating a regular service in East Pittsburgh and regular concerts began in Europe in the same year from The Hague. In the United Kingdom, Marconi's also made a start in 1920, but were checked by the Post Office. Their first regular service went on the air from Writtle, near Chelmsford, early in 1922, and their London station, 2LO, followed three months later.

In the United States, the system was developed by private enterprise; freedom from restraint led initially to rapid growth – and near-chaos. In Britain, the Wireless Telegraphy Act of 1904 vested the power to license all transmitters and receivers in the Post Office, and the first formulation of a government policy on broadcasting was made to the House of Commons on 4 May 1922 by the Postmaster-General of the day, F. G. Kellaway. He began, diplomatically, by saying he hoped the United Kingdom could learn from the American experience. Applications would be considered only from British companies which were *bona fide* radio manufacturers. Kellaway told the House that it would be impossible – and undesirable – to grant the very large number of applications that had already landed on his desk. He therefore proposed to invite those who had applied to come together under the aegis of his department and work out a way of providing 'an efficient service' through cooperation rather than competition.[2]

The manufacturers formed a committee drawn from the 'Big Six' – British Thomson-Houston, General Electric, Marconi, Metropolitan-Vickers, Radio Communication, and Western Electric. There was much tough bargaining over such issues as the pooling of transmission patents, but after five months they came up with the sort of shotgun arrangement required of them. An inaugural meeting was held on 18 October at No. 2 Savoy Hill – the address of the Institution of Electrical Engineers – and more than 200 firms sent representatives. A single company was formed with a share capital of £100,000. Each of the 'Big Six' put up £10,000 and nominated a director; two independent directors were elected by the smaller firms.[3] Dividends were to be limited to 7½ per cent. The Company's income would be derived from half the ten-shilling licence fee and a royalty from manufacturers on sales. The origins of British broadcasting, that is to say, were almost purely commercial.

Installed in his cubby-hole, Reith lost no time in asserting his authority. He had a long talk on 1 January with the Company Secretary, Anderson: 'I discovered he thought he was to be independent of me, but I adjusted that satisfactorily and quickly,' he noted when he got round to bringing his diary up to date.[4] The following day he made his own first staff appointment, and it was an important one: 'Interviewed Miss F. I. Shields and fixed her up as my secretary, after a good talk and explaining exactly what I wanted.'

Miss Shields, a Girton girl, had been recommended by Lloyd George's Frances Stevenson, whom he had met during his brief foray into politics; she was the first of a succession of remarkable women who would serve, organise, advise, cosset, mother and occasionally bully Reith throughout his BBC career and beyond it. They were highly resilient – they had to be; they were frequently driven to extremes of exasperation; they were all fiercely loyal. Reith came to depend on them to a notable degree, as much privately as professionally – he took them out to dinner and he relaxed in their company at the cinema; they went house-hunting for him, offered him advice about anything from the tone of an important memorandum to the education of his daughter. It would be a foolish historian of British broadcasting who failed to take account of the influential role played by that figure of legend, the BBC secretary; Miss Shields was the archetype.[5]

In February another important gap was filled when he recruited Peter Eckersley as Chief Engineer. Eckersley, who had served in the war as a Wireless Equipment Officer, came from Marconi. He was not only a gifted engineer but also one of the band of exuberant young men who had been playing gramophone records and improvising broadcast entertainment from an army hut in a field near Writtle. Such programme planning as there was usually took place about half an hour ahead of transmission in the nearby 'Cock and Bell'. The offerings included a five-minute Children's Hour, signed off with a theme song which Eckersley sang in a high tenor voice to the tune of Tosti's 'Goodbye'. They had dramatic ambitions, and presented the balcony scene from *Cyrano de Bergerac*. They were also pioneers in the broadcasting of live music. Lauritz Melchior came to sing for them, and imagined that the louder he sang, the further his voice would carry. He particularly wanted to be heard at home in Denmark; his opening note shattered the microphone and shut down the generator.

Eckersley's first day at the BBC was a busy one:

On the morning I joined I was summoned to see Mr Reith. He outlined my immediate problems . . . 2LO, the London transmitter, installed on the roof of Marconi House, was interfering with the Air Ministry receivers over the way and must be moved to a new position. I had better be satisfied that the new stations, to be erected at Glasgow, Cardiff, Bournemouth and Belfast, were being properly installed . . . Several of the new technical publications were asking for articles on our future plans: publicity was essential. He suggested I should see the new press man, Smith, who was coming down from Glasgow. Was it necessary for me to live in Essex? Hadn't I better get a house in London at once? And perhaps a better suit of clothes might help . . .[6]

The 'new press man' was a Scotsman called W. C. Smith, a journalist (and former missionary) recommended to Reith by his brother Douglas. He too was flung in at the deep end:

He came down for the day but I took him on at once and he did not go back. I took him to lunch with me at the club and in the afternoon he had to attend a meeting of the publicity managers of the wireless firms. I made him straighten up his collar and tie before he went.[7]

Although he was gratified that the Board was 'leaving it all to him', the BBC's new General Manager soon discovered that he had not been presented with a *tabula rasa*. During the negotiations that led to the setting up of the Company, the Postmaster-General – the 'policeman of the ether', as Reith described him – had come under strong pressure over news broadcasts. The 'Fourth Estate' was nervous, and the news agencies combined with the Newspaper Proprietors' Association and the Newspaper Society, which spoke for the provincial papers, to represent their misgivings. The result was that a month before Reith's appointment as General Manager, the Company had already entered into a highly restrictive agreement with the news agencies, and the Post Office had granted the BBC 'temporary and provisional permission' to transmit news summaries.

The agreement was for six months. In return for a royalty, the BBC was to receive each evening a summary of the world's news of sufficient length to 'constitute a broadcasted message of half-an-hour's duration'. It was to be prefaced by an acknowledgement of the agencies' copyright. The BBC also met the anxieties of the provincial evening papers by agreeing that it would not broadcast bulletins earlier than 7 p.m. The substance of the agreement (though not the seven o'clock rule) was incorporated in the Licence which the Post Office issued to the BBC early in 1923.

Reith had been in the saddle for only a couple of weeks when there was further trouble with the press. The Newspaper Proprietors' Association told the Company that if it wished to have details of its programmes in the papers, it would have to pay for the privilege at the going rate. Reith managed to stiffen his Board and pulled off a considerable coup when the millionaire Gordon Selfridge, who reserved regular space in one of the London evening papers to advertise his department store, offered him the freedom of it to give details of the London programme. The circulation of the *Pall Mall Gazette* rose sharply; after a few days the NPA backed off and said rather lamely that its members must decide individually what they wished to do. 'They have made proper fools of themselves,' Reith wrote in his diary. 'It was our first great victory.'[8] There was an important consequence, because it was during the short confrontation with the NPA that the seed of an idea was planted in Reith's mind: seven months later the BBC launched *Radio Times*.

Having for the time being seen off the press, Reith found himself obliged to square up to the Post Office over the licence fee. There were two issues. The first concerned the very large number of experimental licences that was being handed out. The BBC suspected, probably with good reason, that only a small proportion of these was being issued to genuine wireless amateurs with an interest in scientific experiment; the rest were going to people who were handy with a screwdriver and who were assembling their own receivers from cheap foreign components.[9] The BBC was also concerned about the scale of licence fee evasion and the apparent unwillingness of the Post Office to prosecute.

Reith held no particular brief for the licence fee arrangements; they had been agreed before his appointment, and he had come to the view privately that they were unworkable. By the beginning of March 1923, only 80,000 BBC licences had been taken out, and the issues were no longer being debated solely between the BBC and the Post Office. Lord Beaverbrook was running one of his noisy populist crusades in the *Daily Express*, calling not only the licence fee system but the very existence of the BBC into question. The Company saw those who did not pay a licence fee as 'pirates'; the *Express* depicted them as champions of free enterprise, knights in shining armour tilting against the dragon Monopoly.

Reith, disinclined to waste time on editorial monkeys, sought audience with the organ grinder:

> Saw Beaverbrook about the stunt he was running against us. I was not a bit afraid of him as I imagined he expected me to be. He said I had impressed him very much. He said all he was out against was manufacturers taking control of broadcasting.[10]

The main battle, however, had to be fought with the Post Office. The new incumbent there, Sir William Joynson-Hicks, had a very different political style from his predecessor, and this was not altogether to the BBC's advantage. Bumping into Reith in the street, he told him that he had it in mind to revise the licence system and wondered whether the ten-shilling licence fee might be restricted to crystal sets. He was just off to Norwich; would Reith drop him a line there?

Reith did. It was a long and well-judged letter; Asa Briggs describes it as having 'something of the qualities of an encyclical'.[11] Reith reminded 'Jix' that the manufacturers involved in the new enterprise had come together at the request of the Post Office; the latter, however, had not honoured the contract between them and it had become obvious that new regulations needed to be formulated – and enforced. He rejected the charge of monopoly: the BBC was open to any *bona fide* manufacturer and more than 570 had already applied. He concluded with a number of suggestions – that the Post Office should be tougher on evasion; that experimental licences should be restricted 'to those qualified by real scientific knowledge'; and that consideration be given to a constructors' licence fixed at £1.

The PMG's reply to the BBC Board was unaccommodating. He praised Reith's performance – 'firmness and courtesy beyond praise' – but he went on to issue an undisguised threat:

> If you decline to assent to these proposals, and I admit that under the terms of the Licence you have that power, I am thrown back on my responsibilities to interpret your agreement fairly as between yourself and the general public ... I shall have no alternative but to grant experimental licences to those applicants who have filled up the necessary form.[12]

Up to this point the exchanges between the BBC and the Post Office had been confidential. 'Jix', however, had been giving interviews to the press and there had been a good many leaks, and the Company now decided that it should present its case publicly. This was done in a robust press statement. The

Postmaster-General responded in a combative late-night statement to the Commons two days later. He proposed to ask his staff to examine the 33,000 outstanding applications for experimental licences; he also announced the setting up of 'the strongest Committee I can get' to consider not merely the matter of licences but 'the whole question of broadcasting'.

The series of enquiries into British broadcasting now stretches out like Banquo's posterity. The first of them was presided over by Sir Frederick Sykes, a retired Major-General and Unionist MP who was married to Bonar Law's daughter; the composition of the committee throws interesting light on how the concept of the great and the good has evolved over the years. There were three other MPs (including J. J. Astor and Charles Trevelyan), two senior civil servants from the Post Office, Viscount Burnham, who was Chairman of the Newspaper Proprietors' Association and the President of the Radio Society of Great Britain. Tokenism lay in the future – Joe Public was represented by Sir William Robertson, a former Chief of the Imperial General Staff and the first Field Marshal to rise from the ranks. Their number was completed by John Reith. It would be unthinkable today, but he had actually asked the Postmaster-General to include a BBC representative. After much argument Joynson-Hicks had agreed – provided it was Reith himself. 'As the BBC was in the dock he might have declined,' he wrote in *Into the Wind*. 'I was grateful to him for agreeing; and much relieved.'

When Reith was being interviewed for the General Manager's job, one of the directors had told him that in no time at all he would know everyone worth knowing in the country. One of his first encounters was with Dame Nellie Melba, who had named a fee of 300 guineas – the Reith charm worked, and she agreed to sing for nothing. When he was bothered by dry skin on one of his hands, he consulted Dr Weir, who looked after most of the Royal Family. In the middle of March, after lunching at the Caledonian Club with F. A. Iremonger, the editor of the *Manchester Guardian*, and G. K. A. Bell, then Chaplain to the Archbishop of Canterbury, the latter arranged for him to have an hour with Dr Davidson at Lambeth:

> I wanted his cooperation in some sort of control for the religious side. He had never heard wireless, so, with some diffidence, I asked if he and Mrs Davidson would dine with us next Monday. He looked at his book and said he would be delighted. I thought this would be a very pleasant shock for M. I communicated it to her on the telephone from the office.[13]

When Monday came, however, Reith was stricken by what he described as a 'weird and awful pain' in his back. He took himself off to Dr Weir again: 'He said it was lumbago, and I was most annoyed.' It was the day on which the Company was moving into its new offices at Savoy Hill, just off the Embankment.[14] Reith got through the day as best he could and then struggled home to the flat which he and Muriel had taken in Queen Anne's Mansions in Westminster:

> It was most embarrassing the Archbishop coming as I could not possibly go down to meet them at the door . . . I arranged to be engaged on the telephone so M went down. I was in awful pain but I do not think they noticed anything. Before dinner I was standing talking to them with the wireless set at my back and I pushed the switch without saying anything about it. The set had been given to me by Pease, and was a very fine sideboard affair in mahogany. Nobody could have told that it was a wireless set and there were no aerial connections. The Archbishop and Mrs Davidson got a great surprise – thunderstruck in fact. The whole evening was most successful. There was no piano solo so I rang up Stanton Jeffries and got him to play Schubert's *Marche Militaire* . . .[15]

Another early dinner guest was the Company's chairman, Lord Gainford. Gainford, who had been Postmaster-General briefly during the war, was a member of the 'Quakerocracy' that dominated the economy and society of much of the north-east of England, and his family interests included railways, collieries and a bank. He was a perceptive and kindly man; the word 'workaholism' would not be coined for another forty years, but Gainford clearly knew all about the malady and found a delicate way of referring to the symptoms: 'He said that M. was entitled to my undivided attention for at least one hour every evening,' Reith wrote in his diary.[16]

The Sykes Committee met for the first time on 1 May. Reith found it interesting, but was not over-impressed by Sykes in the chair. The same evening, there was a ceremony to mark the opening of the new studio at Savoy Hill:

> Gainford read a speech I had written. Birkenhead was due to come at 10, but he was dining with a crowd of people at the Savoy and had to be fetched. He was quite drunk, but managed to absorb what Gainford and I told him and made an excellent speech, swaying to and fro in front of the microphone, about the BBC having the right to expect its contract with the government to be honoured.[17]

Reith continued to build up his team – and to improve its quality by selective weeding. In May 1923 he noted in his diary that he had had some conversation with Gainford about Anderson, the Secretary: 'He is quite inadequate for the job, hopelessly so, and should never have been appointed.' He also told the Chairman that he was beginning to feel the need of a deputy, and his mind flickered briefly over what might have been: 'I actually thought of DCB as Deputy General Manager, a job which I suppose he would certainly have had if things had been otherwise.'[18] Things were not otherwise, however, and a month later, at the suggestion of F. J. Brown, an Assistant Secretary at the Post Office, he interviewed Charles Carpendale, a recently retired Rear-

Admiral. The former Transport Officer of the 5th Scottish Rifles (TA) grilled this distinguished product of the Senior Service (Carpendale had been a captain at the age of thirty-four) for two hours: 'He was amazed at the dissecting he got,' Reith wrote rather smugly.[19]

Carpendale, 'a martinet on the quarterdeck but a good fellow in the ward-room', as Peter Eckersley described him, came aboard a few weeks later. He quickly became devoted to Reith, and for the next fifteen years he ran an admirably tight ship for him. 'My early memories of the BBC,' Eckersley wrote, 'picture the Admiral wrinkling his forehead in puzzlement at the strange sort of people and the strange sort of problems he had to deal with.'[20] R. S. Lambert, the first editor of *The Listener*, seasoned his account of 'Carps' with a touch of malice. The Admiral had been describing to him an interview with a young Scot who had applied for a job:

> He talked big to me about his achievements and his prospects, said he had done this, that and the other at Glasgow; and that he had been offered a fellowship at Oxford. Well, I wouldn't let him get away with that! I told him we took no stock of 'fellowships' here; that they were three-a-penny, anyway; and that he would get no bigger salary at Savoy Hill because of it . . . By the way, what *is* a fellowship?[21]

Reith did not drive himself less hard after Carpendale's arrival, but he complained only that the days were too short, never that he had too much to do. His diary continued to suffer, although at the end of July he felt compelled for some reason to fill page after page of it with an extended – and highly tedious – account of what he described as the 'monstrous treatment' he had received from the War Office over an application he had made for a wound gratuity and pension.

The correspondence was not recent – it had begun after his return from the United States in 1917 and had continued sporadically until the previous year. There is nothing to indicate why his sense of grievance about it should suddenly have flared up in this way. It may simply have been provoked by one of his periodic re-readings of earlier volumes of his diary. It is also conceivable that it was triggered by being in touch with Charlie, which for many years was to affect Reith in the way that sunspots affect radio reception. A diary entry in July recorded that Charlie's mother had died:

> I wrote him a brief note expressing sympathy and not, of course, mentioning Jezebel. He replied from the Langham Hotel on the 26th, beginning 'My dear John,' and ending 'Yours very sincerely, Charlie,' and of course dragging Jezebel into the letter.

Whatever the reason, it illustrates how easily, even when things appeared to be going well for him, Reith could topple into that brooding self-absorption that was one of his most salient characteristics.

During those early months at the BBC he was on better terms with Muriel than at any time since their marriage: 'M. always seems very glad to see me home in the evenings and it is awfully nice,' says a diary entry on 19 July. 'I do wish we had our own house and all our gear.' There had been talk of buying a house in Surrey and selling Dunardoch, which had upset his mother. Reith said he had no desire to sell up in Dunblane and would not do so if his mother would live there permanently; he attributed her unwillingness to do so to the malign influence of his sister Jean.[22] In April they moved to an attractive but noisy flat in Victoria Street. The search for a house continued, and during the summer they made a number of sorties out of London:

> Drove to Chobham Heath, which is very fine. Later walked a long way on the river bank in the moonlight. I felt it would be nice to have a friend again, and was still having regrets about Bowser.[23]

There was much activity during 1923 on the publishing front: 'Everything is now in shape for the BBC magazine and from various alternatives I chose *Radio Times* for the title.'[24] The paper was originally contracted out to George Newnes Ltd – the only firm prepared to take the risk. Profits were to be divided, but Reith held out for a payment of £1000 a year to the BBC whether there was a profit or not. The first editor was Leonard Crocombe, who was seconded from Newnes where he edited *Titbits*, and editorial control rested initially not with the BBC but with the publisher.[25] Reith agreed to write a weekly editorial of 1200 words – 'It was rather alarming, but I thought I should rather like it.' The first issue appeared on 28 September, and was sold out. So was the second – 285,000 copies. Reith kicked himself for not having doubled the print order.

That first issue of *Radio Times* is a fascinating period piece. It sold for twopence. In addition to programme information, there was advice from the Assistant Chief Engineer on how to choose a wireless and an article by Sir Ernest Rutherford called 'The Miracle of Broadcasting' – based on his presidential address to the British Association which the BBC had broadcast a few days previously. Crocombe shrewdly gave space to a member of the public, identified only as 'P. J.' of Birmingham, to express a view critical of the Company's performance: 'Do they really think the majority of their "listeners" are really interested in such lectures as the Decrease of Malaria in Great Britain, How to Become a Veterinary Surgeon, etc? . . . Frankly, it seems to me that the BBC are mainly catering for the "listeners" who own expensive sets and pretend to understand only highbrow music and educational "sob stuff".' Most intriguing of all was an article entitled 'The General Manager. By One Who Knows Him':

> Mr J. C. W. Reith, the General Manager of the BBC, is so shy of publicity that apart from inevitable references to him in the daily press in connection

with 'big' BBC matters, he has managed to avoid almost entirely the usual press interviews ... He likes to work standing, and has had a special table fitted up at elbow height (his own), on which stand his telephones and all his more important papers. Thus a first interview is likely to prove rather trying for the interviewer, as, in all probability on entering the room he will find the manager's back firmly turned upon him and until he realises that Mr Reith is at the telephone, he is likely to endure some moments of acute discomfort.

On turning Mr Reith will look quickly at the intruder, sizing him up in one brief but all-absorbing glance of a most dismaying keenness. His manner is abrupt; not with the disconcerting abruptness of discourtesy, but rather the necessary conciseness of a very busy man.[26]

The Board, observing that he had not been hired to run a magazine, suggested that their General Manager should have a percentage of any profits. Reith 'thought it hardly proper' (although later, characteristically, he calculated that the proposition would have quadrupled his salary). It was a significant scruple. The months in which he sat round the table as a member of the Sykes Committee had been an anxious time for him, and he had become aware of a potential conflict of loyalties:

> The trade had put me in office; expected me to look out for them; there was a moral responsibility to them. But I had discerned something of the inestimable benefit which courageous and broad-visioned development of this new medium would yield.[27]

The words have something of the easy grandiloquence of hindsight, but an important idea was taking hold in John Reith's mind in the summer of 1923. Although he was the employee of a combine of commercial firms, he was beginning to see the outline of a higher commission to be performed as a servant of the public.

Piety and ignorance have sometimes combined to write the early history of British broadcasting in the idiom of *1066, And All That*. In this version Reith is portrayed as a latter-day Archimedes, rushing off without his towel to set up something called public service broadcasting between a late breakfast and an early lunch. It was not quite like that. Reith wrote in his memoirs that at the first meeting of the Sykes Committee views were invited on the most appropriate constitutional arrangements for broadcasting:

> I gave a personal opinion – broadcasting should be conducted as a public service and under public corporation constitution. It was not the 1925 Crawford committee which coined either idea or expression.[28]

But no more was it John Reith. In June 1922, for instance, several months before the BBC was set up, the American radio pioneer, David Sarnoff, had written: 'broadcasting represents a job of entertaining, informing and educating the nation, and should therefore be distinctly regarded as a public service', and had gone on to advocate the setting up of 'a Public Service Broadcasting Company or National Broadcasting Company'.[29]

Notions of public service did not in any event detain the Sykes Committee unduly. Although Trevelyan, Labour landowner and great-nephew of Macaulay, entered a minority plea urging that broadcasting should pass out of private ownership, his colleagues were content to suggest that adequate public control would be achieved by the establishment of a Broadcasting Board. Its membership should be such as to 'inspire confidence in the public mind', and it should be the recipient of all proposals – and complaints – relating to the new medium. When the report was published in October, Parliament was in recess and press interest was not strong. The magazine *Popular Wireless* found nothing in it which could not have been decided 'in almost less time than it took Carpentier to knock Beckett into sweet oblivion'.[30]

So far as nuts and bolts issues were concerned, the committee came down in favour of one licence instead of three. It should be set at ten shillings, and the BBC share raised from half to three-quarters. Advertising was ruled out on the ground that it would lower standards. Royalties on the sale of receiving sets should be abandoned.

The BBC Board had been given a preview of the Report, and this last proposal – to which Reith had entered what he described as 'a brief but emphatic reservation' – filled them with dismay. They saw the royalty system as 'the cardinal principle on which broadcasting was established' – which, being translated, meant that it was the bulwark that protected the manufacturers against competition from foreign sets and components. At the end of August, Reith was despatched to see whether he could win any concessions from the new Postmaster-General, Sir Lamington Worthington-Evans, who had succeeded 'Jix' while the committee was sitting.

Reith had several long sessions with Worthington-Evans, two of them at his home in the country, and found him friendly. A compromise was reached. The Company would continue to receive protection from foreign competition until the end of 1924, the expiry date of the BBC's original Licence (the Postmaster-General slipped into his statement at this point a deft reference to the prevailing level of unemployment). Until then, the general licence would remain the same, but the BBC would get 7/6d from it instead of five shillings. Royalties would also remain for that period, although they would be reduced, and a new fifteen-shilling constructors' licence would be brought in; there would in addition be an interim licence, also costing fifteen shillings, and those who had already assembled a set were given fifteen days' grace to acquire one. The effect was dramatic. The number of licences increased from 180,000 to 414,000 in ten days – 200,000 of them of the interim variety. The Company's financial position was eased almost overnight.

All this won Reith golden opinions from his Board. Godfrey Isaacs, the Managing Director of Marconi, telephoned to congratulate him: 'He was tremendously emphatic and said he could not find words to express his admiration,' Reith wrote. 'I was most surprised as he is usually so undemonstrative.'[31] Isaacs also drafted the minute of appreciation which the Directors agreed at their October meeting, and which spoke of Reith's 'consummate ability and tact'. At the same meeting they resolved that he should become Managing Director: 'They also urged me to take a holiday and gave me 10 guineas thereto.'[32] He was thirty-four years old and had been with the Company less than a year.

They were still house-hunting. Reith had now, very reluctantly, decided to sell their house in Dunblane, and on a visit there at the beginning of the month they had packed up their belongings: 'I really felt very sad for many things at leaving Dunardoch.' He did not encounter Charlie on this occasion, but there was gossip about him to be recorded: 'Bowser is away in Nairn. He has two motors and is said to have paid £500 to have his wife's portrait painted. I still cherish no grudge and leave him in my prayers as of old, which is very odd.'[33]

Back in London, he plunged into a new round of activity. The Astronomer Royal came to see him, and he arranged to have time signals taken automatically from Greenwich. The King had agreed to accept a wireless set, and Reith sent Carpendale to the Palace to make the arrangements. The time of the Lord Mayor's procession came round: 'I received an invitation to the banquet, but finding, to my intense indignation, that I had been put in an overflow room with a few others, I went home.'

On 14 November, he made a speech on the occasion of the Company's first anniversary, and there was a passage in it that underlines the direction in which, with Sykes behind him, his mind was turning:

> Although we are idealists, we have commercial obligations, and the business of wireless manufacturers in Gt. Britain depends on our efforts. On the other hand, I believe I have said enough to indicate to you that we are actuated by definite policy and ideals, consistent with which we are determined to make the broadcasting service of as widespread interest and application as possible. The BBC is a public utility service.

At Savoy Hill, he kept a beady eye on everything and everybody: 'Nearly sacked Parker today as the result of his having had too much to drink the night before.'[34] (Reith was unfamiliar with the convivial working habits of Fleet Street – Parker did the Company's liaison with Newnes over *Radio Times*.) Just occasionally he grumbled in his diary about having bitten off more than he could chew: 'My *Radio Times* weekly article is an awful plague. I've also a long Christmas one to do and two for *John O'London's*.'[35] When he wasn't bringing his diary up to date, he was writing letters: 'My very dearest mother,' he wrote on 24 November:

This is the first sheet of writing paper with my name on it, so I am sending it to you – also a spare sheet which you can show Douglas.

I wonder if you heard the opera from the Old Vic this evening. It was sent by wireless across the Thames and then rewirelessed from London . . .

I shall not let any more racing news be included than we can help. We have already cut it down quite a bit.

Ten days before Christmas, Reith and Muriel set off for a foreign holiday. Muriel had had her hair bobbed for the occasion, and Reith thought it 'quite satisfactory'. In spite of all that had passed between him and Charlie, he did not find it possible to shake off the habit of ten years: 'I wrote a letter to DCB saying I was leaving for a few days holiday in Rome and that as I should not be back before the 20th I was sending him a line to wish him, as in every other year, a very happy birthday, Christmas, New Year etc.'[36]

They were seen off to Paris by the faithful Carpendale and continued by train to Rome. Reith's diary accounts of holidays, particularly of holidays abroad, have a certain manic flavour, slightly reminiscent of a Jacques Tati film: 'We went into the catacombs of St Calixtus guided by a priest, who I thought was talking Italian and to whom I said that I could talk French – and then discovered that he was talking English, or thought he was.' After lunch they went to St Peter's, and saw the Guido Reni *Crucifixion*, of which they had a print at home: 'Unfortunately a funeral was on.' Back at the hotel, the hot tap burst: 'I stopped it with a coat hanger and a suitcase. I reported the matter later in voluble French.'

They moved on to San Remo, and on Christmas morning set off for the service in the English Church:

We could not get a seat so sat outside the door at the east end to hear Christmas hymns. We waited for 40 minutes and heard nothing but high-brow chants and were both infuriated; so much so that I wrote to the parson in the evening telling him what I thought about it.[37]

'If the 1923 struggle for survival had been successful,' Reith wrote, 'there was struggle now for place. I wondered what sort of reception Caxton had when he set out . . . Perhaps he too encountered boycotts, oppositions, obstructions, suspicions, jealousies, from the vested interests of the day; from those of whom the silversmiths of Ephesus were prototypes . . .'[38] Reith was happy to take on all comers, whatever their trade, and 1924 was a year of rapid expansion and progress.

On 6 January, the first service from a church – from St Martin-in-the-Fields – was broadcast, and in an article in the *Manchester Guardian* later that month, Reith recorded, with characteristic robustness, his satisfaction with the advances made in religious broadcasting:

We were informed by some folk that they had not bought receivers to have religion thrust upon them. Our reply was that half an hour per week was not excessive, and that if they did not approve there was always the alternative of switching off . . . This recognition of Sunday was made because we conceived it to be right, and in this event opposition ought not to force an alteration of plans conceived on such a basis. But today, and for months past, we have hardly had a letter of complaint. On the contrary there are hundreds of communications of a most appreciative and almost pathetic vein, from invalids and from the aged from whom all such consolations have long been withheld . . . [39]

From Glasgow, in February, came the first experimental broadcasts to schools. In April, BBC microphones were present at the opening of the Wembley Exhibition – the first time that the voice of the King was heard over the air: 'Everything went most successfully,' Reith wrote in his diary, 'including the broadcast which went out all over the country and was the biggest thing we have done yet.'[40] New regional stations were opened during the year at Manchester and Belfast, numerous relay stations were set up, and work began on the high-power transmitter at Daventry.

Archibald McKinstry, the Metropolitan-Vickers representative on the Board, told him in April that he thought he would soon be in line for a knighthood, and at that month's Board meeting his salary was raised by £750 – 'as it dashed well ought to be', Reith wrote in his diary that night. This meant that he now had a salary of £2500, expenses of £250, and a further £200 fee as a director. Even so, he was by no means settled or content in that spring of 1924, and he seems to have poured out his heart in a letter to his brother Douglas, whose no-nonsense reply survives. 'I don't think you should talk or think lightly about leaving the BBC,' Douglas told him briskly, and he continued in a tone that had echoes of their father:

> Your remark about finding a refuge in the busyness of organisation because such busyness acts as an opiate and enables you to forget is the best proof you have ever given me of the great danger you are running on the intellectual and spiritual side . . . To be perfectly candid I do not think that your main interests are really literary or deeply intellectual even though you may suppose they are. I take you to be more a man of action . . . You are intensely ambitious and according to William Ewart Gladstone that's a good thing, but do not let your pride lead you to think that the life of the organiser is a second-best, and that he must or may drown his feelings and disillusionment in an orgy of overwork . . . The temptation to be overbusy is fed by the much more mundane and human desire to have plenty of *material* resources. I pray you to be fearlessly honest with yourself every day in this respect. Say – so much more income, so much less God.[41]

Reith had set aside his earlier Parliamentary ambitions, although it is curious to note that he retained his secretaryship of the London Unionist Committee until the middle of 1924.[42] He had played no part in the previous year's general election which led to the formation of the first Labour government under Ramsay Mac-Donald. The BBC's offer of air-time to the parties during that campaign had been declined, but by the time Parliament was again dissolved in October 1924, the government whips had had second thoughts, and agreed to one broadcast from each party. MacDonald and the Liberal leader Asquith both chose to have speeches relayed from public meetings, which Reith thought a mistake. Baldwin showed himself more amenable to advice. Reith dined with him at the Savoy on the night of his broadcast and then took him round to the studio: 'He gave an excellent twenty minute talk which will, I expect, win the election for him.'[43]

It was the beginning of a cordial relationship by which Reith was to set great store. A few months later he and Muriel were invited to dine with the Baldwins at Number 10. The Prime Minister was in entertaining form about the perquisites of his office, and said he thought he had obtained true eminence the day his car drove down the wrong side of Piccadilly when he was in a hurry. Reith, not to be outdone, countered with the assertion that his ability to broadcast from his own study was also 'greatness in a form', and Baldwin amiably agreed. He also said he would like to have a wireless set at Chequers:

> I said we would supply him with one, or would he prefer to pay for it. He said he did not like sponging on anyone but quite frankly he would like to have it given to him, and that he was overdrawn at the bank. He said he used to be quite well to do but there was no money in his present job.[44]

In June 1924, the Reiths' extended trawl of the property market, which had taken them round most of the Home Counties, came to an end. They found a small house in Barton Street, an agreeable eighteenth-century backwater tucked away behind Westminster Abbey. They also bought a motor car. It was a 23/60 Vauxhall, dark red and with red leather upholstery, and both Reith and Muriel were very excited about it: 'It is really very fine, but we are both scared of it. It was too wet to have the car out after dinner, so we went and gloated on it in the garage.'

In the summer of 1924 Reith was also persuaded to turn author. Sir E. Hodder-Williams, the Chairman of Hodder & Stoughton, had approached him with the suggestion that he should write a 50–60,000-word account of broadcasting. The Board was keener on the idea than Reith was himself, but he began to sketch an outline for it one weekend in June. Never a great man for holidays, he worked at it during their summer break in Rothiemurchus and before the end of August the completed manuscript was in the post.

On their way south, they stayed for the last time at Dunardoch:

> Our last night in what was our first home and I'm quite regretful at leaving it in many ways, but Bowser has ruined this place for us. I hope some

judgement will be meted on Mrs Henderson and Jezebel. I regret giving the house up for mother's sake, as it has been a comfortable refuge for her, but she has not used it nearly so much as she might have done on account of Jean.

They drove on through the Scottish border country, calling at Abbotsford and crossing into England at Carter Bar: 'I felt very sad for some unaccountable reason and lingered on the Scottish side for some time, picking a little white flower which I sent to mother.' They were not far across the English border before an effective remedy for his melancholy presented itself: 'We got nabbed by the police for exceeding the speed limit, and to make matters worse, my driving licence had expired.'[45]

Broadcast over Britain was published in November. Reith appears to have experienced little pride of authorship – 'My wretched book has had an extraordinarily favourable reception.' Stylistically it is rather ponderous. He had not yet evolved that distinctive staccato semi-telegraphese which in later years led someone to compare him with Dickens' Mr Jingle. But although it is nothing like as absorbing as Reith's later autobiographical writings, it provides a useful insight into how his thinking was developing after eighteen months at the helm. 'A remarkable (and cheerful) gospel book for the times,' wrote Asa Briggs, 'setting out a philosophy of broadcasting which cannot be found in the Sykes Report.'[46]

Reith had been with the BBC for almost two years, and had not put a foot wrong. His reputation outside was also growing; over lunch one day a business acquaintance cast a fly over him on behalf of F. G. Kellaway, the former Postmaster-General who had now succeeded Godfrey Isaacs as the Marconi nominee on the BBC board. Kellaway, he was told, would very much like to have him as his right-hand man at Marconi and a salary of £10,000 was mentioned: 'I said I did not want to leave the BBC yet, and certainly would not if any of the Board objected.'[47]

As the year drew to a close his mind turned, as it always did, to Charlie, and he wrote him a note for his birthday. 'Extraordinary reply from Bowser,' reads a diary entry two days before Christmas. 'He says he follows my considerable doings and congratulates me on them.' On New Year's Eve, the Reiths entertained Peter Eckersley and his wife to dinner at Barton Street and then, as midnight approached, they switched on the wireless: 'Big Ben, Auld Lang Syne, Strand noises, St Martin's bells and then the old-time watchman's cry. I was feeling glum about DCB.'[48] He continued to brood about Charlie until well into the new year, and in the middle of February he spent the greater part of two weekends going through old correspondence:

Sunday. Not out all day. Read through DCB's letters from the beginning until 1921. I had kept every one he had ever written me. Today I tore up a few and arranged the others by period. I felt very sad. There was an extraordinary affection between us and we shared almost everything. I suppose that good must somehow come out of it, being disinclined to believe that all this was lost.

Later, however, he changed his mind. 'Of course all's lost,' he wrote in the margin, 'and a very good job too. I have no regrets of any sort.'

Reith's circle of acquaintance continued to grow, and he missed no opportunity to proselytise for the BBC. Early in 1925 Muriel and he were invited to spend the weekend at Canterbury where the Archbishop's former chaplain, Bell, had recently become Dean:

> Lots of people to dinner last night and to lunch today, including a freak professor from Oxford, who did not like telephones or wireless. I soon disposed of him. The dean preached in the evening and made a reference to broadcasting.[49]

The next morning, back in London, he and his newly appointed publicity chief, a Canadian ex-pilot and Rhodes Scholar called Major W. E. Gladstone Murray, went to call on Geoffrey Dawson, the editor of *The Times*, and the following week he had Dawson to dinner at Barton Street and showed him around Savoy Hill.[50] He was to remain on good terms with *The Times* throughout his BBC years. A few weeks later Muriel and he were entertained to dinner by Beaverbrook, who then took them on to *No, No, Nanette* and supper at the Savoy. They sat there talking till one in the morning, and Reith registered that the views of the mercurial Max had veered into a new quarter: 'He said he had made up his mind that there must be monopoly in broadcasting, but that he had to be in it.'[51]

Before 1925 was many weeks old, Reith once again found himself squaring up to the Postmaster-General – the fourth holder of the office he had had to deal with. This latest bird of passage at the Post Office was Sir William Mitchell-Thomson, and he introduced a Bill aimed at removing any uncertainty about his right to collect the licence fee. That didn't bother Reith at all, although he judged the methods proposed – they included the searching of premises – to be heavy-handed. He did, however, take vehement exception to the proposal that the pill should be sugared by a reduction in the licence fee: 'I knew, if the Post Office did not, how much money would have to be spent in technical expansions of the service; in improvements in programmes; in the provision of alternatives.'[52] He found himself in informal alliance with the Labour Party, who took a high line in the House about the 'inquisitorial' nature of the measure, and the Bill was rejected.

There were matters of rather greater moment which would have to be discussed with the PMG before long, because the BBC was moving towards the expiry of its licence. Reith felt it increasingly absurd that broadcasting should be subject to the direction of a junior minister like the PMG, and hoped for a Royal Commission to consider the Company's constitutional future, and at the March meeting of the Board he persuaded them to hold a special meeting to consider what their position should be.[53]

They met a week later, and Reith wrote an exasperated account of their deliberations in his diary:

> The meeting was very stupid, lots of them talking at once. Noble said nobody else could manage the BBC as well as they did, because of their knowledge of wireless, which was of course humbug. It is not a knowledge of wireless that is required; and in any event, they have never managed it. I am very glad they have left me to do so, but I think they should recognise and face up to the position now.[54]

Reith was not entirely well in the spring of 1925. He had been unable to shake off a cold, and his doctor eventually packed him off to bed with a warning about the possibility of lung trouble. A large bunch of roses arrived from the women staff at Savoy Hill: 'I felt quite overwhelmed.' Later in the month he saw the doctor again, this time about the noise in his ear: 'Milligan says it is purely functional and aggravated by the strain of work, etc. He strongly recommended no late hours in the office, leaving at 6 at latest, and no Saturdays.'[55] His mother was down on one of her periodic visits, and he relaxed to the extent of taking her walking in St James's Park. It was the day before Primrose Day, and the sight of Disraeli's statue adorned in the traditional way stirred old family loyalties. 'I wondered why nothing is ever done in this way for Gladstone; it is rather a reflection on the Liberal organisation, he being much more worthy of it.'[56]

Family memories ran strongly in his mind again later in the year when he heard that there had been a great fire in Glasgow and the College and Kelvingrove Church had been burned to the ground. Reith wrote to the Minister, Dr Knight, but although he began with an expression of sympathy – 'I well remember what a grief and shock the burning of the real College Church was to my father' – the letter continued rather less conventionally:

> I never liked Kelvingrove, finding it vastly different in almost every respect from the old College. Later I liked it the less because I never thought they appreciated my father, treated him very badly in the matter of salary and even after all his devoted work promptly forgot about him immediately after his death . . .
>
> I did not intend all this when I began. I was only writing to express deep sympathy with you, but you know I was, in the Biblical sense, extraordinarily jealous for my father and greatly attached to him.[57]

Dr Knight acknowledged this unusual communication, but we no longer know in what terms: a note on Reith's copy of his own letter says simply, 'Replied nicely but incompletely 16/7.'

July saw the opening of the Daventry long-wave transmitter. Its two steel masts towered to a height of 500 feet and it was the highest-powered station in the world. Alfred Noyes wrote a poem to mark the occasion, and Baldwin, in a letter to Reith, said how sorry he was that he had a prior engagement. The new transmitter, the Prime Minister wrote, 'will give no less than twenty million people the opportunity to receive both education and entertainment by means of cheap and simple apparatus: and I look upon Daventry as another milestone on the road to the social betterment of our people.'[58]

In August, Reith took Muriel off for a brief holiday in the West Country. While they were there he sought out the place where Charlie and he were to have stayed in August 1914 when their camping plans were disrupted by the war: 'It was chosen from a map, but is a gorgeous place.' Then they went north, and inspected the house in Dumfries where his mother and Jean had recently gone to live. Reith, predictably, found it 'appalling', and appears to have written to tell his sister so on his return to London. He obviously said a good many other things to her as well. His letter does not survive, but he kept Jean's reply. It throws painful light on the brittleness of their relationship; it is also almost the only occasion on which we do not see Jean through the prism of Reith's dislike and jealousy of her:

Dear John,
I once long ago read and was also taught at school that one of the signs of a good writer was the use of 'simple English words'. Your letter in fact frightens me by its construction alone and leaves me in a semi-petrified and breathless condition by the time I reach the last sentence . . .
The one thing I write this for is to say this. Try beginning once again. 'Let the dead past bury its dead.' . . . The more one broods on past evils the bigger do they become until in the end they simply eclipse all things. Every attempt at reconciliation is made *in the light of old grievances*, which is hopeless.
When you come, whether it's this week or later, *be natural* with me. Say 'How are you?' and kiss me just as you do mother . . . After all, nothing very dreadful did happen, nothing at least that one can't forget if one makes an effort . . .
You say you never looked upon me as a sister. Well, begin to do so *now*, and you will find you haven't made a mistake except that you didn't do it earlier.
Your affectionate sister, Jean.[59]

A week before he performed the opening ceremony at Daventry, the Post-master-General had told Parliament that he was setting up a committee under Lord Crawford to consider the future of broadcasting in 'the widest possible terms'. It was not the Royal Commission that Reith had hoped for, but it was the next best thing:

To such a body one would be glad to present an account of the stewardship; explain and defend the conceptions and the policies by which one had been animated and determined; limn the opportunities and potentialities ahead; in general consolidate the past, pre-empt the future.[60]

The 27th Earl of Crawford and Balcarres had served briefly in the Cabinet in 1916 and 1922 and had a strong interest in the arts. His colleagues on the committee included no fewer than four fellow-Scots – Lord Blanesburgh, Captain Ian Fraser, a young Tory MP who had been blinded in the war, William Graham, who had been a junior Treasury minister in the 1924 Labour government, and Ian MacPherson, who later became Lord Strathcarron. They were joined by the musician and educationist Sir Henry Hadow, the physicist Lord Rayleigh, and the shipping magnate Sir Thomas Royden. The only woman on the committee was Dame Meriel Talbot. Rudyard Kipling was also a member, but resigned through ill health quite early on.

   When Reith came to write his memoirs, he rather glossed over the way in which the BBC made its case to Crawford, saying only that a comprehensive memorandum of information was prepared for them. After setting out a two-page summary of the submission, he wrote, 'Marvellous. That was the way one had to talk in those days.' What he omits to make clear is that this 'Memorandum of Information on the scope and conduct of the Broadcasting Service' was entirely his own work. He asserted, with breathtaking aplomb, that it was 'an impartial statement of the conduct of a Public Service'. It was submitted, he said, 'in the interests of Broadcasting, not of the British Broadcasting Company'.

   Nothing could illustrate more graphically the ascendancy he had established over his Board. When the secretary to the committee wrote to say he assumed the Company would wish to submit evidence, Reith, whose low opinion of civil servants was already well developed, put him right in the most lordly fashion. The Company, he replied, had no wish to make representations. They believed, 'in view of the manner in which public obligations have been discharged', that their interests would be respected. He himself would submit a personal memorandum.

   There was nothing in the document which should have surprised anyone who had read and digested *Broadcast over Britain*, but by the time the Board assembled for its December meeting, some of its members clearly felt that their Managing Director was coming close to biting the hand that fed him:

   It was pathetically dreadful. They are reacting to my evidence, which I do not believe they like at all and are beginning to try to assert themselves. I have no opinion of Noble, Binyon and Burnham. Gray, when sober, has a little sense. Pease is usually sensible, and McKinstry almost invariably so. Bull of course is quite alright. Gainford is often too weak.[61]

Reith had good reason to feel confident. He had kept his ear close to the ground and he knew that things were going his way on the committee, not least because his views on how things should be ordered coincided with those of the Post Office. He had had a chance to present his arguments in person the previous week when he had been called for his first session of oral evidence, although he had walked like a cat around questions of constitutional detail. 'I may have my own views, my own colleagues on the Board, my own Chairman, may have their views,' he said at one point in the exchanges. 'I do not think it would be quite right for me to give my opinion.' 'We will make your mind up for you,' Lord Crawford said easily. 'I do not imply that it is not already made up,' retorted Reith.[62]

Although he was much preoccupied with Crawford, he continued to meet an extraordinarily wide range of people, both professionally and socially. The chairman of the publishers John Lane called, and asked him to write a book on the religion of the plain man. Another visitor to Savoy Hill was the Prince of Wales; he stayed for half an hour and Reith found him 'very amiable'. Reith's diary quite often makes pedestrian reading, but his accounts of some of these encounters can be extremely entertaining:

> After lunch to work of various sorts as usual, inimical to the peace of the Sabbath; and what was more so, a visit from Blackwood, with Sir Harry Lauder in tow. We heard later that Jessie, the parlourmaid, was overcome by this honour, and promised herself much pleasure on returning to Glasgow in the recounting of how she was in the same house as such a hero, and actually made his tea. The little man is very self possessed and egotistical. He gave a short private hearing of a new song relating to one Mackay – for which sort of performance he can apparently make up to £2,000 per week.[63]

The following week, he described a rather different encounter – and recorded for the first time what was to become one of his most tenacious ambitions: 'Saw Professor Gangulee of Calcutta, son-in-law of Rabindranath Tagore . . . Rather bored to start with but became aware that he was not of the ordinary type. He made me think that I might take the Viceroy's job if it were offered to me.'

He also found time that autumn for amateur theatricals. The BBC Staff Operatic and Dramatic Society put on a triple bill of one-act plays and the cast of *The Bishop's Candlesticks*, based on an incident in Hugo's *Les Misérables*, included C. D. Carpendale and J. C. W. Reith, the latter playing a thief. 'The performance in the evening was apparently very successful indeed,' Reith wrote jubilantly. 'It was the first time I have ever acted, but I always knew I could.'[64]

The year had taken a lot out of him. 'Very worried at my inability to recapture in any way the old spirit of Christmas, which I used to enjoy so much,' he wrote on 21 December, and his diary entries over the holiday period reflect a combination of restlessness and unfocused discontent. His return to the office on 1 January seems to have made little difference: 'Feeling indescribably bored and could hardly get any work done. I could do with a voyage round the world.'

The Crawford Committee began to formulate its conclusions in the early weeks of 1926. Reith, who had gone to great pains to cultivate the membership, called on Ian Fraser and came away with a pretty clear idea of what their proposals were likely to be: 'In general things are OK and as I should wish,' he wrote, adding with a touch of impatience, 'I should have been on the committee to keep clearing things up and prevent woolliness and misconceptions. I cannot control this sort of thing from outside.'[65] The Report was published in March 1926,[66] and Reith got very largely what he wanted. The committee, as A. J. P. Taylor later succinctly put it, 'endorsed the moral case for monopoly. Parliament did not demur. Conservatives liked authority; Labour disliked private enterprise.'[67]

Reith had two meetings with the Postmaster-General during March and found him very ready to discuss who the new 'Commissioners' should be.[68] He urged Gainford's claims to the chairmanship on each occasion, but gathered that there was little chance of this: 'Perhaps the Post Office thought he had given me too much power; or was too old; perhaps his being a coal owner was an objection; and a Liberal – since the Conservatives were in power.'[69] The PMG's counter-suggestion was Lord Foster, who had recently been Governor-General of Australia. The proposed remuneration for the chairman was £3000; Reith (whose own earnings had just been increased by £750 to £4450) thought this 'ridiculous'.

These routine exchanges with the Post Office were soon interrupted by events on the broader political stage. For the best part of a year, trouble had been brewing in the coal industry, which employed at the time more than a million workers. Low-priced coal from Germany and Poland had knocked the bottom out of the market, and British coal-owners could see no way to stem their losses other than imposing a longer working day and cutting the miners' wages. When the owners threatened a lock-out at the end of July 1925, the government bought time with the offer of a nine-month subsidy and appointed a Royal Commission under Sir Herbert Samuel to find ways of increasing the industry's efficiency.[70]

Samuel presented his report in March 1926. His longer-term proposals for structural improvements were rejected by the coal-owners; his short-term recommendation for a reduction in wages was rejected by the miners. The government and the General Council of the TUC both failed in their efforts to break the deadlock.

Reith noted in his diary on 23 April that a general strike was brewing, and that he had been in touch with J. C. C. Davidson, who had been detached from his post as parliamentary secretary to the Admiralty to be vice-chairman of the Emergency Committee.[71] A week later, shortly before midnight, a messenger from Number 10 arrived at Barton Street with a request for an immediate announcement to be made about the stoppage that had been called in the coal industry. It was a Friday evening. Jack Payne's orchestra was playing dance music. Reith gave orders for all transmitters to be connected to his private line; at midnight the dance music was cut off and he made the announcement himself from his study. 'Very impressive performance,' he noted immodestly in his diary.

It was the last entry he made for a fortnight, and when he resumed he wrote that the story would have been much fuller and more interesting if he had been able to write it daily. It was his only regret: when he came to summarise this part of his diary seven years later, he wrote: 'I was *most happy* throughout. I do not say that I welcome crises, but I do welcome the opportunities which they bring.'

The opportunities which the General Strike offered to Reith and to the BBC were enormous, but for the nine days it lasted he was also leading his troops through a political and constitutional minefield. The central opportunity arose from the fact that because the printers had joined the strike, most national newspapers had ceased publication. Reith got authority from Davidson on 3 May to broadcast news bulletins at any hour; he promptly arranged for them at ten, one, four, seven and 9.30, and asked Reuters to supply whatever news they had accordingly. The principal danger was that the government might decide to exercise its powers under the Emergency Regulations and commandeer the BBC, with disastrous consequences for its fragile independence.

Lunching as a guest at the Travellers' Club on the first day of the strike, Reith came upon the Prime Minister, who left the group of people he was with and came across:

He said we had the key situation now and everyone depended on us. He asked if we were properly protected and I said we were everywhere. Savoy Hill is hotching with policemen and special constables. He said the Government had no alternative but to break off negotiations on Sunday night and he seemed ready to talk to me much longer. I said he ought to broadcast soon.[72]

Reith had been to the Admiralty that morning with Davidson, whose main responsibility was the control of all news. He formed the view that Davidson had no clear idea of what he wanted from the BBC or indeed of what he was supposed to be doing himself. He also learned that the government was to produce a newspaper of its own, to be called the *British Gazette*, and met an official called Caird from the War Office who was to edit it: 'He apparently thought that the BBC news was to be regarded as a kind of off-shoot to that. I told him I was not going to have that at all.' Davidson came to see him at one o'clock in the morning bringing a copy of the *Gazette*'s first edition: 'He was pleased with it, but I told him I did not think much of it.'

Reith conceded that the early BBC bulletins were 'pretty rotten', but blamed this mainly on the chaotic state of affairs at the Admiralty. By 5 May things were going rather better; he himself was vetting every item of news. (He and Carpendale also took to reading some of the bulletins themselves – 'this to some extent as the result of complaints that our announcers had been sounding panicky,' he noted in his diary. 'Much favourable comment resulted.') He heard from Davidson, however, that Churchill, then Chancellor of the Exchequer, and the Minister to whom Baldwin had given responsibility for the *British Gazette*, wanted to take over the BBC, and the next morning, immediately after breakfast, he went with Davidson to Number 10 to put the Company's case to the Prime Minister.

> He walked up and down the Cabinet Room while Davidson and I leaned against the mantelpiece and explained our views – at least I said what I thought and Davidson joined in. Every time I made a point, the PM stopped in his perambulations and faced us. He said he entirely agreed with us that it would be far better to leave the BBC with a considerable measure of autonomy and independence. He was most pleasant. I was a little scared of being at No. 10, especially at such a time, but was not nervous at all.[73]

Baldwin said that Reith ought to attend the Strike Committee of the Cabinet, of which he himself was not a member. Reith's old sparring partner Joynson-Hicks, now Home Secretary, was in the chair, and he had already been briefed by Baldwin, but he was not the strongest of chairmen, and in Churchill and Birkenhead the committee included two of the Cabinet's most aggressive hard-liners.[74]

> Jix said that as I was there they would take broadcasting first and asked Davidson to start off. He then said that he had been authorised by the PM to say he preferred to trust the BBC, in particular Mr Reith, the Managing Director, to do what was best. He, Jix, agreed with that. Winston emphatically objected, said it was monstrous not to use such an instrument to the best possible advantage. Jix then weakly said he would have it discussed at a Cabinet meeting if anybody felt strongly about it. Churchill then launched out on other matters without asking the Chairman to say anything, and at this stage I thought I had better clear out as they had apparently finished with broadcasting.[75]

It was his first experience of a Cabinet committee and his first experience of Churchill. Reith thought it advisable to buttress his position by getting something down on paper for the Prime Minister. He marshalled his arguments with remarkable assurance and authority, and what he wrote that night remains a classic statement of the case for broadcasting to be independent of government:

> The BBC has secured and holds the goodwill and affection of the people. It has been trusted to do the right thing at all times. Its influence is widespread. It is a national institution and a national asset. If it be commandeered or unduly hampered or manipulated now, the immediate purpose of such action is not only unserved but prejudiced. This is not a time for dope, even

if the people could be doped. The hostile would be made more hostile from resentment. As to suppression, from the panic of ignorance comes far greater danger than from the knowledge of facts. If the government be strong and their cause right they need not adopt such measures . . .

The Cabinet did not, in the event, get round to discussing the BBC when it met the next day; a formal decision not to commandeer the BBC was not taken until 11 May, which was the day before the strike was called off.

The next test of Reith's political and diplomatic skills came when the Archbishop of Canterbury telephoned and asked whether he might broadcast a manifesto drawn up by the leaders of the Churches. This contained the suggestion that the strike should be called off and negotiations opened concurrently, something Reith knew Baldwin had set his face against. J. C. C. Davidson pointed out that to broadcast the manifesto would be to play into the hands of Churchill and those who thought like him; Baldwin, on the other hand, who had seen the text, had not made things easier for Reith by telling the Archbishop that although he would prefer it not to be broadcast, he would not take steps to have it stopped.

The complications did not end there. Reith had unwisely shown the manifesto to his Chairman – one of the few occasions during the strike when he involved the Board in any way – and Gainford had further muddied the waters by writing a letter to the Archbishop off his own bat. 'A nice position for me to be in between Premier and Primate,' Reith wrote in his memoirs; 'bound mightily to vex one or other; at thirty-six years of age.' To his credit, he concluded that the least bad course was to turn the request down on his own authority, and this he sturdily did on the telephone, 'putting it as nicely as I could', and denying, out of a sense of loyalty to Baldwin, that he had been influenced by the Prime Minister's view.

Archbishops were not in those days encumbered with advice from press officers and public relations advisers. Dr Davidson had already told his friends that the 'peace appeal' would be broadcast and had sent the text to the newspapers. He wrote a long letter to Reith complaining that the Churches were being refused a hearing at a great historic juncture. Reith went to see him, and appears to have made no attempt to conceal his unhappiness at what he felt obliged to do: 'He certainly squirmed somewhat at what I said in my letter,' the Archbishop wrote later that day, 'but he appealed to me to realise the difficulty of his own position. It would, of course, be easier for him to let the government commandeer the BBC, but he thought it would be harmful in the public interest.'

Later that day – it was a Saturday – Reith heard that the Prime Minister wanted to take up the suggestion that he should broadcast. He offered 9.30 that evening and said he would call for Baldwin at 9.10, having decided that the broadcast would be better done from his house than from Savoy Hill. They drove back to Barton Street escorted by a police tender with a dozen or so policemen. The Prime Minister seems to have been extremely relaxed. He handed Reith his manuscript, asking him to see what he thought of 'this tripe' and inviting comments or suggestions:

> I put in a word 'presumably' on the first page, and told him that it would have to do. He said he thought of ending with something personal, and I said yes, something about trusting him. Then I said 'What about this – I am a man of peace; I am longing and working and praying for peace; but I will not compromise the dignity of the British constitution.' He said, 'Excellent; write it down if you have a legible hand.'[76]

Baldwin sat at Reith's desk, and at 9.30 Reith began to announce him – 'London and all stations calling – the Prime Minister.' He had to lean over Baldwin's shoulder to get close enough to the microphone, and as he did so the Prime Minister unconcernedly struck a match to light his pipe. Reith retreated to one of the big armchairs in the room (J. C. C. Davidson was in the other) but it creaked rather badly so he got up again:

> Then I began to think of what I had written, and wished that I had had a warning that his speech had no proper ending. I did not like the word 'dignity' in such a crisis, as people might say it was no time to stand on dignity, etc. I wrote this on a bit of paper to Davidson, and he suggested 'safety' or 'security.' The PM had reached the second last page, but I took the last one from under his hand and wrote in 'safety and security.' When he came to this he paused, but almost imperceptibly, and it was certainly much better.[77]

Reith's mother was staying with them at the time. She had been listening outside the study door while the broadcast was in progress. She now tried to escape downstairs, but Reith took her in and introduced her to Baldwin, and she said she was proud to be the first to see him after his speech. The Prime Minister was disinclined to linger – Mrs Baldwin would be worrying about him, he said. In the car on the way back to Downing Street he told Reith that he was very grateful for all the BBC were doing and 'indicated quite clearly that his anxieties were not lessened by some of his colleagues'. Reith returned home well pleased with himself: 'M and I thought we would get a little brass plate put on the desk as the speech was such an important one, and was really instrumental in breaking the strike.'

The colleague who was the principal cause of Baldwin's anxiety was Churchill, and Reith had a second encounter with him the following evening. It had been agreed that the former Foreign Secretary, Earl Grey of Falloden, might make a broadcast on behalf of the Asquithian Liberals. Reith went to pick him up from 11 Downing Street, where he was staying with the Churchills, and was invited in for coffee. His diary entry for this day is a puzzle. He wrote that he had not met Winston before, although they had sat round the table three days previously at the Cabinet committee meeting at the Home Office; his account also suggests that Churchill did not at first recognise him, and that too seems improbable:

> He asked me later if I were connected with the BBC. I said I was the Managing Director. He swung round with, 'Are you Mr Reith?' – almost shouted out. I said I was. He was much interested and said he had been hunting for me all the week. I said I was on the job all the time and he could have asked me to come along, and that he ought to do so when he was feeling indignant with us, and that we could have had a straight argument. He was really very stupid ... His wife backed him up, but Lord Grey approved the idea of keeping the BBC to some extent impartial ... He came to the car with us, saying he was very glad indeed to have met me. He said he had heard that I had been badly wounded in the war. I said that was so, but that had no bearing on my actions at present, which embarrassed him![78]

Reith was still not without embarrassments of his own. They now arose principally from his dealings with the Labour Party, who earlier in the week had pressed him to allow a broadcast by 'a representative Labour or Trade-Union leader'. He had made the case for it, but the government had said no. Labour's feeling that it was not getting a fair crack of the whip was increased by Lord Grey's broadcast, in which he had had some sharp things to say about the unions.

On 12 May, Reith was himself at the microphone reading the one o'clock bulletin when news came through that the TUC leaders had been to Number 10 to tell the Prime Minister that they were calling off the strike. That evening he was in the studio again, and he contrived to invest the proceedings with an air of pure theatre. He read messages from the King and the Prime Minister and followed these with 'a little thing of our own':

> Our first feeling on hearing of the termination of the General Strike must be one of profound thankfulness to Almighty God, Who has led us through this supreme trial with national health unimpaired. You have heard the messages from the King and the Prime Minister. It remains only to add the conviction that the nation's happy escape has been in large measure due to a personal trust in the Prime Minister.
>
> As for the BBC we hope your confidence in and goodwill to us have not suffered. We have laboured under certain difficulties, the full story of which may be told some day ...
>
> In going to work tomorrow or the next day, could we not all go as fellow-craftsmen, united in a determination to pick up the broken pieces, to repair the gaps and build up the walls of a more enduring city – the city revealed to the mystic eyes of William Blake ...

He then launched into a reading of Blake's *Jerusalem*: 'I had an orchestra brought together and just as I began to read the poem, they played in the background. At the end they came in with full orchestra and chorus with the last verse and it was tremendously impressive.'[79]

For a day or two Reith was as high as a kite: 'Letters galore about the *Jerusalem* business.' The Bishop of Winchester said that it was precisely what the nation needed: 'it was a great opportunity for a Christian message and it was greatly used.' Baldwin wrote in warm terms: 'You have your reward in the knowledge that you have given satisfaction and pleasure to an enormous section of the British public, but over and above that, you and all members of your staff may rest assured that your loyal service has earned the warm appreciation of the government.'[80]

The Labour Party was understandably less pleased. Reith, in a very frank memorandum to his senior staff after the end of the strike, conceded that they had ground for complaint, but maintained that the decision flowed inescapably from the declaration in the High Court that the strike was illegal: 'we were unable to permit anything which was contrary to the spirit of that judgement, and which might have prolonged or sought to justify the strike.'[81] Later he repeated a form of words he had used in his message to the Prime Minister – that 'since the BBC was a national institution, and since the government in this crisis were acting for the people . . . the BBC was for the government in the crisis too.' Paddy Scannell, in his *Social History of British Broadcasting*, calls this a 'notorious syllogism', but it is not easy to see how Reith could have formulated it otherwise.

Judgements about the impartiality of the BBC's strike coverage were inevitably coloured by the political standpoint of those making them. In a letter to *Radio Times* the Labour MP Ellen Wilkinson, who had driven more than 2000 miles around the country addressing meetings, was highly critical: 'Everywhere the complaints were bitter that a national service subscribed to by every class should have given only one side of the dispute. Personally I feel like asking the Postmaster General for my licence fee back.'[82] There was some disquiet inside the Company too. Peter Eckersley, the Chief Engineer, was one of those roped in to help in the newsroom, an experience he described years later after he had left the BBC:

My job was to sort out the news as it came in higgledy-piggledy and arrange items under headings. My tidy sheets were sent to the Admiralty where, so we gathered, government censors would pass it for broadcasting. I therefore shared with a few others the staggering experience of comparing all the news as it came in with that which was considered fit for public consumption. Many of those besides myself who had been proselytizing the BBC as the impartial public servant were bitterly disappointed. It was not so much that the news was altered as given bias by elimination.[83]

Asa Briggs' perusal of all the bulletins broadcast during the strike led him to conclude that much news was excluded; in some cases this was attributable to the directive that went out to Station Directors on 7 May – 'nothing calculated to extend the area of the strike should be broadcast.' Messages from the General Council of the TUC were put out, however (they found no place in the pages of the *British Gazette*); labour demonstrations were reported, and so were the speeches of union leaders and of political critics of the government. The two principal services which the BBC performed for the government were to keep the political temperature down and to check the spread of rumour – it was not true, for instance, that there had been a riot at Hyde Park Corner in the course of which a number of society ladies had been struck over the head with milk bottles; nor was it the case that two divisions of the Red Army had been despatched from Archangel and were to be landed at Wick.[84]

Reith wrote later that what he valued most in the aftermath of the strike was that thirteen of his senior staff put their names to a round robin expressing their appreciation of the way he had carried them through the crisis: 'It is your leadership that has made the BBC what it is and therefore able in the emergency to do what it has done . . . You never failed to keep a steady hand on the tiller and gave confidence to us all.'[85]

Reith's performance during the nine days of the General Strike cannot be judged in a vacuum, because he knew throughout that he had unfinished business with the government. The strike took place after the publication of the Crawford Report but before it had been debated in Parliament, and there was still much to be done if the Post Office was to be won over to his way of thinking on a number of outstanding issues. He was not on especially good terms with the Postmaster-General, Mitchell-Thomson, whom he found pompous, but he got on very well with his deputy, Lord Wolmer, and after a dinner party one night at Wolmer's house in Chester Gate he took him back to Savoy Hill and managed to worm out of him the name of the new Chairman. It was to be the Earl of Clarendon, then Parliamentary Under-Secretary for the Dominions and a former Conservative Chief Whip in the House of Lords: 'Wolmer said he thought he would be very nice and suitable and that he would not interfere at all.'[86]

The Postmaster-General told the Commons that the government accepted the main proposals of the Crawford Committee in the middle of July. They proposed that at the end of the year the BBC's service should 'pass over as a going concern' to a new authority. It would be established by Royal Charter and it would be known as the British Broadcasting Corporation (Crawford had suggested 'Commission'). The PMG told the House that he had financial arrangements in hand which he hoped would make it possible for the new body to start 'with an absolutely clean sheet, clear of all liability'.

Crawford had recommended that the Post Office should keep only as much of the licence fee as was needed to cover their own expenses and that any surplus should accrue to them only after the needs of the BBC had been met, but Reith did not find it easy during June and July to get them to pay serious attention to the estimates he had prepared. A diary note for 1 July reads, 'I have the Post Office proposals now – absolutely rotten and ridiculous,' and looking back thirty years later he wrote, 'If they had been dealing with vulpine contractors it might have been understandable.' Later in the month he tried to outflank the Post Office by sending a memorandum to all Members of Parliament. His argument was that if the BBC did not move forward, it would decline: 'The saturation point of productive and efficient expenditure on the Broadcasting Service is not yet within sight.' It was a risky manoeuvre, sourly received by the Postmaster-General and his officials, but it won Reith useful support in the House.

From his Chairman-elect he felt he got no support at all. Clarendon was wheeled into a meeting with the Postmaster-General early in July, but made no contribution to the discussion. Reith rang him up the next day to ask what he thought of things:

> Evidently he did not in the least understand what was happening yesterday about money. I am afraid he is a stupid man and weak. I do not see him taking a strong line on anything as required. If he interferes it would most likely be through fear that trouble might come if he did not. I am afraid he might turn out a nuisance. I think he is a decent enough sort of fellow, but I ought to be very wary of him.[87]

The other issue on which Reith had hoped to win some ground was that of controversial broadcasting. The Sykes Committee had reported in favour of greater latitude, but the Postmaster-General had allowed little besides the three political broadcasts at the last election, and Reith felt the BBC was still in chains. Crawford had recommended that a 'moderate amount' of controversial material should be permitted, provided it was 'of high quality and distributed with scrupulous fairness'. The BBC had put a toe in the water during the General Strike, although it was plain from the tone of the first of these 'editorials' that they were not intended to provoke brawls in saloon bars: 'Many of you will be missing the editorial chat in your favourite newspapers, and I hope you will not think we are presuming if we venture to supply its place with a few words of advice to the ordinary good citizen . . .'

The General Strike ended, but the miners stayed out, and the editorial comment offered each night gradually began to sound less anaemic. Within a fortnight, however, the BBC found itself caught in the sort of crossfire which is an occasional hazard for innocents in Whitehall. The editorials were the work of Gladstone Murray and a member of his staff called Major C. F. Atkinson. They had been receiving a certain amount of rather furtive guidance from J. C. C. Davidson, in his capacity as Assistant Chief Civil Commissioner, the thrust of which was to urge moderation on both sides. The talk on 21 May, for instance, emphasised the importance of reaching agreement on the miners' claim, and four days later listeners were told that the great social problem of the twentieth century was 'how to reconcile or rather how to combine economics with humanity'.[88]

Some newspapers thought the BBC was poaching on their preserves. Some MPs thought it was being soft on the miners. The Postmaster-General (who, as Chief Civil Commissioner, was Davidson's superior in such matters) fired a shot across the Company's bows in the House of Commons. Reith was caught slightly on the hop because he had been away for a long weekend in Norfolk with his mother and Muriel, and when he got back, he gave his publicity aides a roasting:

> What I was angry about was that Murray's judgement should have been so utterly at fault and in spite of the undertaking given me about no controversy over the weekend. I was amazed that he should have let Atkinson write five coal editorials, which, in the latter stages anyhow, were obviously controversial. He tried to make out that they were not and, of course, the things themselves were quite clever.[89]

Over the next couple of days there was a lot of to-ing and fro-ing with Davidson, who clearly felt that he had put his head too far above the parapet; Reith's diary entries about him show a distinct curl of the lip:

> His chief anxiety seemed to be to get back from me the notes on the suggested coal editorials which he had given to Murray last Friday. He made fatuous reasons about their really having been intended for himself only, his writing being well-known, etc – really dreadful ... I gather he has been told to keep off us and does not like to say so.[90]

A letter from the chief permanent official of the Post Office to Reith on 2 June confirmed that things were back to where they had been before the strike began: 'The Postmaster-General considers it right that the existing policy of avoiding the broadcasting of controversial matter should be maintained during the remaining period of the Company's Licence.'

Reith had itchy feet again in the months immediately after the strike. There was a paragraph in the *Westminster Gazette* early in June forecasting that he would get a knighthood, but he noted grumpily in his diary that he was not at all sure that he would accept it: 'Also newspaper yarns about my being offered a radio job in America, and for many things I would not mind going there.'[91] A few weeks later he had a letter from his brother Douglas thanking him for some money he had sent: 'I don't think you should yet be tired of the BBC, especially if it is to become a national thing. But you know best I suppose. In any case, I would make jolly sure of what I was going to before I let slip what I had.'[92]

In the middle of July, Reith's mother returned to Scotland and he wrote her, as he frequently did on such occasions, a long, extravagantly worded letter in which regret jostled with self-pity:

... I am missing you most awfully ... There were so many more things I wanted to do with you ... I went into your little room by myself when I got in this evening at 7 and knelt down beside your bed ... it is really dreadful now that you are gone ... I wish we had been going off to France the day you left so that I should not have felt the lonely house so much ... With ever so much love, darling mother – from your sorrowful and lonely Johnnie.[93]

Muriel and he set off for their motoring holiday a couple of weeks later; 'we are quite proud of the GB at the back.' Reith had made it his business to see most of the senior staff before his departure, and he left a twenty-seven-page memorandum headed 'Loose Ends' for Carpendale. He did not believe in travelling light: 'We managed to get all the gear in nicely, M's big hat box, dressing case and suitcase, my two suitcases and the leather box from the BBC; lunch basket, attaché case, umbrella and two sticks; tennis racquets and rugs.'

It was something of a sentimental journey for both of them (this was the occasion he visited the farm where he had been billeted in 1914). Their first stop was at a British war cemetery near Le Tréport to visit Muriel's brother's grave; then on to some of his wartime haunts: 'We found splendid trenches, three or four shells, bombs, lots of old bully beef and jam tins and barbed wire. It was most thrilling and M was quite overcome.'[94] Later, when they visited the grave of Muriel's first fiancé, Reith did not distinguish himself by his delicacy: 'I said I supposed if he had appeared she would readily go with him and leave me.'[95]

He could never manage much more than a week on holiday without becoming twitchy:

August 3. Dull and rainy. Still no wires forwarded from Armentières, which was rotten. Nothing in the morning, and a three hour walk in the afternoon. A letter from Mother, to which I replied. Idiotic and vacuous people danced to the jazz all afternoon, including the revolting Charleston. Went to the extreme end of the hotel and read Spengler's *Decline of the West*.

They moved on to St Enogat, near Dinard, only to find that here, too, things were not as they should have been, particularly at the English church: 'I do not know that I ever heard the lessons worse read, and the sermon absolutely dreadful.' He returned to Spengler: 'Very interesting and stimulating and I wish I could see myself on the road to working out my destiny. I always thought I was to do something considerable.'

The holiday was cut short by the news that Muriel's father was gravely ill, and he died shortly after their return home. Reith thought his mother-in-law very stupid, but decided that he should cheer her up by treating her 'normally', something he felt other members of the family never did. 'I said that when it was all over she and M could go for a week or two, and she said she might –

to Ramsgate.' The funeral arrangements did not meet with his approval: 'a dreadful one-horse hearse with the driver in a bowler hat ... we had to stop several times on hills.'[96]

They managed another couple of weeks off in September, and went to Scotland, but it was not a visit that afforded him any great pleasure. Douglas had been seriously ill, and Reith was shocked by his physical state: 'His brain works clearly enough, but he acts and speaks as if he is an old man.' They were briefly in Dunblane, and from the Minister of the Cathedral he had news of Charlie: 'He told us that Bowser is now learning farming and goes on a motor bike to Glassingall each morning, which I suppose is better than loafing about as he has been doing for the last four years.'

They moved on to Crianlarich. It was a Sunday, and the roads were busy. The tenor of Reith's observations on his fellow-road-users hovered between misanthropy and dottiness: 'What brutes motoring makes of people. I sometimes wonder that the Lord does not do something to protect the Sabbath Day. It seems strange that this is only possible through human agency, which is not likely to do much.'

He returned to London determined to spend less time in the office and do less work at home, but it was not a resolution that came to much. At the end of October, the Postmaster-General announced the names of the four Governors who with Clarendon were to make up the new Board. Gainford was appointed Vice-Chairman. He was joined by Dr Montague Rendall, who had been Headmaster of Winchester, Sir John Gordon Nairne, formerly Comptroller of the Bank of England, and Mrs Philip Snowden, whose husband had been Chancellor of the Exchequer in Ramsay MacDonald's first Cabinet. Reith met them three days later when they were called to the Post Office and shown draft copies of the Royal Charter and Licence.

The Corporation was to be set up for a period of ten years. The Postmaster-General had to approve the hours of broadcasting, and the Corporation was obliged to accept official announcements by government departments. The Postmaster-General also reserved the right to require the Corporation 'to refrain from broadcasting any matter'; in case of emergency he would also have the power to take the stations over. Mitchell-Thomson told them that his financial proposals rested on a sliding scale. The Post Office would deduct 12.5 per cent of the gross licence revenue for expenses; it would pass on to the Corporation 90 per cent of net revenue on the first million licences, 80 per cent on the second, 70 per cent on the third, and 60 per cent thereafter.

The restriction on controversial broadcasting was to remain. The Corporation was not to be permitted to air its own views on matters of public policy or on matters of political, industrial or religious controversy. Restrictions on news, on the other hand, were to be lifted; the Corporation was to be allowed to engage in news-gathering in any part of the world and to subscribe to news agencies. 'The position is most unsatisfactory,' Reith wrote in his diary that night. 'The new body is not getting any more autonomy than the old, which is a deliberate ignoring of the Crawford recommendations.' The arguments continued for several days. Eventually the Postmaster-General produced a big stick, and to Reith's chagrin the Governors caved in:

> Heard today to my infinite disgust that the PMG had got Clarendon along on Saturday after all my work the evening before and threatened him with getting five other governors if they did not agree. What a sickening affair it is. Clarendon is so weak and stupid that he immediately accepted the terms.[97]

Two weeks later, when the Postmaster-General presented the Charter to the House of Commons as an 'agreed' document, Reith was so incensed that he considered making a public protest:

> I think the PMG and Murray have behaved in a very caddish way, and it is most unfortunate that Clarendon and the others have not more guts to stand out against this treatment. Already I have found it rather irritating to have Clarendon and the new people coming nosing about.[98]

He was clearly not in an ideal frame of mind for the festivities to celebrate the rite of passage from private company to public corporation. His old Board treated him generously. He had had the use of an Austin car belonging to the Company. At their December meeting the directors decided to make it over to him and to present him with 1000 guineas. 'I felt quite embarrassed,' Reith wrote, 'though it is the least they can do.'[99] He responded rather more graciously a week later when Carpendale led him into the General Office. It was crammed with the entire headquarters staff. The Admiral made an amusing speech and presented him with a flower bowl – and four antique silver candlesticks.

That evening there was a dinner at the Hotel Metropole. The Prime Minister sat on Reith's right hand and Mrs Baldwin on his left. Muriel wore a Paquin dress for the occasion. Some thought had been given to enlivening the proceedings. The two soups on the menu were distinguished not as 'clear' and 'thick' but as 'headphone strength' and 'loudspeaker strength'. When the toastmaster intoned 'Mr Chairman, My Lords, Ladies and Gentlemen, pray silence for the nine o'clock time signal', it started off as Big Ben but finished up as a cuckoo clock.

Reith spoke seriously about social purpose and 'commonsense Christian ethics'. The supply of good things, he said, created the demand for more. He ventured to believe that a new national asset had been created, and that down the years it would bring 'the compound interest of happier homes, broader culture and truer citizenship'. Baldwin, between puffs at a pipe which was a recent present from Edgar Wallace, struck a lighter note. 'Your list of guests,' he told Reith, 'seemed to me to represent all those most eminent in the class to which I belong – men of push and go, lovers of the limelight, and the darlings of the press.' He was proud, he said, to pay tribute on their behalf to those 'far more distinguished, silent, anonymous, obscure people who have created broadcasting in these islands'.

Reith went home to Barton Street and wrote up his diary: 'There was much congratulations, but I did not enjoy the thing at all.' He had to go out again the next evening to a staff dance at the Cecil. He was feeling very tired, but after eleven o'clock he suddenly livened up, danced quite a lot and enjoyed himself. His speech at the dinner had gone down very well: 'Miss Matheson informed me that she suddenly felt when I was speaking last night that I was a future Prime Minister. I hope this was genuine.'[100]

On 20 December he noted in his diary, as he unfailingly did, that it was Charlie's birthday. He also recorded that a letter had come to the office offering him a knighthood. Nothing illustrates more clearly Reith's essential perversity than the absurd comedy he played out over the next few days. It was just four years since he had told his mother that he wanted a knighthood for her sake and for Muriel's. But on the day the offer came, he wrote in his diary:

I should have been surprised if it had not come, but was by no manner of means pleased. I am not keen on titles anyhow and a KG would not have been too much for what I have done . . . An ordinary knighthood is almost an insult. The PM has never comprehended the importance of our work . . . I put the letter away and thought no more of it all day.

The next day, however, and the day after that, he thought about it a great deal. He not only thought about it, but discussed it with practically everybody under the sun. Miss Shields sensibly had no view one way or the other. Miss Nash, however, who had now joined him as a second secretary, was very much against it, although after Reith had taken her out to dinner and to a movie she saw some of the arguments the other way. Muriel suggested he should telephone the Archbishop of Canterbury, but this he was reluctant to do; he did, however, ring up his friend Bell, the Dean of Canterbury, who was all for it, 'and could see no prejudice in any direction'.

Miss Matheson was all in favour, and so was Clarendon. Reith even pursued Ramsay MacDonald. This pantomime took so long that there was an anxious telephone call from Sir Ronald Waterhouse, Baldwin's private secretary, who was accustomed to rather prompt replies to that sort of letter. Finally, on 23 December, just before going off to the country for Christmas, Reith wrote 'accepting the wretched knighthood', as he put it in his diary.

The letter that actually went to Waterhouse contained an excuse for the delay that was as flowery as it was implausible: 'I am sure you will understand that the matter which was the purport of your communication required earnest consideration.' It was not what Reith was originally minded to write. The copy of his reply which he kept in his scrapbook has a note on it which reads, 'Carpendale made me alter my original letter, saying it was very snotty.'

Eight

SILLY BERTIE, MUSSOLINI, AND THE RED WOMAN

Yea, even among wiser militants, how many wounds have been given, and credits slain, for the poor victory of an opinion, or beggarly conquest of a distinction!

SIR THOMAS BROWNE, *Religio Medici*, 1642

I am not arguing with you – I am telling you.

JAMES WHISTLER,
The Gentle Art of Making Enemies, 1890

THE FIRST Director-General of the British Broadcasting Corporation soon became reconciled to the indignity of knighthood. 'I am pleased to see you have got a title to your name,' his old nurse, Maggie Raeside, wrote from Glasgow; and from Swarthmore came a letter from Jeannette Laws saying that it gave her a warm feeling round her heart whenever she thought of it. He received in all about 500 telegrams of congratulation and 1200 letters, and spent many hours topping and tailing a multigraphed reply.

The new regime quickly turned out to be much less congenial than the old, and Reith was to find the first three years of the Corporation the most trying of his BBC career. Within days of the first meeting of the Board, Mrs Snowden had written to Clarendon saying that she considered the minutes very unsatisfactory and making a number of other complaints. 'What a poisonous creature she is,' Reith wrote in his diary. Before the month was out he sounded the first note of a theme that was to become tediously familiar throughout his remaining years at the BBC:

Beginning to feel very definitely that I ought not to be long with the BBC, but it is extremely difficult to find what the next job is to be. So few good jobs or ones that I would like at all. What a curse it is to have outstanding comprehensive ability and intelligence, combined with a desire to use them to maximum purpose.[1]

He blamed some of his new difficulties on the Postmaster-General, who had told Clarendon that the chairmanship was likely to take up three-quarters of his time but had given him no guidance on what a chairman was meant to do – and not to do:

What a stupid ass Clarendon is. A letter from him today referring to:

1. A Foreign Office complaint re: the Emperor of Japan;
2. A set for his daughter;
3. A hospital appeal;
4. An ex-butler of the Duke of Portland.

He does not begin to understand what a nuisance his friends can be . . . To have to put up with such a man and with a creature like Mrs Snowden is quite wrong.[2]

Years later Reith wrote in his memoirs that he might have got on with Clarendon ('Silly Bertie' as he was soon calling him) if Mrs Snowden had not been on the Board or with Mrs Snowden if Clarendon had not been Chairman. It is not at all clear why he should have thought so. Ethel Snowden – she was known in the Labour Party as 'Annikins' – was described by Emmanuel Shinwell, who had reason to know, as 'the would-be Sarah Bernhardt of the party'. She was, he said, 'small, buxom, and fearsome when crossed, with an unerring knack of squeezing the last drop of drama out of the most trivial incident'.[3] The Postmaster-General had appointed her without reference to Ramsay MacDonald, and had given her to understand that her duties as a Governor would keep her 'almost fully occupied'.

Before she had completed three months as a Governor, she had concluded that there ought to be a Board meeting every day and reduced Reith to spluttering exasperation: 'Board for two and a half hours and an abominable exhibition by Mrs Snowden. A truly terrible creature, ignorant, stupid and horrid.'[4] This did not exhaust his thesaurus of invective, however, and before long Mrs Snowden was accorded the distinction of a personalised niche in the Director-General's private demonology. Jezebel was still reserved for Charlie's wife, but that left a wide range of Biblical reference. Reith's mind turned to the Book of Revelation. There, in the verses devoted to the Mother of Harlots and Abominations, he came upon the ultimate accolade, and he bestowed it in the course of a railway journey with the Chairman at the end of March: 'Much talk with Clarendon about the Scarlet Woman.'[5]

The Whore of Babylon reciprocated Reith's detestation, although she does not seem to have had a pet name for him – 'Mussolini' was used, but almost certainly not coined, by Clarendon. The tone of an early letter to Lord Gainford indicates that Mrs Snowden was also rather afraid of the Director-General:

. . . It is impossible either to be happy or to contribute one's best if one is to be delivered over bound to the tender mercies of a man whose overwhelming egoism is as distasteful as his character and ability are overestimated . . .[6]

The constant bickering between the Director-General and the Board which characterised the three years of Lord Clarendon's chairmanship makes boring and demeaning reading. In the second volume of his *History of Broadcasting in the United Kingdom*, Asa Briggs seeks to apportion blame for it. In addition to the friction caused by the personalities and undoubted inadequacies of Clarendon and Mrs Snowden, he identifies the variety of the problems the BBC faced in those years, many of them associated with rapid growth:

> In such circumstances, committees of any kind are subordinate to people. They must be. And there may be so much to do on a big scale, so many big decisions to take, that personal authority is essential. In such challenging circumstances, the favourite British arts of committeemanship and sub-committeemanship appear very minor virtues.[7]

It could be argued that that is to let Reith down rather lightly, or at least to see the situation very much through Reithian eyes. Much turns on how much weight is to be attached to the revealing passage Briggs quotes from Reith's own memoirs:

> I have always functioned best when responsibility for decision rested wholly and solely on me. Every faculty is then alerted, mobilised. When, as on a committee, others are involved, it has often been otherwise ... Perhaps I should have made more effort to resist this partial atrophy, whatever the cause.

It was no doubt intensely irritating for someone as quick as Reith that the Board should, for instance, take an hour to decide whether his £6000 a year was to be divided between salary and expenses and whether this should include rail fares. The disagreements between Reith and the Board were seldom over any great issue of principle, although they were sometimes dressed up as such. As is so often the case within organisations, they arose essentially over questions of precedence and demarcation. The old Board had effectively thrown the reins over Reith's back. Now, with new drivers on the box, he found them gathered up in the inexpert hands of a dim peer and a bossy and ambitious woman; to a man of his temperament their uneven tugging was profoundly uncongenial.

February had taken him to Buckingham Palace, and it had amused him to discover that he was to be knighted at the same investiture as Milne Watson, who had offered him a job with the Gas Light and Coke Company in 1919.[8] It had also brought him the flattering news that he had been elected to the Athenaeum under Rule II, which gives the committee discretion to elect nine people a year who have 'attained to outstanding eminence in Science, Literature or the Arts, or for public services'. 'Far be it from me to question their discrimination,' Reith wrote in his diary. 'I thought mother would be pleased.'[9] He was to use the club frequently, and later served on the committee. There were BBC people who came to feel that their Director-General's views on programmes sometimes owed less to what he had heard over the air than to what he had heard over the lunch table.

His tribulations with the Chairman and Mrs Snowden made him think nostalgically of the easy relationship he had enjoyed with the hard-headed businessmen who had made up the old Board. Not, however, to the extent of persuading him to respond positively when he was sounded out about becoming Joint Managing Director of the Marconi Company; Reith, for reasons which are not always entirely clear, consistently drew his skirts away from any executive association with commerce. So he sat tight at Savoy Hill, letting off steam to Carpendale, and to his secretaries, and in the pages of his diary:

I was worried about the future, thinking I ought not to stop longer with the BBC. Of course I should have been Chairman of it with opportunity to do other things ... The Chairman and Board are a humbug.[10]

He was endlessly busy, professionally and socially, on big things and small, on his own account and on other people's. He arranged for a book to be written about his father; he bailed out his brother Robert, who was being threatened with legal proceedings for debt and 'felt the end had come'. His old friend Dr Tuttle came on a visit from Swarthmore, and Reith, ever generous to those he liked, took him to Mappin & Webb's and bought him a gold wristwatch. He kept his political friendships in good repair: 'wrote a good Empire Day speech for the Prime Minister, which I do not imagine he will use'.[11] Visiting the Commons one day in the summer he encountered a politician of a rather different stripe: 'Quarter of an hour's talk with Winston Churchill in a corridor, he sitting on a table and holding forth about controversy in broadcasting. He was glad to find that I was all for it, and I ditto with him.'

Muriel and he were bidden one night to Somerset Maugham's house ('a silly scheme to begin a party at 11.15') and were entertained to Negro spirituals, which he thought 'very well done'. He was also flattered to be asked to lunch in Carlton Gardens by Lord Balfour, although he felt a little out of things, as 'so much of the talk concerned things of which I knew nothing – hunting, etc.' On another occasion that summer, Muriel and he found themselves in a party that was taken off after dinner to watch greyhound racing at the White City. Reith was disgusted: 'The most significant manifestation of public depravity that I have seen, and a reflection on the intelligence of the people.'

The spring and summer of 1927 saw a rapid expansion in the broadcasting of sporting and other public events. A new agreement with the press at the beginning of the year had made it possible to send microphones to Twickenham for the first running commentary on an international rugby match. In March the Grand National was covered for the first time, and in April the Boat Race, and throughout the summer the range of outside broadcast coverage was steadily extended – Essex versus the New Zealanders from Leyton (the commentary was provided by a cricketing parson), Trooping the Colour, tennis from Wimbledon.

Perhaps the most notable event of the year was a musical one. 'Today I fixed up a contract with Sir Henry Wood,' says a matter-of-fact entry in Reith's diary on 13 April. Chappell's, the music publishers, had been consistently unfriendly to the BBC and had submitted evidence hostile to broadcasting to the Crawford Committee; they were also the owners of the Queen's Hall, and it had been rumoured that they were considering turning it into a picture palace. The agreement between Wood and the BBC covered not only his celebrated Promenade Concerts but also provided that he would conduct twenty-five public or studio concerts for the Corporation in each of the next three years.[12]

In July, Reith and Muriel went on holiday to Scotland. Revisiting Dunblane was always a nostalgic experience, and he wrote in his diary that he thought he should like to be living there quietly still. They attended divine service in the Cathedral. Charlie came past, and on seeing them turned to say he was glad to see them back again: 'We shook hands, but very coldly, and were very surprised.'[13] They moved on to the west coast, but found the country round Machrihanish unattractive. There was also quite a lot of rain, which is not uncommon in that part of the world: 'We felt we might almost go back to London. Each year it happens this way, and we do not benefit from past experience.'

He was never able to put the BBC out of his mind for long: 'Wrote to Miss Nash with a good idea about my office, a dark dado about 3' 6" high, and a shelf.' Nor did he have the good sense to tell the office not to disturb him. Accordingly, when a letter arrived from Carpendale complaining about the latest antics of Mrs Snowden, he felt obliged to lock himself away and compose a reply: 'Two hours letter-writing, all owing to the "Red Woman",' he complained in his diary. They played a little whist, and he was torn 'between the desire to win and the desire not to beat Muriel'. Towards the end of their stay, the weather improved, and they were able to bathe and lie in the sunshine. 'We were sad at leaving it,' he wrote, 'but perhaps we shall see it again; perhaps after we are famous.'

Reith had been quick to see that there would be an important international dimension to broadcasting. There is a note in his diary as early as August 1924 about the need for some sort of association which would not only examine questions of copyright but also 'promote the interests of broadcasting generally'. When the Union Internationale de Radiophonie was set up in 1925, Arthur Burrows went off to Geneva to be its first Secretary-General.

Reith's questing mind had also turned early to the potentialities of broadcasting to the Empire. 'All our colonial concerns', he told the London Conference which set up the UIR in March 1925, 'are now looking to us to suggest something from which they will benefit,' and a year later there is an impatient note in his diary on what he saw as a missed opportunity:

> Read the official paper re: Indian Broadcasting Company and am more than disgusted with the matter. I had made two attempts to get things on the right lines, one two years ago with the India Office and then about a year ago with the viceroy . . . There is neither vision nor recognition of the immense potentialities of broadcasting in this affair; no ethical or moral appreciation; just commercialism.[14]

There were two sorts of constraint on broadcasting to the Empire. The first was technical, and related to the quality of short-wave transmissions. Peter Eckersley set matters out in a characteristically crisp memorandum for a Colonial Office Conference in the spring of 1927: 'We stayed our hand so as not merely to put out noises combined with all sorts of atmospherics and inaccuracies and periods of silence and general unpleasantness.'[15]

There was also the small matter of who would pay. Governments traditionally look at the ceiling when such sordid questions are raised. The BBC, on the other hand, which derived its income exclusively from listeners in the United Kingdom, could not easily contemplate financing expensive experiments from its own resources. There were also copyright problems and the likelihood of difficulties with the press over the broadcasting of news. Reith decided to go ahead and argue about money later. The first experimental broadcasts to the Empire were made from a short-wave station at Chelmsford on 11 November. Reception was patchy, but the programmes were greeted with enthusiasm.

So was a speech which Reith made in November 1927 to the Manchester Luncheon Club. It was, at least, by his audience, although some of his staff may have been less appreciative when they read accounts of it in their newspapers. Reith disliked provincial cities and always maintained that he hated public speaking, but it never took him long to have an audience eating out of his hand. 'Don't judge our programmes by children's hours or variety entertainments,' he said on this occasion, to loud laughter. 'I know they are dreadful. I haven't much opportunity of listening in my own room, but there are occasions when I cannot get across the room quickly enough to turn my set off.' This, however, was merely his way of creeping up on his subject, and he was soon launched into a confident and forceful exposition of one of his stock themes:

> In the early days it was said that the Broadcasting Company ought to take showmen and super-showmen into its service because they knew what the public wanted . . . Did the public know what it wanted? Look at the kinema, what it gave and what the public took from it. Those responsible for the control of broadcasting set themselves the task of being a little ahead of the public. They were criticised for it, told they were dictators, and accused of things which were far from their intention . . .

It was a familiar complaint that Reith listened only to such criticism as he wished to hear. He was certainly highly skilled at diverting it into channels which served his immediate purpose. Radio criticism as a *genre* was in any case in its infancy, and it was only occasionally that newspaper readers were offered a view about the output that was either perceptive or penetrating. Toward the end of 1927, the Irish playwright and novelist St John Ervine was given space in the *Daily Express* for a series called 'Open Letters to Celebrities'. One of them was addressed to 'The BBC, through its Director-General', and it provides interesting evidence of how the programmes in the late 1920s sounded to one fairly sophisticated pair of ears.

His opinion of the variety entertainment on offer tallied with Reith's: 'Your concert parties are dire. The funny man in a boarding house is positively comic compared with them.' But he went on to offer a view of the Corporation's more demanding fare: 'Many of the gentlemen who give "Talks" deliver their sentences as if they were committing them to the grave. Sometimes when I listen to a discourse on the Sex Life of the Newt or the Domestic Habits of the Soft Shelled Crab, I begin to imagine from the tone of the gentleman who is talking that he is a member of a jury which has just had to view a very unpleasant corpse . . .'

Ervine concluded by turning his attention to something that was conspicuously absent from the airwaves, and in doing so he did Reith a considerable service. He was, in fact, doing no more than give witty expression to one of the BBC's own arguments, but it was one to which the government had shown itself completely deaf:

> You have a rule that no controversial matter shall be spoken through the microphone. That is a rule which is characteristically English both in its merits and in its demerits. It promotes amiability and allows persons of diverse opinions to meet without hitting each other, but it also makes discussion sterile and reduces debate to a mere exchange of empty compliments. Better a bloody nose than a torpid mind! . . . Every man in this country should periodically be compelled to listen to opinions which are infuriating to him. To hear nothing but what is pleasing to one is to make a pillow of the mind.[16]

Trouble flared again with Mrs Snowden during the autumn:

> The 'Red Woman' surpassed herself today at the Board, making most insolent and unfounded statements. If Clarendon had either guts or decency he would have pulled her up, but he has nothing of either. It was left to me to take exception and be very outspoken and even rude to her. I expect she came ready for trouble as I had naturally declined to give some information she improperly demanded in a letter as to who had been responsible for a certain mistake for which I had already apologised.[17]

The Director-General, in his relentless way, pursued the matter by handing Clarendon a lengthy handwritten letter of complaint. Indignation always tended to complicate Reith's syntax, and it seems unlikely that 'Silly Bertie' took in more than half of what was being conveyed to him, but he said he was terribly sorry and that he would try to be firmer in future.[18]

Mrs Snowden could be every bit as tiresome as Reith when she got her teeth into something, and one of the things she had her teeth into in the autumn of 1927 was No. 21 Thurloe Square. This house had been bought the previous year and the idea was that Roger Eckersley should entertain there on the Corporation's behalf. Reith thought highly of Eckersley, admired his social graces, and had promoted him to be Programme Director. The general view among his colleagues was that he shone more brightly in Thurloe Square than he did at Savoy Hill;[19] when this exercise in corporate public relations came to the attention of Mrs Snowden, however, she was quick to register puritanical disapproval. 'I have definitely decided to oppose Reith's proposal that Eckersley shall entertain on a large scale in a Corporation house,' she wrote to Gainford. 'I shall move at the next meeting that from January 1st 1928 all entertainment allowances cease and our Station Directors, who feel they must entertain some distinguished visitor to their town, shall send in their Bills to Headquarters.'

She sent Gainford and Clarendon a paper headed 'Notes on the Subject of Hospitality in Business'. She asserted that the practice could not be defended morally as it was an indirect attempt to get something for nothing. 'I have reason to believe', she wrote darkly, 'that it is easy to step outside the law in this matter, as it is simply bribery and corruption. Keeping within the law through a knowledge of the necessary tricks is not consistent with either the honour or dignity of the BBC.' She also expressed concern about Eckersley: either his health or his work would suffer – 'our employees should not be exposed to the danger of constant entertainment of people of artistic temperament.'[20]

On this, as on most issues, Mrs Snowden failed to carry her colleagues with her. None of the Board found Reith easy, but for all his gloomy stiffness they generally found him easier to take than their fellow-Governor. 'Poor lady,' says a letter from Rendall which survives in the Gainford Papers; 'she is terribly upset and her health has suffered. But all her conduct appears that of a person (almost a child!) wholly unversed in public affairs. She is amazed and collapses if we don't agree with her. She really means well; but her methods are deplorable: I hope we shall steer safe through Scylla and Charybdis . . .'[21]

Reith was, as it happens, involved in the affairs of a rather different Board at this time, but circumstances alter cases, and there he saw things rather differently. He had for some time been a Governor of his old school, Gresham's. He lunched with his fellow-Governors in the Fishmongers' Hall in mid-November, and at the meeting that followed made a lengthy intervention:

I spoke about publicity, athletics, the chapel, social class, dress and the magazine – obviously creating much embarrassment. The Chairman did not want to have any discussion, but various Governors spoke on the matters. It is all quite farcical, the Governors having no power at all, and their time being taken up in the discussion of trivialities and not in control of policy. I practically made up my mind to resign.[22]

He brooded over the matter for several weeks, and then, at the end of December, he did indeed write a letter of resignation:

> ... I have noted with increasing regret and surprise that matters of policy in connection with the School, or at any rate many matters of high significance, are not discussed by the Board at all ... The headmaster is unreceptive to, and intolerant of, any criticism of the school, and of suggestions contrary to his own opinion ... The Board, I gather, cannot or will not, whether through disagreement or embarrassment, take action in these matters. I find, therefore, that I cannot be of the assistance I had hoped ...[23]

Reith clearly shared Emerson's view that 'a foolish consistency is the hobgoblin of little minds.'

The turn of the year often found Reith brooding over real or imagined wrongs. The festive season of 1927 did little for him. He bought Muriel, who was pregnant, a diamond ring, but she did not seem particularly pleased with it. 'I have no interest in Christmas,' he wrote, 'and Muriel is unhappy.' He also noted that she had taken to snoring, and that this kept him awake. He spent long hours during several weekends early in the New Year sorting out old papers and burning many of Charlie's letters. An earlier clearance two years previously had reduced their number to about 400, but now he got rid of all but twenty. He also returned to Charlie a bundle of photographs, accompanied by what he described as 'an abrupt note':

> I began 'Dear Bowser,' and said that for the benefit of his progeny I was enclosing some photographs of him, of which I knew there were no copies and which were not likely to be of much interest to me in the future. I said I had a few left and that it would interest me to know whether he had kept any relics of our erstwhile acquaintance.[24]

Even that did not get the poison out of his system. At the end of the month he turned his attention to the remaining twenty letters, went through them one last time, and then burned them too:

> The ones read today were written during the Southwick/Bulford period, when he was immensely in love with M. I could not help feeling rather sorry that my friendship with him should have ended as it did. My feelings changed, however, when reading the latest ones after his engagement. I blame myself to some extent, but certainly not sufficiently to extenuate his abominable attitude thereafter. But I still think the horrid Argaty women were responsible, not he. Jezebel and her wretched mother.[25]

He returned to the office in a sour mood, and trouble blew up almost immediately. The Governors had agreed that they would not give individual interviews. Mrs Snowden, however, had spoken to a disgruntled author who felt he had some grievance against the BBC and had then made a statement to a newspaper; the editor made the most of his opportunity and spread an attack on the BBC over two columns. Clarendon at first said that he would ask the Postmaster-General to have Mrs Snowden removed, but then lost his nerve. Reith's rage on such occasions was not always in direct proportion to the importance of the issue. Carpendale, who was a keen skier, had gone off on holiday to Gstaad, but Reith pursued him with a six-page letter giving a blow by blow account of the Board's latest iniquities: 'A feeling came over me, for the first time since my association with the BBC, that I really did not much care, and that it was quite useless to expect anything at all with Clarendon constituted as he is.'

The Admiral's concentration on the hazards of the *piste* must have been seriously tested. Reith, who had few secrets from his secretaries, wrote that Miss Shields and Miss Nash both shared his view of the 'utter futility and hopelessness' of the situation. Indeed, the pair of them had turned up in the office at 9.15 one evening and urged his immediate resignation: 'If I did not do this or something pretty drastic, I should be disloyal to the service and letting it down in such a way as would never enable it to recover.' He very much wanted the Admiral's advice, although he reminded him, rather conspiratorially, that care was needed when communicating *en clair*: 'In either wiring or telephone conversations, "Charles" could do for Clarendon, "Sophie" for Mrs Snowden, and "Others" for the other members of the Board.'[26]

Although it is not clear how seriously Reith considered resignation, he did undoubtedly speak about it a good deal. On the same day that he wrote to Carpendale, he talked to Montague Rendall. Rendall had formed a high regard for Reith during his year on the Board, although he obviously thought him a bit of a prima donna; he now wrote begging him to see things 'in their just proportion':

It cannot be right, in the sight of God or man, even to contemplate throwing it up for reasons which are, as you admitted to me, trivial ... We all have to march through life with a few people whom we would like to discard but cannot ... For some years, I should like to think for many years, you have a great work to do for England, and I ask to co-operate with you as a *friend*, who is proud of this position.[27]

Reith carried his complaints well beyond the confines of the BBC, and one of those he wrote to was the King's private secretary, Lord Stamfordham. Stamfordham and his daughter had lunched with the Reiths at Barton Street earlier in the winter, and Stamfordham, in the course of quizzing Reith about Mrs Snowden, had said that in his opinion she suffered from megalomania.[28] Writing now from Buckingham Palace, he expressed himself more discreetly:

The information given in your letter of yesterday fills me with regret so far as my interest in and appreciation of the work of the BBC is concerned: but on the other hand if there is no longer sufficient scope for your powers in that enterprise you are, in my humble opinion, right to seek for new fields especially at a time of life when those powers are at their best . . .[29]

Reith also told Sir Ronald Waterhouse, the Prime Minister's secretary, that he thought it was time he moved elsewhere, and as a result he had forty minutes with Baldwin early in February. Baldwin thought he would not be happy in a purely commercial job; he quizzed him on what effect his departure would have on the BBC, and Reith told him it would not suffer. The conversation then seems to have become rather discursive. They agreed that Governor-Generalships were not up to much. When asked whether he had anything specific in mind, Reith said that the only ones that seemed suitable were running the Electricity Board or going to Canada as High Commissioner, although later in the conversation he also mentioned going to Washington as ambassador or to India as Viceroy.

Nothing came of this interview with the Prime Minister, but at the end of February Reith wrote in his diary, 'Much enquiry and perturbation about a story in the *Daily Mail* that I was leaving for the City.' There is a certain note of relish in the entry. The report appeared in several papers, in fact, and the *Daily News* even ran a story that the theatrical impresario C. B. Cochrane, who was then managing the Albert Hall, was tipped as a possible successor. The speculation was not dampened by a curious statement from Savoy Hill which said 'as far as is known there is no foundation in the report that Sir John Reith intends to resign in order to take up a post in the City.' Reith had, in fact, lunched a few days earlier with the Managing Director of HMV. 'He virtually asked me to come and work under him for a year or so, so that he could retire soon,' Reith wrote. 'There are few jobs in the country that would give me so much money, but it would never do for me.'[30]

The newspaper stories bear all the marks of something spoken out of the side of the mouth by a BBC publicity officer over lunch with a Fleet Street contact, and it cannot be excluded that they were planted on Reith's initiative. Although he always went out of his way to emphasise his indifference to the press, he had a cunning awareness of how it could be used. The response on this occasion was certainly not unhelpful to him. The BBC's Station Director at Cardiff wrote that his departure would be an irreparable loss to the Corporation – 'the Staff here was staggered as if by a blow.'[31] There was an expression of shock from Sir Henry Wood: 'Our relations have been so cordial, that I cannot bear the idea, after my first season, of working with a stranger.'[32] Most soothing of all, perhaps, was a letter from the Poet Laureate, Robert Bridges, in Oxford: 'It is the universal opinion of those who take the BBC seriously that you were raised up by Providence to be the salvation of the country.'[33]

At the end of January, shortly before he emerged from his bouts of burning Charlie's letters, and just as the rumours of his departure from the BBC had begun to fly, Reith had travelled down to Wales to propose 'The Immortal Memory' at the Cardiff Caledonian Society's Burns Supper. The previous year, a Scottish doctor called Sir James Crichton Browne had published a book which faithful bardolators had seized on as a vindication of the poet's character on medical grounds. Reith used it as a springboard for a vigorous defence of his fellow-countryman. Here, he told his listeners, they saw a genius, if ever there was one: 'burning with aspirations and emotions disruptive of mind and body; conscious of the insistent urge of a mighty power within; of a desire and a longing, first inarticulate but always profound; of an assurance of a supreme purpose and a mighty potentiality . . .'

He was not, of course, speaking only about Robert Burns.

In programme terms, the most important event of 1928 was the lifting of the ban on the broadcasting of controversial material. Reith had sensibly not pressed the issue during the first year of the operation of the Charter, but he had returned to the charge in a letter to the Post Office early in 1928, offering an assurance that if controversy were permitted, it would be 'prudently and tactfully intro-duced'.[34] The Prime Minister told the Commons on 5 March that the restric-tion was to be removed. Although the ban on the BBC's expression of editorial opinion was to remain, broadcasting on matters of political, industrial or religious controversy would now be permitted.

Within a few weeks, Reith found himself being wooed by Winston Churchill. The Chancellor, eager to know what the BBC planned by way of Budget cover-age, asked Reith to go and see him at the Treasury. 'Miss Nash made me go home and change first,' Reith wrote. 'I was there for about an hour, he giving me tea, and being very civil.' He was subjected to a powerful burst of the famous Chur-chill charm: 'He asked if the rumours of my leaving the BBC were true, and said he was very thankful that they were not. He said he thought I had about the biggest job in the country.' What Winston wanted was to have his Budget statement broadcast direct from the House of Commons, something that the BBC was ready to do but which Reith knew Baldwin was not disposed to agree to. Churchill urged him to return to the charge with the Prime Minister, and laid on the flattery with a trowel, telling Reith that he had great influence with Baldwin and that the Prime Minister had a very high opinion of him.

Reith went away having promised Churchill fifteen minutes on the air the night after Budget Day. He collected him himself at the Commons and took him to Savoy Hill. The Chancellor had promised that he would be 'factual and non-controversial', but that was not how it struck the Opposition, and Reith received a protest from Ramsay MacDonald on behalf of the Labour Party. The BBC was launched on its fated career as pig in the middle.

The early summer of 1928 afforded Reith a brief domestic distraction from the party politics of Westminster and the office politics of Savoy Hill. On Whit Sunday he became a father. He was approaching his thirty-ninth birthday and had been married for six years. The child was born at Barton Street, and

Muriel did not have an easy time. 'I felt dreadfully sorry about everything and only glanced in the direction of the infant,' Reith wrote. 'It seemed extraordinarily unprepossessing.'[35] Parenthood proved a somewhat alarming experience. He left the office early once or twice during the following week and went home to have tea with Muriel and the nurse: 'They made me hold the baby for a little, the nurse giving it to me without warning while I was sitting in a chair.'

He was quickly making plans for the infant's future, however. Or rather he set about firming up plans that had been in his mind for some time – a diary entry from three years previously reads 'Decided to send our son to Eton if and when we have one.'[36] Now, within days of the birth, he was scanning an Eton College list and taking advice about houses and prep schools.[37]

It was not only in the matter of his son's education that Reith was aiming high. He had also conceived the ambition of having the child christened by the Archbishop of Canterbury. He accordingly sounded out the Archbishop's chaplain, who thought His Grace might well agree to perform the ceremony at Lambeth provided not more than a dozen or so friends were invited and that no attention was called to the occasion in the press – 'I mention these points quite baldly because I am sure you will see the difficulty in which an Archbishop would be placed if many other friends of his were, on the strength of what they saw or read, to ask him to take their children's baptism too!'[38]

Reith too, however, was placed in a certain difficulty by this latest ambition. Two years previously, Dr Fleming, the Minister of St Columba's, Pont Street, had asked whether he would consider becoming an elder there, and Reith had declined on the grounds that he did not wish to sever his connection with the United Free Church.[39] He clearly now had some explaining to do. Just how he sought to extricate himself from his embarrassment is no longer known, but Dr Fleming's delicious reply survives, and it is plain that Reith was dealing with a master both of psychology and diplomacy:

My dear Reith,
It is very good of you to tell me of Lady Reith's and your own very natural wish that your little Christopher should, if His Grace consents, have the lifelong and precious memory that he was baptised by the first Scottish Archbishop of Canterbury – a privilege which few of his contemporaries could fail, in time to come, to envy.

If I might venture to criticise the Anglican Baptismal service, it has always seemed to me a pity that God-parents – often of very shadowy suitability – should be substituted for parents in the matter of responsibility for the Godly upbringing of the children. But I understand that it would be quite in order that her ladyship and yourself should be the sponsors; and in that case, that difficulty would disappear.

The only other point that occurs to me is, that your boy's Baptism (into the Church Catholic) should not be regarded, through its being celebrated by His Grace, as pledging him to a lifelong or exclusive adherence to the

Anglican Branch of the Catholic Church. His Grace is, I know, too under-standing and large-minded a Scotsman to wish that the Baptism of your child should involve any indelible *denominational* 'earmark'. . . .

In thus indicating – so far as I have a right to do so – my cordial concur-rence in Lady Reith's and your own wish, might I add the possible condition – that I might be allowed the happiness of being present when the Baptism takes place?

Yours always, Archibald Fleming.[40]

The ceremony duly took place at Lambeth Palace on 7 July. Reith's sister Jean had laid her hands on a small bottle of water from the River Jordan, and this was added to the water from the River Dee that had been sent down from Scotland. Reith recorded in his diary his satisfaction with the performance of the two principal actors: 'The Archbishop had on his proper robes with the GCVO ribbon and looked very fine. Christopher John was a little noisy, but on the whole quite good.'

Muriel and he had been discussing giving up Barton Street and looking for a house in the country, but they now decided that for the time being they would stay put, turning the first floor into nursery quarters and converting the dining room into his study. Given that Reith was never happier than when there were things to be moved around, it is curious that there is so little mention in his diary of a question of accommodation that was beginning to preoccupy him professionally at this time. The staff of the BBC had now passed the 1000 mark, and Savoy Hill was bursting at the seams. 'Meeting to discuss Broadcasting House,' he noted in the middle of August; 'the first bit of interest I have taken in it apart from the finance.'

His twin demons of boredom and restlessness were a good deal in evidence that autumn. Miss Nash, never slow to speak her mind, wrote him a long letter in September taking him to task for being bored with the Corporation and telling him that it would have been better if he had left at the end of 1926. One manifestation of his restlessness was the alacrity with which he offered others the benefit of his advice. He went into Savoy Hill one Sunday evening to see the Home Secretary, and in the course of conversation told him that he would have liked to be appointed to the Royal Commission on the Police which was then sitting:

I asked him why he did not get up a proper police campaign against litter and hooliganism and so on. He said he and the Transport Minister were meeting on Tuesday to tackle the noise problem and that soon only bulb horns would be allowed in London . . . He said the police were already so unpopular that he did not want to make them much more so. I said this was largely because they occupied themselves so much with footling things and left the urgent problems alone. This did not seem to have struck him before . . .[41]

He also gave his mind to improving the organisation of Rowntrees, the chocolate concern. He had recently met Seebohm Rowntree, the firm's chairman, who, impressed by Reith's administrative grasp, had asked for his advice:

> I wired him for an organisation chart, and he sent me a big folder about his show, which I spent all last evening reading. I was certain I had got my finger on the chief weak spots and indeed I had. For one thing, he could not give proper orders to the Heads of his Branches over the other Directors, etc. . . . He and his Organisation Secretary, whom he had brought, admitted it all, and were much impressed.[42]

As winter drew on, he succumbed once again to the lure of the footlights. This time it was a production of Ian Hay's comedy *Tilly of Bloomsbury*, and Reith, who was cast as Stilbottle, did not confine his attention to mastering his own part: 'Two hours rehearsal,' he noted on 16 November. 'Tilly herself has improved very much and says it is due to my advice to her, and I expect it is. Gielgud, the producer, is very good and we want to give him a presentation.' Some weeks earlier, at the first run-through, Val Gielgud, then a junior assistant at *Radio Times*, had lived dangerously. Wishing to insist on the importance of starting on time, he began before all his actors had turned up, and when two latecomers arrived deep in conversation he announced that he expected punctuality and that there must be no talking while others were working. It was only at the end of the session that he realised he had ticked off Reith and Carpendale:

> I felt that my prospects of a successful BBC career were at that moment distinctly bleak. As it turned out, however, Sir John in particular seemed immensely to enjoy relief from his official cares implied by playing the part of a drunken broker's man, which he did with great aplomb and success. He made up to the life: bleary-eyed, scruffily-bearded, thoroughly disreputable; and I believe he got as much fun out of acting the part as his slightly bewildered staff got out of watching this reputedly grim and humourless figure letting himself go.[43]

Reith felt that the first night was a tremendous success: 'I seemed to have done very well, making people laugh a lot.' He was so excited afterwards that he had to go for a drive to calm down.

Shortly before Christmas, he went off on holiday to Switzerland – Muriel was unable to join him because her mother had been ill. He admired the scenery and enjoyed the sunshine. He watched some of his fellow-guests waltzing on ice to a gramophone: 'I do not think I ever saw anything so graceful, and wished I could do it too.' On Christmas Day he went to the little English church and afterwards sat on his balcony reading St John's Gospel. The words of a hymn came into his mind – 'Lord, speak to me that I may speak' – and he wrote it out in full in his diary. Then he went out and tried his hand at bob sleighing.

On 5 January he heard that Douglas had died: 'There cannot, or certainly ought not to be, anything here for sorrow or regret.' He wrote his brother's name across the page of his diary, and inscribed the dates of his birth and death: 'He tried hard to help me when I was young.'

When he reached Paris on the way home there was a telegram from Miss Nash asking him to telephone:

> She told me that there was much row on in connection with the publication of *The Listener*. The Red Woman wants a Board meeting called about it of course. Apparently every newspaper in the country is trying to prevent our publishing it. I was not the least bit worried if only the damn silly Governors would keep out of it.[44]

A serious weekly journal had been under consideration for some time, and an editor had been appointed the previous October. The trouble began with the appearance of the second dummy, which alerted the press to the fact that *The Listener* was to contain not only the text of broadcast talks but book reviews, articles on broadcast music, an editorial column, and pictures. Fleet Street felt it had been caught napping by *Radio Times*. It was disinclined to be caught a second time and raised the cry of 'unfair competition'.

The *Financial News* was first into the breach, proclaiming that it was 'an illegitimate stretching of official activity', and the *New Statesman* was not far behind – 'a wholly intolerable and indefensible proposition'. R. S. Lambert, the first editor of *The Listener*, wrote waspishly some years later that one might have expected a Socialist paper to support the establishment of a non-profit-making journal capable of being regarded as an experiment in State enterprise, but that was not the way it looked at the time. In mid-December, the Newspaper Proprietors' Association and its allies asked to see the Postmaster-General. The PMG, however, directed their attention to the Charter. Clause 3(d) was clear and specific, giving it as an object of the Corporation 'to compile and prepare, print, publish, issue, circulate and distribute, whether gratis or other-wise, such papers, periodicals, books, circulars and other such literary matter as may seem conducive to any of the objects of the Corporation.' He declined to see them.

Early in January the Proprietors asked to see the Prime Minister. They now had the support of the Master Printers' Federation and of the Publishers' Association, and on 5 January *The Times* entered the fray with a rather ponder-ous leader: 'There is ground for believing that it will after all be a newspaper in the usual sense of the word ... At bottom, it is a plain question of equity; a State-protected enterprise clearly should not be brought into competition with others.'

This was the point at which Reith returned from Switzerland and plunged into the fray. He asked to see Baldwin and briefed him on the Corporation's position: 'I made a good deal of their not having come to the BBC, which he said was a big point.' The Prime Minister did not need much persuading that it would be preferable if the matter could be settled without his intervention.

Reith's own account of the subsequent course of events is distinctly self-congratulatory. Instead of receiving a deputation at Savoy Hill, he chose to go to the offices of the Newspaper Proprietors' Association: 'I was alone – deliberately so,' he wrote in *Into the Wind*. 'The greater the number that sit on one side of the table the greater the advantage to him who sits alone on the other.' In fact Lord Riddell, the NPA chairman, was flanked by a dozen or more of his associates. For the first hour or so, Reith listened and made notes, but then he laid into them:

> I had to take a strong line, which fortunately I can take, and what a good thing it is that I can say 'I won't have that.' It all came to a most anti-climactic conclusion as to what I would accept . . . Drove back with Riddell feeling mildly pleased that I could put it across such a gathering. But of course it is the Lord helping me.[45]

There was, however, a good deal more pliancy – and uncertainty – to this latter-day Daniel than the lions of the press might have gathered from his performance in their den. It had been agreed that a press deputation should see the BBC Board the following week. Before that took place, Reith wrote to Robert Vansittart, Baldwin's principal private secretary. He gave him a progress report, but he also asked for advice, and the language of the letter itself is even more revealing than the edited version of it he entered in his diary:

> . . . One realised fully and from the outset the difficult position in which the PM was placed and that this must be kept in mind. In view of this, and of our close association with the State, it does not seem improper to ask for some guidance.
>
> . . . If we considered ourselves only, having explained our general attitude, disposed of misapprehensions (calculated and otherwise), and reiterated our readiness to cooperate with them consistent with our public responsibilities, we should have yielded little if anything, and all would probably have been well.
>
> . . . Their appeal to the PM altered the matter, and one is anxious to know whether it would be not only courteous but prudent for us to come to an agreement with them, if possible, even if it involved going rather further than otherwise one would – though still not materially inconsistent with the morality and rationality of our position. That is, ought we to be conciliatory lest Government *force majeure* be exercised, as well as from the desire to save the Prime Minister further trouble?[46]

In the event, things went very much Reith's way. The Board accepted his advice and agreed to a number of contingency concessions. He had another hour alone with the deputation before they went in, and persuaded them to accept the substance of a memorandum he had prepared in preference to the much longer one they had brought with them. They were in and out of the

Boardroom in ten minutes; Miss Nash telephoned Vansittart to tell him that 'all was well'; the first edition of *The Listener* was on the news stands two days later:

It is really a great victory and I have done it all alone, but I cannot say I felt the least elated. There was not a word of appreciation from the Board. I surely prayed for help before going down for the meeting with the deputation this afternoon. I am much burdened with a sense of my own ability, and this is not conceit.[47]

Reith received many congratulations. Baldwin was 'very grateful' that the matter had been settled 'so that he was not bothered', although a month passed before he sent for Reith to tell him so; Reith was pleased, but felt that the Prime Minister 'ought to do something' for him.

Reith's handling of the affair throws a good deal of light on his style of management, and nearer to the coal-face his 'great victory' was viewed with some reserve. Richard Lambert, the paper's editor, was not called into consultation at any point; he therefore had no opportunity of expressing a view about the various compromises that were discussed and how they might affect the viability of the paper. The BBC agreed to recognise a standing committee representing the various publishing interests involved and to bring to its notice any future projects for new publications, although it stated that it had no plans for further newspapers. Lambert and others thought the Corporation was foolish to appear to tie its own hands in this way; its rights in this area were clearly set out in the Charter, and there had been occasional talk at Savoy Hill of embarking on the publication of a daily paper.

Lambert was also exercised by the prospect of the BBC's agreeing to limit the proportion of original contributed matter to 10 per cent, which in his view would have turned *The Listener* into a sort of BBC Hansard. His worries on that score were eased by the addition of the words 'not related to broadcasting', and he and his small team took the formula as a challenge to their editorial ingenuity – a broadcast talk on animal psychology, for instance, was seen as an opportunity to review a book by W. H. Hudson; a wireless performance of *St Joan* was made the peg for a review of a learned work on witchcraft. As an earnest of good will, the BBC also undertook not to accept for *The Listener* more advertisements than were necessary, along with its other revenue, to cover its total costs. This restriction, however, turned out to be a blessing in disguise, because it meant that the BBC was never able to regard *The Listener*, as it did *Radio Times*, as a milch cow for revenue.[48]

The paper quickly established itself, although it was never quite as other periodicals were – in his first five years as editor, for instance, Lambert was not allowed to see the circulation figures. It was to flourish in the broad acres of public service broadcasting for many years; it was not until 1990 that the soil in those fields finally became too sour and thin to sustain it.

There was a rash of resignations from the BBC early in 1929, and some newspapers were quick to suggest there must be something wrong with an organisation that experienced such difficulty in holding on to some of the more gifted members of its staff. The departure that excited the most interest was that of the Corporation's Chief Engineer, Peter Eckersley, who left in the summer, when he was about to become the guilty party in an action for divorce. Years later, when he published a book about his BBC years, he wrote about the episode with dignity and restraint:

> Sir John Reith, as both a Christian and the head of a national organisation, had the right to order my dismissal and the integrity to uphold his convictions. It might nevertheless have been thought that a national conscience which sees no ideological obstacle to an alliance with an officially anti-Christian country, and which permits atheistic schoolmasters to prepare boys for confirmation, might have found a way to accept the services of a technician who only wanted to readjust his private life. The liberty given to more famous and responsible people was, however, denied to me, because I happened to come under the control of that rare individual who acts according to his spiritual convictions.[49]

Eckersley was pursued by the press, but he wrote later that he felt a distaste for 'wearing my heart on a headline' and declined to do more than confirm the fact of his resignation.[50] He believed that some of his former colleagues were less fastidious:

> Rumours were spread by the BBC which hinted that there were 'other things', unmentioned because unmentionable, that really justified a dismissal. The divorce, said these rumours, was only an excuse. Doubtless BBC propagandists thought that they were doing their duty by their chief, but he, I am sure, would not feel that his actions needed the support of lies.[51]

In fact the Eckersley affair caused Reith a good deal of anguish. It was Mrs Snowden who had first told him what many people at Savoy Hill had apparently known for some time, which was that Eckersley had a mistress and that she was the ex-wife of a colleague in the Music Department: 'I could not make out what had happened to him of recent months,' Reith wrote in his diary. 'I felt as if I had known the whole story, but in a code which I had not solved.'

It is plain from his diary that over the next few months Eckersley's matrimonial difficulties became a matter of intense, almost pastoral concern to Reith. There were discussions with Clarendon and with senior colleagues; he even talked about them after lunch at the Athenaeum one day with Lord Byng, the Metropolitan Commissioner of Police. When Reith came to write his memoirs he denied the allegation that in his day divorce was inevitably followed by resignation or termination – 'Never such a rule', he wrote. 'They were judged, as in other public bodies, on the circumstances of the divorce and of the individual's employment.'[52] That is flatly at variance with the account in his diary of his conversation with Byng:

> He said I ought not to keep anyone on in the BBC after being divorced, irrespective of the circumstances, which is what I have felt all along . . . It is quite impossible to differentiate between cases; if one were allowed to stay, another might think himself unfairly dealt with if he were not. There is the bad influence, and one case leads to another.[53]

In Eckersley's case, however, he hoped for a time that the question of divorce would not arise. Without mentioning names, he described the circumstances to Byng: 'He said he thought I might let him stay if I could be satisfied as to the future.' Two days later, Eckersley told Reith that he had resolved to break off the affair. He placed his resignation unconditionally in Reith's hands and assured him that what he cared about more than anything was to reinstate himself in the confidence of his colleagues. Reith, in return, undertook to recommend to the Board that he should be retained on the staff, and this, somewhat to his surprise, they agreed to.[54]

That could have been the end of the matter. Two months later, however, Eckersley came to him with the suggestion that he should be paid a retainer of £1500 or £2000 but allowed to take on outside work. 'I supposed this meant that he was not going to keep his undertaking with regard to the woman,' Reith wrote in his diary. He supposed correctly. Less than two months later, Eckersley told him that he had decided to return to his mistress. The announcement of his resignation was given to the press the same night.

Reith was a good deal taken up with politics in the spring of 1929. The government still had a substantial majority, but the Parliament that had been elected in November 1924 had almost run its term, and Baldwin was eventually to opt for a May election. Reith had drawn closer to Ramsay MacDonald in the three years since the General Strike. With so little support in the press, the Labour leader recognised the importance of political broadcasting. Reith, lunching with him in February, had said that it was for the three parties to agree the details of a rota, and MacDonald told him that Labour was ready to agree to almost anything.[55]

The Conservatives were less amenable. There was much correspondence with J. C. C. Davidson, now Chairman of the Conservative Party Organisation. Reith found him 'obstinate', and grumbled about him, both in his diary and in person to Vansittart. That did not prevent a prompt response when Baldwin wrote to ask for help in classifying his potential listeners. 'What proportion may be working class?' enquired the Prime Minister (he wrote in his own hand). 'Does wireless go to the workman, or is the workman listener an exception?'[56] Reith's reply sheds interesting light on how the BBC saw its audience in those pre-audience research days:

> The social centre of gravity is much nearer the bottom than the top of the social scale. In the broadcast audience it is probably rather lower still.
> ... You will have every sort of individual listening to you, and a large proportion of working-class people, mostly in their homes, not in clubs or pubs. The workman and his wife will certainly be there, but so will the ordinary middle-class fellow and his, mostly at the fireside.[57]

Baldwin came to the studio to make his first broadcast the following week. It was lodged in Reith's elephantine memory that he had turned up during the General Strike without an ending to his speech, so he had prepared a three- or four-minute peroration. The Prime Minister did indeed ask for advice about how he ought to conclude, and Reith produced his draft: 'He was awfully pleased with it, but said it was too good for tonight and that he would use it on his second broadcast before Election Day.'[58]

Reith was eminently even-handed between the parties. Some weeks later, Ramsay MacDonald was to broadcast from Newcastle, and Reith travelled north to be with him in the studio. He found him hoarse and tired: 'A lot of rehearsing and adjustment before he began for which he was very grateful. He spoke for 36 minutes and got very declamatory and bitter towards the end.'[59]

The parties were left in no doubt that although the Director-General of the BBC was at their service, he was in no sense their servant. During the campaign the Liberal chief agent telephoned to say that Lloyd George was very annoyed at not having a date in the same week as the Prime Minister and Ramsay MacDonald and that he wanted Reith to go and see him:

> I said I was not going along to be abused, nor to be kept waiting. He said Lloyd George would receive me at once and be civil, so I went and was there for about half an hour. He was quite amenable but I did not like him or his entourage.[60]

Another politician who was awarded low marks during the campaign was Neville Chamberlain, then Minister of Health. 'He was very poor,' Reith wrote in his diary. 'He said he had had no time to prepare his address. I asked him what more important he could have had to do all week.'[61]

The victory went narrowly to Ramsay MacDonald, and he set about forming his second minority administration. When he came to broadcast his first message as Prime Minister, he told Reith he was having 'an awful time' making up his Cabinet – 'I would realise what it was if ever I had to do the same.'[62] One of his appointments was of Mrs Snowden's husband to be Chancellor of the Exchequer.

There was a bizarre incident during the broadcasting of the results which demonstrated that there was still no aspect of the BBC's activities which escaped the attention of its chief executive. 'The Exacting Wireless Public,' said a headline in the *Birmingham Post*:

> After the last General Election certain constitutionally awkward people wrote to complain that announcers had shown 'bias' by voice inflections when reading the results ... To prevent a recurrence of criticism, the Director-General conceived the idea of having the results read by a comparatively strange voice ... He assumed the task himself and, such is the contrariness of listeners, before long people were telephoning that he was 'indistinct' ...[63]

A journalist on the *Morning Post* had a more enquiring mind than his provincial colleague: 'As the result of a "scene" between Sir John Reith, Director-General of the BBC, and Mr Eric Dunstan, the well-known announcer, on Thursday night, the latter has severed his connection with the BBC.' The *Post* reporter had picked up his story at an election party to which Dunstan had gone after leaving Savoy Hill. The procedure, he said, had been thoroughly rehearsed with the staff on duty, but Reith had turned up during the second news bulletin of the evening and told them that he proposed to announce all the results himself up to 1.30 a.m. The telephone began to ring almost at once, with requests that the results should be read more clearly and more slowly. It fell to Dunstan to convey this to the Director-General. 'I did my best politely to inform him of the position, but all he said was: "I will not read any slower; I am going on announcing," and he turned his back on me.'

Reith had misjudged his man. Dunstan, who had previously been Vice-Consul in Seville, secretary to Mr Gordon Selfridge and ADC to the Governor of the Fiji Islands, marched angrily out of the studio, the building, and the employ of the BBC. It was a good exit, and it was accompanied by a sturdy assertion of the professional proprieties: 'If my resignation has the effect of ensuring that in future people do not interfere on such important occasions, when nerves are taut and the one thing necessary is a cool head and freedom of action, I do not regret it. The listening public wants clear and efficient announcing, and this is the announcer's job and no one else's.'[64]

The statement put out by the Corporation the next day showed that its press and public relations machinery still needed a certain amount of fine tuning: 'The vacancy caused by an announcer's resignation has been filled, and the BBC has no statement to make on inaccurate accounts of the incident which caused it.' There were occasions when Reith's autocratic temper served the Corporation well. This was not one of them. William Blake put the matter very economically in *Auguries of Innocence*, even if he forced the rhyme:

> The strongest poison ever known
> Came from Caesar's laurel crown.

It had long been a source of regret to Reith that he had started to keep a diary only when he was in his twenties, and he now found time in the midst of everything else to begin to dictate to his BBC secretary, Miss Nash, a summary of his life in the pre-diary days. 'I am very glad to be started on this,' he wrote in his diary on 8 April; two days later he recorded that the task had been completed.

Miss Nash seems to have exercised considerable influence over him at this time. Earlier in the year it was at her insistence that he had accepted an invitation to a government dinner at the Mansion House in connection with the British Industries Fair: 'I was much averse to going and when I got there was disgusted with my seat and went home. I shall accept no more invitations until I am sure my position is appreciated.'[65] A diary entry two days later reads, 'Miss Nash made me visit her horologist; an entertaining but extraordinary business. He told me I would have a peerage in 1931 or 1932, might be Prime Minister, etc.'

Although he was now a considerable public figure and came into contact with any number of people in many walks of national life, Reith remained an essentially solitary man. He had a number of cronies, but no intimates – Carpendale, after six years as a close colleague, would occasionally send him mock naval signals – 'From Vice-Admiral Second in Command to Commander-in-Chief' – but still addressed him as 'Sir John'. He had been on quite close terms for some years with George Bell, the Dean of Canterbury, who in May of 1929 was made Bishop of Chichester. Reith heard the news in a less direct way than he felt he was entitled to, and dictated what must have been one of the more unusual letters of congratulation Bell received on his elevation:

> . . . Such a surprise – and shock. I have passed through a variety of sentiments since. Umbrage. High dudgeon. Sympathy. Satisfaction. Gratification . . . I note your reference to your 'friends and wise old counsellors'. I gather my first notification would have been the newspapers if it had not been for the Festival. Hence, perhaps, the umbrage and dudgeon. You used to include me in the first category – rather specially as it seemed, and somewhat to my surprise, as I am not accustomed to be thought a friend of anybody, and do not have many, if any, myself . . .[66]

This was partly what made his diary so important to him. What other men would have got off their chests – and forgotten – over a drink with friends, Reith stored away in the memory-bank of his diaries and scrapbooks – and frequently retrieved. He also went repeatedly back over the life of his father. A diary entry for Good Friday 1929 reads, 'Devoted the whole afternoon and evening to contentedly going through more papers, including father's old letters from 1864 on . . . I burned much in reverent holocaust.'

There was little enough contentment to be found in his relations with the Board. Baldwin had been highly entertained during one of their conversations earlier in the year when Reith had said that 'a thorn in the spirit was worse

hn Reith, newly knighted, at the age of 37

Reith and Ramsay MacDonald

Below: Winston Churchill at the microphone, 1935

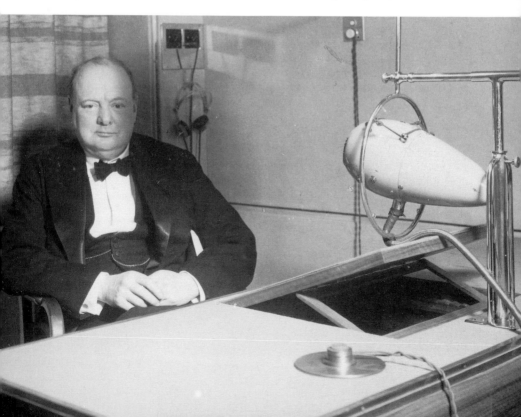

ove: Peter Eckersley at Savoy Hill in 1926
ove right: 'Carps': Admiral Carpendale in 1929
ght: R. S. Lambert, 1937, first editor of *The Listener*
low: Harman Grisewood in his announcing days, 1934

Early days in television:
Madame Karsavina in 1933

Above: Sound effects
at Savoy Hill, 1927

A bridge broadcast
from 2LO, 1927

than a thorn in the flesh', and had asked whether he felt he must burst, but it had not been Reith's intention to amuse. 'I am to an extent responsible for the way in which things are,' he wrote in the middle of May, 'but the abominable Board is responsible for it all. The wells of satisfaction and inspiration were polluted by the wretched woman; the idiocy and futility of Clarendon did the rest.'[67]

Something that irritated Reith beyond measure was that Clarendon and his colleagues had taken to lunching at the Savoy on Board days without inviting him to join them. The week after Eckersley's departure he noted that it had been 'a superficially peaceable Board' and registered surprise that there was no reference to all the press interest there had been in the matter:

> I thought it very odd that they all sneaked off hurriedly at 1.00. I discovered subsequently that they had betaken themselves to Clarendon's house and confabbed there till after tea like mice conspiring against the cat, but without coming to any conclusions. What a miserable lot they are.[68]

A visit to the theatre to see Patrick Hamilton's play *Rope* gave him the notion that he might make some money by writing a play about the Board, and he actually spent some time at his desk trying to flesh out the idea. He also responded to a request for help from Baldwin, who had been elected Rector of St Andrews University and wanted a few ideas for his inaugural address. Reith, never one to do things by halves, overwhelmed him with advice. He might care to read Tyndall's 1870 address to the British Association, and he urged him to study the ideas of Dr Thomas Chalmers, in his view one of the greatest Scotsmen who ever lived – he could send him a pamphlet, a short life, or a four-volume biography. He also offered him a range of texts from Proverbs and the Book of Job, adding a gloss which was plainly autobiographical: 'One of the most severe trials of character and ability comes, I think, to the man who has made his way so far, perhaps very far, and then finds himself definitely and dreadfully prejudiced by the very degree of his ability, compared with that of those around and above him . . .'[69]

Although no reference to it survives in his summarised diary, Reith registered at this time that there had been a change in Charlie's circumstances. He pasted into his scrapbook an undated cutting from a local newspaper in Perthshire: 'Homecoming at Argaty', said the headline. 'Argaty estate employees gave a warm welcome to their new laird and lady, Mr and Mrs D. C. Bowser, on Monday last.' An arch decorated with flowers and evergreens had been erected at the entrance gate, and the Bowsers' car was roped by workmen and hauled up the avenue to the front door of Argaty House. The oldest servant on the estate was on hand to open the car door, and the factor made a speech of welcome.

Charlie replied at some length. They would never forget this home-coming, he said. They had brought their children, and they would seek the constant help of all who worked on the estate in their training and upbringing. From them they would learn of the wild fowl and 'the terrible rabbit', of the beauty of the flowers and the ways of the quiet woods and trees. 'When we realise', he concluded, 'that the birds in their flight seek to rise higher, the flower strives daily to lift its head to the light, and the trees of the forest point ever to the Highest, then in this realisation there seems to me to be no limit to the scope and value of your teaching.'

Reith was overcome during the summer with his customary regrets that he had not made more of his mother's annual visit: 'I shall miss her dreadfully, though in my present miserable state of unsettlement her being here added to the strain.'[70] She had been with him on his fortieth birthday, however, and one day he had managed to take tea with her on the terrace of the House of Commons. Ramsay MacDonald had come by and had been very pleasant: 'Lady Astor spoke to her also and asked if it was from her that I had my Mussolini traits.'[71]

His 'Mussolini traits', Clarendon's obtuseness, and the pertinacity of Mrs Snowden continued to poison the atmosphere at Savoy Hill. There were disagreements about Reith's salary; about whether the Chairman's correspondence should be forwarded to him unopened; about whether Governors should be allowed to visit branch heads, and if so, whether collectively or in pairs; about whether Mrs Snowden should be permitted to broadcast about disarmament. This last proposal raised the Director-General's contempt for his Chairman's ignorance to a new pitch. 'What is said,' Clarendon told him, 'must be heard, of course, in the USA, France, Italy and Japan as well as here' – an arrangement which would have meant opening up the Empire transmitters specially on a Sunday, cancelling programmes already advertised in *Radio Times*, and breaching an agreement governing international relays that had been made with the Foreign Office.

The nadir of absurdity was reached at a meeting between Clarendon and Reith in September. Carpendale, although he told Reith that he thought Clarendon was 'next door to certifiable', had been exerting himself to improve relations between the two. He took Reith off to the United Services Club one night and spent three hours persuading him to go and visit the Chairman at his home the next day. He might have spared himself the trouble.

Things got off to a bad start because Clarendon, after shaking hands, neglected to offer his visitor a chair and Reith, being Reith, towered menacingly over him for five minutes before asking icily whether he too might sit down. By Reith's account, Clarendon began by saying that he wished, as a matter of principle, and before any discussion took place, to find out whether he agreed with his interpretation of the Charter – if not he saw no point in having the discussion. Would he admit the analogy of the Board as the Commander-in-Chief of an army? Reith thought a better analogy would be that the Board was the Cabinet at home while the chief executive was the Commander-in-Chief in the field.

Clarendon became heated at this point and interrupted his pursuit of definitions with a catalogue of specific complaints – that Reith had made a fuss about having to make reports to the Board; that he had objected to their lunching without him at the Savoy; that the Board felt they were spied upon. Espionage? Reith was incredulous. Yes, insisted Clarendon. How else could it have been known that the Board had lunched at his house on a particular day? Reith said he had deduced it from a casual remark of his butler's on the telephone, which Clarendon conceded was a straightforward explanation, but then he produced another instance, and now it was Reith's turn to become heated. The suggestion was either ludicrous or insulting. Did Clarendon believe he had engaged a detective to watch their movements? The Chairman was immune to irony. Yes, he did – or perhaps an agency of some sort.

At this point Clarendon offered Reith a cigarette, and Reith responded by making 'another endeavour to get the matter on a more friendly basis'. The Chairman reverted to the supremacy of the Board. He saw the Director-General's position as similar to that of a permanent secretary in a government department. Reith agreed. The Minister would consult with the permanent secretary but make up his own mind. Reith agreed with that too. At this promising juncture, however, Clarendon's car was announced. He had an appointment in half an hour; 'he had "given me an hour" already, but we might continue some other time.'

Reith returned to Savoy Hill in a furious rage and gave a blow by blow account of what had happened to Carpendale and Miss Nash. By the time he got down to his diary that night, however, he was a little calmer. 'We feel pretty sure of our ground,' he wrote, 'and perhaps in a way we are spoiling for a row. None of us feels there is the least chance of things being satisfactory so long as the Lord is Chairman.'

The next day Nairne managed to convince him that he should write to Clarendon expressing regret for the difficulties that had arisen and saying that in the interests of the service he was ready to do whatever he could to bring about 'a harmonious and satisfactory cooperation'. Reith grumbled, but complied: 'I did not care for the letter at all, it being much too polite, but I sent it off.' Clarendon was not at first disposed to accept this olive branch, but Nairne and Gainford worked on him, and at the end of October things were patched up:

> Letter from the Lord saying he deplored as much as anyone what had taken place recently; that he had had an opportunity of some talk with his colleagues; like them, he was prepared to let bygones be bygones with a view to starting *de novo* in happier circumstances ... People here are pleased about it and I suppose I should be too, but I have always said there was no use in putting a patch on the sore until you have eradicated the poison.[72]

There was one emotional sore of his own which remained obstinately infected. In September he had been briefly in Scotland, and had visited Dunblane. 'Bowser is now living at Argaty,' he noted sourly in his diary, 'and the last shred of independence gone.' A few weeks later he wrote that he had been going through 'relics of DCB' and reducing them drastically. 'I sent him Jez-ebel's letters, keeping only two; it is clear from these that they would never have gotten engaged if it had not been for me.'[73]

At the end of October he lunched at Lambeth with the Archbishop of Canterbury, who said flattering things about his work and told him he had more influence than any man past or present. Reith poured out his troubles and spoke about his ambitions,[74] and the Archbishop assured him that the grass was nothing like as green on his side of the fence: 'He said I would not like his job because he had no power and the clergy could put their fingers to their noses at him.'[75]

A week later Reith captured the headlines when he told a Diocesan Confer-ence at Leamington what *he* thought about the clergy. The Bishop of Coventry, in his letter of invitation, had said they would regard it as an extraordinary privilege if he would tell them something of the principles and ideals of the BBC's religious department, but Reith did not let that detain him unduly. He had not really wanted to attend their conference, he told his audience, but having made the journey, he hoped he would offend them – it was better to go away offended than complacent and lethargic.

There had been little encouragement for religious broadcasting from church-men because there were clergy who were afraid it would diminish their congre-gations. He himself had been brought up to go to church twice on Sunday, but today he rarely did – 'and more often than not my spiritual and mental state is worse on exit than on entry.' He had a low opinion of the Anglican order of service – 'the *Magnificat* and the *Nunc Dimittis* and all the rest of it, and no central theme, no inspiration, no message' – and an even lower one of the quality of English sermons: 'I literally marvel at the exhibitions which some clergymen are content to make of themselves in the pulpit Sunday by Sunday.'[76] The Bishop, in his letter of thanks, courteously turned the other cheek. 'We are all most grateful to you for coming to our conference yesterday and for the stimulant you applied,' he wrote. 'The frank and sympathetic criticism of a non-ecclesiastical layman is not easy to get . . .'[77]

Carpendale, returning from the Continent at the end of November, thought he detected an improvement in morale: 'Dear Master,' says a handwritten note which Reith kept in his scrapbook, 'I just want to say how perfectly delightful it is to come back from abroad and find you in such a very happy mood about work in general – I can't tell you how I enjoyed hearing you talk about the future happy prospect of when we are all in Broadcasting House and you as Chairman . . .'[78] Although Reith continued to express himself in fairly extrava-gant language about Clarendon in his diary, a certain lightening of the tone was apparent. A week before Christmas, the Chairman went away on holiday. 'We profoundly hope the blessed Lord may kill himself in one way or another in Switzerland,' Reith wrote, 'but feel there is not much chance.'[79]

Reith had been fingering the idea that he might succeed to the chairmanship for some time. The thought had grown out of his frustrations with the Board, but it was also an expression of his more general restlessness and of his limitless (if not always sharply focused) ambition. The last volume of Churchill's *The World Crisis* had recently appeared, and Reith was absorbed by it: 'There is no doubt I was built for times like that,' he wrote. 'I feel I shall never have an opportunity of employing all my tremendous abilities; but Muriel thinks I shall.'[80]

An opportunity offered in the first week of 1930. Sir Josiah Stamp told him that he must soon find a technical Vice-President to have charge of 100,000 men in the London, Midland and Scottish Railway. It was a big job. He would have under him the Locomotive Superintendent, the Chief Civil Engineer, the Carriage and Waggon Superintendent, and the Marine Superintendent, who had responsibility for a hundred workshops and all the company's dock and harbour installations. The salary would initially be £7000 – a higher figure, Stamp said, than for the railway's other three Vice-Presidents. As Reith recorded the details in his diary, he brooded over the pros and cons: 'The biggest snag is that I should be junior Vice-President. I really think if I were to be senior Vice-President and if the pay were more, I should go.'[81]

A month later he heard something which, for a time at least, was to drive all thoughts of leaving Savoy Hill from his mind. Gladstone Murray telephoned and told him that one of the news agencies had a story that Clarendon was going to South Africa as Governor-General. Miss Nash, following customary BBC drill, was listening on the parallel line, and Reith heard her gasp. 'I answered quite calmly that I had heard nothing about it, but it would not surprise me. What terrific news! We could not contain ourselves and did not know what to do to show our delight.'[82]

Reith rang up Sir Francis Morgan Bryant, an acquaintance at Buckingham Palace, and squeezed confirmation out of him, although he said that it was 'very private' and not to be announced for some days. Jubilation must be tempered with discretion. Reith picked up his telephone again and passed on 'the amazing news' to Carpendale – in French.

Nine

FULL MERIDIAN

Take the sum of human achievement in action, in science, in art, in literature – subtract the work of the men above forty, and while we should miss great treasures, even priceless treasures, we would practically be where we are today.

SIR WILLIAM OSLER, *The Fixed Period*, 1905

THERE WERE people in London in 1930 who believed that John Reith was mad. They included the Postmaster-General, H. B. Lees-Smith. It had been decided, after a good deal of casting about, that the chairmanship of the BBC should be offered to J. H. Whitley, the former Speaker of the House of Commons. Lees-Smith told him, presumably by way of reassurance, that it was not as daunting a job as it might seem; the Director-General, he said, would not last very long, 'because he will end up in a lunatic asylum'.[1]

Reith was certainly the subject of a good many stories, not a few of them put about by Mrs Snowden, but he was not to leave the service of the Corporation for another eight years – was, indeed, only approaching the mid-point of his BBC career. He was to look back on the Whitley era as a period of 'light, and understanding, and excellent wisdom'; but on the day the appointment was announced he wrote in his diary that it was 'very annoying – another instance I suppose of the damage done by the Red Woman'.[2]

When he heard that Clarendon was off to South Africa, he told Sir Gordon Nairne that he would like to be Chairman himself. There was a disagreement within the government over whether the appointment lay with the Prime Minister or the Postmaster-General, a point settled by the law officers in favour of the Prime Minister. When MacDonald sent for him and asked his advice, Reith at first proposed Gainford, but MacDonald said he would never do. Reith then came clean and said he would like the job himself.

He followed this up with a letter to the Prime Minister urging that there should be either 'a well paid half-time chairman with a chief executive with half my salary' or 'a well paid chief executive and a trustee type of chairman'. He pressed the same advice on Lees-Smith and on the Lord Chancellor, Lord Sankey. He even went to see Lord Stamfordham at Buckingham Palace: 'He said he did not think the King would have anything to do with the BBC affair, but he strongly advised me to do everything I could to protect my own position.'[3]

Immediately he got wind that Whitley was to be appointed, he dashed off a letter to the Lord Chancellor expressing his disappointment and wrote in his diary that he was 'disgusted' with the Prime Minister. An occasion to demonstrate this presented itself a few days later in Westminster Abbey, when Reith attended the funeral of Lord Davidson, the late Archbishop of Canterbury: 'The pall bearers included MacDonald and Baldwin, to the former of whom I directed a glare of malevolence.'[4] There was one small consolation: 'To our immense delight the Lord has been told to resign at once, and he is very angry about it.'[5]

There were changes in Reith's domestic life in the spring of 1930. On 1 March he took possession of Harrias House, a property on Lord Burnham's estate at Beaconsfield, and it was to be his home for the next twenty-five years. The house was described in an article in *Homes and Gardens*:

> Architecturally it has no outstanding quality. It seems to have been originally a bailiff's house attached to a large estate, and subsequently – about 20 years ago – enlarged and altered out of all semblance to its modest beginning. It is now a house of considerable size, designed on what may be called modern Georgian lines, with its rooms most conveniently arranged on two floors.[6]

Reith was not much taken with the district and found the Buckinghamshire countryside flat, but the house had four acres and two cottages and they were to have the freedom of the rest of the estate. He was sad at leaving Barton Street, and retained sentimental memories of it as Christopher's birthplace, but it was now too small, and Muriel and he were both tired of what he described as 'the dirt and confinement' of London. The move did not escape the inquisitive attention of Mrs Snowden, who dropped into Gainford's ear the rumour that Reith was working hard to have Lord Burnham made Chairman: 'He is, I understand, Lord Burnham's tenant. Verb. sap.'[7] Gainford sent a cool reply by return: 'Lord Burnham had a stroke in India and is no longer the man he was, and should not be regarded as a possible appointment.'[8]

At Muriel's prompting, Reith had given up smoking for Lent. He reviewed the experiment in his diary on Easter Day. He had embarked on it, he wrote, for four reasons: 'Christian principle; uxorial amenability; discipline; mental and physical benefit.' It had not been a total success, and Muriel was sorry she had suggested it: 'I gather,' Reith wrote, 'that people have found me more irritable.' There were certainly one or two occasions during the early spring when he appears to have been in highly combative form: 'Welsh MPs deputation on the infernal and absurd Welsh Children's Peace message, but I dealt with them all right; they said I was as bad as a South Wales coal-owner.'[9]

Within hours of the announcement of Whitley's appointment, Reith had a letter from him: 'May I say with what pleasure I look forward to being associated with you in the great work of which you are the creator . . .' The Director-General had not heard much language like that in the past three years, but the outsize Reith ego was still extensively bruised: 'I am very much inclined to leave the BBC,' he wrote broodingly in his diary, 'but what must prevent me apart from anything else is that it would be just what the hag would like.'[10] As he awaited Whitley's first visit to Savoy Hill, he did not pitch his expectations high:

> I did not find him as impressive as I had expected, but he has a quiet dignity and I am not without hope that things will go satisfactorily; he was very nice to me, and although I am sure he has been filled up with all sorts of stories about me, I expect he will try to make up his own mind.[11]

There was one matter on which the new Chairman seems to have made up his mind with remarkable swiftness. Reith makes no mention of it in either his memoirs or his diary, but almost as soon as he arrived, Whitley raised with Gainford the possibility of a secretary to the Board 'who would be under the orders of you and myself' and would be appointed from outside. 'I shall propose nothing in a hurry,' he wrote, 'but this appears to me to be the key to the situation, and to be essential to a fair balance of powers between the Director-General and the Board.'[12] He interviewed at least one possible candidate (a clerk in the Journal Office at the House of Commons) and wrote again to Gainford to say that Reith had 'trotted out all the old objections which I had heard from you . . . He seemed afraid that the proposal came from Mrs Snowden!'[13] Mrs Snowden had indeed made just such a suggestion to Lord Gainford shortly after her appointment; it took him a little longer the second time round, but Reith eventually once again succeeded in kicking the idea into the long grass.

John Henry Whitley was sixty-four at the time of his appointment. His roots were in Yorkshire, and he was a nonconformist. Before entering Parliament as a Liberal he had been a cotton-spinner, and he had given his name to the Whitley Councils, the machinery devised to secure conciliation and cooperation in the Civil Service and in industry. He asked Reith to forgive and forget. 'Being satisfied that he knew how much he was requiring,' Reith wrote, 'I promised to try; and succeeded. Free from internal strife, suspicion and distrust, one was able, undistracted, to get on with the job.'[14]

It was a year of steady development and consolidation. The BBC had recently acquired agency tape machines and begun editing its own bulletins. In March the second of the two twin medium-wave transmitters was opened at Brookmans Park in Hertfordshire, and this made it possible for the first time to offer a full daily service of 'contrasted programmes' to listeners in London and the Home Counties.

It was also at Brookmans Park in the spring of 1930 that an important step forward was taken in the new medium of television. The first BBC thirty-line experiment had been conducted the previous August from John Logie Baird's Long Acre studio via Savoy Hill and the 2LO medium-wave transmitter at Selfridge's. Then, with only one channel available, vision and sound had to alternate; now it became possible, after the close of radio programmes, to transmit experimental sound and vision signals simultaneously. This was followed in July by the Corporation's first attempt at a television play. It was called *The Man with the Flower in His Mouth*, and it was produced by Lance Sieveking and Sydney Moseley.

Later that month, Reith was present in the Central Hall, Westminster, when the newly constituted BBC Symphony Orchestra assembled for its first rehearsal: 'Made them a little speech at Boult's request. They then played *The Flying Dutchman* Overture for me.'[15] Adrian Boult had recently been recruited as the BBC's Musical Director. The orchestra's full strength was 114, and it was the declared aim of the BBC that it should set a standard for English orchestral playing and bear comparison with the finest orchestras in the world.

It was an ambition that met with a crabbed response from the English musical establishment. In his inaugural address as President of the Incorporated Society of Organists, Sir Hamilton Harty said that it was 'morally wrong and quite indefensible' for the BBC to enter into direct competition with private musical interests: 'It was never meant that the BBC should have the trusteeship of large sums of public money in order to use this money to crush and imperil private enterprise.'[16] Harty spoke in much the same tones as the newspaper proprietors had done in the controversy over *The Listener*, and the debate over the nature and role of BBC orchestras was to rumble on down the years. The first concert, conducted by Boult, was given at the Queen's Hall in October. The critics, unconcerned with ideology, were in no doubt about the quality of what they heard: 'The virtuosity of the Orchestra', wrote *The Times*, 'wiped out any reproach Englishmen may feel in the face of visiting Orchestras from abroad.'[17]

Whitley's benign influence was not long in making itself felt. 'Board 11.30 to 1.15,' Reith recorded in his diary on 17 September. 'I am now on quite agreeable terms with the Snowden woman', although he added, 'I told Mr Whitley it was not likely to last long, and that I would really rather be at enmity because one knows where one is.' Whitley had made it a condition of coming to the BBC that he should be allowed to complete his work as Chairman of the Royal Commission on Labour in India, and he went off there for six months at the end of September 1930. He left behind him a Director-General notably happier and appreciably more relaxed than he had been for some years.

The mid-point of Reith's BBC career is a good moment to arrest the beat of chronology and take stock of what he had achieved and how he was regarded, both by outsiders and by those whom he drove forward in the pursuit of excellence. One of the most effective ways of rolling back the years is to browse through the early BBC Year Books. They offer a vivid sequence of sepia snapshots; they are a record not only of what was achieved but of how those who ran the Corporation saw themselves and their task. The introduction to the 1931 edition reviewed the steady increase in licences: 'Statisticians will continue to argue about "saturation points." So far as the BBC is concerned there is no saturation point short of "wireless in every home".' The number of licences then in force exceeded three million, representing about twelve million listeners, or roughly every second home in the country.

A striking feature of the publication is that about a third of its 450-odd pages are given over to engineering matters – a technical directory for those who wanted to know more about cumulative grid rectification or beverage aerials, tips on how to design a crystal set, a definitive dissertation on sidebands and heterodynes. There are articles on piano balance and studio acoustics, a BBC time signal chart, and a summary of the international distribution of wavelengths under the Prague Plan.

The writing about programmes is remarkable for the complete absence of the note of self-congratulation that crept in in later years. The section on drama, for instance, begins: 'The BBC broadcasts something like fifty plays in the course of a year. Of this year's fifty, perhaps a dozen can be reckoned as definite failures.' Tyrone Guthrie is singled out as probably the most promising pure radio dramatist yet discovered: 'Perhaps it is rather to be regretted that he chooses morbid themes and handles them brutally, but none the less his next play is awaited with great interest by those who take their broadcast drama seriously.'[18]

Vaudeville programmes were also passed in brisk review: 'In fairness to variety artists, and in particular comedians, they should not be allowed to appear too frequently . . . Listeners have asked, and not always in the politest terms, why the BBC does not put out fresh talent. The answer is simply that it does not exist.' Listeners received a stern reminder that they had a part to play in the maintenance of standards: 'The public are in no way absolved from responsibility in this matter, as long as they remain content to listen to rubbishy songs and remain satisfied with the poor standard of material offered by comedians.'[19]

Even after the best part of a decade, the Corporation still took a modest view of its role as a purveyor of news: 'The public is naturally anxious to know what is happening in the world, and although the supply of news is mainly the task of the Press, there are certain duties which only a broadcasting service can accomplish' (principally, it seemed, the relaying of news which had arrived too late for the evening papers). So far as speech programmes generally were concerned, the question of whether talks were too highbrow was earnestly weighed, and there was a resigned wringing of hands over the tendency of that elusive quality, personality, to evaporate at the microphone:

The very best Snarks are horribly apt to become Boojums at Savoy Hill. The famous author may stammer through his manuscript in a cockney voice; the well-known actress, radiating personality and perfume through the Studio, may sound on the loudspeaker like a tired school-marm; the famous explorer, with whose name the world is ringing, very possibly can't put two words together before the microphone . . .[20]

Such were the corporate tones – clear, assertive, self-assured – in which John Reith's BBC spoke to its various publics in the early 1930s. For someone who affected such a vehement dislike of personal publicity, the man himself was marvellously adept at generating it. He used to protest that he wished to be as anonymous as the editor of *The Times*, but the evidence of his scrapbooks is that he was as susceptible as the next man to the seductively ambivalent thrill of seeing his name in the papers.

Someone who caught him brilliantly on the wing in those middle BBC years was Harold Laski. Reith himself was sufficiently struck by the socialist academic's view of him (in an article in the *Daily Herald*) to dwell on it for half a page when he came to write his memoirs more than a decade and a half later:

> ... His deep-set eyes look as though, at any moment, they may let loose a tempest. He is vehement, determined, aggressive, masterful. He works easily with you while you agree with him. When you disagree, no one can quite tell, least of all he, what will be the outcome . . . There is a fanatic in him. It is one of his gifts and one of his limitations. It explains his power of work, his energy and his drive. But it means also that he carries about with him a bundle of dogmas – social, religious, ethical, political – and he has a tendency to make them the measure of all things and all men. Sunday is what the lawyers call a *dies non* on the wireless, because Sir John will have it so. Controversy is always a little tepid and half-hearted, because Sir John believes we ought not to go too far . . .

Laski had obviously heard Reith in full flight on public occasions, but as an occasional broadcaster he had also picked up a whiff of the atmosphere inside the BBC:

> ... At a conference, he seems to talk as though he was in charge of the national well-being. He speaks with the urgency of a Pontiff. You too rarely hear from the admirable and efficient staff he has gathered about him. He gives the impression that the BBC pivots too exclusively upon his private sense of right and wrong . . . There is still not a sufficiently comfortable atmosphere at Savoy Hill. He has gathered about him brains in plenty. But he has cramped their usefulness and their creative quality by being too dominating in his governance.

The article had begun by conceding the measure of Reith's achievement in imposing himself on the public to the extent he had in less than ten years. Laski concluded with a perceptive qualification:

> A man as dominating as he could easily be a little more audacious. The big thing for wireless to do is to provoke people into thought. That means Mr Harry Pollitt as well as Mr Baldwin and Mr Morrison. It means Professor Hogben as well as Professor Huxley . . . Let everyone speak, and let everyone be answered. That is the really big thing to do.[21]

Although he was a son of the manse, Reith's religious beliefs were far from orthodox. Kenneth Wolfe, in his survey of the politics of broadcast religion, has described his attitude to religion as 'more than slightly superstitious and certainly not an accurate reflection of his Presbyterian upbringing'.[22] Reith's sabbatarianism, however, was bred in the bone. 'Apart from any puritanical nonsense,' he had written in *Broadcast over Britain*, 'I believe that Sabbaths should be one of the invaluable assets of our existence – quiet islands on the tossing sea of life'; in the Reith scheme of things the quiet of those islands was not to be disturbed by 'sport or motoring or parading about the streets'. He had told the Crawford Committee that broadcasting should not be allowed to assist the process of secularisation: 'The Sunday programmes should be framed with the day itself in mind without being dull – and they should not encroach on church hours.'

The result was a programme schedule that reproduced with almost eerie fidelity the unchanging pattern of the Sabbath in the College Church manse thirty and forty years earlier. It began with a service which lasted from 9.30 till 10.45. There followed a lengthy period of silence, broken at 12.30 by a sequence of talks and serious music (Bach cantatas were much favoured). A second service followed at eight in the evening, and then more music until the Epilogue at eleven.

Some listeners appreciated this more than others. For members of the churchgoing middle classes it was not a matter of great moment; they had other ways of filling the day. Those lower down the social scale had fewer resources. When Seebohm Rowntree carried out his survey of working-class life in York later in the decade, he got people to record what they did on each day of the week. 'Sunday is the worst day in the week, absolutely dead,' wrote one respondent. 'After tea we roll up the carpet, find a foreign station on the wireless giving a dance band, and we dance most of the evening, sometimes playing cards for an hour before going to bed.'[23] It was the day of the week with the largest potential audience; the uncomplicated men who ran Radio Luxembourg and Radio Normandie marvelled at their good fortune.

On the issue of controversy in broadcasting, Reith was caught, as all his successors have been, in a crossfire. Criticism came not only from men of the left like Harold Laski, but from mavericks of the right like Winston Churchill, who in April 1933 was proposing the toast of 'England' at a Royal Society of St George dinner. The speech was broadcast. 'You see these microphones?' Churchill asked his audience, and then he launched with impish glee into a settling of scores:

They have been placed on our tables by the British Broadcasting Corporation. Think of the risk these eminent men are running. We can almost see them in our mind's eye, gathered together in that very expensive building with the questionable statues on its front. We can picture my good friend Sir John Reith, with the perspiration mantling on his lofty brow, with his hand on the control switch, wondering, as I utter every word, whether it will not be his duty to protect his innocent subscribers from some irreverent thing I might say about Mr Gandhi, or about the Bolsheviks, or even about our peripatetic Prime Minister. But let me reassure him. I have much more serious topics to discuss. I have to speak to you about St George and the Dragon . . .

That Reith had, as Laski put it, 'gathered about him brains in plenty' nobody would have disputed. 'I was not much interested,' he wrote in *Into the Wind*, 'in people who applied to the BBC as they might have applied anywhere else for employment. The requirement was men and women who wanted to be in the BBC and nowhere else; who realised its potentialities and were moved and minded to share in their achievement; who realised also how exacting the labours would be.'[24] He saw almost everybody who was being considered for a job. The interviews were always idiosyncratic and occasionally alarming; Reith conducted them with all the rigour of a novice-master interrogating postulants for a particularly austere religious order.

Richard Lambert, later the first editor of *The Listener*, came from a home where the atmosphere was progressive and free-thinking. His heroes were Fox and Cobbett and Cobden. He had been to Oxford, worked for the Workers' Educational Association and the Labour Party, and was a pacifist. When he applied for a junior educational appointment with the Corporation, Reith's first question was, 'Do you accept the fundamental teachings of Jesus Christ?' Lambert was unable to give the unambiguous, multiple-choice-type answer that was clearly expected of him.

The Director-General reminded him of a giant bird, moving restlessly and jerkily on its perch, and his second question was almost as startling as the first: 'Have you any personal disability of character, any weakness, that you know of?' Lambert, being, as he wrote later, neither an introvert, a Roman Catholic, nor an Oxford Groupist, had no answer ready. He also felt that the question invaded his personality in a way that he rather resented, but decided (understandably in the circumstances) that he could own up to occasional nervousness. The barrage of supplementary questions that followed seemed designed to impress on him the difficulties of working in the BBC: 'It produced a sense of mental distress and physical discomfort – I suppose you might call it fear,' he wrote. 'This remained with me throughout my years at the BBC, until near the end, when it fell off my back like Christian's burden at the Hill of Deliverance.'[25]

Some years later, after the move to the BBC's new headquarters, the young Harman Grisewood, later to rise to prominence as Controller of the Third Programme and Chief Assistant to the Director-General, was ushered into the presence for a similar purpose. He had been supporting himself in agreeable fashion since leaving Oxford by working as a radio actor. His cousin Freddie was already established as an announcer, and Harman had been persuaded that he should apply for a vacancy in the same department. Although his friends had marked his card, he confessed later that he was unprepared for the theatricality of the Reithian personality.

The Director-General began by grasping the poker and attacking the coals in the grate. (He had insisted that his new office should have an open fire; it was the only one in Broadcasting House.) 'What am I doing?' he demanded, and when Grisewood replied, 'Poking the fire', Reith echoed him scornfully with 'Fire, fire, fire', rolling the 'r' ferociously.

> 'What is this?' he said next, shaking his cuff-links at me. I knew I should say 'gold' and I knew, too, that he would then correct me by pronouncing the word 'goold.' 'Goold, goold!' he cried testily. 'You've a southern accent – like your cousin.' If he had been playing the part of an ogre I think the Children's Hour producer would have told him to tone it down a bit . . .[26]

Bright young women generally had an easier time of it than bright young men. Early in 1924, for instance, Reith, at the instance of a friend, had seen an Oxford undergraduate called Mary Somerville, who announced in effect that she intended to join the BBC and the sooner the better. Reith told the story with wry affection in a warm obituary tribute many years later: 'At the end of the interview, I said I agreed with her. She *was* joining the BBC, but the soonest would be about 15 months hence, she meantime having taken her degree at Oxford; and I said I hoped it would be a good one.'[27]

When Miss Somerville arrived at Savoy Hill, her first boss was J. C. Stobart, whose empire consisted of talks, news, education and religion; she was soon, in Richard Lambert's phrase, 'swimming round him like a swan round a carp'.[28] She quickly secured privileges for herself, including personal access to the Director-General at any reasonable time and exemption from the rule requiring female staff to resign on marriage. Most notably of all she gained for her staff a concession unheard of in other departments; she argued that because of the affinities between the administration of school broadcasting and the actual work of teaching, they should have additional holidays at Christmas and Easter.

Another young female Oxford graduate who basked in the sunlight of Reith's favour was Janet Adam Smith, the daughter of the Principal of Aberdeen University. She joined as a typist, but before long moved to *The Listener*, and in the early 1930s did distinguished work there as Assistant Editor.

Some of the poetry the paper published brought complaints from readers, and there were also occasional rumblings from inside the Corporation. The issue of 12 July 1933 contained a four-page poetry supplement. The poets represented included C. Day Lewis, Herbert Read and John Lehmann, but pride of place was given to Auden's *The Witnesses*, spread over two pages and illustrated by menacing, elongated woodcuts commissioned from Gwen Raverat. A few days later, 'Jove thundered', and the young Miss Adam Smith was summoned to Reith's office to be catechised on poetry in general and this supplement in particular:

The D-G wanted to know why there was so much that seemed odd, uncouth, 'modernist', about our poems. He was not choleric, like the outraged pundits who wrote to us from the Athenaeum, but puzzled. He made it plain that he wasn't objecting to modern poetry as such any more than to the modern music broadcast by the BBC, but I think he was anxious that poems which appeared in *The Listener* . . . should be recognised as having merit by responsible and informed persons beyond the paper.[29]

In the discussion that ensued, Janet Adam Smith mentioned the name of T. S. Eliot: 'Sir John then suggested that it would be interesting to have *his* opinion of the poems we published. Possibly he had in mind Mr Eliot the critic, the director of Fabers, indeed the member of the Athenaeum, rather than the poet of *The Waste Land*.' The great man was offered a ten-guinea fee and agreed to pronounce. He did not, to Janet Adam Smith's initial disappointment, supply a glowing testimonial. He did, however, provide something which, in terms of BBC politics, turned out to be of much greater use to her – a measured and low-key consideration of the grounds on which a weekly was justified in publishing contemporary verse. He concluded, rather tepidly, that *The Listener* was one of the very few weeklies 'in which he would not dissuade any promising young poet from seeking to appear', and Janet Adam Smith came to recognise that his very lack of enthusiasm was a blessing in disguise:

For the rest of the time that I was at *The Listener* there was still abuse from the Athenaeum, still muttering within the Corporation, and I had to be ready with a glib paraphrase of every poem in case it were challenged by someone in the hierarchy. (I remember trying to explain Dylan Thomas's *Light breaks where no sun shines* to the retired soldier who was a controller of programmes.) But from Jove there was no more thunder . . .

There was one poet who was exempt from all Reith's strictures, and that was Robert Bridges. Bridges was born in 1844 – a contemporary, therefore, of Reith's father – and appointed Poet Laureate in 1913. The two men admired each other greatly. Bridges had been a member, with George Bernard Shaw, of the Advisory Committee on Spoken English set up in 1926, and had given the first of the BBC's National Lectures two years later. Reith never tired of telling people that *The Testament of Beauty* would endure long after most other poetry of the day had been forgotten. An account of Bridges' spiritual philosophy, it had been published on the Laureate's eighty-fifth birthday in 1929, and went through fourteen impressions in a year. Its appeal for Reith lay in its highly romanticised, if not entirely coherent, evocation of broadcasting:

> Science comforting man's animal poverty
> and leisuring his toil, hath humanized manners
> and social temper, and now above her globe-spredd net
> of speeded intercourse hath outrun all magic,

and disclosing the secrecy of the reticent air
hath woven a seamless web of invisible strands
spiriting the dumb inane with the quick matter of life.
Now music's prisoned rapture and the drown'd voice of truth
mantled in light's velocity, over land and sea
are omnipresent, speaking aloud to every ear,
into every heart and home their unhinder'd message,
the body and soul of Universal Brotherhood . . .

Reith's conservative literary tastes were equally evident in his response to what was on offer on the West End stage in the early 1930s. He came away from a performance of *Private Lives* with a low opinion of Noël Coward: 'I do not think I have seen any of his things before and if they are like this I do not want to see any more. Apart from being sickeningly immoral and licentious, I thought it utterly fatuous.'[30] He was much more at home with the less disturbing fare offered to his parents' generation. Two nights after his exposure to Coward, he recorded that he was reading Frances Hodgson Burnett's celebrated (if much derided) *Little Lord Fauntleroy*: 'enjoyed it and was even affected by it in parts'.

One of the most engaging cameos that survives of Reith in those years was painted by his secretary, Miss Nash – it appeared in the BBC house magazine *Ariel* some years after she had stopped working for him when he was leaving to go to Imperial Airways:

. . . Pictures of him working with a speed and concentration I have never seen in anyone else; moments of crisis just before a fight with some deputation or other when, instead of concentrating on what he was going to do, he would be absorbed in something which did not matter in the least; days when, having filled me and the others in the office up with enough work to last a week, and having thereby cleared his own desk, he would suddenly decide that the furniture must be changed round, and we would all work at it till we were hot, dusty and tired, and every telephone had been pulled out by the roots, the loudspeakers dislocated, and all the buzzers put out of order. It was generally after such a bout of physical energy that he would give his famous rendering – in broad Scots – of *The Wee Herd*.[31] And there were days when he would tease and plague us till I could willingly have brained him with his own walking stick; or when he came in on a Saturday morning (quite unnecessarily in my opinion!) wearing a particularly nauseating Harris tweed suit. Great times, happy days.

In August of 1930, Reith set off – none too willingly – to visit Germany. There was a radio exhibition in Berlin, and the broadcasting officials he met told him how much they admired the British system. When his BBC colleagues returned home, Reith permitted himself a few days' holiday, and he was whisked off by the Chairman of the South German Company to his summer retreat on the Bodensee.

Dr Wanner had five flaxen-haired daughters. Reith had never been curtsied to before and was charmed. He thought them all very pretty; and he thought the second-oldest, the eighteen-year old Irene, very pretty indeed. There were boat trips on the lake, visits to Austria and Switzerland, a conducted tour of the Graf Zeppelin. When, after a week, a reluctant Reith announced that he must go home, it was arranged that he should go by way of Heidelberg and Mainz and that Irene should sail with him down the Rhine to Cologne. Wiesbaden and Coblenz and Bonn slipped by, and Reith discovered that he still knew *Die Lorelei* by heart. One evening after dinner they went to the cinema together and walked along the river bank under a romantically full moon. He did not think a great deal about broadcasting.

The train for Calais left at 6.35 in the morning, and Irene saw him off. His brief Rhenish idyll found a place in his memoirs many years later: 'Having taken cordial but decorous farewell I climbed aboard. "Good morning, sir." It was Adrian Boult. Some explanation seemed to be required.'[32] Muriel appeared to think so too: 'M. was a bit huffy about the Rhine trip,' says a sheepish diary entry, 'and about the Wanner girls generally.'[33]

The new house and its garden kept him very busy that summer and autumn – making hay, sawing logs, gathering apples. The word is always relative in Reith's case, but those late months of 1930 do seem to have been a period of some contentment for him. 'Bought a very jolly hen house on wheels,' reads a diary note in mid-November. 'We have about eighteen large pots of chrysanthemums indoors and they make a fine show.' Leaving London had proved an expensive business, costing him something in the region of £2500, but as Christmas approached he resolved to lay out £100 on a new pearl necklace for Muriel, 'even though I am much overdrawn'. The annual audit which he attempted in his diary each 31 December was more composed and settled in tone than it had been for some years: '1930 has been a disastrous year in the country; happy enough for us, and important in our having moved to the country. For the office, the kicking out of the poor creature who was Chairman made things more comfortable . . .'

Early in January 1931, Reith made what he called a 'momentous decision' about his diary. He had by this time filled forty-four loose-leaf volumes with his small, even handwriting. These were supplemented by thirty-five or more 'enclosure volumes' or scrapbooks. They constitute a repository for an astonishing range of material – letters, family snapshots, press cuttings, first-day covers, Cabinet papers, menus, even train tickets. To a man like Reith, gripped as he was throughout life by a passion for order, there could be no more bizarre memorial than this vast jackdaw's nest enclosed in hard covers.

He had come to feel that much of the diary was taken up with trivialities, and that there were a number of things 'which I would not care for people to read now'. It had in truth become something of an incubus. A less self-absorbed man might have decided that the time had come to destroy it and put his leisure time to less corrosive use. That, however, would have offered no scope to Reith's enlarged talent for making complications. He decided instead to set about making a summary: 'The diary may lose some of its interest for me, but there are plenty of other advantages to make up for that. It is a terrible labour which confronts me, but there is no other way for it.'[34]

He finished summarising and condensing the first eleven years in fourteen months. The remaining eight years were to take him until August 1935. Much of the summary was dictated, although for some periods – his time at the front, for instance, and for a part of 1922 – it is in his own hand, the writing so small that he sometimes crammed eighty lines onto each page. Throughout these four and a half years, he continued to dictate his current diary in similar form. Then he was once again to pick up his own pen. Small wonder that in later years his children remembered him as locked away for long hours each weekend in his study.

The re-reading of his diaries involved in this process seems to have prompted an examination of conscience. 'On this day came to various conclusions affecting character, outlook on life, which I think will be very useful and helpful,' he wrote on 18 January. 'I believe, for instance, that sin finds one out to a greater degree than people imagine, and that illicit happiness is succeeded sooner or later by equivalent unhappiness.' His conclusion was that he must 'revert to a more definite ethical code and attitude', and during some later re-reading he added a handwritten footnote: 'This sounds as if I had a lot to reproach myself about!'

He continued to excite a good deal of admiring attention in the press. In *The Strand Magazine*, in a series called 'Pen Portraits of the Prominent' by the novelist Gilbert Frankau, Reith took his place alongside John Masefield and Charlie Chaplin. Frankau thought he was one of the very few after-dinner speakers in London worth listening to – 'Here, at any rate, in an age of almost universal flabbiness, is a leader, a man of forthright competence, who both understands and means to carry on his job.'[35]

Reith had, in fact, along with a number of duchesses, been a guest at one of Sir Philip Sassoon's grand lunch parties a few weeks previously, and there he had met Charlie Chaplin: 'I find it rather difficult to realise that he actually exists. He is the best known man in the world,' he wrote in his diary.[36] At another lunch a few days later he encountered Sir Oswald Mosley, who announced that although he had only two or three supporters in the Commons, he proposed to go ahead with a new party and expected to field 400 candidates at the next election.[37]

About Lloyd George, of whom he also saw something at this time, Reith's feelings were ambivalent. The Welsh Wizard had initially been critical of the BBC, but now declared himself converted and expressed interest in joining the Welsh Religious Advisory Committee. Reith wrote that he could well understand his hold on those immediately around him: 'It is difficult to keep in mind one's indignation, dislike and even contempt for a lot that he does when one is with him.'[38] A couple of months later, Lloyd George came to Savoy Hill to make his first studio broadcast. He was very nervous, and this affected his performance. Halfway through, Reith passed him a card on which he had written in big letters 'TOO SAD', and this simple production device had the desired effect. Lloyd George pocketed the card and said he was going to have it framed.[39]

When they met again at Churt in the autumn, Reith once again felt the magnetism of his personality: 'I always used to feel during the war that if I had got in touch with him I could have had some very big job, for which even then I felt myself capable.' The range of Lloyd George's conversation reminded him of his father, and Reith was flattered but also unsettled by the direction which the talk took: 'He said that he could cure unemployment in the country in a year if I was seconded to work with him. I could not help feeling upset as a result of his opinion of me, feeling that I had lost so much time up to date.'[40]

A visit to the United States and Canada in the early summer had also induced feelings of nostalgia. Whitley had urged him to accept an invitation to a conference on educational broadcasting in New York. He sailed with Muriel on the *Aquitania* and made the acquaintance of many American broadcasters. There was, he wrote in his memoirs, more newspaper interest in the visit than was welcome. '"Microphone Mussolini" Here', said the *Christian Century* of Chicago; 'They say all sorts of things about this strange, rather grim czar of British broadcasting,' said the *Ottawa Citizen*; 'Briton Urges Sales Chatter Modification', the *San Francisco Examiner* informed its readers: 'Sir John C. W. Reith seems to be making a profound impression upon the American radio interests, and one immediate result is likely to be felt in the form of sponsorship modification.'

In Washington he was received by President Hoover and reminded him that they had both spoken at the Scotch-Irish Society banquet in Philadelphia in 1917. Hoover said he remembered the occasion, and asked Reith what he thought of their radio: 'I said good in parts, but that something might have to be done about the number of stations and the sort of stuff some of them put out.'

They went to Swarthmore. 'I had looked forward to this hour for many years,' Reith wrote, 'but before coming here I had got my expectations down to about 50% below par, to avoid disappointment. At the end of the day I felt that the realisation had been 100% above par.' Muriel was astonished at the beauty of the place, and admitted that he had not been exaggerating. When they went to church, 'the whole service was put through with a dignity and precision that quite astonished M, who is usually rather critical of Presbyterian services.'

At supper he sat next to Jeannette Laws, now Jeannette McCabe. 'There is a bit more of her than there was when she was 18,' he noted ungallantly, 'but she was still very good looking.' The evening was not without embarrassment: 'We could have talked a great deal about the old days, and very obviously she had by no manner of means forgotten them.' Reith's diary entry continues with some rather jejune musings about what might have been: 'Sometimes I think

I was rather silly in those days because I never even kissed her. On the other hand I think I was very wise. Far too many people get married. I have sometimes wondered whether I would have been more fond of her if her people had been millionaires; I hope not.'

In Chicago he was presented with a medal struck for him by the Columbia Broadcasting System, and *The Christian Science Monitor* devoted a leader to him: 'The Britons seem to realise more clearly than we the devastating influence of trifling and trashy broadcasting, and their responsibility to keep the wireless clean and respectable, as well as attractive.'[41] Reith's brief acceptance speech at the award ceremony was broadcast, and created a powerful impression – 'A matchless example of public speaking,' the *Monitor* thought. 'One regretted that the Britisher's time was limited to a few minutes.'

Nowhere more so than in Swarthmore, where his audience included his devoted old friend Dr Tuttle. Reith kept the enthusiastic letter he received from him: 'I do so wish a door, wide and effectual, might open for you in America. There is no sort of doubt that you are badly needed here.'[42] Bathed in an agreeable glow of adulation, Reith and Muriel sailed for home in the *Empress of France*.

Reith always had a keen sense of his own worth and was never slow to translate it into financial terms. One of Whitley's first discoveries when he returned from his six months in India had been that his Director-General was consumed with resentment over a matter relating to his salary. He had been promised annual increases of £750 in Clarendon's time, but these had not materialised. The new Chairman raised the matter with his colleagues, but Reith was only partly mollified by the outcome:

> Whitley came back after lunch and with some diffidence told me they had approved my salary being raised to £7500 as from 1st April. On hearing that they did not propose to do anything to make up for the past wretched treatment owing to Clarendon I told him that I was surprised and disappointed, and that I might not accept the increase.[43]

He embarrassed Whitley early in May by announcing that this left him £3750 down on what he had been promised, and that the Board 'had lost a great chance of making me feel happy with them'. The Chairman told him how anxious he was that he should regard him as a friend and expressed the hope that he would now let the matter drop. 'Probably I shall say nothing more, which will leave him guessing,' Reith wrote boorishly in his diary.[44]

In other respects, his relations with the Chairman were easy and cordial.[45] Whitley listened sympathetically to his difficulties and frequently sought his advice – 'he is almost the antithesis of the silly ass Clarendon.' Toward the end of 1931, Whitley was asked to go and see the Prime Minister about new appointments to the Board. He invited Reith to draft a document setting out the responsibilities of Governors – 'which I naturally did with much pleasure'. The Chairman accepted it as it stood, and so did the government (the Postmaster-General was now Sir Kingsley Wood). It became known as the Whitley Document, and for the next twenty years it was put in the hands of all new Governors on appointment. Lucid and magisterial, it remains the *locus classicus* of how things should be ordered in a public service broadcasting organisation:

> The Governors of the BBC act primarily as trustees to safeguard the broadcasting service in the national interest. Their functions are not executive. Their responsibilities are general and not particular. They are not divided up for purposes of departmental supervision. The suggestion sometimes made that Governors should be appointed as experts or specialists in any of the activities covered by the broadcasting service is not regarded as desirable. The Governors should as far as possible be persons of wide outlook and considerable experience of men and affairs, preferably with previous public service of one kind or another; and there should be included also a person or persons with financial and commercial experience . . . With the Director-General they discuss and then decide on major matters of policy and finance, but they leave the execution of that policy and the general administration of the service in all its branches to the Director-General and his competent officers . . .

Only a man of Whitley's exceptional qualities of mind and character could have safely given Reith his head in the way he did. Reith was constantly surprised by him, finding in this wise and dignified man in his mid-sixties the heart and spirit of a boy. He once told Reith that he had always regarded himself as being exceptionally quick on the uptake, but that since coming to the BBC the boot had been on the other foot – 'he had never met anyone, he said, with such a quick working mind as mine – twice as fast as his.'[46] It said much about Whitley and about the rare working harmony he forged with his prickly Director-General that he never permitted an announcement to be made in the name of the Board. 'We are one body,' he said, 'Governors, Director-General and staff. The Corporation; the BBC.' Like all classical moments, it was of brief duration, but it was during the four years of John Whitley's chairmanship that John Reith was able to give the fullest and most rounded expression to his concept of what broadcasting as a public service should be.

By early 1932, Reith's revision of his diaries had taken him up to the time of the war, and this Sisyphean pursuit ate heavily into what other men might have regarded as leisure time.[47] One Sunday in February he had broken off from re-recording the past and resumed his attempts to eliminate it:

> I cleared out a few more photographs of DCB, sending them to him. I have now only two or three left. I put in a note, without beginning or ending, explaining that the photographs which I had sent him periodically had not come to light accidentally, that I was much too tidy for this, but that it was an eliminating process. At the foot of the brief note, I put 'No reply', but I

had a sententious letter from him this morning, which neither M nor I can make sense of. Cockburn from Dunblane called unexpectedly, on his way from Geneva. He told me that C. was now a member of the County Council, and he spends a lot of his time travelling about inspecting buildings. When he said he was sorry we had not joined the Friends of the Cathedral scheme, I said that I was put off anything to do with the Cathedral, for reasons that he knew – referring to Bowser.[48]

A good deal of time was taken up in the early months of the year with preparations for the move to Broadcasting House. He met the architect there early in March, telling him he did not like the design for the mantelpiece for his room and that he was even less taken with the proposed wall lights: 'Miss Nash made a good suggestion for lessening the extreme hideousness of the balcony door. It is really a very ugly room.' Eventually Muriel took a hand too. The colour scheme was of buff and old rose, the furniture reproduction Chippendale. A painting of Tayside by David Farquharson was inset in the Tasmanian oak panelling above the fireplace; Reith told a journalist that his only regret was that it was not a painting of Deeside.[49]

During April, Reith had two major distractions on the domestic front. The first was that while he and Muriel were sitting at dinner one night, cat burglars put a ladder against the wall of Harrias House and ransacked their bedroom. In the commode stand beside Reith's bed they found nothing more interesting than a chamber pot and his service revolver, but they made off with clothing and most of Muriel's jewellery, worth several thousand pounds.[50] A week later, Muriel went into extended labour. Reith walked her slowly through the upstairs rooms. Last thing at night he turned on a concert by the Orpheus Choir which was being broadcast from the Queen's Hall. They sang the 124th Psalm and Reith stood below in the hall, conducting vigorously: 'M said it was most moving, and it certainly was quite thrilling to me.'

When he woke the next morning, Muriel had given birth to a daughter. They had both had a rough time. The child weighed eleven and a half pounds, and it had taken the doctor twenty minutes to get her breathing. She was born on Reith's mother's eighty-fourth birthday. When she was christened at the end of May, she was given the names Marista Muriel. Marista was doubly unusual – they had asked a friend for a list of old Scottish names and they had misread Mariota. The ceremony took place in the little church at Kingston Buci where they had been married, and was performed by the Bishop of Chichester, with Reith, Muriel and Mrs Whitley as godparents. The *Aberdeen Press and Journal* reported that water from the River Dee had been used; it also announced, rather oddly (the phrase could only have come from Reith himself), that 'this ceremony does not in any way mean that Sir John has any intention of being other than a Presbyterian.'

Back in Beaconsfield, Muriel thought she would like to be churched, so Reith telephoned the local vicar: 'His wife said he was out playing bridge, which I thought an extraordinary occupation for a clergyman on Saturday night. We both went to church next day and his sermon certainly bore out his occupation of the evening before.'[51]

The move to Broadcasting House had been in progress since the beginning of the year ('by instalments and in plain vans,' *Punch* said). When Reith's turn came he felt that an era was passing:

> I packed the little things in my room and bade it an affectionate farewell. It has been the scene of an enormous amount of work and I suppose considerable achievement. It really has a kind of romantic interest and the only period I should like to forget is that during which the miserable Clarendon was a visitor.[52]

The 1931 Year Book had described the ideal the BBC was setting itself in its new headquarters: 'More numerous and better-proportioned studios, perfectly isolated from one another and immune as far as possible from the invasion of sounds from the City.' It was a tall order. One 'City sound' that the engineers had failed to get the measure of was the rumble of the Bakerloo Line. Reith conceded that it was a great improvement on the improvisations and congestions of Savoy Hill, but he never had much affection for the building. He missed the bustle of the river, and the views of Lambeth Palace and Cleopatra's Needle and the Tower.

The new headquarters of British broadcasting did not excite universal admiration. The *Architectural Review* wrote of 'the labyrinthine pokiness of the interior'; the building was indeed too small for the BBC's multifarious purposes from the start, and staff began almost immediately to spill out into other premises.[53] There was no garage accommodation and, apart from the canteens, nowhere to meet for social purposes. Broadcasting House was also originally 'dry'. In the summer of 1932, a party of a hundred or so journalists was given a guided tour. If lunch had not been moved, at the last minute, to a nearby hotel, the new building would have got a very bad press indeed.

The famous Latin dedication over the lifts in the entrance hall (*Templum Hoc Artium et Musarum...*), with its quotation from the Epistle to the Philippians, was the work of the scholarly Rendall. Mrs Snowden had argued for English to be preferred to Latin and objected to the inclusion of Reith's name, but Whitley overruled her.[54] The inscription attracted a good deal of comment, and some of it, as Reith rightly suspected, was sarcastic. 'It informed those classically educated that its foundation was due to God and Sir John Reith,' wrote the feline Richard Lambert; 'the coupling of the two names matching the majesty of the one with the modesty of the other.'[55]

The letters of the inscription had been sculpted by Eric Gill, who was also responsible for the symbolic figures of Prospero and Ariel on the face of the building above the main doors. These became the subject of much lewd merriment, and there was even a question in the House of Commons to the Home Secretary: a Labour member, Mr G. G. Mitcheson, felt that the statue

was offensive to public morals and decency – would he instruct the Metropolitan Police to remove it?[56]

It all had to do with the size of Ariel's private parts. BBC folklore has it that
the Governors were invited to climb up onto the scaffolding to consider whether
Gill's sense of proportion was defective. All eyes turned on Rendall, who had
been designated 'the ultimate authority in matters of decoration at Broadcasting
House'. He could also, as an ex-Headmaster of Winchester, be expected to
speak with authority on such matters, and he did: 'I can only say, from personal
observation, that the lad is uncommonly well hung.' Gill was invited to take
up his hammer and chisel and emulate Michelangelo.

Reith addressed a general staff meeting in the Concert Hall on 3 May. There
is a recording of what he said in the BBC's Sound Archives; it is rather a
stilted performance, and it is plain that he was not hugely at his ease on such
occasions.[57] He said that he had had three main functions since he joined the
BBC: to repel external attacks, to push out the frontiers, and to watch over
the health and happiness of the staff. It had, he said, been 'a perpetual distress'
to him to pass people in the corridors and not be sure whether they were
members of staff; he made the alarming announcement that he proposed to
remedy this in the next few weeks by visiting everyone in their offices.[58] He
also reminded them that there was 'more in the BBC than just broadcasting':

> Some of you may not have realised that we constitute, in fact, a new and
> vitally important experiment in the management of a public utility service.
> In my own view, before so many years are out, you will find public services
> such as the Post Office, which are now run entirely by the government, and
> others which are run by private enterprise, taken over by bodies constituted
> somewhat similarly to the BBC.

This was an idea which Reith elaborated in an address to the Royal Institution
later in the month, and which attracted a good deal of press attention: 'No one
can accuse Sir John Reith of being a socialist,' wrote *The Weekend Review*:

> . . . His bold declaration last weekend in favour of the 'nationalised rational-
> isation' or 'rationalised nationalisation' of railways, coal mining, steel indus-
> tries and other services is a significant sign of the times . . . A fresh drive
> to develop the public corporation principle under the National Government's
> auspices is clearly called for.[59]

Reith's ideas about public corporations had grown out of a decade of practical
experience at the BBC. When he stepped beyond the bounds of public administration and ventured into the realm of political theory, offering a sequence of
loosely articulated observations about the nature of democracy, he was in less
familiar territory:

I suggest that the BBC is serving – and as one gathers serving fairly well – a high democratic purpose by means which, in the literal sense of the term, are certainly not democratic, and this in democratic days, when means which are not democratic are the objective of quick and bitter hostility. And, I enquire, can democratic principle and democratic purpose best be served – can they, in the long run, be served at all – by democratic means as we understand them?

He invited his audience to look around England and to form their own conclusions 'as to whether we are not badly in need of definite, even drastic, centralised action in many different fields'. The recent break-in at his own home – and what he saw as the ineffectiveness of the Buckinghamshire Constabulary – were clearly still fresh in his mind: 'What are we coming to that bandit gangs can, with impunity, raid our homes and places of business and hold us to ransom on the King's highway?' The highly charged rhetorical tone has echoes of some of the speeches he made in the United States during the war:

> What of the spoliation of the countryside, desecration stalking unchecked on road and meadow, the old character and amenities destroyed? . . . There is no point in saying that this or that must stop. We have said so long enough. We need more central authority and central determination. How is it that we have become so tolerant, even of monstrous wrong? Is it laziness or timidity, or is it just another instance of the mediocrity which comes from a misunderstanding of real democracy?

Speeches in this vein were a commonplace in Italy and Germany in the early 1930s. They were less familiar in Britain, except from Mosleyite platforms, and it is plain from an entry in Reith's diary that he knew he was being controversial. (He had shown his text to Whitley but, characteristically, he had done so two days after delivering it rather than two days before.)

> Next day he told me, to my surprise, that he thought there was no objection from the BBC point of view. I had thought there would be a racket about my unconventional views . . . I am not dissatisfied with it myself, and am glad that I can after all still produce a thing of this sort, in spite of being so much occupied with business affairs. It worries me, however, inasmuch as it makes me realise how much I could do in this line if I had the time.[60]

Reith's impatience with what he saw as the inadequacies of 'democratic means' was not confined to the British political scene. Two years later, when what was to become the India Act of 1935 was being drafted, he was called in for discussions with the Secretary of State:

> It was an unsatisfactory meeting, as England has obviously given up all idea of governing India . . . I said it was rather discouraging to have such a

hopeless attitude to start with and that as broadcasting was quite new surely in the new Statutes it could be reserved for the federal Government, or even for the Viceroy ... Graves and I came away very depressed, I particularly so as I have been reading an interesting book about Rhodes.[61] It would be interesting to trace the development of the democracy inferiority complex in Imperial affairs ... and far too much lip service prematurely to democratic methods.[62]

Two days earlier, he had registered in his diary his approval of someone closer to home than Africa who was unencumbered by such complexes:

I really admire the way Hitler has cleaned up what looked like an incipient revolt against him by the Brown Shirt leaders. They gave Röhm an opportunity to commit suicide, which I think was rather beastly, but otherwise I really admire the drastic actions taken, which were obviously badly needed.[63]

Reith's scepticism about 'democratic means as we understand them' also found domestic expression within the BBC, and was well illustrated by his attitude to staff representation; the arrival of Whitley as Chairman had brought him welcome relief on a sector of the front where he was beginning to feel hard pressed.

It was another of the many issues that had brought him into conflict with Mrs Snowden. She had proposed the setting up of a staff association. There were to be five councils, and the object was 'to enable the staff to make direct representations to the Board on any matter concerning their work, conditions of service, status, etc.' The draft scheme stipulated that there should be at least one woman representative on each council. If the ballot did not produce this result, the woman receiving the largest number of votes would be automatically returned. This early attempt at positive discrimination held little appeal for Reith.

His senior management colleagues had as little time for the idea of a staff association as he did, and Carpendale and the other members of the Control Board drew up a statement. They pointed out that those who worked in the Programme and Information Branches were a very mixed bunch – musicians, dramatists, educationists, novelists, journalists, artists, 'and some who might have been *dilettanti* had they not found their *métier* in the BBC'. Such people, they asserted, were individualists, and any form of representative council 'would be alien and repugnant to their whole outlook'.[64]

Whitley decided that the case for a representative council had not been made, and the issue did not bubble up again until early in 1934, when newspapers owned by Rothermere and Beaverbrook were engaged in one of their periodic 'press rackets', as Reith called them – attacks not just on the Corporation but on him personally. One of the more comical of these appeared in the *Daily Express*, which had sent a reporter and photographer down to Beaconsfield to try and interview him. They were intercepted on the road to Harrias House by a policeman on a bicycle, who warned them that Sir John did not like strangers passing his house, and that the property was guarded by two ex-members of the Metropolitan Police and 'a large and savage Airedale dog'. The men from the *Express* returned to Fleet Street without their interview, but were given quite a few column inches to describe the rest of their evening – 'a burly figure wrapped up to the chin in overcoat and muffler came towards the gates. At his heels was a huge dog which leaped against the bars and tried to reach us . . .'[65]

The *Express* wanted an interview because Reith had been invited that day to address the 1922 Committee of Conservative backbench MPs. 'I had purposely looked less austere than normally,' he wrote in his diary. He spoke for less than ten minutes and answered questions for the best part of an hour. Towards the end he brought off a characteristically theatrical coup. One backbencher wanted to know whether morale at the BBC was really as low as had been alleged: 'What about the reports of Prussianism at Broadcasting House?' Reith murmured modestly that that was not the kind of question he could well answer personally, but passed the Chairman a document which had been handed to him as he was leaving Broadcasting House.

It was a round robin. It had been organised by Miss L. Taylor, a junior member of the Accounts Branch, and she had collected 800 signatures. Morrison read out the memorial to which they had put their names:

> The undersigned members of the staff of the BBC, thoroughly disgusted with the false and malignant statements about the Director General being published in certain newspapers, wish to record their detestation of the action and methods of the newspapers concerned and to reaffirm their loyalty and gratitude to the Director General.

'Director General Cheered after Explanation', said the headline in the next day's *Morning Post*. 'Sir John Reith Plays Daniel,' said the *News Chronicle*, 'but the Lions were all tame!' Reith wrote in his diary that the press had executed 'an incredible volte-face', and expressed himself astonished. The less surprising fact of the matter was that the meeting was not open to the press and that the account of it that was later given to journalists was concocted by the Chairman and Secretary of the Committee, one other MP – and Reith himself. He was showered with more than fifty telegrams and letters of congratulation – from the Belgian Ambassador, from the editor of *Punch*, from the Marchioness of Douro, from the Regimental Association of the British South African Police.

The Beaverbrook rat-pack had their instructions, however, and did not immediately fold their tents; a few days later there was another *Express* cutting for Reith to paste into his scrapbook. 'Sir John Reith's Watch on the Sky', said the headline. 'Airmen who fly over Sir John Reith's country house in Buckinghamshire are just as suspect as pedestrians who enter the grounds.' The paper had dug up an aerial photographer, a Mr A. W. Hobart of Croydon.

Having a job to do at Uxbridge, he had also flown over Gerrards Cross and Beaconsfield, taking speculative photographs of country houses. When these were printed and despatched to the owners, he was visited by a detective from the Buckinghamshire force; Reith had apparently made a connection between the sight of a low-flying aircraft and the recent burglary at Harrias House.[66] Some months later, he was bidden to lunch with the Beaver at Stornoway House. 'He said he wanted to know whether I had any complaints against any of his newspapers,' Reith noted in his diary. 'I could hardly tell him that I never read any of them.'[67]

In spite of Whitley's emollient presence, Reith still restlessly scanned the horizon for new challenges, although his ambition was no more precisely focused than it had ever been. He dined one night at the Athenaeum with the novelist John Buchan, who was a Conservative MP at the time. The creator of Dick Hannay made some casual observation about the tremendous shortage of men for big jobs, and asked whether Reith would consider a governor-generalship or the Washington Embassy, hinting that Baldwin and MacDonald had talked to him about the matter.[68] Some weeks later, when he was lunching with Geoffrey Dawson, the editor of *The Times*, the conversation took a similar turn. Dawson spoke about the governorship of Bombay, and elicited a typically Reithian response: 'I said the chief difficulty in that job from my point of view was that there was a viceroy over the governor.'[69]

Reith made a lengthy record of another such conversation in the autumn of 1933, this time with Sir Maurice Hankey. It was not the first time he had shared his anxieties about his future with the Secretary to the Cabinet:

> Hankey was very decent and told me that my name had been mentioned more than once in connection with some big appointment, but that people had then said I had no experience of Parliament, etc. . . . The same thing more or less applied to the Washington post, but he thought I might quite likely be asked to take on something like railway nationalization, and he mentioned cotton too. I told him the sort of job I might take if offered and mentioned the Post Office if there were to be a permanent postmaster-general . . . I also told him I thought I ought to know exactly what I would have to do in the event of another war, or even a national emergency like the general strike. He asked me if I wanted a mobilization job, and I asked him 'Would I not be minister of munitions, or something of that sort?'[70]

Relations with 'The Scarlet Woman' had improved dramatically. (She was now Lady Snowden, her husband having been made a viscount, and Reith's various terms of abuse for her no longer appeared in his diary.) In the summer of 1932 he even escorted her to the final night of the Wagner opera season, dining at the theatre beforehand. The thousands of miles that now separated them did nothing to lessen the animosity he felt towards his principal *bête noire*, however. In the summer of 1933 he attended the opening of South Africa House by the King: 'The wretched Clarendon is on six months leave in this country. I saw him in the distance and felt much inclined to hit him on the sleek head with a stick.'[71]

Clarendon's successor continued to show an almost feminine understanding of Reith's hunger for recognition and reassurance and praise. When the Director-General went into the Chairman's room one day, he noticed that Whitley covered something with a sheet of blotting paper. Shortly afterwards, his secretary brought him a letter written in Whitley's own hand. It was to congratulate him on the issue of the five millionth listening licence:

> . . . To very few men there comes a chance of such a definite and clear-cut achievement for the good of humanity. Broadcasting in Great Britain would, no doubt, have been born and have grown without you; but it would have been something very different from what it is today.
> So, go forward rejoicing![72]

There was another illustration of how well Whitley knew his man a few weeks later. Lord Grey had proposed that Reith be given an Oxford DCL, but the recommendation had not attracted sufficient support. With characteristic directness, Whitley showed Reith the letter from Grey conveying this unwelcome news; before doing so, however, he tried, not altogether successfully, to find ways of softening the blow:

> Whitley made quite a speech to me to the effect that I should be the happiest and proudest man in England, and that no one of the great figures of the past, such as Gladstone, could feel that they had done so much good . . . He thought the Oxford affair was a thing to laugh about, and said they would have taken the same line with Caxton and others. I wish I could look at it this way. As a matter of fact I was very angry and disappointed and felt I would never want to go near the place again. I told the Archbishop about it and he seemed indignant.[73]

There was some consolation in a letter two months later from the Vice-Chancellor of Manchester University offering him an honorary LLD: 'Moberley in his letter said that he was very proud that his University should be the first to recognise my work. I was much more pleased with this letter than with the cause of it.'[74] Shortly afterwards, Aberdeen followed suit, and this pleased him even more, particularly because of the association with his father. He travelled north to receive the honour and, at the reception afterwards, Janet Adam Smith's sister Margaret coaxed him into an eightsome reel: 'I felt much exhausted and very hot afterwards, but very pleased with myself.'[75]

His secretary Miss Nash had also succeeded in getting him onto the dance floor earlier in the winter during the festivities marking the BBC's tenth anniversary. Seven hundred and sixty members of the London staff sat down to dinner at Grosvenor House (the Corporation's forty or so office boys were accommodated in an adjoining room). Reith made everybody laugh a good deal with his speech, and they all sang 'For He's a Jolly Good Fellow'. *Radio Times* carried several pages of congratulatory messages – from the Prime Minister, from the Archbishop of Canterbury, from Marconi, from Sir Henry Wood, from Percy Merriman, the leader of the famous 'Roosters' Concert Party which had first broadcast in 1922.

There was more than one view about the actual date of the anniversary, and many of those who sent telegrams from around the world plumped for 14 November. 'It isn't really,' Reith wrote in his diary. '2LO began 14.11.22, but the BBC birthday is really when I joined – December 26!' A little closer to the proper date, after tea with some of his senior colleagues, Carpendale made a short speech and presented him with a silver model of Broadcasting House which had been made by the Goldsmiths and Silversmiths Company. 'I felt horribly embarrassed by the whole thing, and was most uncomfortable and awkward,' Reith wrote. 'It is a most costly thing and very beautiful workmanship. I am very annoyed with myself that I cannot feel enthusiastic about it.'[76]

At the end of 1932, Board changes were announced, Lord Gainford, Dr Rendall and Lady Snowden giving way to R. C. Norman, Lord Bridgeman and Mrs Mary Agnes Hamilton. Although Reith was 'profoundly relieved' at Lady Snowden's departure, he recorded that he was 'very dubious indeed' about her successor; by the time the new team had their first meeting in the New Year, however, he had changed his mind:

> The Board meeting was almost rowdy, certainly quite amusing. Mrs Hamilton was very articulate . . . They passed a resolution about a foot long with respect to my ten years service, and asked me to accept an oil painting for myself with a replica to hang in the Board Room or Council Room.[77]

The choice of painter fell on Oswald Birley, then in his middle fifties and as yet unknighted. Birley had studied under Marcel Baschet in Paris and later, in Madrid, executed a remarkable series of copies from Velasquez; he had painted King George V for the National Museum of Wales in 1928. He portrayed Reith in a strikingly alert pose, seated at his table; he is in semi-profile, and it is the unscarred right cheek which is presented to the viewer. The picture hangs over the fireplace in the Council Chamber at Broadcasting House to this day.

Reith was much preoccupied in the early months of 1933 with questions of reorganisation. The staff now numbered more than 1500. He felt that he himself was still burdened with too much 'of a footling order' (he was not open to the idea that much of it was self-inflicted) and he had thought for some time that Carpendale (who had been knighted the previous year) was not performing as effectively as he should as his second-in-command.[78] The idea began to form in his mind of a sharper differentiation between 'output' and administration; Carpendale would remain in charge of the latter, but would work in tandem with a new senior figure who would have responsibility for the programme side. It also seemed to him that this important new post would have to be filled from outside the Corporation.

He accordingly embarked on an exhaustive process of what would today be called 'executive search'. The idea of drafting a job description, inserting it in the press, and selecting the best candidate at interview does not seem to have detained him for a moment, although it was the way he himself had been appointed. He lunched at the Athenaeum with Ernest Barker, then Professor of Political Science at Cambridge. 'He had a weird idea that the appointments of our staff should be done in some way as civil service appointments are,' he wrote. 'I convinced him that this would be quite impracticable for a long time.'[79]

Reith resorted instead to the upper reaches of the old boy network. 'Got Geoffrey Dawson to come and see me to consult him about our new big appointment.' The suggestions made by the editor of *The Times* included W. S. Morrison, later Speaker of the House of Commons and Governor-General of Australia. Reith went to see him in his chambers: 'I was not much impressed and not surprised when his first question was "what is the job worth?"'[80] Later the same day, he went to consult the Archbishop of Canterbury, both about 'the big job' and about somebody to look after religious broadcasting: 'He was very affable indeed. He said he regarded me as one of the great potentates of the Country and was as complimented as if the Prime Minister had consulted him about Cabinet appointments.'

A number of academics were considered – among them Kenneth Pickthorn, the Cambridge constitutional historian who later became a Tory MP, and P. C. Vellacott, who was Headmaster of Harrow and then Master of Peterhouse, Cambridge. Another was the Oxford historian J. C. Masterman, later Provost of Worcester and University Vice-Chancellor. His path and Reith's were to cross a good many times. In 1933 he seems to have formed a shrewd idea of what life in the BBC would be like and decided that it was not for him: he did not feel, he wrote, 'the sort of crusading zeal – the missionary impulse to do something great which you would be entitled to expect from your second-in-command'.[81]

Although he was sniffy about the Civil Service appointments machinery, Reith had nothing against picking the brains of those who operated it, and a conversation with Sir Herbert Creedy of the War Office threw up more names, including those of the Headmaster of Merchant Taylors and of Sir James Grigg, the Chairman of the Inland Revenue. Reith also got in touch with Lord Eustace Percy, a son of the Duke of Northumberland, who had been in the Cabinet in the 1920s as President of the Board of Education: 'When I phoned him the other night and told him of our need for a big man I wondered whether he might do himself. But I do not think so, as he is so much associated with politics and unpopular with the Labour Party, and probably very difficult and opinionated.'[82]

In the end, the job went to a professional soldier. Alan Dawnay had originally been suggested by Masterman. Etonians always had a head start with Reith; Dawnay was not only personable and well connected but had also been a friend of Lawrence of Arabia's. 'It is dreadful to have been in the position of having so magnificent a job in one's gift,' Reith wrote rather sententiously. 'I could not help taking account of the fact that an incalculable amount depends on this decision, to me personally, to the BBC, and to the country generally.'[83]

Another senior appointment, that of Director of Religious Broadcasting, had also been absorbing Reith's attention. He eventually settled on the Rev. F. A. Iremonger, who before taking orders had edited the *Manchester Guardian*. Not, however, before putting him through the hoops: 'Saw Iremonger again and gave him a Bible reading audition, finding his voice bad. I told him he read the Bible thoroughly badly and was typically parsonic. (Note: he improved enormously as a result.)'[84]

The Iremonger appointment was a success. He stayed for six years, going off in 1939 to be Dean of Lichfield and subsequently writing a notable biography of Dr Garbett. He used to tell people that he always sat on the edge of his chair on Monday mornings – he was waiting for the three short rings on the telephone that meant that the Director-General was on the line and that he was about to get the benefit of his comments on the previous day's programmes. 'I never had the shadow of disagreement with him,' Reith wrote thirty years later, 'except that he did not like old-fashioned hymns like "Rock of Ages" and I did.'[85]

Dawnay fared less well. When he reported for duty in September 1933, he found himself unexpectedly in charge of the entire BBC for four days: Carpendale had been called away to Switzerland, and Reith, who was on holiday in Scotland, sent him a cheerful telegram – 'Hail Caesar and good luck'. Back in London, Reith's initial impressions of his new protégé were favourable, but it was a short honeymoon. The ordered certainties of the War Office were a poor training for the programme side of the BBC, where, even in Reith's day, an instruction tended to be regarded as little more than a basis for discussion. Dawnay simply wasn't up to it. His health broke down and within two years, on the orders of his doctor, he was back where he belonged. Carpendale was then made Deputy Director-General, and the next layer of management down consisted of four Controllers – of Programmes, of Public Relations, of Engineering, and of Administration.

Reith's eagerness to force the pace in most areas of radio development stood in contrast to his much more reserved attitude to television. This relative lack of enthusiasm for the newer medium was shared by several of his senior colleagues and by a number of radio pioneers in other countries – as late as 1940, for instance, Gerald Cock, who had run the BBC's fledgling service before the war and was now working in New York, was startled to hear the great David Sarnoff of RCA say that television 'would have to make its own future'.[86]

There was more than one reason for the BBC's coolness. In the early years, Reith leaned heavily for technical advice on Peter Eckersley, and he was initially sceptical: 'The Baird Apparatus', he wrote, 'not only does not deserve a public trial, but also has reached the limit of its development owing to the basic technical limitations of the method employed.'[87] The attitude of Gladstone Murray, the Assistant Controller in charge of Public Relations, was even more negative. In October 1928 there was a demonstration for the BBC's top brass, and the following day Murray circulated his view of it to his colleagues: 'Keeping in mind the fundamental fact that the intrusion of Baird transmissions into the broadcasting band will gravely disturb our normal service and prejudice the Regional Scheme, I think it is our duty to resist or delay the suggestion in every reasonable and possible way.'[88]

There was also the question of cost. When, in the early thirties, Carpendale instructed Gerald Beadle to prepare a financial estimate for a television service, Beadle, not wishing to clutter the Admiral's mind with complicated figures, gave him a four-word reply – 'Sound multiplied by ten.'[89] In those years of economic depression, when the BBC was being pressed by the government to make a financial contribution to keeping the ship of state afloat, that was an eloquent and forbidding equation.

Although the Corporation continued to insist publicly on its genuine interest in the medium, there was some feeling that it was dragging its feet: 'The attitude of the BBC in regard to this amazing British invention is absolutely incomprehensible,' spluttered *The People* early in 1929. After a good deal of prodding from the Post Office, the BBC's first experimental television programme went out in August 1932. Four years later a number of rather primitive programmes were televised to and from the Radiolympia Exhibition; regular television broadcasts, the first in the world, began from Alexandra Palace on 2 November 1936, the Baird system quickly giving way to the superior system developed by EMI.

Years later, long after he had left the BBC, Reith said that he had always been 'afraid of television', a phrase received with some incredulity. 'It is hard to believe that this Cromwellian character has ever been afraid of anything,' Gerald Cock wrote in 1962. 'I interpret his remark to mean that he had foreseen the present calamitous abuse of TV throughout the world.'[90] Reith had certainly been quick to grasp that television would develop very differently from radio: 'It is only in terms of real interest and entertainment that the new service will succeed,' he had told the Selsdon Committee in 1934. He wrote very little about television in his diary, but the impression remains that he never ceased to regard it as a cuckoo in the nest – in moral terms the lesser medium, and one likely to prove resistant and even hostile to those elevated values with which he had sought to imbue radio.

To the idea of broadcasting to the Empire, on the other hand, Reith brought unqualified enthusiasm. He always believed that a great opportunity had been lost in 1924 when he had failed to persuade the India Office of the potentialities of radio. His view that the subsequent history of the sub-continent might have been different if broadcasting had been organised then on a public service basis was undoubtedly exaggerated, but the strongly proconsular emphasis which runs through Reith's thinking about broadcasting is as impressive as it is consistent.

The BBC had been given permission by the Post Office as early as May 1926 to establish an experimental short-wave station at Daventry; the aim was 'to ascertain how far it would be possible – if such a course were found to be desirable – to establish a wireless link for the purpose of transmitting British programmes to the Dominions and Colonies.' Experiments began at the end of the following year, but it was another four years before the BBC announced that it was to go ahead with an Empire Service. There had been technical obstacles, but they were less formidable than the financial ones; having established that there was no prospect of assistance from the government, the BBC finally decided to proceed on its own. 'The British listener's direct interest in the project is, of course, nil,' said the Corporation's Year Book for 1933, adding, rather grandly, 'but the question of national interests had to be looked at more broadly.'

The service was inaugurated on 19 December 1932, and it was given a powerful boost when King George V made the first of his Christmas broadcasts the following week. Early in the New Year the programme allocation was doubled – from £100 to £200 a week. Within six months broadcasting hours were increased from ten a day to fourteen and a half. Reith noted in his diary in August 1934 his belief that the Empire Service must be developed much more quickly and intensively 'because of competition in other countries, particularly Germany'.[91] Italy was active, too, and so were the United States and the Soviet Union, the latter causing concern in the Foreign Office by the propaganda it was beaming to Palestine and the Persian Gulf. None of this persuaded the Treasury to loosen the purse-strings. Earlier talk of colonial subvention came to little – the Gold Coast and Sierra Leone each set aside from their budgets the sum of £15.

In 1934, General Hertzog, the Prime Minister of South Africa, unhappy with existing commercial arrangements, invited Reith to advise on how broadcasting should develop in the Union. Muriel went with him, and they were away from early September till mid-November. They sailed on the *Windsor Castle*, but Reith found the millionaire's suite disappointing, even though they had installed a specially lengthened bed for him – 'very primitive compared with the Atlantic style'. The orchestra played 'infernal jazz' till 11 p.m., he had to bang on the window at 1.55 one morning to stop people talking outside and when they went ashore at Madeira they were 'pestered by miserable mendicant children'.

Reith briefed himself with immense thoroughness: 'The Postmaster-General was surprised that I was able to tell him where I ought to go and whom to see at each centre.' The details of his tour were settled within two hours of his arrival, and he threw himself into a punishing schedule; one minister told him there had been complaints from civil servants about the hours he worked. He met pretty well everybody who was anybody (except for Smuts, who was abroad), and the exchanges were not confined to broadcasting: 'Saw the Prime Minister at 10 for about an hour. He most heartily agreed with my usual observations on democracy; he said they would have to reduce the franchise if they were going to get anywhere in South Africa.'[92]

He concluded after a fortnight that there were 'hardly two coincident opinions on anything in this country'. The British High Commissioner was very pessimistic about the British connection; Reith quickly decided that, as a Scot, he felt an affinity with what he called 'the Dutch mentality'. He encountered no one with whom he enjoyed talking more than the editor of the republican *Die Burger*, and he was received with great courtesy at Stellenbosch University, the cultural heart of Afrikanerdom. He admired the Cape Dutch architecture, found people friendly but provincial, envied them their material possessions and the breadth of their landscapes. There was no escape from an audience with Clarendon: 'I treated him with formal deference as if I had never met him before.'

Then, fortified by a tin of biscuits and a carafe of iced water, he polished off his report in an all-night session in his hotel suite, signing it two hours before boarding the *Caernarvon Castle* for home. He compressed what he had to say into eleven pages. What he recommended was in effect a South African BBC. He emphasised the potential of broadcasting as an agent of national union and education, drawing together English and Afrikaner, town and country, black and white. There were a number of characteristic bravura flourishes: 'As the assegai to the naked hand, as the rifle to the assegai, so and much more is broadcasting, rightly institutionalised, rightly inspired, rightly controlled, to any other instrument or power, in the service of wisdom and beauty and peace.'

One of his own Governors called it 'a State document of absolutely first-class importance'. More to the point, it was as warmly received in South Africa by the Dominion right as by the Republican left, and accepted without reservation by the government. Reith had been invited to name his own fee for his services, but had declined on grounds of propriety. Later in life, in his ritual tirades against the iniquities of the honours system, he used to instance his South African report as one of many contributions to the public weal which had gone without recognition.

He had, in fact, managed to make heavy weather of a proposal to honour him during the summer of 1934 when a letter had arrived offering him the GBE. He wrote to Ramsay MacDonald asking that the name of Noel Ashbridge, the BBC's chief engineer, might be substituted for his, but it is clear from his diary that his motives were not as pure as he would have had the Prime Minister believe – 'In any event, apart from Ashbridge, I did not think a GBE was good enough.'[93]

From Ramsay MacDonald, on holiday in Lossiemouth, there came a lengthy reply which, in the nicest possible way, put him firmly in his place:

There is a growing assumption that Honours are attached to offices. I think it is a thoroughly bad principle, although the custom has become so strong that I cannot stop it . . . Your Chief Engineer is, no doubt, a first class man and the BBC a most important public institution, and I daresay that one day there will be a Prime Minister who will add it to bodies like Medical Councils, the Civil Service and so on, but I hope that will not happen in my time . . . Therefore if you were now to decline for the very laudable reasons which you express in your letter, that will not mean that the other distinction will be granted, because the one does not hang on the other. I am giving no BBC distinction. I am offering what I consider to be a badge for worthy service and public spirit . . .[94]

'An extraordinarily nice letter from the PM which complicates things greatly,' Reith wrote in his diary. He resolved for some reason not to discuss the matter with Muriel, but he showed the letter to most of the Governors. Norman was enthusiastic, Mrs Hamilton less so, although she thought he ought to accept if only to keep on good terms with Downing Street while the terms of the new Charter were being discussed. Whitley was ill – too ill to see anyone – but that did not deter Reith from sending him the correspondence, and if he had ever had any genuine doubts, they were dispelled by the Chairman's reply: 'For yourself, it will be a splendid answer from the King and his ministers to the pinpricks of the gutter press,' Whitley wrote. 'For the BBC and for the world of broadcasting it means a recognition that our chief *has* done and (thank God) *is* doing, a work comparable with that of a great Viceroy or a great Commander. All our staff – to the messenger boys – will feel an inch bigger on June 4th!'[95]

Whitley also, characteristically, wrote to Reith's mother: 'When a strong man emerges from the ruck to unfurl and hold high a new standard, there are always some curs to snarl at his heels; but it is not often that they get their answer so quickly and so emphatically as this. King George has once again unerringly spoken for His People!'[96]

Mrs Reith was now advancing into her late eighties. She had, to Reith's jealous displeasure, gone on living in Dumfries with Jean. Her hearing was poor, but she was otherwise in reasonable health, and she made it her business to keep a watchful eye on the health of her celebrated son: 'Let me know that you will rub something on your chest and take some linseed and licorice mixture if you have a cough – ¼ lb of whole linseed and ½ stick of licorice boiled for 2 or three hours.'[97]

A letter she wrote to him the following Christmas was less soothing in its effect: 'In a recent letter from Mother she enclosed me a copy of one she had written to Bowser on December 19th, stung to indignation by a Christmas card from him and Jezebel, about friendship.' Mrs Reith had told Charlie that she would be glad to receive his good wishes if he could express some regret for the way in which he had behaved towards her son: she had gone on to indicate that this was something that still concerned Reith, and told Charlie that Reith still kept a photograph of him on the wall of his dressing room:

I am very sorry that she said this because I do not care a scrap about him now and the last relics of that association disappeared more than a year ago. He sent a weird letter in reply – he 'accepted what she said with real regret but with affectionate regard'; he was 'ever prepared for a natural re-birth of the association and had already twice moved towards this'; . . . he harboured no feelings of resentment or bitterness (why should he?); . . . he repeated that he was 'ever on the lookout for the end of the bridge which spans the break', and that when he found it he would 'not be wanting in strength to set out', but was satisfied that the bridge should not be reconstructed by either of us, but he is sure it exists, and that 'we shall find it or not as is willed.' I never heard such rot, and was very angry and inclined to write and tell him to go to the devil.[98]

His edginess in those early weeks of 1935 was compounded by anxiety. Whitley was dying of cancer. When Reith visited him in the nursing home three weeks before the end, he said he had enjoyed his four years as Chairman more than anything that had gone before. He asked that his ashes might rest for a few moments beneath the dedication in Broadcasting House and then be left over-night in the Religious Studio.

Reith found the service at the Golders Green crematorium depressing, and disapproved of the Congregational minister's blue suit and blue tie. At Broadcasting House, and at all Corporation premises throughout the country, he ordered flags to be half-masted until after the memorial service in St Martin's, and for the first time in its history the BBC went into black-edged paper. Reith felt Whitley's death almost as keenly as that of his own father. The tribute which he broadcast had all the sonority of a funeral oration in the high Roman style:

> . . . Thou art a living purpose, being dead,
> A fruit of nobleness in lesser lives,
> A guardian and a guide. Hail and farewell.[99]

In his diary, more simply, he wrote, 'It seemed that one of his main objects was to make me happy, and if he did not succeed I suppose it was because nothing would make me happy.'[100]

Ten

'J. C. W. REITH – LATE BBC'

From morn
To noon he fell, from noon to dewy eve,
A summer's day; and with the setting sun
Dropt from the zenith, like a falling star.
JOHN MILTON,
Paradise Lost, 1667

FROM 1935 on it was no longer a question of whether John Reith would leave the BBC, only of when. He got on well enough with Whitley's two successors,[1] and no man with a remotely normal appetite for work would have considered himself under-employed – the challenge of a new Charter and Licence loomed, as did the question of how the BBC should prepare for war. The evidence of Reith's diary for these years, however, is that he was increasingly restless and discontented; he spoke about resigning so frequently that it is a wonder he stayed as long as he did.

He was slow to shake off the fatigue and depression that settled on him after Whitley's death, and 1935 was not to be a good year. 'Stayed in bed till teatime,' says a diary entry in March. 'I have not been sleeping well at night, irritating kind of dreams.'[2] When he saw his doctor a few days later, he was told he had a heart murmur and should get off to Scotland as quickly as possible. 'I am completely bewildered at the idea of going off for a fortnight to a lonely place like St Fillan's,' he wrote, but off he went – without enthusiasm, and burdened, by way of reading matter, with three volumes of his diary.[3]

One day, in lashing rain, he walked to Lochearnhead and back, and was hugely pleased with himself at covering the sixteen miles in four hours. He also went to Comrie, and climbed the Monument Hill: 'There were, to my regret, no apparent traces of previous visits – on the seats I had stamped my name in 1913 and DCB his.'[4] He went home by way of Glasgow, and found himself, as always, in the grip of conflicting emotions:

Despite my hatred of Glasgow and Glasgow people (so much of it on dear Father's account) there is no doubt of its hold on me. Things are horribly changed, however: swarms of dirty children in all parts of the Park and about the streets, and so much litter in the Park too. How one longs for old days to return.[5]

Then on to Dumfries. He had not seen his brother Ernest for many years, and it was to be their last meeting; he also paid a brief visit to his mother and Jean:

> The stair carpet to the top floor was thick with dust – In two or three rooms there were piles of rubbish, and in one corner I found all the BBC publications since 1925 . . . I am sure if I had a day or two in the house about one half of the contents would go out. In the basement I found a packing case from Harrods which had not been opened, and also a huge package sewn up in canvas. Innumerable cupboards were crammed full of boxes of Jean's. She is evidently worse at hoarding than Mother.[6]

Dr Milligan pronounced his heart much improved on his return to London and now identified indigestion as the root of the trouble. 'I believe the holiday has done me some good,' Reith wrote in his diary, 'because I am trying to take a more optimistic and less discontented view of things in general, a result perhaps of the magnificent scenery of the great open spaces of the Highlands.'[7]

Reith was never able to leave work behind for long, and some of his reflections on his lonely Highland walks had been about the suggested terms of reference for the Ullswater Committee – the village postmaster at St Fillan's had never had to handle so many telegrams and telephone calls in his life. Reith had, in fact, been giving his mind to the renewal of the Charter since the end of 1933. He had hoped initially that another public enquiry could be avoided and that the necessary work could be done by a Cabinet committee. The Postmaster-General, Kingsley Wood, was unaccommodating, however, and Reith had come away from a meeting with him at the Post Office in June 1934 resigned to the idea that the plant was once more to be pulled up so that its roots could be examined.

The chairmanship of the committee of enquiry was offered to Lord Ullswater, a former Speaker of the House of Commons already in his eightieth year. 'He seemed quite friendly,' Reith wrote, 'but the whole affair is quite outside his comprehension, I am afraid.'[8] The membership was not fully in place until shortly before it began its deliberations in May 1935. Clement Attlee and Lord Selsdon had both served as Postmaster-General, and the Committee also contained a former Assistant PMG – Reith viewed it as a packed house. The appointment of Selsdon (Mitchell-Thomson as was) was particularly galling. Reith had not forgotten the events of 1926 and 1927: 'Everything that bothers us in the Charter and Licence he is responsible for,' he wrote to Sir Donald Banks, the Post Office's Director-General.[9]

His mood lightened briefly early in May when he heard that Oxford was to give him a DCL – 'It is of course the greatest academic honour in the world,' he wrote, 'and a very gratifying *imprimatur* from such a quarter on our work.'[10] At the encænia in June, Reith's fellow-recipients included the Duke of Alba, Baron Georg Franckenstein, who was the Austrian Minister in London, and Edouard Herriot, three times Prime Minister of France. His mother went with him to the ceremony; she was so excited that she could not eat her breakfast. Returning at midnight from a Christ Church gaudy, he found a note on her door asking him to wake her; Reith donned his scarlet robe and velvet hat and went in to her.[11]

His pique over the handling of Ullswater did nothing to impair the vigour with which he set about marshalling the Corporation's evidence. The BBC submitted a first brief memorandum early in May – fifteen crisp pages covering every aspect of its operations. No great powers of literary detection were required to establish the authorship of the introduction: the Corporation, it informed the Committee, 'had aimed at providing a service somewhat ahead of what the public would demand were it possible for such demand to be made articulate and intelligible'.[12]

Reith gave oral evidence three times in the first half of the month. The first occasion was friendly until 'the miserable cad Selsdon' posed some hostile questions about the BBC's suggestion that ministerial responsibility should pass from the Postmaster-General to the Lord President of the Council.[13] Reith returned for further sessions the following week, and found them most enjoyable, although he recorded that 'Attlee shows his hand very much as a left-winger and tried to put across trade-unionism for the BBC.'[14] His diary makes plain, however, how tired and jaded he was in that early summer of 1935. Dining with Lord Iliffe one night, he felt himself so strongly inclined to throw it all up that he occupied himself during dinner drafting a letter of resignation,[15] and an entry two days later indicates that the mood had not lifted: 'I feel that the BBC is such an all-absorbing monster – no home life and no time for any interest in wife or children, or in pursuits or interests of one's own.'[16]

It was not only Ullswater that was getting him down. There was also the question of the role of the BBC in the event of war. The previous summer, he had attended a meeting in the Cabinet Office with Sir Maurice Hankey, the Secretary to the Cabinet, and Sir John Dill, the Director of Military Operations and Intelligence. He had gone, he wrote, 'prepared to be somewhat bristly', but had found Dill 'so very civil and friendly' that this had not been necessary: 'Not only do they fully realise our importance in time of war or civil emergency, but they had also come to the conclusion that we should be properly represented and as a part of the family so to speak.'[17]

When Reith and Bridgeman, his new Chairman, called on the Postmaster-General a few months later, however, things assumed a somewhat different complexion. Kingsley Wood told them he had been appointed chairman of a committee to advise on the control and use of broadcasting in war, and when Reith asked whether the BBC was to be represented on it, the answer was no:

> We had a thoroughly unpleasant twenty minutes, with for the first time a definitely and openly hostile attitude on both sides . . . I indicated that if we were not put on the committee I did not feel disposed to give a bunch of colonels and civil servants the benefit of all our knowledge and experience.[18]

Further unpleasantness on this front was averted by a ministerial reshuffle. Kingsley Wood went off to be Minister of Health; Reith found the new Postmaster-General, Major Tryon, 'very civil', and was gratified to hear from him at their first meeting that 'the personal publicity which his predecessor had indulged in was not at all in his line.'[19] A month later he sent Tryon what he called 'our War Memorandum' – a long paper entitled *The Position of the BBC in War*. Reith expressed the view that the Board of Governors would not find it easy to exercise collective responsibility in time of war, and recommended that on the outbreak of hostilities it should be abolished. He also urged the importance of establishing beyond doubt the responsibility and reliability of the BBC's News Service – though he conceded that in practice 'accuracy could not amount to more than the nearest approach to absolute truth permitted by the overriding war conditions including censorship.'

Reith was not completely mollified on the question of contingency war plans until October 1935, when he had 'a very nice letter' from Hankey. It was marked 'Secret and Personal' and it invited him to join a sub-committee of the Committee of Imperial Defence which was to prepare plans for the establishment on the outbreak of war of a Ministry of Information.[20] At its first meeting a week later he had an insight into the distribution of muscle in Whitehall: 'I asked what had happened to the other silly committee which K. Wood had said it would not be proper for us to be on. The reply from Hankey was that it had been short-circuited.'[21]

Although Reith's health had been indifferent for much of 1935, he had subjected himself to a punishing social round. He dined privately with J. J. Astor ('I envied him the fine house he lives in'); he gave lunch to Koussevitsky at Claridge's ('He said there was no doubt about our orchestra being the best in Europe'); he attended a Royal Command concert at the Albert Hall ('To my indignation, we were taken to a box over the platform, so of course we immediately left'). In June there was a Buckingham Palace Ball ('How I hate myself in Court dress!'); in July, he was Lord Stanhope's guest at Chevening ('I did not feel a bit friendly towards Rudyard Kipling, and definitely disliked his wife'). In October he lunched with Dr Marie Stopes ('not nearly as alarming as I had expected'); in November, he entertained Marconi at the Carlton:

> I told him I had always admired Mussolini immensely and I had constantly hailed him as the outstanding example of accomplishing high democratic purpose by means which, though not democratic, were the only possible ones. I didn't say what I believe – namely that if I had been Foreign Secretary I could, I believe, have got Musso to stay his hand in Abyssinia . . .[22]

The new organisational structure devised after the failure of the Dawnay experiment came into operation at the beginning of October 1935. Over lunch a couple of weeks earlier, Reith had remarked to Mrs Hamilton that he was 'perhaps not the type to keep things going after they had been put more or less on an even keel',[23] and there are several references in the diary during that autumn to his not having enough to do: 'I am beginning to feel that I have organised and developed myself out of a job. This is very satisfactory in one sense but I don't know how I shall get on as I probably can't reconcile myself to slack days.'[24]

He had warned his senior colleagues that under the new dispensation he was likely to take much more interest in programmes than he used to, and they quickly discovered that he meant it: the Controller of Programmes received a 'strong memo' from him about jazz and about vulgarity in Variety programmes – 'Germany has banned hot jazz and I'm sorry we should be behind in dealing with this filthy product of modernity.'[25] Privately, however, he was thrashing about:

> I keep wondering what I'm to do. I should like to retire and live much more simply than we do (as of course we would certainly have to!). Living even in the style we do doesn't appeal to me at all, and actually we don't anything like get the value from it we should. There's so much that I want to write, but I don't think I'll ever do it if I'm in a job ... I have been such a ghastly mediocrity compared to what I wanted to be and could have been.[26]

He was still sleeping badly, and he noted in his diary that he hadn't had a night clear of bad dreams for months. Then, early in December, after a string of barium meals and X-rays, he was told he had an ulcer: 'I have only an "erosion" in the duodenum and quite a slight diet is required. I certainly was relieved and grateful.'[27]

On 12 December he received a note from his mother, enclosing a Churchman's Almanac and two small calendars. Concerned by the shakiness of the writing (she had used a pencil) and by her uncharacteristic brevity, he dashed off a reply – 'What is wrong? I do not think you would be ill if you were here.' The next evening his sister telephoned to say that Mrs Reith had suffered three heart attacks. 'I have dreaded this for years,' Reith wrote. 'Muriel and I think she would have lived for years yet if it hadn't been for Jean and her temperament and methods.' He was distraught; just how distraught emerges from a poignant diary entry:

> Mu was very kind to me. I broke down over it all, and I didn't know what to do, and I'm not well myself at all ... Miss Nash rang and thought I should go north tonight. This settled me. It was no reflection on Muriel that I had felt so bewildered all day and not knowing whether to go north or not ... I got Mansbridge to go out with a torch to pick any violets she could see. She made a little bunch – all buds.[28]

He arrived too late to deliver them. All he could do was kneel by the bedside: 'I kissed the dear forehead and put my ring to her lips.' He was consumed with remorse at what now seemed all his impatience and unkindness to her: 'These I could feel so terribly, so terribly, that I could almost lose my reason ...' It was the 3rd Sunday in Advent. 'O mater, mater dilectissima mea,' he wrote. 'This is your day now and for always.'[29]

On the day of the funeral, the Dumfries undertaker got the rough edge of his tongue: 'Gibson had assured me that he would do it all as well as Wylie and Co. of Glasgow. The hearse was a wretched affair with the name of a garage on the back . . .' His mother had left an envelope for him, and the note inside it bore a succession of dates and addresses going back to 1923: 'My very dear Johnnie, I know that you will do all you can to carry out my wishes expressed or unexpressed – be very kind and helpful to Jean – she has taken great care of me . . .' That did not prevent what he described as 'a trying scene' in their mother's bedroom on the day of the funeral. 'Oh mother,' he wrote in his diary, 'help us both'; he certainly needed it, especially after he discovered that Mrs Reith had left everything to Jean.

He received more than 400 messages of tribute and condolence. They included a telegram from Ramsay MacDonald: 'Deepest sympathy on death of your Mother my venerable and venerated friend.' There was a letter from Charlie, and after much hesitation, Reith sent a brief and formal acknowledge-ment – 'simply because I thought mother would like it. I added "Many Happy Returns".'[30] From his brother Archie, now rector of West Halton in Lincoln-shire, there came, less conventionally, a letter complaining about the promin-ence given to Reith in the obituaries:

. . . There is somewhere, possibly in moments withdrawn from secular affairs and thoughts of worldly advancement you may recognise it as from a religious source, a saying to effect: 'The first shall be last.' It is a saying you would do well to ponder in view of the Final Judgement – that is, of course, if you believe in God. When I recall Father's intense dislike of the Church of England and of the English Public Schools and your professed affection for him in his lifetime I wonder where the filial relationship so vaunted in the Press comes in as I think how, deserting your father's church you call in dignitaries of the Church of England to baptise your offspring and arrange for public school education? It might be well and only fair if you drew the attention of those whose duty it seems to be to advertise you in the press to the fact Mother had other sons – truly sons, though nobodies – and a daughter, who gave years of her life to devoted nursing of that Mother. Fair is fair, and I do not think either you or your wife have ever sacrificed yourselves either for Father or Mother as Jean has done. I have written remonstrating with the various editors concerned . . .[31]

'Incredibly beastly,' Reith wrote in his diary, 'the product of an unbalanced if not a diseased mind; and he a minister, too.'[32] Back in Beaconsfield on the Sunday before Christmas, he read a book on St Francis which his mother had given him in 1928, and went twice to the local Congregational church – 'I enjoyed it, and was very glad to spend Sunday as of old.'

Late on Christmas Eve, however, an advance copy of the Ullswater Report was delivered to him: 'It gives all we want but it is a wretched document with several silly and annoying things in it.' Years later he wrote in his memoirs that children of seven and three could not be expected to understand why, even at Christmas-time, their father had so little time or thought for them: 'They and their mother have much to forgive all down these years.'[33] What they had to forgive on this occasion was that he disappeared into his study at 10.15 on Christmas morning. By lunchtime on Boxing Day, the report had been filleted to his satisfaction: 'I went through it all critically, hypercritically; made a hundred notes where the wording might have been different; eliminated ninety and wrote a memorandum for the governors about the residual ten.'[34] By early afternoon the fruits of this explosion of misplaced zeal had been delivered to the Chairman of the Governors – by motor cycle.

In his memoirs, Reith wrote that in December 1935 he had been asked if he would like to be considered for the chairmanship of a 'vast organisation', which with associated directorships would have been worth about £20,000 a year. It was, in fact, Cable and Wireless. 'An attractive appointment,' he wrote; 'answer in the negative.' Now, before the end of the year, came a letter from Cosmo Lang, the Archbishop of Canterbury: 'I must not say more about your own dream of escape to the West Highlands to think and write. You have a great work in hand which is infinitely worth doing however tired you may sometimes be or annoyed with the obtuseness of those with whom you have to deal. God bless you in doing it.'[35] It was time to consider his annual audit:

A sad year has passed. I hope 1936 will be a happier and better one. Mother will help to make it so and I pray for health for all of us and freedom from cares and anxieties, and that I shall be very much kinder to dear Muriel.[36]

His hopes for the New Year were not immediately fulfilled. 'It is monstrous that the King hasn't given me a GCVO,' he wrote on 1 January, 'and I should also have had a KCMG for the South African Report.'[37] The King, as it happened, was dying (Reith had attended a meeting in the Cabinet Offices to consider 'arrangements for the demise of the crown' two months previously). On the evening of 20 January, the BBC's domestic and Empire transmitters were brought together and the chief announcer, Stuart Hibberd, intoned the famous bulletin: 'The King's life is moving peacefully to its close.' (The form of words had been drafted on the back of a menu card at Sandringham by the King's doctor, Lord Dawson of Penn.) It was repeated at fifteen-minute intervals. Just after midnight, Reith himself went to the microphone and read the final bulletin: 'Death came peacefully to the King at 11.55 p.m.'

The Prime Minister was to broadcast from 10 Downing Street the next evening, and asked Reith to go along. He dined alone with the Baldwins and noted that there was 'much talk and jesting', although to his embarrassment his top dental plate came loose and bothered him all evening. After dinner, Baldwin, as usual, invited comments on his script and Reith, as usual, was quick to respond: 'I made various suggestions and changed bits of the typed stuff – bringing in the moral authority, honour and dignity of the throne being enhanced.' Reith was well up on all the gossip surrounding the new King's attachment to Mrs Simpson; it was his idea that Baldwin should insert the phrase 'God guide him aright'.[38] The broadcast was done from the Cabinet Room at 9.30, Mrs Baldwin sitting in an armchair at the fire. 'It was good but nothing to what it might have been,' Reith wrote. 'I do wish he would prepare.'[39]

One measure of the complexity of John Reith's character was that his sense of humour found expression in so many different registers. He could be extremely charming – and extremely hurtful. He could at one extreme be extraordinarily childish, at the other grimly sardonic to a degree that was almost Swiftian. Small wonder that people frequently did not know how to take him. In those early months of 1936, with his mother's death and uncertainties about his future both weighing oppressively on his spirits, some of his acquaintances clearly found him very odd indeed. By Reith's own account, one who undoubtedly did was Lord Dawson of Penn. A few weeks after the death of the King, he bumped into Reith in the Athenaeum and enquired how he was. Reith noted their conversation in his diary and wrote it up years later in *Into the Wind*:

> Ill; a serious disease. His medical interest and sympathy were aroused; what was the disease? Accidie. 'Accidie?' he queried, his encyclopædic medical knowledge rumbling in his brain. He had to admit that he had never heard of it; probably wondered if he had missed something in a recent issue of the *Lancet*. I assured him it was a well-known disease; he ought to know it. He withdrew from the conversation chagrined; he said he would go and look it up. But perhaps it is more of a sin than a disease.[40]

Something that was most certainly impaired at the time was Reith's judgement. He continued to allow the Ullswater Report to exercise him to an unreasonable degree. When Mrs Hamilton described it as 'reptilian and contemptible' he thought he had found an ally: 'I was beginning to think I had got things out of proportion, but she is much more indignant than I.'[41] The Chairman and Vice-Chairman, on the other hand, both felt that his strictures were exaggerated, and they were undoubtedly right; they still, however, permitted him to put out a statement in the Board's name which took tedious issue with the Report on no less than fifteen specific points.

When the Report was published in March, the BBC got a very favourable press, but Reith took a jaundiced view of the decision to refer it to a special committee of the Cabinet. A month later, hearing that the Labour Party had chosen to initiate a Commons debate on the subject, he telephoned Attlee and offered to brief Lees-Smith, who had been Postmaster-General in the Labour government: 'I told Lady Bridgeman that it was distasteful to me and something improper to be scheming with the Labour opposition,' he wrote in his diary, 'but it is the Cabinet's fault.'[42] He could have saved himself the trouble. One of the most vehemently anti-BBC interventions in the debate came from Sir Stafford Cripps on the Labour benches.

Reith continued to expend excessive quantities of bile on Ullswater for the rest of the year – 'To the GPO at 11.00 with all the governors. PMG was accompanied by assistant PMG, ex-pawnbroker and looked it . . .'[43] The Cabinet committee was chaired by 'the little cad Wood', and when the government published a White Paper at the end of June it emerged that it had rejected two BBC proposals which Ullswater had incorporated in its recommendations – that the Lord President of the Council should have responsibility for broadcasting policy instead of the Postmaster-General, and that the BBC's monopoly should effectively be extended to cover wireless exchanges. (The BBC's real objection to rediffusion was that relay stations broadcasting commercial programmes threatened the Corporation's monopoly. In its evidence to Ullswater it had found a more sophisticated way of putting it: 'In their comparatively unregulated state the proprietors are in a position materially to damage the Corporation's programme policy by taking a large proportion of programme material from foreign sources . . . and so upsetting the balance upon which the Corporation's programmes are constructed.')

The Chairman remarked one day that he thought Reith was as angry with the Governors as with the Postmaster-General. He plainly felt that every man's hand was against him, and there is a diary entry at this time which indicates a state of distress bordering on the paranoid: 'I daily and more than once in the day ask God and Father and Mother to bring me through all the present critical and very trying times, when so many forces and individuals are doing their utmost to overthrow me in some way or other.'[44] The prospect of soldiering on at Broadcasting House was increasingly unattractive to him: 'Very disgusted with everything and feeling that I cannot stand things longer in the BBC,' he wrote.[45]

What he hoped for in his more realistic moments was that he would find some senior role in the government's defence preparations. Dawnay, who was now back in the Army, had sounded him out about his interest early in February, and in March there was an item in the Peterborough column in the *Daily Telegraph* which could only have been planted by someone friendly to Reith's interests:

I heard yesterday a new name in connection with plans for coordinating defence . . .

It is suggested in one quarter that should Sir Maurice Hankey be retained as Secretary to the Cabinet, Sir John Reith would be an admirable choice as Secretary of the Committee of Imperial Defence.

He has a strong personality and has had considerable experience of large-scale organisation at the BBC.

The advocates of this appointment contend that the fact that Sir John has had no previous career in Whitehall would be a positive advantage, since new men and new methods are required for the solution of the present problem.[46]

Nothing came of it. Sir Thomas Inskip joined the Cabinet as Minister for the Coordination of Defence later that month, and the functions of permanent secretary were exercised by Hankey. Reith was still a member of the CID sub-committee. At one of its meetings in February 1936 he had been offered the Director-Generalship of the Ministry of Information in the event of war, but declined: 'I have either greater or lesser ideas for myself for the next war if it comes.'[47]

The only thing that can be said with confidence about those ideas is that they were confused. He had not abandoned his dreams of a place in the Cabinet or a senior embassy, and these were fed from time to time by the odd remark dropped by an acquaintance, though none ever too odd to be rehearsed in the private confessional that was his diary. One day in the autumn of 1936 he lunched at Claridge's with Lady Reading, who had just returned from the United States and Canada:

> I said that I thought I might like to be British Ambassador at Washington. She said if I were, Anglo-American relations would be very different in a short time; but that she had another job in mind for me. 'What's that?' I enquired out of politeness. 'Dictator of England,' she replied![48]

Two days later, after spending some time with a couple of visitors from Johannesburg, he was off on a quite different tack – 'I really think I would like to be governor general of South Africa – not what I would choose, but what else is there?'[49] To this rhetorical question, the only sensible answer would have been 'not a great deal'. It was not simply that Reith, as he well knew, was not universally popular in Whitehall and at Westminster;[50] it was much more that given his views on the process of government, he was totally unfitted to play any part in it:

> I reflect sometimes on 'politics'. The whole horrid technique should be abolished. Government of a country is a matter of proper policy and proper administration, in other words efficiency. It need not be different in nature from the government of a business – only in degree. And the policy should be set according to the Christian ethic. I wonder if I shall be called to this. I do not wish to be a dictator, but I should appreciate this chance of magnifying Christ, and father and mother would be there to help me – but of course I am not fit for this.[51]

Perhaps it is not surprising that his diary at this time shows occasional flickers of interest in Moral Rearmament.

There was an abortive attempt to portray Reith on the London stage in 1936. *The Times* reported that 'a good-humoured burlesque' of the Director-General of the BBC had been banned by the Lord Chamberlain. The character was to have appeared in a revue called *All Wave* at the Duke of York's Theatre. When the script and description of characters were submitted to the Lord Chamberlain's office, the producer was asked whether the resemblance to Sir John Reith was intentional. 'We admitted frankly that it was,' said an assistant, 'and although we pointed out that the characterisation was in the best possible taste and in the friendliest spirit, the censor said no.'[52]

Reith had found brief relaxation during the summer by once again indulging his penchant for acting. The BBC Amateur Dramatic Society put on Ian Hay's *The Sport of Kings* at the Fortune Theatre. 'Disguised by a reddish wig, and looking uncommonly like Boris Karloff at his most sinister, Sir John Reith spent three hours last night in being a perfect butler,' wrote Margaret Lane in the *Daily Mail*. She pointed out that Bates was a Cockney in the text, but said that Reith had found the accent beyond him (he played it in broad Scots). 'Not true,' Reith wrote in the margin of the press cutting. 'My idea at second rehearsal.' One of his lines raised a big laugh: 'I have no desire, sir, to dictate to the staff, nor to interfere in their private lives.'

Relaxing on holiday was something he found much more difficult. 'I hate not to be with Muriel and the children for their five or six weeks at the seaside,' he wrote in July, 'and yet it's not a bit the sort of holiday I ought to have. It is dull and provincial.' He grumbled about Muriel's unwillingness to leave the children and go off somewhere with him alone. (Christopher was now eight and Marista four.) 'I expect I shall just stay at Thorpeness,' he wrote resignedly, and that is what he did: 'We play ping-pong usually each day, and have actually begun a fearful jigsaw of 2,200 pieces . . . People play tennis opposite whenever it is fine and everybody seems to know everybody else; but we know no-one.'

Early in the holiday, in a mood of gloomy introspection, his mind ran on ambition and the honours that had come his way – his Grand Cross and his Oxford DCL. 'Damnation,' he wrote:

> I wanted these things when I was so young that no one could have believed I had them. Have I ever been young? Not since the war anyhow. And the war didn't make me old. I made myself so by longing for the responsibilities and authorities of twice my age . . . A few years ago I still had ambitions. Now none, but an aftermath of ambitions which makes me dissatisfied and if anything big came now I should only feel that it was the sort of thing I ought to want to take because I once wanted it.

Winding down was always painfully slow. After a week he wrote that he was unable to think without horror of going back to the BBC at any time: 'How I wish this was my retirement to my own new-built home on Deeside or wherever it is to be.' Pipe-dreaming is a common enough holiday pastime, but as Reith sat in the warm sunshine on the Essex coast, he actually sketched out an architectural plan – 'quite different from anything previous, and excellent now. M liked it very much.'

Aldous Huxley's *Eyeless in Gaza* had just appeared, and he began to read it

– 'a filthy book, but of course very clever.' C. A. Lewis, who had been with him in the early Savoy Hill days, had also just gone into print with an account of his days with the Royal Flying Corps, and Reith's own ambitions in that direction were rekindled: 'This is what I've wanted to do for so long,' he wrote (though he added, 'I don't much like being thought to follow his example'). These literary stirrings did not make him an easier holiday companion. Driven from the beach one morning by 'filthy jazz and crooners' from a gramophone in the next-door hut, he plunged into work on his book; never easily diverted once he had set his hand to something, he continued his labours during the family's afternoon picnic.

By the third week his patience with the children was wearing thin: 'I have to keep on telling Christopher John to keep his mouth shut; it makes all the difference to his appearance, but it is very trying.' Although the weather was very hot, Reith, feeling energetic, set off one day to walk along the coast as far as Sizewell: 'M came, but was sorry later. So was Rufus.' (Rufus, an English setter, and Sandy, a Cairn terrier, had been Reith's birthday present to Muriel five years previously. Sandy had developed a tendency to yap, and Reith had decreed that he should no longer accompany them on holiday.)

Before the month was out he was writing to Lady Bridgeman telling her he was concerned about the future and floating the idea that he might succeed Norman as Chairman and have time for other things outside the BBC. When the time came to go home, he decided that there had been some happy times at Thorpeness and was filled with regrets: 'Of course, I haven't been half so nice as I wanted to be, but perhaps not *very* bad,' he wrote. 'Last ping-pong game and I let M win it!'[53]

Something that added greatly to the gaiety of the nation during 1936 was what became known as the case of the talking mongoose. When it first came to public attention in the early spring, it sounded like a silly-season story at the wrong time of year. By November, the hilarity had subsided and some damage had been done to the reputation both of the BBC and of Reith.

Richard Lambert, the editor of *The Listener*, did not confine his interests to broadcasting. He was, with the consent of the BBC, a Governor of the British Film Institute; he had also collaborated with one of his *Listener* contributors, a member of the Society for Psychical Research, in the writing of a small and not altogether serious book about a mongoose called Gef which was said to haunt a farmhouse in the Isle of Man. This unusual animal was said to be eighty-three years old and to come from India. As well as English, it apparently had a knowledge of Russian, Manx, Hebrew, Welsh, Hindustani, Flemish, Italian, and Arabic. It was clairvoyant; had an extensive knowledge of medical terms and of various makes of motor car; it was also something of an arithmetician and claimed to be the Holy Ghost.

The trouble arose when a man called Sir Cecil Levita made some disparaging remarks about Lambert. Levita's wife was a fellow-Governor of Lambert's at the BFI, and over lunch one day with Gladstone Murray, who had been Lambert's boss, Levita tapped his forehead and expressed doubts about his suitability to sit on the BFI board. Murray obligingly relayed this to Lambert, who promptly demanded an apology and withdrawal and threatened legal action.

Levita happened to know Norman – they had sat on the LCC together – and tried unsuccessfully to get him to lean on Lambert. Reith seems to have kept an uncharacteristically low profile in the early stages of the affair – something he later regretted. Lambert was summoned instead by Sir Stephen Tallents, his new chief, who presented him with a memorandum. He was urged to take a week's leave. (This was in early March.) He was told that if he persisted he 'would make the Corporation doubt his judgement' and would seem to be placing his own interests 'in priority to those of the Corporation'. Lambert, not unreasonably, heard in these words the disagreeable sound of the corporate knuckledusters being slipped on – his lawyers subsequently told him that the production of this document at the trial probably added a nought to the amount of his damages.

The matter got further out of hand in April during the Commons debate on Ullswater. Sir Stafford Cripps' strictures on the BBC included an attack on what he called Reith's dictatorial staff policies. He cited the Lambert case as an instance of 'autocratic control over private lives'. It was, he said, a grave scandal.[54] Lambert also found support in a less likely quarter. An elderly Tory peer, of extreme right-wing views, invited him to his house in the country. Lambert discovered that he was a generous subscriber to the conspiracy view of history and believed that an unholy alliance of freemasons, occultists and Bolsheviks was intent on the destruction of civilisation; the editor of *The Listener* came away with a loan of several hundred pounds towards his legal costs.

The Director-General did not see him until the second week in June. 'He was very nervous to start with,' Reith wrote, 'but I dealt gently with him . . . I see now it was a great mistake my not dealing with the matter from the beginning . . . If I had, I don't think any of this trouble would have arisen. He was very civil and respectful and said things about me which he obviously meant.'[55] When this is set beside Lambert's account, it is difficult to believe that they were describing the same occasion:

> He was more nervous than I had ever seen him before, smoking continually and rubbing his hands together incessantly. The interview lasted three and a quarter hours, the longest time I have ever spent in his company. It was entirely abortive . . . He talked on and on, hour after hour, using hypothetical and involved language. He suggested that the governors, who had originally desired to have my action stopped, now thought that it would be best for it to take place . . . But he went on to say that possibly he personally might hold a different opinion. Did I trust him in his personal capacity? If so, would I care for him to give me advice – still in this personal capacity – which might lead to a settlement . . . After three hours my head swam round, and I felt as if I was slowly being mesmerised into agreeing to a settlement,

without gaining any concrete assurance of where I would stand. It was most bizarre behaviour for a chief executive.[56]

The case of *Lambert v. Levita* began on 4 November. Lambert had retained Sir Patrick Hastings, one of the most celebrated advocates of the day. The defendant had paid into court the sum of £105 – his estimate of the possible damages if the case went against him. Two days later, after an hour's absence, the jury awarded damages of £7500. 'Quite amazing and monstrous,' Reith wrote in his diary. 'How rotten the jury system is.'[57] Norman, more alert to the potential damage to the Corporation, immediately wrote to the Prime Minister suggesting an official enquiry; because he had not been called, there had been no opportunity to correct erroneous impressions of his conduct as Chairman of the BBC.

Baldwin set up a three-man board. The chairman was Sir Josiah Stamp, chairman of the LMS Railway. His colleagues were Sir Maurice Gwyer, First Parliamentary Counsel to the Treasury, and Sir Findlater Stewart, Permanent Under Secretary of State for India (Hindustani had been one of the mongoose's languages, after all). The chairman told Lambert that it was not him that was on trial but the BBC, but that was not the impression he formed from the way the proceedings were conducted: 'The atmosphere of the inquiry was that of an informal court-martial, with Sir Maurice Gwyer playing the part of prosecuting counsel, Sir Findlater Stewart that of impartial assessor and Sir Josiah Stamp the genial role of "prisoner's friend".'

Their report was critical of both Lambert and the BBC. Of one particular memorandum which the former had addressed to Reith they wrote, 'we have not often read one more unfortunately phrased.' They exonerated the BBC of exerting undue pressure, but found that the formal warnings issued to Lambert had been expressed without sufficient regard to the strength of his case. It did not follow, they said, that because the Governors and officials of the BBC were honest in what they did, they were also wise.[58] The Committee felt that the BBC might with advantage study Civil Service practice: 'A tradition and a technique in dealing with staff matters has to be established in the controlling authorities: on the staff side a code to determine how far individual freedom of opinion and action are consistent with the paramount responsibilities of the Governing Body must be built up and accepted *ex animo* by the staff.'

This was not at all music to Reith's ears. A year earlier, when the Ullswater Committee had asked for a memorandum about staff associations, he had taken soundings. 'A very few thought it might be advisable as I would leave the BBC some day,' he wrote in *Into the Wind*. 'But I came on great opposition to the idea; they felt it would be taken as a reflection on myself.'[59] He decided to put the matter to what he called a free vote of all the staff, and he got exactly the sort of result he wanted – nine per cent voted in favour, ten per cent were doubtful, eighty-one per cent were against.

Not everybody accepted that the vote had been entirely free, however. Richard Lambert characterised it some years later as 'a fantastic plebiscite'.

He described how each department had met and voted under the chairmanship of its own official head:

> At some of these meetings the most deterrent warnings were given. The establishment of a Staff Association, it was said, would cause the individual to lose his existing right of personal appeal to the DG, or would lead to petty interference in his personal affairs by the Association's committee or officers. So it was no wonder that stenographers, engineers and clerks voted in their hundreds against the heretical proposal.[60]

Even if one aims off for a degree of animus on Lambert's part, the proceedings do seem to have had a whiff of guided democracy about them.

Broadcasting detained the Commons one last time in the week before Christmas 1936, and *Lambert v. Levita* and the Stamp Report both served as ammunition dumps for those who had the BBC in their sights. Lees-Smith, the former Labour PMG, was critical of the delay in setting up a staff association. 'If I talk to any employee of the Corporation,' he said, 'I am made to feel like a conspirator.' Lees-Smith did not believe in understatement: the BBC, he asserted, was 'an autocracy which has outgrown the original autocrat . . . a despotism in decay . . . the nearest thing in this country to Nazi government that can be shown.'[61]

'I do not remember to have read the debate,' Reith wrote loftily when he came to write his memoirs. His memory (refreshed by his scrapbook) served him better in the matter of favourable press comment at the time – one that particularly pleased him drew a comparison with Baldwin, and said that he might soon come to regard a crisis 'as merely evidence of his indestructibility'.[62] In fact the debate marked the end of one of the longest rearguard actions of his BBC career; in his summing-up, the Postmaster-General had announced that a staff association would be set up. Lambert, in his account, wrote that from this time on the BBC became more and more like an extramural department of Whitehall: 'fair, decorous and slow-moving – having lost much of its original *élan*, but also much of its original roughness'. It no longer bore to the same extent the stamp set upon it originally by its Director-General:

> In fact, Sir John Reith seemed largely to efface his personality from the administration, and to withdraw into a kind of seclusion. We saw and heard less of him than ever before; and it was common talk that he had had enough of broadcasting, and was contemplating transferring his energies to new fields of work.[63]

During December 1936, the public mind had been occupied with matters of greater moment than the way the BBC treated its staff. Reith's diary for that month is dominated by the events leading up to the abdication of Edward VIII. His close links with No. 10 meant that he knew as much as anyone about what was going on. Two days after the *Yorkshire Post* had brought the matter into the open, Sir Godfrey Thomas, the King's private secretary, asked if he might come urgently to Broadcasting House. Reith suggested he give his name as Smith: 'His call made me do what I had never done in office hours before. I got a whisky and soda sent up for him; he needed it.'[64]

Ostensibly, Thomas had come to ask how quickly a broadcast could be arranged from Windsor, but he sat for some time, talking compulsively. The King, he said, was quite 'insane' on the issue. He told Reith that he had been surprised, after all the stories about Mrs Simpson's familiarity with the King, at the propriety of her behaviour in public, where she curtsied and called him 'Sir': 'in fact if she hadn't had a husband and hadn't had a voice like a peahen, he wouldn't have seen anything wrong.'[65]

Reith brooded in his diary on the possible outcome: 'It might be the end of the monarchy; or we might have the King as a sort of dictator, or with Churchill as PM, which is presumably what that worthy is working for.'[66] But it is plain that he enjoyed every minute of his involvement in the unfolding drama. He was in and out of Downing Street to see Sir Horace Wilson, and the Prime Minister was in and out of Wilson's office from the Cabinet Room next door. Baldwin implored him not to keep on getting up: 'He said I seemed never to be going to stop. I said I was sorry about my length but I liked to show respect.'[67] The next night, at dinner, he was informed that he was wanted on both telephones – Buckingham Palace was on one line, the Home Secretary was on the other. Sir John Simon wanted to tell him that the new King 'was very particular that his brother should be called HRH Prince Edward'.[68]

The drive to Windsor took twenty-five minutes. Godfrey Thomas had established that the ex-King wanted him to be there by himself. 'Good evening, Reith,' Edward said. 'Very nice of you to make all these arrangements and come along yourself.' For a voice test, Reith got him to read from an evening paper; he turned the pages carefully to the racing news so that he couldn't read anything about himself. As Edward moved into place after the announcement, he kicked the leg of the table, and this was clearly heard over the air. Reith was asked later whether he had been expressing an opinion by slamming the door.

When he got home at 11.30, he found, much to his annoyance, that a neighbour, Lady McKinnon, and her daughter had been with Muriel to hear the broadcast, and had stayed on hoping to learn more: 'They soon realised that what they had heard on the wireless was all they were going to hear.' That Sunday, somewhat unusually, they went *en famille* to the small and ancient church at Hedgerley. Reith felt as if a cloud of depression had lifted: 'Poor Edward. But thank God he and his ways have passed and there is a new King and Queen ... It seemed as if the old England was back.'[69]

It was a provision of the second Charter and Licence which came into force at the beginning of 1937 that the Governors should be increased from five to seven. One of the newcomers was Dr J. J. Mallon, the Warden of Toynbee Hall. 'All I hear of Mallon is good,' Reith wrote. The other addition to the Board was the blind Conservative MP Ian Fraser, who had sat on the Crawford Committee and had now been knighted. This was not an appointment which Reith welcomed, and he was irritated by his performance at his first Board: 'Fraser is a damn nuisance,' he wrote. 'Being blind he is anxious to show he isn't prejudiced, and so bothers about things that they wouldn't. And I have always felt he was on the make, which is the thing we should avoid in Governors.'[70]

His relations with the other Governors remained friendly. The historian H. A. L. Fisher, who had joined the Board the previous year, invited him to Oxford for the weekend and clearly needed no lessons in ear-stroking: 'He pleased me by saying (quite incidentally) that I had read very widely and was "highly cultivated." I had sometimes wondered what a man like him would feel about me in this respect.'[71]

The Corporation was growing fast – the staff now numbered well over 3000 – and Reith was preoccupied in the early part of the year by the impending retirement of Charles Carpendale. The *Daily Mail* ran a campaign alleging pro-Republican bias in the reporting of the Spanish Civil War, which had broken out the previous summer. This prompted a number of questions in Parliament by what Reith called 'backbench nonentities'; he went the rounds of the parties at Westminster as he had done in 1934 and gave a good account of himself. He also discussed Spain with Sir Robert Vansittart, who was now the permanent head of the Foreign Office: 'Very apprehensive lest Franco (owing to *The Times* and BBC) feels unfriendly to this country and so is dominated by Italy and Germany . . . He would like us to get pro-Franco in our news and even stop using the word "insurgents".'[72]

Television was getting into its stride. Wimbledon was covered for the first time, and so was the Service of Remembrance at the Cenotaph; a recently escaped lunatic interrupted the two-minute silence, but the disturbance was not shown on the screen; worried listeners and viewers telephoned the BBC to ask about the unexplained noise.

The big broadcasting event of the year was the Coronation; it was broadcast worldwide by radio, and the return of the procession from Westminster Abbey was televised at Hyde Park Corner. Reith was much involved in the preparations. He had heard in January from the second secretary at the Palace that the King, because of his stammer, was more bothered about his Coronation Day broadcast than anything else, and wondered whether it would be possible to record. He was at the Palace twice in the week before the Coronation as the King went through the painful process of rehearsal with Lionel Logue; 'speech therapist' had obviously not yet established itself firmly in the language – Reith described him as 'the King's stutterer curer'.[73]

There was a period of several days when Muriel saw her chances of witnessing the great occasion receding; Reith thought the places they had been allocated in the Abbey were 'hopeless' and sharp words were exchanged. In the event they had an excellent view – 'but were of course not where we should have been if the blasted Earl Marshal's office hadn't muddled things. We were among nonentities.'[74]

Reith was invited to dine at Windsor the following April. After dinner, the King spoke to him of left-wing influences, and urged him to talk to the American ambassador, Joseph Kennedy, who believed American journalists got their information from the London School of Economics. Reith confirmed to the monarch that it was indeed 'a plague spot'. Shortly before Christmas, there was a letter to say that the King would like to give him the coveted GCVO for his work in connection with him, his father and his brother. 'Very nice,' Reith wrote, 'as not many have this decoration.'[75] For once, the Honours List escaped his anathema.

He had pressed on with his war book in the early months of 1937, and by early April he was revising the first typescript of it during his daily train journey to town.[76] He also gave his mind one last time to drafting a speech for Baldwin, who in the week after the Coronation was to address an audience of young people in the Albert Hall – one of his last engagements as Prime Minister before handing over to Chamberlain. When he listened to the speech on the night, Reith was only moderately flattered by the result: 'I thought he would have done better to stick to what I gave him but he went off on the brotherhood of man.'[77]

Reith's mood in that early summer of 1937 was relatively benign. He was invited to view the Coronation naval review from a P & O ship, and it was in the train on the way back from Tilbury that someone showed him a newspaper story headlined 'The fleet's lit up'. The BBC staff commentator had been Lieutenant Commander Thomas Woodrooffe, and it had quickly become plain to the audience that his former shipmates had entertained him all too royally before he went on the air; he was every bit as lit up as the fleet. The broadcast was scheduled to last for twenty minutes, but the announcer on duty (it was the young Harman Grisewood) faded it out after five – with some reluctance, he later confessed, because it was highly entertaining. The entire performance was, however, preserved on one of the immense and cumbersome Blattnerphone machines which represented the state of the art of recording in those days, and was played back at the subsequent enquiry. Reith took the affair seriously, but not as seriously as some of his lower-deck detractors maintained: 'Damnable, but funny, too,' he wrote in his diary.[78]

Something that gave him inordinate pleasure shortly after Spithead was an invitation to spend some days aboard the battleship *Barham*, the flagship of the Mediterranean fleet. After watching manoeuvres from the compass platform, the Captain asked if he would like to take charge: 'I thought he was joking. He wasn't. He told the Watch Officer to stand down and sent a message to the Flag Lieutenant: "Sir John Reith is in charge of the ship." I really think this was the most thrilling moment of my life.'[79] When he left, the Commander-in-Chief said they had never had a guest who took such an interest in things. It was, he wrote, 'a frightful come-down' to rejoin an ordinary P & O ship and to find himself once again among mere civilians. When they sailed out of Gibraltar, he trained his glasses on the *Barham* and saw that she had hoisted a signal: 'Of course I didn't know what it was, but did "RD" in semaphore from the upper deck in case they could see me.'[80]

In July the Reiths celebrated their sixteenth wedding anniversary. They exchanged rosebuds from the garden at breakfast, and in the evening went out to dinner at the Dorchester. He felt the time had come for decisions to be made about Christopher's education, but he did not find it easy. 'On Thursday night I asked God for guidance between prep schools,' he wrote. 'Finally, because I believe God gave me the sign I wanted, we decided on Sandroyd.'[81]

They went off on holiday to the seaside again, this time in Cornwall. Apart from the occasional swim, which he combined with a patrol along the beach to pick up litter, he spent almost all his time on his war book. One day the family urged him to take the afternoon off, and they set out for a picnic – Muriel at the wheel, Reith reading his manuscript in the passenger seat, the children, Rufus and a nurse in the back.[82] On the way to Bodmin they collided with a lorry at a crossroads. The off-side of the car was torn away. Marista's face was cut; Muriel escaped with a bruised arm, but was severely shocked. Reith himself came off worst with crushed ribs, an injury to his left leg, and a cut over one eye.

The local telephone exchange told him next morning that thirty-six newspapers had asked to be put through during the night. He was deluged with letters and telegrams – from the US ambassador, who was at sea on the *Empress of Britain*; from Beaverbrook, who was on holiday at Deauville; there was even what Reith rather archly described in his memoirs as 'a gracious enquiry from a Highland castle'. He found it difficult to sit down and stand up for a few days, but the X-rays showed that nothing was broken.

Back in London, he read a magazine article which said that to find a parallel to the BBC Charter and the powers granted to its Director-General, it was necessary to go back to the days of the English East India Company – 'Sir John Reith is as firmly seated in the saddle as Clive or Warren Hastings.'[83] He was also told by C. H. G. Millis, the BBC's new Vice-Chairman, that he had heard his name mentioned in connection with the chairmanship of Imperial Airways.[84]

The vacancy arose because of the recent death of Sir Eric Geddes, but this was not the first mention of Imperial Airways in Reith's diary. 'Imperial Airways is getting bigger and bigger,' he had noted six months previously, 'and must be an interesting show to run.'[85] It so happened that IA's managing director, G. E. Woods Humphery, was an old acquaintance – they had served their apprenticeship together in Glasgow, and Reith had been his best man when he got married during the war. He was sufficiently intrigued by the rumour retailed to him by Millis to seek Humphery out. They lunched together in the middle of October, but Reith seems to have pumped him without disclosing his interest: 'Can't make out whether he knows about my being run for Imperial Airways chairmanship. He said he wouldn't have a full-time chairman!'[86]

Reith was more than usually at odds with himself in the late months of 1937; the only thing from which he derived any pleasure was his election to the King's Bodyguard for Scotland (the Royal Company of Archers). He fretted throughout the autumn about his war book, which he had decided to call *Wearing Spurs*. He showed the manuscript to an enormous number of people, from newish friends like Mrs Hamilton to old ones like Jack Loudon. Sir Cyril Radcliffe liked it, but thought it should be amended. The Chairman found it 'intensely interesting', but felt that publication would do him a lot of harm; Iremonger, the Head of Religious Broadcasting, said he hadn't been able to put it down, but that it was 'the most complete personal revelation since the Confessions of Augustine.' Sir Warren Fisher took a similar view – he declared himself 'quite thrilled', but didn't think it 'seemly' that he should 'bare his soul' in public. Reith, curiously enough, took all this like a lamb. 'It is awfully disappointing that I can't do anything with it,' he wrote. 'It would have been such fun, and the money, too!'[87] He seems to have hoped that he might make anything up to £10,000 out of it.

At the office, he was intensely irritated by what he saw as the Board's slowness in coming to a decision about the deputy director-generalship, and the day before they actually made up their mind to appoint Cecil Graves he told the Chairman that he was 'fed up with the whole business and wanted to clear out at the end of the year'.[88] A month later, when he was off ill for a week or so, he actually offered his resignation in writing to the Chairman, and Norman read the letter out to the Board: 'Apparently everybody was very complimentary and didn't take the offer seriously!' That had possibly been part of the object of the exercise.[89]

Things were not exactly going swimmingly on the domestic front, either. 'How unsettled I feel,' he wrote in the middle of October. 'Of course it would have been far better if I had never been married.' An entry the next day conceded that he was not giving Muriel an easy time: 'She is awfully overburdened and we're in a bad patch.'[90] Muriel's burden was not made lighter by Reith's frequent attempts to adjust it for her: 'It seems impossible for M to keep her papers tidy. I spent some time sorting things out for her on Saturday, but they just get bunged back again.'[91] Muriel had an additional reason for being in low spirits. Although she was now forty-four, she had very much wanted to have another child and had consulted a number of specialists; now came confirmation of their advice that another pregnancy would be inadvisable.

Reith and Muriel had both been deeply upset when Christopher went away to school at the end of September. Reith sought relief from the ache of separation in writing letters. He was to bombard both his children in this way throughout their years at school and university; in the course of Christopher's first eleven weeks away from home, Reith wrote to him twenty-five times.

The guidance which he believed he had received about prep schools turned out to be defective in one respect; the Almighty had not seen fit to let him know that Charlie had also decided to send his son to Sandroyd. When Reith discovered this in the course of Christopher's first term, he was intensely indignant, and much against Muriel's wishes, decided that he must remonstrate. 'Dear Mr Bowser,' he wrote, 'We didn't know children of yours were at Sandroyd until after we had decided (on various recommendations) to send our son there. If any of us chance to meet there (or anywhere for that matter) can't it be as strangers.' Once launched, he could not restrain himself; another old sore must be fingered:

> There's something I meant to write about long since. I happened to see a copy of a letter from my late mother to you and your reply. Hers was written after receipt of a Christmas card of yours on the *motif* (apparently) of friendship. It seems to have vexed her; but she made some inaccurate, unfounded and indeed incredible remarks which even this late I want to correct. She wrote that I still (i) had photographs of you in evidence (ii) felt friendly towards you (iii) regretted the termination of an acquaintance (iv) desired its resumption. I can't imagine where she got any of this from. All nonsense. And there hadn't been a photograph nor any relic of you in my possession for years before that – e.g. even a ring was sold for its gold equivalent. In your reply you said you were 'ever on the look-out for a bridge' and that if you found it you 'trusted to have strength to cross it' – this apropos a renewal of acquaintance. Whatever does this mean – anything at all? No reply required – but you will (I hope) understand my desire not to have wrong ideas on this matter current.

Charlie disagreed about the necessity for a reply, but kept it brief. 'Dear Sir John Reith,' he wrote on 3 January, 'Your letter of Boxing Day has been duly received and is hereby acknowledged.' This did not give Reith a great deal to get his fingers into, but he did his best: 'He can't write even a formal letter without awkward phrases,' he wrote sourly in his diary. 'I don't myself regret that mine to him was posted except that it was doing what Muriel didn't want. Personally I don't mind how cruel mine was and I hated the idea of his thinking I still had any slightest feeling for him.'[92]

'I am not at all happy about our religious life,' he had written a few days earlier as he cast up his accounts for the old year. 'There is so little of it . . . God be with us and our beloved children, keeping us all well physically, morally and spiritually in 1938.' A diary entry seven days later made it seem that the first part of the petition might have been garbled in transmission:

> To my intense disgust and sorrow and almost fury, CJ was in bed with a temperature of 102 and Mara also stayed in bed. I was too sick to go along and see them even and was rather beastly with Muriel on leaving and on the telephone. It was particularly wretched with tomorrow Saturday and no one to play with in the garden.

'No one to play with in the garden.' Halfway through his forty-ninth year, the man echoed the cry of the child of eight, swinging on the inner gate of the manse at Rothiemurchus in the year of Queen Victoria's jubilee.

Reith had recently made the acquaintance of Montagu Norman, the Governor of the Bank of England and brother of the BBC Chairman, and shortly before Christmas Norman had suggested that the Reiths should join his wife and him on a five-week cruise to the West Indies – 'as a duty to yourself and as a pleasure to us,' he wrote. 'Please don't fail. The passengers are a dull lot – but orderly. Yours hopefully . . .' When Muriel said she could not be away from the children for so long, Norman turned up for tea at Harrias House on Christmas Eve and tried to get her to change her mind: 'He was very genial and rather amusing,' wrote Reith, 'but I can't help being rather frightened of him.' Muriel stuck to her guns, however, and on 19 January Reith sailed off with his new friends for Curaçao and the Panama Canal.

He was, as always, diligent in the matter of homework, although Froude's *The English in the West Indies*, which he took with him, had been published in 1888. When they got to Panama they were given the full treatment. They were taken the length of the canal by rail motor, motor launch and motor car, were shown the control tower, the spillway and both sets of locks, and were received by the Governor; Reith thought it was as interesting a day as he had ever spent – 'except for those in *Barham*'.

He spent quite a lot of time on board ship in the company of a young woman called Helen Moir, and continued to see a good deal of her on his return. He noted in his diary that there had been an argument with Muriel about what he rather obscurely termed 'my new attitude to life'. A few days later it was Muriel's birthday. He bought her a bunch of red tulips and a large box of fruits from Fortnum and Mason. They dined at the Savoy Grill and went afterwards to see Ian Hay's play *The Housemaster*, but the evening ended badly: 'M not in good form. Said in effect that the mildest and shortest bit of flirtation offset any and all good and kind things.'[93]

This did not divert him from what he described as his 'new policy of greater sociability', which found expression the following week in his giving Miss Moir dinner at Boulestin's. He had declined to go with Muriel to the sports day at Christopher's school – this was partly because he had come to dislike the Headmaster and his wife, but principally to avoid the Bowsers. He went off instead with Jo Stanley, who had now succeeded Miss Nash as his senior secretary; he shoe-horned himself into her Austin 7 and after lunching at a pub they spent the afternoon at Kew. 'Oh, how I wish Muriel would be happy,' he wrote the next day. 'She has no cause for worry or concern whatever.'

Muriel thought differently. They dined in town together on the eve of the anniversary of their engagement, and Reith presented her with eight carnations, but once again she was not, as he put it, 'in good form': 'I was sorry not to be going home with her and wanted to do so, but she said not.' Reith spent the evening of the anniversary itself in a party with Helen Moir; supper at 'an amusing place in Soho' and then on to the revue *Nine Sharp*. They were at the theatre together again early in May when he took her to the Apollo to see *Idiot's Delight*.

He stayed at his club quite a lot during the week at this time: 'I was hoping there would be a crisis on,' he wrote on the day after the German annexation of Austria, 'and that I should have to go up to Town.'[94] At home, his temper was even more uncertain than usual, and one day he stormed out over lunch because he thought the children were paying no attention to him. A curious diary entry early in May also indicates that he had broken the habit of a lifetime:

> Sir Ernest Benn to see me distressed to hear from one of his sons who had been at the Tuesday dinner that I had given up being teetotal. Very odd and touching it was. Sir John Reith 'away up there' had just come down a little nearer ordinary people.[95]

Carpendale had retired at the end of March, and Reith saw to it that he should be seen off in style. He had originally enquired whether they might fly a Vice-Admiral's flag or a White Ensign above Broadcasting House for the occasion. On the day, however, the Admiralty went one better and supplied two buglers and four bosun's mates. After 'Carps' had made his farewell speech, they filed on from either side of the Concert Hall platform. Everyone rose to their feet. Reith chronicled the ceremony with ecstatic economy: 'Attention – Admiral's call – first pipe as he stepped off the platform – second as he left the hall. It was simply terrific – most moving – almost too much so.'[96]

Very shortly now he would be piped over the side himself, with rather less ceremony but a good deal more drama. He had some satisfaction in those last few months from an extension of the BBC's activities that was to be as important for the country as for the Corporation. He had for several years been urging the need for broadcasting in foreign languages – 'the projection of England', as he called it; Whitehall was prodded into an awareness of the possibilities only when the Italians began to broadcast to the Arab world from Bari.

When Reith and Norman were belatedly invited to a Cabinet committee meeting in the autumn of 1937, they made a number of forceful representations – that if there was to be foreign language broadcasting it should be done by the BBC, and that as people could not be expected to listen to news alone, there would be a need for sustaining programmes. Most important of all, they argued that the BBC must have the same freedom *vis-à-vis* government departments as it enjoyed in its domestic service. Reith's view prevailed. It was his last assertion of moral authority as Director-General. Without his craggy insistence on the distinction between news and propaganda, the reputation of the BBC in the world could not have been the same. It was perhaps the richest of many legacies. He broadcast a message himself when the Arabic Service was inaugurated early in 1938; programmes in Spanish and Portuguese for Latin America came on the air two months later.

The case for broadcasting in foreign languages had been easier to make because of the perceived drift to war; that same drift contributed greatly to Reith's restlessness and anxiety about his own future. His conversations with Montagu Norman during their winter cruise had done nothing to make him less unsettled – Norman had told him one day that he should stay at the BBC 'only till my new job turned up', but no such job materialised. When he dined at Windsor in April, he told the King he wasn't busy and wanted to do something else: 'When he asked what, I said I imagined it would be what the PM or himself wanted.'[97]

Imperial Airways had been back in the news at the beginning of March, but not in a way that increased Reith's interest in being associated with the company. The report of a committee chaired by Lord Cadman was highly critical both of the board and of Woods Humphery's performance as managing director: 'I was less inclined than ever to go there,' Reith wrote.[98] He called on the Military Secretary at the War Office to enquire about joining the Territorial Army if war came, and was given a form to complete. A few days later, however, at a dinner given by the American ambassador, he bumped into Leslie Hore-Belisha, the Secretary of State for War, and this led to a proposition that interested him greatly. Hore-Belisha told him that the whole organisation of the War Office badly needed looking into – would Reith take it on? He would have him made a major-general for the purpose. Reith was greatly excited, although he professed a preference for doing it without rank or publicity: 'I could go to the BBC for an hour or so daily and work at the War Office all the rest of the day, and most of the night if required.'[99]

It came to nothing. Hore-Belisha had made the proposal off his own bat; when he went to see Warren Fisher to clear his lines with the Cabinet, he was asked to lay off and told that Reith was probably going to be offered the chairmanship of Imperial Airways. Reith heard this on 29 May. On 3 June, Gerald Beadle, then Controller, West Region, was up from Bristol for the day. He put his head round the Director-General's door and proposed lunch at his club. Reith said that would suit him very well as he had an early-afternoon appointment. In the taxi he told Beadle that he was going to see the Prime Minister. 'It looks like the sack,' he said.[100]

Reith's appointment was in fact with Sir Horace Wilson: 'It was as feared. The Prime Minister and the Secretary of State for Air had authorised him to "instruct me to go to Imperial Airways – tomorrow if possible".'[101] It would be a full-time job, and there would therefore be no question of outside interests. Reith wriggled, but was uncomfortably aware that he was not wriggling very effectively. After fifty minutes he played a last despairing card:

I managed to collect myself to the extent of telling Wilson that if the Prime Minister wished me to do this or that I would presumably, in such days as these, do it; but I must have it direct from him, especially as I was so utterly reluctant. There was the clue to the monstrous pusillanimity. If the Prime Minister wished me to do something I must do it. Atrophy of self-interest and intelligence.[102]

The conversation with Chamberlain was rather absurd: 'I asked if he was instructing me to go. He said he wasn't using that word. So I asked if he wanted me to go. He said again that was maybe too strong but that if I went he would be very glad.'[103] This exercise in logic-chopping lasted no more than four minutes. Reith then went off to the Athenaeum to discuss details with Sir George Beharrell, the Imperial Airways acting chairman.[104]

Andrew Boyle, in his 1972 biography of Reith, advanced the theory that he was eased out of the BBC by some sort of informal establishment conspiracy in which the Norman brothers, senior members of the Whitehall *mafia* like Warren Fisher and Horace Wilson, and the Prime Minister himself all played a part. Charles Stuart, when he published an edited version of the diaries three years later, found this 'more ingenious than convincing' and thought that no particular intrigue was necessary to persuade Reith to leave when he did. Asa Briggs, in the extended essay called *Governing the BBC*, which appeared in 1979, lent some support to Boyle's thesis, but found it 'a little more firm in its outlines' than the impressions he had derived from a day's talk with Norman a year or two before he died.

The evidence for anything coherent enough to be labelled a conspiracy is not strong. Certainly, there was more than one view about Reith in the Chamberlain Cabinet. A spirited exchange with Lord Halifax the year before about the Christian ethic had sent the future Foreign Secretary away convinced that he had been arguing with a Socialist; when Reith had sat beside the Prime Minister's wife at a Newspaper Society dinner a few weeks before his fateful interview, he had given her the benefit of his view on what he saw as 'the lack of aliveness of the Conservative Party', and this had got back to Chamberlain.[105]

Nor did all members of the BBC Board view their Director-General uncritically. Mary Agnes Hamilton admired him greatly, but it was an admiration laced with strong reserve: 'While I was at the BBC,' she wrote in her memoirs, 'we talked and thought too much about the DG and too little about broadcasting.' The accent of that talk, she said, was 'a fascinated mixture of affection and repulsion'. At once domineering and morbidly sensitive, he struck her as 'one of those who never grow up out of the illusion Carlyle denounced so passionately: the illusion that the universe is made for them.'[106] The concern of Ronald Norman, as Reith's Chairman, was of a more practical nature, as he explained years later to Andrew Boyle: 'A chief executive whose desk was cleared early enough each day to permit undue and sometimes pointless interferences with the work of senior subordinates can all too easily become an embarrassment. This, I'm afraid, was the case with Reith before the end of 1937.'[107]

That leaves us some way short of a well-documented conspiracy. It is in the nature of large organisations – BBC numbers were creeping up to the 4000 mark – that they generate gossip, and it is not unusual for this occasionally to become mildly regicidal in tone. Almost all of those who took part in these events are now dead. Their papers yield no pointers as to whether Reith slipped or was given a friendly push. What we know for certain is that he had been announcing for years that he was going to jump.

The manner of his going raises one point of great psychological interest, and it relates to Reith's attitude to authority. There is a clue to it in the curiously self-critical note which occurs in his account of his 3 June interview with Wilson; the reference to his own 'pusillanimity' has already been quoted, and there is another line in which he says that he was later 'unable to explain or excuse my own idiotic, incredible fatuity'.[108] Mary Agnes Hamilton could have helped him to see the reason: 'In many ways,' she wrote, 'he is an Ibsen character; one of those strong men who look stronger than they are.'[109] He had, in fact, flinched in this way before – his father, his Headmaster at Gresham's, the Brigadier in France in 1915 had all in their different ways represented a superior authority to whom Reith found himself making reluctant submission.

There was no objective reason why he should not have declined to do as the Prime Minister asked. He was the chief executive of a public corporation operating under royal charter. At least two people to whom he spoke in the days immediately after his meeting with Chamberlain clearly thought there was nothing inevitable about a move to Imperial Airways and did not believe that he had committed himself irrevocably. Hore-Belisha, for instance, telephoned three days later and told him that he had had two further meetings with Warren Fisher and the Prime Minister: 'His great idea turns out to be that I should be under-secretary of state – head of the War Office! (£3,500 vice £10,000). He said W. Fisher approved and that it would happen if I turned down Imperial Airways.'[110] The next evening he went to see Montagu Norman, who was ill with shingles: 'He was very keen on my going to IA but advised me to insist that Woods Humphery resign first and that the government support me in turning the concern into a public utility – also on proper conditions for myself.'[111] This makes it plain that things were very far from signed and sealed.

The next day he told the BBC board what had been going on. There were expressions of shock at the prospect of his departure; one member asked whether he might not be seconded, and there was also some discussion of the possibility of his succeeding Norman as chairman (Norman was already some months into his second extension of office, and the search for a successor had been under way for some time). That evening there was a belated farewell dinner to Carpendale at the Savoy, attended by past and present Governors and some senior members of staff: 'Melancholy and rather ironic that I should have to make a farewell speech when I myself was also departing,' Reith wrote. 'I spoke for about 15 minutes – with two or three veiled references to my own departure ... I quite enjoyed the whole affair but I don't know how I shall get through my own departure.'[112]

As things turned out, he got through it very badly. In a letter to Sir Stephen Tallents a month later, he wrote of being to some extent 'under a kind of anaesthetic'; his diary account of those weeks occasionally gives an impression of a man walking in his sleep. When he surveyed the period a decade later in his memoirs, he wrote that he had still been hoping against hope 'that a last minute salvation might come from some quarter – Hore-Belisha, BBC governors, the Almighty, anywhere'.[113] His talks with Beharrell were not going well; as he was to be an executive chairman, he could not understand the Imperial Airway's board's insistence that there was still a role for Woods Humphery. Nor did he like some of the suggestions he was hearing about who should succeed him at the BBC; there was support in Whitehall for the idea of a senior civil servant – the permanent head of the Post Office was suggested, and so was Vansittart.

His sense of timing was appalling. Having finally decided that he would write to the Prime Minister to ask whether he might retain a BBC connection, he left doing so until the day his appointment was announced in the House of Commons. He had gone – for the first time in his life – to Ascot; he noted that the letter to Chamberlain was signed 'in the place where people send notes to their bookies!' He recorded rather cryptically in his diary that his draft was amended by Warren Fisher – 'Not to move Norman, I a governor' – which suggests that he had originally proposed himself for Chairman. In its final form the letter simply asked that he be put on the Board. 'It would lessen the regret I feel,' he wrote, 'and would be, I think, acceptable to the staff and to governors.'[114]

During Ascot, Reith was the guest of Lord Camrose at Hackwood Park. Professional anxieties did not affect his appetite: 'At breakfast I took three helpings of chicken kedgeree and then bacon and egg . . .' For all his years close to the centre of things, he was still in many ways an innocent abroad: 'I suppose you've stipulated for preferment,' his host remarked. Reith did not know what he meant, never having heard the term used outside the Church: 'He said he supposed I was to have a peerage. That, evidently, is what other people would have done.'[115] When the Secretary for Air made his statement in the Commons, Aneurin Bevan enquired slyly whether Reith's appointment was due to his well-known opposition to trade unionism at Broadcasting House; once the news was out, he received something like a thousand letters and telegrams, and for a day or two he was buoyed up by what he called the 'tremendous splashings' in the newspapers.

Punch had a full-page cartoon entitled 'The Transit of Mercury'. 'Sir John can leave Broadcasting House,' intoned *The Times*, a little fruitily, 'with the knowledge that his pioneer work, now brought to maturity, has not to wait for the approval of posterity.' Atticus, in the *Sunday Times*, observed less fulsomely that he had been fortunate in his enemies: 'They attributed to him the brutality of Ivan the Terrible, the methods of the Ogpu and the general malevolence of Dr Miracle in *Tales of Hoffmann* . . . Like Lord Baldwin and many other eminent men, he has been deeply indebted to those who tried to destroy him.' In the *New Statesman*, Sagittarius had fun with the question of the succession:

> The BBC expects a sign. Rapt in a sacramental hush;
> The brooding Governors decline
> To rush.
> But to the millions listening in,

> Somehow a wordless rumour's broached
> That God has tentatively been
> Approached.

The Governors were, in fact, aiming rather lower than that, and not in directions of which Reith approved. He succeeded in scotching the idea of a civil servant, but failed to persuade them that Graves, whom he himself favoured, was the best man for the job. At the Board meeting on 22 June they asked him to sound out F. W. Ogilvie, the Vice-Chancellor of Belfast University, who had been recommended to Norman by the Warden of All Souls. In his diary he described the Board's proceedings as 'quite fatuous'; that evening he telephoned Warren Fisher and withdrew the suggestion that he should be made a Governor.

Most of the weekend was spent answering letters: 'The staff ones are too harrowing for anything,' he wrote, 'and I am feeling more miserable than ever.'[116] The next day he went to Wimbledon – again, a first visit – and sat in the Royal Box; in the evening he went to a party given by Carpendale at the London Casino – 'most elaborate cabaret and the most undressed I have ever seen.'[117]

It had never crossed Reith's mind that there could be more than one view about the wisdom of his being involved in the choice of his successor. He was due to leave on the last day of the month, and the Board was to continue its deliberations the day before that. In the early afternoon, an obviously embarrassed Norman came into his room and said that some of his colleagues felt they should decide the succession by themselves:

> He said he didn't approve, but there it was. I said I thought it was dreadful. I was already annoyed enough by having heard that some of them thought it wouldn't be fair to my successor if I were on the Board – what a reflection on the successor. He was in an awful stew and when I said I wouldn't come to the Board he begged me to. I would perhaps have done so but I got more upset and broke down later. He came in two or three times and it was awful.[118]

Towards the end of the afternoon, Muriel came in to collect him; they were going to a party to mark Lord Cromer's retirement as Lord Chamberlain: 'Unfortunately I realised that this was her last visit to my room where she had been so often – and this completely overcame me and I cried like anything.' Eventually he composed himself and they left. Muriel shook hands with the lift attendant, Kilroy, and with Plater, the chief commissionaire. As they left the building, Reith was once again in tears.

A further meeting with Norman the next afternoon did nothing to mend matters. Distress had now given way to anger. Reith told the Chairman that he had given instructions for his wireless and television sets to be recovered and for his name to be removed from the distribution list of BBC publications.

He vetoed any ideas of farewell presentations; the message that went out to section and departmental heads in London and the regions was, in fact, drafted by his secretary, something which the faithful Jo Stanley kept to herself for more than fifty years.[119]

He took Miss Stanley with him that night on one last strange BBC journey. Cecil Graves went too. They drove to Droitwich to the high-power transmitter, and there, at midnight, Reith closed down one of the big oil-engines – 'and it was not necessary,' he wrote, 'for the engineers to tell me what to do.' He also signed the visitors' book: 'J. C. W. Reith – late BBC.' The satisfaction derived from this rather stagey exit soon evaporated. He brooded incessantly over the events of recent days and felt impelled to write a stiff, reproachful letter to the Chairman; in a second letter he made a further ill-judged attempt to influence the Board in favour of Graves.[120]

Norman told him in reply that he had had a miserable weekend and regretted that he had not shown greater foresight and wisdom: 'But a lot of foresight was needed,' he concluded, 'and I doubt whether the lack of it was so serious an offence as to have drawn down on me the Dear *Mr* Norman in your "personal and private" note.' In the middle of July, Norman wrote again to say that the Governors had gone firm on Ogilvie; they had also resolved that 'having regard to the pre-eminent services rendered to the Corporation and to broadcasting generally by Sir John Reith', he should be awarded an *ex gratia* payment of £10,000:

> He said (I having raised this point with him) that he was sure I wasn't technically entitled to the year's security payment but he was sure that didn't now matter. It mattered a lot. I felt quite furious and if I had had the decision verbally I should most certainly have declined it, and with some asperity. Damn them . . .[121]

The following week he had a telephone call from Norman. A Governor had pointed out that his resignation had not been put in writing at any time – would he mind tidying up that small detail for them? This request roused Reith to a new pitch of rage and bitterness and the reply he dashed off was full of savage mockery:

> 'Just for tidyness' sake,' you said – well, my desire for tidyness is often thought to be exaggerated, but no tidyness issue seems to warrant any risk of an extension of the misunderstanding and unpleasantness which have gathered round my departure . . .
>
> Having tonight announced your betrothal to the attractive young suitor of your choice, were you fearful that the morning would find a dissolute old wretch on the doorstep claiming restitution of his rights?
>
> Now then –

I resign
I shall resign
I have resigned.
There it is – in all three tenses . . .
Is that sufficient? Or should there be another sentence renouncing all and every claim on the body and absolving it from liability of every sort? . . .[122]

The following day he entered his fiftieth year. He lived until he was eighty-one, but there would be nights even in extreme old age when he dreamt that he was back in Broadcasting House.

Eleven

ADRIFT

My loneliness and my unemployment – these two awful trials. I
asked to be made patient and to wait in trust.

JOHN REITH, DIARY, 6 October 1939

WHEN REITH was made a Doctor of Laws at Manchester in 1933, the
university orator compared him to Prospero: 'I present to you in the flesh, his
magic garment plucked from him, the chief of the magicians by whose agency
"this isle is full of noises, sounds, and sweet airs that give delight and hurt
not".' That magic garment had now been roughly plucked from him a second
time, and he had been banished from his island. There was little in his life in
exile that he found congenial.

Imperial Airways had its offices in an old furniture depository near Victoria.
On the second floor, down a narrow and dark passage, he found a door marked
'Managing Director'. He had inherited Woods Humphery's secretary. The first
piece of paper she handed him related to a £50 bonus; the second was a request
for authorisation of £238 to be spent on passengers' lavatories at Croydon.
This he declined to sign. 'It seemed I was to work in very low gear,' he wrote;
'I doubted my capacity.'

He took stock of his new kingdom, measuring it grimly against what he had
known. He was staggered to discover how much of a one-man band it had
been: 'When I left the BBC no one need have noticed it. Without Woods
Humphery, no one in Imperial Airways knew where they were.' Equally disturbing was the impression he formed of the philosophy of the board. It had
been articulated for him by one of Beharrell's colleagues, Sir Hardman Lever,
in a conversation before he joined, and it had made Reith realise that he was
moving into a world of alien values:

> He had been on a great many boards – and he had never let any shareholders
> down. So that had been the *passe-parole*. Not the importance of this national
> service; the extension of its routes and services; the linking of Empire; not
> that 'the globe-spread net of speeded intercourse' should be of British weav-
> ing; not that through the seven skies, as once upon the seven seas, British
> airlines, crews and craft might ply supreme. Shareholders. But neither would
> I let any shareholders down; I would let them out; and get good terms for
> them in their going.[1]

Reith, rather as Montgomery would do, set about tidying up the battlefield.
On his third day he started conversations about setting up some sort of executive

management committee on the lines of the BBC Control Board. Before the end of his first week he also served notice that it was his intention to bring about an amalgamation between Imperial and British Airways and establish a public corporation:

> There was an impropriety in subsidies at one end and high dividends at the other; here the dividend motive was, in my view, incompatible with the public service motive; here it seemed to have operated to the prejudice of efficiency and contentment.[2]

In August, he took a two-room flat at Marsham Court to serve as a base during the week. The rent was seven guineas a week, and the view from the bedroom window was of a slum tenement – 'very rackety and dirty'. He was plagued with lumbago and not at all in good form – 'frightfully lost and lonely and bewildered', he wrote. That did not prevent him from driving ahead with what he had set himself to do – his aim was to have a statute introduced by the end of the year.

He made an early call on Clive Pearson, the Chairman of British Airways, and after two hours felt he had overcome all his objections. On 15 August he dined with Montagu Norman: 'Told him what I was doing and of my plans for getting out of Imperial Airways.' (He had been there every bit of six weeks; Miss Stanley had just resigned from the BBC to join him.) Norman told him that somebody had to give 'blood and tears' to make Imperial Airways come right: 'I said that I didn't see why this should be me and that anyhow I would have done a great deal before I left.' By the end of the month he had informal approval for his plans from the Secretary of State for Air. The scheme went before the Cabinet in October, and an announcement was made in the Commons on 11 November 1938. He had got what he wanted in four months.

Thoughts of the BBC ran constantly in his mind, though with no thread of consistency. In September, for instance (this was shortly before Munich), he decided that he was not sorry to be out of it as it would be so subservient to the Ministry of Information in time of war. A few weeks later, meetings with Graves and Carpendale and their wives brought old memories flooding back: 'Feeling very uncompanionable and saying dreadful things about the BBC,' he wrote. 'I said I thought I would like to smash it.'[3] He approved of Chamberlain's visit to Hitler – 'just what I have been thinking all along I would do if I had been PM or even Foreign Secretary.' He responded sourly, however, to the acclaim which greeted Chamberlain on his return. 'It is all annoying to me as I have so much more ability than these PMs,' he wrote. 'I ought of course to have been dictator.'[4]

The emotions which the prospect of war aroused in him varied from one day to the next. At the end of September, he was suddenly filled with apprehension at the thought of Muriel and the children being exposed to any danger. A couple of days later it dawned on him that they might have 'East End refugees' billeted on them – 'This was a real and ghastly horror of war far exceeding any other!' The threat had been real enough for trenches to be dug in Hyde Park and for Reith to have arranged for a pantechnicon to evacuate supplies from the office to Pembrokeshire. When the threat appeared to be receding at the beginning of October, he reflected glumly that his chances of the sort of job he hankered after were probably receding with it.

He was eager to be clear of the executive functions of his chairmanship at Imperial Airways as soon as possible, and set about recruiting a managing director. Graves recommended Leslie Runciman, a director of Lloyds Bank and the LNER as well as of his family shipping business. He joined at the beginning of December, and he and Reith set about organising the new corporation; they never, Runciman said years later, exchanged a cross word.[5]

By the summer of 1939, after much discussion with the Air Ministry and the Treasury solicitors, a detailed plan was circulated for comment. Reith had drawn heavily on his BBC experience, and described the basic principle of organisation as 'functionalism tempered by a considerable measure of regionalism'. The work brought him little satisfaction. A June diary entry reads: 'I have been trying lately to forget, as it were, that ever I had a place of influence and dignity,' and again, four days later, he wrote:

> In very bad form – frightfully depressed about the future. Contributing to this is the new fact that Kingsley Wood is taking all the credit for the Airways Bill and also for the Civil Aviation Planning committee which was of course *entirely* my idea. Self-seeking little cad.[6]

His departure from the BBC had increased his already prodigious sensitivity to real or imagined slights. A chance remark by an acquaintance in the middle of April made him realise that for the first time in ten years he had not been invited to the Royal Academy dinner. He brooded for a week and then wrote to the Secretary to ask why. The reply offered apologies and expressed the hope that he would nonetheless come – an invitation which Reith promptly declined. It was only when the President himself – at that time Sir Edwin Lutyens – wrote him a note in his own hand that he was persuaded to change his mind. He did not particularly enjoy the evening: 'Spoke with various bigwigs whom I don't think bigwigs at all.'[7]

He had also been brooding over what Lord Camrose had said to him at Ascot in June about asking for a peerage, and he now wrote a convoluted and rambling letter to Sir Warren Fisher which concluded by doing just that: 'I should like to go to the House of Lords; and do not mind saying so. I should like the additional interest, and it would lead to others.'[8] It didn't work. Sir Samuel Hoare, the Home Secretary, thought highly of Reith and was keen to see him made Minister of Information in the event of war, but he told him that it was impossible for a minister of any importance to be anywhere but in the House of Commons.[9]

Shortly before he started at Imperial Airways, Reith had been cheered by a visit from Sir Donald Banks, now the permanent head of the Air Ministry: 'He wanted me to think of the job as a far bigger one than I had imagined it; sitting at the centre of a vast aerial communication system, almost as if I were chairman of all the English shipping companies. I hope he is right.'[10] Civil aviation was growing fast – the United States and the Netherlands had been particularly quick to see the opportunities, notably in the Pacific. Banks had dropped a seed in fertile soil; Reith began to see the British Overseas Airways Corporation (the title was of his devising) not as a purely United Kingdom concern but as a partnership owned and managed by all the members of the Commonwealth. He sounded out the Indian and Australian High Commissioners, the Finance Minister of New Zealand, the Prime Minister of Southern Rhodesia – all responded favourably. Kingsley Wood agreed to reserve seats on the new board for the Dominion governments. Reith began to feel that it was 'all rather exciting', but his dreams for such developments fell increasingly under the shadow of the approaching conflict with Germany.

When the Airways Corporation Bill received the Royal assent on 4 August, Reith was in mid-Atlantic on board the *Queen Mary*. The drama of his departure from the BBC the previous year had meant no summer holiday and a trip to Canada had been planned to make up to the children for their disappointment. He had made the arrangements in the spring, noting with satisfaction that Cunard had offered him 'the courtesy of the line' (i.e. a free passage) and minimum rates for the family,[11] but as the date of their departure approached excitement was mixed with apprehension; Vansittart had procured a diplomatic visa for him, but also advised him not to go.

They travelled in some style. Reith had a dressing room next to their double cabin, and the nurse, Worthington, shared another cabin with the children. They had with them three trunks, six suitcases, three hat boxes, one sack and six other pieces including Muriel's work box. During the voyage he read Bernard Pares' *The Fall of the Russian Monarchy*, and managed ('to my natural intense annoyance') to throw a £1 note overboard by mistake. 'I felt that I really wouldn't mind if we were not returning,' he wrote.[12]

They visited the New York World's Fair as the guests of the National Broadcasting Company, spent a week in Maine, and set off for the Canadian Pacific coast. On 25 August he received a coded message from Horace Wilson which told him that he should return home at once, with the family, by sea.

They went back to New York by way of Niagara and their baggage was put on board the *Aquitania*. Reith consulted the British ambassador in Washington, the consul-general in New York, the High Commissioner in Ottawa, the Air Ministry in London; almost till the moment of sailing, he could not master his indecision about whether to expose Muriel and the children to the risks of the crossing: 'I knelt down in the bathroom and asked God to show us the way,' he wrote. Shortly before six o'clock he kissed them goodbye and their luggage was put ashore.

On the table of his saloon there was a basket of red, white and blue flowers from Jeannie McCabe and her husband Tom: 'Red for courage,' she had written on the card, 'white for peace and blue for everlasting friendship.'[13]

That evening, as they headed out into the Atlantic, the ship was blacked out; they heard that children were being evacuated from London and that the fleet was at battle stations. At lunch on 3 September came the news that war had been declared: 'I did not write it now in capitals as on 29.7.14.'

No outgoing radio messages were permitted. Reith started on a never-ending letter to Muriel – thirty-nine pages by the second day. Before he was dressed the following morning, the second steward came to fit him with a gas mask. Reith thought this ridiculous, and could not see what this would do for him in a torpedo attack; the steward told him that the *Athenia*, ahead of them on the same course, had been torpedoed off Ireland that morning. He kept his watch 'on dear Muriel's time'; by the time he got to Southampton on 6 September, his letter to her had grown to 104 pages, and the air-mail postage came to fifteen shillings.

The first news he heard on landing was that Lord Macmillan had been made Minister of Information. He had a high regard for him, but doubted the wisdom of the appointment: 'No experience of the tortuous ways of propaganda, press procedure, public relations; and too much of a gentleman for what would here be entailed. No message from anyone; I was not required.'[14] Airways House was deserted, the staff all evacuated to Bristol; Runciman said he would welcome his company there, but that there was effectively nothing to do – civil aircraft production had stopped; civil aviation was totally subordinated to the military.

Reith, desolate without Muriel and the children, went home and waited for the telephone to ring: 'I wonder if I can stand this much longer,' he wrote a week after his return, '– inactivity and separation. Prayed and called on God for rescue.'[15] H. J. Wilson said that he had suggested him for both the Information and Supply Ministries, 'but "they" wouldn't have it.' Montagu Norman told him there was clearly some prejudice against him, but urged him to have patience and keep quiet.[16] It was not advice which Reith found easy to follow. One day he took himself off to Kensington Gardens:

> Walked round and round and up and down from 12.30 to 2.45 wrestling with myself. I tried to establish contact with God and with father and mother. I went over all my sins of past days asking forgiveness; thought so much of darling Muriel and of the so many unkindnesses to her ... My loneliness and my unemployment – these two awful trials. I asked to be made patient and to wait in trust.[17]

One offer of employment did come – the Lord Mayor of London telephoned to say he wished to see him on an important matter. Hope turned to indignation when he was asked if he would take charge of raising money for the Red Cross by the sale of jewellery and the like.

He decided to bring the family home for Christmas and then, against strong official advice, improved on the idea by resolving to go and fetch them. He sailed on a Dutch liner at the end of November; his fellow passengers included the Governor of British Guiana, a former Canadian Prime Minister, and several hundred Jewish, Polish and Czech refugees. He had retained his childish delight in unannounced arrivals. Jeannette McCabe installed him in her library at Swarthmore and ushered in Muriel and Marista with the words 'Here's the gentleman from Imperial Airways.' Reith wrote in his diary that it was the most tremendous thrill of his life: 'I wish the exultation and joy of this reunion might stay with us always.'[18]

He bought Muriel a diamond bracelet, visited old friends, dredged up from his elephantine memory an old debt: 'Telephoned Mrs Friend – this by way of expressing regret for not having asked their little girl of five or six to say the 23rd Psalm to me 22 years ago. Been on my conscience ever since.'[19] They sailed home on calm seas under blue skies; the voyage became eventful only when they anchored off Ramsgate and were taken ashore in an Admiralty drifter through waves that were eight feet high. For a few days the relief of their homecoming drove thoughts of his under-employment from his mind; they celebrated Christmas with the biggest tree they had ever had, its top just missing the ceiling.

On 3 January 1940 he went to Bristol. He and Runciman sat up half the night discussing the state of civil aviation, and they agreed that Reith should set off on a tour of all Imperial Airways routes; it was not at all what he would have imagined himself doing in wartime, he wrote in his memoirs, but a journey round the world would at least get him away from 'the exasperations of idleness'. When he got home and told Muriel, she did not like the idea one little bit, but her disquiet was short-lived. As he was dressing for dinner, the Prime Minister's secretary rang to say that Chamberlain would like to see him at eleven the next morning:

I knew what he wanted; it was not what I wanted. 'I am sure', said my wife, 'you should do whatever you are asked to do.' There it was again.

Twelve

MINISTER OF THE CROWN

> There is nothing so easy but that it becomes difficult when you do
> it with reluctance.
>
> TERENCE, *The Self-Tormentor*, 163 B.C.

WHAT REITH wanted was to be Secretary for War. What Chamberlain offered
him was the Ministry of Information. He did not accept it very graciously, and
his brief tenure – he was there for only four months – was undistinguished. If
he had known that until the day before their interview the Prime Minister had
intended to appoint somebody else, it is conceivable that he might not have
accepted at all.

The Ministry of Information had been the subject of much criticism both
in Parliament and in the press. Chamberlain told Reith that he wished to
replace Lord Macmillan so that the Minister should be able to defend himself
in the House of Commons, but that was only part of the story. Something that
had been exercising Chamberlain much more was the friction between the
Commander-in-Chief, Field Marshal Lord Gort, and his imaginative, assertive
but not universally popular Secretary of State for War, Leslie Hore-Belisha.
The Prime Minister had come to the view that the latter must be found another
place on the political chessboard. He had decided that if Hore-Belisha went
to the Ministry of Information, he could be replaced at the War Office by the
President of the Board of Trade, Oliver Stanley – 'the greatest contrast in
temperament I could find'.

He had already arranged to see Hore-Belisha when the idea was torpedoed by
the Foreign Office. The Foreign Secretary, Lord Halifax, stayed behind after
that morning's Cabinet meeting and entered strong objections: 'He thought',
Chamberlain wrote to his sister, 'it would have a bad effect on the neutrals both
because H.B. was a Jew and because his methods would let down British pres-
tige.'[1] Hore-Belisha was accordingly offered the Board of Trade (which would
be vacated by Stanley). He refused, and effectively passed out of political life.

Reith knew none of this when he met Chamberlain in the Cabinet Room
the following afternoon and was greeted, as he thought, 'without cordiality'.
He asked whether it was essential that he should enter the Commons. The
Prime Minister said that it was, but that this need have no political implication:
'I said there would need not to be since although I was more his way of thinking
than any other, I wouldn't be in line on all points. I was a Gladstonian Liberal
– as my father was.' Reith then tried to establish what precisely it was he was
being asked to do:

Of course I had remarked how different the job was now from what it was at the beginning of the war, but as to what support he would give for a reassembly of the hived off parts, he was very 'cautious' – rather shockingly so. Timid. He hoped there wouldn't be a 'brawl' about it. Obviously he isn't going to oppose Churchill or the Service Ministries. He thought I might look around and then tell him what I recommended. He would see what he could do. (Quite likely nothing.) Most unsatisfactory it all is.[2]

Reith asked whether the job carried War Cabinet rank and membership of the Privy Council; the answer to both questions was no. When Chamberlain spoke about the BBC, he appears, for the Prime Minister of a nation at war, to have carried devotion to the cult of the amateur and to the ideal of fair play to eccentric lengths: 'There was a great deal of dissatisfaction with it; but he hoped I would be gentle with it, and not use my knowledge of it to do things that another minister could not do.'[3]

Press reaction was favourable. To *The Times* the qualities most needed at the Ministry were grip and drive. Reith's appointment was an obvious, but also a courageous one, and suggested that the Prime Minister did not always choose his colleagues with an eye to peace and a quiet life. The paper's sole reservation was a perceptive one: 'The one doubt about him is whether his long enjoyment of an independent command may have rendered it difficult for him to collaborate in a team.'[4]

His first official call on a fellow-member of that team was on the First Lord of the Admiralty; it was with Winston Churchill and his staff that the Ministry of Information seemed to be most at odds – Charles Stuart, the editor of Reith's diaries, has a happy phrase about the 'secretive particularism' of the service departments. Churchill began in combative style by observing that he remembered Reith chiefly as the individual who had kept him from broadcasting about India when he wanted to; before he left, however, he was offering him friendly advice about the House of Commons.[5] It had been arranged that Reith should be returned unopposed for Southampton. The seat was held by Sir Charles Barrie as a National Liberal; he was to retire with a peerage, and Reith was to stand as a National candidate.

He was to be adopted in Southampton on 20 January, and he travelled down with Muriel in time for lunch. In the lobby of the Polygon Hotel there were several officers standing about in battle-dress. One of them said, 'Good luck, John.' It was Charlie. Reith took off his hat and after a slight hesitation they shook hands. Charlie was a captain in the Army Service Corps and was just going overseas. Reith's diary entry for that day makes plain that the encounter had upset him: 'I had been thinking of him a few minutes earlier when passing troops just leaving for the front and remembering how I had been so sad to leave him in the last war.'[6]

He was introduced into the Commons on 6 February. The *Daily Telegraph* noted that he took the customary three steps with an expression of 'granitic seriousness'; the *Glasgow Herald* reported that the ILP Member for the Gorbals

invited the new Minister to 'give us your signature tune.' Reith exchanged
some badinage in a Glasgow accent with Clydeside MPs on the benches opposite; then, as Churchill and others had advised him, he hurried off to try and
win friends and influence people in the smoking-room.

He had confessed to Churchill that he was feeling rather frightened of the
Commons. 'Not nearly so frightened as they are of you,' came the reply. In
fact he made a not unpromising start. Herbert Morrison told him he had a lot of
friends and some enemies. R. A. Butler, then a junior Foreign Office minister,
volunteered that he was getting on 'very nicely' in the House and that people
were surprised that he was so friendly. Baldwin wrote him a long letter full of
shrewd and friendly advice: 'Every House has its own distinctive character and
every man of position has to make good (or not!) in a new House. You come
in like a new boy at a new school and you must learn its ways . . .'

If he had things to learn in the Commons, he felt that there was one area
in which his new colleagues were in need of instruction. Something that irked
him greatly was the poor quality of the speeches – and broadcasts – made by his
fellow-ministers. This prompted the thought that he ought to be broadcasting
himself, possibly on a regular basis, but Chamberlain was not receptive to the
idea, and said that he should not do so more frequently than his colleagues.[7]
Reith did, however, make one broadcast in his ministerial capacity – to France.
'Sir John Par-r-r-le Bien le Fr-r-rançais,' said a headline in the *News Chronicle*.
He sounded, the report said, like an ambitious West End actor impersonating
a French university lecturer addressing English students.[8]

Summoned to a meeting of the War Cabinet for one item of business, he
was impressed by Chamberlain's chairmanship: 'Conducted in quite a smart
way so far as I saw, and really rather reminiscent of my old Control Boards.'[9]
After a month in office, however, he was already restive and despondent at the
sluggish response to his own efforts to construct a coherent information
machine: 'There was still in fact no information in the ministry except in its
title.' The Press and Censorship Bureau led a life of its own, and there was
no News Division of any sort. Propaganda in enemy countries was the preserve
of the Foreign Office; Postal and Telegraph Censorship was the responsibility
of the War Office; control over the BBC was minimal:

> What would Dr Goebbels have thought of it all? I had been hailed as his
> opposite number, counterpart, arch-enemy. How he would have laughed –
> if he could have believed a tenth of what was happening here.[10]

He received conflicting advice on how to proceed. Baldwin wrote across the
top of his letter of advice 'PATIENCE First Last and All the Way', and
Montagu Norman and Horace Wilson similarly urged him to work for what
he wanted 'on the quiet'. Leo Amery, on the other hand, not then in office
but still influential,[11] had more beguiling counsel to offer. Amery sat in the
chair each week when a small group of anti-Munich Conservatives met over
dinner. He told Reith that the government could not afford to have a row with

him, and advocated an 'ultimatum of requirements' – he was bound to get what he wanted. It was a siren voice which appealed powerfully to a man of Reith's temperament:

> Ultimatum procedure would have come easily and naturally to me; it would have been justified; it was hard to refrain. But, however ridiculous, even monstrous, the position, however little support the Prime Minister was giving me, I did not think it would be decent ... Though I did not realise it, it was a critical moment in my life. In deciding to try to gain the objective gradually and quietly, I made a wrong decision; wrong for the country, wrong for me.[12]

By Easter, for all that, he felt that he had achieved a degree of order and method in the Ministry, and the sort of executive control board he had been aiming at was in place – the model, once again, had been the BBC. At divisional controller level, he had assembled a formidable array of talent – the general division, which looked after broadcasts, films and advertising, was under Kenneth Clark; neutral propaganda became the responsibility of Ivone Kirkpatrick. There was also the future Lord Radcliffe, already a luminary of the bar, who had originally been brought in as deputy to Walter Monckton in the Press and Censorship Bureau; in his case, Reith's first impressions were not entirely favourable:

> As irritating an interview as I think ever I had with Radcliffe KC, said to be one of the cleverest men in England, though I should have said one of the stupidest, about Press Division work. His trouble was that he took the narrow legalistic view that it was just his job to interpret censorship regulations, not to argue with the Services about censorship and not to try to extract more news than they wanted to give. Also he thought an event wasn't news till the press got it! Weird and infuriating. Save us from lawyers.[13]

After the Easter break he was sent for by the Prime Minister. Chamberlain had had a weekend's fishing, and told Reith he was pleased not to be feeling stiff after it. He also said he thought propaganda was not being taken nearly seriously enough, and described the behaviour of some sections of the press as 'abominable'. This gave Reith his cue:

> I told him the Ministry of Information was now organised for its work; it could do an immense amount of good if it were given proper authority; otherwise he might as well abolish it. Was he so inclined? I could, if he liked, put up a plausible case for its abolition ... the Ministry was an exotic; it pertained to dictatorship; special measures had to be taken to graft it on to the democratic system; they had not been taken here. He said what he had never said before: 'I'm going to support you, Reith.' There it was, at last, though not how, nor to what extent.[14]

Reith had won the confidence of the Prime Minister too late. Just before Whitsun, in the course of a debate that was nominally about the withdrawal of British troops from Norway, Leo Amery rose from the Conservative benches and repeated Cromwell's words to the Long Parliament: 'You have sat too long here for any good you have been doing. Depart, I say, and let us have done with you. In the name of God, go.' In two days Churchill was busy forming his first Cabinet.

The names of the new War Cabinet were announced on Saturday evening, Churchill retaining the Defence Ministry for himself. The news that Reith had been replaced by Duff Cooper came through as he sat in Monckton's office at the Ministry the following evening: 'Things had run true to form to the very end,' he wrote sardonically in his memoirs; 'the Minister of Information was late with his final bit of information.' He shook hands with his staff, gathered up his things, and within minutes was on his way home to commune with his diary: 'How filthy this treatment – and what a *rotten* government.' He was not much mollified by the call he received later in the evening from the new Prime Minister's PPS:

> Brendan Bracken telephoned me at 10.15 or so to say I was 'to blame for all this' owing to my having no address in *Who's Who* and I would find a very nice letter from the PM at the Athenæum. Bracken said the PM thought very highly of me and had one if not two jobs to suggest. He said there certainly was no suggestion that I hadn't done my job very well, nor that I wouldn't be asked to do another at once. What to believe? A dirty business every way.[15]

Churchill sent him to Transport – a disappointment, as he had thought it might be Shipping or the new Ministry of Aircraft Production, which went to Beaverbrook. Reith spent the next morning with his predecessor, Euan Wallace, who gave him the unwelcome news that he had not found himself particularly busy – the railways more or less ran themselves through the Railway Executive Committee, and there were Port Emergency Committees to deal with anything that came up in the docks. Early conversations with his new officials reinforced this: 'Explicitly, though politely, I was assured that all was very well; implicitly, still more politely, asked not to interfere. Magnificent, if incredible.'[16]

The manner of his removal from the Ministry of Information had been a blow to his self-esteem, but it had also shaken his self-confidence. His attitude to the new Prime Minister was ambivalent. He frequently expressed his dislike and mistrust of him, but there was also an unmistakable fellow-feeling, even an attraction: 'I wanted a job,' he wrote in his memoirs, 'that would bring me into direct and constant touch with Churchill. That was how I felt, or was prepared to feel, towards him when he became Prime Minister.'[17]

The conviction grew on him that he had been moved to a backwater. He heard the news that the British Expeditionary Force was to be evacuated from

France from his officials: 'Very odd, I thought, that this information should reach me from below.'[18] He was no better pleased, however, by what was offered from above. The following week, he attended one of Churchill's meetings for ministers:

> Nothing to it and I disliked it very much. Sycophantic remarks by so many of them and Beaverbrook preening himself and being flattered for increase of production for which he is probably not at all responsible. Oh, so lonely, so jealous and so unhappy.[19]

The following day this sour despondency betrayed him into absenting himself from one of the most memorable and stirring occasions in British Parliamentary history: 'Wish I had had to make the sort of speech Churchill did yesterday,' he wrote. 'I felt I couldn't go to hear it. Jealousy. I *could* speak.' He could perhaps have matched the Prime Minister's mood of sombre defiance, but only a man of Reith's quite uncommon conceit could dream of rivalling the mastery of the Commons which Churchill displayed on that June afternoon in 1940.

During the preceding eight days, more than 330,000 British and Allied troops had been landed in England from Dunkirk. 'We must be very careful not to assign to this deliverance the attributes of a victory,' Churchill told the House. 'Wars are not won by evacuation.' In public and later in secret session, he articulated the resolve of the British people to fight on. The famous closing passage of the speech proved, as he later wrote, a 'timely and important factor' in United States decisions about entering the war: 'We shall fight on the beaches, we shall fight on the landing grounds, we shall fight in the fields and in the streets . . .' They were words to set beside those which Shakespeare's Henry V spoke before Agincourt. John Reith, sulkily excluding himself from the nation's finest hour, appears inescapably as a small man in the presence of great events.

He was also a man in a state of acute mental distress. A diary entry in the middle of June shows someone very close to the edge:

> When I think how badly, very badly, I have been treated by Chamberlain and then by Churchill and how unhappy I am in my present state, I think I would despair if I didn't keep always in mind that the Lord God omnipotent reigneth.[20]

The following day (the day, as it happened, on which France capitulated) his mood was calmer: 'I ruminated a good deal today on the future. I was wondering whether God wouldn't show his hand now in some unmistakable way. I believe he may.'

He was anxious about the family. The McCabes sent a cable saying they would love to have the children, but Reith was scornful of those who packed their children off to the safety of the United States (he noted that they included Lord Louis Mountbatten, Duff Cooper, and the editor of the *Daily Express*).[21]

Evacuation at home was a different matter, however, and one day over lunch he sounded out the Bishop of Lichfield about finding some quiet country rectory in Shropshire where Muriel and Marista might go as paying guests.[22] He came more and more to dislike leaving home each day to travel to London; every morning, in the tunnel before Marylebone, he recited to himself the Lord's Prayer and the 23rd Psalm. It didn't do much good. 'It is dreadfully difficult to trust in God as I should,' he wrote on 5 August. 'I feel all deteriorated.'

That deterioration was nowhere more apparent than in the near-atrophy of his much-vaunted management skills. Soon after his change of ministry, he noted that he was 'greatly missing the nice fellows from the other place'. The senior officials at the Ministry of Transport – the Permanent Secretary was Sir Leonard Browett – must have found their new political master distinctly odd: 'I told Browett the other day that I disagreed with his organization but that I did not want to say in what way as it was obvious he didn't expect me to interest myself in it.'[23]

One of the few people with whom he felt an affinity was the Chief of the Imperial General Staff, Sir John Dill. This was partly because Dill shared his low opinion of Churchill, but Reith discovered that there were other matters on which their views coincided. One of his few pleasures at this time was his regular visits to Dill's flat in Westminster Gardens for dinner, where the conversation seems occasionally to have taken a distinctly Falangist turn:

> Much talk about leadership. Dill doesn't think success will come to us till we have our stand on moral issues and our outlook and intentions clear. Of course this is what I feel strongly, and always have ... He finds the PM very trying of course. I told him that if there were anything of a dictatorship here it would be with Army support and that would be his look-out.[24]

He wrote later in his memoirs that with the fall of France 'there came an increasing sense of things to be done, but I was nowhere near the planning or the doing.' His mind turned instead to the future:

> Not having enough to do in helping to win the war, and feeling sure that sooner or later some form of nationalisation would be imposed on railways and other means of transport, I put my mind to work on that subject. I was accused later on by one of the railway chairmen of 'trying to nationalise us behind our backs'.[25]

Attlee, then Lord Privy Seal, liked the memorandum he produced, and reported that the Prime Minister had made encouraging noises. He had further conversations with several Labour members of the Coalition, including Herbert Morrison, and produced a paper for presentation to the Cabinet in early September: 'To a meeting with Attlee and Greenwood at 5.00. Went over points for me to make about railway public ownership next day at the Cabinet. They clearly want me to take all the responsibility and odium.' The next morning, however, before he was called to the Cabinet, he had another meeting:

> Saw Beaverbrook in his garden (telephone and bell-push being carried about after him) 10.00 till 11.00. Weird the influence he now has – deputy PM of course. He said he recommended me for political promotion and was very anxious that I shouldn't spoil myself by the public ownership business, which, of course, I know to be the right course.[26]

He emerged from the Cabinet meeting dissatisfied with his performance: 'I had to hedge, to my disgust, between Attlee and Beaverbrook and so was indefinite in recommendation.' The occasion still rankled the following day: 'Feeling very disgusted with the Churchill-Beaverbrook regime and their atti-tude to government ownership,' he wrote. 'Wondered if I might not resign on this – a convenient peg.'[27]

He was also irritated to be at the receiving end of a number of Churchill's celebrated Personal Minutes with their red labels enjoining 'Action This Day'. 'With me anyway this emblazoning was unnecessary,' snorted Reith; 'A junior should not have to be stimulated or frightened into answering quickly a note from the boss.' His officials were stimulated into producing a draft reply to the first of these missives (it was about bottlenecks in the ports) in an hour and a half, but they discovered that their Minister had beaten them to it with a composition of his own. It was a third of the length, and consisted of a number of staccato, numbered sentences: 'The style was new to them and they thought it abrupt; but they had no criticism of the content.'[28]

Early in September, the Germans began their aerial bombardment of London. Buckingham Palace was dive-bombed, and Reith's own ministry was set on fire. He made frequent excursions to view the devastation, but appears to have viewed the plight of the victims with some detachment: 'Visited Holborn Tube,' he noted on 20 September. 'Ghastly crowd of refugees, mostly horrid Jews it seemed. Five thousand there they reckoned.'

As the month wore on, Reith began to feel that his stock with the Prime Minister might be rising. The Germans were expected to invade within days. Bomb damage to the docks and the railways was severe, and Reith made a case for having a number of bomb disposal squads under his own command. Anderson, the Home Secretary, and Eden, now Secretary for War, both opposed the idea, but Churchill ruled that Reith's request was a reasonable one, and telephoned him at home at midnight to ask whether the matter had been satisfactorily resolved. 'This is your war now, you know,' the Prime Minis-ter said, and added that he had great confidence in him. This revived Reith's hopes that Churchill, possibly influenced by Beaverbrook, intended to offer him a bigger job: 'I wished he would; and that he would ring me again or summon me at midnight – every midnight.'[29]

Although he had been in the Commons for nine months, he had not yet spoken in the Chamber. In the middle of September the House went into secret session for a debate on transport. The opening speech was made by Emmanuel Shinwell, and Reith had to reply. Maiden speeches are not often made from the front bench. He spoke for forty-five minutes: 'Bloody good,' said Margesson, the Tory chief whip, when he sat down, and Shinwell, not known for such courtesies, tossed a note of congratulation across the floor.

His first speech in the Commons was also his last. Two weeks later, Churchill called him into the Cabinet Room and told him he wanted him to move to the Ministry of Works – and go to the House of Lords:

> I told him I didn't think much of it and that I thought I might have stayed in the House of Commons after the war. I said I wanted a Service ministry and he replied that the war might go on for a long time, with Japan and America in. I said I had wanted to be more in touch with him and that he didn't really like me.[30]

Churchill bridled at this; he had, he said, a great admiration and respect for Reith's qualities, and repeated that the war might go on for a long time yet:

> I rose; said I was not happy about either the job or the Lords but supposed I ought to take both as an order. That suited him. 'Yes,' he said, getting up and shaking me warmly by the hand, 'I command you.' I wondered if I would ever walk out of that historic room with any sense of elation; with any real satisfaction in what had been put on me; taxed to the limits of capacity and endurance.[31]

He was sworn as First Commissioner of Works and Public Buildings at a Privy Council on 4 October. 'I hope you like your new job,' Beaverbrook wrote. 'You can become the building arbitrator of Great Britain.'[32] The *Daily Express* dutifully echoed its master's voice: 'Peer-to-be is Minister of Britain-to-be'; another paper expressed the hope that he would not rebuild London in the style of Broadcasting House. Beaverbrook also said in his letter that he would have a big administrative job before long, and Reith, a consistent ringer for the dog in the fable, wrote in his diary, 'Maybe he was referring to India.'

Baron Reith now, but Baron Reith of where? He played with a number of place-names in and around his birthplace – Carron? Invercarron? Carron Water? Fetteresso? Wisely, he took local advice: 'Spoke to a Stonehaven doctor about Kincardineshire topography; he said the Carron Water wasn't a salubrious stream . . .'[33] Muriel didn't like Fetteresso, and Arduthie, which was another possibility, was also ruled out – he felt it would be mispronounced, and he also discovered that there was an estate of that name – 'which would scarcely do as I don't own it'. On 7 October, therefore – the twenty-fifth anniversary of what he frequently described in his diary as 'the day I was killed in 1915' – he visited Garter King of Arms and settled for Lord Reith of Stonehaven. That was how he was announced when he was received by the

King a fortnight later, and he thought it 'really sounded rather well.' It was not the only note of satisfaction in his diary that day: 'Muriel wrote The Honble C. J. Reith on a letter and parcel today!'[34]

One of the most thoughtful comments on his appointment came from Clough Williams-Ellis, in an article in *The Spectator*. He quoted D. H. Lawrence: 'The English may have great spiritual qualities, but as builders of splendid cities, they are more ignominious than rabbits.' Hitler, he wrote, had clumsily and painfully inured them to large-scale destruction; it was now for Reith to show what dynamite could do when selectively applied in the service of town planning, civic regeneration, and human well-being generally:

> The last great chance for exchanging the haphazard sprawl of London for something fine, gracious and efficient was, of course, given by the Great Fire, a chance notoriously and disastrously missed. If Sir John's immediate function is no more than to act as a sort of burly commissionaire, restraining the queue of property-owners from pushing past him to set about rebuilding incontinently on their shattered sites, that is a very necessary task that will need all his relentless strength of purpose.[35]

For the moment, however, more immediate matters clamoured for attention. He was being chivvied by Beaverbrook to find bomb-proof strongholds for Churchill and other ministers: 'We crashed about looking at steel-framed buildings, to the great perturbation of their inhabitants – New Scotland Yard and Vine Street police station included. Broadcasting House only just escaped.'[36] An alternative meeting-place for Parliament had to be provided in Church House, Westminster; the job was completed in three weeks – 'a triumph of hustle', Reith called it, and so it was. And there were endless meetings (and some confrontations) about cement supplies: 'One of Churchill's women snoopers was over yesterday for two hours badgering Beaver and Wolmer about cement – his Gestapo. Disgusting it all is.'[37] (These ladies were less sinister than Reith makes them sound – they were members of the statistical department run for the Prime Minister by Lord Cherwell.)

There was also the small matter of his terms of reference. Much ink had already been spilt over these before Reith's arrival. When he saw what was proposed he had their announcement deferred, principally because there was nothing in them about post-war planning and reconstruction. There followed several weeks of argument, mainly with the Ministry of Health. The upshot was a form of words, drafted by Attlee, which charged the new ministry with responsibility for 'consulting the departments and organisations concerned with a view to reporting to the Cabinet the appropriate methods and machinery for dealing with the issues involved'. The Circumlocution Office could not have done better – though Reith wrote in his diary at the time that the formula was 'pretty comprehensive' and that he felt pleased about it. When he published his memoirs nine years later, however, he had the benefit of hindsight: 'Airways, Information, Transport, Works – all the same sort of tale.'

When he took his seat in the Lords on 6 November, his sponsors were Lord Gainford and Lord Wigram. A week later he attended Neville Chamberlain's funeral: 'I thought Churchill and Attlee anyhow among the pall bearers couldn't be feeling very proud of themselves.' He had seen Chamberlain for the last time early in September when he returned briefly after illness:

He was in the chair at a meeting, sitting in the big bow window of the Lord President's room in the fragile Treasury building, glass half-way round him, when his secretary came in to announce imminent danger. Chamberlain thanked him; carried on with the meeting. The secretary was agitated; asked if he would not adjourn downstairs. No, he said, not unless anyone there so desired. The secretary began to draw the heavy curtains across the window; was checked. 'Let's have the daylight while it's there.'[38]

Early in December, the death of Lord Lothian, the ambassador to Washington, affected him rather differently. 'I would like this post more than I can say,' Reith wrote. 'Laid my desire before the Lord.' He also, after some hesitation, confided in Beaverbrook, and in R. A. Butler, who said he would mention his interest to Halifax, the Foreign Secretary. He thought about little else for the next ten days: 'Trying to be in touch with God about this USA business,' he wrote on 18 December. 'I ought not to ask to go, but having said I want to go, ask to be reconciled to God's will.'

It was an improbable ambition. Churchill felt that Britain's relations with the United States at that time called for an ambassador who was 'an outstanding national figure and a statesman versed in every aspect of world politics'.[39] With Roosevelt's approval, he offered it first to Lloyd George, 'our foremost citizen'. When he declined on grounds of age (he was now seventy-seven), Churchill turned to his Foreign Secretary: 'When I made him this proposal, which was certainly not a personal advancement, he contented himself with saying in a simple and dignified manner that he would serve wherever he was thought to be most useful.'

Reith seems to have mastered this disappointment fairly quickly, and in the early months of 1941 buckled down to his work in the Ministry with something approaching enthusiasm. In January he received a deputation from Coventry, led by the Lord Mayor. 'I did not know what authority I had,' he wrote in his memoirs, 'but I would not allow this high-powered civic deputation to return to their battered city with a tale of Whitehall gruntings and wafflings, telling their wives it was all waste of time and that they had gotten nowhere.' When their formal business was concluded he took them to lunch in a private room at Claridge's. He told them that if he was in their position he would plan boldly and comprehensively and that he would not at that stage worry about finance or local boundaries. The Mayor said that in twenty years of coming on deputations to Whitehall he had never received such treatment; Reith sent them home each carrying two or three daffodils from the lunch table. 'After all,' he wrote, 'the daffodils "come before the swallow dares, and take the wind of March with beauty." They were meant to be symbolic of a city's resurrection.'[40]

He began to find the Upper House not uncongenial, and towards the end of the month he spoke again, this time on the problems of physical reconstruction. He said that he had been authorised to make three assumptions: that the principle of planning would be accepted as national policy and that a central authority would be needed; that a positive policy would be worked out for agriculture, industrial development and transport; and that some public services 'would require treatment' on a national basis, some regionally, and some locally. This made him very much the flavour of the month with those professionally concerned with planning and architecture; *The Architects' Journal* said that his speech was probably the most inspiring message that had ever reached architects and town planners from the Lords,[41] and in April he was elected an honorary fellow of the Royal Institute of British Architects.

His responsibilities ranged widely – from the maintenance of 14,000 official buildings to the construction of munition factories, from ancient monuments to Duck Island in St James's Park. His officials had to discover what the departments wanted, and what the various branches of the building and civil engineering industries could – or would – do: many of the larger contractors had built up what were virtually private armies, and these constituted powerful inducements to the award of further contracts. Reith quickly got the measure of how great the gulf was between what was wanted and what was possible:

> Here the dilemma: on the one hand a monstrously inflated programme; on the other a declining and largely immobile labour force; serious doubts about materials, unorganised industries, bombs and more bombs. And, to crown it all, the reluctance of old-established departments to submit to anything that looked like control from an upstart ministry, their attitude ranging from the vaguely unhelpful to the positively obstructive.[42]

He had been joined by Hugh Beaver, a partner in the firm of Alexander Gibb. Beaver told Reith that the speed at which he moved was 'rather shattering to the average person', but he himself was far from average, and he soon came up with the suggestion that the system of priorities which they had inherited should be scrapped and replaced by a system of labour allocation to departments. Steps were taken to prevent the coincidence of labour peaks. 'By July 1941,' Reith wrote later, 'there was order and system in place of chaos.'[43]

To matters outside his own immediate sphere, however, he paid recklessly little attention. 'Budget – though I didn't know about it,' says a diary note on 7 April. 'There was a meeting of ministers to hear details but I had the American Ambassador at the time and I wouldn't have gone anyhow.' This self-imposed isolation did nothing to help him in his struggle to establish his ministry as the central authority for post-war planning, and increasingly he was to find himself in conflict with both the major parties within the Coalition. Charles Stuart put the matter well:

The Conservatives feared that he would undermine the rights of property in land; the Socialists that in so doing he would steal their thunder. The Conservatives wanted nothing done; the Socialists nothing done save by themselves. Yet John Reith stood, above all, for getting things done and in his own way; so a collision was inevitable.[44]

At the end of January, Reith had announced the setting up of a committee under Mr. A. A. Uthwatt, KC. He told the Lords that its terms of reference made it clear that the government did not intend post-war reconstruction to be hampered or prejudiced by speculative transactions in advance. The committee was asked to explore means of stabilising the value of land for development and to consider what powers were necessary to enable the acquisition of land by the public on an equitable basis.

After a good deal of inter-departmental in-fighting, Reith was allowed to announce the government's intentions for post-war reconstruction, such as they were, on 17 July: 'I apologised for the delay; I was good at that by now.'[45] The government accepted the Uthwatt recommendation that land should be pegged at 31 March 1939 values and promised legislation to secure orderly planning, especially of devastated areas. Reith was to chair a council of ministers to 'coordinate this work of forward planning'; the official statement that he had to read out doffed its cap to the idea of a central planning authority at some future date, but said that the Minister of Health and the Secretary of State for Scotland would continue to be responsible for any new legislation implementing the interim report of the Uthwatt Committee.

Whenever he could, he escaped from the frustrations of Whitehall and Westminster by accepting invitations to visit heavily devastated areas and meet the city fathers. He went to Southampton, to Portsmouth, to Liverpool, to Glasgow and to Plymouth, and in each place he offered the same advice as he had to Coventry. In Plymouth he witnessed something remarkable – 2000 people dancing in the open air on the Hoe:

Below them was spread the awful havoc lately wrought on their city; not far away across the sea the enemy. As they danced the summer evening into night I saw a coastal forces flotilla steam out from their Devonport anchorage in single line ahead; there was business for them to do, and they would probably do it all the better for what they could see on the Hoe. I envied the commanding officers of those little men-of-war; envied their chance of glory or of glorious death.[46]

One day in August he lunched with Julius Southwood, the chairman of Odhams Press, who asked if he did not think it heroic of Churchill to cross the Atlantic to meet Roosevelt. (The Prime Minister had sailed from Scapa Flow a couple of days previously to meet the US President off Newfoundland.) 'Nice for a minister to be told this by a press man,' Reith wrote, 'but I let on that I knew.'[47]

He was even more indignant a month later when his ministry was asked to pick up part of the bill:

> I have been asked to approve £450 odd for wines etc. on the *Prince of Wales* for Churchill and Co., under guise of entertainment of foreigners. I wonder how much of it Roosevelt drank. Today I was asked to approve £1,300 for a special train for Beaverbrook and Co. going to the north of Scotland en route for Moscow. I hope Beaverbrook gets killed en route. It would be a splendid release and escape for this country.[48]

The intemperance of his language about Beaverbrook at this time ('to no one is the vulgar designation shit more appropriately applied') was occasioned by a dispute over the removal of park railings; Churchill was variously 'an impostor' and 'a menace'. He and Dill continued to dine together and nurse their dislike of the Prime Minister and his entourage. The CIGS had accompanied Churchill on his visit to Roosevelt, and when he got back he showed Reith an album of photographs:

> I shuddered with anger and irritation and disgust at the pictures of Churchill and Beaverbrook. Dill said, 'Our empire is worth saving. We must save it if we can from what others may do to it.' – 'What do you mean?' I asked. There was a picture of Churchill on the page before us. He stabbed it with his thumb. 'That.'[49]

Reith's move into government – he received a ministerial salary of £3500 – had not been good for his bank balance. His agreement in 1938 with Imperial Airways had provided for his appointment for eleven years at £10,000 a year plus director's fees, and a sum of £38,000 was to be payable at the age of sixty or on his death. The circumstances of his resignation were obviously not envisaged when the agreement was drawn up, and Reith seems to have turned his mind to the financial consequences of leaving IA only belatedly. He had already been Minister of Information for some months before he got round to writing to Sir Alan Barlow at the Treasury to say that he felt entitled to receive £38,000, although he acknowledged that any payment made to him would ultimately constitute a charge on public funds and said that he would accept Barlow's advice in the matter. Barlow was unable to find any Treasury precedent to guide him, and Reith had eventually agreed to accept one-eleventh of the £38,000 for every complete year of service. This, Barlow said, was 'handsome and public spirited, and as such we recognise and will remember it'.

Public spirit did little towards paying Christopher's fees at Eton or maintaining a large establishment; Reith began to feel that Harrias House was too much for them and started to keep an eye open for something smaller. His eye also wandered in search of diversion. A note in early August records that he had met an ATS staff officer called Christie who was, he thought, 'rather amusing'. He was naïvely surprised when Muriel thought differently – 'Funny talk with M about taking a girl out to lunch or dinner'[50] – but he went on seeing 'Christie' for several months; for some curious reason he never referred to her in his diary by anything other than her surname.

Muriel was also struggling with the sort of difficulties which all housewives face in time of war. Reith conceded that she was 'working far harder than any slavey of olden days', though he also grumbled that she made things harder for herself than they need be.[51] The servant situation got steadily worse: 'A blasted charwoman was to have come yesterday and didn't. I put a curse on her.'[52] Domestic preoccupations, continuing frustrations at the Ministry, regrets about the past, a chance glimpse of Charlie at Euston – here were the ingredients for a highly explosive brew, and as the end of the year approached he was at the lowest ebb: 'Thinking about a "suicide" speech,' he wrote, '– suicide politically or anyhow as a member of this government.'[53] The following Sunday, just four days before Christmas, everything boiled up to produce an explosion of helpless rage:

> It was a horrid day – cold and wet. Both children have colds, so didn't go to church – anyhow what's the good. M and I went but I was in a vile temper over the hopelessness of things at Harrias House and in the office, and I was particularly infuriated by the thought of what Ogilvie had done (and the blasted board who appointed him) with the BBC ... I had some fun with the children but I feel I am really of no use whatever to them. Oh, awful it all is ... I was feeling in dreadful bad form, inclined to scrap my whole diary. I kicked this volume across the study last thing at night.[54]

The mood of black dejection continued into the New Year, and sometimes its effect was physical:

> Miserable day. I went to lunch at the Athenæum but was in too bad form to have it. Disgusted almost beyond endurance and very unhappy. I often wish I were dead. What leadership is needed – and I might have given it – a lot of it, but I don't feel I want it now, nor able.[55]

The general course of the war seemed to concern him hardly at all. Six weeks previously, the US Fleet had been shattered at Pearl Harbor and the *Prince of Wales* and the *Repulse* had been sunk off Malaya with the loss of 600 lives. 'War with Japan now,' he noted baldly in his diary. 'Parliament met but I didn't know of it.'[56] On 11 February he was at last able to announce in the Lords that his ministry was to have extended powers and be restyled the Ministry of Works and Planning.

It was his last act as a politician. At the end of the following week, Churchill, under strong pressure to conciliate public opinion, made changes in his War Cabinet and carried out a substantial reshuffle in the lower reaches of the administration. This time the letter went not to the Athenaeum but to Harrias House. Reith opened the door to a despatch rider at 7.30 on Saturday evening:

'My dear Reith, I am very sorry to tell you that the reconstruction of the government which events have rendered necessary makes me wish to have your Office at my disposal ...' In later years he compared the shock of what he read to the impact of the sniper's bullet on that October day in 1915: *The Germans wouldn't heave a cricket ball at me. What could it be?*

He had himself driven to London and spent an hour and a quarter with Sir John Anderson, the Lord Privy Seal. Anderson, a dry and kindly fellow-Scot, had tried to school him in the ways of Whitehall, telling him that he thought his memoranda were 'too abrupt and harsh' and cautioning him against appearing to treat his ministerial colleagues contemptuously. His advice now was that he should put his resignation in the Prime Minister's hands without delay, but Reith pondered one last, mulish gesture: 'I wondered if I should not do nothing, in which case I should have to be dismissed by the King.'[57] Yielding reluctantly to Anderson's persuasion, he went off to his office in Lambeth Bridge House. 'I never wrote a harder letter,' he said in his memoirs:

> Certainly my office and I are at your disposal.
>
> It has been a privilege to be associated with the government at such a time.
>
> I wish I could have been of more help to you personally in your tremendous and splendid task.

Left to himself, he would have sent only the last sentence. The first two were written at Anderson's dictation.

Reith was to brood for the rest of his life over the reasons for his dismissal. Jealousy and resentment at the growth in power of his ministry, perhaps?

> I have no doubt that we were moving too fast and too far for other ministers concerned, so that they could cabal about lack of team spirit and such like. No doubt about it – the good work and growing authority of the Works side with consequent interference with freedom of other people – *delendus est*. Similarly with the planning side – still more *delendus*. And taken together the job was obviously very important and the most important of all after the war – so why should I have it – *delendus* urgent.[58]

He also attributed it to hostility within the Conservative Party. He was told by Lord Balfour of Burleigh that some of the more right-wing members of the 1922 Committee had urged their chairman, Erskine Hill, to press for his removal; they did not like the effect some of his proposed policies would have on the building industry and believed that he might be moving towards land nationalisation. When Hill declined, they had gone direct to James Stuart, the government Chief Whip. This version was confirmed to him a year later by the American ambassador, John G. Winant, who told him he had had it from Churchill.[59]

Many years later, his friend Lord Selborne, in what Reith described as 'an extraordinarily kind letter', tried to persuade him to view the matter in a less conspiratorial light:

> I think you take Churchill's dropping you in 1942 too seriously; and are you sure it was at the behest of a *Tory* cabal? I have always thought it was simply because he was head of a coalition and had to find places for the 3 parties represented in the coalition, and people like yourself, not attached to any party, had no one to fight for them. I thought it was very ungrateful treatment, but he did the same to other people . . . But although 'Politics is an accursed trade' as my grandfather Lord Salisbury once exclaimed, I think some allowance must be made for a PM leading a coalition in a war where the nation's existence was at stake.[60]

Reith was unpersuaded by Selborne's patrician detachment, but he was, in truth, as ill suited to the 'accursed trade' as it was possible to be. Mary Agnes Hamilton, who had been in the Commons herself before becoming a BBC Governor, saw very clearly why it was that the messy and devious subtleties of the political game were beyond him:

> For his own convictions one can see him going to the stake, but like too many potential martyrs, he has little patience with the differing convictions of others. Others in fact represent his Achilles heel; he blocks his own vision and deflects it dangerously. Generous and unfailingly kind to those below him, warmly considerate of their welfare, ready to put himself to endless pains to serve them, he lacks, tragically for himself and for his fellows, capacity to collaborate on terms of equality.[61]

Thirteen

BUSINESS IN GREAT WATERS

The tallest trees are most in the power of the winds, and ambitious
men of the blasts of fortune.

WILLIAM PENN, *Some Fruits of Solitude*, 1693

FOR SEVERAL weeks after his dismissal, Reith spoke to hardly anyone other
than Balfour of Burleigh and Anderson. 'Hard, isn't it?' he wrote to the latter.
'I was always sorry for Moses on Pisgah, but he was 120 years old. What do I
do?' Anderson's advice was to sit tight and wait for something to turn up. Six
days after his dismissal something did:

> Invitation from that bloody shit Churchill to be Lord High Commissioner.
> I saw that there was a letter from his office but I didn't open it; took it up
> to Muriel in bed with the others. Next time I went up she told me there was
> something for Miss Stanley to refuse – 'from that cur'.[1]

To represent the monarch at the General Assembly of the Church of Scotland
was an honour that Reith had long coveted. He wanted it because it would
mean living in state at Holyrood Palace. He wanted it for his father's sake. If
he did it in 1942, he would probably be asked to do it in 1943 as well, and
that was the centenary of the Disruption, rich in association with his hero
Thomas Chalmers.

Anderson urged him to accept, pointing out that to refuse would look like
pique: 'If you accept it will not stand in the way of anything else that may come
along.'[2] The idea of accepting anything from Churchill stuck in Reith's craw,
however; once again it was the patient Anderson who helped him to compose
a more gracious and more sensible letter than he was capable of writing himself:
'I am very loath to ask to be excused from doing what you suggest . . . But I
am passionately anxious to contribute directly to the war effort to the utmost
of my power . . .'[3]

A few days later there came a second suggestion, this time from Brendan
Bracken, who was now Minister of Information: would he take on the
coordination of the ordering of wireless apparatus under the Ministry of Supply?
'Chickenfood,' said Anderson contemptuously, and advised him to have nothing
to do with it.

Reith was now in a state of considerable mental disturbance: 'Feeling absolutely awful,' an entry for 10 March reads, 'and on razor-edge of frenzy'; a
week later he fell quite seriously ill and was in bed for more than a week with

a high temperature. 'Dreaming about politicians and all the rest of it,' he wrote
when he was able to resume his diary:

> What put me to bed was a very sore throat but it was my recent shock which
> made me liable and of course that has prevented recovery. Always listening
> for the telephone . . . Muriel's kindness and gentleness and cheerfulness
> and care I could never describe.[4]

When he was better he went to see Anderson, who was shocked by his appearance. Anderson told him that the war situation was extremely serious; he had
thought that Churchill might have been out of office by that time, and felt that
any major disaster such as the loss of Ceylon or a naval defeat in the Bay of
Bengal might still bring that about. He hoped Reith would refrain from attacking the Prime Minister in the Lords, 'though he admitted I could say a few
things'.[5] Reith went home and thought he might kill time by starting to write
his memoirs: 'I tried; made nothing of it; not with a war in progress.'

He lunched once day with the editor of *Picture Post*, who tried to persuade
him to 'create a nuisance value' for himself, but Reith told him that wasn't his
line. He travelled to London quite frequently, although he had no particular
reason to do so: 'I went up this morning, quite unnecessarily of course – as
every day, but "just in case" like other kinds of unemployed visiting daily the
bureau.'[6] After three months, he could bear the inactivity no longer. Someone
whom he had known since the late 1920s had recently been appointed chief
staff officer to the Rear-Admiral Coastal Forces:

> Phoned Charles Meynell to see if he could get me into Coastal Forces as a
> warrant officer – chief clerk or storekeeper or something like that, at a post
> where there was excitement and danger. He phoned me in the evening to
> say he had spoken to his Admiral and they wanted me to come and organize
> the command but I would need to be RNVR sub-lieutenant. I said I couldn't
> have a commission.[7]

By early June these Lawrence of Arabia-like scruples had been overcome. He
had, to his satisfaction, been passed medically fit for executive, seagoing service,
and was in uniform as a lieutenant-commander RNVR – a 'two-and-a-half
striper', as he liked to describe himself. He wrote later that he felt rather elderly
and foolish. He had the rank of a young man and a uniform 'which, when
covered with the regulation blue burberry, made me look, except for the cap
badge, exactly like my own chauffeur'. He was paid 27/2d a day, plus allowances, which meant that his income was one-thirtieth of what it had been two
years previously.

It was all rather different from his days as Director-General or a Minister
of the Crown, when there were always secretaries in the outer office and official
cars at the door. On one of his first days he set out to go to the Athenaeum
for lunch, but the underground defeated him; he managed to go twice from

Baker Street to Paddington, and the journey finally took him more than an hour.

He was installed in an office ten foot square up the Finchley Road. The first job he was given was to organise a special liaison service to cut down delays in the repair of the new craft that were coming into service with coastal forces. He soon discovered that he had not been included on the night-duty roster – probably out of deference to his years – and to this he took exception:

I was put on the list all right; it thrilled me to make signals on my own – hoping nobody would criticise them in the morning; to answer urgent telephone messages; to be informed by the petty officer of the watch that the ship was darkened and revolvers loaded – the ship being a block of flats in Hampstead.[8]

Although Anderson had urged him not to make life difficult for Churchill by attacking him in the Lords, he had also advised him to find an occasion to speak there as soon as he could – 'on the principle, presumably,' Reith wrote dryly, 'that if one is badly thrown from a horse the sooner one mounts a horse again the better'. He accordingly put down a motion in which he asked the government whether they were giving immediate attention to the future constitution, control and management of the essential public services. He spoke on 17 June, feeling 'very jittery' beforehand. He gave an outing to a number of his favourite hobby horses – the superiority of the concept of the public corporation, his reservations about the civil service ('the strongest trade union in the country'), his doubts about the adequacy of democratic method in achieving democratic purpose.

The part of his speech that attracted most public attention was his advocacy of a national transport corporation, covering the railways, road transport, canals, coastal shipping, and internal air services. The speech was much praised by his fellow-peers, but came in for a good deal of critical scrutiny in the press. 'Socialism in the House of Lords,' said a headline in the *Railway Review* – 'or is it Fascism?'[9] The *Morning Advertiser* resorted to irony: 'It is not at all clear why Lord Reith's Corporation is not to include all the cycle and car manufacturers, to say nothing of the makers of perambulators and roller skates.'[10]

Back in Hampstead, Reith's second achievement was to organise his admiral and the chief staff officer who had recruited him out of their jobs and get the supply side of this important functional service established as a department within the Admiralty. Admiral Kekewich took it like a man: 'He might have felt some animus against me, or at least a regret that he had taken this cuckoo into his nest. Nothing of the sort.'[11] When Reith moved on after eight months, Kekewich sent him a copy of the flattering confidential report he had written. 'It must be strange for you to think of being reported on,' he wrote in a personal note. 'It is even stranger for me to have to report on a privy counsellor . . .'

The work kept him busy, but he was nothing like fully extended. He kept a jaundiced eye on the political scene. Anderson frequently assured him that

Churchill was well disposed, but although the hope that he might yet be summoned to some great task occasionally flickered into life, his hatred of the Prime Minister was by now obsessional. In October, Churchill was given the freedom of Edinburgh: 'Damn blast the bloody swine,' Reith wrote. 'He is the greatest menace we've ever had – country and Empire sacrificed to his megalomania, to his monstrous obstinacy and wrongheadedness.'[12] As so often with him, his mood darkened as the year drew to a close and painful memories jostled with present miseries: 'Bowser's 46th birthday, the swab,' he wrote on 20 December. 'I was horrid to everybody. Poor children.'

On the last day of the year he went to see Anderson:

> I was there for over an hour and it might have been five minutes for all I can remember of it. I was in a terrible state this evening. I would welcome death. I wondered if I might not start again and go through *King Alfred* [a naval base where officers were trained] with a view to going to sea. The most terrible New Year's Eve I have ever had. Feeling utterly hopeless and in despair.[13]

The Admiral thought he was too old to be trained for going to sea, and in the early days of the New Year he struggled to pull himself together. 'I am still an Olympian,' he wrote on 6 January; 'I reflected a lot on this today and was considerably comforted.' Muriel, who stood as much in need of comforting as he did, might well have felt that her married life was being lived not on the slopes of Olympus but on the lip of Vesuvius. When her fiftieth birthday came round in March, it fell by ill chance on the day after one of Churchill's broadcasts, and Reith was in such a black mood that he barely spoke to her: 'I was horrid to poor M because of the state I was in, and I thought I had better stay in Town for the rest of the week.'[14]

In the middle of February he had transferred with the reconstructed materials section of Coastal Forces from Hampstead to Westminster. The move did not increase his workload:

> I look at my empty table and take up a pencil or my pen but have nothing to write, or I go out of the room as if I were going somewhere, walk down the corridor and then turn back; and I don't like to be out of the room for long in case my telephone rings . . .[15]

On that particular day his telephone had rung, as it happened. It was Miss Stanley, who had returned to BOAC after he left the government, to tell him that many of the staff would like to see him back; a round robin was circulating to that effect and a telegram had been sent to the Secretary of State for Air. Reith did not wish to return: '– not from any point of view except money'. He did, however, take part in a Lords debate on the affairs of the Corporation the following month, making a plea for the separation of civil aviation from the Air Ministry, and for BOAC to be allowed to have civil aircraft designed. He also argued that it should be allowed to advertise – American airlines were doing so on a grand scale, and openly saying that they were going to use the war to win the peace.

Anderson suggested that he write to Churchill: 'It would be the most distasteful thing I ever did and humiliating but I suppose I must try.' He sat up all night over the draft, but Anderson didn't like it – Reith had even proposed, rather pathetically, to enclose a copy of Kekewich's confidential report on him. Once again it was a form of words suggested by the older man which was sent. Churchill's reply was courteous but non-committal: 'You may be sure that I will try my best to find suitable employment for your well-known energy and capacity . . . It would certainly be a great pleasure to me that you were pulling your full weight in the war.'[16]

Shortly after this he was transferred to the staff of Admiral Sir Frederick Wake-Walker, Third Sea Lord and Controller of the Navy. The first thing he asked Reith to do was examine his organisation and tell him what was wrong with it. His second task was to devise a new policy for the training and utilisation of technicians. The Controller liked his report, but was afraid it was too revolutionary for him to put to his colleagues on the Board of Admiralty. These two assignments absorbed his attention and kept desperation at bay for the best part of eight weeks, although he found himself carrying out his new duties in a part of town that he would have chosen to avoid:

> My room looked across Horseguards to No. 10 and the cabinet room. I would often see the Prime Minister's car waiting for him at the garden entrance; which was about the last thing I wanted to see. And in this area one was continually sighting former colleagues; they drove by in priority-labelled cars. I wished people would help me to forget, or anyhow not hinder.[17]

'Salvation, or a measure of it, was at hand,' Reith wrote in his memoirs. He had been cast down in the middle of June 1943 by the news that Lord Wavell had been made viceroy – 'so that has gone again' – but at the end of the month the Controller handed him a file about combined operations and asked him to draw up terms of reference for a new combined operations material department:

> What I produced meant, in fact, the establishment in this single new department of a miniature of the Controller's total sphere, almost a miniature Admiralty, less the staff side . . . It was to be responsible for all technical training – that is training other than actual sea-going; for the appointment of all combined operations technical officers ashore and afloat throughout the world.[18]

The proposals were bold and unorthodox. Reith justified them on the ground that if an invasion of Europe was to take place in 1944, desperate measures were necessary. They were accepted as they stood. When the search for someone to do the job proved difficult, Reith proposed himself. Before the matter was finally settled, he heard that the First Lord of the Admiralty, A. V. Alexander, had referred his appointment to Churchill. This prompted a thought: 'If he says yes,' Reith wrote, 'it carries the devastating significance that I am off his agenda and in this job for the duration.' And so he was. He was promoted Captain RNVR, and for the next seventeen months had enough on his plate to satisfy even his gargantuan appetite.

The new department was accommodated in a 'ghastly building' between Holborn and Tottenham Court Road without daylight or natural air. Reith went to work much as he had done in France thirty years earlier, and by mid-August the Directorate of Combined Operations Material was installed in the old Paymaster-General's building with a front door on Whitehall and a garden on Horseguards. 'The department,' he wrote, 'was the object of curiosity elsewhere and of good-humoured envy: "Of course you can do as you like. You're in DCOM".'

There was an illustration of the truth of this early the following year. The department had outgrown its quarters. Reith wanted to solve the problem by having a large hut erected where a bomb had cleared a space, but there was an *ukaz* from Churchill that no temporary buildings were to be put up in Whitehall without his express permission. Reith watched for his opening:

> Churchill was in Marrakesh. A note to Attlee was delivered at 9.30 one morning. At 9.45 he telephoned to say he would come round and see for himself. It was very obliging of him. I pointed out that by building up a wall on the Whitehall pavement the large hut required could be erected and no one be any the wiser. He authorised it at once; it was built in a few days.[19]

'I was happy,' Reith wrote in his memoirs; 'little time to think of anything but the job in hand.' He certainly put in very long hours; characteristically, he kept a record of when he left the office during the first three months, and it averaged out at 1.15 a.m. Frequently he worked all night, 'then repairing, exultant, for a hot bath and breakfast at the Athenæum'.[20] The picture that emerges from the diaries, however, is not so much of a happy man as of a man anaesthetising himself with work. Occasionally, the anaesthetic wore off: it had certainly done so on a day in late August when he poured out his unhappiness in a rambling, despairing diary entry and in a letter which, to the recipient, Lord Woolton, must have made startling reading:

> . . . I told him of the children wanting me to come and play with them and of my wanting to shout at them that I wished to God they'd never been born, and that we had to break up this home . . . Of course I shall have the most ghastly remorse about all this. I've not done my duty by the children. I never spend the sort of times with them that I had expected and hoped. It isn't all

avoy Hill at night

elow: Reith locking up at
avoy Hill for the last time,
Iay 1932

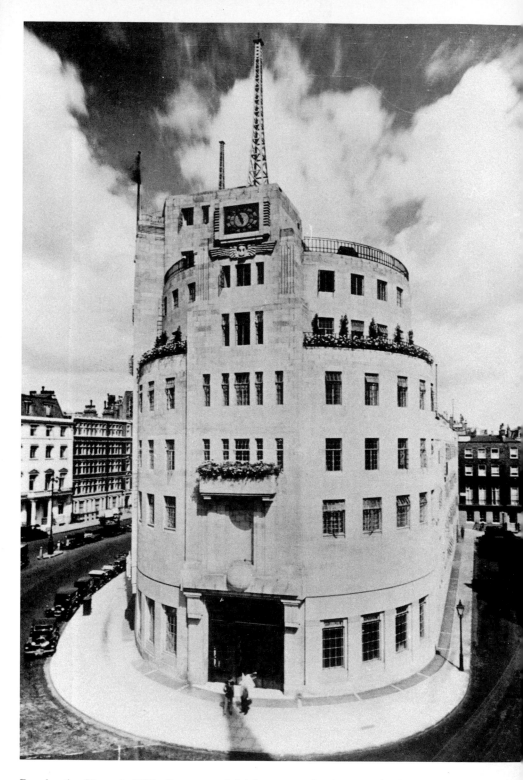

Broadcasting House in 1932 – Prospero and Ariel are not yet in place over the doorway

Mary Somerville in 1937

Below: Jo Stanley in 1937

'Ariel between Wisdom and Gaiety' – sculpture by Eric Gill on the west front of Broadcasting House

Below: 'This temple of the arts and the muses' – the Latin inscription in the entrance hall of Broadcasting House

DEO · OMNIPOTENTI
TEMPLVM·HOC·ARTIVM · ET·MVSARVM·ANNO·DOMINI·MCMXXX
RECTORE·IOHANNI·REITH·PRIMI·DEDICANT·GVBERNATORES
PRECANTES·VT·MESSEM·BONAM·BONA·PROFERAT·SEMENTIS
VT·IMMVNDA·OMNIA·ET·INIMICA·PACI·EXPELLANTVR
VT·QVAECVNQVE·PVLCHRA·SVNT·ET·SINCERA·QVAECVNQVE
BONAE·FAMAE·AD·HAEC·AVREM·INCLINANS·POPVLVS
VIRTVTIS·ET·SAPIENTIAE·SEMITAM·INSISTAT

my fault. They're fond of me, but I am no use at all to either of them. Here is the home and grounds they have enjoyed so much, and in which Christopher has worked so hard, passing from us. We should have left it long ago. My overdraft is now about £3,000 and it mounts up every month. It seems the end of all things ... I wish a bomb would eliminate us all. It is the only way out. And all of this, or most of it, is due to that loathsome cad Churchill. I feel like disposing of all my books, burning my diaries and selling most everything we have. God Almighty, whatever that or he may mean, has completely cut us off ... The Crichton people write to ask if I will pay £22 for dentures for Ernest. It all comes still on me. I suppose I am nearer to lunacy than ever he has been. I find I still can't contemplate suicide, chiefly because things would be so muddled and difficult for the family. But I surely do wish to God I'd never married ...[21]

The family was much affected at this time by the loss of Rufus, the retriever. (Sandy, the Cairn terrier, whom the master of the house had never much liked, had been given away some years previously.) Reith, who could be immensely sentimental, wrote out an epitaph for him, enclosing his pedigree and membership ticket of the Kennel Club: 'Rufus, 1929–43. Given to us by his owners in 1930, put to sleep 24.8.43, owing to old age, the infirmities, disabilities and inconveniences thereof. Buried under the pink hawthorn tree by the gate in the south west meadow. We all loved him and he was part of the family for 13 years. A gentleman among dog ...' The whole family signed it, and Reith sealed the envelope with the seals of the BBC, the Airways Corporation, the Office of Works, and the family coat of arms and crest.

At the Admiralty, he made himself so busy that there was a period of three weeks when he did not write a single line in his diary – the longest gap since his earliest days at the BBC. When he resumed, he noted that he had lost a stone in weight in little more than a month: 'I am dreadfully thin and haggard and bony. I feel almost lost in my clothes now.' He began to take cod-liver oil and malt, and his doctor gave him a note entitling him to an extra pint of milk. The very occasional slack day disturbed him, because it gave him time to think, but they were few; most of the time he drove things forward with ferocious energy, usually master of his brief, an accomplished and shameless bluffer when he was not:

Took the chair at a meeting about ships' spares. I was not sure what was happening, or meant to be happening, nor what I wanted, nor what I got; but I got what I wanted and the minutes will make it clear.[22]

He usually had draft minutes ready in advance; always formulated and sometimes recorded the desired decisions. On one occasion this had the effect of drastically shortening the course of a meeting called to discuss the Pluto cross-channel oil pipelines. The admiral in the chair took Reith's briefing so well that after a few words about each item on the agenda he simply read out the decision which Reith had suggested he should aim at.[23]

He devoted much energy in his first month to acquiring a secretary, enriching in the process the store of Whitehall gossip about his weakness for a pretty face. He was intent on securing the services of a girl whose family lived in Dunblane; the only obstacle was that she was serving in the ATS, and the Army was not disposed to release her. A sequence of testy diary entries in July and August charts the ascent of Reith's request through successive layers of War Office bureaucracy: 'The blasted Adjutant-General has refused to let Joyce Wilson leave the ATS. Of course I ought to have gone and seen him.'[24]

What Reith could not know was that the file had gone even higher, and been placed before the Secretary of State, the waspish Sir James Grigg, who embellished it with a note in his own hand: 'I will not have my officers, ATS, shunted about to suit the convenience of John Reith, who somewhat late in life has discovered the art of fucking.'[25] Grigg eventually relented, and by the end of August Reith had what he had plainly exerted himself to get: ten days later he gave lunch to Lady Grigg – 'by way of thanking her for getting Joyce Wilson'.[26] The Secretary of State's coarseness was misplaced. The episode confirms that Reith was an innocent, but does not prove that he was a philanderer. His relationship with his secretary sometimes seemed imprudent, and was the subject of much ribald speculation, but there is no evidence that it was adulterous.

In the middle of December he was elected to the court of directors of Cable and Wireless and its associated companies. This was good for morale, and also eased his financial situation, as it brought in emoluments of £1500 a year plus tax at 5/6d in the pound. He toyed with the idea of cutting back on expenditure by removing Christopher from Eton, where he was not getting good reports: 'He seems quite unintelligent and there's nothing to be done about that. Muriel says he gets it from her. I was bad at school work – but no one ever said I wasn't intelligent.'[27]

Early in February 1944, Reith was given a document 'with the most secret markings of all'. It was the first instalment of the invasion plans: 'Thrilling, and rather awful to have this in one's hands ... Here anyhow I knew what very few indeed of my late ministerial colleagues knew.'[28]

In the month or so before the invasion, busy as he was, he dipped into a particularly deep trough of despondency and alienation: 'I really feel I could contemplate killing myself,' he wrote. 'I don't know how to do it decently. I am absolutely at the end of my tether and am making things terrible for poor Muriel also.' He was concerned about three things – his future, his financial situation, and the house at Beaconsfield. He was normally so self-absorbed that he found it almost impossible to stand outside himself, but there is a long diary entry in the middle of May 1944 that leaps out from the page:

I suppose I am and always have been almost completely self-centred and that nothing interests me at all except what I am concerned in. I expect it is too late to change. I have no ordinary human kindness or tolerance. I have brilliance, intellect and all sorts of things like that, energy, conscientiousness and thoroughness. About the only passion I show is in reviling politicians, Churchill especially. Never rise to any heights. Scornful of patriotism and honest efforts to serve the country. Loathing the common people. I will rarely admit greatness in others. This is the kind of thing that might be said of me. A good deal is true. I am obsessed by my own fate and by a desire for revenge for my treatment; by a sense of injury. Is my ambition just lust for power? (I don't think so; I never have.) I think no one is so unhappy or has had such hard treatment or is in such a bad way. The greatness that used to be there never now appears – nothing that shines. I only show a hopelessness and almost an acceptance of my own shortcomings. I have always known I had a horrid character and disposition. And now I am querulous and embittered and small and shrunken and can't see even the near horizon. Believing nothing and without faith or hope; stifled and strangled and submerged by the pettiness of my own preoccupations. The inspiration and domination of my personality are gone.[29]

The effect is electrifying – as though one were overhearing, through the wall of a confessional, one of Francis Bacon's terrible screaming popes. As so often with Reith, however, things are not what they seem. This is no unflinching self-portrait. He was not here describing what he saw in his mirror in those despairing weeks before D-Day – he was copying, like a child on a school bench, from a lesson that had been set before him.

It is a bleak and devastating judgement, the more so because it was written by the person who at that time stood closest to him. The original text is tucked away, out of sequence, at the back of one of Reith's post-war scrapbooks. It is headed simply, 'Verdict on JCWR by Joyce Wilson.'

On the night of 5 June 1944 he found it difficult to go to bed. The number of British landing-ships involved in the invasion was 126, as well as 777 major and 1570 minor craft. On D-Day he had a telephone call from the Controller to congratulate him on the serviceability percentage achieved. The Admiral had expected between seventy-five and eighty per cent; the actual figures had been ninety-eight per cent for craft and ninety-nine per cent for ships.

A few days later he was flattered and excited to be included in a party of senior officers who crossed to Normandy; they toured the beaches from Courseuilles to Port-en-Bessin and saw the beginnings of one of the two huge prefabricated harbours code-named Mulberry.[30] On a second visit he was able to stay longer, and one day lay in bed watching an air attack on the ships in the British sector through open french windows: 'It was a French billet again; and war; and a German attack. I imagined that it was as thirty years earlier – and wished it were.'[31]

On the sudden death of Sir Kingsley Wood the previous September ('No loss that, at all,' Reith wrote unfeelingly in his diary), his place as Chancellor had been taken by Sir John Anderson, and Reith now decided to re-open with him the question of his financial arrangements when he left Imperial Airways. He did not, he wrote, insist on the full sum which he believed was due to him, but felt that the Treasury should now make a 'fair and reasonable proposal'.[32] He saw Anderson a fortnight later and was told it couldn't be done: 'He had the cheek to say that what I had got out of the contract was good payment for the short term.'[33] Shortly afterwards, when he was going to France by air for the day, he returned to the charge in a manner that at least had the merit of originality: 'I left a letter for J. Anderson putting it flatly up to him to look after the family financially – £15,000 and a Viscount [sic] for CJ – if I didn't come back from tomorrow's trip.'[34]

He was a good deal in the company of Joyce Wilson. She had been a guest at Beaconsfield over Easter, but that had not been a great success: 'She was so frightened of Muriel's disapproval, which was made obvious last time she was here, that she wouldn't take any sherry or gin, though I had got them out.' His own manners as host did little to mend matters: 'I have been very unfriendly to JW all weekend,' he wrote the next day, adding, a touch sourly, 'The Colonel makes up for it' – they had a number of American servicemen boarding with them at the time, and he had observed, during one of her earlier visits, that Colonel Holt seemed to be 'much taken' with Miss Wilson. In July he had a long discussion with her about whether she should go with him to his next job; he also noted that he had given her some of the early volumes of his diary to read. The following month she celebrated her thirty-third birthday, and Reith took her to lunch at the Savoy and to dinner at the Carlton Grill.

At the end of October, when he was invited to the launch of a tank landing-ship at Swan Hunter's Neptune yard in Newcastle, he decided she should accompany him. This prompted the gallant suggestion by the management that she should perform the launching ceremony, which pleased Reith greatly, although there was some awkwardness when an admiral who had also been invited decided to bring his wife. Wartime austerity dictated that a bottle of red wine should do service for the traditional champagne. Miss Wilson was presented with a bouquet of carnations and with a brooch. Reith thought it very pretty, but recorded that they later had an argument about its value.[35]

'Increasingly hard in the late summer of 1944 to concentrate on the job and keep one's thoughts from drifting off to what might have been,' Reith wrote in *Into the Wind*.[36] Once the invasion was launched, the work of his department was largely completed, and he felt disinclined to stay much longer in the Admiralty, although he told his superiors that he would if they made him logistics admiral for the Far East. The tribute that he valued most came from his Vice-Controller, Admiral Tower:

I am convinced that one and all recognised you as a real leader and put all they had into their work for that reason alone ... If you had not been director the whole Overlord operation would, at the very best, have been far less efficiently done than it was, and might not have been done at all.[37]

His last day in uniform was 18 December. His work received formal recognition in the New Year's Honours List when he was made a Commander of the Bath. He wrote in his memoirs that he learned about it as he read *The Times* in a jolting tube train on 1 January, but that was a bit of embroidery – Joyce Wilson had brought him in a signal about it one day in September.[38] It was on the Prime Minister's recommendation. Reith was particularly proud of the fact that it was a military CB, a distinction, he noted, not previously achieved by any civilian, Privy Counsellor or ex-minister.

Two things took the gilt off the gingerbread. The first was that the announcement was in very small type – 'hardly anyone will see it.' The second was that Lord Portal, who had succeeded him as Minister of Works, became a viscount. 'This is really absolutely shameful,' he wrote. 'But of course he is a friend of Churchill's . . .'[39]

Fourteen

AROUND THE WORLD IN FIFTY-TWO DAYS

Hear him debate of commonwealth affairs,
You would say it hath been all in all his study.
WILLIAM SHAKESPEARE,
King Henry V, 1598

THE CIVILIAN assignment for which Reith left the Admiralty arose from his directorship of Cable and Wireless. There was concern in Whitehall about the relationship between the company and the Dominions, and there was friction between C & W and the Commonwealth Communications Council – the new name for the old Imperial Communications Advisory Committee. The dominance of Cable and Wireless – London-based and commercially owned – was the cause of considerable resentment elsewhere in the Commonwealth. There was much talk of drastic organisational change, and Reith had not been on the C & W board many months before he conceived the idea of some sort of imperial corporation – a telecommunications equivalent of what he had envisaged for civil aviation.

His views were well received within Cable and Wireless, and the government asked them to put the scheme to the CCC. The presentation did not go well, however, and shortly afterwards the Council endorsed an alternative proposal from Australia and New Zealand for a looser arrangement – public corporations in the United Kingdom and each of the Dominions would be associated through interlocking directorships and there would be a degree of coordination by the CCC. Nobody in Cable and Wireless, the Treasury or the Post Office thought it would work; shortly before Reith left the Admiralty, the War Cabinet gave its approval to the idea that an emissary should visit the member countries to explain the United Kingdom position. This was the mission for which Reith was now preparing himself.

Reith being the man he was, there had inevitably been much discussion about terms and conditions. The bruising experiences of the past two and a half years made considerations of status even more important than before: 'I wondered,' he wrote, 'whether I could be minister without portfolio but with a less silly name – I ought to have ministerial status anyhow.'[1] He tried the idea out on Anderson, but the Chancellor didn't like it. In talking to his friend Lord Balfour of Burleigh, he said revealingly that it was not purely a question of status with the Dominion governments, but of 'my need to be reinstated with myself'.[2]

The government view was that he should resign as an ordinary director of Cable and Wireless and be reappointed as a government director, but this did not go down well with the company, so he simply resigned – 'Once again from the point of view of financial futures I was acting stupidly,' he wrote in his memoirs.[3] The Treasury agreed that he should be paid at the rate of £5000 a year, and that he should have appropriate allowances and entertainment expenses.

Reith's diary for this period shows a revival of something of his old spirit and makes for much crisper and more interesting reading. He sometimes toyed with the idea of throwing everything up and trying to earn a living by his pen. It is not clear what subjects he would have found outside himself, but he could certainly write both graphically and entertainingly. His accounts of his travels are often vivid, and the diary is enlivened by agreeably sardonic cameos of those he met socially or in the way of business. Shortly before he went off on his world tour his fellow-guests at a dinner at Claridge's included the widow of Lord Willingdon, the former Viceroy of India: 'Lady Willingdon took a cigar for her son, bones for her dogs and a shilling from me for the cloakroom.'[4] A few days later, briefing himself for his mission, he called on Clement Attlee in his room in the Commons: 'He was very friendly, but beyond urging a cure for air-sickness he had nothing specially relevant to say.'[5]

He took with him the director-general of the Censorship Department, the assistant director-general of the Post Office, and a member of the War Cabinet secretariat. He also took Joyce Wilson, who was extricated from the Admiralty with greater ease than she had been from the War Office. They left Northolt on 22 January in a Consolidated Liberator of RAF Transport Command; the former chairman of Imperial Airways thought the party would get better attention from the Air Force than from a civil airline.

As one of the main objects of the exercise was to explain why the UK government could not fall in with the so-called Anzac scheme, it seemed sensible to head first for Australia. On the second day out, he was jolted by a message that his brother Ernest had died: 'Now he is with Father and Mother and Beta and Douglas,' he wrote in his diary. 'He was extraordinarily unselfish and kindly dispositioned.' In Washington, Reith dined with an agreeable young counsellor at the British Embassy who had been at Gresham's. He was called Donald Maclean, and his name was to flash round the world six years later when he levanted with his fellow-traitor Guy Burgess. On to San Diego and Hawaii; it was some years before Reith was to announce his celebrated discovery that 'life was for living', but possibly he was set on the road to it during that trans-Pacific flight: 'Bought a pair of fancy Honolulu bathing pants. Never been in such warm sea.'[6]

In Canberra, Reith listened with admiration to the 'impressive imperial pro-nouncements' of the Australian Prime Minister, John Curtin: 'If everybody's to take a purely national view, then it's good night to hopes of peace, leagues of nations, security, fraternity, and all the rest of it. Nothing but bloody tanks and guns.' Six days and 110 hours of discussion later, they reached a compro-mise agreement and moved on to New Zealand, where he found the capital dull but the Prime Minister and Minister for Finance accommodating.

Reith was getting about four hours' sleep a night and thriving on it. They headed for India. The pilot brought the Liberator down to 2000 feet and circled twice round the Taj Mahal. Then to Delhi and to what Reith described as 'the splendours of viceregal lodgement'. He was given the Irwin suite, which the Viceroy and his wife had originally occupied; 'my bedroom is about 70 feet by 35 and the bed about 8 feet broad.'[7] He found negotiations with the Indians 'very slow going', but by the time the party moved on to Kenya they had come into line and accepted the document that had been signed in Canberra.

When they dined with the Viceroy, a gorgeously attired Punjabi stood behind each chair. Government House in Nairobi fell short of this standard of service; their stay in Kenya was brief, and it was perhaps just as well: 'I didn't like either Governor or wife – she almost spherical, common in all her ways, with a cigarette hanging from her mouth. I had nothing to say to them, nor they to us; nor had they the decency to get tea for us.'[8] Reith made up for this when they moved on to Salisbury, in what was then Southern Rhodesia: 'This morning at breakfast I had an orange, kedgeree, bacon and eggs, cold ham. If I had seen the cereal I should have had that also.'[9] On the way south, their air commandant made a detour and took them even lower over the Victoria Falls than he had done over the Taj.

Reith knew that South Africa and Canada were going to be the hardest nuts to crack. In Cape Town they saw the Prime Minister, Field Marshal Smuts – 'My *dear* Lord Reith, you are most welcome to South Africa' – but dear Lord Reith failed to budge him. It was the first real failure of the tour: 'I was disgusted with him and wanted to be away,' he wrote. 'What a country; I should be frightened to live here.'[10]

The last leg of their journey took them by way of Ascension Island, Brazil and Trinidad to Canada. When there was nothing to look at, Reith slept – a seven-foot sofa had been installed on the Liberator for him. For diversion there was the backgammon board which Joyce Wilson had brought. When the tour was over, it was inscribed with a lengthy and somewhat bizarre account of their odyssey:

THIS BACKGAMMON BOARD is a very unusual
Backgammon board . . .
It has done what no other backgammon board
Ever did before or since.
It has travelled round the world
In a record and epic flight . . .

Reith later gave over the best part of a page in his memoirs to reproducing the inscription word for word.[11]

He was already beginning to worry about what he was going to do when he got home: 'It's simply awful to imagine oneself racketing in tubes and buses again.'[12] But first he had to work on the Canadians; their position was peculiar in that their external communications linked up with those of the United States, and they were therefore less dependent on the Commonwealth system. The party had flown direct from the tropics, and Ottawa lay under deep snow; the day after they arrived, Reith went down with severe sinus trouble. The British High Commissioner at the time was Ramsay MacDonald's son, Malcolm, and when he reported to the Secretary of State for Dominion Affairs on the visit, he was full of praise for Reith's performance: 'I understand that his tactful handling was to no small degree responsible for the extremely cordial atmosphere which prevailed.'[13]

MacDonald had known Reith since the days of his father's premiership, and had been looking forward to gossiping about old times. Years later he told Andrew Boyle that he had been startled to discover that when he was not caught up in the negotiating sessions, Reith allowed Joyce Wilson 'to monopolise all his available time, attention and affectionate interest'. His insistence that Joyce Wilson should be in on everything also caused the High Commissioner headaches in the field of protocol. 'It was a trying interlude,' he told Boyle:

I had, of course, heard past whispers of his friendships with women while I was still in Whitehall. This particular manifestation admittedly took me by surprise. It complicated things in the circumstances and gave rise to some awkwardness.[14]

Reith had been bombarding Sir John Anderson with progress reports from each capital on their route, and was piqued to find no message from him when he returned to Northolt. Anderson invited him to call a week later; it was a month before the Dominions Secretary did the same. Characteristically, Reith finished his report overnight and had it printed within seven days – six pages, thirteen appendices. 'A party of this sort cannot travel and make such contacts,' he wrote, 'without being recipients of interesting and possibly important comment; nor without forming some conclusions on Commonwealth and Empire affairs.' He was greatly offended when nobody took him up on this – although he also won a five-shilling bet with a Treasury official that nobody would.

Anderson liked his report and promised to give it a fair wind in Cabinet; Beaverbrook and others, however, were suspicious of Reith's suggestion that the proposed central corporation should be strengthened by vesting in it the 'oceanic assets' of Cable and Wireless. The Cabinet finally agreed – but only just – to the calling of a conference. It was to meet in London, and Reith was invited to chair it. Before that could happen, the wartime coalition was dissolved and the Prime Minister set about forming his 'caretaker' administration. 'The cad Churchill is making up his new government,' Reith wrote. 'I suppose I should really like to be offered a job – if it were a decent one – but I don't think it would be good for me to take it.' He was not put to the test, and when the sixteen names in the new Cabinet were announced, he was almost philosophical: 'The only job I know I want is ambassador to USA – or viceroy though what I saw of India put me off that a bit.'[15]

At a more mundane level he made his debut that summer as a magistrate on the local bench:

> Tilbury, a housepainter, is chairman, and no use, the talking being done by one Horace Walker, KC, an octogenarian. There was a case about under-weight for coal and a bastardy case – a girl of 19 and an Australian; she was trying to pin fatherhood on him but it was dismissed. Most unsavoury and an indication of what is happening in war – particularly with Americans.[16]

Reith made practically no mention in his memoirs of the closing stages of the war, but there are occasional diary references to it: 'I saw a war map today, and was delighted to see that the Russians are a third of the distance from Berlin that the US and British are. I suppose I hope the Russians will get there first – which is dreadful but it's a factor of my hatred of Churchill.'[17] He pondered the death of Mussolini: 'What an extraordinary end. He did wonders for his country and then went wrong.'[18] Reports early in May that Hitler, too, was dead prompted a more than usually bizarre diary entry:

> If Churchill had any inspiration or imagination or spiritual vision in him, he could make an immortal utterance about Hitler and Mussolini. It's utterly beyond him – witness his feeble Roosevelt tribute. I would do it on the lines of an additional canto to Dante's *Inferno*.[19]

The general election campaign was a source of considerable irritation, and the attention paid to the Prime Minister provoked him into taking liberties with the language: 'Newspapers and the BBC', he wrote, 'are sycophanting to such an extent that one almost expects to hear how he goes to pump ship.' One other piece of election news came to his attention: 'Heard that Bowser was to stand as a conservative in Perth! He has certainly changed his politics.'[20] Peers, like lunatics, had no vote; Muriel, after listening to a party political broadcast by Lady Violet Bonham-Carter, decided that she would vote Liberal for the first time.

For most of May and June, Reith had busied himself with preparations for the conference: 'I never came on anyone with such capacity for orderly and comprehensive drafting as myself,' he wrote immodestly.[21] He certainly made an immensely thorough job of the physical arrangements. He was determined that visiting delegations should not be scattered across London in hotel suites and High Commission offices, and he managed to lay his hands on 5 Old Palace Yard, which looked out on the Houses of Parliament on one side and on the Henry VII chapel of the Abbey on another. Within a matter of weeks the building had been cleaned up and decorated. A large room was provided for each delegation, and their country's coat of arms was painted on the door.

It was decided late in the day that the UK delegation should consist entirely of officials. Reith tried to smooth ruffled Commonwealth feathers by arranging for a number of ministers to be present at the opening ceremony:

> The visitors were apparently concerned as to what they should wear on this occasion. The South African minister consulted me about it; they proposed black coat and striped trousers for the opening but less formal dress thereafter; was that right? Quite right; but as chairman I would appear in formal rig throughout. So we were all in our Sunday suits to receive Chancellor of the Exchequer Anderson when he arrived to open the proceedings in light tweeds.[22]

Before the conference ended, the election results had been declared and it was a Labour Chancellor of the Exchequer who presided at the farewell dinner. Reith had been giving his mind to an appropriate send-off for the Commonwealth delegates: 'I had thought it would give them a particular thrill to be embarked under the white ensign; to visit France and see something of war devastation there.'[23] The First Lord of the Admiralty obliged, and a frigate and a destroyer were laid on to take them to Calais and Dunkirk. On the way home, a division of motor torpedo boats manoeuvred at speed round them, and the ships fired pom-poms and star shells – 'all exciting and beautiful', Reith wrote. To round the day off he took them to Canterbury, where he had arranged for them to be received by the Archbishop; then they all sat about in deck chairs in the garden of one of the canons and had supper.

The end of the conference left him with nothing to fill his days. He took the family off on holiday to Wales, and it was there that he heard of the Japanese surrender. 'I do not feel the least elation about anything,' he wrote. 'The only way in which it might affect us is that Christopher may not have to join the Navy . . . I wish we could have a house in Scotland with a burn beside it.'[24]

The Attlee government announced their acceptance of the conference proposals in October 1945, and a bill giving partial effect to them was introduced the following May. 'Yesterday it was coal; today it is cables; the Socialist advance therefore continues,' boomed Hugh Dalton, the Labour Chancellor. Reith was outraged – 'the bill neither derived from nor was inspired by Socialism' – but not on purely ideological grounds:

> Dalton paid a long and fulsome compliment to Sir A. Duncan [the chairman of the Iron and Steel Federation] when introducing the Steel bill. When he introduced the Cable and Wireless bill, for which I am entirely responsible, he never even mentioned my name.[25]

Fifteen

BRAVE NEW WORLD

Join the party and you get a peerage and jobs.
JOHN REITH, *Diary*, 1 January 1947

THE 1945 ELECTION produced a massive swing to Labour and Churchill was swept from office. 'There was no question about my jubilation on this score,' Reith wrote, 'however little confidence I might have in Attlee and Co.'[1] That lack of confidence did not lessen his interest in the possibility of a job from the country's new political masters.

Dalton pressed him to accept the chairmanship of the CCC, which would lead to that of the new board and be worth £3500 a year. Reith's instinct, as so often, was to play hard to get, but that was not a game which his financial position allowed him to play with much assurance:

I made it quite clear that I wasn't keen on the job, but agreed to do as he wished, subject to his trying to keep my income up and to my not being prevented (or prejudiced) from taking other jobs.[2]

At the end of August, Lewis Silkin, the new Minister of Town and Country Planning, offered him the unpaid chairmanship of a committee to consider the development of New Towns. During September he noted that he had had a pleasant talk with Lord Addison, now Secretary of State for Commonwealth Relations, and that he had promised to talk to 'Clem'. They met again at a reception at South Africa House a couple of months later. The Foreign Secretary, Ernest Bevin, had just announced the setting up of a joint UK/US commission to inquire into the future of Palestine and the plight of the Jewish victims of Nazi persecution, and Reith registered his interest. Addison said he would pass that on; he also appears to have issued a fairly direct invitation to Reith to join the Labour Party.[3]

Reith brooded about this for several weeks. When he eventually wrote to Addison on the first day of the New Year, he began by asserting that he had never been a Tory, but then rehearsed a jumble of considerations that made him hesitate to throw in his lot with Labour. 'I am wholly in sympathy with Labour principles – and other parties have none,' he wrote:

My best service might be in loose rather than close association with the party, but with no doubt as to sympathy on all major issues. Because I have said publicly for years what I felt on such matters as nationalization and because I have shown in my work (BBC, Airways, politics and telecommunications) the direction in which my allegiance lies, I have destroyed any chance of being offered the few private enterprise sort of appointments I might have considered. I am therefore dependent on your people – and unfortunately they know this.[4]

Reith wrote another letter on 1 January 1946. It was to Winston Churchill. He marked it 'Personal and Private', and it began, 'This is a letter I have wanted to write to you for more than two years. There is nothing you can do about it now, but I felt I must send it.' It was the most extraordinary letter he ever wrote, and perhaps also the most poignant.

He chronicled his career since the beginning of the war – the call to duty as Minister of Information at a time when that office was 'in notorious disrepute'; the financial sacrifice entailed; his reluctance to leave the Commons; the 'utter shock' of Churchill's letter of dismissal in 1942. He told of his pride in his work at the Admiralty. He noted that others who had been dismissed 'were given sufficient alternative employment and income . . . there was nothing for me.' This extended catalogue of reproach, addressed to the wartime leader of the nation, was unusual enough, but it was less remarkable than the great shout of pain with which the letter concluded:

I have (like you) a war mentality and other qualities which have commended themselves to you. Even in office I was nothing like fully stretched; and I was completely out of touch with you. You could have used me in a way and to an extent you never realised. Instead of that there has been the sterility, humiliation and distress of all these years – 'eyeless in Gaza' – without even the consolation Samson had in knowing it was his own fault.

Churchill, on his way to the United States on the *Queen Elizabeth*, sent a reply which even Reith conceded was 'quite decent'. His letter, Churchill wrote, had grieved him; he had always admired Reith's abilities and energy, but on the occasions he had considered him for various posts, he had encountered opposition on the ground that he was difficult to work with:

I am unfeignedly sorry for the pain which you felt which I understand very fully, as I was myself, for eleven years, out of office before the war, during the past six of which I earnestly desired to take part in the work of preparation . . .
    If you think I can be of service to you at any time, pray let me know; for I am very sorry that the fortunes of war should have proved so adverse to you, and I feel the State is in your debt.[5]

Early in 1946, Reith found cause to be displeased with Churchill's successor. He judged a speech which Attlee made at the United Nations to be 'four times too long and utterly banal'. It was, he wrote, 'the sort of thing I could have

produced a kind of Lincoln Gettysburg speech for.' He became so agitated
that he rushed from the house at 9.30 in the evening and walked almost as far
as Penn, 'unbearably worried about what I was going to do':

> I tried to get in touch with God, with mother and father, being so desperately
> in need of help. I am near the end of my tether in every way. I am very
> near wishing I could die; I simply don't see any way out of my difficulties. I
> know I might still be rescued but the time is getting short. Sands running
> out.[6]

Undeterred by the fact that nobody had suggested it, he turned over in his
mind whether he might not like to be Secretary-General of the United Nations
– 'starting up something new is my line and of course I could have made of it
what I did of the BBC.' Then his attention switched to the bursarship of
Wellington College which had just been advertised. He took the view that the
chairmanship of the new Coal Board would be well within his competence and
felt he ought to have been approached – 'but I shouldn't be at all keen on
it, knowing nothing about mining.' Meeting the Bishop of Gloucester in the
Athenaeum, he told him he would like some honorary job in a cathedral close
in return for a house.

His failure to find employment was not the only reason for his distress in
those early weeks of 1946. His relations with Muriel were going through a bad
patch once again, and it is plain from his diary that Joyce Wilson was part of
the reason:

> Muriel in bed for breakfast but I didn't say anything to her when I got up,
> nor all day. I don't think JW is likely to come here again and I'm not
> surprised. It is a most awful atmosphere for anyone; and awful for Marista
> also; it is really well that she goes to school in September.[7]

He craved the affection and company of his children, for all that, and was still
capable of exerting himself to divert and amuse them: 'Marista and I made a
big snowman in the style of Epstein's Genesis.'[8]

Early in March, after a Prime Ministerial broadcast, he thought he saw an
opening, and wrote to Attlee:

> Since last summer, I have not had two days' work a week and if it had
> not been for Silkin's New Town Committee I would have had nothing to
> do at all. It does not seem right, especially in such times. And it is hard
> to bear.[9]

Attlee, famous for his economical way with words, sent a two-sentence reply
in his own hand – 'You may be sure that I have you in mind as one whose
services are not being fully utilized at the present time' – but nothing came of
it, and he had to content himself with his New Towns Committee, which took

up two days a week at the outside, and with his occasional appearances as a magistrate: 'More satisfactory today than ever before in sending a woman thief to prison for six months. If I hadn't been there it would only have been three or four.'[10]

The end of March saw the publication of the interim report of his New Towns Committee. It dealt with the type of agency that should be responsible for the creation of the new towns. Its principal – and totally unsurprising – recommendation was that there should be a government-sponsored public corporation financed by the Exchequer, with local authority corporations and authorised associations as the alternative. Reith wrote a sonorous introduction in which he said that their task far exceeded the mere devising of machinery for the ordered laying of bricks and mortar: 'Our responsibility . . . is rather to conduct an essay in civilisation, by seizing an opportunity to design, evolve and carry into execution for the benefit of coming generations the means for a happy and gracious means of life.'[11]

The *New Statesman* said that the report talked a great deal of sound sense in a few pages.[12] Praise did not come only from the left, however. Gilbert McAllister, MP, writing in *The Spectator*, reminded his readers that when Reith had become Minister of Works and Planning he had asked for men 'with wings to their minds'. The phrase, he wrote, had been received with little understanding and more than faint ridicule: 'Few people know their Aristophanes today; but Lord Reith was right both in period and in mood.'[13]

In April, the work of the committee took him briefly to Sweden. When the Swedish Crown Prince was in London the following month, Reith and Silkin were asked to pick him up at the Embassy and take him on a conducted tour of Welwyn. Reith was horrified by the appearance of the chauffeur – 'thoroughly untidy and no gloves'. Worse was to follow:

Silkin had no hat or gloves and didn't say 'Sir' once. A shabby parish clerk met us on the main road and guided us to the UDC office the door of which was only half open. There was some waffling on the pavement, then more inside, then a man came nonchalantly down the stairs and shook hands with the Crown Prince with his other hand in his trouser pocket . . . Really ghastly and I wish I could have stage-managed the whole business – Swedish flags and motor cycle policemen and such like. Damnable.[14]

In the summer he lost the services of Joyce Wilson, who had decided to go back into the Army. 'Wrote "hints for Joyce in her new job",' he noted in his diary. 'I feel I've not been at all kind to her all these years she has been with me and now she's gone.' He was very cast down at her departure, and felt the need to share his feelings with Muriel:

I said (not by way of reproach) that I didn't think I would ever have let her go if she (M) had felt differently to her. M said she had never liked our association and that I had so much companionship with her, whereas she herself was only the cook housekeeper.[15]

The following month they celebrated their silver wedding. Muriel gave him fifteen volumes of de Quincey. Unusually, he did not record his present to her.

Early in July, Silkin asked whether he would take on the chairmanship of one of the New Town corporations. Reith thought he would be of more use as a general commissioner with oversight of all the corporations, a suggestion which the Minister said he would consider.[16] A few days later, shortly before the publication of his New Towns final report, Reith's colleagues on the committee gave a dinner for him at the Savoy, and in proposing his health one of their number, F. J. Osborn, paid witty and affectionate tribute to his chairmanship. He was anxious, he said, for the report to be printed quickly before he reflected too much on what he had put his signature to:

> What have we done? We have told the most urban country what towns should be; the pioneers of the first Industrial Revolution how to conduct a second; a nation of shopkeepers to have fewer shops; of tea-drinkers to take wine with its meals; of dog-lovers that it must not go to the dogs . . .

The report was an intriguing social document. It ranged widely over the detail of size and social structure, zoning layout and landscape treatment, and Reith's fingerprints were all over it, especially in the section dealing with social life and recreation:

> Without being repressive, the agency should seek to prevent ugliness, rowdiness and squalor in all places of assembly and amusement . . . Care must be taken to ensure that camouflaged drinking saloons are not allowed . . . Greyhound racing . . . would bring in its train consequences likely to be specially objectionable in a new town because displeasing to a large proportion of the residents.[17]

He dithered about whether to accept a New Town chairmanship, partly because he hoped that he might get a 'proper job', partly because he thought the corporations would be too much under Civil Service influence. While on holiday in Scotland in August he read some speculation in *The Scotsman* that he might be considered for the chairmanship of the new Iron and Steel Board, and his hopes soared. It turned out to be no more than gossip, and when he returned to London he told Silkin that he would take on the chairmanship of Hemel Hempstead.

Joyce Wilson was working in Germany, and Reith had been in frequent touch; he now wrote to Sir Edward Bridges, the head of the Treasury, recommending her for an OBE.[18] Then, after he finally made up his mind about Hemel Hempstead, he telephoned to ask whether she would come back to him. She rang the next day to say she would. Two weeks later she was once again installed in his office, and in a one-room service flat in Marsham Court; by the end of the month, Reith, constitutionally deaf to wagging tongues, had moved into a larger flat at the same address and began to use it for the inside of each week.

Christopher had now come to the end of his time at Eton and had been called up for national service in the Navy; Marista had gone away to school for the first time at St George's, Ascot. Reith was in his fifty-eighth year, and his mind turned more and more insistently to writing his memoirs. He had lunched with Geoffrey Faber just before leaving the Admiralty a couple of years previously and had been offered an advance of £750. Now he began to talk to Hutchinson, who first mentioned a figure of £1000 for the British Empire rights, an offer subsequently increased to £2500. In December he agreed to deliver a manuscript by the end of the following July, and plunged into his pre-1914 diaries, the bit firmly between his teeth.

In the course of 1946, Reith also slowly began to get back on terms with the BBC. For years he had held himself stiffly aloof, refusing to attend the twenty-first anniversary celebrations in 1943 ('The lunch should have been given *to me*') and declining an invitation to become an honorary life vice-president of the BBC Club.

In 1944, when William Haley became Director-General, Reith's reaction to the appointment had betrayed a strand in his make-up which was not simply childish but downright primitive. For several months he played a silly trick in his diary of affecting not to know Haley's name – 'I wonder what I would do if Bailey, the new sole director-general of the BBC, made any approach to me,' one entry reads.[19] It was a bit like sticking pins into a wax image, a form of jujuism that allowed him to deny something too painful to accept. Indignation was a great help in clearing the brain, however, and by the beginning of 1946 he was no longer in doubt about what his successor several times removed was called – 'Haley in the BBC is a KCMG after about one and three-quarter years service there – simply shocking.'[20]

Then it was reported to him that Haley had made some highly complimentary remarks about him; the man was clearly not all bad. Reith wrote offering to meet, and Haley responded warmly – 'It is a source of great pride to me to be trying to carry on the great traditions you founded ... Diffidence kept me from approaching you ...'

Lunched at Manetta's with Sir William Haley! He gave an awkward sort of bow when I went in ... He expressed on several occasions the utmost admiration for me and my work and said he wanted nothing better than to carry on what I had done and bring the concern back to what it had been. He was sure, however, that he wouldn't be there long if I were chairman. I had made it clear to him that my letter to him had nothing whatever to do with the vacancy for chairman.[21]

In the event the chairmanship went to Lord Inman – 'a Labour peer no one has heard about – miserable choice,' Reith wrote. He had been told at a dinner party a week previously that it had not been offered to him because he was 'too strong for Attlee'. He still held out against the idea of improving his chances of preferment by joining the Labour Party, however. When somebody told him at a sherry party that they had heard he had done so, Reith responded with a notable conversation-stopper: 'I said I had also become a Muslim.'[22]

He returned Haley's hospitality with lunch at the Carlton Grill: 'He was at great pains to assure me that he had nothing to do with my not being offered the BBC chair.'[23] They talked a great deal about organisation and personalities. A week later, BBC engineers turned up at Harrias House and installed a combined sound and television receiver. After dinner on Christmas Day, the king over the water permitted himself to unbend a little in front of the small screen.

Early in 1947 he had to recognise that one of his most cherished ambitions would never now be achieved. India was moving rapidly towards independence, and the Attlee government announced the timetable for the end of the Raj:

What upset me far more than their decision to evacuate by June 1948 was that the playboy Mountbatten had been made viceroy, Wavell being dismissed. So that is the job I most wanted on earth gone for good . . . More can be done by the viceroy in the next year than in the last hundred, and they choose that fraud and counterfeit.[24]

He threw himself into his memoirs. He made a considerable corvée of it, fretting over a title and working in furious bouts that frequently went on into the small hours. He was heavily dependent on Joyce Wilson, who took dictation and produced drafts. At the end of March she was suddenly taken ill. Reith found her behind screens in a public ward at Caterham Cottage Hospital; she remained dangerously ill for several days, but responded to treatment by penicillin and was told that she must convalesce for up to two months. 'I expect she won't be back at all,' Reith wrote glumly. 'What I'm to do, I simply can't imagine – and how can I do the memoirs?' Luckily for him, he was able, as so often over the years, to command the unswerving loyalty of Jo Stanley, and she was soon hard at work in her spare time deciphering Joyce Wilson's shorthand.

He continued to be in touch with Haley, who succeeded in persuading him to go to lunch in his old room at Broadcasting House. 'Of course I was enormously envious of Haley with all the circumstances and amenities of a big office and organization,' he wrote. 'I don't know that I was as much "on the job" as I might have been, because it was so harrowing.'[25] Haley rang him in the middle of April to say that Inman was to be Lord Privy Seal, and that the chairmanship was therefore once more open. They both lobbied vigorously, and for some weeks his hopes ran high; then after supper on Whit Sunday Haley suddenly

appeared at Harrias House, and Reith knew from his manner that someone
else had been chosen. (It was, as it turned out, another Labour peer, Lord
Simon of Wythenshawe.) 'The last straw it seemed,' he wrote. 'It wasn't just
a "job" that might be offered and wasn't, like so many others. It was in a class
by itself. I fell I absolutely *must* get away from this country.'[26]

This was more than talk. He considered writing to Smuts to explore the
possibility of settling in South Africa, and he wrote to Vincent Massey, then
the Chancellor of the University of Toronto, about opportunities in Canada.
The result was a letter from Massey offering him the position of Dean of
the Faculty of Engineering and Applied Science, and Reith wrote expressing
qualified interest: 'I must also, of course, have some regard to mundane points
such as income – where would that put one socially and economically? And is
there a house?'[27] The idea grew on him when he was in Scotland on holiday
in August, but early in October the opportunity dematerialised: 'Letter from
Massey, most apologetic and embarrassed. I am too old. So that's that.'[28] His
reply expressed surprise, but conveyed hurt; he was so offended that he could
not bring himself to write to Massey again for several months.

Haley exerted himself constantly to keep his spirits up and make him feel
wanted. After the disappointment over the chairmanship, he wrote him an
eloquently consoling letter in which he said that his conception of broadcasting
remained the driving force of the BBC, and that this was felt even by those
who had never had the privilege of working for him:

> I hope you will not let weaken the links that bind you to the BBC. They
> are stronger than any formal attachment. Our work of rehabilitation and
> regeneration will encounter many obstacles. We need your sympathy and
> understanding. An easy and natural relationship would enrich us and – if I
> may say so – would enrich you as well. I believe that from such an association
> much happiness could flow.[29]

When Haley told him a few weeks later of the plan for a series of lectures
named after him, he affected not to like the idea, but was not a little flattered.[30]
The Corporation's Silver Jubilee celebrations were approaching; Haley tried
unsuccessfully to persuade him to broadcast but won his agreement to reading
the lesson at a service. He also accepted an invitation to dine with the Governors. It was to have been at Claridge's, but was transferred to Broadcasting
House because of a strike. The BBC's first Director-General was not
impressed: 'I felt disgusted at their doing it in this scudgy way,' he wrote. 'They
should have had a big party with, I should have thought, the Prime Minister.'
Nor did he much like the moral he drew from his conversation with the new
Chairman: 'Simon of Wythenshawe told me he had offered to do some job for
Attlee; nothing came of it; then he joined the Labour party, was made a lord
and given the BBC.'[31]

July had always been an improbable deadline for his memoirs, and he was
still hard at work on them as autumn turned into winter. As he wrote, he

relived some of the episodes he was describing with painful intensity: 'The story of the Clarendon/Snowden troubles fair makes my blood boil,' he noted at one point. 'At times I felt I couldn't go on.'[32] He sometimes worked through the night. There are occasional complaints in the diary of feeling 'very buzzy in the head'; he seems not to have made the connection between this and the large amounts of benzedrine with which he had taken to dosing himself.

The postscriptum with which the memoirs conclude is heavily tinged with purple. 'Periodically, in writing these closing words,' reads a passage on the last page, 'I have been conscious of speech and music from some nearby loudspeaker', and he harks back by nostalgic association to his childhood:

To the haunting tune of Crimond the metrical version of the 23rd psalm is being spread over all the world from the Abbey of Westminster; from the wedding of the king's daughter:

> The Lord's my shepherd, I'll not want;
> He makes me down to lie . . .

That age-old song of presbyterian Scotland, the national anthem of its faith. I see my mother trace its lines for me to read. I hear my father's voice: 'John, can you say the 23rd psalm yet?' I hear it sung at family worship in the manse; in the College Church in Glasgow; in the little highland conventicle of halcyon summer holidays. The abbey of Westminster dissolves to the Kirk of Rothiemurchus . . .[33]

His diary paints a less lyrical picture of his mood on the day of writing: 'Miserable Royal wedding day,' he wrote. 'Completely out of phase with everything and everybody through not being asked to the Abbey or anywhere.'[34]

With work on the memoirs advanced to that stage, he no longer had enough work to keep Joyce Wilson fully occupied. Over lunch with Haley at Broadcasting House, Reith broached the question of finding her something at the BBC: 'I don't suppose he would risk making her secretary to the resuscitated management committee because of jealousies caused . . .'[35] He had accepted Haley's invitation with some reluctance, because he was beginning to find the renewed association with the old firm unsettling: 'I don't really think I want to keep up this contact. Does me more harm than good.' He went off home, and while the rest of the family played rummy, he shut himself away to write letters and bring his diary up to date: 'The old year is nearly over . . . It seems that everybody has now accepted my absolute negligence – nothing and nobody.'[36]

The reason for Reith's growing ambivalence about the renewal of contact with the BBC was not far to seek. He was not a man who could ever be content with the sound of music in the next room. He attended further Silver Jubilee celebrations in Birmingham and Glasgow in the course of 1948, though with no great enthusiasm or enjoyment. The Scottish anniversary fell in March, and

Reith contributed a bizarre piece to *Radio Times* in which he wrote about himself in the third person:

> ... Much of what he himself did in the days of his charge derives directly from a Glasgow manse and from his own frequent nocturnal perambulations along the High drive of the West-end Park – particularly when the winds blew strong. The winds seemed to be saying things to him, but he never quite understood what they said . . .[37]

During the family's Scottish holiday in August he noted that he was dreaming almost every night that he was back in the BBC, and in December, as he sank into his customary mid-winter depression, he wrote to Haley to say that he could not go on with 'a superficial and intermittent involvement' in BBC affairs.[38]

Haley, as always, responded with tact and delicacy, although he either did not fully grasp – or wisely chose not to address – the true reason for his predecessor's unhappiness:

> ... While I can understand your feeling that because by the very nature of your work you once knew everything down to the smallest detail you are now conscious of all you do not know, I do wish you to appreciate that I have derived great help from you, that I should be distressed if because of your dissatisfaction we were to grow apart . . .[39]

It was, of course, Reith's passion for 'the smallest detail' which lay at the root of the trouble. The itch to get his fingers into any aspect of the BBC's activities was uncontrollable. Early in the year he recorded that he had lunched with George Barnes, newly appointed to the strangely styled post of Director of the Spoken Word (it meant he was in charge of radio). 'Gave him most excellent advice,' Reith wrote, 'his terms of reference and all. It was worth a great deal of money.'[40] Some weeks later he was offering guidance at a different level: 'Joyce W is having a very busy time; I produced some notes for her.'[41]

He made two further appeals to Attlee during the year, reminding him that the chairmanship of Hemel Hempstead and of the Commonwealth Communications Council occupied 'only a small fraction of the week and of my energies'.[42] Attlee mislaid his first letter ('I should hesitate to put any blame on my secretary'), but then invited him to No. 10 and listened patiently for half an hour while Reith told him how he felt about his 'idleness'.[43] When Herbert Morrison made the mistake at a party of asking him how he was, Reith told him, and with mathematical precision – 'fifteen per cent occupied'.[44]

Christopher had now completed his national service and discovered, somewhat to his surprise, that his father had decided he should go to Oxford. There were discussions about whether he should study estate management or forestry, and Reith set about trying to get him in, trading heavily on his acquaintance with J. C. Masterman, who was now Provost of Worcester. Christopher had signed on at crammer's, and Reith took him to Oxford to meet the Professor of Forestry and to lunch with Masterman. 'He will take CJ to oblige me,' he wrote. 'He has turned down about 1,000 fellows but said his conscience was quite clear because of what I had done for the country.'[45] Christopher, who was not academically inclined, had to have two goes at Responsions. When the news came that he had passed, Reith was beside himself with excitement: 'It was almost too good to be true,' he wrote. 'I rang a tremendous peal on the ship's bell.'[46]

Marista was now a spirited and intelligent girl of sixteen, with a generous allocation of Reith genes. She had done well in her School Certificate, gaining distinctions in two-thirds of her subjects and credits in the rest; when she read the lesson in chapel on Good Friday, the chaplain told her that he had never heard an ordained man do better. In one of her letters home, she asked advice about two essays she had been set – on 'Art for art's sake' and 'Democracy in an industrial civilisation'. 'Silly subjects,' Reith rumbled. 'Wrote a long letter to her with full answers and essays.'[47] In December she was confirmed in the Royal Chapel in Windsor Park by the Dean. Reith already entertained substantial ambitions for her: 'Wrote Marista about being first woman PM. I am sure she can and should be something very considerable.'[48]

Although she might seek advice about a school essay, Marista's recollection in later life was that asking questions at home was not a profitable exercise:

> Questions were not invited because he made statements which were beyond question. You also knew that if you were so bold as to ask a question, you would be given an answer that was obscure. So any kind of discourse was oddly discouraged. It was excluding. It was a hothouse atmosphere – the fresh air didn't get in. And there was all the precariousness of being surrounded by glass.[49]

The glass was under fairly frequent threat. Domestic storms could brew up with dramatic suddenness and over matters of no great moment. Christopher had for years worked like a Trojan in the garden, and made himself extremely knowledgeable about what needed doing and how it should be done, from the felling of trees to the laying out of new flower beds. There was a reminder in that July of 1948 that none of this was protection against summer thunder:

> Annoyed with CJ at breakfast, arguing with me on the extraordinary contention that there was nowhere in the garden to begin a manure heap. I therefore went to town by myself and he by bus. Missed the train I went for and had to wait for the 9.15.[50]

At some stage during the year, for reasons which do not emerge from his diary, Reith decided to acquire a literary agent and to ask him to find a new publisher for his memoirs. The agent approached both Collins and Hodder & Stoughton, and Reith preserved in his scrapbook an undated four-page report by Hodder's chief reader:

... There is little need to draw attention to the author's prose style. It is enough to make the Brothers Fowler turn in their graves. But it never gets out of hand ... I note, with relief, that I need not concern myself with possible libel. (A layman, of course, would say that a good deal of the book was solid dynamite.) This really is a remarkable book by a remarkable man.

Reith, who was rather impressionable in literary matters, seems to have taken the remarks about his style to heart, and there is an uncharacteristically contrite note in his diary: 'Finished the first volume of memoirs referring to *Fowler's English Usage*, which I should have been to before.'[51]

He was not the only man in England who had been busy with memoirs. Winston Churchill had just published *The Gathering Storm*, the first volume of his majestic six-part account of the war, and Reith devoured most of it in one long evening. Five years later the work was to win for its author the Nobel Prize for Literature, but all that John Reith could find to say that night in his diary was, 'There's no reference to me or broadcasting.'[52]

Reith added a third job to his portfolio in 1949. He was asked to go and see the President of the Board of Trade, Harold Wilson. Wilson – 'aged 33 but looking ten years older' – asked whether he would be interested in the chairmanship of the National Film Finance Corporation, the body charged under the recent Cinematograph Film Production Act with the allocation of £5 million for loans for the production of British films. The salary was only £1500, but Wilson said that the scope of the job was potentially much bigger than the terms of the Act indicated. Reith accepted the offer at a further meeting some days later (on his way there he 'invited the aid of the Almighty'). He asked for one paragraph in the draft letter of invitation to be altered (he didn't care for a phrase about 'mutual cooperation' between him and the corporation's managing director) and said that so far as salary was concerned he would prefer to deal direct with the Treasury.[53] Another small ray of financial sunshine pierced the clouds when his agent secured £1000 from the *Sunday Express* for the serialisation of extracts from his memoirs.[54]

Reith had once or twice over the years allowed his interest to be engaged by the Moral Rearmament Movement, and there are indications in his diary that he was being badgered by them at this time. Some months previously he had helped them draft a letter of complaint to the BBC, and he was now approached by two of their officials called Wilson and Lean: 'Former told me his guidance had told him that my biggest life's work was still to come and that I might be instrumental in causing a Christian revolution in this country.' Reith was not entirely persuaded: 'I wish I might have some guidance direct,' he wrote.[55]

The MRA did not give up, and there was a further approach, this time from someone more senior:

Their more or less head man in London had the following guidance recently
. . . 'He is a chosen vessel – meant to restore moral and spiritual values to
Britain. The greatest part of his life lies ahead of him. You need him at Caux
for planning of your world Christian strategy together. Urge him strongly to
come – to cancel other dates if need be and to make this a priority.'[56]

Reith sensibly left his priorities unaltered and cancelled no dates. He had a
most important one at Henley. Christopher had been doing well on the river
at Oxford, and his Worcester crew had a good first day at the regatta. Reith
was so excited that each time they won, he rushed to the mobile Post Office
and sent a telegram to Marista. On day two things went less well – Bedford
School beat them by a canvas, and First and Third Trinity by a length. 'I think
I feel it much more than CJ will but I was so very, very sorry for him,' Reith
wrote. 'There was even an element of selfishness in it! I was getting a personal
lift out of CJ's success.'[57]

There was a flurry of activity on the telecommunications front during the
summer. The Commonwealth Telegraphs Act became law on 31 May, and
this established the Commonwealth Telecommunications Board as the successor body to the CCC. In August there was a conference between all the
Commonwealth governments and the United States; the Americans wanted to
rescind the 1945 Bermuda Agreement about rates and increase them. Reith,
in the chair, drove the proceedings forward at a cracking pace and eventually
a compromise was agreed. He was gratified to be sent, later in the year, a
copy of the report which the Chairman of the US Federal Communications
Commission had sent to Dean Acheson, the Secretary of State:

> It soon became evident that the conference was most fortunate in having
> Lord Reith selected as our Chairman. He took command at the outset and
> set a pace which, although rather breathtaking, served to preclude much
> useless argument. On several occasions Lord Reith, through his extreme
> tact and able diplomacy, succeeded in bringing agreement on matters which
> had appeared irreconcilable.[58]

In late August there was the annual family pilgrimage to Scotland, this time to
Torosay Castle, on the Isle of Mull, which functioned at the time as a cross
between a country house and a hotel. One day they crossed to Iona, where
'the great George Macleod' was waiting to show them around. 'He was very
attentive,' Reith wrote. 'I hadn't met him since I more or less offered him the
Scottish directorship of the BBC about 20 years ago.' Later there was a more
strenuous outing:

> Today I did what I've often wanted to do, but was beginning to doubt my
> capacity to do . . . I set out at 10.30 in lashing rain and strong wind . . . 28
> miles, and with no training; extraordinary . . . After dinner I did Gay
> Gordons, Petronella and Dashing White Sergeant till 11 – two hours of it.

I enjoyed it greatly, but it's very upsetting; I so badly want to do them all well.[59]

There was a special reason why Reith so badly wanted to do them well. Staying at Torosay with her parents and brother there was a pretty dark-haired girl of nineteen. She first appears in the diary as 'the Mackay girl', but then she becomes 'Dawn', and it is clear from the frequency with which she is mentioned that Reith had begun to seek out her company. The day after his epic walk, the two families went on an excursion together.

For the first time that week there was a break in the weather. They boarded a launch at the jetty and made for the Isles of the Sea, where he recorded that they visited the grave of St Columba's mother and that he and Dawn sat on the top of a rock together. 'A really wonderful day,' he wrote in his diary. 'After dinner instruction in Hamilton House and Scottish Reformer.'[60] The next day was a Sunday, but Reith was now so carried away with the desire to shine on the dance floor that he mislaid his sabbatarian scruples and joined in more reel and country dance rehearsals in the library after dinner. More than thirty years later, Dawn Mackay did not remember him as an especially apt pupil: 'He wasn't a very relaxed person. I think you've either danced reels from your cradle or you haven't – he wanted diagrams laid out on the floor, with graphs of who went where when . . .'[61]

The following day he set off on another marathon walk. He went off suddenly, and rather late in the day – Dawn Mackay thought he had had a 'monumental up-and-downer' with Muriel. He was away so long – he had gone as far as Lochbuie, at the south-east of the island – that Muriel became anxious. Mr Mackay, who had known Reith for some time, went out in his car to look for him. He had some difficulty in persuading him to accept a lift and they were not back at Torosay until 8.45.

After dinner there was to be a dance. Marista and Christopher were dressed and ready and soon went down, and so, a little later, did Muriel. Just why, after all the pleasure he had taken in the rehearsals, Reith did not follow them his diary does not make clear. He may simply have lost his nerve. Possibly he had over-taxed himself on his walk. There seems to have been some sort of further altercation with Muriel. At any event, he stayed put in his room, although as he sat there with his diary before him he was tempted by the strains of the music to change his mind:

I wasn't sure that I wouldn't dress and go down to the dance; a little persuasion from Dawn would probably have made me do so . . . Anyway it's over now. I heard the last eight and foursome reel that I might have danced with Dawn . . .[62]

The next day his spirits had revived. The sun shone, and he succeeded in monopolising Miss Mackay's attention for most of the afternoon: 'After lunch talked to Dawn till tea.' The sentence is underlined in the diary, and so is another which says 'Dawn came to the entrance to the wood.' The holiday was coming to an end. The two families made a last excursion together up Loch Linnhe to look at the seals: 'I was glad to have this last trip on the blue sea,' Reith wrote:

> Dawn rushed off for a 4 pm hair appointment on our coming alongside. When she went off to the Duart dance last night she had found her catapult in her coat pocket and had asked me to keep them [sic] for her. I had meant to give them to her at the station ... I was feeling ghastly. It's a relief in some ways to be going south.[63]

In the south, real life reasserted itself. Christopher had to be ferried back to Oxford; an invitation to chair a Foyle's lunch for Wilfred Pickles had to be indignantly declined. There was a new Standard Vanguard car which Hemel Hempstead had supplied to be grumbled about, and proposals about premises for the National Film Finance Corporation to be resisted: 'I am absolutely against going to Soho Square on the score of dignity.' Idyllic Highland memories slowly faded, and for a period of some years the members of the Mackay family appear only infrequently in the pages of the diary.[64]

Into the Wind was published in November. Reith grumbled a little when he heard that Hodder were printing only 6000 copies. Malcolm Muggeridge, reviewing it in the *Daily Telegraph*, homed in waspishly on Reith's assertion that he and Churchill were temperamentally alike: 'a classic example', he wrote, 'of a one-way resemblance. By the same token St Pancras Church is like the Erechtheum in Athens, but indubitably not vice versa.'[65] The *Glasgow Herald* handed it to Tom Johnston, Labour's Secretary of State for Scotland, and he concentrated on the author's propensity, during his brief years in Whitehall, for treading on political toes: 'Even Lord Reith could not take on all the parties and some of the ministerial staffs single-handed.' The review in *The Times* (unsigned, as was the practice in those days) made a highly perceptive observation – 'it suggests that the diary from which the book is quarried may be a dangerous document.'

The idiosyncratic prose style attracted a good deal of attention. Walter Allen, in the *New Statesman*, found that it did not make for easy reading: 'Lord Reith has retained a staccato note-form which falls at times into a curious sub-Carlylese.' Edward Hodgkin, in *The Spectator*, saw a prose model in Dickens: 'The narrative is not helped by being written in a series of short snorts, rather as though Mr Jingle had got hold of a dictaphone.'

The reviews all went into the scrapbook, and so did two letters. One of them had been sent not to Reith but to the Bishop of Gloucester:

> How I wish Lord Reith might know that down the years his example and clear thinking is still shining a guiding light, even though it may be to the most insignificant of secretaries tucked away in West Region. I have always recognised that the BBC had something which other corporations would

appear to lack, namely the pride of belonging – and now I realise to what source this may be traced.

The other was from Mary Somerville, now very much the *grande dame* of educational broadcasting, and it showed how good his judgement had been when he recruited her all those years before:

... I'll be honest and say I wish you had waited. Oh I'm grateful enough to have the story, but I could shake you till your teeth rattle for ending on that obituary note! Of course there will be a new chapter, but you'll not get again the old sense that God is using you if you just sit girning that the state doesn't! ... You know your Bible. When was it not so? And did that ever stop the prophet of the Lord?

Sixteen

ANYTHING LEGAL CONSIDERED

'Isn't there some big job you would like me to do? I could do such a lot, you know.'

JOHN REITH, *Letter to the Prime Minister,*
August 1950

ONLY A MAN of Reith's intensely romantic disposition (and unsophisticated literary taste) could set at the head of his memoirs the opening lines of Longfellow's ode *The Building of the Ship*:

> Build me straight, O worthy Master,
> Staunch and strong, a goodly vessel,
> That shall laugh at all disaster,
> And with wave and whirlwind wrestle.

Although the words are, in fact, those of a merchant placing a commission with the master of a shipyard, it is entirely conceivable that Reith understood the first line to be an invocation to the Almighty. He certainly still saw himself as a vessel in the other sense, and he was no less eager in his seventh decade to be taken and used for some high purpose than he had been as a young man. In his less exalted moments, however, he knew well enough that the sort of jobs he was interested in came mostly from governments and political parties, and this thought was in his mind as the country voted in the general election of February 1950. 'I simply don't know which I dislike more, Labour or Tory,' he wrote on polling day – but he added, 'nor which, if either, would be any better for my doings.'

Labour retained power, and the only immediate effect of this was that in his Hemel Hempstead job Reith had to deal with a new Minister of Town and Country Planning:

Saw Dalton at 3.00 in his House of Commons room. Oh, gosh – couldn't have been more cordial. Very delightful that *'nous deux'* being friends should have this new association now ... How I dislike and distrust him; he couldn't have been more civil – nor more insincere.[1]

The previous month he had been concerned when William Haley was taken ill and had to go into the London Clinic, and he was greatly moved by a letter which Haley wrote before he went into the operating theatre:

> Whatever happens it will set my mind at rest more this night to have written you one word: of thanks for your friendship to me at all times; of appreciation of the unsparing way you have been ready to give time to me even when it may have been inopportune to you; and lastly, for your inspiration. One doesn't, perhaps, thank you for that. It is a natural phenomenon.[2]

Haley had been urging him to give evidence to the Committee on Broadcasting chaired by Lord Beveridge. The timetable had been disrupted by the general election, but Reith appeared before the committee in the middle of April: 'Beveridge had the courtesy to come out and fetch me in,' he wrote. 'Quite interesting; very hard work and rather harrowing of course.'[3] He followed this up with a memorandum on what he saw as the major issues. He urged the committee to recommend a fifteen- or twenty-year term for the new BBC charter, informed them that listener research on the scale to which it had grown was a waste of time and money and 'wholly subversive', and asserted that there was too much regional material. He also let them have it with both barrels on the question of monopoly:

> It was the brute force of monopoly that enabled the BBC to become what it did; and to do what it did; that made possible a policy in which moral responsibility – moral in the broadest way; intellectual and ethical – ranked high. If there is to be competition it will be of cheapness not of goodness. There is no reality in the moral disadvantages and dangers of monopoly as applied to Broadcasting, it is in fact a potent incentive.[4]

By the time Beveridge and his colleagues had digested all this, Reith was on holiday in Argyll, and a letter inviting him to meet the committee a second time followed him there. One Sunday the whole family went to church in Ardrishaig. Reith approved of the choice of hymns and paraphrases; there was a good congregation and he thought the singing was splendid. Even more unusually, he approved of young Mr McCormick who took the service:

> The text was from the last verse of Zechariah VIII and the minister referred to the awful need for leadership, finishing by substituting 'Scotsman' for 'Jew' – 'we will go with you for we have heard that God is with you.' Impressed and moved me very much, this ending. I wondered if this text today was the heralding of real work and service, like Dr Ivor Roberton's text about the end of 1922.[5]

Signs and portents were all very well, but it was by no means certain that everyone was equally alert to them. Before the holiday ended, Reith took the precaution of sending a note to Attlee: 'Isn't there some big job you would like me to do?' he wrote. 'I could do such a lot, you know.' He returned home in an edgy and restless mood, and although there was a friendly acknowledgement from the Prime Minister, the benefits of his holiday were swiftly dissipated by domestic irritations: 'The damblasted charwoman who should have got the house ready for us sent a note saying she had "company" and therefore couldn't come. A thousand curses and damns on the cad she is . . .' Marista appears to have taken the charwoman's part, and this led to a 'sickening row' over supper: 'I don't suppose we'll speak to each other for a long time,' he wrote.[6]

He had sent Churchill a copy of *Into the Wind*, and Churchill replied that he looked forward to studying it. He also acknowledged the comments Reith had sent him about the second and third volumes of his own memoirs – these had ranged from putting the former Prime Minister right about who was responsible for war damage during Reith's tenure at the Ministry of Works to telling him that he had misquoted the hymn 'Eternal Father, strong to save'.[7]

Throughout September and early October he was sunk in morose introspection – the only cheerful note was struck by a visit to the BBC's Paris Cinema in Lower Regent Street to see Kenneth Horne and Richard Murdoch in the last edition of the programme *Much Binding in the Marsh*.[8] He was sleeping badly, and the past rose up frequently before him. A service of hymns broadcast from Glasgow stirred memories of his father: 'Sometimes I can hardly bear the thought of him and mother. How I long to be near them.'[9]

He spent time tidying the letters and notes he had kept from Muriel over the years since 1919: 'Oh how terribly sad to read how she loved me then and often later,' he wrote. 'Of course I am pretty sure I was pretty beastly to her all along.'[10] Neither of the children responded to his desire to be involved in their activities: 'Marista I am sure is finding me more and more irritating and is getting close to a positive dislike.'[11] And there was another painful old chapter which could still spring obstinately open from time to time:

> Wrote Minister of Dunblane Cathedral saying they could throw out the alms dishes I gave in memory of father; also to Helen Lamb telling her to remove my name from the list of members. Absolutely ridiculous to have Bowser as patron with me around.[12]

Then, in the middle of October, he was summoned to Downing Street. Attlee offered him the chairmanship of the Colonial Development Corporation – a full-time appointment at a salary of £5000. Reith was not altogether happy at giving up his other activities and distinctly unhappy at the prospect of a drop in income of £2500.[13] Not for the first time, he took refuge in suggesting that he should discuss financial details with Bridges of the Treasury: 'The PM said yes – with relief in his voice.'[14]

The question of his salary went in the end to Hugh Gaitskell, who had just succeeded Sir Stafford Cripps as Chancellor. He ruled that there could be no advance on £5000, but there had never been a serious prospect of Reith turning the offer down on that or any other ground. A sentence was inserted in the official announcement to say that the appointment involved him in 'considerable financial sacrifice'.

The CDC's office was in Dover Street, and Reith was installed there in a matter of days. He met his predecessor, Lord Trefgarne, and found him 'alert and intelligent': 'He has a Humber Pullman for his own use alone, and he takes it anywhere he wants to, including Ascot!'[15] The following week, Reith was the subject of the *Observer* profile, and thought it 'very well done':

> In its long history, the British Empire has owed a great deal to a few men of genius. They were not easy men, nor were they the type that succeeds in the give-and-take of our domestic political system. But it was men like Raleigh, Clive, Hastings, Gordon, Livingstone, and Rhodes who made ours the most successful of the empires of modern times . . .
>
> Where, in our mild, modern community, could one find a man possessing the technical and social standards of today and the peculiar cast of mind of the great imperial pioneers? In selecting Lord Reith to be Chairman of the CDC, Mr Attlee has shown great insight of the man and the job . . .[16]

Mary Somerville had been right; there was to be a new chapter – of sorts. It would last for nine years, and Reith would gladly have had it last as long again.

Reith began, as he always did, by shifting the furniture, and not only metaphorically: 'Saw the Finance Director today,' says a diary entry in his first week. 'Heaved out Trefgarne's enormous desk which cost £380!'[17] Getting the organisational furniture the way he wanted took longer, but as he had done at Imperial Airways and elsewhere, he set about replicating the management structure he had devised at the BBC. He listened with what patience he could muster to the advice offered by ministers:

> Saw Herbert Morrison at No. 11 – and this was really funny – he read me a little lecture about public corporation chairmen in their relationship with ministers – me! Everything he was tactfully suggesting I had known and practised for twenty-five years . . . Ye gods![18]

By Christmas he had made his number with Alan Lennox-Boyd, the Conservative shadow Colonial Secretary. By mid-January he had abolished the regular meetings with the Colonial Office which he had inherited. He had also inherited heavy financial losses, and an organisation which he considered top-heavy and over-centralised: 'Each day I seem to come on some new sickness in CDC,' he wrote five months after his arrival, '– some new underestimate, disloyalty, grumble, failure.'[19] Towards the end of April he recorded the arrival of an administration controller of his own choosing: 'It was a comfort to know that another brain of some calibre was at work on the mess.'[20] Then, in the middle of May, he dropped a major piece of the jigsaw into place: 'First meeting of Executive Management Board – six months that has taken me. I feel great relief and satisfaction over this.'[21] It was almost like old times.

Busy as he was reshaping the CDC, he still found time to have a view about Lord Beveridge's proposals for reordering the BBC. There was much in his report with which Reith profoundly disagreed. Herbert Morrison, then still Lord President of the Council, invited his comments, and Reith expressed himself forcibly and at length. Beveridge, he asserted, had been prejudiced and motivated by a desire to uncover abuse. The position of the chief executive would be rendered impossible: 'In that great office,' he wrote, 'there would in future be found only a harassed corrector-general.' He also laid about him on programme policy, criticising the committee for not attacking those aspects of it of which he himself disapproved:

> ... The Third Programme, positively and negatively, is objectionable. It is a waste of a precious wavelength; much of its matter is too limited in appeal; the rest should have a wider audience ... The Third Programme was introduced as a sop to moral conscience, a sort of safety valve. Odd that this vital issue has been ignored.[22]

The White Paper issued in July was not at all to his liking. He put his name down to speak in the Lords, but on the day of the debate changed his mind; much as he disliked the government's proposals, he harboured even darker suspicions about the intentions of the Tory opposition. Before there was time for legislation, however, Labour was defeated in the October general election, and Churchill's new Conservative administration set up a Cabinet committee to consider broadcasting as a whole.

For the rest of 1951, Reith's attention was fixed mainly on programmes. Much of his critical fire was directed at Haley, who, understanding and sympathetic as always, returned better replies than some of Reith's diatribes deserved. 'I acknowledge the difficulty of making the true equation between liberty and standards,' he wrote in one letter, 'but one of the responsibilities of the BBC seems to me to be to preserve tolerance.' He concluded by reading Reith a courteous lecture on distinguishing means from ends:

> I am as anxious to have as high and serious a moral system of broadcasting in this country as you are. But I seek to do it within the concept of an agreed serious body of opinion, both inside and outside the BBC, and not by means of purely personal predilection or ukase.[23]

Later in the year, *The Times* marked the fifth anniversary of the Third Programme with a leader. Reith pronounced himself 'very disgusted', but appears for some reason to have held Haley responsible for it, and instead of simply addressing a letter to Printing House Square, he fired off yet another salvo in the direction of Broadcasting House. Haley's reply, in his large and

schoolboyish handwriting, covered twenty-one pages. He told Reith that nothing that had happened for a very long time had been such a blow as his letter.
The 'Third' had been very much Haley's baby, and he gave a patient account
of its genesis:

> When I took over in 1944 (and even more in 1945 when people's minds
> began to turn away from the war to other things) the BBC did not have any
> longer the *Times* circulation among its audience. They wanted nothing of
> what we had to offer except perhaps the news bulletins. The two great
> universities had grown unconscious of us. They neither listened nor, in the
> main, contributed to our programmes ... I do not believe the climate of
> opinion in those post-war years would have allowed the BBC to carry through
> so large an influx of high and serious material into the existing programme
> compass ...[24]

Haley might have spared himself the effort. All he got was a rather inconsequen-
tial reply saying that the standards of the Home Service and the Light Programme were not what they should be. 'He either doesn't mind,' Reith wrote
in his diary, 'or just isn't able to give the necessary orders to bring things
right.'[25] The two men were not speaking the same language. They were not
even discussing the same subject. The Director-General of the BBC was
talking about broadcasting. His predecessor was essentially thinking aloud
about himself.

'All happy families are alike, but an unhappy family is unhappy after its own
fashion.' It is not known whether Reith ever read *Anna Karenina*, but the
unhappiness of his family life was fashioned on the anvil of his own temperament. For a time at least the family were the beneficiaries of the new interest
offered by his work at the CDC. As 1950 ended he had been extremely worried
about Muriel, who had caught measles, and he began the New Year in a mood
of almost mellow contrition, kneeling by the sofa in the study and 'commending
us all to God's care in all our special needs'. 'I wish so desperately that I was
more patient and more kind with them,' he wrote. 'I love them so, I love them
so ...'[26]

These sentiments quickly frayed round the edges, and his relations with
Marista, in particular, began to deteriorate. In the spring he made heavy weather
of her plan to spend a week with friends on the Broads: 'I don't think much
of the business at all – with some questionable company, in a hired boat
none of them can sail.' On the morning of her departure, Marista seems to
have responded to his disapproval with a display of family temperament: 'She
had to be asked by Muriel to say goodbye to her father. Terrible it is. I was
sorry I hadn't wished her a good time so had the old porter give her a message
at the station.'[27]

He was made miserable by the prospect of her approaching departure to university. As with Christopher, although with less need, he had tapped into the old-boy net to try to smooth her path to Oxford, and had been greatly excited when the last obstacle was removed by a credit in Latin. During the autumn, however, she had decided she would rather go to St Andrews, and this became a strand in the conviction forming in Reith's mind that she was growing away from him.

> Intolerably sad to look back two or three years only; she was a little girl and so happy and friendly and attractive; and now she seems suddenly to have become so indifferent and reserved and remote. I do not know what has gone wrong; I have tried so hard; and I am so very, very fond of her. Oh dear, oh dear.[28]

What had gone wrong, of course, was simply that Marista was no longer a little girl; in the process of growing up, this intelligent and attractive young woman was becoming restive at the discovery that there were, as she put it many years later, 'so many delays in becoming an autonomous person'.[29] Charlie Bowser had made the same discovery almost thirty years previously.

After six months or so, the challenge posed by the new horizon of colonial development had already lessened, and Reith was no less restive at the unmanageability of Harrias House. 'Desperately anxious to get into a small place,' he wrote in July. 'I wish I could decide if it's worth hanging on in the south and in CDC kind of work in case the one worthwhile job comes; or whether I should give up and go and live somewhere in Scotland and write.'[30]

That year's Scottish holiday was not a success, however. The weather was poor and the hotel unsatisfactory; one night Reith caught a drunk urinating over the cars in the garage and called out the proprietor: 'The vileness of man is more and more obvious and revolting every day.'[31] He spent much of the time on the great mass of CDC paper he had taken with him, but this did little to lighten his misanthropic mood: 'Very sad and serious that I dislike and distrust most everybody at the CDC, or at any rate find them so unreliable and inefficient.'[32] He slept badly, and in one of his dreams was back in his old room in Broadcasting House.[33]

Marista went off for her first term at St Andrews in October, and Reith was in considerable distress:

> I have had such disturbed and distressed nights dreaming about Marista. I've done everything I can think of to make her happy and comfortable; nothing I want so much as to help her – my darling little daughter. I am so pathetically pleased if she takes anything of mine – one of my blotting books last night, and a loose leaf book tonight. I wanted so much that we might have had a prayer together as of old, but, though I hung about, there was no response.[34]

After they had seen her off at King's Cross, Reith returned home, his eyes 'sore with tears'. In the days that followed he fired off a fusillade of letters to her; by 21 October he had already written twelve, and by early December the tally had risen to forty. In November, Muriel and he went north to see how she was getting on:

> I shall never forget the way dear Mara ran along the platform to M – it was exactly like the old days on the platform at Beaconsfield; simply wonderful it was and I felt that nothing in the weekend could be better than that. Dinner and then to the cinema – *The Lavender Hill Mob* – and both it and the thing before it made us laugh greatly; thoroughly successful . . . Thanked God for the happy time.[35]

On their return, they went to look at some flats in a conversion in Eaton Square. Reith's desire to leave Beaconsfield was strengthened by the state of Muriel's health. He wrote in his diary that she was plagued by rheumatism, but it was more probably arthritis; X-rays of the spine and pelvis showed that her condition had deteriorated, and she was put on a stringent diet. Reith was full of remorse: 'I've done so little for them, and been so often bad tempered and unkind. Oh I hope we shall all be happy together after this world has passed for us.'[36]

On Boxing Day, they entertained the Haleys. Friendship did not preclude envy: 'It upsets me so dreadfully to think that anybody has the job I created,' Reith wrote in his diary. He did not follow his usual practice of reviewing the year, and his diary for the first days of 1952 gives an impression of a man caged in misery and irrationality. He was again much exercised by his financial situation: 'Feeling I simply must try to get some money,' he wrote on 4 January, 'and I am entirely ready to leave the CDC.' The next day, he applied to present unhappiness the poultice of past bitterness: 'I was feeling most desperately sad about Marista's going off tomorrow. She doesn't seem to have any feelings for me at all. Read 1921 diary about Bowser and his miserable Jezebel.'

Thoughts of writing ran in his mind again. He had meant to enter for the story competition run by the *Observer* before Christmas, but had missed the deadline. Now he became more ambitious: 'Very nice weather today, cold and clear,' he wrote on 13 January. 'I must write some novels.' But he found it impossible to leap off the treadmill of diary and letters. A complaining letter to Haley elicited a response of almost saintly restraint. It included a paragraph of lavish praise for his work at the BBC – 'If only you could ever realise . . . what a towering legend you are' – and ended with words of gratitude for his friendship: 'It is a gift, and those lesser mortals, like myself, who come into contact with it, and feel its radiance, can only praise God that it exists . . .'[37] For once, Reith had the grace almost to be abashed: 'Haven't got over the amazingly kind letter Haley sent me a few days ago; I don't know what to do about it; I am much more used to being underrated than overrated.'[38]

He was never short of things to feel aggrieved about. During the Easter holidays, Muriel and Marista settled down one Saturday to watch the Boat Race on television. Reith could not bring himself to join them: 'Because of CJ not being in the VIII I had no interest; would really have preferred Oxford to lose because he wasn't in the crew.'[39]

The former Foreign Secretary Lord Halifax also earned his displeasure at this time. There had been rumours that the new Conservative government was contemplating some form of sponsored broadcasting, and Halifax had written to *The Times* to say that this would lower standards: 'we have in the BBC something quite unique, which every other country admires and most other countries envy.'[40] Reith wrote to say that his letter should do much good and bring things to a head, but could not restrain himself from adding a word of reproach; 'In the circumstances of the letter, I should have appreciated a word of commendation from you of all people, and in *The Times* of all places. It seems, however, from two sentences in the middle of your letter, that you feel that what you so commend and so desire to preserve has just "grown gradually" . . .'[41] Halifax sent him a more gracious reply than he deserved.

Reith gave the first account of his CDC stewardship in the annual report for 1951, which appeared in March. The report in *The Times* reflected something of the scepticism which many people felt about the task Reith had set his hand to:

It is hard to decide how much the Corporation's failures have been due to mismanagement and how much to the nature of its terms of reference. It is difficult to see how any one organisation, however efficient, can collect under its roof an expertise many-sided enough to deal with such a diversified functional and climatic field, ranging from fisheries in the Seychelles to hotels in Belize. Another point which comes out is the inconsistency between the Corporation's activities as an investment trust and in supplying managerial skill . . . It operates in the half light between private commercial enterprise and the frankly 'gift' expenditure of colonial development and welfare funds.

Several newspapers remarked on the distinctive style of the report. The *Manchester Guardian* detected a Biblical flavour – 'like Lord Beaverbrook's directives, which are based on the same model'. Reith made it plain that in his view he had so far done little more than roll up his sleeves: 'Most of 1951 went in redding-up; in examining and assessing; in adjustments and abandonments; a vexatious occupation when there was so much positive work clamant to be done.' The *Glasgow Herald* reported that the Scottish term 'redding-up' had foxed some English journalists, but that one of Reith's aides had offered a tactful translation: 'By and large, it's what the charlady does after you gentlemen leave.'

Spring came on, but Reith, as an April diary entry demonstrates, did not hold conventional views about the passing of the seasons:

I definitely prefer winter to summer, not just because of the fires in the grate but because a considerable proportion of humanity goes to its smelly earth and so we're relieved of the pestilence of their presence.[42]

On the same day that he wrote this, he discovered that William Haley had been offered the editorship of *The Times*. Reith wrote that he envied him enormously going to such a job – 'one of the very few worth having'. When they lunched together in the Lords the following week, it was of the editorship that they mostly spoke: 'I said it was *sui generis* in the world, and whether the BBC director-generalship was at nadir or zenith, I could not imagine his hesitating.' But Reith also found time, with inimitable candour, to cross-examine his friend:

I asked him if he had nothing at all on his conscience about the smash up of the BBC – which looks like coming; and went over the main issues I have with him – the lack of programme policy or control, and the failure to plan as for a military campaign against the present troubles.[43]

The White Paper setting out the government's plans for a system of commercial television which would break the BBC's monopoly was published three weeks later, and when it was debated in the Lords it was Reith who led the attack on it, speaking from the Opposition despatch box. 'The speech of the debate was Lord Reith's,' wrote the Parliamentary Correspondent of the *Manchester Guardian*. 'Nothing quite like it has been heard in the House of Lords. It was more like the utterance of a prophet, and it was clear from the faces on the Government front bench that prophets are an embarrassment to them.'

His opening was unprophetically colloquial: 'Look at it, and let us congratulate the writers, for it is clever – Oh! yes, it is clever. Stand off to starboard and you will see it is green; and to port you will see it is red. Very clever – on a superficial viewing . . .' He had worked all night on his speech, and he spoke for twenty-eight minutes: 'I suppose some of your Lordships might think me incapable of unbiased consideration of the issues here involved . . .' Whether they did or not, they greatly enjoyed much of what he had to say, particularly when he turned his attention to the plethora of advisory panels which was proposed:

These panels were somehow or other – not specified – to be representative of the local authorities, and from them there were to be 'drawn' – presumably out of a hat provided by the Office of Works – [laughter] – three of the eight members of the National Councils . . . and after all the agonies of conception, gestation, incubation and delivery in plain vans – [laughter] – these poor fellows were not to get any pay. The chairman did, but by the time their councils were formed, they probably would not be fit to draw it. [Loud laughter.]

In his peroration he spoke about what he had done at the BBC – and why: 'I tried to do as I had been taught in the Manse of the College Church in Glasgow':

> What grounds are there for jeopardising this heritage and tradition? Not a single one is suggested in the White Paper. Why sell it down the river? Is there leadership and decision in this White Paper; or compromise and expediency – a facing-both-ways? A principle absolutely fundamental and cherished is scheduled to be scuttled . . . Somebody introduced dog-racing into England; we know who, for he is proud of it, and proclaims it *urbi et orbi* in the columns of *Who's Who*. And somebody introduced Christianity and printing and the uses of electricity. And somebody introduced smallpox, bubonic plague and the Black Death. Somebody now is minded to introduce sponsored broadcasting into this country . . .

He concluded – inevitably – with his favourite quotation from Kant ('the starry heavens above me, the moral law within me').[44] It was, the *Guardian* said, a remarkable performance, and the only one in the debate which would have been worth televising.

If it was inevitable that Reith should quote Kant, it was equally inevitable that in winding up for the government the Lord Chancellor, Lord Simonds, should quote from Milton's *Areopagitica*. 'I yield to nobody in my admiration for Lord Reith's work,' he continued silkily:

> I believe he was at the BBC for 16 years. It so happens that under the Patent Law 16 years is the term that is granted for an invention which is worthy of a patent – if it is a remarkable one it can be extended for a further term of years. The noble Lord, Lord Reith, did remarkable work, and he served for the full period of a monopoly of sixteen years. The monopoly was extended in favour of some of his successors, but the time has now come for the monopoly, like all other monopolies, to come to an end.

Reith, less happy at the receiving end than when handing it out himself, expressed himself 'very very disgusted', and thought the Lord Chancellor was 'talking like a socialist on the hunt for votes'.

He then did something which demonstrated yet again that his intellectual equipment did not include political antennae. He wrote to Churchill. Two days earlier, he had been accusing the government of betrayal and surrender, comparing their proposals for broadcasting to the introduction of dog-racing and the bubonic plague. He now airily invited the leader of that government to reconsider his position: 'I am sure, from every point of view, that there should be second thoughts. Perhaps you will ask me to come and see you sometime; the last occasion was ten and a half years ago.'[45]

It so happened that Churchill's doctor, Lord Moran, who took an interest in broadcasting, had missed the debate because he was in hospital. He read *Hansard*, however, and a few days later, he wrote to *The Times* saying that he had been unpersuaded by the Lord Chancellor's defence. He described in his memoirs a visit to Churchill on the morning his letter appeared:

CLEMMIE: Have you read Charles's letter in *The Times*?
WINSTON: It is not a subject I feel very strongly about. I do not worry about it as I do over the solvency of the country.
MORAN: But is not the issue fundamental?
WINSTON (peevishly): I don't see why it is fundamental. It is not at all fundamental.

It was plain that he did not want to discuss the question; he was not interested in abstract issues. And then, on the spur of the moment, he said:

'But I am against the monopoly of the BBC. For eleven years they kept me off the air. They prevented me from expressing views which have proved to be right. Their behaviour has been tyrannical. They are honeycombed with Socialists – probably with Communists.'

He spoke hotly; his detachment had quite gone.

'I first quarrelled with Reith,' he went on, 'in 1926, during the General Strike. He behaved quite impartially between the strikers and the nation. I said he had no right to be impartial between the fire and the fire-brigade.'[46]

Reith, not waiting for a reply to his letter, repeated some of his views in an article in the *Observer*, with references to 'the freedom of the ether' and 'the brute force of money': 'Must the politician submit everything to the criterion, as he sees it, of the next election vote?'[47] This provoked Churchill's son Randolph, a veteran of newspaper polemics, to enter the fray: 'Those who have suspected Napoleonic gropings in Lord Reith's idiosyncrasy will find ample confirmation in his literary style,' he wrote. 'Nervous, staccato, interrogatory – he contrives to be simultaneously obscure.' Only Reith could have been surprised at the curt tone of the letter he received from the Prime Minister a few days later. Churchill wrote that he had now had time to read both his speech in the Lords and his *Observer* article: 'In view of these I cannot feel that an interview between us would be useful at the present time.'[48]

The BBC's Governors were now in search of Haley's successor, and the government had to find someone to follow Simon of Wythenshawe, whose term as Chairman had expired. Reith looked on balefully from the sidelines. On his sixty-third birthday, in July, Haley telephoned to wish him many happy returns. Something that pleased him less was to hear from his friend that the new BBC Chairman was likely to be Sir Alexander Cadogan – a choice to which Reith could instantly muster at least four objections:

Having been quite ineffective at the Foreign Office he was sent to be UK representative at the United Nations; having been quite ineffective there he was brought home, given £5,000 p.a. for life from the Suez Canal and the OM – which of course was a bad let-down for the OMs and the first time a civil servant got it. And now the BBC; absolutely *shocking*. Spoke with Clark of the *Observer* and I hope he can start some trouble about this.[49]

Early in September he set off on the first of his overseas tours as CDC chairman. He dipped into his own pocket and took Marista with him. They flew to East Africa by Comet and visited Uganda, Kenya, and what were then Tanganyika and Northern Rhodesia. 'See-It-All Reith Puts on a Double Act,' said a headline in the *Daily Express*. He was, their Nairobi correspondent reported, having a wonderful time playing the two roles he loved – 'the human dynamo and the invisible man'. The human dynamo was at the Corporation's offices at 8.30 a.m., 'questioning, pronouncing, putting notes in a beautiful neat hand in a little black book'. From time to time, Corporation officials emerged, wilting under the pressure. The invisible man took over whenever Reith saw 'the glint of a press camera lens or the pencil of a newspaperman'.[50]

He had not lost his ability to establish an easy rapport with other ranks. At a mine in southern Tanganyika, accompanied by the Governor's wife, he encountered a group of African charge hands:

> I had Lady Twining make a speech to them in Swahili; then she and I shook hands with each, she asking each what tribe he came from and what work he did. About two miles from Ngaka I received the head road ganger, an elderly man who had served in the German army, so some conversation was possible; at the end of it, imploring us to wait, he rushed off to his hut, returning with a basket of eggs.[51]

They flew to Livingstone, where the provincial commissioner showed them the site of a proposed CDC hotel and took them to the Victoria Falls. Reith recorded with satisfaction that they saw in one and a half hours as much as most people would see in one and a half days: 'This is an experience rather than a spectacle; stupendous and awful; and it is fitting that the statue of David Livingstone has its back turned on the jazz band of the Victoria Falls Hotel.'[52]

On his return from Africa, Reith learned that Haley's successor was to be Sir Ian Jacob. They did not take to each other. Although Jacob had been Controller of the Overseas Service, he had not been with the BBC in Reith's time and did not feel the same urge as some of the older hands to genuflect in the presence. He had also committed the grave offence of serving Churchill during the war, when he had been deputy secretary of the War Cabinet. A Cambridge-educated professional soldier, he was less marked by the distinctive BBC ethos than some of his colleagues. The director-generalship of the BBC was certainly an important job, but it was not the first important job he had done; his attitude to the first man who had done it was a good deal less reverential than his predecessor's had been.

He wrote to Reith inviting him to dine with the Board of Management early in the New Year, but Reith bridled at a sentence in his letter which seemed to suggest that the Board had been inaugurated by Haley. His letter declining the invitation was not notably gracious, and he could not refrain from adding a postscript: 'Actually the Management Board was established 30 years ago (in February 1923), not just six years ago. It lapsed from 1940 to 1947.'[53]

Reith was not having a good winter. Largely at Marista's urging, he had allowed himself to be nominated for the Rectorship of St Andrews University, but he came only third in a field of five, behind the Earl of Crawford and Balcarres and the Rev. Michael Scott, a liberal Anglican clergyman who had been prominent in the Campaign for Nuclear Disarmament. 'Of course,' he wrote, 'I wouldn't have done it but for dear Marista, instinct and inclination being entirely against it.'[54]

St Andrews was generally regarded as the most conservative of the Scottish universities; a contest in Glasgow or even in Edinburgh might have reflected a question that was generating some heat in Scotland at the time. Since the death of George VI earlier in the year, there had been controversy over whether his daughter should be Elizabeth I or Elizabeth II. Those of a Nationalist persuasion argued, logically but perversely, that the first Elizabeth had ruled only England and that the style Elizabeth II for the first queen of that name after the Act of Union was both incorrect and insulting to her Scottish subjects. Reith might have lived among the English for many years, but the old adage held – 'Scratch a Scot and you find a Nationalist.' 'I was glad to hear', he wrote in his diary, 'that the first pillar box in Edinburgh marked ERII had been painted black in the night and a sham bomb put in it.'[55] A week later *schaden-freude* had given way to confusion:

Applications by Lords to the halfwit Earl Marshal should have been made before now by those wishing to attend the Coronation. I have not applied. But I'm terribly worried about dear Muriel because I think she wants to go, and I am absolutely hating the whole business, and yet so unwilling not to do what she would like. But I don't know that we would necessarily be asked to anything. It's absolutely damnable; and I'm utterly miserable.[56]

The weather was wet and cold and he sought refuge in his study:

Nothing of any interest all day. I wrote and worked. How I wished we might have some games, and that M could come out of that terrible kitchen; her being there from morning till night is like an absolute and impenetrable pall on the house. No conversation, no fun, no noise; as bad in its gloom as the Manse at home; no friendliness even.[57]

30 December was an important day for him. It was thirty years since he had started at the BBC. Nobody remembered. He turned down another invitation from Jacob, this time to lunch at Broadcasting House, and when the Scottish

Controller asked him to go to Glasgow for their thirtieth anniversary celebrations, he turned that down too: 'I thanked him but said I could have nothing to do with it; there was practically nothing of policy, procedure or practice as I had put them there.'[58] When he did finally agree to be Jacob's guest for lunch, the occasion was something of a comedy:

> Lunched with Sir I. Jacob at Army and Navy Club. I hadn't at all been looking forward to this; felt much inclined to call it off. We met at 1.10 (he being ten minutes late) and parted at 2.35 without mention of broadcasting or the BBC. This is exactly what I had wanted and what Muriel had suggested; I was afraid that if broadcasting had come up I should be rude.[59]

What Reith didn't know was that Jacob had formed precisely the same resolution. He recalled the occasion with clarity almost forty years later. 'I said, well, I'm not going to mention the BBC unless he does – we've got plenty of other things to talk about. Well, he didn't, and the BBC wasn't mentioned from start to finish – but he did explain that what he really wanted to be was Minister of Defence.'[60] The two men did not meet again in 1953, and Reith's disillusion with the BBC continued to fester. When he heard from the Welsh Governor, Lord Macdonald, that George Barnes, who was now running the television service, wanted to televise dog racing, he wrote savagely in his diary, 'That's fine; the degradation and prostitution is confirmed in this particular act.'[61]

He was still troubled by strange dreams. His diary records that one night at the end of February, 'feeling most wretched', he had gone early to bed without supper:

> Queer dream that I was trying to get to an accustomed road and asked a yokel; he misunderstood and pointed to a sea wall affair stretching out into a stormy sea with no end visible, and very narrow for walking; also it was nightfall. 'But does that go to the other side?' I asked. He was somewhat embarrassed – 'Oh no, I couldn't get to the other side,' he said.[62]

It reads almost like a parody of Bunyan – 'The Pilgrim's Progress from this World to that which is to come.' His mind turned frequently to the past. When he read a book based on Earl Haig's diaries he wrote in his own, 'I wished I could be back in the 1914 war.' Out of the blue there came a letter from a member of his Transport section in France for whom *Into the Wind* had stirred old memories:

> I don't know if you realise, even now, what you meant to those Glasgow fellows. The older elements like Shadow and Bobby Warwick had probably never cared much for anyone in their lives; their main affection being horses, whisky, beer and thick black tobacco. The younger were only half-baked boys whose affections for anyone in authority were non-existent. With you it was different . . . I remember the last dreadful morning when we had been

assembled in the meadow because you wished to speak to us ... It was a very disconsolate section that went on with its usual work of grooming, etc. As big Jimmie Mackie said to me: 'I feel like greetin.' And for once, Willie Dowell's appalling obscenity (worse than usual) ceased to be a matter of amusement and became the expression of everyone's feelings.[63]

Reith had been trying for some months to get the Colonial Secretary's approval to his accepting outside directorships (he had been approached by both Tube Investments and the Phoenix Assurance Company). Lyttelton was not against the idea in principle, but said it would mean a reduction in what he was paid, and this was discussed around Whitehall for some time: 'Really wicked the *pro tanto* reduction the Treasury swine arc insisting on,' says a diary note in March. A compromise was reached. Reith's CDC salary came down to £3500, and he attended his first Tube Investments board meeting on 1 April.

These new arrangements were not made public until May, however, and they caused a squall both in Parliament and in the newspapers. The Beaverbrook press was first out of the trap with a leader in the *Evening Standard*: 'If a fireman, while putting out the flames, were to take time off to do a crossword puzzle, the reaction of onlookers would be angry.'[64] The Peterborough column in the *Daily Telegraph* was also critical:

> Few will admire the sense of timing with which Lord Reith made a recent request to the Colonial Secretary ... Whatever the merits of permitting such highly paid state servants to engage in outside activities, one point is indisputable. The CDC seems at the moment to be in need of every minute of Lord Reith's working day.[65]

At Question Time in the Commons, Lyttelton defended the decision on the ground that it would keep Reith in closer touch with the business world outside. This was greeted with ironical cheers from Labour, but Mr R. D. Williams, the Tory member for Exeter, took some of the wind out of their sails by pointing out that Reith's predecessor, the Labour peer Lord Trefgarne, had remained on the board of three companies when he was appointed to the CDC in 1947. The Colonial Secretary enlarged on his reasons when Labour returned to the attack a few days later. He told the House that Reith had almost completed his reorganisation of the Corporation, both at headquarters and in the regions, and that he would now concentrate on major policy questions. Labour managed a further ironic cheer when he said that Lord Reith had assured him that he would still regard the Corporation as having the first claim upon his time and energies.[66]

The affairs of the CDC received more reasoned scrutiny in the Lords at the end of July. Lord Winster, initiating a debate on its latest report, said that it would be useless to deny that 'very grave misgivings existed about this Corporation'. Up to the end of March it had invested some £44,500,000 in colonial industries, but by the end of the financial year 1951–2 its consolidated

loss was over £8,250,000, of which £3,500,000 represented losses on abandoned projects. Winster was critical of the paucity of information in the report
about specific projects, and questioned the sort of advice the Secretary of
State appeared to be giving the Chairman – 'the Corporation should go into
enterprises and incur great risks, but always where there is a prima-facie possibility of making a profit.' That, Lord Winster said, was to echo the woman in
the nursery rhyme:

> Mother, may I go out to swim?
> Yes, my little daughter,
> But hang your clothes on a hickory limb,
> And don't go near the water.[67]

Reith missed most of the fuss, because he had set out at the end of May on a
second African tour, this time to the southern part of the continent and accompanied by Muriel. They sailed on the *Winchester Castle*. A special seven-foot-
long bed had been installed for him; it was taken out in Cape Town and fitted
in the *Capetown Castle* for the return voyage.

There was a chance to visit Mafeking, which 'rather thrilled' him, although
he did not approve of what he saw in the old fort which had been one of the
defended posts in the siege: 'It was all overgrown with weeds and in a shocking
state of neglect, although one would expect to see it treated with respect.'[68] It
pleased him on their journey through Bechuanaland to see a railway station
pillar-box with 'VR' on it.[69] Elsewhere in the protectorate, notably at the Bechuanaland Cattle Ranch, there was less cause for satisfaction: 'This job is one
with as disgraceful a story as any in the Corporation, utter incompetence and
criminal extravagances especially in machinery.'[70]

These foreign trips always unsettled him, and on his return he did not adjust
easily to the English summer: 'How disgusting London is in hot weather,' he
wrote, 'the usual rig for the man being no collar or jacket but definitely braces;
boys in bathing pants and females more or less in what I suppose is called
beach costume.'[71] He was inordinately pleased, however, when Marista asked
him to read a logic primer in the hope that he might be able to help her: 'I
should be so *awfully* pleased if I could; I feel I have been of such little use to
the children. Began on the logic book at once.'[72]

He was soon plunged in depression again, however, brooding over what he
had done to make himself so much disliked by his children. He even found
cause for self-reproach in a letter from Jeannie McCabe: 'They have a 41'
twin diesel cabin cruiser; what an utter idiot I've been working for the state
instead of making money so that the family could be happy and comfortable.'[73]

They took a late holiday in the Highlands, at Rothiemurchus, and for a few
weeks he came as near as he ever did to relaxing, savouring sights that took
him back to his childhood: 'Saw the old manse, and the gate I helped to
decorate for the Queen's jubilee 56 years ago.'[74] At the post office at Feshie
Bridge he met the niece of a woman who had given him a piece of the chocolate

which Queen Victoria sent to the soldiers in South Africa in 1901: 'It was a fine place to be, with the loch where we bathed every day; so much that was in memory of those olden days.'[75] One day they visited Insh, and he was much taken with the inscription on the gravestone of a young girl: 'Lost in the hills she loved'.[76]

At the beginning of October, the CDC's controller of finance, William Rendell, was appointed general manager, and Reith handed over his executive responsibilities to him. Two months later, in a letter to Vincent Massey, now Governor-General of Canada, Reith wrote that he sometimes wondered whether he would have taken on the CDC if he had had any idea of the state it was in. 'Perhaps I would,' he added, 'for I have always been very stupid. Anyhow I have been more liquidator than chairman and it has been a rather sickening time, but things are nearly in shape now.'[77] The period of 'redding up' was at an end, and Reith hoped that the work of the Corporation could move into a more positive phase.

Broadcasting now claimed Reith's attention once again. Since his lunch with Sir Ian Jacob at the beginning of the year, he had effectively sulked in his tent. Then, towards the end of 1953, the government published its proposals for commercial television. At first he affected indifference – 'I am so disgusted with the BBC that I don't care' – but he was fairly quickly drawn back towards the flame and spent a good deal of time caballing with those of his fellow-peers who shared his views. He eventually decided not to intervene in the Lords debate, but he wrote an article for the *Observer*. This was printed on the centre page under the rather portentous title 'The Precedence of England', Reith arguing in it that the champions of independent television were 'trying to promote commercial interests under the guise of Miltonic precepts and at the cost of this country's precedence in a vital sphere'.[78]

This prompted Sir Ian Jacob to have another go at restoring diplomatic relations. 'We are all trying our best to maintain the standards you set,' he wrote to Reith early in 1954. 'Can we not try to dissipate these misunderstandings by meeting and talking?'[79] They lunched at the Connaught, and talked till four – the arrangements were made through Miss Singer, who had sat in Reith's outer office all those years before and now sat in Jacob's. This time they did talk about the BBC, but there was no meeting of minds. It seemed to Jacob that Reith was urging him to run the BBC the way Beaverbrook ran his newspapers. They parted amicably enough, but later Reith telephoned Miss Singer to say how disappointed he was; he had made a point of putting on a Royal Engineers tie and the Director-General hadn't noticed.[80]

The meeting had, in fact, irked Reith very considerably. 'Not worth taking the space and time to describe the conversation,' he wrote contemptuously that evening, but he rehearsed it constantly in his mind and eventually, two weeks later, Jacob received a bitterly accusatory letter from him:

... I do not think I ever lost half an hour's sleep in all the vexed sixteen years of my association with the BBC, but I have in the last fortnight.

... There is nothing left in broadcasting of what I put there and cared mightily about, is there? ...

If there is nothing left, if you are entirely satisfied, if we do not agree fundamentally, well there is nothing I can do to help you, is there; or the BBC, or broadcasting; and no point in any contact.

Tell me if I am mistaken.[81]

They lunched again toward the end of March, and Jacob told him just that, but he was wasting his time, and Reith came to the angry conclusion that he was doing the same. He dug out the copy of his 5 March letter and scrawled on it, 'lunch 23rd, but it was a farce and an intolerable bore. I shall see him no more. He is utterly wooden and very jealous.' That suited Jacob entirely well. He had a public corporation with a staff of almost 13,000 to run.

On his sixty-fifth birthday, Reith looked in for twenty minutes on the report stage of the television bill in the House of Lords. It was not good for his temper: 'Absolutely nauseating ... And the three palsied old hags, Woolton, Swinton and Salisbury, yapping away on the front bench. I left in disgust.'[82]

Apart from what Charles Stuart described as 'occasional keening references to the decline of standards', broadcasting was now virtually to disappear from Reith's diary for four years. He permitted himself one more letter to Sir Ian Jacob, drawing to his attention that Sir Charles Carpendale was approaching his eightieth birthday. Jacob was grateful, and proposed to mark the occasion – he hoped very much that Reith would join them. Feelings for his old lieutenant were not as strong as present animosities, however:

I replied thanking him but please to excuse me. Letter from Miss Singer asking me earnestly to reconsider which I did and wrote attitude unchanged and that it would be horribly insincere to go to Broadcasting House feeling as I do.[83]

Reith was much exercised during 1954 with getting away from Harrias House. Buckinghamshire had never held much appeal, and he liked it less and less as the years went by: 'What a beastly place Beaconsfield is now.' His mind turned increasingly toward finding somewhere in Scotland, and although he had little idea of what he wanted, he had lines out to agents and acquaintances in various parts of the country.

He got quite excited in February about a house with a stream near Moffat, and shortly afterwards there was a farm at Dunscore, also in Dumfriesshire, which briefly roused his interest. Early in May he noted that he had spoken to Melville Dinwiddie, the BBC's Scottish Controller, about finding something in the Borders. They went north to look at a number of properties, including one in Melrose, but concluded that it was an 'utter waste of time'. Christopher had now firmly decided that he wanted to be a farmer, and the search in Scotland was therefore also directed to finding a place for him. The strength of Reith's concern to see him established may be judged from a diary entry at the end of September:

> Then forsooth to see Bowser, with whom to make matters far worse, was Jezebel, at Brown's Hotel. And that needs a bit of explaining. It was the result of my feeling I mustn't let my hatred and despising of him and his wife prevent our getting some good farm chance for CJ. So there had been quite an exchange of letters, he professing to be very ready to help.

Nothing seems to have come of the meeting, although there was some further correspondence. Reith did not feel that a readiness to accept help from Charlie imposed any sort of obligation – so far as he was concerned, their relationship remained as bitterly set in amber as it had been for the past thirty-two years: 'Contemptible I thought him.'[84] Contemptible or not, Charlie still rose up unbidden in his mind as each year drew to a close: 'The wretched Bowser's birthday tomorrow – 58 he is – and what a poor feeble creature he is; if we're to be in Perthshire I must try to forget his existence.'[85]

The hunt was also on for a flat in London. They looked at one in Westminster Gardens and another in Dean Trench Street, nostalgically close to their first London home in Barton Street. Albany was another possibility. Over lunch in September, William Haley mentioned that he had been offered a flat at Lambeth Palace. Reith made immediate enquiries and Muriel and Marista went up to town with him three days later: 'Straight to Lollards Tower; there for over an hour, and tremendously taken with it they both were. Means the two third-floor flats at £700 p.a. but I think it's worthwhile as they like it so well.'[86]

'Primate takes in £7 a week "lodgers"', said a headline a few weeks later in the *Sunday Express*:

> They will occupy four luxury flats built at his official residence, Lambeth Palace. But though he has to approve the choice of each of them personally, the Archbishop will not benefit from the rents. They go to the Church Commissioners, owners of the Palace . . . An official of the Church Commissioners told me, 'Lambeth is a white elephant' . . .[87]

Reith, always on his best behaviour where archbishops were concerned, wrote at length to Dr Fisher to thank him for approving the tenancy:

> I have been trying to write for about a fortnight, but in longhand. I am old-fashioned (and perhaps stupid) enough to feel there is a courtesy in longhand even though it is more troublesome . . .
> There is something slightly ironic in my living in 'Laud' flat, for I was brought up with an intense regard for the Church of Scotland and its history; and have remained a member of it.

You can imagine what we thought of Laud in Scotland – his efforts to stamp out Presbyterianism and the persecution of the Covenanters.

However, both our children were baptised by Anglicans – our son the last baby baptised in Lambeth Chapel by Dr Davidson, and our daughter by George Bell in the little Sussex church where my wife and I were married – and later confirmed (the children, I mean).

We are a quiet and peaceable family.[88]

His Grace might have doubted it if he had been a fly on the wall at Harrias House a few weeks later:

Awful arguments and distresses about Christmas cards and where to spend Christmas. I had the card done with the air photo of this place and HAEC PER ANNOS XXV ERAT DOMUS but Muriel thought it would irritate people. And I was putting Laud Chambers, Lollards Tower as the new address – Christopher didn't approve of that. So both ideas I thought so much of are dropped.[89]

In the event, the festive season passed off peacefully enough. Reith made amends for his boorishness to Carpendale at the time of his eightieth birthday by inviting the Admiral and his sister-in-law to lunch on Christmas Day: 'Unfortunately the Carpendales didn't go till 3.35, so I had to listen to the Monarch for the first time; didn't like her voice.'[90] Reith was going off to the Caribbean on CDC business immediately after the holiday, and as was frequently the case, the prospect of separation induced a flow of rather maudlin reflection about his relations with Muriel and the children:

It's such a crushing awful unspeakable remorse that comes on me when I think how far I've failed in my duty and privilege as husband and father. I love them so terribly, and I am utterly sure that, whatever may happen in this world, we shall be together for ever in circumstances we can't now conceive. I hope they may forgive me and love me. However I have acted and seemed I have always loved them all beyond any words to tell. I have a horrid and most troublesome disposition . . . Oh God give me opportunity and skill and grace to make up to them in some measure – my darlings – the best and greatest and most precious of all – Muriel, Christopher, Marista . . .[91]

He flew off the next morning on a three-and-a-half-week tour that took him to the Bahamas, Jamaica, British Honduras, Trinidad, Barbados, and British Guiana – '38 take-offs and 38 landings in all sorts of aircraft, trying to be intelligent and well informed as to the continually shifting panorama of people and places and things.' In Nassau he stayed at Government House:

After dinner, having made clear that I could not and would not play bridge, I was introduced to a word-making game called Scrabble from which after much humiliation but tactfully assisted by the ADC, I actually emerged winner. Thereafter, I being hungry, the governor's wife, ADC and I went to the kitchen in search of biscuits. I have never seen so many nor such large cockroaches; I was thoroughly frightened.[92]

He called on Lord Beaverbrook, was caught up, *en route* for Jamaica, in a carnival in Miami, tut-tutted in Honduras over the neglect of broadcasting in the Colonial Empire. He was briefly in Caracas. The British ambassador took him to church, and he was invited to read the lesson:

I am always rather scared of reading lessons since reading desks usually seem to be heighted for dwarfs or near-dwarfs; but I was relieved to note that here there was a movable book rest. I moved it up about a foot from its normal and naturally tightened the thumbscrew to prevent accident in mid-passage. Afterwards, in the hymn before the sermon I was horrified to realise on looking for the pulpit that the reading desk was also pulpit; and the clergyman was a small man; his head would be visible below the desk instead of above it, and unless he were strong in the fingers he would not be able to loosen the thumbscrew . . .[93]

In Barbados, he encountered a mysterious Colonial Office official who did not altogether seem to fit the part; he turned out to be the head of Special Branch from Scotland Yard, on a reconnaissance for a forthcoming visit by Princess Margaret. He said that Reith would not remember having met him before, but he did not know his man. 'Yes,' said Reith, 'thirty years ago when twenty pounds was stolen from my secretary's desk at Savoy Hill.'[94]

In British Guiana, when he flew up to the site of a CDC hydro-electric project at Tumatumasi, there hardly seemed room for the aircraft to come down on the Potaro river:

After a false start, the river bank looming too close, we made for the Kaiteur Gorge despite some mist, the captain 'pretty sure I can find the entrance to it'. He found it all right – precipitous bastions, and as we flew up the gorge it seemed that the aircraft's wing tips must scrape the precipices on either hand. In twenty minutes the Kaiteur Falls came in sight, higher than Zambesi and Niagara combined.[95]

For the rest of 1955, CDC affairs did not bulk large, although Reith had preliminary talks with Sir Godfrey Huggins, the Prime Minister of the Central African Federation, and with Sir Roy Welensky, the Prime Minister of Southern Rhodesia, about plans for hydro-electricity, and these later matured in the Kariba dam project. He was assiduous in his board duties at the Phoenix and did good work at Tube Investments, where he helped to restore the aluminium division to profitability. For most of the year, however, he was preoccupied with family affairs – with settling in at Lambeth and with the continuing search for a place for Christopher. He was also increasingly concerned with Marista's future. She was now in her last year at St Andrews, and Reith did not at all like what he heard of her plans – or what he saw of some of her friends.

In February they went to look at Glenfarg House in Perthshire, which had been designed by Sir Robert Lorimer, but it was not suitable. Then the search switched for a time to England, and Christopher inspected a farm at Crewkerne in Somerset. Marista was very keen on Scotland; Christopher had no strong views either way; Muriel would far rather be in England. Reith had no regrets about leaving Beaconsfield, although initially not everything went smoothly at Lambeth. He was in a great fury just before Easter when he was told that he might not keep a car in the service yard, and considered following his usual practice of taking a complaint immediately to the top. 'Blasted cads,' he wrote in his diary. 'I nearly made a signal to Fisher on the way to South Africa.'[96]

The next day was Good Friday, and Reith occupied himself in writing a letter to Churchill, whose resignation had been announced a few days previously.

'Here's someone who worked faithfully and well for you, but whom you broke and whose life you ruined. You were kind enough, some years later, to agree that you had misjudged; you wrote that you were very sorry, and that the State was in my debt. I couldn't remind you of this while you had opportunity to put things right; but I can now. And say that I'm sorry to feel as I do.' Of course people would say it was awful to have written such a letter, undignified and all the rest of it. But if I hadn't done it I should be much more bothered than I'm likely to be having done it. Much relief.[97]

He did not have a great deal of time for Churchill's successor, either: 'Heard the wretched Eden announcing a general election on May 26th; a most horrible affected voice he has, and utterly namby-pamby like his rabbit teeth.'[98] He listened to some of the election broadcasts, deploring what he saw as the emphasis placed on benefits and the lack of any suggestion of duty or service. The Conservatives were returned with a comfortable majority: 'How sickening,' he wrote, 'that a hollow third-rater like Eden should be Prime Minister for some years now.'[99]

He seems to have taken curiously little satisfaction from being able to announce, in the CDC's report for 1954, that for the first time since the Corporation was set up, there was a small net income from its continuing projects. The Times ran a complimentary leader: 'Year by year the CDC, under the direction of Lord Reith and his colleagues, is cutting out diminishing quantities of the dead wood left by the former regime.'[100]

Early in June he was grumbling in his diary that throughout her four years at university, Marista had been 'too much engrossed with other things to write proper letters'. A month later he heard that she was thinking seriously of going to work for the Student Christian Movement in Sheffield for two years:

'Horrified I was, and sad.' Ten days after this it was Reith's birthday – his sixty-sixth – and there is an ominous diary entry that reads, 'There was no reference to it by request in Lollards Tower.' He was brewing up for an extended bout of misanthropic rage, and the only sensible thing to do was stand well clear. Muriel did, in fact, take herself off to Sandwich on holiday – it is not clear whether this had been planned or was a response to his behaviour. On one of the days she was away – it was a Sunday – Reith left the flat and roamed the streets for long periods: 'Went out not even washed till about 4. Went out again at midnight, returning at 3 a.m.'

In September, matters deteriorated further. He wrote in his diary that he had been greatly looking forward to Marista's return. He was at King's Cross in good time to meet her, and noted with his usual precision that the train was twelve minutes late:

> To my amazement the wretched leechlike Leishmann was with her, dressed of course in shabby tweed jacket and grey trousers and with a foul filthy rucksack on his back and another similar receptacle. I was so disgusted that I could hardly speak – and of course it meant that Marista had had to travel 3rd. We went to the hotel for a taxi and of course had to give him a lift. Then to add good measure I heard Marista saying she would fetch him next day . . .[101]

Murray Leishman spelt his surname with one 'n', not two, but he was to get the Haley/Bailey treatment for some years and soon became accustomed to it. It was not his first meeting with his future father-in-law; he had already bobbed up in the diary a year previously during one of Reith's visits to St Andrews. Marista had brought him to dinner, and Reith had noted then that he was the President of the Student Christian Movement and much taken up with the work of the Iona Community. The realisation that Marista had formed a strong attachment outside the family had the effect of depressing and agitating him simultaneously:

> Feeling that I have now forfeited any right to another life. I don't think I want to see my mother and father again, and my children wouldn't want to see me again; nor Muriel. And if this is a permanent sentiment presumably I have no more concern with or interest in religion, Christian or other . . . It's entirely my fault and Muriel's that Marista is all hooked up with this Student Christian Movement, and is going to Sheffield. And ditto that Christopher has no aspirations above labouring, it seems. Poor Christopher, poor Marista to have had me for father. God Almighty what a crime committed that I should ever have married, or had any children. Poor Muriel. I wonder if in my reason and my health I shall survive this crisis.[102]

Another cause for agitation at this time was the inauguration of independent television. Reith had lunched with the BBC Chairman, Sir Alexander Cadogan, the previous month, and had told him that he had been approached to broadcast an inaugural message. Cadogan had said he could not see how this could be reconciled with his previously expressed views about commercial broadcasting: 'He had the answer – that the BBC no longer deserved its monopoly,' Reith wrote, 'and I told him why.'[103] Nothing came of the proposed broadcast – Reith appears to have named a fee of £5000, which at £1000 a minute struck even the BBC's new rivals as a shade too commercial. The tone of his diary entry for the day on which the BBC was finally driven out of Eden was one of brooding self-pity: 'As commercial television starts tonight, the monopoly which I defended and held against hard odds is broken. I wondered on the way to the office whether anyone in all England (or Scotland) would give me a thought of sympathy today.'[104]

As it happens, one person did. A letter came from Norman Collins, who had resigned as Controller of BBC Television in 1950 and was an architect of the new system:

> I feel that the least that I – as one of those in some measure responsible for this revolution – can do is write acknowledging the immense debt that this country will always owe to you as the only begetter of the traditional form.
>
> You *were* the BBC; and I secretly suspect that if you had gone on being the BBC, tonight's upheaval would never have occurred at all.[105]

It is highly unlikely that Collins, who had left the BBC when he was passed over in favour of George Barnes, believed any such thing, but the compliment was elegantly turned and Reith was touched. 'I try hard not to let myself think about the British Broadcasting Corporation or anything relating thereto,' he wrote in reply. 'It was a gracious and kindly act on your part, which I very much appreciate.[106]

At the tail-end of 1955, Reith had a conversation with the Colonial Secretary, Alan Lennox-Boyd, and noted that he had 'more or less agreed' to carry on at the CDC for a further three years from the beginning of April 1956. 'It wasn't a coherent talk at all,' he wrote, 'and I was a bit disgusted with it.'[107] He rapidly became more disgusted still, and for the next two years he was involved in a number of major disputes with the Colonial Office about the extent of the CDC's mandate.

Contention first arose over the statutory right of the Corporation to be involved in house- and road-building. The Law Officers had ruled that there was a need for amending legislation to provide retrospective authorisation for a number of projects on which the CDC had embarked. Reith was at first resistant to the idea that he and his officials should make any contribution to this process: 'All that is required is some courage and strength on Lennox-Boyd's part.'[108] By the early summer, however, he had come round, and the bill to validate existing projects received the royal assent on 2 August.

The next day, he flew off on another of his overseas tours, this time to Central Africa. His senior secretary at the CDC at this time was a young woman of twenty-three called Molly Cotara, and she accompanied him. It is clear from his diary that they had been a good deal in each other's company during this period, and that the relationship was not altogether to Muriel's liking. Miss Cotara had spent an evening at Lollards Tower in the early summer: 'M. was very unfriendly and sarcastic to her,' Reith wrote, 'and I wouldn't think she would want to come again.'[109] In July, when he was sixty-seven, Miss Cotara took him out to lunch at the Dorchester; later in the year, when her twenty-fourth birthday came round, he returned the compliment by entertaining her to both lunch and dinner.

There was no question, during the Central African trip, of her being tucked discreetly away in a back room with her typewriter. The arrangements made for her were much more those appropriate for the wife of a visiting dignitary than for his secretary; in Salisbury, when Reith was entertained to dinner by the Prime Minister of the Federation, Lord Malvern, Miss Cotara had her place at the table.

He was taken to see the site of the Kariba dam, then within a year of completion. In Mzuzu, he was entertained to lunch by the provincial commissioner; Reith was delighted to discover that he knew a lot about Livingstone, and even more delighted to find that he had on his shelves a book called *Among the Wild Ngoni*, which he remembered from his childhood.[110] On a visit to a nearby estate he attended a tea party for African senior staff. They were lined up to be presented, which Reith thought odd and unnecessary, but he walked down the line, shaking hands and finding a few words for everybody. He found them all very civil and friendly, but felt that too much time was taken up by a non-employee, 'a local agitator and vice-chairman of the Congress party'. Reith, who exerted himself, as always, to master everybody's name, got the designation of the 'agitator' slightly wrong – he was, in fact, the secretary-general of the African National Congress. He got the name right, though – the man was called Kaunda. Eight years later, when Northern Rhodesia became independent as the Republic of Zambia, he became the country's first President.

Back in London, Reith quickly became embroiled in further disagreements with the Colonial Office, who construed the new Overseas Resources Development Act as limiting the areas in which the CDC might operate. Reith felt that the exclusion of all territories that had been given self-government was retrograde. He was particularly incensed by the government's insistence that no assistance should be extended to the Rhodesian Iron and Steel Commission; he argued that as discussions had begun long before the amending legislation was mooted, the British government was under a moral obligation. He asked the new permanent under-secretary at the Colonial Office, Sir John Macpherson, if he was prepared for board resignations, and described a Colonial Office letter on the RISCOM row as 'a real shocker of equivocation and deceit'. All his old dislike of politicians and civil servants welled to the surface: 'As I have often said, civil service and politician morality carries an automatic discount of fifty per cent on what applies among decent people.'[111] A few days later he ostentatiously cancelled his acceptance of an invitation to a lunch where Lennox-Boyd was making a speech about help to colonial territories.[112]

As was so often the case, reverses in Reith's work marched in step with frustrations in his domestic life. They combined in the autumn of 1956 to exclude from his diary practically any reference to events in the greater world, even though those events included the Suez crisis and the crushing of the Hungarian uprising. Yet another expedition to look at a house – this time at Aviemore in Invernessshire – proved abortive, and in his disappointment Reith lashed out wildly: 'Ghastly swarm of people from Dundee apparently under the tutelage of a man in a kilt who wore the same shirt all day and evening with no collar or tie. Beastly.'[113] He also lashed out at the Student Christian Movement, because Marista had raised the possibility of continuing to work for them for a third year: 'I am getting to hate the SCM because they take advantage of MM almost fraudulently,' he wrote, 'and because they're third-raters and most inefficient. Quite unworthy of anyone with MM's ability, personality and character.'[114]

In the week before Christmas, his indignation was suddenly swept away. Marista, playing the organ at an SCM service in a London church, suffered an epileptic attack and collapsed over the manuals: 'I certainly prayed for forgiveness for all my own faults,' Reith wrote, 'and for our dear daughter's clearance of this affliction.'[115] That prayer was answered, but a diary entry for the last day of the year showed that one affliction had been replaced by another:

> Marista said she was in love with some minister of her own age whom she had known for three years; and maybe he with her. George Macleod knew all about it, and thought it was absolutely splendid.[116]

It was not the first word that occurred to Reith. The need to mention Murray Leishman was so painful that on this occasion he could not even bring himself to misspell his name. Marista had another four days' holiday, but her father did not succeed in making them happy either for her or for himself:

> She won't talk to me about anything, never consults me, never shows the least affection. I am most desperately sad about it, and I've tried over and over again in the last five years to get on to friendly terms with her . . . Each night lately I've tried to get something from her, but she seems utterly indifferent and stony.[117]

His black mood did not lift quickly, and he seemed almost resentful of anything that seemed likely to dispel it: 'Noticeable increase of daylight,' he wrote on 12 January, 'and this I don't like at all.'[118] On the same day – it was a Saturday – he heard that his loyal friend and lieutenant of BBC days, Cecil Graves, had died of a stroke. He immediately telephoned Lindsay Wellington, the Director of the Spoken Word, to establish whether he had arranged for the house flag to be flown at half-mast over Broadcasting House on Monday: 'It hadn't occurred to him, and he was very grateful.' There was less reason for corporate gratitude the next day when Reith telephoned the BBC's Controller in Scotland and gave an effortless demonstration of how to combine pettiness, poor taste and bad manners in one short phrase:

> Rang Dinwiddie to ask him to arrange for some flowers for poor Graves for tomorrow, and I asked him to write on the card 'From the first director-general of the BBC in grateful memory of the man who should have been the second.'[119]

His spirits had not improved greatly by the end of the month: 'Wishing I could have some objective for the remaining part of my life, which can't be very much,' he wrote. 'I wish I could make dear Muriel happy; that would be a good objective. I have really come a most awful crash in life.'[120] His energy was still prodigious, but he expended it without much discrimination, and the victories he won were small: 'I got the temporary bus stop post shifted from beside the Tower door in the wall because swine seem specially to spit while waiting for buses.'[121]

Marista was now thinking of enrolling at New College, Edinburgh, to prepare for a Bachelor of Divinity degree. Reith was quite taken with the idea, but admitted to her that he would be in favour of almost anything that got her away from the SCM. He wrote a bizarre letter about her to the Bishop of Sheffield:

> ... I wonder what you think of her future activity? Complete surprise to me; complete approval also in my mind in the space of five seconds or so; for my mind usually moves monstrous quick*; and betwixt that particular saddle and the ground I had consulted my father and grandfather and Dr Thomas Chalmers and a Church of Scotland brother deceased and also myself, and had emerged slightly dizzy but content. (You've heard about Dr Thomas Chalmers, haven't you? Anyhow I've got to write an article about him shortly.)
> *A lot too quick for most people; wholly undemocratic and undesirable; will be legislated against by the Tory government if they (or it) lasts long enough. Frightful liability.[122]

Marista found a small flat on The Mound, and in August Muriel and Reith were in Edinburgh to help her get it in order. He was pathetically eager to please her: 'Yesterday I got the books very nicely arranged into five chief categories.' Something was also at last in prospect for Christopher, and they moved on to Perthshire to inspect a farmhouse which had come on the market. Their route took them through familiar countryside: 'Through Dunblane and by the road to Argaty where I launched a curse – both coming and going – on the wretched Bowsers.'[123]

Whitebank Farm, near Methven, was derelict, and Reith found it most unattractive, but Christopher took possession of it toward the end of August. Tom and Jeannie McCabe had put up $30,000 to help him acquire it. Reith wrote that he was 'thankful beyond words' that Christopher had a farm of his own at last, but words came easily enough to describe the state in which they found it: 'I have never seen such criminal negligence and beastliness of filth and disorder and rubbish as all over this place. The cattle court is 3 ft. deep in water at one end.'[124]

He appears for once, in that summer of 1957, to have left his professional preoccupations behind him in London. The sparring with the Colonial Office had continued through the spring and summer. The Ghana Independence Act, which had given independence to the former Gold Coast in March, had the effect of excluding it from the CDC's area of operations. Later that month, the Colonial Office asked for all reference to the Rhodesian Iron and Steel Commission and to emergent territories generally to be removed from the CDC Report for 1956, which was then in draft. Reith refused, and when the report was published in May, its clipped conclusion was thought to be provocative:

It is surely commonsense that the now-established, efficient and profitable CDC should be permitted to invest in emergent and emerged territories: CDC has been assured on behalf of both the Ghana and Malaya governments that it would be a great pity if emerging members of the Commonwealth were, at a critical stage, to be deprived of help of the experienced CDC personnel; of course 'Colonial' would have to come out of CDC title.

Both Dr Kwame Nkrumah and Tunku Abdul Rahman Putra had written letters to support Reith's case, but as Miss Mandy Rice-Davies famously observed on a later occasion, 'They would, wouldn't they?' The Colonial Office was sufficiently stung to issue what was in effect a rejoinder to the report, including a sentence describing the CDC comments about Ghana and Malaya as 'over-stated'.

In November, Reith set out to tour CDC operations in Nigeria, which was not to attain independence for another three years. A diary entry during his stay in Kano, in the Muslim north, gives a tantalising glimpse of how well he could write about travel:

At intervals, but without obvious reason, a man from the sands tilted a seven-foot bugle and put cacophony on the air. After twenty minutes he shuffled indignantly from the scene; but five minutes later, reappeared mounted on a camel with another one in tow. At his first salute thereafter at least three parties gave him alms; he had been trying to do his act without the scheduled props; the public had not responded; something had been accomplished in Nigeria.[125]

He got on well with the Federal ministers in Lagos, less well in some of the regions. When he got to Enugu, expecting to meet Dr Azikiwe, the Eastern premier, he was told that he was unwell, but Reith preferred to believe that the mercurial 'Zik', who was said to be in Port Harcourt on the south coast, was merely 'ingratiating himself with the riverain tribes'. As Reith was leaving, the acting Prime Minister thanked him for coming and again expressed regrets for the Prime Minister's absence, repeating that it was due to ill-health. 'I asked if the Premier had sent any message to me. After more whispering it seemed he had not. I said could I send one to him; Acting PM said, "Oh yes please". "Tell him", I said, "I hope he will soon be better".'[126]

Warmed with the satisfaction of having evened the score in this Byzantine manner, Reith flew on to the Muslim north. It was two days before he realised that he had left behind in Government House, Enugu a rather unusual piece of personal equipment in the shape of a blackjack – a six-inch lead cosh at the end of a short leather rope 'which was given me by a thug in America in 1916 and which usually goes with me to strange places':

I wondered whatever a Government House would make of such an item when found; and thought I had better get a message sent. Of the previous half dozen occupants of the bedroom they had thought me the most likely to be the owner. In due course it arrived in the diplomatic bag in Kaduna.[127]

In Kaduna he saw the Prime Minister and twelve of his ministers. He found that they talked less easily than in the south, but it was a pleasant and friendly meeting with a good deal of laughter. At one point he asked which of them was responsible for a particular matter and two ministers sitting together each pointed to the other. He in turn was asked his opinion about whether members of the House of Assembly should be on the board of public corporations. He explained what the position was in England, but was not prepared for the minute of the exchanges which he was later shown:

Lord Reith stated that he felt the present membership of Northern Region Development Corporation was open to criticism ... He pointed out also that in the UK politicians were prohibited from membership of public boards. He added that this did not apply to members of the House of Lords because they were popularly regarded as being mentally defective.[128]

Back in London he prepared to travel north for Christmas – they were to put up at an inn close to Whitebank and be together during the day at the farm. He had been 'terribly distressed and hurt' to hear from Marista in October that she was abandoning her BD course. Then, shortly before he left for Nigeria, there had been a letter from her to say that she was considering becoming engaged to Murray Leishman. 'It was the biggest shock I ever had,' Reith wrote. 'Muriel is as shocked as I, but very sad at my reactions.' At Muriel's request he had written to Marista, 'imploring her to think again', but he clearly had little confidence in his powers of persuasion, because he added, 'It may do more harm than good.' Now, on his return from Africa, he could no longer thrust the matter out of his mind: 'In normal circumstances it would have been wonderful to be going to spend Christmas and New Year with the family all together. But because of Marista and her infatuation for the rucksack man I'm dreading it.'[129]

It was an exceptionally awful Christmas even by Reithian standards. Marista announced on Christmas Eve that Murray Leishman was getting a few days off and that later in the week she was going to Edinburgh, where his parents' home was, to spend some time with him. Reith's response was to say that if he had known she was not to be there he would not have come north, and the next day he saw to it that things went rapidly from bad to worse:

> After tea I asked MM quite quietly if she really intended going off the next day and she said yes; I said it seemed that she was preferring this man to her father and mother and brother; she said to put it that way if I liked. After a bit of thinking I said I really wanted to go back to London tonight and I really did most urgently mean it ... I went upstairs but CJ came imploring me not to go off. Muriel seems unable to do one single thing to help. I didn't speak to anybody for the rest of the evening. They had the distribution of Christmas presents. What a shocking farce ... Christmas Day 1957 finished as it had begun – without goodnight.[130]

Everybody had a thoroughly wretched time. Christopher was understandably upset, and so was Muriel; Reith had formed the view that she had no understanding of his feelings and did not speak to her for several days. A great deal of the time was spent letting off steam in his diary – partly about Marista and 'the wretched man', partly about the state in which the previous tenants had left the farm: 'The wretched swine that were here ought to be put in gaol; they cleared the accumulated rubbish of years out of the loft in the house by filling up the drainage ditches ...'[131]

Marista made an attempt to inject some normality into their relations at the end of January by coming south for the weekend – 'just to talk,' she said on the telephone, 'not about anything special.' Reith's initial pleasure at the proffered olive branch was short-lived:

> As the time approached I found myself afraid of it – that no ordinary communication or relationship was now possible between us ... Yes, I am unforgiving to those who have wronged and hurt me, and who have not asked for forgiveness, who have expressed no sort of regret ... Muriel talks as if it were all quite simple; nothing required from MM at all; I must just behave normally ...[132]

He did not find that easy. They went to meet her at King's Cross, but while Muriel and Marista embraced, he could only say 'Good evening' and take her bag. Silence in the car was followed by silence over tea in the flat: 'I couldn't bring myself to speak at all. And when Marista went off to have a bath Muriel reviled me for my disgraceful behaviour.' It was two days before 'the wretched man' came up in conversation:

> She said any engagement was entirely hypothetical. She didn't express any regret for the Christmas tragedy; and took it all very casually and as of no account that we had been so terribly distressed.[133]

The family barometer remained at stormy. Marista went back to Scotland, and Reith turned his mind to the affairs of the CDC. The Corporation was now operating profitably. The improvement in relations with the Colonial Office had been sustained, and in the early months of 1958 he began to hope that his term as chairman might be extended until his seventieth birthday, or even beyond. He had an agreeable dinner at the Commons with the Colonial Secretary in February, and a satisfactory meeting a month later with the Secretary of State for Commonwealth Relations, Lord Home, who told him that he wanted 'every sort of contact' with the CDC.

During the summer Reith's fellow-directors tried hard to persuade Lord Perth, the Minister of State at the Colonial Office, that his chairmanship should be extended. He spent August at the farm in Perthshire – 'our new home, as I think it is' – rigged out in sea boots, corduroys and a sports jacket, and when he returned to London two of his colleagues told him they thought they had made some impression. They were badly mistaken, as Reith was to discover on the afternoon of 23 September:

> Saw the squalid Lennox-Boyd at 5. I knew from his manner that I was to be given *congé* . . . Abruptly and crudely he said he had better tell me what he had to say. By next March I would have been eight and a half years in CDC; that was quite a long while; did I not think it was time for a new long-term appointment? Of course there was no reflection on me; I had done very well for CDC; he was grateful; but he thought the time had come for a change . . . It was a horrible experience. I have wondered how I got through it. I don't think I can carry on till the end of the term nor do another hand's turn for CDC . . . I did ask God that everything should be working for the best.[134]

The most pressing 'hand's turn' was a tour of CDC projects in the Far East, for which he was due to leave in little more than a week. Although he initially made noises about cancelling it, it is unlikely that he seriously considered doing so; apart from anything else, he had promised to take Molly Cotara with him. They set off on 2 October, and almost immediately his spirits rose:

> Frankfurt at 1230 GMT for an hour. Here spoke with Sir Cyril de Zoya, President of Ceylon Senate, rescuing him from a German policeman with

whom he was in unilateral altercation through not having secured a receipt
for a magnum of eau-de-Cologne bought in airport shop. Made much of
this; by saving him from jail we hoped we had cemented the bonds of what
used to be called Empire.[135]

Three days later they were in Singapore, and he was still in excellent form,
watching 'a very inferior cabaret' in the Cathay restaurant and tucking into ten
courses – diced chicken skin with pine seeds, shark's fins in brown sauce,
bird's nest stuffed in whole chicken, abalone in oyster sauce . . .

> I soon achieved relative dexterity with chopsticks; but though I tried very
> hard there was much trouble otherwise, for the muscles of one's throat
> seemed set on rejecting almost everything that came to them . . . And I was
> getting more and more hungry. Fortunately item ten was a fraud: a splendid
> Lyons cake of which I had three slices.[136]

He was endlessly curious, eager at every stage of the journey to see not only
what figured on the itinerary but whatever else could be packed into the day.
In Kuala Lumpur he gave the Malayan Prime Minister, Tunku Abdul Rahman,
the benefit of his views on how to revise the constitution of the railroad. At
Tawau, in North Borneo, he embarked on the Governor's new yacht, *Petrel*,
which was to take him to a CDC estate at Kunak, and London seemed agreeably
far away:

> The Celebes Sea, blue sky and sunshine, every prospect pleasing. One felt
> that the Colonial Office and Treasury would probably disapprove; would
> find a clause in Overseas Resources Development Act which, turned upside
> down, would make it an offence for any officer of CDC – chairman in
> particular – to go to sea in a governor's yacht; and that made the sea bluer
> and greener still.

The serenity of the day was briefly clouded, but only by his own concern for
form and protocol. About noon a 4–5000-ton ship appeared on the port bow.
It was plain to Reith that the other vessel would salute the Governor's yacht.
The question was, did the captain of the *Petrel* know the drill? It was, of course,
the Governor's yacht, and he was a visitor; an oblique approach was called for:

> 'What ship's that?' I asked, appearing just to have noticed. '*Marudu*, my lord.'
> 'Thank you,' I said; and did a turn around the deck. '*Marudu* will probably
> salute you, won't she?' That surprised the captain; it hadn't occurred to him;
> he was worried. 'I suppose,' I said, 'conventions are the same in this sea as
> in the west, are they? She'll give you a blast on her whistle and dip her red
> ensign to your blue; and then you will acknowledge in the same way. Is that
> right?' 'Yes,' he said; but it was an unconvincing affirmative.

Ex-Captain Lord Reith, RNVR, decided that he must make some arrangements of his own. He went below to fetch a hat, coming on deck again just as they drew level, and was 'vastly relieved' to see that a sailor had been stationed below the gaff from which *Petrel*'s ensign was flying and had the sheets in his hand. There was a tremendous blast on the whistle of the other ship, and she dipped her ensign: 'No whistle return from *Petrel*; I could have pulled the rope myself but did not.' What he did do, however, standing just outside the bridge-house, was ceremoniously remove his hat; and, training his glass on *Marudu*'s bridge, he saw two figures salute in return. The Governor's honour had been saved: 'But for the rest of the day my ears were haunted by the *Petrel* whistle which was not blown . . .'[137]

In Kuala Lumpur he was put up in the Istana Tetamu, a vast house that in former days had been the residence of high commissioners. He was greatly taken with Malaya: 'I was sorry to be leaving this agreeable, friendly and interesting country – all the more agreeable that the Colonial Office has nothing to do with it.' On his last morning he got up early and watched the sun rise:

> I could see tracks climbing and disappearing into jungle; and I wondered if, forgetting everything and everybody of the past, I might climb up one of the tracks and leave the rest to Osiris and the Sun. But here were the boys with breakfast.[138]

It was his last major CDC trip. He was to make a brief journey to East and Central Africa in February and March, but by then his heart was no longer in it. He had quickly become aware that pressure was being put on his co-directors to stay on with the CDC after his departure, and that his deputy, Sir Nutcombe Hume, was being asked to take over the chair on a caretaker basis: 'Obviously he is hopelessly outwitted by the crooks on the other side and they have him all smarmy and anxious to please just as they want it – except that he hasn't retracted on his refusal to stay if I go.'[139]

Reith took the view that as his colleagues had all put their names to successive annual reports, they should now stand by him – believed, indeed, that they had undertaken to do so – but he was fighting a losing battle. On 5 March, Molly Cotara handed him a letter saying she was very sorry to be giving it to him. It was from Hume. He wrote that the Colonial Office would not take no for an answer, but that what had influenced him much more had been the urgings of the directors and the general manager that he should carry on:

> I tore the letter into bits. I think I have never read so disgusting a bit of hypocrisy . . . What a filthy, caddish trick to play – all because of his wretched wife, of course, who wanted him to be chairman of CDC. It's an endorsement of Colonial Office attitudes to me . . .[140]

There was one last matter to be resolved – the CDC Annual Report for 1958. Reith's original inclination was to have nothing to do with it, but that went against the grain. On Palm Sunday (it was also Muriel's sixty-sixth birthday) he sat brooding at home: 'I am extremely reluctant to let the filthy politicians and civil servants and the filthy traitors on the board get away with it. On the other hand I don't want to be beaten on it.' He leant heavily on Molly Cotara for advice on how to proceed; he had great respect for her judgement, and she seems to have exercised a moderating influence, persuading him to try to secure Hume's agreement to the terms of his draft.

Four days later he chaired the CDC board for the last time. His colleagues had seen the Report only late the previous afternoon. Reith told them that he would consider any suggestions that were not of fundamental principle, but all but one of them said that they were willing to sign it as it stood:

> I told him he would be expected to resign if he did not sign. He asked for the weekend to consider. I said No, it must be settled now and I asked him to sign. So he did. I think it was extremely good chairing on my part. And that is that. I went off without saying anything.[141]

He was reading from the same script as in 1938, and he departed, as he had done then, with bitterness and a singular lack of grace.

J. C. W. Reith – late-CDC.

Seventeen

LIFE IS FOR LIVING

Most men that do thrive in the world do forget to take pleasure during the time that they are getting their estate, but reserve that till they have got one, and then it is too late for them to enjoy it.

SAMUEL PEPYS, *Diary*, 10 March 1666

Qu'as-tu fait, ô toi que voilà
Pleurant sans cesse,
Dis, qu'as-tu fait, toi que voilà
De ta jeunesse?

PAUL VERLAINE,
Sagesse, 1881

WHEN REITH shook the dust of the CDC from his feet he was four months short of his seventieth birthday. The past months had been a strain, but physically he was in pretty good shape. He had been bothered before Christmas by a certain huskiness in the throat, and had seen a specialist: 'He said my blood pressure and system were applicable to a man twenty to thirty; I should live into the nineties.'[1] Leaving the CDC meant a drop in income of £5250 a year, but he still had his directorships at the Phoenix and Tube Investments, and to these he had added three years previously a seat on the board of the British Oxygen Company, which gave him the use of a Rolls Royce and a chauffeur.

His departure from the CDC coincided with a revival of interest in the affairs of the BBC. It is true that when he heard, in August 1958, that the Corporation was broadcasting betting prices, he wrote, 'that is about the last trace of my management gone.' That his interest was submerged, however, not extinct, was shown by a remarkable incident in the late 1950s of which he made no mention in his diary. A newspaper report had suggested that Sir Ian Jacob might be in line for the secretary-generalship of NATO. He was startled to receive a letter from Reith – if the speculation was well founded, might there be a prospect of his returning to Broadcasting House in Jacob's place?[2]

In August 1958, Reith had received a letter from the Vice-Chancellor of Oxford. Would he see a Professor Briggs, formerly a don at Worcester College, now at Leeds, who was embarking on a history of the BBC? 'I'm not in the least wanting to see him,' Reith wrote in his diary, but he did in fact lunch with him at the Oxford and Cambridge Club some weeks later. Asa Briggs had clearly done his homework, and also had the advantage of having known Christopher at Worcester: 'What he said was absolutely satisfactory to me,' Reith wrote, 'so I said I would give him whatever help I could.'[3]

Reith had also recently met Sir Arthur fforde, who had succeeded Sir Alexander Cadogan as Chairman of the BBC. fforde's background was different from that of most of his predecessors; a classical scholar, he had previously been both a solicitor and headmaster of Rugby. When he wrote, rather diffidently, saying he would like to talk, Reith responded by treating him to what Charles Stuart called a 'summary of his resentments' over the past twenty years:

> I was glad when I heard of your appointment, though I wondered whether the ill had not gone far beyond recovery. It began three months after I left when the evil machinations of a particular individual brought my successor to say at the microphone that 'We are here to give you what you want' – a negation in half a line of everything I had stood for . . .
>
> When the Beveridge Committee reported – with the wretched Selwyn Lloyd in a minority of one – I told the then DG that a pip-squeak like that would not have gone into a minority of one unless he had been assured of the support of his party, or had been acting on its instructions . . .
>
> Nothing whatever was done; the BBC went the way of all flesh; to the flesh-pots of the vote. The wretched shopkeeper Woolton was primarily responsible for this surrender and betrayal – *stigmam qui meruit* . . . ; I wish some mark of the beast could be put on his forehead . . .[4]

They did not meet until the following July, when fforde, unwisely, allowed the conversation to get onto the question of who should succeed Jacob as Director-General. A fortnight later, on Reith's seventieth birthday, there was a letter from fforde to say that the decision about the new Director-General was one of which he would not approve. The job had gone to Hugh Carleton Greene, brother of the novelist Graham Greene, a former *Daily Telegraph* journalist and at that time the BBC's Director of News and Current Affairs. fforde had accurately gauged Reith's reaction:

> I wrote that the appointment of a divorced man, remarried and an unbeliever would be an immense delight and encouragement to those set on the paganization of the country. I said I thought his letter had been a greeting on my seventieth birthday and that there had been a lunch-party in Broadcasting House on my sixtieth . . .[5]

Reith also wrote in his diary on his seventieth birthday, 'I suppose one of the unhappiest days of my life.' It is not clear whether this was due to general depression, fforde's letter, or his deep disappointment that Marista neither wrote nor telephoned; she marked the occasion by sending him a book with a card inside which said 'many happy returns and love'. Since giving up the idea of taking a BD at New College, she had been working for George Macleod, the leader of the Iona Community, who had taken on the convenorship of the Church of Scotland church extension committee.

Marista clearly did not volunteer a great deal about her private life, and Reith appears to have thought – he certainly hoped – that the 'wretched infatuation which ruined our Christmas holiday in 1957 was over'. This belief did not survive a letter he received the day after his birthday. It came from his sister Jean, who now lived in Edinburgh, and wrote to say she had had a visit from Marista 'and her lad Murray'. This prompted Reith to telephone and ask whether Marista and 'this Leishmann' were engaged. (Jean thought not.) A few days later, Christopher rang and said that Marista was in Perth teaching 'her lad Leischmann' to drive. 'We are very bothered about it,' Reith wrote in his diary – as was indeed evident from his renewed assault on the spelling of Murray's name.[6] Marista earned a further black mark a month later: 'Discovered that she wasn't teetotal – but of course never a word to me.'[7]

Although he had determined to cut himself off from all his Commonwealth interests, there were two occasions during the summer when he derived a measure of bleak satisfaction from matters relating to the CDC. The first was in June, when the last Annual Report to carry his signature appeared and his strictures on the government were made public: 'Unfortunately 1958 was not a happy year; many irritations; no capital reconstruction; as the CDC came to real terms with itself in its task, relations with government departments became such that the Corporation felt frustrated and discouraged.' The *Observer*, which he had always been able to rely on for admiring support, had an article with the headline 'Laurel for Reith':

As Chairman of the CDC he converted an embarrassing national liability into a valuable asset. His only known misdemeanour is that of achieving this success by treading fairly heavily on some important Whitehall corns, and speaking frankly when he thought the Government was wrong.

His kind of bold but responsible leadership is precisely what is needed if the CDC is to be fully effective; it could become Britain's small-scale version of the World Bank.[8]

He was also gratified by the findings of the committee which the Colonial Secretary had set up shortly after his departure to examine the financial structure of the CDC. The committee believed that the CDC could not continue to finance marginal and essentially risky projects in underdeveloped territories under the existing system of fixed-interest repayable loan capital. *The Economist* said that the report applied a convincing logic to the reconciliation of statutory aims and appropriate means of finance: 'The vociferous demands for special treatment made by Lord Reith during his chairmanship have thus won the committee's endorsement.'[9]

If this was balm to a hurt mind, it did nothing to make Reith think more kindly of his former colleagues; his successor was still 'the viper Hume' and he was still guilty of 'black treachery'. He declined the gift of a picture from the CDC staff: 'I wonder what the Board actually contributed,' he mused meanly in his diary. 'What of course they should have done was to give me a dinner party with two presentations, one from CDC funds, from which every Director has had £20 worth of books, and one personally from themselves and four or five old Directors . . .'[10]

In July and August he spent several weeks in Perthshire. The old desire to extend himself physically was still very strong. Some time before his seventieth birthday, he had made a proposition to Janet Adam Smith and her sister – would they help him mark the day by joining him in an ascent of Cairngorm? They need have no worries about his fitness. There were forty-odd steps to the flat in Lollards Tower. He had calculated how many times they went into the height of Scotland's fifth-highest mountain and had gone into proper training. This, however, was to be no mere exercise in Munro-bagging: 'I've a feeling I may meet my father again at the summit. I'd like to die up there and go away with him.' Janet Adam Smith, as the daughter of a distinguished Biblical scholar, knew all about the strange things that could happen on mountains; she was also, as an Aberdonian, severely practical. 'Who's going to carry you down?' she enquired.[11]

In the end, three weeks after his birthday, he had to settle for Christopher as a climbing companion. The events of the day remained clear in his son's mind more than thirty years later: 'There was a great deal of preparation the night before, and ringing up various weather forecasting stations – and I think the AA, though I'm not quite sure what they had to do with it. It was planned like a military operation.' They set off from the farm at six in the morning. Muriel went with them. Christopher parked the car at a pleasant spot by a burn, and they left her there with a supply of books and papers. They reached the summit in four hours. Reith was irritated to find that now there were roads where previously there had been a wilderness: 'I can remember when there was nothing here except heather,' he grumbled. His left knee bothered him a little on the way down and he was glad to get back to the car, but apart from feeling stiff he was none the worse.

Mere physical exertion was not enough, however, and he found his relative inactivity difficult to endure. 'It is very odd having no contact in London at all,' he wrote at the end of July while he was at the farm. 'Awful. I feel myself to be up on a very high shelf.'[12] Partial relief came from his nomination to the board of the North British Locomotive Company. He was elected on 10 August and made vice-chairman a week later. 'Gosh,' he wrote, 'I wish I were chairman.'

The company had been hard hit by the switch from steam to diesel engines, and Reith and the new chairman, Tom Coughtrie, inherited among other difficulties an overdraft of almost £2.75 million. An article in the *Investors' Chronicle News Letter* noted that they had also inherited a working agreement of some standing with the General Electric Company, which had lent the company £500,000; the Treasury had granted a loan of £1.75 million, and the Clydesdale and North of Scotland Bank had come up with £1.5 million. The *News Letter* observed that institutions like these would scarcely offer the company backing on this scale unless they had confidence in the ability of the board to turn it to good use, and felt that NB £1 ordinary shares at thirteen shillings could prove a useful recovery stock.[13]

Back in London at the end of August he was pleased with his newly decorated office at the British Oxygen Company and pleased to have his Rolls changed for a two-year-old dark green one with only 13,000 miles on the clock.[14] He was not altogether well, however. 'I often have difficulty in remembering where I am,' said a curiously phrased diary note in the middle of September, 'or in which direction moving.' Some weeks later, after noting his regret that the Tories had been returned in the general election, he added, 'Feeling absolutely lost and alone', and a few days later there is an entry that ends with the words, 'Oh how welcome would be death.'[15]

Molly Cotara had gone off to another job when he left the CDC, and he missed her greatly. For her twenty-seventh birthday in October he bought her a handworked silver bracelet decorated with moonstones at Georg Jensen's. A few days later he went to Burns & Oates, bought her a small crucifix and chain, and took it into Westminster Cathedral to be blessed. He found the little ceremony quite moving: 'And God bless you, too,' said the priest as he left.[16] He took her out to dinner, took her to the theatre, took her to supper at The Ivy. She appears to have been going away or abroad for a time, because after noting that she had dropped him at the end of Lambeth Bridge at 1 a.m. he wrote, 'and that's that till March 12th.' The next day in his diary he wrote: 'Decided to exclude alcohol for five or six months. Also took to wearing a black tie. Can't remember where if at all I had lunch.'[17]

He threw himself into the affairs of North British Loco. A statement went out to stockholders in the middle of October, and there would be no mistaking its authorship even if it had not spoken about 'redding-up'. It made no attempt to dress up the range of skeletons that had been found in the cupboard – technical production problems, serious after-delivery service difficulties, costs so high in almost all departments that there would be little or no profit on current orders. The balance sheet and trading account as at 10 July showed a loss for the half-year of almost £1 million. 'There has been an overhaul of accounts in conjunction with the company's auditors,' the statement concluded. 'Stockholders now know the worst.'[18]

Muriel was now spending a good deal of time in Scotland helping Christopher at the farmhouse, and although Reith was up and down there were increasingly periods when he had to fend for himself at Lollards Tower. Solitude did not suit him. 'Gradually realised it was Armistice Day Sunday,' he wrote on 8 November. 'I walked round and round the park from 10.30 till 2.30. Nothing to eat all day. Terrible it was.' In his loneliness he took to telephoning people with whom he had had no contact for many years – Cissie

Murray, May McQueen and May Murray all received calls. He also got in touch with the Mackay family, and this brought him a long letter from Dawn:

> Apparently she is teaching the monarch's children dancing, making 'lots of money'. 'Very busy, very important and very trying,' she said she was. She also said she was 'very happy and thoroughly enjoying life.'[19]

There had been a period in his life when he might have said that of himself, and he was carried vividly back to it at this time by an article in *Punch* which he stuck into his scrapbook. It was by Mary Adams, who had joined the BBC before the move to Broadcasting House. It had a one-word title – 'Technique'; it was something she began learning, Mrs Adams wrote, the moment she arrived at Savoy Hill one sunny Monday morning:

> . . . The doors opened before me. Everyone sprang to attention as I entered. Charwomen rose from their kneeling, little lads saluted, striped trousers knocked at the knees. When I got into the lift I saw the reason why. I had preceded the boss: John Reith himself, in a frock coat. . . .
>
> Mr Reith was the Corporation, and the Corporation was Mr Reith. Queen Victoria, Genghiz Khan, Leonardo, rolled into one. He was Headmaster, Field-Marshal, Minister, Permanent Secretary, Commissar, Captain of the ship, Father, wielding a cane, a baton, a pen, a telephone, a secretary, with effortless ease. Around him we were all dwarfs working with secateurs. But what a Man for a Master![20]

Reith could never read too much of that sort of thing, but it unsettled him, too, because it reminded him of days when he also had a small daughter who mostly did his bidding and ran eagerly along the station platform to meet him . . . As Christmas approached, he made a number of attempts to reach some accommodation with Marista over how she was to divide her time over the holiday, but he set about it so clumsily that the effort to improve relations was doomed to failure. It was now rooted in his mind that 'our darling Marista', for whom he prayed every night, regarded him not simply with indifference but with dislike. 'What have I done to bring this most supreme sorrow on me?' he wrote after they had dined together one evening in Glasgow.[21]

He had in fact already begun to seek the affection he craved elsewhere. The renewal of contact with the Mackay family had led to an invitation to visit them at Finchampstead in Berkshire, and one Sunday early in December Reith went to Waterloo and caught a train – 'a thing I haven't done for long years.' It was a nasty day, but the countryside was a revelation to him. The house was off an avenue planted with Wellingtonias – 'a magnificent sight it was.' After lunch there was coffee in front of a fine log fire, and then Dawn took him for a walk: 'Really wonderful country, with fine trees, and a big lake, and fine views.' He

stayed for tea, and then the Mackays' son George drove him back to town.[22]
His sister had celebrated her thirtieth birthday a few days previously.

The only thing Hugh Greene and John Reith had in common was their
immense height. Greene nevertheless judged it politic, on the day before he
moved into the Director-General's office at Broadcasting House, to write to
his illustrious and prickly predecessor:

> Although I did not have the honour of serving under you myself, I have
> always during my years with the BBC been impressed by the feeling of
> loyalty which you still inspire among those who did. It would be a great
> satisfaction to all of them if we could have you with us from time to time.[23]

Greene knew that the BBC would shortly once again find itself under scrutiny
by a committee of enquiry. It was just conceivable, in what was likely to be a
patch of rough water, that Reith could be of some assistance; on a more cynical
view, it was only prudent to identify any potentially loose cannon and do what
one could to secure them. His letter was well judged, and had the desired
effect, although Reith initially viewed the renewal of the BBC association with
some wariness. The two men lunched in a private room at the Dorchester in
the middle of February: 'We had quite a good meal,' Reith wrote, 'and, I
suppose, quite a good conversation.'[24]

Gradually, over the next few months, his contacts with the Corporation
became more frequent. He went to a party at Hugh Greene's house, and agreed
to have his name restored to the circulation list for BBC publications. He was
entertained to lunch at Bush House by Sir Beresford Clark, the Director of
External Broadcasting: 'I seemed to give them great amusement, particularly
in exchanges with Hodson who, they said, was not accustomed to being worsted
in argument.'[25]

On some of these BBC visits he was accompanied by Dawn Mackay. He had
been frequently in her company since the beginning of the year. He now often
spent the weekend in Berkshire, and they were much together in London – he
took her to dinner at the Ecu de France and at the Dorchester, and she sometimes
went back with him afterwards to Lollards Tower. They lunched at the House
of Lords, and he got hold of a ticket for her for Princess Margaret's wedding. He
took her to the Royal Navy tattoo and he took her to Ascot, where they were
entertained by the BBC. Leonard Miall, then Head of Television Talks, met
them in the box on Gold Cup Day. The champagne flowed freely, and Reith
was in effervescent form. The guests also included some knowledgeable racing
contacts of the BBC's from Newbury and Cheltenham:

> They seemed to know precisely which horse was going to win each race and
> kindly marked our cards. Reith and I went off together to the tote and
> placed our bets and throughout the afternoon we were seldom disappointed.

Between races we sipped whisky and soda and chatted with the charming girl Reith had brought with him. My mental picture had been of a rather dour son of the manse who would not allow drinks to be served on BBC premises or starting prices to be broadcast. I drove home considerably better off than when I arrived and with all my preconceptions of Lord Reith shattered . . .[26]

Dawn Mackay was working at the time for the legendary Madame Vacani, 'teacher of dancing to the nobility and gentry for more years than she will confess to', as the *Sunday Times* put it in a 1953 profile. Madame Vacani (Mrs Marguerite Rankin in private life) had taught not only Prince Charles and Princess Anne but their mother and aunt before them. She had studios in the Brompton Road, but also despatched her assistants to various girls' schools and to conduct 'country classes' deep in the shires:

> . . . Although her work now is chiefly that of organising this widespread system of imparting the elements of deportment, ballroom manners and the Court Curtsy, she will still illustrate her conversation in her own Mayfair drawing-room with a neat little *chassée*, a polka step or – more disconcertingly – by putting her interviewer into the first ballet position and coaxing him into a graceful movement of the arms – *so!*[27]

Dawn Mackay was to look back on her twelve years with the eccentric Madame Vacani with unalloyed pleasure: 'An excellent training for life, and very useful in dealing with the old boy.'[28] She shared a small flat at the top of a house in Ennismore Gardens – Reith didn't like it because there was no lift. He was in the habit of introducing her as his goddaughter: 'I shall be delighted to meet your goddaughter,' Hugh Greene said in a handwritten note in April. 'I feel very grateful to her after reading what you say about the part she played in recent events' – a reference to the apparent reconciliation which had come about since the beginning of the year. Greene was perfectly aware that she was not his goddaughter; Harman Grisewood, who was his Chief Assistant at the time, recalled thirty years later that it used to amuse Greene to speculate coarsely with his cronies on the true nature of the relationship.[29] On one occasion Greene overstepped the mark, and made a suggestive remark of some sort to her. Miss Mackay parried it coolly by saying that he should not judge others by himself: 'I really detested him. He was a very unpleasant man – he looked exactly like a shark. His lordship was convinced he was a communist.'

A letter that survives in one of the scrapbooks throws revealing light on how Reith regarded Miss Mackay at this time. It is from Marmaduke Tudsbery, who was for many years consulting civil engineer to the BBC, and whose relations with Reith were quite different from those of most of his colleagues – he was, for instance, the only BBC associate who ever addressed him as 'Walsham', and he seems to have enjoyed a degree of familiarity, even of licence, which Reith permitted to very few. Tudsbery had been a central figure in the planning of Broadcasting House, and when it was completed he had presented Reith with a golden key to the building. Now, thirty years on, when it had entirely gone out of most people's minds, Reith wrote to remind him of this agreeable symbolic gesture and to make a request. Tudsbery's elegant reply indicates that he was a man of both charm and delicacy:

My dear Walsham,
I am flattered that you still have the key, and to know that you didn't rid yourself of it when you shook the dust of Broadcasting House from your feet – as did your namesake cast aside the great seal when he left his kingdom! . . .
  If, having passed the allotted span, you are determined now to rid yourself of belongings of sentimental value, (Why the haste? Abraham was several hundred years older than you when he 'begat'!!) it will certainly please me to see you pass it on, on May 20th, to Miss Mackay – who unlocked for you, after all these years, the gate that you have kept so firmly shut. She will preserve the key, I am sure, as a memento of her godfather, who will ever be remembered as the founder of Broadcasting.
  Yes, do give it her, but don't get yourself fitted for a coffin yet!!!
                    Ever yours, Marmaduke.

The occasion on 20 May was a visit to the television studios at Lime Grove, where Reith and Miss Mackay lunched with Tudsbery and another old colleague, Gerald Beadle, now the Director of the Television Service. Afterwards they were shown over the new BBC television centre then in course of construction. Dawn Mackay's recollection of the episode is that she expressed some reluctance to accept this unusual gift:

The golden key? Oh, yes, I told him he had no right to, but at that precise moment I think if I hadn't had it in my custody it would have gone into the river, which I thought would have been a pity. He had two or three times threatened to throw it off Westminster Bridge . . . On one occasion I know he had it in his hand and was threatening to throw it across the terrace of the House of Lords, and it would have been a pity if it had gone into the mud of the Thames.

Miss Mackay did not accompany him when he went to present the prizes at Glasgow Academy a month after his visit to Lime Grove, but she figured prominently, if anonymously, in his address to the boys of his old school. The *Glasgow Herald* carried an extended report. Reith told his audience that the previous evening he had been talking to a very young friend for whom he had both great admiration and great affection:

I said, 'You should be able to give me a message for the boys of Glasgow Academy,' and she replied (loud laughter, during which the speaker said 'an intelligent audience, Mr Chairman') – 'Tell them LIFE'S FOR LIVING.'

I said 'That's a cliché, isn't it, and you know how I hate clichés.' This was her reply: 'It is *not* a cliché; it's my own original invention; and even if it were a cliché you were never given it when you were young, and you haven't learnt it yet . . .' There's the message for you – that life's for living. And she was right that I had never been told it when young, and that I haven't fully learnt it yet; but at least I now realise how much I've missed, and how many mistakes I've made . . .[30]

Much of Reith's diary for 1960 is taken up with charting his attempts to slide down that learning curve, mainly under Miss Mackay's tutelage. One weekend in Berkshire he was coaxed onto the tennis lawn: 'I was enormously averse to this,' he wrote, 'chiefly, I suppose, because I didn't want to make a fool of myself,' but in the event he played for two hours and felt as full of energy at the end as at the beginning:

I think I played as good a game as ever I played in my life . . . I had long since given up any thought of playing again, but with great regret, because I always enjoyed the game so much and all the circumstances of it are so pleasant (I used to feel this in Dunblane days, at Invercauld).[31]

The circumstances were decidedly less pleasant whenever he had occasion to meet Marista. Getting off the night train from Scotland toward the end of January, he spotted his chauffeur waiting to take his bag. Reith was about to move off towards the car when the man said, 'There is somebody here hoping you will recognise them.' It was only then that he saw Marista:

I took off my hat; she said Hello; I asked how she knew I was on the train, and instead of answering she beckoned to a youth a yard or two off, and there, to my fury, was the wretched man that we are all afraid she was going to marry. He had on corduroy trousers, a dirty burberry, and a cloth cap. He could not have escaped the look that I gave him, of surprise and irritation, and I nearly said that if my daughter were going to meet him he ought to dress properly. He took his glove off, but then saw that I was not going to shake hands with him. However, eventually I did hold out my hand, but said nothing to him.[32]

Marista's birthday fell on Palm Sunday. 'She is 28 today, but has no message or present from me,' he wrote in his diary. He seems to have had some aware-ness of what he was doing to himself. When he was in Glasgow on business in May he drove along the Great Western Road and glimpsed the towers of the College Church: 'I am far off my father and mother now,' he wrote. A week later, he recorded the inevitable:

Letters from the man Leishman, Marista Muriel Reith and Dr George Macleod, informing me that the long expected engagement is now actuality.

I shall not even acknowledge receipt of any of them, and I suppose 50 years ago I should be solemnly ruling the name Marista Muriel Reith from the family Bible.[33]

Marista Leishman later came to believe that her father never fully recovered from the trauma of her engagement, although it is plain that he had already suffered a good deal of psychic injury before it took place. Reith's behaviour in the seven months leading up to the wedding was certainly that of a man whose mental balance was severely disturbed. When the engagement notice appeared in *The Times*, those who offered Reith congratulations were told that it was 'a matter of distress' to other members of the family.

Business took him to Glasgow at the end of the month, and as he went through the revolving door at NBL, a young woman got up from a bench and spoke to him: 'I looked at her vaguely and in surprise for half a second or so, then recognised Marista; I imagined that the extent to which I have felt that she had written herself off as a member of the family had had this extraordinary effect, that I was beginning to forget what she looked like.' Marista found him totally unyielding, and he found the conversation completely pointless: 'She was wearing an engagement ring, and it looked as if it might have come from a cracker,' he wrote sneeringly. 'What is more she was not wearing the signet ring which she has worn for a great many years.'[34]

Over tea at the farm the following weekend, he pursued the question of the signet ring with manic fixity. When Marista said that she couldn't wear it next to her engagement ring, he retorted that she could wear it on the fourth finger of her right hand. When she explained that she had taken it off to avoid damage to her engagement ring, he quickly became exasperated:

I had to point out to her that there were no diamonds round the ring, only a single blue stone in the middle with some very little diamonds round it, and that the signet ring couldn't possibly touch any of them; moreover, that in an issue between gold and diamonds it is the gold that gets worn. I told her, politely but definitely, that I presumed either she or her fiancé objected to the signet ring, either because it would be objectionable to socialists, or because it had been given to her by her father and mother . . .[35]

It became possible over time for Murray Leishman to look back on these painful events with admirable detachment and even with some amusement (later, when he worked as a psychotherapist, his experiences with his father-in-law took on a certain professional interest). He was greatly helped by two older men who were his friends and mentors. The Rev. W. A. Smellie was the minister of St John's Kirk in Perth and served for a time as a religious adviser to the Independent Television Authority. There came a moment when Murray felt that he must expostulate with Reith, and he showed what he proposed to write to Bill Smellie. 'That's a splendid letter,' Smellie said. 'Now put it in a drawer for a year. The essential thing to remember is that you've got the girl,

you've won – allow him to have his tantrums.' That restored Murray's perspective: 'You had to see him as a wee boy who had got into a tantrum, and who
was at the same time intelligent and splendid. But having that sort of bi-polar
perspective, I found, was essential for survival.'

George Macleod was also a great help. A baronet, Macleod was an unusual
ornament of the Scottish ministry. A large, self-confident man, he had read law
before going into the Church, and had the useful advantage of not being remotely
afraid of Reith. This was partly a matter of temperament; Marista maintained
that her father sensed it, and was uneasily aware that Macleod knew how to argue
and that he didn't.[36] The two men had met over dinner soon after Marista had
taken up her Church of Scotland job. Reith, convinced that Macleod was
exploiting his daughter, had remonstrated by saying he had told her that most
people had weekends off. For Reith, the remark was untypically crab-like;
Macleod countered it suavely by saying he understood Reith himself didn't take
his weekends off and that Marista was very like him.[37] Macleod did much in those
difficult days to bolster Murray Leishman's morale. 'What you've got to remember,' he would boom cheerfully, 'is that only the fourth person of the Trinity
would be good enough for Reith's daughter.'[38]

Reith had now acquired an additional business interest. At the end of January
he had been appointed chairman of the State Building Society, one of four
directors chosen by the Chief Registrar of Friendly Societies – this followed a
court appearance by the society's managing director on charges of aiding and
abetting in the fraudulent conversion of more than £3 million, and of falsifying
the minutes of a board meeting with intent to defraud. Reith told shareholders
at the annual general meeting that he and his colleagues regarded themselves
not as undertakers hired 'to bury away the past of the society as quickly as
possible' but as a team of salvage men. This went down well. A report in *The
Times* said that in striking contrast to the angry scenes at the previous AGM,
the proceedings had been pervaded by a quiet good humour, and that this had
been generated by Reith's 'confident manner'. By June, he was able to send
out a circular announcing that shareholders would have 10 per cent of their
holding returned the following month.

He was seeing more and more of Dawn Mackay, and he was now a frequent
visitor to her parents' home at weekends. They must have been exceptionally
tolerant hosts, because in most houses the behaviour on any one of a number
of occasions of this improbable *cavaliere servente* would have ensured that he
was invited no more. Once he lost his temper and flung his coffee cup across
the verandah. On another occasion the family had planned to go to early
communion, and Mrs Mackay went in to Reith with morning tea. 'Janet,' he
intoned mournfully from his bed, 'I cannot come. I am not in a state of grace.'
Mrs Mackay produced a brisk and memorable return of service. 'In that case,'
she said, 'you'd better get up, get shaved and get yourself *into* a state of grace
– and you've got fifteen minutes.' Reith, whose experience of the receiving end
of ultimatums was limited, complied.

He and Dawn were frequently seen about together in London during the

week, dining at Boulestin's or the Hyde Park buttery, going to the theatre –
he took her to see Noël Coward's new play *Waiting in the Wings*, and found it
'absolutely first class'. At the end of July he was introduced to Madame Vacani:
'rather an old humbug, but extremely astute'. The next night, after dining
together, he and Dawn travelled on the night sleeper to Edinburgh, and after
breakfast at the North British Hotel drove to Fossoway, where she had a
goddaughter. Reith more than once put it to Christopher that he should invite
Dawn to the farm, a proposition which he received with a total lack of enthusiasm. She did eventually pay one brief visit, but when Reith told Muriel he
would be very glad if Christopher were to marry her, the suggestion led to
'some acrimony'.[39]

Marista's wedding had been set for 3 December, in Perth. At the end of
September, Reith wrote to Andrew Stewart, the BBC's Controller in Scotland,
with a seemingly casual enquiry:

> Could you very kindly let me know what a man LEISHMAN does on the
> Edinburgh evening paper *Dispatch* – or something such?
>
> I have been variously informed that he is joint editor, assistant editor,
> news editor, and reporter.
>
> I am mildly curious to know, as it seems that his son is to marry my
> daughter.[40]

When he acknowledged Stewart's prompt reply he told him he would not be
going to the wedding.[41] Andrew Stewart was one of the old school. He had
been recruited by Reith in 1926, worked for him during the war at the Ministry
of Information and admired him inordinately. He now took a deep breath and
wrote to say that in his view it was Reith's Christian duty to attend the wedding.[42] William Haley was another who urged him to go, and George Macleod
also weighed in. Reith was still making a show of canvassing opinion on the
matter at the end of October, and the advice he got from Christopher brought
him up short: 'Everything was ghastly enough already, and I should only come
if I were prepared to bury the hatchet. I was very surprised and disappointed
at his taking this line.'[43]

Disappointed or not, he was moving towards a decision, although he was
reluctant to admit it even in his diary. Three weeks after that conversation with
Christopher, there is the briefest of entries: 'Huntsman about wedding rig,' it
reads, 'in case I go to Perth on the 3rd.'[44] It also seems likely that a conversation
over lunch at the Mackays' had some influence on him. He was the only guest.
Dawn Mackay remembers that when the conversation turned to the wedding,
Reith announced flatly that he had no intention of being present, and the
atmosphere became rather charged: 'Marista is no daughter of mine!' he
informed the table. 'Good gracious!' Dawn interjected. 'Lady Reith must have
been carrying on with the milkman, then.' This produced an exclamation of
shocked reproof from her mother, but quickly reduced the rest of the family
to uncontrollable laughter. Reith eventually managed to join in, and this allowed

Mr Mackay, for whom Reith had quite a respect, to say, 'Well, John, if you don't go, you are certainly not the man I thought you were.'

Reith's renewed contact with the BBC had been maintained on two levels. He had a number of meetings with Harman Grisewood, the Chief Assistant to the Director-General. These were ostensibly to discuss public relations and preparations for the Pilkington Committee of enquiry which had by then been set up, although Grisewood also recalled an appeal from Arthur fforde to be friendly to Reith, whom he said was very lonely and unhappy and needed friends. Grisewood had a house near Much Hadham in Hertfordshire, and somewhat to his surprise Reith accepted an invitation to lunch there; on another occasion he went to Lollards Tower, which he found half shuttered and extremely gloomy. Reith offered him sherry, which Grisewood remembered as dark brown and tasting of cough mixture. Reith then startled him by saying, 'Would you pray with me?' and when Grisewood, who was a Roman Catholic, assented, he was led off towards the chapel:

> Before we knelt down, he turned to me in rather a fierce and melancholic way, and said, 'I'd have you know that I'm a very bad Christian.' And I had almost the same sort of feelings I had when he interviewed me many many years before, that this somehow was an exhibition that was meant to be impressive in some way ... But there it was, and he knelt down, and we prayed, not aloud, I'm glad to say, but we certainly prayed – I fervently, if rather nervously.[45]

Reith made his television debut in 1960. He had agreed earlier in the year to appear in the *Face to Face* programme and answer questions from John Freeman. Dawn Mackay went with him to the BBC on the night, and they were shown around the studios. In one area, carpenters were at work. Most of the locker doors were decorated with what she remembered as 'the most dreadful sort of *Sun* pin-ups' – all except one, which had a picture of a Henry Moore sculpture. 'A Third Programme carpenter, forsooth,' growled Reith.

He was not in the easiest of moods, and Dawn Mackay remembered feeling apprehensive. She and Gerald Beadle sat on a sofa in an adjacent room, watching the performance on monitors. Beadle said that he had never before seen Freeman display the slightest sign of nerves; Freeman was not to know that his subject had got slightly cold feet after being shown how he had put Adlai Stevenson and Sir Roy Welensky through their paces.

In the event Reith felt that the 'long-dreaded day' had passed off entirely well. He gave nothing away about his famous 'black list' of people he had it in for in a big way (except that it was not carved in stone and that the names on it changed from time to time) and he remained coy about the big jobs he would still like to do – 'I could name one, but it would be awfully improper to, wouldn't it?' (It was the chairmanship of the British Transport Commission.) His answering technique caused some amusement, and might have thrown a less experienced interviewer: 'Have you got that, Mr Freeman?' he would say occasionally. 'That answer your question?' Sometimes it did and sometimes it didn't. Was he ambitious? Only to be fully stretched. What about his height? An affliction. His greatest defect of character? An inability to tolerate slow-wittedness. A happy man? Oh no. A successful one? Not that either. At the end, Freeman dug up what he had said in his Glasgow Academy speech the year before – what was it he had missed out on? By now, that was an answer that needed no rehearsal – 'that life was for living'. But he wanted to be sure that his interviewer had grasped his meaning, so he added, 'Is that clear?'

He got 200 fan letters, and made a seven-page summary of them in his scrapbook. One was from Norman Collins: 'It is always a joy to see a Man stand out among the faceless ones. The fact that I think you are wrong in no way detracts from my admiration.' Another was from Mary Somerville. 'The question Freeman did not ask rose to *my* lips afterwards,' she wrote. 'Why did you not stretch *yourself* – for the Lord's sake!'

Two weeks before she was to be married, Marista wrote to Jo Stanley thanking her for the blue Corsican tablecloth she had sent as a wedding present. 'I am very sorry about Papa,' she wrote:

I have a feeling that over the years the thing will heal, even if only a little, and that it's probably at its worst just now. One cannot keep up a perpetual barrage against someone getting married after they have been settled for some time; on the other hand I don't pretend all the trouble is on one side. But I do insist on hoping for the best![46]

It was raining in Perth on the day, and when Reith got to the Station Hotel, he discovered that he had forgotten to bring a white shirt. The hotel manager quickly found him one, but the sleeves were far too short. As Reith would not dream of appearing in public showing anything but the conventional length of cuff, there was nothing for it but to attack the sleeves with a pair of scissors. Muriel then stitched the severed cuffs inside the sleeves of his morning coat. This at least gave Marista something to laugh about on the way to church, but meant that he couldn't stretch his arms out properly for the rest of the afternoon.

The service was conducted by Bill Smellie and George Macleod. After he had taken Marista up the aisle, Reith retreated to the front pew on the north side and looked stonily ahead throughout. He and Muriel shook hands with about 200 people, of whom he knew only fifteen or twenty. George Macleod made a speech. When he said that the bridegroom was the most popular man of his time in college and was to be congratulated on bringing politics into his religion, Reith left the room. Shortly afterwards, leaving Muriel behind, he abandoned the proceedings altogether. He changed out of his wedding clothes and drove to the house of Dawn's friends at Fossoway. The local garage man then drove him to Edinburgh Airport and he flew south to spend the rest of the weekend with the Mackays.[47]

He returned to the farm for Christmas, feeling 'unsettled and unhappy'. He refused to accompany Muriel and Christopher when they went to see Marista's new house on Christmas Eve. On Christmas Day, just as they were finishing the plum pudding, the bell rang:

> There, to everyone's amazement and my intense disgust, were Mr and Mrs Leishman. Marista came in as if she were delighted to see me and were going to give me a kiss, which she hasn't done for about 7 or 8 years. I shook hands with her formally, saying 'Good evening', and that was all. Then the man came in, and though I gave him a formal bow, which ought to have put him off, he walked over to me, holding his hand out. I shook hands with him also, but with still more unwillingness. Then I went out of the room up to the bedroom . . . It was a most trying experience for me, and I would have been saved it if Muriel had done as I had asked and made sure yesterday that they didn't come over when I was at the farm.[48]

His behaviour angered Christopher, who was also 'very hostile' when he heard from Muriel where Reith was proposing to spend the New Year weekend.[49] They travelled south by train. Reith saw Muriel off to visit friends in Reading. He himself followed the well-trodden path that led to the Mackays.

It is not uncommon for elderly people to think of death. Reith thought about it a great deal, but also talked about it, and not only to his familiars. Early in 1961 he took the chair at an All Souls discussion group which met at the Athenaeum, and a text survives of his opening remarks. 'To die in the hills we love is surely to find a more romantic, congenial, lovely place of exit than anywhere else on earth,' he told his hearers:

> But of course it does not come out like that at all. For, so dying – whether by exposure or sudden fall – an immense amount of trouble is inevitably caused in the search for the corpse and in its transportation to wherever it has to go. I have always felt that one should die efficiently if one can – giving as little trouble as possible . . .
>
> Often of late I have wished there were a recognised, easy, maybe even lawful, way to walk where death would be standing waiting for us; where, overjoyed, we would greet it as a friend . . .[50]

Two people were particularly well placed to appreciate how severely depressed he was at this time. One was Dawn Mackay, the other was his secretary. Barbara Hickman had first worked for Reith in CDC days, as a junior to Molly Cotara. 'The Hick', as Reith called her, came from a modest background. It was her

first job, and for quite some time Reith's stormy insistence on excellence at
the first attempt came near to overwhelming her. In 1959 she went off to
Canada, returning to work for Reith at British Oxygen early in 1961. He
informed her almost at once that his life was now different. He was, he told
her, frequently down in Berkshire at weekends. He revealed to her that he had
made an important discovery, although its terms had been amplified since he
had revealed it to John Freeman and the boys of Glasgow Academy: life, he
told Miss Hickman, was for living – and for loving.

It rapidly became clear to 'The Hick' that Reith's interest in Dawn Mackay
was obsessional – 'it took over his whole life, nothing else mattered.' This was
not simply a matter of observation. She had come to work at British Oxygen
as a secretary, but in no time at all her role came to resemble that of *confidante*
in a drama by Racine. She was not simply called upon to book tables in
restaurants or buy tickets for the opera or telephone Lady Reith to say that he
would not be home. Nor was it simply a matter of typing up the lengthy
outpourings of his feelings intended for his diary; before ever he settled to
dictation she would already have heard an extended rehearsal of them. This
took up great slabs of the working day, and there were occasions when she felt
guilty about it – she was, after all, employed by British Oxygen. What she
transcribed from her shorthand read like confused despatches from a war zone
where instinct did daily battle with higher principle, and she was exposed to a
heavy fall-out of frustration and guilt.

From 'The Hick', as from almost all his secretaries, Reith got not only the
total commitment that he demanded but a substantial unearned bonus of affection. It was, for all that, a considerable strain, both morally and emotionally.
Almost thirty years later, working as a probation officer at Wormwood Scrubs,
she was still not entirely sure why she had endured it so long (she stayed until
1966): 'I suppose it was about my need to be wanted. It flattered my ego.' The
first time that she unburdened herself to any extent was during a meeting with
Marista in the late 1980s.[51]

Barbara Hickman remembered Dawn Mackay as warm, generous and spon-
taneous – 'attractive in a *Country Life* portrait sort of way'. Reith showed her
all the letters which passed between them – his full of endearments, hers
displaying fondness, although without exposing her emotions to the extent that
Reith did. There were also a great many letters from Mrs Mackay, and these,
too, Reith shared with his secretary. Sometimes, when dictating for the diary,
he spoke about sexual desire. He quite often reverted to one particular occasion
when he had experienced an almost overwhelming sexual urge in Dawn's
presence and had had to struggle to suppress it, and it was this that made
Barbara Hickman confident that they never had sexual relations. 'My understanding was that the relationship wasn't improper,' she said. 'There always
seemed to be some sort of boundaries which somebody had erected. It always
seemed that he was pushing against those boundaries.'

Those who knew him less well assumed that he had gone beyond those
boundaries. Certainly most of those he encountered on their various excursions

to the BBC believed that Dawn Mackay was his mistress. Rather naïvely, this high-spirited young woman does not seem to have realised this at the time:

> I felt very sorry for him and I did have great affection for him, but if you mean was it ever a physical relationship, no – good gracious, no. Nothing could be further from the truth, or less likely, frankly. At his best he was a very good companion. He could be very funny and very amusing – he did have a great sense of humour when you could dredge it up to the surface. I went to places and did things that I wouldn't otherwise have done, and I learned a lot from him. I learned a lot about public life, for instance, because if you asked him a question – I asked him once about the Monopolies Commission, and I got 15 pages to read the next day . . . I don't think I was altogether real, you know. I was a sort of fictional being, a fantasy composition of things that he had always wanted, bits of what he would have liked Lady Reith to be, of what he wanted Marista to be, only I didn't have Marista's brains . . .

Reith spilled out to her his views and feelings about everything under the sun, not excluding his exasperation at what he saw as his wife's inadequacies. Muriel had clearly never found it easy to assimilate the elaborate briefing notes which her lord and master was in the habit of preparing for her, and her social aptitude had not increased with the years; Reith maintained that if, say, she found herself at dinner beside some BBC luminary who had been with the Corporation since time began, she was quite capable of saying, 'And tell me, Mr So-and-So, have you been with the BBC long?'[52] She was, Reith was in the habit of announcing, 'no suitable consort for me'. After one of these disloyal outbursts, Dawn enquired why he had ever married her in the first place. Reith seemed momentarily taken aback: 'Nobody has ever asked me that before,' he said. 'Well, I'll tell you. Somebody else that I didn't particularly like was interested in her, so I thought I would see if I could cut him out.' Although she had no means of knowing how much truth there was in this reply, Dawn was nonetheless chilled by it. 'It was the only time I ever actually hated him,' she said.

Dawn Mackay said that she had not been aware of the dissensions which her friendship with Reith caused within the family, and registered disbelief that Muriel could have been jealous of someone forty years her junior: 'She *couldn't* have been! You couldn't be jealous of somebody that age who really didn't take anything seriously.' Reith once told her that 'he had had some physical satisfaction with a secretary, though he had never had a relationship with her', a confidence which she found understandably baffling. He also spoke to her about Charlie, although he never identified him. He had been the only real friend he ever had, the one person in his life to whom he had been able to talk about absolutely anything; he also told her that there had been those who thought the relationship too close.

Reith was frequently in a state of distress at this time, and found it difficult to contain his emotions. When he was in a rage he could be violent, throwing flower pots across the office and breaking telephones. This did not go unnoticed, particularly after British Oxygen moved to new open-plan offices in Hammersmith. Apart from writing to Miss Mackay and pouring out his feelings in his diary, he would pursue her compulsively on the telephone. If he failed to reach her, he would talk at length to whoever else he was able to raise. He almost always rang Barbara Hickman in the course of the evening. If she was going out, he insisted that she should leave a number; if he rang her at the flat she shared and the line was engaged he would become enraged and get the operator to interrupt the call. His unwillingness to go home meant that his chauffeur, Phillips, was sometimes still sitting in the Rolls outside Hammersmith House at 11 p.m. or later. He could get through quite a lot of whisky during these evening sessions. He also ate a great many biscuits. If Barbara Hickman went home without seeing to it that his tin was full, she was in trouble.

There were times when she registered disapproval – of his drinking, for example, or when she felt compromised by being asked to tell Muriel less than the whole truth – and there is evidence of some sensitivity to this: Reith used to call her his *custos morum*.[53] Sometimes he talked to her about suicide, his mind usually turning to the river. She remembered one occasion when he did not go home at all, but passed the night walking endlessly to and fro across Waterloo Bridge.

Something Dawn Mackay never told Reith was that she gave up some of her leisure time to working as a Samaritan. One night she and her flatmate had been to a ball. Shortly after they got home – it was about two in the morning – Reith telephoned. He was in a state of great agitation. He was alone at Lollards Tower, and told her that he had a gun in his hand. 'I didn't *think* he would commit suicide, because I thought he was too arrogant,' she said, 'but there was always the danger of a dramatic gesture.' After the best part of two hours on the phone, her Samaritan repertoire exhausted, she finally said, 'Well, if that's what you want to do, it's perfectly easy – just pull the trigger.' There was a tremendous crash at the other end of the line:

I thought, 'Oh, my God!' – but all that had happened was that he had dropped both the gun and the telephone, and that was the end of it. The next day my father rang him and said, 'You'll kindly get into your car and you'll come down here.' He drove down like a lamb and handed over the gun to Daddy.

The troughs of depression were kept apart by the occasional manic peak. Reith would sometimes enliven the end of the afternoon by reciting from the Bible or launching into 'The Darkies' Sunday School' (*Jonah was an immigrant, so runs the Bible tale . . .*). He could also reel off lengthy passages of *Paradise Lost*; alternatively Miss Hickman would be invited to join him in singing a hymn:

> Behold! the mountain of the Lord
> In latter days shall rise
> On mountain tops above the hills
> And draw the wondering eyes.

Three decades later she could still not hear Scottish Paraphrase No. 18, sung to the tune of 'Glasgow', without a pang.

There was a particular reason for Reith's obsessive concern that every nuance of his feelings for Miss Mackay should be recorded. He had tried for a time to persuade her to take all the diaries and scrapbooks into her care, but she had laughed and gestured round her small flat: 'Where on earth would I put them?' It remained an *idée fixe*, however, that she should one day read all the extravagant things he had written in the volume dedicated to her, and he extracted an undertaking from Barbara Hickman that after his death she would get it to her. So long as the entries which she typed up were locked in the bottom drawer of his desk at British Oxygen, this posed no difficulty, but there came a time when they were removed to Lollards Tower, where they were kept in a locked attaché case. Miss Hickman was provided with a second key.

In the middle of May 1961 a curious advertisement appeared in the personal column of *The Times*:

LORD REITH SEEKS ADVICE. He has kept a diary, not a day missed, for over 50 years . . . He is more and more minded to destroy it because: 1. he does not wish to put a burden on either of his children by leaving it to them; 2. he does not like to think of it lying in some library for a hundred years and then being scrapped (he would prefer to scrap it himself); 3. he does not want there to be such records of himself. Has anyone any kindly advice? Write Box J 261, The Times, EC4.[54]

The advertisement aroused great interest. Reith was in Scotland that weekend; he was pestered by reporters on the telephone and pursued by photographers on the train. He declined an invitation to appear on *Panorama*. He received more than 300 replies, and catalogued them neatly in his scrapbook. Many of them urged him not to destroy the diary. Offers of custody came from the BBC, the National Library of Scotland, and the Universities of Auckland, Glasgow, London, Keele and York. Nuffield College, Oxford expressed an interest, and so did the Tottenham Public Libraries and the London School of Economics. Two jokers suggested that it should be sealed and deposited under water or land for later discovery and conjecture.

There were enquiries from literary agents, newspaper editors, publishers, and would-be biographers.[55] Asa Briggs, who had recently embarked on the second volume of his history of British broadcasting, wrote, 'I will gladly do something with it myself, safeguard it, edit it, place it and so on rather than see it cast on one side or destroyed.' From the replies that Reith sent out it is possible to see how his mind was working: the alternatives, he wrote, seemed to be outright sale, 'in which case I would lose control, so the price would certainly have to be considerable', or arranging for someone to prepare an edited version.

Lord Beaverbrook sent round the literary editor of the *Evening Standard*, Harold Harris, and he spent two days at Lollards Tower leafing through the material before deciding it was not for them: 'You mentioned the possibility of having them destroyed,' he wrote, in a rather oily letter. 'I do beg you never to give in to such a wanton impulse. Imprisoned in these volumes, like a statue in a block of marble, is a whole man, public and private, in all his variety . . .'[56] Reith asked Asa Briggs what he thought he would be likely to get if he sold the diary outright, and Briggs said at least £75,000: 'This was entirely in line with my own theory – that I would expect £100,000, but would hesitate a good deal over £50,000.'[57]

Barbara Hickman was aware of Dawn Mackay's mother being very much in evidence at this time, and that is confirmed by the diary. In the course of 1961 she was quite often included in excursions to the theatre or to Covent Garden (Reith enjoyed *Tosca* less than *Aida*), and on one occasion he recorded a conversation he had with her about Dawn's future: 'We both feel she should finish with the Vacani business, have a decent holiday, get into an entirely new activity and away from the wretched lodgings in which she now is.'[58] He also made guarded enquiries at the Phoenix about life assurance for her, and the company actuary sent him details of a policy 'suitable for a Lady aged 32 next birthday'.[59]

Reith lavished presents on Miss Mackay – books, records, pieces of jewellery from Cartier. He sometimes asked for things to be sent round to the office on approval. 'Anything she wanted she could have,' said Barbara Hickman. 'The slightest hint, and she would have it in the post next day.' It was a demanding form of generosity, however, and if the recipient said the wrong thing, the donor was quite capable of coming round and taking the latest present back again. Miss Hickman remembered most of the jewellery coming back in one go when the relationship was at an end – 'I have this vision of having them all over the desk.'

In the middle of July, Reith suddenly realised that a present for Muriel would be in order as their fortieth wedding anniversary was approaching. Miss Hickman told him that this was known as a ruby wedding ('which I had not heard of before'). She went out to Mappin & Webb for him and chose a gold brooch with rubies and diamonds. Reith had taken Dawn Mackay and her mother to *Swan Lake* a few days previously, but his arrangements for entertaining Muriel on their anniversary were more modest; they lunched at home, and in the evening he took her to the cinema to see *Ben Hur*.

Committees of enquiry always induce a healthy bout of self-examination in those being enquired into, and as Sir Harry Pilkington and his colleagues got into their stride, the BBC began to wonder whether it needed to do something to tone up the quality of its senior and middle management. It decided to embark on a series of management training courses. These were residential, and lasted a fortnight. After a successful pilot in Sussex, they were held at the Uplands conference centre in Buckinghamshire, not far from Disraeli's house at Hughenden. Each was attended by a couple of dozen members of staff – controllers, departmental managers, programme editors. They were directed by Oliver Whitley, who was now the BBC's Controller of Staff Training and Appointments, and it was he who was instrumental in persuading Reith to go down in the early 1960s and address the troops.

He went for the first time in March 1961, and Sir Arthur fforde took the chair. Reith spoke only for about ten minutes, and there was then a lengthy question and answer session. The questions were slow to come, and were of uneven quality. Reith's instinct, if he did not find a question particularly inter-esting, was to cuff it aside rather than reply to it, and it was not long before this happened. The questioner was an engineer, and his neighbour, also an engineer, attempted to retrieve the situation. 'I think, Sir,' he began, 'that the point my colleague was getting at . . .' That was as far as he got. 'Oh, I under-stood very well what he was getting at,' purred Reith. 'I'm very intelligent, you know.' Before he left, the members of the course formed up in the bar, and Reith went down the line shaking hands and interrogating people about their jobs. To one or two, he posed the all-important supplementary question: 'And are you fully stretched?'

He paid a second visit in June, and was induced to play his first game of croquet, which had become something of an Uplands ritual. The evening session had not finished until 10.15, so that before long they were smashing the balls about the lawn in darkness. Reith was partnered by Hugh Greene, who played a vicious attacking game. Their opponents were the Director of Administration and the Controller of Television Programme Services, but the promotion prospects of these worthies were never remotely en-dangered. 'DG and I won, three up and one to play,' says a satisfied note in the diary.[60]

These were enthralling occasions for the BBC staff who were present, most of whom had joined ten and twenty years after Reith's departure. In the main he reminisced, but he did not confine himself to broadcasting matters, and was quite prepared to talk about his disappointments and his ambitions, past and present. He was, for instance, much preoccupied at that time with events in Central Africa. The previous year he had suggested himself as governor-general to Sir Roy Welensky,[61] and more recently, after a conversation with Julian Greenfield, the Minister of Justice in the Central African Federation, he had once again convinced himself that he had a contribution to make:

If I were suddenly asked what I could suggest towards some settlement of the frightful confusion and the really dangerous, or anyhow intolerable, situ-ation that has arisen, I would say to send me out with plenipotentiary powers as governor of all three countries.[62]

Shortly after his first visit to Uplands, Reith gave evidence to the Pilkington Committee, and here too he did not think much of the questions, most of which were put by the chairman himself. 'Good afternoon, Lord Reith,' Pilkington began. 'You are the first person who has come all alone and unsupported.' 'Ought I to have brought someone?' Reith enquired. Pilkington told him that the programme companies had explained that their main purpose in life was to put out as many serious programmes as possible. 'Is that hypocrisy or merely humbug?' asked Reith. It is unlikely that he helped the committee a great deal. They were charged with charting a way forward, but Reith could only point backwards and assert the superiority of what had been, much as he had done ten years previously to Beveridge.

He gave an engagingly frank account of the beginnings of audience research: 'I much dislike the system of cadging round from door to door,' he told the committee, although he conceded that he had been a party to the starting of it: 'I said at last that it might be experimented with – provided care was taken that the results confirmed what I knew to be so.'[63] The committee membership included Richard Hoggart, and he recalled that afternoon's evidence in his memoirs thirty years later: 'The towering and anguished-looking Lord Reith spoke as though his words were being cut out of granite during a thunderstorm.'[64]

The British Transport Commission job which Reith had so much wanted had gone to Dr Richard Beeching, and in the late spring Reith lunched with him: 'Of course I told him that I envied him enormously, and that it would have taken twenty years off my age if I had been given this job.' He followed this up with a rambling letter emphasising his availability. Beeching had clearly found him rather odd, and sent a non-committal reply: 'I shall certainly have it in the forefront of my mind, although, frankly, I do not see how to fit you in in any satisfactory way.'[65]

He also lunched at the Garrick with Robert Lusty, who had recently become a BBC Governor, and who wanted him to write a book for Hutchinson's, of which he was chairman. Lusty also had something to tell Reith which he was sure would give him pleasure. A cartoon that Max Beerbohm had done of him toward the end of his time as Director-General had recently come up at Sotheby's, and the BBC had been the successful bidder. 'The BBC bought that?' said Reith. 'But my agent was the other fellow left bidding when the rest dropped out.' It hangs in the Governors' dining room at Broadcasting House to this day, with a note from Max to Lady Colefax: 'Here it is, dear Sybil, and I think I have captured the essentially poetic (but also queerly pre-Raphaelite) appearance. But I know I have failed to get the steely and practical eye.'[66]

The eye remained remarkably steely, even in his seventy-third year, and it continued to range restlessly in search of great endeavours. Moral Rearmament still came alongside from time to time. One of their senior men called on him the day after their leader, Dr Buchman, died, ostensibly to seek his advice about complaining to the BBC over their news coverage, but there was, as always, a second purpose:

Of course he also told me that God had told him that the best years of my life were still to come, more or less, if I only went to Caux. I said I thought it was time that God declared himself directly to me if I were to do anything.[67]

Later in the year he was approached by Hugh Gaitskell, the Labour leader:

He asked if I would take on a sort of royal commission on money expenditures during elections. I said I would but that I would want Tory members as well as Labour and I tried to point out to him how much more valuable this would be. He was very scared and not at all intelligent.[68]

This evolved into a commission of enquiry into advertising on behalf of the Labour Party. *The Times* said that Reith, in accepting the chairmanship, had made it known that it should not be thought to indicate any party political attachment on his part.[69] The commission did include one or two people who were not Labour sympathisers, but there were those who thought that Reith was naïve and allowing himself to be used. The news was not well received at Lollards Tower: 'M very vexed with me for not telling her about my "new job"; I said I just hadn't thought of it; there was no deliberate withholding.'[70]

During a visit to Glasgow in the autumn, he had gone back to the old Hydepark works where he had served his apprenticeship, but it was not a sentimental journey from which he derived any comfort or pleasure.

I went and stood in a particular spot where I was only a few inches off a sudden and most messy death. Somehow or other the heavy chain had fallen off an overhead crane and had crashed down about two feet from where I was standing. I wish to God it had fallen on me, just as I have so often wished that October 7th 1915 had been the end.[71]

In the early autumn, Reith noted that he had given dinner to Miss Dodds, the headmistress of Heathfield School. He had first been introduced to her by Dawn Mackay, who was an old girl, and this had led to an invitation to read the lesson at the school's carol service. On the day, he managed to stumble over one of the legs of the chapel's old brass lectern. He therefore resolved that the school should have a new (and grander) one, which he presented to the school to mark Dawn's time there; he and the Mackay family had attended the dedication service the previous year.[72] Now, over dinner, Miss Dodd told him that she had been asked to resign. She appears to have asked for his help, and Reith offered to act for her.

He took himself off to see the headmaster of Harrow, Dr James, the chairman of the Heathfield governors, who had with him the school's solicitor. They told him that they had been concerned about increasing unpunctuality on the headmistress's part, neglect of correspondence and inaccessibility to parents. There had been a great many complaints. They also, after some hesitation, mentioned two other matters which weighed with them – Reith did not enlarge on them in his diary, describing them only as 'matters of rumour or conjecture'. He later gave Miss Dodds an account of the meeting, saying that it was his impression that the school council wished to treat her 'decently'.[73]

It is not clear where the initiative for this came from, but Reith also now began to involve himself in the search for a successor to the unfortunate Miss Dodds. He seems for a time to have given his mind to little else: 'Very busy and a bit fussed about Heathfield doings,' he noted on 16 October. 'Most difficult to keep things in hand and sensible.' Three days later he drafted a press announcement about Miss Dodds' departure: 'What an amazing trouble this has given me.'[74]

The fuss and trouble were clearly out of proportion to their cause, and Reith realised that he was in need of medical attention. On 18 November he consulted a psychiatrist: 'I went to Bell and Croydon myself to get yellow pills, and they certainly made me feel and behave very queerly.' He stayed in bed the next day, and was visited by his own doctor, who gave him what he described as 'a high-powered injection': 'Dr Sturridge wanted me to go into St Thomas' Hospital for three weeks, but eventually agreed to the electric business (which I do not understand at all) being done twice weekly.' He returned to the office, noting that he had to see the doctor every day that week for an injection and that he felt 'awful'. He nonetheless travelled out to Harrow that afternoon for an hour's conversation about Heathfield with Dr James. 'He was quite ready to consider Dawn Mackay for the headmistress,' he wrote in his diary that night. 'I think she could do the job.'

His twice-weekly electric-shock treatment took place at the Royal Waterloo Hospital: 'All I can remember is taking my shoes and jacket off, a nurse standing beside the bed; and then I wakened up about two hours later.' To find a word to describe how he felt when he got back to Lollards Tower, he reached back into the vocabulary of his Scottish childhood: 'I felt a good deal shoogly, and went straight to bed.'[75] He went on feeling 'shoogly' for several days, and his sleep was disturbed by a recurrent nightmare that he had lost his pocket book. Miss Mackay, meanwhile, was winning all hearts at Heathfield. She had been interviewed by Dr James, and as Reith began to surface, he had a telephone call from one of the school governors: 'We're all quite excited by this Miss Mackay.'[76]

That excitement was sustained for a further two months. At the end of February, Miss Mackay was the unanimous choice of the Heathfield governors to be their new headmistress. Reith met the board on 6 March ('disposed of several important points during lunch') and she was formally offered the job that afternoon.

Investigative journalism was not fully up to speed in Britain in the early 1960s, but there was a certain twitching of the nostrils in Fleet Street. The *Sunday Express*, describing Heathfield as 'the exclusive girls' school for royalties, aristocrats and those who wish to make influential friends', said that it was a most intriguing appointment:

Miss Mackay has apparently no scholastic degrees whatever and no experience of school teaching at all. She is a Heathfield 'old girl' who when she left school took a secretarial course.

Disliking secretarial work, she gave it up to join the staff of a fashionable dance academy where she has been for ten years. I gather that she didn't apply for her new job. Friends put her name forward. Influential friends obviously.[77]

Miss Mackay was discreet and modest, saying she gathered that a member of the school council had put her name forward: 'I wouldn't have dreamed of applying for the post,' she was reported as saying, 'and when it was offered to me my instinctive reaction was to turn it down.' She had not in fact initially taken the idea remotely seriously, although she had recently met a couple of the school's governors at a dinner party and told them that she thought standards were slipping. She had hesitated before accepting Dr James' invitation to lunch, but Reith rang and announced that he was sending Phillips round in the Rolls:

So I arrived at Harrow, and I liked Dr James very much, and after lunch he said, 'I don't believe you've got the slightest idea of why you're here, have you? Somebody suggested you'd be a possible new headmistress.' I fell off the sofa I laughed so much.

She was reluctant to see the other governors, but James pressed her: 'So I did, and that was great fun, because they all took me out to lunch or dinner, and I had a wonderful time, and that was that and I went off to South Africa.' By the time she returned the job had been advertised, but the board had not found what they were looking for. Reith was not the only one urging her to accept. 'Darling,' said Madame Vacani, '*of course* you have to.'

Reith appears to have abandoned his electrical-shock treatment at the end of the first week. He was still clearly far from well in those early months of 1962, although the diary contains little specific detail about his health. His family life had now effectively fallen apart, and the rare diary references to his wife and children almost invariably make painful reading: 'Muriel was informed last night about 7.30 that Mrs Leishman's baby had begun its exit, and at 11 that it had been born – a son. I felt no interest whatever.'[78] He refused to go and see Marista and the child, and did not attend the christening.

Blood was still marginally thicker than water, however. When Marista wrote to say that the car he had given her two or three years previously had now been driven into the ground and that they could not afford a replacement, she received a cold telephone call to say that she might buy what car she wanted and send the bill to him.[79] There was a warm letter from Marista some weeks later in which she thanked him for 'a magnificent present'. She also extended a small olive branch: 'The issue of a ring is not so important, I find, as the bargain it entails. Perhaps we could do without that.' Reith reproduced the text in his diary, but wrote, 'I don't know what she means.'[80]

In April he went off briefly to Southern Rhodesia, where he had been asked to open the Central African Trade Fair. He stayed at Government House with Sir Humphrey Gibbs, and was a sharp-eyed guest: 'I told Lady Gibbs that His Excellency had his decorations on wrong – two bad mistakes. She had him alter them at once.' If Reith's audience in Bulawayo the next day were expecting the sort of speech they had had on the same occasion from the Queen Mother two years previously, they were in for a surprise. 'Anti-Colonialism Damned by Reith', said the headline in the *Rhodesia Herald*. What he offered them was a robust hymn to Empire:

There has been much disparagement and denunciation recently of British imperialism and colonization; and presumably it will miserably persist so long as there is a single island called colonial. Perhaps nothing – in conception policy or execution – has ever been subject to such vicious fabrication and distortion wherever chance or mischance offered scope – stygian and satanic . . .

It is not certain that his audience understood all the words, but they loved the tune:

I do not believe that transference of full Westminster democratic institutionalism and practice all at once will solve the outstanding problems . . . Both the old Africa and the new Africa are authoritarian; and before any realistic and definitive policy can be settled and established, it is essential authoritarianism must be recognised . . .[81]

Towards the end, the rhetoric became cloudier. The first requirement, he told his audience – he omitted to say for what – was 'the fear of the Lord which is the beginning of wisdom'. He ended with a verse from a metrical psalm, and as he walked the fifty yards back from the speaker's dais to the Royal Box they all stood up and applauded: 'I could not help wondering whether the applause would last out. Actually it did last the whole time.'[82]

He was on his feet again ten days later, this time in a debate on commercial television in the House of Lords. He had put down a motion after reading a book called *Pressure Group* which had been published the previous summer. It was the work of a Princeton professor called H. H. Wilson, and it gave a detailed account of the breaching of the BBC monopoly.

Reith spoke for about thirty minutes, and was heard in absolute silence. As proof of tenacity of memory for old grievances, the speech would have done credit to a Pole or an Irishman. 'Using, so to speak, a bulldozer rather than a shovel,' said the Parliamentary report in *The Times*, 'he shocked the House with his directness of language. It disconcerted a large number of peers to find Lord Reith describing commercial broadcasting as an incredible evil and saying, with absolute self-confidence, that if his was the supreme power it would be killed off tomorrow.' There was stronger meat to come, because Reith – 'hunched, mountainous, and speaking with a kind of controlled ferocity', said *The Times* – went on to deliver a sustained personal attack on Lord Woolton, sitting not ten paces from him. The words came tumbling out in a welter of mixed imagery. The noble Lord, he asserted, had sold the BBC down the river; it was an action comparable to the introduction into England of bubonic plague and the Black Death; it had been a disreputable conspiracy.

Reith had written to Woolton several weeks before the debate, although his letter amounted to a fairly minimal observance of the Parliamentary niceties.[83] When Woolton rose to speak, he said that he would not reply in detail to Reith's 'torrent of vulgar abuse', but he wished to know what was intended by the phrase about 'selling the BBC down the river'. Was there a suggestion that there had been some sort of financial transaction? 'This is usually the point,' *The Times* said, 'at which peers swiftly jump up to disclaim any such implication. Not so Lord Reith: "If the cap fits, my Lords, let him wear it," he said dourly, and the silence in the House became almost palpable.'[84]

A number of his fellow-peers congratulated him, although a breach of the conventions of the House on that scale does not normally go down well. Opinion beyond Westminster divided on predictable lines. Mary Stocks, who had been a member of the Beveridge Committee, wrote to say that she took a pessimistic view of the outcome of Pilkington, feeling that commercial interests would 'leap to their prey like a tiger chained with cobwebs'. There was, she said, 'comfort in hearing one mighty voice raised in wrath against the commercial interest. More power to its owner!'[85]

Dawn Mackay's translation from Madame Vacani's establishment to Heathfield meant that Reith saw less of her, at least during the week, but he was still busy on her account: 'Wrote a report to DM about the four possible bursars she was to see; very full and careful, and also several questions about procedure when she had made up her mind between the applicants.'[86]

Reith had got the names of several likely candidates from John Arkell, the BBC's Director of Administration, whom he had met in the course of his visits to Uplands,[87] and had characteristically assumed that he was the only source of advice on the matter. A telephone conversation a couple of weeks later disabused him. The 'Heathfield HM', as he had taken to calling Miss Mackay in his diary, said that one of her governors had also been active, adding for good measure that she hadn't much liked one of Reith's candidates (a retired admiral) and that in any case they couldn't afford him. Reith registered shock, and wrote that it was 'a most difficult and most unhappy situation'; the following day's entry reads, 'Nightmares and awful anxiety dreams every night.'[88]

Towards the end of June the sun forced its way briefly through to him – he had a letter from the Provost of Worcester College to say he had been elected an honorary fellow as from Midsummer Day: 'And the new Provost is Lord Franks, whom I always disliked!' He rang Christopher to share the good news: 'Unfortunately it didn't mean anything to him; and he has such an awfully unfortunate way of speaking on the telephone – so abrupt and chilling.'[89] He quickly sank back into his now habitual gloom: 'Sorted up the instructions on my demise,' he wrote on 5 July, 'which I profoundly hope will soon be required.' When Barbara Hickman was away from the office for a fortnight on holiday, there were vexations to be endured there – 'Had a very poor day with the locum, a St Andrews MA who had never heard of John Knox.'[90]

The Pilkington Report had been published in June, and the sharpness of its reflections on commercial television angered the government almost as much as it did the companies. Reith wrote little about it in his diary and declined an invitation from the *Evening Standard* to comment. He took the view that he had been vindicated by it, however.

He was very touched during the summer of 1962 by several kindly and sensitive letters from Sir Arthur fforde. Reith and Muriel had been his guests at lunch at Broadcasting House, and he had evidently been concerned at Reith's state of mind: 'It is a grief that you should continue to suffer this distress at "not being properly occupied",' he wrote:

. . . Believing as I do that God in his mercy really does decide things in his own time, however hard it is for us at times to see it – it was in my mind to ask whether this your distress can be anything but preparatory to a ΤΕΛΟΣ not yet seen? and whether when you say
(a) I want a job that will stretch me to the limit, and
(b) I want to be so busy that I have no time to think about my distress, the message may not be, 'the time is now accomplished during which you were to serve Me in those busy ways. You are being stretched by your distress. You are being stretched of a purpose. When you can stop thinking in the former categories, this new purpose, in new categories, I will shew you.' And as for wanting not to have time to think, what then becomes of Philippians IV, 4–8?[91]

Reith seems to have been genuinely grateful for this 'really wonderful letter' and to have derived comfort from it: 'I will do the best I can to submit to the will of God,' he wrote, 'and first to believe it is the will of God that I should be in this desperate state.' But he added, 'It really is inhumanly hard.'[92]

William Haley also tried to help, and took advantage of a session with the Prime Minister, Harold Macmillan: 'I told him straightforwardly of your desire,' he wrote to Reith. In another letter at this time, Haley tried to influence his thinking about his diaries:

You said to me at the Ritz that *all* you wanted was a large lump sum that you could put into trust five years before your death could reasonably be expected.
. . . Now I do not know what is in the diaries – there may be nothing you would object to being published before or after your death. I am possibly jeopardising our friendship by suggesting there may be. But I care deeply

for your name and fame now and hereafter. I am most anxious that this generation and posterity shall see you in a fair light.

. . . I think you believe you can have the best of both worlds – get a good sum and retain control . . . It seems to me it is a case of 'Your money or your life.' And I think you will want the life saved for history.[93]

Reith's brother Archie had died earlier in the year at the age of ninety, and shortly before Christmas there was a letter from his widow, Cissie. 'Dear old John,' she wrote, 'why is it that we can solve other people's muddles and problems and never our own? I can see a little harassed look come over your face . . .' She had a favour to ask him. Could he not invite Marista to be with them at the farm at Christmas? 'Life is uncertain,' she wrote. 'If we throw away an opportunity, it may never come again. Do please try and do what I ask.'[94]

He did try, but it was a pretty miserable effort. The Leishmans arrived at about six o'clock on Christmas Day. Reith had never seen his grandson, and had seen neither of the parents for more than two years. He shook hands with them, but did not speak: 'And I hardly looked at either of them all evening – especially I didn't want to look at Mrs Leishman because I didn't want old memories to come surging back; I was so very fond of her when she was a child; and I had such great hopes for her.' When they got up to go at 9.45, he managed to break his silence – by asking her whether she still had her signet ring, or whether she had sold it for scrap . . . 'Goodnight, Sir,' Murray said as they left, 'and thank you for your splendid hospitality.' Next morning, Reith wrote his son-in-law a letter:

> Dear Mr Leishman, You thanked me, on departure last night, for the hospitality of the occasion, but the hospitality to you and Mrs Leishman was my son's, as this is his house . . .

'Of course,' he wrote superfluously in his diary, 'it was a wretched Christmas – for everybody, I suppose.' The next day he had the grace to be ashamed. He had given Marista no present, and she had brought him a nicely mounted picture of Dunnottar Castle. He wrote her a short note, and enclosed £25. One thing, however, he could not bring himself to do: 'I didn't use her name Marista, the name that we had such great pleasure in; and I don't suppose I ever shall again.'[95]

Reith attended several celebrations of the BBC's fortieth anniversary. The main in-house event was a dinner at Broadcasting House – 'This, I think, is the part of the celebrations which I most feared.' He was placed opposite his own portrait, which he found 'not very congenial'; before the speeches he asked for all the lights to be turned off except for two in the centre, and thought that a great improvement. He was presented with a television receiver and a set of the Oxford English Dictionary; he recorded that the volumes were ranged in order at Lollards Tower before he went to bed that night.

The next night there was a dinner at the Mansion House. The City Chamberlain led the procession – Reith envied him his clanking spurs. All the BBC people Muriel spoke to said how wonderful the previous evening had been, and what a hold he had on them all – not just during the ten minutes of his speech, 'but seemingly through all the years'. He could never quite believe it, however often he heard it, and old enmities and jealousies lurked close to the surface; when he heard that there had been a party in Broadcasting House to unveil Sir Ian Jacob's portrait, he told Sir Arthur fforde that if it was to hang in the Council Chamber, he would like his to be removed.[96]

Reith calmed down, but trifling though the incident was it underlined the essential brittleness and shallowness of his relationship with the Corporation. He found it increasingly difficult to discern any continuities between the instrument he had created and the organisation that Hugh Greene was now leading into the swinging sixties. He went to Uplands again in April, but when Oliver Whitley raised the question of another visit in June, he registered reluctance.[97] He was busy going through some chapters which Asa Briggs had let him see from his second volume, eventually published two years later under the title *The Golden Age of Wireless*. He did not at all like what he saw: 'The more I read of it, the more irritated I get by the boosting he gives to pip-squeak press critics, so called, of broadcasting, and to all the critical books that have been written by stupid self-centred malcontents.'[98]

His relationship with Dawn Mackay continued to bring him more pain than pleasure. Toward the end of April 1964 he went to Oxford to dine with Sir John Masterman. An extraordinary letter survives which he wrote to Barbara Hickman late that evening. 'I am very very grateful to you,' he wrote, 'and very sorry that you should be so bothered. It seems utterly unreal and inexplicable that I should be here this evening when there is only one matter in my head or heart and when there is such terrible uncertainty and calamity at every throw.' The letter, which runs to several pages, is scrawled in pencil on Worcester College letter paper and is not notable for its coherence, although that may partly have been due to the hospitality at high table. He appears to have asked Miss Hickman to act as an emissary and go down to Crowthorne with a letter for Dawn – a letter which he first wanted both 'The Hick' and Mrs Mackay to vet. ('Will she be able to read it? She has only one eye.')

It's not clear what the purport of this second letter can have been. Dawn had apparently gone off to Italy, which clearly distressed and agitated him, and he badly wanted to know whom she had gone with; he also expressed distress at the thought of her going on one of their favourite walks (presumably in Berkshire) and gathering primroses with someone other than himself. The letter is one great rambling shout of pain: 'I can't contemplate severance, even with all the cruelty there has been. It really would be too dreadful for me . . . Does this letter read as if I wanted to break off? I don't, I don't. I can't face life without her, even if I cannot face it as things are now . . .'[99]

The range of Miss Hickman's duties would have surprised British Oxygen's Personnel Department. Because Muriel was now so much in Scotland, Reith very often had to fend for himself at Lollards Tower, and it fell to Miss Hickman to keep him stocked up. She was astonished that he did not succumb to malnutrition, because his diet consisted largely of biscuits, bananas and marmalade (which was kept, like everything else, in the refrigerator and quickly became congealed). There was, however, one delicacy of which he was inordinately fond – a brand of breast of chicken made by Shippams. One evening he felt unwell, and concluded that the jar he had opened for supper must have gone off. He therefore left a note by his bedside saying that if he should die in the night, the coroner need look no further than the chicken. He survived to tell Miss Hickman all this next morning, and to dictate a letter of complaint to Shippams – to the chairman, naturally. The latter was quickly on the telephone to enquire after his lordship's health. Shortly afterwards Miss Hickman took delivery of a whole hamper of chicken breasts.

In the summer of 1963 Reith was taken ill in the BBC box at Ascot. Not chicken breasts, but acute appendicitis, and he was admitted to King Edward VII's Hospital for Officers. 'Feeling very annoyed at what happened,' he wrote to the managing director of the Phoenix, 'and to be told that it was very unusual for an appendix operation at my age didn't make things any better.'[100] His scrapbook contains the usual exhaustive catalogue – it covers four foolscap sheets – of who enquired after him, who sent gifts (and what they were), who sent flowers, who sent telegrams, who wrote to Muriel and who came to visit.

He went to convalesce at the farm, and while there recorded laconically a piece of family news: 'Omitted to say that on the 11th the man Leishman rang in the morning to say his wife had had a daughter.' He made a rapid recovery from his operation, and he was able to celebrate his seventy-fourth birthday on the river at Henley as John Arkell's guest. In August his doctor gave him a thorough examination; 'He said a big and difficult job was what I needed to have to get me out of the depression and frustration, and that I was entirely fit in every way to have such a job.'[101]

His disaffection with the BBC grew steadily. He neither watched not listened to much of the output, but did not regard that as a disqualification from having a view, and he was quick to pass on complaints and criticisms which came to him at second hand: 'If I were not committed (as it were) to friendliness with the DG,' he wrote, 'I am pretty sure I would make a serious attack on the BBC in the Lords.'[102] Instead he wrote a 'long and rather angry' letter to Sir Arthur fforde. The reply did nothing to reassure him:

> He seems to agree with everything I say, but to be too weak or frightened to give orders to the staff. The BBC, particularly in television, has utterly discarded everything I did, and the vulgarity of the *Radio Times* week by week makes me sorry I ever started it.[103]

The approach of autumn found him in generally low spirits: 'Cowper's hymn – or is it Whittier's? – "When on my day of life the night is falling" – has been much in my mind of late,' he wrote towards the end of September. 'I do often think of my earthly end, and of what's beyond; and a great deal about Father and Mother.' His brother Robert had been in failing health for some time and Reith, when he had heard earlier in the year that he had been taken into hospital with pneumonia, had written, 'How I envied him.' Now news came that he had died, and was to be buried at sea. Reith noted his passing with two words: 'Tragic life'.[104]

He went off in October on what was to be his last foreign tour for British Oxygen. Tidy-minded as always, he checked before leaving that everything was in order with the arrangements he had made with a rather up-market firm of undertakers. One of its directors acknowledged his cheque in a note intended to be breezily reassuring: 'I most certainly hope that you don't have to redeem (hope that is the right word) your crematorium policies while you are on tour, for while you may be intensely dissatisfied with your own life you do not give other people that impression . . .'[105]

He was away for the best part of a month, in Pakistan, India and the Far East. His first stop was in Karachi and, as always, his sardonic curiosity about people and places lifted him out of himself:

> The nadir of this afternoon was not exactly a slum, but it certainly was a slummy exhibit. A holy place of some sort, I gathered, and part of the holiness was a muddy pond, around which, maybe in some simulation of worship, were a hundred or so men, women and children, with a glazed fixity, intensity and inanity of concentration – almost equal to that achieved by the television addict – gazing at godhead perhaps, or rather godheads; for here in what might have been elemental slime were a dozen or so wretched crocodiles . . .[106]

In Delhi he was received by the President, Dr Radhakrishnan: 'One wished that all presidents were such as he, with his tremendous background of philosophical learning.' The President also had a gratifyingly long memory: 'The last time I heard your voice, Sir John – I beg your pardon, Lord Reith – you said, "This is Windsor Castle, His Royal Highness the Prince Edward".'

He continued to Ceylon, to Malaya, to Singapore, to Hong Kong, flying home by way of Tokyo, Honolulu, and the United States. Back in London, he soliloquised about his journey: 'Is there too much of me and too little about British Oxygen's interests in this?' In a diary entry while he was away he had confessed to a feeling of something approaching fraudulence:

> I do all I can on these occasions to talk about Oxygen and not (repeat not) about BBC, BOAC, CTB, CDC or anything else irrelevant. I do not feel uncomfortable when being questioned about fundamental problems of organization, for one can easily bring in British Oxygen; often, though, I am almost saying, 'Hoi, will you remember what I am and not what I was?'

'What I am and what I was.' The grievous disjunction still turned constantly in his mind, and even the patient William Haley seemed to despair of finding a remedy:

Your attaining serenity is something I have longed for desperately. So far, nothing I seem ever to have said on this score has had any effect. It makes one doubt the old adage: 'Great is truth and it shall prevail.' For it is truth. And a wide circle know it is. Why cannot you?[107]

The inevitable breach with the BBC began to open up early in 1964. He signalled it in his diary on the first day of the year: 'I don't think I am going to have anything more to do with Carleton Greene or Lady – as she has become today.'[108] He relented to the extent of accepting an invitation to lunch with her one last time at the St Ermin's Hotel, but he used the occasion to make clear that he thought the gulf between them unbridgeable:

> I lead; he follows the crowd in all the disgusting manifestations of the age ... Without any reservation he gives the public what it wants; I would not, did not and said I wouldn't. I am very annoyed that I ever got on to terms with him.[109]

Shortly afterwards he wrote to Oliver Whitley, declining an invitation to Uplands and making the bizarre assertion that the programme *Juke Box Jury* was a manifestation of evil. He also lashed out at Whitley in personal terms: 'You have elected to side with the regnant lord. All right. But I wouldn't think it profitable or effective to essay irreconcilables – e.g. the O. J. W. of today and of twenty or thirty years ago.' Whitley, a man much admired and respected by his colleagues, was widely regarded as the Reithian conscience of the BBC. He was also, if anything, even slower to wrath than his father had been. He wrote a long reply, but then tore it up. When he was feeling calmer he tried a second time, and told Reith his fortune in a way that few other men would have dared:

> I simply tried to say, and I say again, that there is something wrong when you, not apparently having any direct knowledge whatever of a programme, e.g. *Juke Box Jury*, accept that it is 'EVIL', a very strong word, because someone, of whose identity you don't even seem to be very sure, said so.
> ... Rather than admit the possibility that he and you may be wrong, you begin to attribute to me in your mind such things as transfer of loyalty, change of attitude, abandonment of principle. I, who spend a good deal of time in practical concern and action for young people and what is good or not good for them. I whose father would have got a good laugh out of the idea that this programme is 'evil'.
> Why do you do this, I wonder? The reason seems to me to be that you are determined to make the evidence fit your picture of the BBC and the DG, rejecting any suggestion of good and accepting any suggestion of bad.
> So distressed about this had I become that I thought it better to risk a rift

Above: 'May God bless her and all who sail in her': Swan Hunter's Neptune Yard on Tyneside, October 1944. Reith's secretary, Joyce Wilson, swings a wartime bottle of red wine to launch HMS 020

Right: Dawn Mackay

Television début, October 1960: Reith in the 'Face to Face' studio with John Freeman (back to camera) and the producer, Hugh Burnett

Below: 'The only thing they had in common was their immense height': Hugh Carleton Greene welcomes Reith to BBC Television's twenty–fifth anniversary

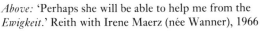

Above: 'Perhaps she will be able to help me from the *Ewigkeit*.' Reith with Irene Maerz (née Wanner), 1966

Right: Irene aged 18: a picture taken in 1930

Below left: 'Her most lovely eyes looking into mine; and what could I be thinking, and what she?' Barbara Maerz, 1966

Below right: Irene in the 1960s

Royal Scottish Academy Annual
Exhibition, May 1967: Reith and the
President, Sir William MacTaggart,
contemplate an exhibit in the
sculpture court

Below: 'Slipping into vice-regality':
the Lord High Commissioner,
observed by John Knox, processes
into the Assembly Hall of the
Church of Scotland in Edinburgh

between you and me than to watch in silence while you mix up with legitimate criticisms and anxieties about the BBC and/or its DG a whole lot of absurd ones, which needlessly distress you, which seem ludicrous to reasonable people who are your friends and admirers . . .

It was a magisterial rebuke. Reith made no reply to it. A friendship of almost thirty years was at an end. Four months later he put a more recent friendship in jeopardy with an intemperate letter to Sir Arthur fforde:

> . . . The BBC has lost dignity and repute; in the upper reaches of intellectual and ethical and social leadership it has abdicated its responsibility and its privilege.
>
> Its influence is disruptive and subversive; it is no longer 'on the Lord's side'.
>
> I am sorry I ever had anything to do with it.[110]

This was a remarkable letter for more than one reason. The first was that fforde had been forced by ill-health to retire from the BBC more than a month previously.[111] The second was that in a letter to William Haley, Reith appears to have suggested that he would himself be willing to be drafted in to succeed fforde as Chairman. Haley's reply was a model of delicacy:

> . . . I would welcome such an appointment as I would no other. So would most people who care desperately about what the BBC can do for the education, culture and moral health of the country. But, alas, so often in public affairs – and above all in public appointments – the right thing is not done. So do not set your heart on it too much. I would not have you heartbroken.[112]

The job went to Lord Normanbrook, who as Sir Norman Brook had been Secretary to the Cabinet. At a Buckingham Palace garden party in July, Reith fell into conversation about him with the Queen's private secretary, Sir Michael Adeane:

> I said if this Normanbrook had had the sense to write to me on appointment this would have committed me to help him. M.A. immediately said, 'Is it too late now?' Before I could answer some female burst in on us . . .[113]

Reith sent Adeane his answer the next day. He would be ready, he wrote, 'to respond favourably' to an approach from Normanbrook – on the assumption that Normanbrook 'was sorry he had not made overtures to me in the first place'. To Reith's astonishment, Normanbrook came up to him at the re-opening of the Whitehall Banqueting Hall two months later – 'most polite he was' – and the two men were to remain in touch over the next eighteen months or so.[114]

Although he had no occasion to travel during 1964, Reith maintained his interest in Commonwealth affairs, even if this sometimes found rather eccentric expression. He lunched one day with the Metal Box Company, and one of his fellow-guests was the Southern Rhodesian High Commissioner:

> He told me he had been tremendously pleased by the little note I had sent him about the casino to be erected near the Victoria Falls; that it was an insult to Livingstone, the Almighty, and the god of the river. He said he had sent it on at once to the Prime Minister with a covering note . . .[115]

Reith's interest in politics had always been spasmodic, and anyone searching for a thread of consistency in his views would have needed keen eyesight. In October he noted that if he were an American he would certainly be voting for Senator Barry Goldwater, the right-wing Republican;[116] a month later he wrote offering his services to Harold Wilson, recently installed as Britain's first Labour Prime Minister for thirteen years: 'I do not belong to any Party, as you know, but I am more than ready to help you – the more difficult the job the better.'[117]

He had as sharp an eye as ever for real or imagined slights. He kept in his scrapbook a copy of a comically absurd letter he wrote to the Marquess of Cholmondeley, the Lord Great Chamberlain. Earlier in the year he had subscribed to the idea of a painting of the House of Lords in action, and had agreed to pay £5, presumably as a contribution to the commission. When a picture of the painting appeared in *The Times*, Reith observed that he did not figure on it, and established that the criterion for inclusion had been a minimum of twenty-four attendances during the Parliamentary year 1961–62:

> . . . Is no credit given, or allowance made, for those who are simply too busily occupied, quite possibly largely on public work, to achieve the required 24 attendances? And is no sort of past service – BBC foundation (by way of illustration and example only, as the lawyers say), ministerial offices, privy councillorship – of any relevance? Nothing at all?
>
> In India, 'failed BA' used to be seen on calling cards. Perhaps one should add to one's *Who's Who* record that one was not considered worthy of inclusion in the House of Lords picture of 1961/62.[118]

Very little escaped his attention. This was the era of the first pirate radio stations, and Radio Caroline was claiming audiences of six or seven million listeners. An article appeared in the *Oldham Evening Chronicle* headed 'The Jolly Roger Flies Again': 'Lord Reith might well turn in his grave,' it said, 'but the fact remains that millions of people, provided with hour after hour of pop music, are getting just what they want . . .'[119] This earned the editor of the *Chronicle* a sharp note of correction: it bore the signature of Barbara Hickman, but the stylistic fingerprints were those of her employer:

Might I point out:

1. That Lord Reith is still alive;
2. that, if he were not, he would still not be in a grave;
3. that if he were in a grave, he would not achieve the cliché you suggest.[120]

He could still, in his lugubrious way, be very funny, and he turned the episode to good effect when he was the guest speaker at the Independence Day Dinner of the American Society in July. He did not mind references to 'the late Lord Reith', he said, but he took vehement exception to reports – 'deriving usually from animadversions on the BBC' – that he might be turning in his grave. 'I will never be in a grave,' he told his audience. 'Here in my hand is my cremation certificate, available in about 120 establishments throughout the world . . .'[121] However idiosyncratic the performance, he could still charm the birds out of the trees when he chose to, and cast a powerful spell. In the autumn he was entertained by Bill Paley of the Columbia Broadcasting System and a group of his senior executives: 'They were all very nice to me indeed; one of them said it was "like having lunch with a legend".'[122]

Legend or no, he did not respond with any great enthusiasm to a request from John Snagge that he should record some extracts from *Into the Wind* – these to form part of an obituary feature. After reflecting on the matter for a fortnight, he wrote to the producer, Francis Dillon; the letter not only confirmed that he would not himself take part, but aimed a torpedo at the whole enterprise: 'I ought to mention that, in the instructions as to what is to be done on my demise, there is a clause asking the BBC not to halfmast any flag anywhere, and not to have any obituary talk about me.'[123]

He was happy enough, however, to record a modest sign of fame which came his way during the summer from the Oxford and Cambridge Schools Examination Board. Somebody sent him the paper on 'The Outline of English History from the Roman Conquest Onwards', drawing his attention to question number 35: 'Discuss the historical importance in 20th-century Britain of two of the following: electricity; women's suffrage; professional football; the cinema; Lord Reith; Edward VIII; "appeasement" in the 1930s; the National Health Service.'

He was at last able during 1964 to bring the saga of the State Building Society to a satisfactory conclusion. A communication went out to shareholders: 'The enclosed formal letter is complicated and long. In brief you are being offered all your money back plus an extra 1/- in the £. My co-Directors and I advise you to accept.'[124] His efforts were appreciated. Just before Christmas, he heard from a Mr Neil Brown of Finchley: 'Dear Sir, I hope you will accept these few cigars in the spirit in which they are sent. I had only £100 in the State Building Society, but I have been fascinated by your tireless efforts to get my money back!'[125]

Muriel had figured in the diary only at the beginning of the year when she had been seen by a vascular specialist and undergone an operation. In Scotland, things had not been going at all well at the farm. Christopher had been obliged to plough and sow several fields twice over in the spring, and Reith's concern at this run of bad luck made him superstitious: 'It would be particularly dreadful if he thought there were a curse on the place, presumably the result of the wretched previous farmer, Smith. I have got the length, however, [of wondering] if I should get a Catholic priest up to exorcise the curse.'[126] So far as Marista was concerned, there were modest signs in the course of 1964 of an improvement in relations. The Leishmans had spent a weekend at Lollards Tower in the summer; on a visit to Perthshire in September, Reith noted that 'without any warning I suddenly found myself being gazed at by my grandson Mark'; in December, when the family moved into a new manse, he sent them a telegram and a pot of azaleas.[127]

Early in 1965, Reith was able to strike one name off his blacklist. The body of his old enemy Winston Churchill lay in state in Westminster Hall. Reith noted that a whole string of lavatories had been erected almost opposite Lollards Tower, and large crowds moved along the Embankment to file past the catafalque. Peers and their wives were invited to go between ten and eleven: 'I was not there, nor am I going,' Reith wrote loftily in his diary, but it wasn't true – he had himself driven there with 'The Hick', never reluctant to jump a queue by pulling rank. He did not, however, take up the two seats in St Paul's to which as a peer he was entitled, although he knew that Muriel would dearly have loved to have attended the funeral: 'She likes to see the eminent people,' he wrote, 'which is precisely what I do not like to see when I feel I am or ought to be as eminent myself.'[128]

A few days previously there had been a Lords debate on broadcasting, but Reith did not intervene (he wrote to Normanbrook afterwards to say that his silence was attributable to 'decency to yourself and a sense of dignity for myself'.) The debate was wound up by the Parliamentary Secretary to the Ministry of Technology, Lord Snow (the novelist C. P. Snow), and he paid Reith a handsome tribute:

> He began with a vision which I must say I do not entirely share but which I deeply respect, of what can be done with such a medium. In the process of carrying out his vision, though many of us disagreed with him, often violently, he raised the tone of our national life. Of this we are quite clear. We are not so sure that the same vision is so easy to sustain at present.[129]

In his letter to Normanbrook, Reith challenged a recent statement by the BBC's head of radio drama that it was the BBC's duty to reflect opinion, 'not to dictate or mould it'. Normanbrook dissociated himself from that particular formulation, but went on to say that it troubled him that so much of the current debate about the BBC was conducted from extreme positions. 'On the one side,' he wrote, 'are those who disregard all the changes which have taken place in our society in the last thirty years and seem to believe that the BBC could proceed today as it did in the days when there was no television and the Corporation had a complete monopoly of broadcasting . . .' He did not name names, but that was a very precise description of Reith's own position.[130]

It so happened that Reith was giving lunch to Harman Grisewood on the day he received this. He showed him the correspondence, describing Normanbrook's reply as jesuitical, though he remembered his manners sufficiently to apologise for using the term to a Roman Catholic.[131] To Normanbrook he sent a brief note saying that as their disagreement was 'so complete and vehement' it would be better for him to say no more.[132]

A few weeks later, however, there was a dramatic illustration of how jealous Reith still was for what he saw as the well-being of his creation. A sketch in a television series called *Not so much a programme, More a way of life* made offensive references to Roman Catholic views about birth control, and two Conservative MPs tabled a motion calling for the immediate replacement of Sir Hugh Greene. Reith, four months short of his seventy-sixth birthday, gave full rein to his unrivalled capacity for fantasy-building:

> I concluded, without hesitation whatever, that if in fact the director-general were dismissed, and if inconceivably I were offered the job, I would take it; and I could do what was required more or less in my sleep. I would insist on being director-general, not on the board. I think this would be better and wiser than my being executive chairman even.

Hugh Greene, entirely predictably, lived to fight another day, and for the rest of the year Reith paid little attention to broadcasting matters, although at Harman Grisewood's suggestion he offered during the summer to put his experience at the disposal of the new Labour government. He did so in a letter to Herbert Bowden, the Lord President of the Council: 'The writer is REITH,' he began, 'who used to have a good deal to do with broadcasting and the BBC.' Bowden sent him a polite, non-committal reply, and he heard no more.

There were also now fewer calls on his advice from Ascot. He had been seeing progressively less of 'the Heathfield headmistress'. When he visited the school early in March, he noted that it was the first time he had seen her for more than six months. A few weeks later, just after Marista had given birth to a daughter, Reith fell to musing about children's names: 'Susannah is very high on the list with me if not at the top,' he wrote. 'Once upon a time I would have put Dawn high, though I was never quite certain whether the name was not considerably enhanced by my liking an individual who carried it.'[133]

The individual in question had been showing altogether too many signs of independence for Reith's liking, but that was not the sole reason for her fall from favour – she had also formed an attachment to the man whom Heathfield had taken on as bursar. In May, Miss Mackay resigned the headship and announced that she was to be married. Two months later she invited Reith ('ungraciously', in his view) to the last Evensong at Heathfield before her departure: 'I wrote today that I could not attend; I don't expect to hear from her again.'[134]

He was mistaken – he had a telephone call from her the following month. The path of true love had not been running entirely smoothly for Miss Mackay. In May her private life had been splashed over the front page of the *Sunday Express* – 'I admit there was a time when the major and I talked about getting married,' she was reported as saying, 'but we only talked about it. I have no plans to get married now. Not now or ever.'[135]

There had clearly been further talk with the Major, however – and a further change of mind, because what she now rang Reith to ask was whether he could help her to secure the withdrawal of a marriage announcement which was due to appear in *The Times* the following morning. He could and he did. When they spoke again later in the day, she sounded tearful, and asked Reith to say nothing to her parents. He noted in his diary that he had spoken to Mrs Mackay only the previous evening: 'She was awfully worked up and distressed at the way her daughter was behaving, and for the first time, she said there was no truthfulness now – which I've been sure of for years.'[136]

Reith had once again begun to think of finding a place in Scotland, and there was some discussion of building on Christopher's land. Muriel and he visited the offices of the Norwegian Export Council to enquire about a system-built log house, but all they could produce was a drawing of one small bungalow; they also went to see what the English Colt Company had to offer. Then a cottage came up in Argyll which they liked, and Reith entered into negotiations for it with a firm of solicitors in Oban; having acquired it, he decided to turn it over to Marista.[137] The search for property led Christopher on many a wild-goose chase:

It had to have a burn to begin with. It had to be away from the road, and yet not too far from the road. It had to have views. It had to be cosy, secure, all sorts of things. I looked at many places, and there were one or two I thought were just possible. When I saw something, I would say, 'I think if you were interested you need to be fairly quick.' And he would say, 'How much is it going to cost?' I think at that time the ceiling was between £10,000 and £15,000 . . . Most of what I looked at was well below ten, but I remember something that was 14 or 15: 'Far too expensive – and far too busy to come up, anyway.' So that was that.[138]

There was another reason why Scotland was in his mind during 1965; he had been approached in the spring by the Scottish National Association of Glasgow University to ask whether he would stand for the Lord Rectorship. They had first approached him three years previously, with an assurance that he would also have the support of the Liberal and Labour clubs; there had been the prospect of a straight fight with Edward Heath, and Reith had subsequently regretted shying away from it. This time he accepted, though as a non-party candidate; in addition to the Nationalists, his supporters included the Dramatic Society, the Literary Society, the Folk Song Club, and a group known as the Distributists. The Liberals and Labour combined to put up Lord Caradon, who as Sir Hugh Foot had been a colonial governor and was now Britain's permanent representative at the United Nations; the Conservative candidate was the former Health Minister and Tory Party chairman, Iain Macleod.

Interest in the contest was not confined to Scotland. 'Why should men of such eminence in different walks of life be prepared to risk the indignity which all too often seems to be the most notable badge of office?' asked a *Times* leader. 'The memory of Mr R. A. Butler assailed with flour and eggs during his installation address remains vividly in the mind.' The incentive for office had been more obvious when the Rectorial was a popularity contest among the champions of the political parties – Gladstone, Disraeli, Rosebery, Asquith and Churchill all figured on the roll of past Rectors at one or other of the Scottish universities. Although the Rector was only the third-highest officer in the University, he presided at meetings of the University court. Perhaps a more important consideration for Reith (a paradoxical one, given his views about democracy) was that the Rector was exclusively the choice of the students – a symbol of the belief in student self-government which was such a strong strand in the Scottish university tradition.

The Reith camp conducted a vigorous campaign – there was no strong tradition of aiming above the belt. 'Which of the three candidates has caused the most civil wars?' they enquired in a Rectorial quiz (Lord Caradon, the most amiable and unwarlike of men, was a former Governor of Cyprus). They identified the main threat as Iain Macleod, the outwardly anglicised son of a Highland doctor. 'Which "Scotsman" studied ENGLISH law at Cambridge? Who was rejected by the Scottish electors and then fled to a safe English seat?' (Macleod had contested the strongly Labour Western Isles constituency in 1945 before being returned for Enfield.) Reith's election literature asserted that he was the only candidate pledged to do the job properly – he would attend every court meeting; he would be available in Glasgow to any student representative or individual wishing to see him; he would defend student interests at all times.

Polling took place in November. In a turnout of just over 50 per cent, Reith won convincingly – he got 1857 votes to Macleod's 1239 and Caradon's 750. By Glasgow standards, the election was relatively peaceful – the police made only five arrests. For the first and only time in his life, and in his native city, Reith was a beneficiary of the democratic process he so much despised.

His gradual estrangement from Dawn Mackay had affected him deeply and contributed to the depression and world-weariness that weighed on him for most of the year. A diary entry in July speaks of 'longing for the time whistle', and in September he wrote that he was in great sorrow and anxiety, and 'longing more than ever for release'. He did not seek medical advice, but sometimes believed that he was ill: 'I feel my head throbbing so often, and such pressure and tension that I think I must be near a stroke – particularly after I find myself to have worked up an indignation about this or that, or this and that and that.' There was a period in late September and early October when he was taking alarmingly large numbers of sleeping-pills. The whole of one weekend was spent in an extended drugged sleep. A few days later, noting that he had gone to bed at 8 p.m., he wrote, 'Something has happened to me, I'm almost sure, in the last month or so. I have suddenly become old.'[139]

He was more than ever obsessed by thoughts of how little he had done in his life, and there are one or two distinctly dotty diary entries in which he tries to express this mathematically:

> Did some writing today, including a letter to Jean Mauzé in which I gave him a mathematical substantiation of a remark I had made that the percentage over my life was 15 to 20. He had immediately and strongly asked me for the percentages applying to the BBC, Navy and CDC. My reply was that my personal stretch, having regard to the circumstances of the time, what I did, and what I might have done was: $16 \times 40 + 2 \times 7.5 + 10 \times 7.5 = 730$ units – the first figure in each group being years, the second the percentage achievement. I said to the 28 years above had to be added 22 (to make up an effective 50 years (25 to 50)), and the percentage for the 22 was 7.5, so add 165 units to 730, total 895 units of achievement compared with the total possible – 50×100; and that makes 17.9 per cent, which is confirmation of 15 to 20 per cent.[140]

In the autumn, Lord Normanbrook received a letter from him:

> I am writing to ask you to be so kind as to communicate, on my behalf, either an instruction or a request – whichever be the more proper and the more likely to be observed – that, when I depart this life, there should be no reference to me on the BBC, except – if it be desired – a simple factual statement of departure in a dozen words or so; but no special tribute of any sort; no symposium of opinions, which I know has been obtained from many old associates; no half-masting of any flag.[141]

Normanbrook was concerned by this peculiar request, and asked if they might meet. Over lunch he exercised his skills of persuasion to such effect that Reith agreed to leave a decision to his discretion: 'I know that in thanking you for giving me this latitude,' Normanbrook wrote, 'I can speak on behalf of all your friends and admirers in the BBC.'[142] Rather surprisingly, Normanbrook made no use whatever of that latitude and chose to accede to the quite improper request Reith had made of him. The bureaucratic fall-out inside the BBC was awesome, and over the next five years or so the matter consumed a phenomenal number of managerial man-hours.

In the summer of 1966, Frank Gillard, the Director of Sound Broadcasting,

LIFE IS FOR LIVING 377

addressed a confidential memorandum to his Assistant Director and to the Head of Talks and Current Affairs (Sound):

> Lord Reith is insisting that when he dies there shall be no obituary pro-
> grammes and no memorial service. The most that he will permit is a short
> broadcast by the Chairman of the BBC.
> Work is therefore to stop on all obituary projects. But what has been
> done so far is to be preserved, in case he is later persuaded to change his
> mind . . .[143]

Two years later, when Reith was in hospital with heart trouble, Oliver Whitley, now Chief Assistant to the Director-General, wrote to the BBC's Head of Publicity suggesting that if he were to die, 'it would be most desirable that we should explain publicly that it is in deference to his express wishes that we are not broadcasting the kind of documentary tribute programme with which we often mark the death of notable people.'[144] The matter was also discussed at the BBC's weekly news and current affairs meeting. The Editor of News and Current Affairs reminded his colleagues of what had been laid down, and it was agreed in discussion not to interrupt programmes with an announcement of death.[145]

The minutes of the meeting disclose that by the following week a disturbing thought was stirring in the mind of the Head of Radio News:

> H.R.N. said that the BBC would be in an embarrassing position if an ITV
> company flashed the news of death and the BBC waited until the next
> bulletin. E.N.C.A. did not think it likely. H.T.C.A.(R) suggested that ITA
> should be told of Lord Reith's wishes concerning symposia of special tributes,
> bearing in mind that one of the programme companies (Scottish Television,
> for instance) might otherwise mount an imposing programme of that
> kind . . .[146]

Two years later (this time the discussion was prompted by Reith's eighty-first birthday), the meeting again went into theological conclave and heard a ritual reading of what had become the BBC's most important standing instruction after that relating to the demise of the Crown. It was only in 1971, a matter of months before Reith's death, that the question that had been lurking in even the muddiest minds around that large table found halting expression: 'Was the ruling as it stood at present,' asked the Head of Talks and Current Affairs Group (Radio), 'somewhat too restrictive?'[147] The Director-General (Hugh Greene had been succeeded two years previously by Charles Curran) said that he would look at the original papers. A fortnight later, back down from Sinai, he imparted his conclusion to his colleagues:

> The BBC's interpretation of Lord Reith's wishes still ruled out items in
> sequences and current affairs programmes, but there was no objection to

quoting what was being said elsewhere or to reflecting and taking part in subsequent public discussion . . . The BBC was not to *start* the discussion.[148]

The episode proves different things to different people. To uncritical admirers of Reith, it serves as evidence of how powerful his influence remained within the BBC thirty years after his departure. It is also possible to see it as a manifestation of corporate flaccidity – a trait not apparent in his own time as Director-General, but just conceivably one which his masterful style of leadership did something to implant in the genes of those who came after him.[149]

Dawn Mackay was no longer there to tell him that life was for living, but by the late summer of 1965 he had found other company in which to continue testing the proposition: 'Lunch with SW on her 19th birthday,' says a diary entry on 14 August. SW was Sarah Whitcombe. She had just left school, and was about to start a three-year course at the Chelsea School of Art. Her mother was the daughter of an old naval acquaintance of Reith's, and Reith had used his influence to arrange a job for her father at British Oxygen. They lived in Astell Street in Chelsea. Reith now became a frequent visitor there, and there were equally frequent outings to lunch or dinner or to a concert. Sometimes her mother came, too, and he would accompany them back to Chelsea to listen to records.

Sarah was a descendant of Lord Grey of the Reform Bill, so one day, after entertaining her to lunch at the Lords, Reith took her to see his bust and to explore the Lord Chancellor's garden. Afterwards they took a taxi to a shop in Pentonville Street to buy drawing materials: 'Great fun – compasses specially and several other instruments that went into a box something like my old BBC one that I had given her.'[150] Two nights later, after dinner at the Whitcombes', they sat listening to Chopin and Tchaikovsky and Sarah sketched him: 'Very good indeed it was. Then Mrs W made me read the Postscriptum from *Into the Wind*. I felt considerable embarrassment in doing this.'[151] His embarrassment soon wore off. A few weeks later, after they had been listening to Elgar's Second Symphony, he read them the sequence in his memoirs about the composer and Bernard Shaw, and at the end of the evening, he presented Sarah with his own leather-bound copy of *Into the Wind*.[152]

On Advent Sunday, they spent a long day in Cambridge. (Reith, precise as always, noted in his diary that they were together for thirteen and three-quarter hours.) 'It was an incredibly beautiful day in every way,' he wrote. They explored King's College and sat for a time in the early winter sunshine: 'SRW took some photographs of me and I wanted to take some of her.' They lunched with some of her friends: 'The host wanted to put me on the right, but I said that was SRW's place.' They attended Evensong in chapel, met Alec Vidler, the Dean, and later dined with him: 'Continuous talk through dinner, and I was so proud of SRW . . .'[153]

Reith's semi-domestic arrangements with the Whitcombes continued through the winter. The sketching sessions after dinner had now acquired a purpose. Robert Lusty had recently heard of the existence of *Wearing Spurs*, read it at one sitting, and proposed publication. Reith, in the process of revising the manuscript, had conceived the idea that Sarah should design the dust-jacket and do a sketch for the frontispiece, and he persuaded Lusty to agree. His infatuation with the girl was complete. She was Charlie at Comrie, Irene cruising down the Rhine, Dawn Mackay at Torosay, Marista as she might have been – 'paragon of all infallibilities'.

She was going on a short trip to Brussels, and Reith badly wanted to buy her an overcoat. Mrs Whitcombe drove them to a shop in the King's Road where she had seen something she liked: 'It was such fun. We tried to get a scarf to suit the panchromatic colouring of the coat, but couldn't. Walked back, I carrying the coat.' On the day she left he was there to see her off on the Golden Arrow with Suchard chocolate and white carnations. When a woman at Hutchinson's pronounced her first sketches unsatisfactory, he naturally couldn't begin to understand why.

Reith had attended his first meeting of the Glasgow University court at the end of November. When a reporter from *The Scotsman* asked him where he was going to live, he said, 'We did buy a place up Appin way, but it is a bit small so my daughter is living there. But we shall be getting a place here.'[154] The news item was picked up by other papers, and Reith felt that he owed his notional landlord a word of explanation:

Dear Lord Archbishop,
. . . Because you and Mrs Ramsey have been so kindly disposed to us, we wanted you to know what the position is – if I can get near to defining it myself. In fact we don't know what the position is . . .
    We have been looking for a bolthole in Scotland – following the example of the eel – because at my age I didn't think new work would come to me in London, and because I imagined that I would find what's left of life less troublesome away from the scenes of former activity of all sorts.
    The Rectorship has, I suppose, given impetus to the idea of finding a house in the north . . . There we are at present – in a waffle, anyhow in unstable balance between north and south . . .[155]

He was right about new work in London, although the 'bolthole' in Scotland was to elude him until the last year of his life. From now on, however, the balance began slowly to tip in favour of the north.

Eighteen

HILLS OF HOME

Be it granted me to behold you again in dying,
Hills of home! and to hear again the call;
Hear above the graves of the martyrs the peewees crying,
And hear no more at all.

> ROBERT LOUIS STEVENSON,
> *Songs of Travel:*
> *To S. R. Crockett,* 1895

REITH WASTED a good deal of his own and Lord Normanbrook's time early in 1966 when he took issue with something the BBC Chairman had said in a public lecture. The question was whether Reith had publicly advocated the concept of a public corporation in the formal evidence which he gave to the Crawford Committee more than forty years previously. When Normanbrook, following Asa Briggs and Lincoln Gordon,[1] said that he had not, Reith wrote to say he was astonished. When Normanbrook coolly stood his ground, Reith began to lose his temper and cast unwise aspersions:

> I have no doubt that the Civil Service for years has been anxious to soft-pedal what I did in managing the BBC, in creating the first public corporation, and in having a great deal to do with the creation (and operation) of many others . . . (And I have other proof of this malignity if it would interest you.) . . . Do remember that I've kept a diary for 56 years; and, equally important, that my memory is still efficient . . . Does somebody advise you, or do you yourself wish to denigrate me and what I did?[2]

Normanbrook replied with some acerbity that he was not in the habit of reading out what others had written. He also observed that whereas autobiographers were generally subjective (Reith had quoted *Into the Wind* at him), there was an obligation on historians to be objective. It therefore seemed natural to rely on Asa Briggs, 'a reliable historian who had access to all the relevant documents – including I gather, your own diaries.'[3] The evidence is that Reith, for once, had not plunged into his voluminous archive for chapter and verse. If he had done so, he would have discovered that his memory was less efficient than he claimed. On 1 February 1926 he had written in his diary, 'It must be put on a public service basis, but I cannot say this definitely in evidence.' He wrote a final, ungracious letter to Normanbrook terminating the correspondence.

His sourness of temper may have been partly due to the fact that his time with British Oxygen had just come to an end. Any loss of activity was always profoundly unwelcome, and in this case it also meant that he no longer had the use of his Rolls and his chauffeur. Lunch with Haley at the Ritz only made things worse: 'He is one of the most important and influential people in the country, I who once was in a similar position, am now nobody and nothing and nowhere – Reith is now only a wraith.'[4]

The habit of work was so deeply ingrained that he was unable to modify the routines associated with it, even when there was little to do:

> At my table all day, and in awful anxiety and perplexity about what to do, and not getting on at all with M. I knelt in the chapel for quarter of an hour in the dark. God help me. I simply can't . . . imagine how to get through another day.[5]

He was still frequently in the company of Sarah Whitcombe. When he heard the fee proposed for her work on *Wearing Spurs*, he pronounced it 'scudgy' and persuaded Hutchinson's to agree. One night she took him to see *Parsifal*. He thought it an unforgettable experience: 'Especially the final scene – most moving; it brought tears to my eyes.' Reith took her to see *Oedipus Rex* and *Man and Superman*. She also accompanied him to the opening of Parliament, where the Earl of Longford admired her hat.

Sir Gerald Kelly had expressed a wish to paint him – he thought he had 'a very fine head' – and early in April Reith began to go to his studio for sittings. After a few months, it occurred to him that even though Sir Gerald was a Past President of the Royal Academy, a little advice from Miss Whitcombe might not come amiss, and she called on him two days after her twentieth birthday. Kelly, a man of delicate sensibility, sent Reith home feeling proud of his protégée: 'Apparently she made a great many suggestions which he was very glad to have.'[6]

Reith sank into one of his familiar troughs of depression in the spring of 1966, weighed down by a sense of the loneliness and purposelessness of life and raging against the world about him. He walked one Sunday from Lollards Tower to Westminster, and did not like what he saw: 'Utterly disgusting, dirty, depraved young men with long hair and prostitutes are in much evidence . . . They wouldn't be allowed by Hitler, and there's a mighty lot that he might do to clean up this country . . .'[7]

He went to Perthshire for Easter, but it was not a happy time. On Easter Day they went to the Episcopal church in Comrie; Reith was irritated by the 'uneducated' pronunciation of the minister and enraged by the playing of the harmonium: 'The fat formidable female who operated the machine blared out several "organ pieces" before service, finishing with Handel's *Largo* which in fact took about ten minutes to finish.'[8] More seriously, there were uncertainties about the future of the farm, where profits had dropped from £1000 to less than £100, and he was plagued by his continuing inability to get on terms with Marista and her husband:

> Many years since the 'beloved family' were together and alone at a meal, and most unfortunately I cannot be ordinarily natural and friendly with her, let alone the least bit affectionate. I can't, and I suppose will never get over my indignation and hurt at the way she treated us all – e.g. leaving her family to spend Christmas (two or three times) with the Leishmans; and of course her rejection of any friendliness with me from 17 up; and of marrying a man whom we all disliked . . .[9]

The black mood persisted on his return to London. 'I felt myself very near to the ultimate breakdown,' he wrote on 18 April. He wondered whether a change of medication might do something for him, and visited a chemist in the Horseferry Road: 'I have now another lot of the anti-suicide sort.' They had little effect: 'Oh so longing to be taken away,' says an entry four days later. Although he had little to occupy him, he had a sense of being overwhelmed, and of having far more to do than he could manage. He wrote that he felt as he had done on his return from the United States in 1916 – 'from being somebody to being nobody'.[10]

At the end of May, accompanied by Muriel, he went off to Austria. He had kept in touch with the Wanner family, and now Irene, with whom he had sailed so blissfully down the Rhine in the 1930s, had invited them to her chalet in the mountains, between Innsbruck and the Italian border. They were met at Munich by Irene's husband, Dr Maerz. The house lay more than 3000 feet above sea level. The air was magnificent, and Reith was captivated by the views of the Bavarian Alps. He was also quickly captivated by Irene's daughter, Barbara, and his diary for the following week describes an infatuation even more intense than he had experienced for her mother thirty years previously.

There were excursions up the Zillertal and shopping expeditions to the local town. Reith bought the girl a gold bracelet (and recorded that it had cost him 335 marks). Sometimes in the evening they played bowls. Reith kept a careful note of the score, and was particularly pleased when he and Barbara beat Irene and Muriel by 52 to 38. 'I think more and more of her,' says a diary entry on the fifth day of their stay; 'she must have tremendous bravery.'

The emotions that Barbara aroused in him included pity, and perhaps a certain fellow-feeling – three years previously a wig she had been wearing at a fancy-dress party had caught fire and her neck and the lower part of her face were badly scarred. Even better than beating Irene and Muriel at bowls was to play alone with Barbara and let her win: 'I enjoyed it simply enormously; it seemed to be one of the happiest hours of my life. Such fun and so much laughing, and Barbara most awfully attractive. I had her to myself for this hour . . .'

After a sleepless night he got up at five, heavy with thoughts of returning home. That day they took the aerial railway to the top of the Wallberg, and Reith thought it the happiest day of all:

Barbara yesterday and today was dressed in a Royal Stuart kilt and a white blouse, with my gold bracelet showing, looking most awfully smart . . . M and Irene were walking some way ahead of B and me, and we were talking about all sorts of things, and I told her about the Horace odes book which was my most precious book possession, it having been bought by my father in 1846 I think, and having been used by him such a tremendous lot. I said I had often wondered whatever would happen to it after I departed, and that now I had decided to give it to her, and that I was awfully pleased about this. She asked about CJ and MM and was reassured by what I said; and then she made that sudden move again, and her arm round my neck holding me close, and she kissed me on the cheek. I put my arms round her, and there we were standing together like lovers in that most beautiful spot. I suppose if M or Irene had happened to look round they would have been surprised, though I don't think Irene would have been . . .[11]

That evening Barbara sat beside him on the terrace as he brought his diary up to date. He allowed her to read what he had written. It was the last evening of their stay:

When bedtime came, for the first time I kissed her on the lips. On the study calendar slip for today I wrote (underlining 7 a.m.) 'Heute und Immer, Benedicat tibi Dominus et custodiat te, For Barbara, the very dear, the very lovely, the very brave, from John, und aller aller Liebe.' . . . Last night, after I had kissed her, she ran up the stairs and then we had a grasp of the hand which I shall always remember. But oh so much that I will always remember – little exchanges between us. Often, from the second day here, there have been eye to eye, and eye held by eye, her most lovely eyes looking into mine; and what could I be thinking, and what she?

The next day was Sunday. He was up at five again, and after breakfast Irene drove Barbara and him to church (Irene had remained a Protestant, but Barbara, like her father, was a Catholic). Change the names, and Reith's diary entry for that early June day in 1966 could be mistaken for an account of the precious times spent with Charlie fifty years earlier:

It came on me with a great joy and wonder that B and I were alone, and that she was in my charge, and that we were going to church together. After some quiet discussion we went into the third pew from the front – a most extraordinarily uncomfortable one, very difficult to kneel and very difficult to get up . . . There was an unfortunate scene as we were going down the aisle: two children came out from a seat and stood staring at B. Oh horrid it was; I immediately went in front of her and walked down beside her so that she couldn't be looked at . . . Irene was there – I had hoped she might have been delayed so that I could have walked further with B . . .

Irene drove them to Munich. Muriel went ahead into the departure lounge, but Reith went back to the car, said his farewells to Irene and saw her into the driving seat:

> I put my arms round Barbara and kissed her and held her for a few moments. 'Goodbye my Darling,' I said. 'Gott sei mit dir.' I was in control of myself throughout this last scene – which I certainly was not on the drive. B got in, and the roof was open, I kissed her hand, and she jumped up and kissed me on the forehead, a final clasp of the hands, and she was away. She waved to me and I to her all the time the car was in sight.[12] I held my arms open, and waved and waved and the air was full of the kisses she blew to me.[13]

They flew home by Comet. Reith telephoned the Maerzes to announce their arrival and rang again the following day. *'Nur gestern'*, he wrote in his diary, *'Nur gestern'*. He went to the Scotch House and bought Barbara a Cairngorm pin to go with her kilt. When Sunday came round, he went into the chapel at Lambeth – 'in memory of the 11 to 12 service last week in Rottach.' London was in the grip of a heatwave. When the longest day came, he wrote in his diary, 'I suppose I might be more unhappy than I am, but I can't imagine it short of insanity. And I'm not far from insanity now maybe.'[14]

After that, there are fewer and fewer references to the Maerz family, although a brief entry in September indicates that he had not forgotten one important date – 'Telegram to Barbara Maerz on her 14th birthday.'

Shortly after his return from Austria, Reith finally saw the publication of his much-delayed Advertising Report, which had been in the hands of the Prime Minister since the beginning of the year. The principal recommendation was that there should be a National Consumer Board with powers to check the standards of all products advertised; a rather more curious suggestion was that wealthier newspapers should pay a levy which would be used to subsidise their less popular rivals. A leader in the *Western Mail* said that the report 'has strayed, with left-wing banners flying, into territory it clearly does not – or does not wish to – understand'.[15]

Muriel went off to Scotland, and Reith picked up the threads of his London existence. He was once again much in the company of Sarah Whitcombe. One morning he got up at 5.30 to accompany her and her mother to an early service at St Luke's, Chelsea;[16] a few Sundays later she picked him up on the Embankment and they went together to All Souls', Langham Place, which reminded him very much of the original College Church in Glasgow. Before the service he had pointed out to her the windows of the Director-General's office at the front of Broadcasting House, and afterwards he took her into the front hall so that she might see the Latin inscription.

Never happier than when pulling strings, he got in touch with John Snagge and arranged for her to have a summer job at the BBC. He gave her dinner in the revolving restaurant on top of what was then the Post Office Tower, and lunch in the House of Lords, plying her with a double portion of honey and brandy ice-cream. After another visit to the Post Office Tower a couple of weeks later with some of her friends, they ended up doing a sixsome reel on the pavement outside her parents' house – 'tremendous fun,' Reith thought. One of the few mentions of Muriel at this time occurs when he records that on telephoning her at the farm one evening there was an 'acrimonious exchange' about his diary[17] – it is possible she had come across his account of their stay with the Maerzes; indeed it is not out of the question that he had shown it to her.

At the beginning of September, *Wearing Spurs* was published. It was widely and favourably reviewed. 'It is not easy to put one's finger on just what gives the narrative its unique quality,' wrote Malcolm Muggeridge in the *Observer*. 'I should say, myself, its truthfulness. People lie habitually about war, as they do about sex and about money. War literature is a kind of power-pornography . . .'[18] The review in the *Daily Telegraph* was by Sir John Elliot. 'John Reith was born with a claymore strapped to his side,' he wrote. 'The only thing his good fairy forgot was to give him a scabbard for it.'[19]

Reith was so busy answering letters about the book that he got a fortnight in arrears with his diary, although this was partly because the list he had drawn up of those who were to receive complimentary copies contained more than a hundred names. He was hugely pleased – and genuinely surprised – by the tributes paid to the literary merits of the book. 'And what a cracking good soldier,' added his fellow-Scot, the novelist Eric Linklater. 'His hundred-horse-power zeal must have been like a Rolls Royce engine condemned to drive a wheelbarrow.'

In November, he was the guest of honour at a Foyle's Literary Lunch at which William Haley took the chair. He confessed in his speech that he was unhappy both about the working of democracy in Britain and about the oper-ation of the welfare state, though he favoured both in principle. 'But can we give the young of today the stimulus with which the young of 60 years ago went to war?' His own contribution to the stimulation of the younger generation was to see to it that Sarah Whitcombe was invited and to mention her in his speech. Mrs Whitcombe and Muriel were also present, but it was Sarah who was seated in the place of honour between Reith and Haley, and it is to her that the book is dedicated.

Quite a few recordings of Reith survive in the BBC Sound Archives, and they make an interesting study. He had a fine voice – light and clear and resonant. In his prime it had been a good deal anglicised, but as he advanced into old age, his speech became markedly more Scottish again. There was certainly no mistaking his origins when he delivered his Rectorial address in Glasgow University's Bute Hall in late October.

It was not a conventional opening. 'Well . . . ?' he began. 'Amn't I far too old to be Lord Rector of this University?' The hesitation after the first word did not indicate any doubt about how to continue – the pause, like every single word in the six pages of his typescript, had been minutely calculated and endlessly rehearsed. And it achieved the intended effect – laughter, cries of 'Yes!', and an appreciative drumming of feet. He had caught his audience's attention in less than ten seconds, and he held it effortlessly for the next twenty minutes – the student body, the robed members of the University Senate, special guests like Sarah and Mrs Whitcombe.

He talked of his father and grandfather, paid tribute to Gladstone, recited a verse of Burns. It was a shamelessly theatrical performance, much of it delivered in the sort of parsonical drone he had himself so often deplored. He had nothing particularly original to tell his hearers. Many of the themes and tags which had served him in speech and writing from the earliest years were recalled to the colours – the importance of being fully stretched, the insidious nature of *accidie*, the message he had once thought the wind was bringing him from the everlasting hills . . . 'One of the sad things in life', he said, 'is that youth can only be enjoyed by the young and when you're a bit older, anyhow my age, you'll know what I mean by that.' He offered them a Latin tag in free translation: 'Without love and a bit of fun, life is not worth living.' He told them it was from Horace, but it is not certain that he was thinking of so venerable an authority.

There was a sombre passage about achievement, stylistically a cross between one of the minor prophets and Charles de Gaulle: 'Will you take something from me as to the success of any individual, only herself or himself can judge – their judgement is absolute . . . *C'est moi qui parle.*' He raised his customary two cheers for democracy, inveighed against the 'tyranny of licence', directed his audience's attention, as he never failed to do, to the 'immortal witness' of Immanuel Kant. In his coda, he dwelt on the mystery and magic of the Indwelling Christ, and the plain prose sense of what he wished to convey became elusive.

The applause was generous, for all that. It had been a Rectorial address like no other – arresting, obscure, corny, strangely moving. Reith recorded his relief. 'And so this day is past – which I had dreaded, or anyhow had had in awe, for a whole year.'[20] The speech was widely reported, and Reith had a lot of correspondence, much of which he stuck into his scrapbook – letters from bishops and retired ambassadors, and a request for a text from His Excellency Commander Prince Alexander Desta, Commander-in-Chief of the Imperial Ethiopian Navy.

Before returning to London, he went to Dunblane and attended morning service in the cathedral: 'The wretched Bowser, looking very aged, came to shake hands with me, I not knowing who he was.'[21]

Reith's doctor detected signs of heart strain early in 1967, and arranged for him to see a specialist. Reith also noted glumly that halfway through his seventy-eighth year, his memory was beginning to play tricks on him:

Periodic signs of senility: great bewilderment over 4 keys suddenly observed on the mantelpiece here. Enquiries made in all directions – but twelve hours later, suddenly wondering where my GU [Glasgow University] keys were, realised that these were they. This really was a milestone.[22]

Such gloomy reflections were driven from his mind ten days later by a phone call from Marista (he recorded that she had reversed the charges). She had spoken that afternoon to the Moderator-Designate of the Church of Scotland – the Queen Mother, convalescing after illness, would not be able to take up her appointment as that year's Lord High Commissioner, and Reith was to be invited in her place. Confirmation came two days later in a letter from the Prime Minister: 'I was sorry that Father and Mother hadn't lived to see this letter,' Reith wrote.

Within days he had had a first meeting with Alistair Blair, the Edinburgh lawyer who then held the office of Purse Bearer – in effect adjutant to the Lord High Commissioner. Reith had prepared a list of questions a page long, and felt that Blair gave him satisfactory answers to all of them, except that relating to what he called 'kit allowance': 'I heard that Parliament had approved £7,500 for expenses of all sorts, but a wretched civil servant (as usual) at St Andrews House had only passed about £6,500. I told AB what I thought of this and asked him to put it across the civil servant.'[23]

While the Assembly is in session, the Lord High Commissioner ranks third in Scotland, taking precedence over all members of the Royal Family except the Queen and the Duke of Edinburgh. The prospect of this exalted station drove most other things from Reith's mind over the next few months – including the fact that Muriel's birthday fell on 21 March. Marista, for once, fared rather better, and when she was thirty-five in April he sent her £120 to buy clothes; in choosing his suite for the Assembly, Reith had resolved that his daughter should be Extra Lady-in-Waiting.

He had also decided to invite his son-in-law to be his Chaplain, although dark clouds gathered for a time over this appointment when it came to Reith's ear that 'the man Leishman', who continued to take a keen interest in politics, had signed a petition protesting against the decision of the current Moderator to go aboard a Polaris submarine:

I thought at once 1. this was a ham-handed foolish thing to do; 2. it was very discourteous to me; 3. it might make it quite improper for me to have him as chaplain.[24]

There were problems with Christopher, too, who telephoned a month before the Assembly to ask why Reith had let the Purse Bearer invite him to Holyrood for two nights when he had said he didn't want to come even for one – he disliked any sort of party, and the thought of formal dinner parties was especially unappealing. 'I thought he was very unjust to me over this deplorable incident,' Reith wrote. 'And it certainly cast much gloom over me.'[25]

As he pondered his arrangements for Holyrood, a thought came into Reith's mind of which no mention remains in the diary – he picked up the telephone to Dawn Mackay and asked if she would care to be a member of Muriel's suite. Twenty-five years later, Mrs Hargreaves remembered very clearly how she had replied. 'You must be joking,' she told him. 'How tactless can you get?'[26]

The absence of any reference to this in the diary is not in itself of particular significance. It is notable that the entries generally have become very much shorter – a reflection, possibly, of his continuing depression and lassitude or of his growing dissatisfaction with the diary. There is, however, a second reason for the conspicuous brevity of the entries during this period – the diary volumes now deposited in the BBC Written Archives at Caversham have been pruned of an enormous amount of what Reith dictated or wrote during much of the 1960s.

A letter which Miss Hickman received from Reith as late as the spring of 1967 (she was by then no longer working for him) makes it plain that the diaries in their original form were still intact at that time, and that despite the ending of his relationship with Miss Mackay, his original intentions for them had not changed:

Dear Barbara,
The locks of the attaché case which have some things under their special care are so troublesome that I have today transferred the thing to a newish, cheap, not leather case, a key of which I send herewith ... You would abstract this case, wouldn't you? Not the same day as my removal, but very soon after the burning. You might say you don't know more as to contents than some papers you were going to clear up and dispose of for me. Don't have the key in your pocket. Thank you very much.
Love, John C.W.R.

That letter was written on 9 April 1967. At some date after that, the diary entries for the period between January 1960 and February 1966 were severely edited and retyped. In the original version, Barbara Hickman's typescript (she used an electric machine of the 'golfball' variety) was interspersed with occasional passages in longhand which Reith wrote himself at weekends. For most of the revised version an old-fashioned manual typewriter has been used.

Barbara Hickman is clear that in the years of his infatuation with Dawn Mackay something of the order of 90 per cent of what went into the diary was devoted to her. The entries were not only about what Reith and she had done together, or what she had worn, there were also lengthy passages about the nature of his feelings for her: 'Often he just poured out his troubled soul.' Almost nothing of this survives. Miss Hickman recalls that Reith told her, after the relationship had petered out, that he had asked Jo Stanley, who still helped him with the scrapbooks, to edit the diary so that all references to Miss Mackay were removed. More than a quarter of a century later, Miss Stanley, overcoming an initial reluctance to cast her mind so far back, acknowledged that she had indeed carried out such a process of revision – 'out of kindness to all concerned'.[27]

Miss Mackay, as has been seen, did not in the event become a total non-person. Miss Stanley carried out her task of doctoring the record with less than complete thoroughness (and does not seem to have directed her attention to the scrapbooks, where a number of photographs survive). The result achieves a bizarre symmetry with the period four decades earlier when the Director-General of the BBC sat down to write Charlie Bowser out of his life's story – but could not entirely carry it through.

In Glasgow, meanwhile, the university Rectorship was not affording Reith scope for the rather grand ambitions he had brought to the office. Prickly as always, he had been quick to take offence, within weeks of his installation, at an imagined slight:

> I discovered, after the event, late this afternoon that there was an Annual Student Carol Service at 3 pm in the chapel. That explains why the Principal told me he was sorry he couldn't go to the Lord Provost's lunch, but he deliberately suppressed the reason, knowing I would go, and so he would lose his seniority in the readings. Contemptible this is.[28]

Andrew Stewart, whom he had appointed as his assessor, did his best to smooth the ruffled rectorial feathers, pointing out that as a note about the service appeared on page 138 of the University diary, there would be a general assumption that everybody knew about it. Reith, always reluctant to abandon conspiracy theory, was only partly mollified, and as spring came on his dissatisfaction with university affairs once again came bubbling to the surface:

> There is no satisfaction nor interest now that I have become so much aware of the deceitfulness and weakness of Wilson, and the way in which I am carefully, even if courteously, prevented from doing anything.[29]

'Wilson' was Sir Charles Wilson, the University Principal. There were certainly things which he 'courteously prevented' the Rector from doing, but they were things with which the Rector should not have been concerned in the first place, such as making nominations for honorary degrees, which was exclusively the preserve of the Senate. Andrew Stewart, whose function it was to represent him on the University court, was conscious of 'an awful feeling of being pulled apart':

> There were the two camps, and I had this awful feeling of having to support Reith on the one hand, and at the same time having to try and protect the university from him, if I can put it that way. Charles Wilson said to me, 'You know, all he's got to do is say to me, "I'd like so-and-so to get a degree." I chair the Senate, and I'm pretty certain I could put anything he wanted

through.' But oh dear no, he wouldn't do it. Too grand to do that, you see. And it got to the stage when he wasn't speaking to the Principal, or indeed to anybody.[30]

Reith had told the Purse Bearer that he wanted to have as few outside engagements as possible during the General Assembly, partly because he thought they were mostly silly and boring, partly because the ministers and elders expected to see a good deal of the Lord High Commissioner. On the evening of his arrival in Edinburgh, there was the ceremonial presentation of the City keys. The next morning, after a service in St Giles, there was the opening of the Assembly. Reith wore the dark green and gilt court uniform of the Queen's Bodyguard for Scotland (The Royal Company of Archers). A splendid photograph appeared in the papers which captured the moment at which the procession passed the statue of John Knox in the courtyard of the Assembly Hall. This caught the fancy of the Duchess of Buccleuch, who had been a guest at the previous evening's banquet at Holyrood: 'I am glad to see that his Grace more than competes with John Knox,' she wrote to Muriel in her bread-and-butter letter.

Reith reminded the brethren in his opening address that in 400 years he was only the second son of the manse to be honoured with the Lord High Commissionership, but he was the first son of a former Moderator. He closed with a story about his great hero, Dr Chalmers:

> At the age of 18 he was engaged in a big house in the neighbourhood of his home to act as tutor to 7 children, working all day long, and generally treated as a rather inferior menial of the establishment. In due course he felt he had to make a gentle demur against his treatment. The head of the house received it thus: 'You have far too much pride, Mr Chalmers.' And this is the reply he had from Thomas Chalmers, aged 18: 'Sir, there are two kinds of pride; the first lords itself over inferiors, the other rejoices in repressing the insolence of superiors. The first I have none of; the second I glory in.'

Reith himself certainly gloried in his brief season as the Queen's representative. 'I find myself thinking about Holyrood occasionally,' he wrote when it was all over, 'and I realise that it was the only time in my life when I was adequately circumstanced; extraordinary how completely naturally I slipped into vice-regality.'[31] There was at least one occasion when his concept of vice-regality came into conflict with the requirements of good manners. As the official car drew up one morning, Lady Reith made as if to step in first, but a long arm restrained her. 'D'ye not yet realise, woman, that I'm the Queen's representative in this land?' said the Lord High Commissioner.[32]

The Lord High Commissionership was very good for morale: 'One was just out of a dream,' he wrote. 'Things had been happening that could only happen in a dream.' At the end of June he was received by the Queen to present his report. He spoke for fifteen or twenty minutes, mentioning the various bodies which had specially sent messages of loyalty and devotion: 'I asked once if I was boring her and she said No, indeed.'[33]

To say that John Reith mellowed as he approached the end of his eighth decade would be to exaggerate, but he did now sometimes seem a little more detached, a shade less vehement. Indignation flared briefly in the summer of 1967 when he heard who Lord Normanbrook's successor was to be – 'Almost incredible news – that the new BBC Chairman was the vulgarian Hill of Luton, forsooth' – but within a year he yielded to a plea from Lord Muirshiel[34] and agreed to a meeting:

> We started at Boodles, then went to a private room at the Turf Club and talked till 11.30. Hill was most forthcoming; he had decided that the Direc-tor-General would have to go, and Kenneth Adam also. Greene is to be up for another divorce – also adultery – and Hill was apparently most reluctant to give him notice now in case there was a press row about it . . . Hill said he was very glad to have met me, and when, after a good deal of thought and very mildly, I said I was prepared to help him, he said he was most grateful both for this meeting tonight and for this offer.[35]

The offer was never taken up. Reith nursed his resentment for two years and then wrote a long letter of complaint to Jack Muirshiel: '. . . And would you not have thought that the Lord Hill might have said something to me about getting that terrible McKinsey firm in, and to have asked me to discuss their report with him?' he concluded. 'I am most sorry that I offered to help him.'[36]

His memory was getting no better: having forgotten Muriel's birthday in March, he also managed to forget their forty-sixth wedding anniversary in July – she mentioned it to him at bedtime. 'I find myself more and more slipping into ruminations about the past,' he wrote.[37] Some of his diary jottings at this time convey a distinct air of dottiness. He was greatly interested in two articles by Sir Bernard Lovell about the solar system and the universe: 'I believe I might make a contribution to these tremendous problems,' he wrote.[38] During a party at the University in Glasgow he startled a Dr Gillespie by asking him whether 10^{78} meant anything to him: 'He said it was the total number of particles in the world – which was quite good . . .' A few days earlier, Reith had written in his diary, 'Profoundly anxious to cogitate seriously on 10^{78} and all therein involved. I wish I could talk to A. E. Eddington. I wonder, I wonder if I, if *I*, am to be given something to do in this incredible context . . .'[39]

He still gave his mind to more mundane matters, however. He was constantly making enquiries about houses or cottages in various parts of Scotland, all of which, for one reason or another, proved to be unsatisfactory. He also returned from time to time to the question of what should be done with his diaries. During one of his occasional lunches at the Ritz with William Haley, he told him that if Christopher agreed, he thought they ought to go to Worcester College, and that he would like Haley to have control of any editing or pub-lishing.[40] A few weeks later he was off on a different tack: 'Wondering if I could get a good price for my diary in the USA; and I wrote to ask Christopher if he would mind.'[41]

Alone in London, he had little to occupy his days – he had not seen Sarah Whitcombe for more than six months. 'Looking forward all afternoon to ringing Muriel at 6 o'clock,' he wrote one day. 'A large daddy-long-legs was walking and flying about; it seemed as if it were lonely and came to me, and stayed near me for company. I felt I was getting some company from it.'[42] He was briefly back in Perthshire in mid-October, but slept badly and was concerned by Christopher's melancholy: 'He looks so miserable and answers dully in monosyllables; there's a dreadful depression in the house . . .' 'I am trying to be in touch with dear Mother,' he wrote, 'and that she might help me.' One day he drove out into another part of the county, but old ghosts rose up and his pleasure in the autumn landscape was blotted out by bitter memories:

> Passed the very ugly house that the County Convener, D. C. Bowser (for-sooth and to hell with him) has had built for himself, he having passed over Argaty and the King's Lundies to his son. Amused to see pictures of himself (and his beastly wife) being introduced to the Monarch at Dunblane a few days ago.[43]

Back in town, he telephoned Admiral Carpendale to wish him well on his ninety-third birthday – 'He sounded in very good form' – but his own health now began to give some cause for concern. One morning in late October he woke up feeling very ill, and thought he must have had a slight stroke: 'I couldn't remember names, and I didn't know how to get about.' He remembered well enough, however, that it was on that day in 1917 that Bob Wallace had been killed.[44] Early in November he conceded in his diary something that it had previously been a fierce point of honour to deny:

> There is no doubt about it, but that I have reduced almost to nil the difference between my de jure age and my de facto age. Each morning it seems that I should stay in bed till the hearse comes to take me to the burning.[45]

He still went on endlessly, in correspondence and on visits to Glasgow, about the need for the Rectorship to be 'rationalised and institutionalised', but apart from the discreet and kindly Andrew Stewart, nobody paid much attention. People did, on the other hand, pay quite a lot of attention to three fifty-minute television programmes called 'Lord Reith Looks Back' which the BBC broad-cast towards the end of the year. He had recorded them with Malcolm Mug-geridge earlier in the year, in his office at the university and in the old manse, and now found himself something of a national celebrity, with dozens of letters arriving by each post. 'The whole of Scotland has been talking about your programmes,' wrote Elizabeth Whitley, the wife of the minister of St Giles. 'Your pauses were pulverising. I wish you would come home, and give a lead to the next generation. I believe they would listen to you here.'[46] Muggeridge wrote to say that he had had a lot of letters, too; one of them suggested that Reith should disclaim his peerage, enter the House of Commons and take over the conduct of the nation's affairs.

A letter which came in Reith's own postbag could have re-opened an old and deep wound. It was from Gerald Cock, who had done so much to build up the television service in its early days. There was a time when its contents would have roused Reith to a frenzy of telephoning and correspondence; he received it now with something approaching equanimity. 'About your leaving us – can you bear to hear what follows?' Cock wrote:

> I think it was in the spring of 38 that there was some talk that the Government had decided you were growing too powerful, and that no one could get along with you; that you were to be levered out of the BBC.
>
> It happened that I was on intimate terms with a Cabinet Minister of that time. So, dining with him one evening I indiscreetly asked him if that was true. He smiled at this and changed the subject. That seemed to me not perhaps confirmation but pretty close to it. At that time our relations were a bit frigid and I didn't want to risk a snub by telling you something you might already have known. Later, before the time of that awful farewell dinner to dear old Carps, I was told that Kingsley Wood was the hatchet man; that you were being led down the garden via Imperial Airways with suggestions of greater things to come – bogus of course.[47]

Reith made no comment on the letter in his diary, but appears at least to have acknowledged it, because Cock wrote again three months later, and in this second letter he softened the terms of his story:

> ... In an effort to condense the squalid events of 1938 I'm afraid I gave a wrong impression in one particular aspect. *The story was* that certain people decided to take advantage of your ambition for higher office to side track you into a position of political impotence in Imperial Airways. Even the least intelligent of the cabal must have known they couldn't jack you out of the BBC unless you wanted to go. (If ever anybody had a life job you had it as DG and later perhaps, as a very active Chairman.)
>
> If I'd had – how to describe it – easier entrée to your office in BH in those days I should have reported the story to you – I was on the point of doing so at least twice.[48]

During one of his visits to Scotland towards the end of November 1967, Reith was the guest of the Royal College of Physicians and Surgeons of Glasgow. He sat beside Sir Douglas Haddow, the head of the Scottish Civil Service, and over dinner, crab-like, he broached a question to which he was desperately eager to know the answer: Would the Queen Mother be going to Holyrood the following spring? Oh no, Sir Douglas replied. The strain would be too much for her – he could expect a letter from the Prime Minister within the month . . .

Harold Wilson's letter of invitation came three days later. Reith, in a re-run of the comedy he had played over his knighthood forty years earlier, sat on it for more than a fortnight before he replied, but there was as little doubt as there had been in 1927 about what that reply would ultimately be.

Early in 1968, Reith's heart began to trouble him quite seriously. By the middle of February the writing in his diary has become wobbly in the extreme and peters out in near-illegibility; at the end of the month he was admitted to the King Edward VII Hospital for Officers and stayed there for nineteen days. The Archbishop of Canterbury came to visit him, which he thought a great honour: 'A very nice little prayer at the end. He said he had no doubt whatever that I would get through the Edinburgh business.' The doctors were less sure, however, and Reith told them he was unimpressed by their performance: 'I had to be able to go to Edinburgh on May 17th, so what were they going to do about it?'

Two days later he was moved to the National Heart Hospital and a pacemaker was fitted. While he was there he heard that Charles Carpendale had died. The doctors said there was no question of his being able to attend the funeral and he lay fretting about the arrangements:

I wanted there to be a BBC flag flying from the church; the BBC made a fixture for this, but apparently without going to take any measurements and it could not be put up anywhere; there was no Governor there, and no member of the Management Board, which was quite shocking.[49]

Reith was in hospital for six weeks in all, and he demonstrated during his stay that he had retained his ability to strike up improbable friendships:

By this time I had got on terms with several of the other patients, there being in particular a young man, with long hair, aged 23, one of the immensely wealthy pop singers, or rather pop managers; he was really quite funny sometimes, and the whole ward was often laughing at the interchanges between him and me.[50]

He was allowed home at the beginning of April, and sat in the early spring sunshine in the gardens at Lambeth; he was greatly touched when Michael Ramsay came running out of the Palace, waving his arms in greeting. After a few weeks, Muriel took him off to continue his convalescence at the Royal Crescent Hotel in Brighton. He still suffered from giddiness, but it is apparent from the tone of his diary entries that he was rapidly returning to form: 'The hotel seems to be quite full for the weekend, many ghastly people appearing. I wish it could be made compulsory for people to hold their knives and forks properly.'[51]

They arrived in Edinburgh on 18 May, and were met by the Rolls-Royce which he had insisted should replace the previous year's Austin Princess. When he made his opening address to the Assembly three days later, he was in fine apocalyptic form. 'Scotland is in desperate need of such a conversion as amounts to a revolution under the Cross,' he told the fathers and brethren, 'and such a conversion in Scotland would not be limited to Scotland . . . Something of the Dothan sort could happen in our day; it may well be that we shall see the mountain full of horses and chariots of fire.'[52]

It was not the only time that Reith struck a martial note during his second Lord High Commissionership. His old regiment, the Cameronians, had recently fallen victim to the government's latest round of economies in the armed forces. It had been formally disbanded only the previous week, at Castle Dangerous in Lanarkshire, at a spot only half a mile from where it had first been raised 279 years before.[53] At the Holyrood banquet the following evening, just before it was time for the loyal toast, Reith hit on the idea of proposing an extra toast to the Cameronians; he passed a note to the resourceful Alistair Blair, his Purse Bearer, and in a matter of minutes the military band in the quadrangle below struck up 'Within a mile o' Edinburgh Toon', which was the regimental march. 'It was almost too much for me,' Reith wrote. He had six Cameronian generals among his guests that night, and it was almost too much for them, too: 'They were immensely affected by the inspiration of mine.'[54]

At the close of the Assembly he sent the commissioners on their way with a passage from Isaiah: 'Go through, go through the gates; prepare ye the way of the people; cast up, cast up the highway; gather out the stones; lift up a standard for the people.'[55] His second term of vice-regality had run its brief course; he knew that convention precluded a third. 'In the Queen's name, and rather sadly, I bid you farewell,' he said. 'May the Master be with us all the way.'

He returned to an everyday life which was becoming increasingly featureless. In June the time came for him to retire by rotation from the board of the Phoenix, and he did not seek re-election. His colleagues presented him with a fine copy of Spottiswood's *History of the Church of Scotland* of 1659. Lord de L'Isle, the Phoenix chairman, knew his man, and took the advice of the College of Heralds about a suitable Latin inscription.

When he was in Glasgow in June he was surprised to be approached by four young men from the Scottish National Party who tried to get him to stand again for the Rectorship: 'I said I was too old and it was against my principles to stand again as I was extremely critical of there being neither rationality nor institutionalisation of the office.' He followed the campaign, for all that, and confided his preferences and prejudices to his diary: 'I hope G. Macleod gets in rather than the Elliot woman whom I dislike so much; but I suppose I would put the Communist man from Denmark or Holland above all others; it would do the Principal and the Senate Clerk and a few more an immense amount of good.'[56]

The 'Communist man from Denmark or Holland' was, in fact, Daniel Cohn-

Bendit, a German-born student of sociology at the Sorbonne, but Reith's subversive hopes for him were not realised and George Macleod carried the day.[57] Reith's views about events on a wider stage were equally idiosyncratic. On the day after the Soviet invasion of Czechoslovakia he wrote: 'Nothing will come of all the raging against the Russian – the UN and all forsooth – unless there is a direct intervention by the Almighty.'

From the middle of 1968, gaps begin to appear in his diary. He thought a great deal about death. In the middle of August he spent most of one day working on what he called his 'Demise file', and recorded with satisfaction that he had got it into much better shape.[58] 'In looking through and reading my father's words of 70 to 80 years ago, tears come to my eyes,' he wrote, 'and I so often look at dear Mother's picture on my writing table, and his. And I think it cannot be long before I see them again. I wish we (dear Muriel and I) might go together.'[59] His mood could change very quickly, however: 'Wondering if God maybe had some tremendous work for me to do, even at 80,' says another entry only days later, and when his doctor called at the beginning of September, Reith asked him whether he was likely to live long enough to justify spending money on a house in Scotland.

Dr Sturridge's answer was reassuring: 'He said I certainly should have another five years, possibly more . . .'[60] This led to renewed discussion of whether they might build on Christopher's land (Muriel thought he should not be asked to give up any of it – he had only about 150 acres), and when they were in Scotland at Christmas they went to look at a small system-built bungalow near Glenalmond and at some Norwegian log houses. They liked neither. 'Poor Muriel tries hard to get me to come to some decision about a cottage in Scotland,' he wrote the following February, 'and I keep subconsciously shying off it . . . Odd that all my life I have gone so quickly to a decision, and yet be so dithery in this most important issue.'[61]

Later that week, he was called on to make a decision about something quite different. There was a letter from Buckingham Palace to say that it would give the Queen much pleasure to appoint him to the Order of the Thistle. He had affected to dither about honours in the past, but his pleasure at this distinction was unalloyed: 'I feel great thankfulness to God for the KT,' he wrote. 'I really do. I am sure my father and mother will be amused and pleased.' He was received in audience at the end of the month: 'She said it was very good of me to do the Lord High twice. I nearly said we would do it a third time if she wanted us to.'[62]

Another visitor to Buckingham Palace that week was Richard Nixon, recently elected to the US presidency. Reith had watched the television coverage of the proceedings with mounting disapproval:

He didn't give any sign of respect to the Queen; not even the courtesy that Americans normally show to a female. If he hasn't gotten the Lord with him in exceptional degree he will be the poorest edition of the office we have yet seen.[63]

He soon had occasion to demonstrate that in the matter of courtesy to females he was himself not invariably beyond reproach. In the middle of March there was a telephone call from Christopher:

> He said he had some news to give, and when I said what was it, he said 'I'm engaged to Ann Morris,' and he said it all excited like. My mind went scouting round the district, hoping to find someone whose engagement to my son and heir I would welcome, but I had to ask 'Who's she?' ... The last time I had heard about her I had understood from him that all her pertinacity had no effect on him and that he had finally (so he thought) boomed her off ...[64]

Reith quickly managed to make a considerable drama of the affair. 'This engagement of Christopher overshadows everything,' he wrote. 'I don't suppose I shall ever sleep in the farmhouse again.'[65] The news that the wedding was to be in the Episcopal church in Perth led to an acrimonious exchange on the telephone with Christopher over the Easter weekend: 'It would be most sad for me with my connections with the Church of Scotland, and my father's, and all the line for hundreds of years.' This came oddly from the man who, forty years previously, had exerted himself so eagerly to have his son and heir baptised by the Primate of All England, but Christopher was too delicate to remind him of that.

He did not take against 'the Morris woman' with quite the same ferocity he had displayed towards his son-in-law, although he wrote disobligingly about her after their first meeting and announced that he did not wish to attend the wedding: Christopher's decision to marry increased Reith's agitation over their failure to find a house in Scotland, and he became quite maudlin:

> I have handled my life and poor Muriel's awfully badly, that we have no place to go and spend the remaining years. Quite dreadful – none so ill shod or ill roofed as the shoemaker and the thatcher.[66]

He noted at the end of April that he seemed to be 'more and more sleep-desiring'. He occupied himself by beginning to read Fichte, whom his mother had greatly admired, and his parents were more and more in his mind: 'It's natural that, as the day comes near, I should have some idea or some wish as to how I would think the page might turn,' he wrote early in May:

> I imagine my father and mother, or one of them, coming into the room in the ordinary way and saying they had come to fetch me. They would seem to me to be more or less as they were when in life, and that there would be no special moment at which they and I put off the earthly form and the earthly speech – it would just come naturally and quietly, and I would realise that all was changed, and that soon all would be known to me, and that I would see Christ.[67]

At the end of the month he travelled with Muriel to Edinburgh and was installed as a Knight of the Thistle at St Giles. They dined at Holyrood, and he sat on the Queen's left hand. They stayed at the George Hotel, and one evening, as they strolled round the block, they were spotted by the duty commissionaire at the BBC and invited inside. There was not a great deal to see – in those days the Queen Street premises consisted of three rather fine old houses none too expertly knocked together – but Sergeant Whyte, a short, sturdy Orcadian, had been a Corporation commissionaire for thirty-one years and knew what the occasion required of him. The best thing in the building was a high old concert room which still had a box on one wall. It was now used as a television studio, and was cluttered with equipment, but when they got there Sergeant Whyte, with a certain sense of theatre, switched on all the lights, showing the room to best advantage. The tour was at an end. Not a great deal had been said. As the Sergeant escorted his guests towards the front door, he felt a hand on his arm, and some way above his head a voice said, 'Don't forget the lights, now.'[68]

It was the eve of Christopher's wedding, and also his forty-first birthday. The family had finally talked Reith round. They were to be driven to Perth the following morning, and they offered a lift to Margaret Cockburn, the daughter of James Moffat, the translator of the New Testament. Margaret Cockburn's mother had been a cousin of Reith's – had, indeed, bathed him as a child, and had therefore never been intimidated by his subsequent eminence. Her daughter was similarly disinclined to be overawed, but she acknowledged years later that the day did not begin well:

> He had put out his shoes to be cleaned, and somebody had nicked them. You can imagine trying to get a pair of shoes his size on a Saturday morning in Edinburgh – poor Muriel, I thought she was going to have a nervous breakdown. However in the end he got something to put on his large feet, and off we went. I thought it would be nice in the car because Muriel and I could have a pleasant chat and let John go to sleep or whatever. Not a bit of it. He put us one each side of him, and he sat in the middle like the Rock of Gibraltar. So Muriel and I talked across him for some time and then suddenly, out of the blue, John said, 'I'm not looking forward to meeting the bride's mother. They tell me she looks grim.' Well, I'd had it by this time, so I looked at him and said, 'Well, that'll make two of you.' Muriel shuddered, and I thought, 'My God, I've gone absolutely too far.' And John turned to me and said, 'Do you think I look grim?' And I said, 'By God you do. I mean, here you are, going to your dear son's wedding, and you look as if you were going to a whole load of family funerals.' And do you know, from that time on, he was as nice as pie.[69]

The rest of the year was not easy for him. Visiting his old school at Holt he rashly agreed to a game of squash with one of the junior boys. He had never been in a squash court in his life, and within a couple of minutes he went crashing to the floor. A few days later, he had a second and much more serious fall. He had been unveiling a statue at the Sir Frederic Osborn School at Welwyn Garden City, and as he was making for the car he tripped over a step and fell heavily. The muscles of his left knee were badly torn, and he was in St Thomas's for almost six weeks, which meant cancelling an engagement to take the salute at the Edinburgh Military Tattoo. It also meant that he celebrated his eightieth birthday in hospital, and that Muriel had to acknowledge the messages of sympathy and greeting that came in – there were about 170 of them.

Although the enforced inactivity made him miserable, the nursing staff were clearly charmed by him; the special treatment and diet sheet they made out for him on his birthday survives in his scrapbook – 'One happy birthday all day + one injection of good spirits hourly = many more touchdowns in the Sea of Tranquillity.' He was also gratified during his stay in hospital by a letter he received from Charles Curran, who had recently succeeded Hugh Greene as Director-General of the BBC:

> It was with great pleasure that I heard from John Arkell on Tuesday that you would be prepared to meet me – provided that you could be convinced that I had a genuine interest in listening to your views on the current state of the BBC . . . You will not expect me to say that I should agree in advance with everything that you might put to me. No D-G would ever make such a prior concession! But I think that there must be much common ground between us, because we share a Christian faith which has not always been in the forefront of the BBC's public image in recent years.[70]

When he was allowed home in the middle of August, morale was not good. He had become very deaf, and he realised that full recovery from the severe injuries to his knee would be slow:

> Very depressed and distressed, feeling that I am now almost wholly *passé* . . . I have an hour's rest (and sleep) each day after lunch, and that's surely a very old man's device.[71]

There was further cause for distress early in September when he heard that Irene Wanner had died. 'I had so hoped that she and Barbara would be able to come to our house in Scotland when we had managed to find one,' he wrote.[72] Irene's death affected him deeply; a pathetic diary entry the following day reads, 'Perhaps she will be able to help me from the *Ewigkeit*.'

He now constantly revisited the past – thoughts of the manse and of the College Church and of old friendships were frequently in his mind. He had a sudden desire to write to Connie Harley, who had lived in Australia for many years, and sat at his desk for three hours on end one morning covering page after page: 'A most interesting and extraordinary letter she will find it,' he recorded. 'It tells an immense amount about me as a young man, but it's not complete; it doesn't mention the ghastly five years in Springburn.' That recollection of his apprenticeship prompted one of the very few entries, in all the millions of words he had written over six decades, which sounded a note that was critical of his father: 'I am sometimes very much surprised at the insensitiveness of my father to any signs of greatness or capacity in me . . .'[73]

Early in 1970, Reith's search for a home in Scotland came to an unexpected end with the offer of a grace and favour residence in Edinburgh. The Queen's House in Moray Place had been presented to the Queen in 1954 by the Lords Provost of Edinburgh, Glasgow, Perth, Dundee and Aberdeen. It took him ten days to make up his mind to accept:

> My father was right in saying I would come back with my tail between my legs – though I do wish he hadn't used such a silly and cheap cliché. Even though coming back to Scotland to a grace and favour house makes the forecast the more ill-judged, I still say there was truth in the forecast.[74]

Before they moved north in the autumn, he had one final meeting and a brief exchange of correspondence with the latest occupant of his old chair at Broadcasting House. 'The conversation went all right once I had got properly started,' Reith wrote. 'Curran was very civil to me and said it had been a great honour to have had a such a talk.'[75] A few days later, however, he sat through several hours of a debate on broadcasting in the Lords, and his feelings about the BBC and all its works veered back into a more familiar plane:

> The whole thing was despoiled of any effect by the concentration on the wretched Third Programme instead of dealing with the general utter surrender of any principle in ethical or intellectual standards. Terribly sad – and some appreciable degree of responsibility is with me in leaving the concern in 1936 (or 35 was it?)[76]

It had, of course, been in 1938. Over the ensuing months there was further evidence of how rapidly he was ageing. One day he wrote an angry letter to Charles Stuart, who was now busy editing his diaries for publication: a few days later he could no longer remember who Charles Stuart was. At the end of May, Muriel accompanied him to a reception at the Tower of London. They arrived the best part of an hour early, and as they sat outside in the car someone came over and spoke to him. Reith was deeply embarrassed – he could not remember whether it was Field Marshal Lord Festing or Field Marshal Lord Templar, and could therefore not introduce Muriel. He was so upset by the incident that he announced he wanted to go home.[77]

His handwriting had now become very uneven and unsteady, and from the end of May onwards the diary peters out as a continuous narrative of daily happenings. By the third week in June, his doctor had become seriously concerned by the decline in his mental faculties:

Dr Sturridge put an 'alienist' on to me, without warning . . . I told him about
an extraordinary dream I had of being taken captive in the Tower by some
organisation, and trying to get the police in to rescue me, shouting from the
window, and a strange road sweeper who didn't pay any attention to me . . .
I had a male day nurse and a female night nurse for two weeks or so, and
it seemed as if I had been acting oddly, and was 'confused'. The girl sat up
in my room all night, and this gave me a sense of protection.[78]

They moved to their new home in the New Town of Edinburgh in the autumn.
Before they left London, Muriel told the faithful Jo Stanley that relations
between them were once again as they had been in the old days, something
borne out by several of the fragmentary entries that fill the last few pages of
his diary: 'This morning I gave dear Muriel what I had so much been looking
forward to – a New Year present, which I had managed to buy on Wednesday
at Hamilton and Inches, a little gold rose branch in gold; she was greatly
pleased with it.'[79]

Muriel too was feeling her age. She had had an operation for varicose veins
in 1964, and was now plagued with foot trouble, but would not agree to further
surgery, and Reith fretted about her:

I am most awfully worried about dear Muriel's leg; I don't know what to do.
I am very anxious indeed to arrange a really good holiday for her. Several
times this evening, when she was laughing, I thought I had never seen her
looking so pretty.[80]

His mind turned insistently back to his days as Transport Officer during the
First World War, and to Bob Wallace: 'I am wondering if RBW will come to
help me over the river,' he wrote. The Edinburgh winter was cold and wet, and
he wondered whether they had done the right thing in uprooting themselves. He
found it increasingly difficult to walk, and there were days when he did little
other than sleep.

Sometime in March Reith read an article about the military historian Basil
Liddell Hart. It finished with a passage which he said 'pleased and comforted'
him greatly. The author, Ronald Lewin, had remarked on Churchill's inability
to draw into his entourage Liddell Hart's 'brilliant and creative brain':

It was a time of 'tout le monde à la bataille', yet in a total war which is
inevitably governed by dictatorial personalities there are bound to be losses
on the side, and Churchill – like Hitler and Stalin and Roosevelt – hand
picked his advisers carefully, if not always with discrimination. Who, for
example, can tell what benefits might have flowed had Churchill been able
to attach to his war machine the dynamo called Reith? But merely to mention
Reith is to indicate why Liddell Hart would never have fitted into Churchill's
team. They were both essentially loners, rogue males independent in spirit
and action.

Reith copied out the passage and added, 'I shall certainly have something done in my memoirs with that.' They were the last words he ever wrote in his diary.[81]

His deafness affected his balance, and he had a number of falls. Early in May, as he was going out of the door of his study, he somehow caught one foot over another and crashed backwards full length, severing all the ligaments in his knee and breaking the thigh bone close to the hip. After hospital treatment, he was transferred to the Officers' Nursing Home in Belgrave Crescent, and he died there on 16 June. 'On his special injunction,' said the death notice in *The Times*, 'the funeral will be private.'

One of those who attended was Janet Adam Smith's brother, Alick, and he described the ceremony in a letter to his sister:

> We gathered at The Queen's House, the family, the lawyers, the doctor and myself. We went up to St Giles and into the Thistle Chapel, about 20 in all. The coffin was in the middle. George Macleod came in and started the service by saying that John wanted no eulogy, and that eulogies in prayers at funeral services were a bad idea. And so he started with a recital of all that John had done. I looked to see the coffin heave. Otherwise, a pleasant simple service, consisting of a reading from the Authorised Version and two prayers, the second of which contained a eulogium. It was a most moving service, and very fitting. A good Scottish benediction, with both hands raised . . .[82]

After the cremation, the party reassembled at the Queen's House. It was George Macleod who broached the question of whether Reith's wishes about a memorial service should be disregarded. The discussion was brief, and four weeks later the blue and white Cross of St Andrew flew from the tower of Westminster Abbey.

Before the service, there was unaccompanied music from the BBC Chorus: Purcell's 'Thou knowest, Lord, the secrets of our hearts' and Parry's 'My soul, there is a country'. Murray Leishman read from the Wisdom of Solomon and the Director-General of the BBC from the Epistle to the Philippians. The BBC Symphony Orchestra under Sir Adrian Boult played Vaughan Williams and Elgar and accompanied the Abbey Choir when they sang 'In Paradisum' from Fauré's *Requiem*. The collegiate body had been preceded by the Archbishop of Canterbury in the procession, but it was the Moderator of the General Assembly of the Church of Scotland who was conducted to the pulpit to give the memorial address. He compared Reith to David: 'A man who established a kingdom, yet in his heart wanted to build a shrine . . . A man of vision who complained that he had never been given a big enough job to do.'

The congregation joined in the singing of the metrical version of the 23rd Psalm, and at the end of the service the Abbey Choir sang Orlando Gibbons' 'Amen'. The dying notes were picked up by a piper. The golden doors in the sanctuary were opened, and Regimental Sergeant-Major Thomas Anderson, formerly of the Cameronians, came from the Chapel of Henry VII. The music he played was 'The Flowers o' the Forest', the traditional lament for Scotland's defeat by the English on Flodden field:

I've heard them lilting, at the ewe milking.
Lasses a' lilting, before dawn of day;
But now they are moaning, on ilka green loaning;
The flowers of the forest are a' wede away . . .

The solitary figure moved slowly down through the Quire, and the old lament filled the hushed Abbey and then was gradually lost as he passed through the West Cloister Door.

The College Church could hardly have done it better.

'We brought nothing into this world, and it is certain we carry nothing out.' John Reith left estate in Britain valued at £76 net, £6,155 gross. Not all the instructions that he had laid down in his 'demise file' were disregarded. A week after the funeral, Christopher took the ashes for burial to the tiny ruined church at Rothiemurchus in Invernessshire; in July, on the fiftieth anniversary of her wedding, he drove his mother there. Muriel lived on for another five years; latterly her children arranged for her to have a room in an old people's home in Perthshire, where she was able to have some of her own things around her. 'She was very much calmer and more together at the end,' Marista said, 'and a much happier person; she had borne a lot with extraordinary stead-fastness.' Christopher continued to farm Whitebank. A year after his father's death, and after much discussion with his wife and mother, he renounced the title.

John Reith's name passed not only into history, but also into the language: 'Of, pertaining to, or characteristic of Reith or his principles,' said Volume III of *A Supplement to the Oxford English Dictionary* when it appeared in 1982; 'especially relating to the responsibility of broadcasting to enlighten and educate public taste.' Over the years, the word was to acquire shades of meaning, not least in the BBC, which gradually, for reasons good and bad, became a broader church than its chief architect intended. In the early 1980s, the present writer was the Controller of Radio 3. He gave it as his opinion one day that a play that was under consideration was remarkable only for the scatological fixation of its author. 'The trouble with you,' one of his drama department colleagues said amiably, 'is that you are just an old Reithian fart.'

Charles Stuart's edition of the diaries was published in 1975, and he prefaced it with a perceptive short account of Reith's life. He noted his ability to give excellent advice to all but himself, and the frequency with which he relied on instinctive judgement:

The tragedy of his public life was not, as he often claimed, that he had failed in achievement, but rather, in the words of his great enemy, Winston

Churchill, when writing of the French General Michel, that 'his personality and temperament were not equal to the profound and penetrating justice of his ideas.'[83]

Certainly there are few who have been so grievously maimed by their own temperament; Stuart's words capture the man with precision. Beside them, in the best tradition of BBC impartiality, may be set those with which *The Times* concluded a leading article on the day after John Reith died:

The corporate personality of the BBC still gets, and will continue to get, a twitch on the thread from that angular Scots engineer, of unabashed earnestness and unbending strength, who, having survived a sniper's bullet in 1915, felt himself to be elected by Providence to do something great in the world. He did.[84]

Not a bad epitaph for the old puppet master.

Notes

CHAPTER I

1 The history of the Church in Scotland is a bewildering chronicle of secessions and unions. In 1843, headed by Dr Thomas Chalmers, 451 ministers (out of a total of 1203) resigned their livings and formed the Free Church.
2 J. C. W. Reith, *Into the Wind*, Hodder & Stoughton, London, 1949, p. 6.
3 *Ibid.*
4 Letter preserved in Scrapbook.
5 Pre-Diary Narrative.
6 John Kyrle (1637–1724), 'the Man of Ross', was born in Gloucestershire. On coming down from Balliol, he settled on the family property at Ross in Herefordshire, living very simply and devoting his surplus income to charity. There is a portrait of him in Pope's *Epistle to Bathurst*, the third of his four *Moral Essays*, published between 1731 and 1735. The Society was founded in 1877.
7 *Into the Wind*, p. 5.
8 It is not only the Jesuits who recognise the efficacy of 'catching them young' – John Reith remained a militant abstainer until well into middle life. When he was general manager at Beardmore's after the First World War and was guest of honour at a Burns Supper in the factory, the men made it a teetotal occasion in deference to his views. (Diary, 28 January 1922.)
9 Letter preserved in Scrapbook.
10 Pre-Diary Narrative.
11 *Ibid.*
12 *Ibid.*
13 *Ibid.*
14 *Ibid.*
15 *Ibid.*
16 In 1900 the Free Church and the United Presbyterian Church had united to become the United Free Church.

'Wee Frees' is the name applied colloquially to the small number of Free Church congregations, mainly in the Highlands, which remained outside the union and retain the name of Free Church.
17 Pre-Diary Narrative.
18 Andrew Boyle, *Only the Wind Will Listen*, Hutchinson, 1972, p. 37. Boyle was relying on information from the broadcaster René Cutforth, who had interviewed a number of Reith's school contemporaries while gathering material for a television profile. The programme was never broadcast, and I have been able to find no reference to it in the BBC Archives. Cutforth and Boyle are both now dead.
19 Reith had been given the middle names Charles Walsham after the clergyman of that name who had the charge of Holy Trinity, Westbourne Terrace, when his mother was a girl. She had been confirmed there.
20 John Reith, *Wearing Spurs*, Hutchinson, London, 1966, p. 14.
21 Pre-Diary Narrative.
22 *Into the Wind*, p. 9.
23 Pre-Diary Narrative.
24 *Into the Wind*, p. 11.
25 The proof of this is to be found in Reith's own scrapbooks. A few years before he died, he pasted in a piece of paper which had recently come into his possession and wrote beside it in pencil, 'This document was salved from a heterogeneous mass of papers in the flat of the wretched Jean Reith (ob. 1966).' What his sister had preserved was their father's record of where the family had spent its summer holidays in every year from 1870 (the year of his marriage) until 1911.

CHAPTER 2

1 Pre-Diary Narrative.
2 *Into the Wind*, pp. 11–12.
3 *Ibid.*, p. 12.
4 Summarised Diary, 17 January 1912.
5 *Into the Wind*, p. 13.
6 *Wearing Spurs*, p. 14.
7 *Ibid.*, p. 15.
8 *Ibid.*, p. 18.
9 *Ibid.*, p. 17.
10 Pre-Diary Narrative.
11 *Ibid.*, 21 January 1912. 'Semet' (more usually 'semmit') is an old Scottish word for a vest.
12 *Ibid.*
13 Summarised Diary, 18 June 1912.
14 Scrapbook. The date '9.vii.67' has been added by Reith in pencil.
15 Pre-Diary Narrative.
16 Summarised Diary, 6 January 1913.
17 *Ibid.*, 30 March 1912.
18 *Ibid.*, 19 January 1912.
19 'The lad with the scones' is how James Moffatt rendered the parable of the loaves and the fishes in his translation of the New Testament. Dr Moffatt was married to a cousin of Reith's. As his schooldays receded, Reith became increasingly attached to Gresham's. When the school celebrated its 250th anniversary, he sent them a telegram – in Gaelic.
20 Summarised Diary, November 1912.
21 *Wearing Spurs*, p. 146.
22 Hamilton had been elected to the chair of logic and metaphysics at Edinburgh in 1836, and his lectures appeared in 1859–60, after his death. In his reading, as in much else, the influence of Reith's father is apparent. The lectures were published during Dr Reith's student years.
23 By Angus McNeill. This was a pendant to *The Unspeakable Scot* by T. W. H. Crosland, which had been published by Grant Richards in 1902 – a *Punch*-type article at book length which had offered the Scots a certain amount of homely advice about how to behave among the English. Rule IV was 'There is nothing specially creditable in having been born on a muck heap. Do not boast about it.' Rule X was even more direct: 'IF WITHOUT SERIOUS INCONVENIENCE TO YOURSELF YOU CAN MANAGE TO REMAIN AT HOME, PLEASE DO.'
24 Summarised Diary, 17 February 1914.

CHAPTER 3

1 Diary, 14 November 1937.
2 Summarised Diary, 26 July 1913.
3 *Ibid.*, August 1913.
4 Letter from father, 6 September 1913.
5 Summarised Diary, 16 December 1913.
6 *Ibid.*, 19 December 1913.
7 *Ibid.*, December 1913.
8 *Ibid.*, January 1914.
9 Reith was capable of taking off at any hour of the day or night and walking prodigious distances by himself. He recorded one such feat in his memoirs, when he left home at 2.35 a.m. and returned at 7.35 p.m. 'I had walked the twenty-eight miles to the foot of Ben Lomond; climbed to the summit; walked back. Probably a record.' (*Into the Wind*, p. 16.)
10 Summarised Diary, February 1914.
11 *Into the Wind*, p. 13.
12 Later the King George V Dock.
13 Letter to his mother, 20 February 1914.
14 Letter from his father, 20 February 1914.
15 Letter to his father, 22 February 1914.
16 Summarised Diary, February 1914.
17 Letter to his father, 5 March 1914.
18 *Ibid.*
19 Summarised Diary, June 1914.
20 *Ibid.*, May 1914.
21 *Ibid.*
22 Thomas Chalmers, who had become the first Moderator of the Free Church after the Disruption, was a particular hero of Reith's. He left among his papers an unpublished essay on him which he wrote in the 1950s, and he frequently directed the attention of acquaintances to the importance of Chalmers' writings. These ranged widely over theology, political economy and scientific development, and were published in thirty-four volumes after his death.
23 Summarised Diary, June 1914.

24 *Ibid.*, August 1914.
25 *Wearing Spurs*, p. 22.
26 Summarised Diary, August 1914.
27 *Ibid.*
28 *Wearing Spurs*, p. 29.
29 Summarised Diary, September 1914.
30 *Wearing Spurs*, p. 29.
31 *Ibid.*, p. 30.
32 Summarised Diary, September 1914.
33 *Wearing Spurs*, p. 33.
34 *Ibid.*, p. 37.
35 *Ibid.*, p. 41.
36 *Ibid.*, p. 42.
37 Summarised Diary, November 1914.
38 *Wearing Spurs*, p. 44.
39 *Ibid.*, p. 45.
40 *Into the Wind*, p. 23.

CHAPTER 4

1 *Wearing Spurs*, p. 47.
2 *Ibid.*, p. 48.
3 Summarised Diary, 6 November 1914.
4 *Ibid.*, 30 July 1926.
5 *Ibid.*, 13 November 1914. He received his first letter from Charlie the same day.
6 *Wearing Spurs*, p. 51.
7 Summarised Diary, 8 November 1914.
8 Letter to parents, 26 November 1914.
9 *Wearing Spurs*, p. 57.
10 *Ibid.*, p. 63.
11 *Ibid.*, p. 65.
12 Summarised Diary, 22 November 1914.
13 *Ibid.*, 24 November 1914. Years later, when he came to write *Wearing Spurs*, Reith gave a different version: 'It was odd to think that he would be in London next day; that the day after that my father and mother would be reading my account of the last eventful fortnight.' (p. 67.)
14 *Ibid.*, 1 December 1914.
15 Letter to father, 21 December 1914.
16 Rather inconsistently, he noted the arrangement in his diary.
17 Letter to mother, 18 December 1914.
18 *Wearing Spurs*, p. 77.
19 *Into the Wind*, p. 29.
20 Summarised Diary, 12 December 1914.
21 *Ibid.*, 16 December 1914.
22 *Ibid.*, 21 December 1914.

23 *Ibid.*, 31 December 1914.
24 *Ibid.*, 13 January 1915. An entry in the diary for the following day reads: 'Letters from home and from Kitty Muirhead which bored me horribly.'
25 *Ibid.*, January 1915.
26 *Wearing Spurs*, p. 107.
27 *Ibid.*
28 *Ibid.*, p. 110.
29 Letter to mother, 28 February 1915. Years later, during one of his ritual re-readings of his diary and enclosure books, he annotated this passage: 'cf. BBC 1932–38'.
30 *Wearing Spurs*, p. 112.
31 During his illness, the Transport corporals sent a note to Charlie, and had a reply.
32 *Wearing Spurs*, p. 114.
33 *Ibid.*, p. 123.
34 *Into the Wind*, p. 37.
35 Summarised Diary, 29 January 1915.
36 *Wearing Spurs*, p. 130.
37 Summarised Diary, 13 February 1915.
38 Reith wrote in *Wearing Spurs*: 'My brother and I dined in Town that evening', but this was not so. It is plain from the diary that Douglas had tea at the Bowsers', but then went off by himself, reappearing at Euston shortly before midnight. The fact is that by the time the war diary came to be written up with publication in mind, Charlie had become a non-person. Reith adopted the technique that had served for the likes of Trotsky in the Stalinist era and simply painted him out of the picture.
39 *Wearing Spurs*, p. 131.
40 *Ibid.*
41 Summarised Diary, 15 February 1915.
42 *Ibid.*, 20 February 1915.
43 *Ibid.*, 28 February 1915.
44 *Wearing Spurs*, p. 140.
45 Summarised Diary, 27 March 1915.
46 Letter from father, 30 March 1915.
47 Letter to father, 3 April 1915. A sense of missed opportunity stayed with Reith throughout his life. 'To visit Oxford or Cambridge in after years was (and is) an irritation, for it brings a longing for what had been missed.' (*Wearing Spurs*, p. 150.)
48 *Wearing Spurs*, p. 143.

49 *Ibid.*, p. 154.
50 Summarised Diary, 2 April 1915.
51 *Ibid.*, 7 April 1915.
52 *Ibid.*, 9 April 1915.
53 *Ibid.*
54 *Wearing Spurs*, p. 164.
55 Summarised Diary, 10 April 1915.
56 *Ibid.*
57 *Ibid.*, 11 April 1915.
58 *Ibid.*, 12 April 1915.
59 *Ibid.*
60 *Into the Wind*, p. 45.
61 *Wearing Spurs*, p. 171.
62 *Ibid.*, p. 180.
63 Summarised Diary, 17 April 1915.
64 *Ibid.*, 23 June 1915.
65 *Ibid.*, 25 April 1915.
66 *Ibid.*, 3 May 1915.
67 *Wearing Spurs*, p. 180. Charlie was ill, too. He had German measles and had to stay in bed for two weeks. 'I felt awfully sorry for him,' Reith wrote. 'Just as he had a chance of the first XI, too.' (Summarised Diary, 15 May 1915.)
68 Summarised Diary, 29 May 1915.
69 *Wearing Spurs*, p. 189.
70 *Ibid.*, p. 188.
71 Summarised Diary, 16 June 1915.
72 Letter from father, 12 July 1915.
73 *Into the Wind*, p. 49.
74 *Ibid.*
75 Summarised Diary, 4 August 1915.
76 *Wearing Spurs*, p. 206.
77 Summarised Diary, 7 August 1915.
78 *Wearing Spurs*, p. 205.
79 The author was Gabrielle Margaret Vere Campbell, who wrote under the pseudonym of Marjorie Bowen. The book had been published by Methuen in 1913.
80 Summarised Diary, 22 August 1915.
81 *Ibid.*, 28 August 1915.
82 *Into the Wind*, p. 53.
83 Summarised Diary, 13 September 1915.
84 *Ibid.*, 19 September 1915.
85 *Ibid.*, 20 September 1915.
86 *Ibid.*, 23 September 1915.
87 *Into the Wind*, p. 54.
88 *Wearing Spurs*, p. 216.
89 Summarised Diary, 2 October 1915.
90 *Ibid.*, 7 October 1915.
91 He wrote, for instance, that the opening lines of a children's hymn – 'Above the clear blue sky/In Heaven's bright abode' – came to mind; also that he considered writing in Latin the message that he had really wanted to send. (See *Wearing Spurs*, p. 223.)
92 The telegram form is preserved in Reith's scrapbook. He wrote in both *Into the Wind* and *Wearing Spurs* that the news had come in an official telegram stating that he was badly wounded, but that is not so. This telegram, from the officer in charge of Territorial Forces Records, is also in the scrapbook, and the phrase used was 'degree not stated'. A second telegram to the manse from Charlie two days previously had said, 'Safe field hospital, not serious, doctor pleased'.
93 *Wearing Spurs*, p. 233.
94 Letter to mother, 11 October 1915.
95 *Wearing Spurs*, p. 16. Azrael, the angel that watches over the dying, had no doubt figured in his father's sermons.
96 Summarised Diary, 17 October 1915.
97 *Ibid.*, 12 November 1915.
98 *Ibid.*, 24 November 1915.
99 *Ibid.*, 1 December 1915.
100 *Ibid.*, 8 January 1916.
101 His application for release was refused, however, and he was killed at the front shortly afterwards.
102 Summarised Diary, 18 January 1916.
103 *Ibid.*, 13 February 1916.
104 *Ibid.*, 16 February 1916.
105 *Ibid.*, 19 February 1916.

CHAPTER 5

1 *Into the Wind*, p. 62.
2 His mind turned frequently to his life at the front. 'I would give a good deal to hear a shell come screaming overhead,' he wrote rather perversely to his father in a letter from New Haven. 'It would be the homeliest sound I have heard for many months.' He also still brooded over his treatment at the hands of the Adjutant and the Colonel: 'I get very mad when I think of those two. It's not good for me to remember them, as time is making no difference. If I were aged I should have an apoplectic fit of fury periodically!' (Letter to his father, 25 March 1916.)

Later in the year, he was able to record in his diary that one of his old enemies had been removed from the scene: 'Heard that Colonel Douglas had been killed, which I thought almost incredible, unless it was by a shell some way back.' (Summarised Diary, 24 July 1916.) This was unjust. The Colonel had fallen victim to a sniper's bullet.

3 Summarised Diary, 28 March 1916.
4 *Into the Wind*, p. 61.
5 Summarised Diary, 11 March 1916.
6 *Ibid.*, 8 May 1916.
7 *Into the Wind*, p. 66.
8 Summarised Diary, 4 July 1916.
9 *Ibid.*, 16 April 1916.
10 There is no indication of which paper this appeared in: Reith quite often failed to date and identify the source of the cuttings he pasted into his scrapbooks. Although this article is obviously based on an interview with Reith, he was never a great lover of the press. 'Frightfully angry at American newspapers,' he wrote to his father. 'They are the very last word in vulgar lying sensationalism. The headlines are in such rotten grammar and so slangy that I can't understand them often. I never buy a paper.' (Letter to his father, 18 June 1916.)
11 Scots were thick on the ground in Philadelphia. Reith had recently stayed with a family who were eager to show him that part of their garden immediately in front of their dining room: it was laid out in boxwood hedges and narrow paths in the same pattern as behind Robert Burns' cottage in Ayr.
12 Letter to his father, 1 June 1916.
13 Robert Riddell, a bibliophile and antiquary, was a friend of the poet's to whom Burns promised a manuscript collection of some of his pieces, and Riddell provided him with two calf-bound quarto volumes embossed with his family crest for the purpose. They passed through many hands in the nineteenth century, and there was a public outcry in 1913 when they were sold for £5000 and crossed the Atlantic. It was at that year's meeting of the St Andrew's Society that Gribbel

spoke of his disapproval of the way in which they had been hawked around and announced his gift. The volumes were handed over to the National Library of Scotland in 1926.
14 *Into the Wind*, p. 68.
15 This is what Reith wrote in his diary. In a letter to his father he said they sang 'It's a Long Way to Tipperary'. Perhaps they sang both.
16 Letter to his father, 18 June 1916. In the same letter he told his father that there was to be a reception of some kind for the new minister in Swarthmore: 'I may go. I am pretty pleased to find that he wears a gown and a minister's collar, which so few do here. The majority wear grey ties or white ties with ordinary collars and they look a beastly fishy crew.'
17 He was intent on arranging much more than an agreeable holiday for his parents. 'I can guarantee you an LL D from Lafayette and Princeton or a DD,' he wrote to his father later in the year. 'These are the two greatest Presbyterian colleges in USA.' (Letter to his father, 28 September 1916.)
18 Reith saw the letter after his father's death and pasted it into his scrapbook. 'You have made your mother and me very, very happy, during these last years,' Dr Reith wrote, 'and God will reward you for it. I hope you will have a useful and honourable career before you, and will be spared for many, happy years. But once again let me remind you that life is for the service of Christ, Who did everything for us, and I would rather know that you were a devoted and loving follower of him than a millionaire. You will be kind and thoughtful for your mother, I know: and I would like you to be the same to your brothers and sisters, and keep in close touch with them all. I would like to think that all of you were united, and loved one another deeply. Show the example.'
19 Summarised Diary, 1 September 1916.
20 *Ibid.*, 24 November 1916.
21 *Ibid.*, 3 November 1916.
22 The nine Churches in question were the Roman Catholic, the Protestant

Episcopal, the Presbyterian, the Methodist Episcopal, the Congregationalist, the Dutch Reformed, the Reformed Church of North America, the Baptist, and the United Presbyterian.

23 Andrew Carnegie (1835–1919), the Dunfermline-born philanthropist who built 2505 libraries, believed that world peace could be bought as easily as knowledge. Between 1903 and 1914 he had endowed four foundations and built three imposing 'temples of peace' at a cost of more than $25 million. The deed of the Carnegie Endowment provided that 'when the establishment of universal peace is attained, the donor provides that the revenue shall be devoted to the banishment of the next most degrading evil or evils, the suppression of which would most advance the progress, elevation and happiness of man.'

24 *Philadelphia Public Ledger*, 1 January 1917.

25 Summarised Diary, 29 December 1916. Ellis had sent what he termed 'a confidential memorandum by an American Friend' to the Ambassador two weeks previously, just after the publication of the German peace proposals and when the Church declaration was still in draft. He offered 'some practical considerations upon methods for counteracting this most formidable of all the German strokes of propaganda', and he said in his covering letter that he was writing at Reith's suggestion. Copies of both memorandum and letter are preserved in Reith's scrapbooks.

26 Letter to his father, 22 March 1917.

27 Letter to his father, 25 February 1917.

28 Letter to his mother, 22 March 1917.

29 Letter to his mother, 14 June 1917.

30 Summarised Diary, 10 April 1917.

31 Letter from Bayard Henry, 1 May 1917.

32 *Into the Wind*, p. 69.

33 Summarised Diary, 20 June 1917.

34 *Ibid.*, 2 July 1917.

35 *Ibid.*, 3 July 1917. Years later, when he was writing his pre-diary narrative, Reith noted that each sister eventually

inherited £2 million: 'I think there is some credit to me in that I did nothing about this,' he wrote. Helen married John G. Winant, who became the United States Ambassador in London.

36 *Ibid.*, 11 July 1917.

37 Letter from L. W. McCarthy, 8 August 1917. McCarthy later became a Roman Catholic priest. They met again when Reith visited the United States as Director-General of the BBC in the 1930s.

38 Letter from Jeannette Laws dated 19 July 1917. Years later, when he came to summarise his diaries, Reith wrote, 'I was dreadfully scared of her because she was so fond of me. She was very pretty and about 19, and I suppose anything could have happened there if I had been otherwise constituted.'

39 Summarised Diary, 14 August 1917. A scribbled note at the bottom of the page says, 'I never have – but I tried several times – 25/11/34, 21/12/52, 11/6/62'.

40 Captain Beith was the writer Ian Hay, who had been in the States on a lecture tour and had in fact spoken a great deal more than Reith.

41 *Into the Wind*, p. 69.

CHAPTER 6

1 Summarised Diary, 27 September 1917.

2 *Ibid.*, 17 October 1917.

3 *Ibid.*, 25 January 1918.

4 Summarised Diary, 15 April 1918.

5 *Ibid.*, 16 July 1918.

6 *Ibid.*, 26 May 1918.

7 *Ibid.*, 15 June 1918.

8 *Ibid.*, 21 September 1918.

9 *Ibid.*, 7 September 1918.

10 *Ibid.*, December 1918.

11 *Ibid.*, 31 December 1918.

12 Letter from his father, 19 January 1919.

13 Summarised Diary, 25 January 1919.

14 *Ibid.*, 30 January 1919.

15 *Ibid.*, 20 February 1919.

16 *Ibid.*, 20 February 1919.

17 *Ibid.*, 3 March 1919.

18 *Ibid.*

19 *Ibid.*, 11 March 1919.

20 *Ibid.*, 24 March 1919.

21 *Ibid.*, 1 April 1919. Years later Reith annotated this entry: 'And why have we so seldom had a prayer together since? Nearly 10 years since we did, and no family worship.'

22 *Ibid.*, 5 April 1919.

23 *Ibid.*

24 Letter to Mrs Reith, 10 April 1919.

25 *Into the Wind*, p. 75. He was clearly in the habit of going on about being under-employed in his letters home. 'Did you ever read or hear,' Dr Reith enquired guilelessly in reply, 'that many of those who have risen to distinction have done so by the use they made of their leisure time? It occurred to me that as you complain of having only 10% occupied in your work why should you not throw the remaining 90% into some valuable access to your learning? Take a period of English Literature, such as Brooke's Primer will show you, and make a complete study of it . . .' (Letter from his father, 11 May 1919.)

26 Summarised Diary, 5 August 1919.

27 *Into the Wind*, p. 75. His path and Milne-Watson's were to cross once more: eight years later they were knighted on the same day at Buckingham Palace.

28 Summarised Diary, 28 August 1919.

29 *Into the Wind*, p. 75.

30 Summarised Diary, 9 May 1919.

31 *Ibid.*, 6 June 1919.

32 *Ibid.*, July 1919.

33 *Ibid.*, 20 July 1919.

34 Thoughts about judgement ran strongly in Dr Reith's mind in these last few weeks of his life. 'I am trying to fix my thoughts on the end which cannot be very far away,' he wrote in one of his last letters to Reith. 'This means the effort to imagine myself in the presence of my judge, with all the vanity of this world and its make-believe stripped away, and nothing left but reality. Under a sense of sin and unworthiness I hide myself beneath the righteousness of my Saviour.'

35 Letter from his father, 10 October 1919.

36 Summarised Diary, 10 December 1919.

37 Two months previously Reith had had a letter from Archie's wife saying that he wished to leave the Church and asking for help in finding him a job. Reith also suspected that Archie was the sender of an anonymous message which Jean received after the funeral wishing her 'eternal remorse'.

38 Summarised Diary, 26 January 1920.

39 *Ibid.*, 14 March 1920.

40 *Ibid.*, 19 March 1920.

41 *Ibid.*, December 1919.

42 Letter from his father, 22 October 1919.

43 Summarised Diary, 24 March 1920.

44 *Ibid.*, 8 April 1919. Bryce was born in Belfast of Scottish parents. He had been Regius Professor of Civil Law at Oxford before going into the Commons. He served in the administrations of Gladstone, Rosebery and Campbell-Bannerman.

45 *Ibid.*, 17 June 1919.

46 Clynes was a former President of the National Union of General and Municipal Workers. He had entered Parliament in 1906 as the member for the Platting Division of north-east Manchester. He was defeated by Ramsay MacDonald for the leadership of the Party in 1922. Later he became Lord Privy Seal and deputy leader of the House of Commons.

47 Summarised Diary, March 1920. In his memoirs Reith wrongly places this correspondence with Clynes two years later, in April 1922.

48 Letter dated 12 April 1920.

49 Summarised Diary, 5 April 1920.

50 *Ibid.*, April 1920.

51 *Ibid.*, 22 April 1920.

52 *Ibid.*, 6 May 1920.

53 *Ibid.*, May 1920.

54 *Into the Wind*, p. 79.

55 Summarised Diary, 4 June 1920. His interest in psychology persisted, and was still strong when he came to do his Christmas shopping six months later; his present to his mother was two books on insect psychology.

56 *Ibid.*, 1 July 1920.

57 *Ibid.*, 6 August 1920.

58 *Into the Wind*, p. 80.

59 Summarised Diary, October 1920.

60 *Ibid.*, September 1920.

61 Beardmore received a peerage in the New Year's Honours List shortly after this, and took the title of Lord Invernairn. Reith sent him a letter of congratulation signed by heads of department and shop stewards. 'I suppose a case has been made for him for his war work,' he wrote in his diary, 'because certainly he has done nothing since the war to merit it.' (Summarised Diary, January 1921.)

62 Summarised Diary, 5 April 1921.

63 *Ibid.*, 21 April 1921.

64 *Ibid.*, 27 April 1921.

65 *Ibid.*, 29 April 1921.

66 *Ibid.*, 13 May 1921.

67 *Ibid.*, 17 May 1921.

68 *Ibid.*, 22 June 1921.

69 *Ibid.*, 25 June 1921.

70 *Ibid.*, 21 July 1921.

71 Douglas was slightly misremembering his Shakespeare: 'It is the star to every wandering bark,/Whose worth's unknown, although his height be taken.' The lines are from Sonnet 116: 'Let me not to the marriage of true minds/Admit impediments.'

72 Letter dated 18 July 1921.

73 Summarised Diary, 26 July 1921.

74 *Ibid.*, 30 July 1921.

75 *Ibid.*, 2 August 1921.

76 *Ibid.*, 12 August 1921.

77 *Ibid.*, 23 September 1921.

78 *Ibid.*, 19 October 1921.

79 *Ibid.*, 22 October 1921.

80 *Ibid.*, 27 October 1921.

81 *Ibid.*, 20 December 1921.

82 *Ibid.*, 31 December 1921.

83 *Ibid.*, 4 January 1922.

84 *Ibid.*, 6 January 1922.

85 *Ibid.*, 14 January 1922.

86 *Ibid.*, 15 January 1922.

87 *Ibid.*, 26 January 1922.

88 *Ibid.*, 10 February 1922.

89 *Ibid.*, 23 February 1922.

90 *Ibid.*, 24 February 1922.

91 *Ibid.*, 28 February 1922.

92 *Ibid.*, 1 March 1922.

93 *Ibid.*, 2 March 1922.

94 Letter dated 3 March 1922.

95 Summarised Diary, 14 March 1922.

96 *Ibid.*, 21 March 1922.

97 Letter dated 23 March 1922. Douglas wrote, rather incongruously, on Glasgow High School for Girls letter paper. He was earning a little money there by invigilating at examinations.

98 Letter dated 29 March 1922.

99 Summarised Diary, 2 April 1922.

100 *Ibid.*, 21 April 1922.

101 *Ibid.*, 7 May 1922.

102 Letter from his mother dated 20 May 1922.

103 Two years later, in November 1924, the talk which he gave at Gresham's was published in *John O'London's* and Reith received a fee of £100 for it.

104 Summarised Diary, 7 June 1922.

105 *The Reith Diaries*, edited by Charles Stuart, Collins, London, 1975, p. 46.

106 A few weeks previously, when they were in Jersey, he had written, 'Muriel is really one in ten thousand. She is so gentle and kind and sweet tempered.' (Summarised Diary, 23 May 1922.)

107 Summarised Diary, 19 August 1922.

108 *Ibid.*, August 1922.

109 *Ibid.*, 21 August 1922.

110 *Ibid.*, 8 September 1922.

111 *Ibid.*, 14 September 1922.

112 Chamberlain's position had been weakened on the morning of the meeting by news of a by-election result at Newport. A Labour victory had been expected, but the seat was won by the Conservatives with an anti-Coalition candidate.

113 Bull showed him a letter from Horatio Bottomley, then in Wormwood Scrubs, saying he had persuaded all the warders to vote for him. Unfortunately it turned out that they were not in the right constituency.

114 Andrew Boyle, *Only the Wind Will Listen*, p. 116.

115 Summarised Diary, 30 October 1922. Pacing up and down later became a much-remarked habit of Reith's.

116 *Ibid.*, 2 November 1922.

117 *Ibid.*, 3 November 1922.

118 *Into the Wind*, p. 82. Reith arrived at the figure of £15,000 by adding receipts and payments together. When he presented his final accounts to Sir William Bull in July 1924, expenditure

came to £7642. The largest single payment to an individual was £650 to Lord Birkenhead. Lloyd George's reputation in the matter of honours was a useful lubricant. Bull told Reith that Major Isidore Salmon, the Chairman of Lyons, was 'bothering him for a knighthood'.

119 Summarised Diary, 13 December 1922.

120 Asa Briggs records that Kellaway, the former Postmaster-General, and the journalist John Gordon were both thought to have turned it down. (Briggs, *The BBC: A Short History of the First Fifty Years*, Oxford University Press, 1984, p. 45.)

121 Summarised Diary, 28 December 1922.

122 *Into the Wind*, p. 87.

123 Summarised Diary, 30 December 1922.

CHAPTER 7

1 *Into the Wind*, p. 89.

2 *Hansard*, vol. 153, col. 1600, 4 May 1922.

3 One of them was Reith's political patron Sir William Bull, who was a director of Siemens.

4 Summarised Diary, 1 January 1923. He also discovered that Anderson wished to be known as 'Major'. 'He was only a legal officer,' Reith wrote disdainfully, 'and never near the front.'

5 Miss Shields stayed with Reith for five years. 'It was always "Mr Reith" and "Miss Shields",' she recalled in old age. 'I admired him enormously, we all did, but he was a very difficult man to get along with, especially when he didn't have enough to do. He thought I was a lost soul because I went to the cinema on a Sunday – the only time I could go because I was so busy.' (Miss Shields, who sometimes sported a monocle, did, however, find time to drive a Bugatti at Brands Hatch.) She eventually married and live in Paraguay for some years. Reith was godfather to one of her daughters. (*Dorset Evening Echo Weekly Review*, 22 October 1975)

6 P. P. Eckersley, *The Power Behind the Microphone*, Jonathan Cape, London, 1941.

7 Summarised Diary, 1923. Smith did not stay long. He went off after two years to organise publicity for the Liberal Party.

8 *Ibid.*, 21 February 1923.

9 When Reith joined the Company, the number of licences issued stood at 35,774, of which some 6000 were experimental.

10 Summarised Diary, 9 April 1923.

11 Asa Briggs, *The History of Broadcasting in the United Kingdom*, Vol. 1, Oxford University Press, London, 1961, p. 153. It seems likely that Peter Eckersley, Reith's gifted Chief Engineer, helped him to draft the 'Norwich Letter'.

12 Letter from the Postmaster-General to the Directors of the BBC, 13 April 1923.

13 Summarised Diary, 16 March 1923.

14 Reith had shrewdly taken an option on about four times as much accommodation as they needed.

15 Summarised Diary, 19 March 1923. H. M. Pease, an American, represented the Western Electric Company on the Board. L. Stanton Jeffries, the director of music, was another Marconi recruit. Mrs Davidson enquired whether it was necessary to keep the window open.

16 *Ibid.*, 7 February 1923.

17 *Ibid.*, 1 May 1923.

18 *Ibid.*, 26 May 1923. It is plain from the diary that thoughts of Charlie still ran quite frequently – and sourly – in his mind. Earlier in the year he had returned to Dunblane for the weekend to see his mother: 'Feb. 18. Breakfast in bed. It was snowing. Meant to go to church; I thought it would be amusing to see how DCB carried off his eldership at Communion with me watching him, but mother did not want me to go.'

19 *Ibid.*, 14 June 1923.

20 P. P. Eckersley, *op. cit.*, p. 56. Eckersley penned a number of memorable cameo portraits of the Savoy Hill days; another was of 'Aunt Sophy, demure

and intact, who smilingly filled an interval with a precise piano.'

21 R. S. Lambert, *Ariel and All His Quality*, Victor Gollancz, London, 1940, p. 27.

22 It was not the only thing Jean had to answer for: 'Little Billy, our cat, has disappeared from Dunardoch,' says a diary entry for 11 June, 'driven from home by Jean's brute of an Irish terrier. I wrote to Smith, the old gardener, and asked him to try and find it. We are very sad about it.'

23 Summarised Diary, 18 August 1923.

24 *Ibid.*, 10 September 1923.

25 Crocombe had edited *Titbits* since 1918 and continued to do so until 1945.

26 *Radio Times*, Vol. 1 No. 1, 28 September 1923. 'One Who Knows Him' was, in fact, Miss Shields.

27 *Into the Wind*, p. 90.

28 *Ibid.*

29 G. L. Archer, *Big Business and Radio*, New York, 1939, p. 31. Sarnoff began his broadcasting career as an office boy with the American Marconi Company in 1906 and had become the first commercial manager of the Radio Corporation of America when it was set up in October 1919. He later became RCA's president; his ascendancy in broadcasting in the United States stands comparison with that of Reith in Britain. The two men thought highly of each other and became friends.

30 Georges Carpentier (1894–1975), world light-heavyweight champion in 1920 and the idol of the French boxing public, had recently for the second time floored the British boxer Joe Beckett by a knock-out in the first round.

31 Summarised Diary, 3 October 1923.

32 *Ibid.*, 9 October 1923.

33 *Ibid.*, 1 October 1923. The portrait in question, which shows Maysie in a yellow gown, is a rather striking one and calls in question Reith's various and disobliging descriptions of her. The artist was the Hungarian-born Philip de Laszlo (1869–1937), a fashionable portrait painter of the day who had studied in Munich and Paris

before settling in London in 1907. The painting now belongs to Charlie's son David. Some years later Charlie and Maysie commissioned de Laszlo to paint their daughter Hope.

34 Summarised Diary, 15 November 1923.

35 He had been writing without payment for *Radio Times*, but in December Newnes persuaded him to accept six guineas per 1000 words, retrospectively.

36 Summarised Diary, 14 December 1923.

37 *Ibid.*, 25 December 1923.

38 *Into the Wind*, p. 95.

39 *Manchester Guardian*, 24 January 1924.

40 There was one canker in the rose – what Reith saw as the Company's contribution to the success of Wembley was not reflected in the June Honours List, and he sent a rambling and disgruntled letter to Lord Gainford: 'Probably I shouldn't be writing this letter at all and no doubt will regret having done so, but I am feeling very disgusted . . . The BBC *ought* to have had recognition . . . To be ultra-veracious it's about 5% personal and 95% for the great benefit that would accrue to the BBC . . .' Gainford filed the letter away, scrawling cryptically across the top, 'Wants an honour!' (Letter dated 3 June 1924. Gainford Papers, MS 100.)

41 Letter dated 2 May 1924.

42 Set aside, but perhaps not abandoned. It is not always easy to distinguish between ambition and fantasy. On a visit to Dunblane in the spring of 1924, Reith was in the Cathedral when the organist was playing Scottish songs and psalm tunes. 'I sat at the back and enjoyed it tremendously,' he wrote. 'I think when I am Prime Minister I shall come and do this sort of thing. Some of the magnificent old psalm tunes resounding through the cathedral are enough to strengthen any man and any religious sentiment.' (Summarised Diary, 2 May 1924.)

43 Summarised Diary, 16 October 1924.

44 *Ibid.*, 27 March 1925. Reith also got to know Ramsay MacDonald at this time, and, although he had not been

impressed by his performance at the general election, liked him and found him interesting. When his mother was down on a visit, he took her to meet him, and the Labour leader gave her tea in his room at the House. (Diary, 13 March 1925.)

45 *Ibid.*, 9 September 1924.

46 Asa Briggs, *The BBC: A Short History of the First Fifty Years.*

47 Summarised Diary, 21 November 1924.

48 *Ibid.*, 31 December 1924.

49 *Ibid.*, 11 January 1925.

50 *Ibid.*, 20 January 1925.

51 *Ibid.*, 23 March 1925.

52 *Into the Wind*, p. 97.

53 Summarised Diary, 12 March 1925. At the same meeting the Board approved an increase of £750 in Reith's salary. It was not particularly graciously received. 'It was not as much as I expected,' he wrote, 'and I felt annoyed', though he added, 'To have £3700 at 35 is not bad and I wish I could appreciate it better.'

54 *Ibid.*, 19 March 1925.

55 *Ibid.*, 18 April 1925.

56 *Ibid.* The pleasure he got from walking in the Royal Parks tended to be intermittent. 'Walked in Hyde Park till lunch,' says an entry later in the year. 'Glorious day and quite enjoyed it. Visited the beastly Epstein memorial to W. H. Hudson – an offence to intelligence and decency and an outrage on the amenities of the Park.' (Summarised Diary, 25 October 1925.)

57 Letter to the Rev. G. A. Frank Knight, DD, 9 July 1925.

58 Letter dated 21 July 1925.

59 Letter dated 9 September 1925.

60 *Into the Wind*, p. 99.

61 Summarised Diary, 10 December 1925.

62 Oral evidence to the Crawford Committee, 3 December 1925.

63 Summarised Diary, 25 October 1925.

64 *Ibid.*, 5 December 1925.

65 *Ibid.*, 26 January 1926. Fraser believed that one good turn deserved another. An entry in Reith's diary in April reads: 'Ian Fraser called, still on the hunt for one of the Commissioners' jobs.' He

was in fact appointed a Governor in 1937.

66 Cmd 2599 (1926) *Report of the Broadcasting Committee, 1925.* Committees of this sort did not run away with a great deal of public money in those days. Sykes had cost £320; Crawford cost £106 7s 1d.

67 A. J. P. Taylor, *English History 1914–1945*, Oxford, The Clarendon Press, 1965.

68 The word 'Governor' was adopted later in the year.

69 *Into the Wind*, p. 105.

70 Samuel, who later became leader of the Liberal Party, had been Postmaster-General and Home Secretary during the First World War and had just completed five years as High Commissioner in Palestine.

71 Davidson was also, as it happened, a neighbour in Barton Street. He was officially styled Deputy Chief Civil Commissioner. He later became Chairman of the Conservative Party Organisation, and was made a viscount.

72 Summarised Diary, 4 May 1926. 'Hotching' is an old Scottish word meaning 'swarming'.

73 *Ibid.*, 6 May 1926.

74 Birkenhead was Secretary of State for India.

75 Summarised Diary, 6 May 1926.

76 *Ibid.*, 8 May 1926.

77 *Ibid.*

78 *Ibid.*, 9 May 1926. Reith thought that Grey spoke well – 'I gave him some points in the car going to Savoy Hill.' Then he took him back to Barton Street for tea 'as I knew mother would be very interested to meet him'.

79 *Ibid.*, 12 May 1926.

80 The Programme Correspondence Department's tally showed that 176 people wrote in critical terms of the BBC's service during the strike; the number of letters of appreciation received was 3696.

81 Memorandum from Reith to senior staff, 15 May 1926.

82 *Radio Times*, 28 May 1926. Reith was able to start mending fences with Labour within two days of the end of the strike when J. H. Thomas

telephoned to ask whether he might broadcast an appeal to railwaymen to return to work. Reith cleared his lines with Davidson and Downing Street and then told Thomas that it would be all right 'if he said something nice about the employers and sent in his MS'. (Summarised Diary, 14 May 1926.)

83 Eckersley, *op. cit.*, p. 157.

84 BBC Written Archives, Caversham, Files CO 31/1–11: British Broadcasting Company, General Strike, News Bulletins.

85 Memorandum dated 17 May 1926 from Carpendale, Gladstone Murray and others.

86 Summarised Diary, 23 June 1926.

87 *Ibid.*, 3 July 1926.

88 BBC Written Archives, Caversham, File CO 24: British Broadcasting Company, General Strike, Editorials.

89 Summarised Diary, 25 May 1926.

90 *Ibid.*, 27 May 1926.

91 *Ibid.*, 11 June 1926.

92 Letter dated 5 July 1926.

93 Letter dated 14 July 1926.

94 Summarised Diary, 30 July 1926.

95 Muriel's fiancé had been a pilot in the Royal Flying Corps. After his death she managed somehow to acquire the propellor of the plane in which he had been shot down. It hangs to this day on the wall of an outhouse at Christopher's farm.

96 Summarised Diary, 17 August 1926.

97 *Ibid.*, 1 November 1926.

98 *Ibid.*, 16 November 1926.

99 *Ibid.*, 9 December 1926.

100 Hilda Matheson was one of Reith's bright young women who had joined the staff in 1926 as the first Director of Talks. She had previously been Lady Astor's private secretary.

CHAPTER 8

1 Summarised Diary, 25 January 1927.

2 *Ibid.*, 12 February 1927.

3 Andrew Boyle, *op. cit.*, p. 215. Strike out 'small' and 'buxom' and it would serve as a description of Reith himself.

4 Summarised Diary, 9 March 1927.

5 *Ibid.*, 31 March 1927. Reith's animosity to Mrs Snowden was also

no doubt sharpened by the knowledge that she had addressed anti-conscription meetings during the war.

6 Letter dated 1 May 1927. Gainford Papers MS 100.

7 Briggs, *op. cit.*, Vol. 2, p. 427.

8 Milne Watson seemed a little cool at first. It turned out that he had received a telegram signed 'Reith' congratulating him on his knighthood and saying that it was presumably because he had supplied the King with coal. It was the sort of joke that would have appealed to Reith's rather schoolboyish sense of humour, but he assured Milne Watson that he was not the culprit.

9 Summarised Diary, 1 February 1927. When he was shown over the club on his first visit, he discovered that the Secretary was a brother of Sir Maurice Hankey, the Secretary to the Cabinet: 'I thought him too subservient and nervous for an Athenaeum Secretary.' (Diary, 21 February 1927.)

10 Summarised Diary, 16 April 1927.

11 *Ibid.*, 14 May 1927.

12 The BBC tried to get Wood to agree to a clause that would have prevented him from accepting outside engagements 'where it is agreed between us that the organisers are taking such a hostile attitude towards broadcasting as to be inimical to the cause'. Wood sensibly declined this invitation to take part in other people's battles.

13 Summarised Diary, 31 July 1927.

14 *Ibid.*, 10 April 1926.

15 Memorandum by the Chief Engineer on Empire Broadcasting, 6 May 1927.

16 *Daily Express*, 22 November 1927.

17 Summarised Diary, 12 October 1927.

18 *Ibid.*, 24 October 1927.

19 This was certainly the view of his brother Peter, for whom he had initially worked in a junior capacity. 'Roger's charm would melt a heart of stone,' Peter wrote. 'Gentleman Roger! never expressing an opinion, seeing both sides of every question and, with these safe supports, floating upwards to a resting place near, but never too near, the top.' (Eckersley, *op. cit.*, p. 58.)

Between leaving Charterhouse and joining the BBC 'Gentleman Roger' had tried his hand at the law, run a couple of golf clubs and dabbled in chicken farming.

20 Letter dated 3 October 1927. Gainford Papers MS 100.

21 Letter dated 3 February 1928. Gainford Papers MS 101.

22 Summarised Diary, 17 November 1927.

23 *Ibid.*, 29 December 1927.

24 *Ibid.*, 8, 9, 15, 16 and 22 January 1928.

25 *Ibid.*, 29 January 1928.

26 Letter to Carpendale dated 12 January 1928.

27 Letter dated 14 January 1928.

28 Summarised Diary, 7 November 1927.

29 Letter dated 21 January 1928.

30 Summarised Diary, 23 February 1928. In spite of his protestations, Reith was interested enough to drive out to HMV at Hayes to lunch again six days later and to spend several hours looking at the books (their turnover was £5.5–6 million) and inspecting their latest gramophone, which could handle twelve records. (Summarised Diary, 19 February 1928.) There was a further meeting early in May, when Clarke, the Managing Director of HMV, gave him lunch at the Reform Club. 'He is very anxious for me to succeed him,' Reith wrote, 'and he is now making £40,000 a year.' (Summarised Diary, 3 May 1928.)

31 Letter from E. R. Appleton, 27 February 1928.

32 Letter dated 27 February 1928.

33 Letter dated 11 April 1928.

34 Letter to GPO, 16 January 1928.

35 Summarised Diary, 27 May 1928.

36 *Ibid.*, 16 September 1925.

37 *Ibid.*, 5 June 1928.

38 Letter dated 17 June 1928.

39 Summarised Diary, 31 January 1926.

40 Letter dated 25 June 1928. Fleming was anticipating. It had recently been announced that Rendall Davidson was to be succeeded by the Archbishop of York, Cosmo Gordon Lang, who had been born in Aberdeen and was the son of a former Moderator of the Church of Scotland. Lang was not consecrated until November, however, and the ceremony was performed by the retiring Primate.

41 Summarised Diary, 30 September 1928.

42 *Ibid.*, 24 October 1928.

43 Val Gielgud, *Years in a Mirror*, Bodley Head, London, 1965. Shortly afterwards, the BBC was looking for a new drama director. Reith sent for Carpendale. 'This fellow Gielgud will do,' he said. 'If he can be rude to me, he ought to be able to tell a lot of actors what to do.'

44 Summarised Diary, 7 January 1929.

45 *Ibid.*, 11 January 1929.

46 Letter dated 14 January 1929. For the Diary version, see Stuart, p. 146.

47 Summarised Diary, 11 January 1929.

48 See Lambert, *op. cit.*, p. 96 et seq.

49 Eckersley, *op. cit.*, p. 152.

50 A diary entry of Reith's suggests that Eckersley was not initially minded to behave so accommodatingly: 'We stopped him giving any press interviews, but he is acting in an abominable way and not really responsible for what he is doing.' (Summarised Diary, 6 June 1929.) How Eckersley was persuaded not to talk to the press is not known. Possibly he was reminded that the Corporation regarded his severance terms as generous – he was to be given £1000 on leaving and a further £1000 for at least one year as a consultant.

51 Eckersley, *op. cit.*, p. 153.

52 *Into the Wind*, p. 140.

53 Summarised Diary, 2 February 1929.

54 Very much over Mrs Snowden's dead body, however. 'The Director-General's extraordinary desire to retain him', she wrote to Gainford, 'explains in a way I had not understood his condonement of the most flagrant offence against decency and discipline of which a responsible individual can be guilty.' (Letter dated 28 April 1929, Gainford Papers MS 101.)

55 Summarised Diary, 14 February 1929.

56 Letter dated 13 April 1929.

57 Letter dated 14 April 1929.

58 Summarised Diary, 22 April 1929.

59 *Ibid.*, 28 May 1929.

60 *Ibid.*, 30 April 1929.
61 *Ibid.*, 16 April 1929.
62 *Ibid.*, 8 June 1929.
63 *Birmingham Post*, 1 June 1929.
64 *Morning Post*, 1 June 1929.
65 Summarised Diary, 18 February 1929.
66 Letter dated 20 March 1929.
67 Summarised Diary, 14 May 1929.
68 *Ibid.*, 12 June 1929.
69 Letter dated 6 August 1929.
70 Summarised Diary, 31 July 1929.
71 *Ibid.*, 23 July 1929.
72 *Ibid.*, 30 October 1929.
73 *Ibid.*, 27 October 1929.
74 He mentioned the ambassadorship to the United States, but shortly afterwards he noted in his diary, 'Another job for me has gone as Sir Robert Lindsay has gone to Washington.' (13 November 1929.)
75 Summarised Diary, 29 October 1929.
76 This account is from a press cutting dated 7 November 1929 which Reith kept in his scrapbook. The paper is not identified.
77 Letter dated 6 November 1929.
78 Letter dated 26 November 1929.
79 Summarised Diary, 21 December 1929.
80 *Ibid.*, 30 November 1929.
81 *Ibid.*, 7 January 1930.
82 *Ibid.*, 7 February 1930. Not everyone shared Reith's view that Clarendon was simply an aristocratic dunderhead. He was descended on his father's side from the Villiers family, who were close friends of the Stuart kings, and on his mother's from a daughter of Oliver Cromwell; *The Dictionary of National Biography* said that heredity produced in him 'a blend of Roundhead integrity with the gaiety and tolerance of the Cavaliers'. During his Governor-Generalship he appears to have impressed all sections of political opinion in South Africa by his impartiality and straightforwardness. The *DNB* article is equally complimentary about his later period as Lord Chamberlain: 'His integrity, courtesy, and good manners, together with a gentle and tolerant understanding, made him many friends in the theatrical and literary professions.' Clarendon's views about Reith and the BBC died with him. His grandson, who succeeded him in 1955, confirmed that he left no diaries or papers relating to his chairmanship. (Letter to the author from the Earl of Clarendon, 10 January 1992.)

CHAPTER 9

1 Andrew Boyle told this story in his biography of Reith without disclosing a source for it. The present author had it from Whitley's son Oliver, who joined the BBC in the 1930s and retired as Managing Director of the External Services in 1972.
2 Summarised Diary, 21 May 1930.
3 *Ibid.*, 3 March 1930.
4 *Ibid.*, 29 May 1930.
5 *Ibid.*, 28 May 1930.
6 *Homes and Gardens*, February 1932. It is now an old people's home. Forty yards away the M40 motorway (happily in a culvert at this point) slices its way through what used to be the garden.
7 Letter dated 5 May 1930. Gainford Papers MS 102.
8 *Ibid.*
9 Summarised Diary, 27 March 1930.
10 *Ibid.*, 2 June 1930.
11 *Ibid.*, 11 June 1930.
12 Letter dated 11 June 1930. Gainford Papers MS 102.
13 *Ibid.*
14 *Into the Wind*, p. 132.
15 Summarised Diary, 21 July 1930.
16 Speech at Torquay, 30 August 1930.
17 *The Times*, 23 October 1930. The BBC had embarked on public concert-giving as early as 1924. A detailed account of how its policy had developed may be found in 'The BBC Symphony Orchestra, 1930–1980', by Nicholas Kenyon, BBC, 1981.
18 *The BBC Year Book 1931*, p. 192.
19 *Ibid.*, p. 207.
20 *Ibid.*, p. 212.
21 *Daily Herald*, 31 March 1931. A more admiring piece of writing – a 'character sketch' by Louise Morgan – appeared in the magazine *Everyman*. 'How Carlyle would have loved him!' she wrote. 'He is the type of "hero" – dictator, if you will – that the time is

throwing up in answer to an abysmal need.' (*Everyman*, 19 November 1932.)

22 Wolfe, *op. cit.*, p. 4.

23 B. Seebohm Rowntree, *Poverty and Progress*, Longman, Green & Co., London, 1941, quoted in Scannell and Cardiff, *op. cit.*

24 If a sense of vocation had continued to be an essential qualification for BBC employment, several distinguished careers would have been nipped in the bud. Reith's successor several times removed, Alasdair Milne, recorded that when he came down from Oxford in 1954 he applied to the BBC only after being rejected by Tootal Ties, Yardley's Lavender, and a large advertising agency. (Alasdair Milne, *DG: The Memoirs of a British Broadcaster*, Hodder & Stoughton, London, 1988.) More recently, John Birt appeared for a time to think that there was nothing inappropriate about 'offering his services' as Director-General through a private company.

25 Lambert, *op. cit.*, p. 9.

26 Harman Grisewood, *One Thing at a Time*, Hutchinson, London, 1968, p. 90.

27 *The Times*, 6 September 1963.

28 Stobart had been recruited from the Inspectorate of the Board of Education. He was the author of *The Glory that Was Greece* and *The Grandeur that Was Rome*. He was credited with an encyclopedic knowledge of orders of precedence and styles of address. Reith was much impressed by his *savoir vivre* and relied heavily on him in matters of etiquette.

29 Janet Adam Smith, 'T. S. Eliot and "The Listener"', *The Listener*, 21 January 1965.

30 Summarised Diary, 17 October 1930.

31 A version of this party piece of Reith's survives in the BBC Sound Archives – recorded, oddly enough, in Germany; he performed it during his visit to Berlin in August 1930 described below. It was written by Charles Murray (1864–1941), Scotland's best-known vernacular poet of the early part of this century. Murray spent his working life as an engineer in South Africa, but drew heavily in his poetry on the rural Aberdeenshire of his childhood. 'The Whistle', as the poem is properly called, first appeared in *Chambers' Journal* in 1906 and quickly found its way into the anthologies.

32 *Into the Wind*, p. 138.

33 Summarised Diary, 7 September 1930.

34 *Ibid.*, 8 January 1931.

35 *Strand Magazine*, March 1931.

36 Diary, 21 February 1931.

37 *Ibid.*, 24 February 1931.

38 *Ibid.*, 19 March 1931.

39 *Ibid.*, 31 May 1931.

40 *Ibid.*, 15 October 1931.

41 *Christian Science Monitor*, 6 June 1931.

42 Letter dated 11 June 1931.

43 Diary, 29 April 1931.

44 *Ibid.*, May 1931.

45 Whitley's closeness to Reith caused some restiveness among the other Governors. An interesting letter from Rendall to Gainford survives from the middle of 1932: 'It seems to me that a dangerous heresy is growing up, that there are two Governors only of the BBC, viz: Whitley and Sir John . . . Whitley is so wise and tactful that it doesn't do much harm now: but it is *wrong* . . . Lady S is right in saying that we are apt to be ignored . . .' (Letter dated 29 June 1932, Gainford Papers MS 102.)

46 *Into the Wind*, p. 176.

47 It was at this time that he conceived the idea of writing up his war experiences in book form.

48 Diary, 17 February 1932.

49 *The Birmingham Gazette*, 14 May 1932.

50 Reith became very security conscious after this. When they went away on holiday that summer he nailed up all the windows of the house. See also pp. 201 and 202–4.

51 Diary, 29 May 1932.

52 *Ibid.*, 2 May 1932.

53 Gainford wrote to Clarendon in the autumn of 1932 giving him news of the new building: '. . . everything is working according to plan except that our big Hall, which was intended to be large enough to seat 800 people and afford ample room for our best BBC

Orchestra, has now proved to be quite inadequate . . .' (Letter dated 29 September 1932, Gainford Papers MS 102.)

54 Letter from Rendall to Gainford, 25 September 1931, Gainford Papers MS 102.

55 Lambert, *op. cit.*, p. 33. Reith became so sensitive about the inscription that he asked Marmaduke Tudsbery, the Corporation's Civil Engineer, whether it could be removed. For many years it was accessible only to classical scholars, but there is now a small plaque with an English translation: 'This Temple of the Arts and Muses is dedicated to Almighty God by the first Governors of Broadcasting in the year 1931, Sir John Reith being Director-General. It is their prayer that good seed sown may bring forth a good harvest, that all things hostile to peace or purity may be banished from this house, and that the people, inclining their ears to whatsoever things are beautiful and honest and of good report, may tread the path of wisdom and uprightness.'

56 *Hansard*, vol. 276, col. 325.

57 He found Corporation social occasions something of a trial, too. In the summer of 1933, he went down to the BBC sports ground at Motspur Park for the day: 'Having bowled the first ball in a Ladies' cricket match, I thought I would like to umpire, so did this for the whole second innings . . . It gave me something definite to do, which I am glad of, always finding these staff affairs rather embarrassing and lonely.' (Diary, 1 July 1933.)

58 A self-reproachful note in the diary in September indicates that he had still not made a start on this exercise in staff relations.

59 *The Weekend Review*, 21 May 1932.

60 Diary, 15 May 1932. These ideas of Reith's were given wider currency when he contributed an article in almost identical terms to the 28 May issue of *John O'London's Weekly* under the title 'Ten Years of Broadcasting Democracy in Theory and Practice'.

61 This was Sarah Gertrude Millin's biography which had been published that year.

62 Diary, 4 July 1934.

63 *Ibid.*, 2 July 1934. Hitler had been worried for some time by the threat posed by the *Sturm Abteilungen*, the armed force of the Party. The previous weekend, Ernst Röhm, the SA leader, and a large number of his Brownshirt commanders had been rounded up and liquidated.

64 Control Board, *Statement on Proposed Staff Association*, 27 May 1930.

65 *Daily Express*, 19 March 1934.

66 *Ibid.*, 23 March 1934.

67 Diary, 15 January 1935.

68 *Ibid.*, 7 December 1932.

69 *Ibid.*, 30 January 1933.

70 *Ibid.*, 19 September 1933. Privately, he entertained all manner of other fancies, too. On a visit to Eton, the Vice-Provost told him that after his appearance at the Political Society there all the boys had said they would like him for their new Headmaster. 'I have often thought I would like this job,' he wrote, 'but I should not actually do so, partly because of the dreadful house, but more because the Headmaster is junior to the Provost and Vice-Provost.' (Diary, 3 June 1933.)

71 *Ibid.*, 20 June 1933.

72 Letter dated 30 October 1932.

73 Diary, 17 November 1932.

74 *Ibid.*, 18 January 1933.

75 *Ibid.*, 29 March 1933.

76 *Ibid.*, 21 December 1932.

77 *Ibid.*, 11 January 1933. By the time the summer came, he was dining with Mrs Hamilton at the Carlton Grill and accompanying her to the Russian ballet at the Alhambra; she told him this was a 'humanising experience' for him. (Diary, 19 July 1933.)

78 He had voiced his criticisms to Carpendale some months previously when they had gone together to visit Hartlebury Castle near Worcester. 'He was very glum and morose all day.' (Diary, 19 May 1932.)

79 Diary, 23 February 1933.

80 *Ibid.*, 24 March 1933.

81 Letter dated 17 March 1933.

82 Diary, 27 March 1933.

83 *Ibid.*, 26 May 1933.
84 *Ibid.*, 22 April 1933. Others interviewed included Henry Willink, then a barrister, later Churchill's Minister of Health and Master of Magdalene College, Cambridge.
85 Note by Reith, June 1963, quoted in Briggs, *op. cit.*, Vol. 2, p. 243.
86 Quoted in Gerald Beadle, *Television: A Critical Review*, George Allen and Unwin Ltd, London, 1963, p. 41.
87 BBC Written Archives, undated memorandum headed 'Terms of Reference'.
88 W. E. G. Murray, BBC internal memorandum, *Note on 'Yesterday's Television Test'*, 10 October 1928.
89 Beadle, *op. cit.*, p. 38.
90 *Ibid.*, p. 41.
91 Diary, 28 August 1934.
92 *Ibid.*, 25 October 1934.
93 *Ibid.*, 18 May 1934.
94 Letter dated 20 May 1934.
95 Letter dated 23 May 1934.
96 Letter dated 2 June 1934.
97 Letter dated 19 December 1933.
98 Diary, 13 January 1935.
99 Reith was quoting from an elegy on the death of Sir Stanley Maude, the British army commander in Mesopotamia who died of cholera at Baghdad in 1917. The poet was one of Maude's junior officers, James Griffyth Fairfax, then a lieutenant in the Army Service Corps. Australian-born and Oxford-educated, he was later briefly a Conservative MP.
100 Diary, 3 February 1935.

CHAPTER 10

1 Lord Bridgeman, already ill when he was appointed at the age of seventy in March, died after six months. He was succeeded by R. C. Norman, the brother of the Governor of the Bank of England.
2 Diary, 10 March 1935.
3 *Ibid.*, 11 April 1935.
4 *Ibid.*, 22 April 1935.
5 *Ibid.*, 24 April 1935.
6 *Ibid.*, 25 April 1935.
7 *Ibid.*, 26 April 1935.
8 *Ibid.*, 28 March 1935.
9 Letter dated 26 April 1935.
10 Diary, 8 May 1935.
11 *Ibid.*, 26 June 1935.
12 *Memorandum of Evidence Submitted to the Broadcasting Committee by the BBC*, May 1935.
13 Diary, 8 May 1935.
14 *Ibid.*, 16 May 1935.
15 *Ibid.*, 24 May 1935.
16 *Ibid.*, 26 May 1935.
17 *Ibid.*, 1 June 1934.
18 *Ibid.*, 30 April 1935.
19 *Ibid.*, 25 June 1935.
20 Letter dated 18 October 1935.
21 Diary, 25 October 1935.
22 *Ibid.*, 29 November 1935.
23 *Ibid.*, 16 September 1935.
24 *Ibid.*, 12 November 1935.
25 *Ibid.*, 14 October 1935.
26 *Ibid.*, 24 November 1935.
27 *Ibid.*, 9 December 1935. Muriel hadn't been in the best of health, either: 'Muriel saw Sir Stanley Hewett on Wednesday – fatness, rheumatism, indigestion and lassitude. He has put her on a trial diet and pills – glands apparently. I do hope she gets much better.' (Diary, 8 November 1935.)
28 *Ibid.*, 14 December 1935.
29 *Ibid.*, 15 December 1935.
30 *Ibid.*, 21 December 1935.
31 Letter dated 17 December 1935.
32 Reith heard again from his brother the following summer: 'Can't you get your publicity man to give us a rest from the incessant paragraphs and photographs about yourself?' he wrote. 'I see no way of relief except to change my name by deed poll. I propose asking my solicitor about the procedure when he comes to see me on Wednesday . . .' This time Reith was amused: 'A magnificent letter from the Rev. Archibald,' he noted in his diary, and it joined the other in his scrapbook. (Diary, 15 June 1936.)
33 *Into the Wind*, p. 245.
34 *Ibid.*, p. 247.
35 Letter dated 28 December 1935.
36 Diary, 31 December 1935.
37 *Ibid.*, 1 January 1936.
38 A diary note six months previously records lunching with Lady

Constance Milnes-Gaskell, who was to be Woman of the Bed Chamber to Queen Mary from 1937 to 1953: 'Talked of the terrible way the Prince of Wales carries on. It is indeed very tragic. Mrs Simpson has been figuring in *Time*. It is damnable.' (Diary, 20 June 1935.)

39 Diary, 21 January 1936.

40 *Into the Wind*, p. 255. It is possible that Dawson was simply baffled by Reith's idiosyncratic pronunciation. He was still going on about accidie thirty years later when he gave his rectorial address at Glasgow University. A recording survives in the BBC Sound Archives, and the word comes out as 'aksiday', with the stress on the first syllable.

41 Diary, 3 January 1936.

42 *Ibid.*, 24 April 1936. Lady Bridgeman had been made a Governor after the death of her husband.

43 *Ibid.*, 13 May 1936.

44 *Ibid.*, 3 June 1936.

45 *Ibid.*, 22 June 1936.

46 *Daily Telegraph*, 4 March 1936.

47 Diary, 28 February 1936. Some of his fantasies were of the 'I-want-to-be-a-train-driver' variety. He went on one of the *Queen Mary*'s trial trips that spring and was introduced to the Commodore. 'How I envy him his job,' he wrote. 'I asked him if he would like to change places with me.' (Diary, 17 April 1936.)

48 *Ibid.*, 16 October 1936.

49 *Ibid.*, 18 October 1936.

50 He had most recently had confirmation of this over lunch with Ramsay MacDonald: 'He agreed that the Cabinet was jealous of our power and efficiency and that some of them were jealous of me, though he said it was more that I was a good lightning conductor.' (Diary, 6 May 1936.)

51 Diary, 29 November 1936.

52 *The Times*, 23 November 1936.

53 Diary, August and September 1936.

54 *Hansard*, vol. 311, cols 974–80, 29 April 1936.

55 Diary, 12 June 1936.

56 Lambert, *op. cit.*, p. 258.

57 Diary, 6 November 1936.

58 *Report of the Special Board of Inquiry*, Cmnd 5337 (1936).

59 *Into the Wind*, p. 230.

60 Lambert, *op. cit.*, p. 159.

61 *Hansard*, vol. 318, col. 2370, 17 December 1936.

62 *Into the Wind*, p. 262.

63 Lambert, *op. cit.*, p. 303.

64 *Into the Wind*, p. 264.

65 Diary, 3 December 1936.

66 *Ibid.*, 6 December 1936.

67 *Ibid.*, 10 December 1936.

68 *Ibid.*, 11 December 1936.

69 *Ibid.*, 13 December 1936.

70 *Ibid.*, 15 January 1937.

71 *Ibid.*, 20 February 1937. Fisher had been brought into politics as President of the Board of Education by Lloyd George, and was the author of the Education Act of 1918.

72 *Ibid.*, 9 March 1937.

73 *Ibid.*, 4 May 1937.

74 *Ibid.*, 12 May 1937. His temper had not been improved when he discovered that he did not figure in the Honours List that had appeared two days previously. He was 'infuriated, amazed and disappointed'; he had expected a GCVO at the very least. (Diary, 10 May 1937.)

75 *Ibid.*, 20 December 1938.

76 *Ibid.*, 7 April 1937.

77 *Ibid.*, 18 May 1937.

78 *Ibid.*, 21 May 1937. Woodrooffe survived to commentate another day. He was next heard of eating his hat after predicting the wrong result at the 1938 Cup Final. The Spithead recording was kept under lock and key in the Recorded Programmes Department and was not heard again until 1948 when it was featured in a programme called *Mirror of the Month* produced by Michael Barsley.

79 *Ibid.*, 11 June 1937.

80 *Ibid.*, 14 June 1937.

81 *Ibid.*, 26 July 1937.

82 *Ibid.*, 20 August 1937.

83 Article by George Slocombe in

Nash's Magazine, September 1937.

84 Diary, 14 September 1937.

85 *Ibid.*, 5 March 1937.

86 *Ibid.*, 15 October 1937.

87 *Ibid.*, 7 October 1937.

88 *Ibid.*, 12 October 1937.

89 *Ibid.*, 10 November 1937.

90 *Ibid.*, 18 and 19 October 1937.

91 *Ibid.*, 22 November 1937.

92 *Ibid.*, 4 January 1938.

93 *Ibid.*, 22 March 1938.

94 *Ibid.*, 12 March 1938. He had been to a party at the German Embassy two nights previously and noted that he had quite enjoyed himself: 'I told Ribbentrop to tell Hitler that the BBC was not anti-Nazi, and I invited them to have my opposite number come over to visit us. I said I would "put the flag up for him".' (Diary, 10 March 1938.)

95 *Ibid.*, 5 May 1938. A diary entry the following year indicated that he had reverted to being a teetotaller 'after a year and a quarter otherwise'. (Diary, 15 May 1939.)

96 *Ibid.*, 1 April 1938.

97 *Ibid.*, 16 April 1938.

98 *Into the Wind*, p. 307.

99 *Ibid.*, p. 310.

100 Boyle, *op. cit.*, p. 292. 'Many years later he chided me for not having insisted over the lunch table on his staying with the BBC,' Beadle wrote in his memoirs; 'but who was I to throw my weight about in a matter of such high politics?' (Beadle, *op. cit.*, p. 27.)

101 *Into the Wind*, p. 311.

102 *Ibid.*, p. 312.

103 Diary, 3 June 1938.

104 Wilson had made an arrangement for Reith to go and see Beharrell in his office. Reith insisted that Beharrell should come to him.

105 Diary, 3 May 1938.

106 Mary Agnes Hamilton, *Remembering My Good Friends*, Jonathan Cape, London, 1944, p. 285.

107 Boyle, *op. cit.*, p. 289.

108 *Into the Wind*, p. 311.

109 Hamilton, *op. cit.*, p. 286.

110 Diary, 6 June 1938. Fisher later said that he had told Hore-Belisha that the idea was fantastic.

111 *Ibid.*, 8 June 1938.

112 *Ibid.*

113 *Into the Wind*, p. 315.

114 *Ibid.*, p. 313; Diary, 14 and 15 June 1938.

115 *Into the Wind*, p. 316.

116 Diary, 25 June 1938.

117 *Ibid.*, 28 June 1938.

118 *Ibid.*, 29 June 1938.

119 Conversation with Miss Stanley, December 1991, at Salwayash, Dorset. The text appears in *Into the Wind*, p. 319. Reith made only one change in her draft, which ended with the words '*Au revoir* and thank you'. 'Of course I wasn't going to let the *au revoir* implication stand,' he wrote. (Diary, 1 July 1938.) It was altered to 'Goodbye'. One small point of style would have roused the suspicion of an alert textual critic – Reith was incapable of writing two paragraphs that did not contain a semi-colon.

120 Letters dated 3 July 1938.

121 Diary, 13 July 1938. It was September before Reith finally accepted the payment. When Norman wrote at the end of July to ask whether he might release the cheque, Reith tore up his letter and sent no reply. (Diary, 28 July and letter dated 8 September 1938.)

122 Letter dated 19 July 1938.

CHAPTER 11

1 *Into the Wind*, p. 328.

2 *Ibid.*, p. 329.

3 Diary, 16 October 1938. The previous month, however, he had written: 'What I miss appallingly is the class of man and capacity of man which one had there.' (Diary, 28 September 1938.)

4 *Ibid.*, 15 September 1938.

5 Boyle, *op. cit.*, p. 298.

6 Diary, 15 and 19 June 1939.

7 *Ibid.*, 27 April 1939

8 Letter dated 24 April 1939.

9 Diary, 5 May 1939.

10 *Ibid.*, 24 June 1938.

11 This reduced the cost from £373 to £199. (Diary, 14 March 1939.)
12 Diary, 2 August 1939.
13 Tom McCabe was now Chairman of the Federal Reserve Bank.
14 *Into the Wind*, p. 345.
15 Diary, 12 September 1939.
16 *Ibid.*, 21 September 1939.
17 *Ibid.*, 6 October 1939.
18 *Ibid.*, 5 December 1939.
19 *Ibid.*, 8 December 1939.

CHAPTER 12
1 Iain Macleod, *Neville Chamberlain*, Frederick Muller, London, 1961, p. 286.
2 Diary, 5 January 1940.
3 *Into the Wind*, p. 352.
4 *The Times*, 6 January 1940.
5 Diary, 15 January 1940.
6 *Ibid.*, 20 January 1940.
7 *Into the Wind*, p. 367.
8 *News Chronicle*, 3 April 1940.
9 Diary, 16 January 1940.
10 *Into the Wind*, p. 367. Reith also believed that the British Council and Chatham House (the Royal Institute for International Affairs) should be under his ministerial direction.
11 Amery, who had covered the Boer War for *The Times*, had been First Lord of the Admiralty and Colonial and Dominions Secretary in the twenties; he served as Secretary of State for India from 1940 to 1945.
12 *Into the Wind*, p. 360.
13 Diary, 6 April 1940.
14 *Into the Wind*, p. 373.
15 Diary, 12 May 1940.
16 *Into the Wind*, p. 385.
17 *Ibid.*, p. 383.
18 Diary, 27 May 1940.
19 *Ibid.*, 3 June 1940.
20 *Ibid.*, 15 June 1940.
21 *Ibid.*, 15 July 1940.
22 Letter from the Bishop dated 20 June 1940.
23 Diary, 19 July 1940.
24 *Ibid.*, 3 July 1940.
25 *Into the Wind*, p. 390.
26 Diary, 3 September 1940.
27 *Ibid.*, 4 September 1940.
28 *Into the Wind*, p. 395.

29 *Ibid.*, p. 401.
30 Diary, 2 October 1940.
31 *Into the Wind*, p. 403.
32 Letter dated 6 October 1940.
33 Diary, 5 October 1940.
34 *Ibid.*, 22 October 1940.
35 *The Spectator*, 18 October 1940.
36 *Into the Wind*, p. 411.
37 Diary, 27 November 1940.
38 *Into the Wind*, p. 400.
39 Winston S. Churchill, *The Second World War*, Vol. 2, 'Their Finest Hour', Cassell and Co., London, 1949.
40 *Into the Wind*, p. 424. The line is from *The Winter's Tale*.
41 *The Architects' Journal*, 6 March 1941.
42 *Into the Wind*, p. 414.
43 *Ibid.*
44 Stuart, *op. cit.*, p. 273.
45 *Into the Wind*, p. 431.
46 *Ibid.*, p. 428.
47 Diary, 8 August 1941.
48 *Ibid.*, 16 September 1941.
49 *Ibid.*, 2 October 1941.
50 *Ibid.*, 12 October 1941.
51 *Ibid.*, 16 July 1941.
52 *Ibid.*, 30 September 1941.
53 *Ibid.*, 14 December 1941.
54 *Ibid.*, 21 December 1941.
55 *Ibid.*, 16 January 1942.
56 *Ibid.*, 8 December 1941.
57 *Ibid.*, 21 February 1942.
58 *Ibid.*, 1 March 1942.
59 *Into the Wind*, p. 445–6.
60 Letter dated 20 November 1956.
61 Hamilton, *op. cit.*, p. 285.

CHAPTER 13
1 Diary, 27 February 1942.
2 Letter from Anderson dated 2 March 1942.
3 Letter to Churchill dated 2 March 1942.
4 Diary, 29 March 1942.
5 *Ibid.*, 31 March 1942.
6 *Ibid.*, 9 May 1942.
7 *Ibid.*, 16 May 1942.
8 *Into the Wind*, p. 455.
9 *Railway Review*, 26 June 1942.
10 *Morning Advertiser*, 20 June 1942.
11 *Into the Wind*, p. 459.
12 Diary, 12 October 1942.

13 *Ibid.*, 31 December 1942.
14 *Ibid.*, 22 March 1943.
15 *Ibid.*, 24 March 1943.
16 Letter dated 20 April 1943.
17 *Into the Wind*, p. 471.
18 *Ibid.*, p. 472.
19 *Ibid.*, p. 476.
20 *Ibid.*, p. 477.
21 Diary, 22 August 1943.
22 *Ibid.*, 8 October 1943.
23 *Into the Wind*, p. 479.
24 Diary, 6 August 1943.
25 Boyle, *op. cit.*, p. 324. Boyle had this story from Grigg himself. The Ministry of Defence, now the custodian of War Office records, confirmed in 1991 that Joyce Wilson's service file still existed, but it had been weeded by a delicate hand and no longer contained Grigg's crude minute. (Letter dated 6 November 1991.)
26 Diary, 7 September 1943.
27 *Ibid.*, 22 December 1943.
28 *Into the Wind*, p. 485.
29 Diary, 20 May 1944.
30 The name had no significance. It happened to come next in rotation on the Admiralty's List of Ships' Names then available for use.
31 *Into the Wind*, p. 488.
32 Letter dated 1 July 1944.
33 Diary, 13 July 1944.
34 *Ibid.*, 31 July 1944.
35 *Ibid.*, 31 October 1944.
36 In his diary at this time he noted without comment that Charlie's elder son, a lieutenant in the Coldstream Guards, had been killed in action. (Diary, 3 August 1944.)
37 *Into the Wind*, p. 491.
38 Diary, 21 September 1944.
39 *Ibid.*, 1 January 1945.

CHAPTER 14
 1 Diary, 18 November 1944.
 2 *Ibid.*, 5 December 1944.
 3 *Into the Wind*, p. 501.
 4 Diary, 11 January 1945.
 5 *Ibid.*, 17 January 1945.
 6 *Ibid.*, 26 January 1945.
 7 *Ibid.*, 18 February 1945.
 8 *Ibid.*, 24 February 1945.
 9 *Ibid.*, 27 February 1945.

10 *Ibid.*, 5 March 1945.
11 *Into the Wind*, p. 503.
12 Diary, 7 March 1945. The reality was even worse than the imagining. 'I simply cannot stand the crowds of typists, shopgirls, sluts, prostitutes, hooligans and suchlike which crowd the streets,' he wrote a month later. 'I ought never have to be jostled about by such as these.' (Diary, 20 April 1945.)
13 Letter dated 22 March 1945.
14 Boyle, *op. cit.*, p. 332.
15 Diary, 26 May 1945.
16 *Ibid.*, 26 June 1945.
17 *Ibid.*, 5 April 1945.
18 *Ibid.*, 30 April 1945.
19 *Ibid.*, 2 May 1945.
20 *Ibid.*, 10 May 1945.
21 *Ibid.*, 3 June 1945.
22 *Into the Wind*, p. 516.
23 An earlier outing to Windsor by charabanc had not been a success. The guide turned up forty-three minutes late, and the Dominion party was soon more than doubled in size 'by the adhesion of all and sundry'. The Head of Government Hospitality was attending the Potsdam Conference. Reith wrote a blistering letter of complaint to his deputy. (Diary, 28 July 1945.)
24 Diary, 15 August 1945.
25 *Ibid.*, 29 May 1946.

CHAPTER 15
 1 Diary, 26 July 1945.
 2 *Ibid.*, 8 October 1945.
 3 *Ibid.*, 15 November 1945.
 4 Letter dated 1 January 1946.
 5 Letter dated 11 January 1946.
 6 Diary, 12 January 1946.
 7 *Ibid.*, 3 February 1946.
 8 *Ibid.*, 2 March 1946.
 9 Letter dated 9 March 1946.
10 Diary, 12 March 1946.
11 *Interim Report of the New Towns Committee*, Cmnd. 6759, March 1946. A second interim report, published on 9 April (Cmnd. 6794), dealt with such matters as the acquisition of land, the process of

settlement, the provision of public services and finance.

12 *The New Statesman and Nation*, 6 April 1946.

13 *The Spectator*, 5 April 1946.

14 Diary, 21 May 1946.

15 *Ibid.*, 30 June 1946.

16 *Ibid.*, 11 July 1946.

17 *Final Report of the New Towns Committee*, Cmnd. 6876, July 1946.

18 Diary, 15 September 1946.

19 *Ibid.*, 10 April 1946.

20 *Ibid.*, 1 January 1946.

21 *Ibid.*, 30 September 1946.

22 *Ibid.*, 4, 9 and 14 December 1946.

23 *Ibid.*, 16 December 1946.

24 *Ibid.*, 20 February 1947.

25 *Ibid.*, 3 February 1947.

26 *Ibid.*, 24 May 1947.

27 Letter dated 17 July 1947.

28 Diary, 3 October 1947.

29 Letter dated 4 June 1947.

30 When the first series was broadcast the following year, Reith gave it his critical attention: 'Listened to the first "Reith Lecture" by Bertrand Russell, forsooth. He went far too quickly and has a bad voice anyhow. And it was actually recorded which depreciated its value greatly. However, I wrote him a civil note which is more than Mr Romanes or Mr Rede could do.' (Diary, 26 December 1948.)

31 Diary, 11 November 1947.

32 *Ibid.*, 17 and 18 May 1947.

33 *Into the Wind*, p. 531. He was clearly rather proud of this passage. When he read it in proof to Muriel and Christopher some weeks later, however, he recorded with exasperation that 'neither got the point of it.' (Diary, 30 January 1948.)

34 Diary, 20 November 1947.

35 Aspiring BBC secretaries were not normally seen by the Director-General or even the Director of Administration. Miss Wilson was seen by both and began work in the latter's directorate two months later. She left at the end of the year to return to the ATS.

36 Diary, 31 December 1947.

37 *Radio Times*, 5 March 1948.

38 Diary, 15 December 1948.

39 Letter dated 28 December 1948.

40 Diary, 20 February 1948.

41 *Ibid.*, 9 March 1948.

42 Silkin, the Minister of Town and Country Planning, had invited him to take on Stevenage in addition to Hemel, but he was not attracted to the idea: 'All very well that I should have to clean up all the dirty work there.' (Diary, 24 February 1948.)

43 Diary, 28 May 1948.

44 *Ibid.*, 21 October 1948.

45 *Ibid.*, 13 April 1948.

46 *Ibid.*, 25 September 1948.

47 *Ibid.*, 2 October 1948.

48 *Ibid.*, 6 December 1948. He also at one time wanted her to be chief WREN. (Conversation with Marista Leishman, Edinburgh, March 1990.)

49 Conversation, Edinburgh, March 1990.

50 Diary, 29 July 1948.

51 *Ibid.*, 3 October 1948.

52 *Ibid.*, 4 October 1948.

53 *Ibid.*, 30 March, 5 April 1949.

54 *Ibid.*, 7 April 1949.

55 *Ibid.*, 30 May 1949.

56 *Ibid.*, 30 June 1949.

57 *Ibid.*

58 *Ibid.*, 7 October 1949.

59 *Ibid.*, 9 September 1949.

60 *Ibid.*, 10 September 1949.

61 Conversation with Mrs Charles Hargreaves, London, June 1992.

62 Diary, 12 September 1949.

63 *Ibid.*, 14 September 1949.

64 The families remained in touch, however, and the following year Reith agreed to propose the toast at Dawn's twenty-first birthday party at the Hyde Park Hotel. At the last minute he telephoned to say that he wasn't coming, and Muriel, Christopher and Marista went without him. 'I was told that he was fully dressed, sitting waiting for somebody to go and fetch him.' (Conversation with Mrs Charles Hargreaves, London, June 1992.)

65 *Daily Telegraph*, 17 November 1949.

CHAPTER 16
1 Diary, 16 March 1950.
2 Letter dated 5 February 1950.
3 Diary, 19 April 1950.
4 *A note on some of the major issues for the Broadcasting Commission*, memorandum dated 21 June 1950; copy preserved in Reith's scrapbooks.
5 Diary, 13 August 1950. See p. 114.
6 *Ibid.*, 17 August 1950.
7 Letter dated 10 September 1950.
8 Diary, 13 September 1950.
9 *Ibid.*, 24 September 1950.
10 *Ibid.*, 6 October 1950.
11 *Ibid.*, 30 September 1950.
12 *Ibid.*, 5 October 1950.
13 He was getting £3500 from the CTB, £2500 from the NFFC, and £1500 from Hemel Hempstead.
14 Diary, 16 October 1950.
15 *Ibid.*, 6 November 1950.
16 *Observer*, 19 November 1950.
17 Diary, 13 November 1950.
18 *Ibid.*, 20 December 1950.
19 *Ibid.*, 16 April 1951.
20 *Ibid.*, 24 April 1951.
21 *Ibid.*, 18 May 1951.
22 *Notes on Beveridge Committee's Report sent to Mr Herbert Morrison*, memorandum dated 31 January 1951; copy preserved in Reith's scrapbooks.
23 Letter dated 4 June 1951.
24 Letter dated 2 October 1951.
25 Diary, 6 October 1951.
26 *Ibid.*, 31 December 1950.
27 *Ibid.*, 30 and 31 March 1951.
28 *Ibid.*, 14 May 1951.
29 Conversation with Marista Leishman, Edinburgh, March 1990.
30 Diary, 1 July 1951.
31 *Ibid.*, 4 August 1951.
32 *Ibid.*, 6 August 1951.
33 *Ibid.*, 10 August 1951.
34 *Ibid.*, 3 October 1951.
35 *Ibid.*, 3 November 1951.
36 *Ibid.*, 16 December 1951.
37 Letter dated 24 February 1952.
38 Diary, 2 March 1952.
39 *Ibid.*, 29 March 1952.
40 *The Times*, 21 March 1952.
41 Letter dated 21 March 1952.
42 Diary, 19 April 1952.
43 *Ibid.*, 25 April 1952.
44 Marista, who heard the quotation many times over the years, believed it was the only line of Kant which he knew, but that it would have gone very ill with anyone who had said, 'That's very interesting, John, now would you please expand on that?' (Conversation with Marista Leishman, Edinburgh, March 1990.)
45 Letter dated 25 May 1952.
46 Lord Moran: *Winston Churchill, The Struggle for Survival 1940–65*. Taken from the diaries of Lord Moran, Constable, London, 1966.
47 *Observer*, 15 June 1952.
48 Letter dated 20 June 1952.
49 Diary, 20 July 1952. This was William Clark, who later became Sir Anthony Eden's press officer. He resigned over Suez, and subsequently went to work for the World Bank in Washington.
50 *Daily Express*, 18 September 1952.
51 Diary, 20 September 1952. Until 1918 Tanganyika had been German East Africa. Charles Stuart surmised that the man had presumably seen service there under General von Lettow Vorbeck during the First World War.
52 *Ibid.*, 30 September 1952.
53 Letter dated 19 December 1952.
54 Diary, 5 November 1952.
55 *Ibid.*, 9 December 1952.
56 *Ibid.*, 17 December 1952.
57 *Ibid.*, 20 December 1952.
58 *Ibid.*, 21 January 1953.
59 *Ibid.*, 20 February 1953.
60 Conversation with Sir Ian Jacob, Woodbridge, Suffolk, September 1990.
61 Diary, 17 March 1953.
62 *Ibid.*, 28 February 1953.
63 Letter from Peter Hay dated 6 April 1953.
64 *Evening Standard*, 13 May 1953.
65 *Daily Telegraph*, 14 May 1953.
66 House of Commons *Hansard*, 10 June 1953, vol. 516, cols 209–11.
67 House of Lords *Hansard*, 30 July 1953, vol. 183, cols 1189–97 and 1198–1201.
68 Diary, 20 June 1953.

69 *Ibid.*, 22 June 1953.
70 *Ibid.*, 24 June 1953.
71 *Ibid.*, 12 August 1953.
72 *Ibid.*, 26 August 1953.
73 *Ibid.*, 4 September 1953.
74 *Ibid.*, 14 September 1953.
75 *Ibid.*, 16 September 1953.
76 *Ibid.*, 18 September 1953.
77 Letter dated 7 December 1953.
78 *Observer*, 22 November 1953. It was not only the precedence of England which concerned Reith at this period. A letter survives in his scrapbook from Sir Anthony Bevir, at that time the Prime Minister's Appointments Secretary. Reith had written to him about 'a friend' who had asked for a viscountcy; the friend is clearly himself. (Letter dated 2 September 1954.)
79 Letter dated 15 January 1954.
80 Conversation with Sir Ian Jacob at Woodbridge, Suffolk, September 1990.
81 Letter dated 5 March 1954.
82 Diary, 20 July 1954.
83 *Ibid.*, 28 August 1954.
84 *Ibid.*, 28 September 1954.
85 *Ibid.*, 19 December 1954.
86 *Ibid.*, 30 September 1954.
87 *Sunday Express*, 31 October 1954.
88 Letter dated 25 October 1954.
89 Diary, 17 November 1954.
90 *Ibid.*, 25 December 1954.
91 *Ibid.*, 26 December 1954.
92 *Ibid.*, 28 December 1954.
93 *Ibid.*, 9 January 1955.
94 *Ibid.*, 11 January 1955.
95 *Ibid.*, 17 January 1955.
96 *Ibid.*, 7 April 1955.
97 *Ibid.*, 8 April 1955.
98 *Ibid.*, 15 April 1955.
99 *Ibid.*, 27 May 1955.
100 *The Times*, 29 April 1955.
101 Diary, 13 September 1955.
102 *Ibid.*, 23 September 1955.
103 *Ibid.*, 3 August 1955.
104 *Ibid.*, 22 September 1955. Reith does not seem to have been invited to the inaugural banquet at Guildhall. The Chairman of the BBC and a number of senior staff were. All initially declined, but Cadogan and Sir Ian Jacob were eventually present on the night. (See Bernard Sendall, *Independent Television in Britain*, Vol. 1, Macmillan, London, 1982, pp. 127–8.)
105 Letter dated 21 September 1955.
106 Letter dated 22 September 1955.
107 Diary, 21 November 1955.
108 *Ibid.*, 12 March 1956.
109 *Ibid.*, 3 June 1956.
110 The author was Walter Angus Elmslie. In the fashion of the day, the book carried a long explanatory sub-title: 'Being some chapters in the history of the Livingstonia mission in British Central Africa'. It was published by Oliphant & Co., London and Edinburgh, 1899.
111 Diary, 25 October 1956.
112 *Ibid.*, 29 October 1956.
113 *Ibid.*, 29 September 1956.
114 *Ibid.*, 5 September 1956.
115 *Ibid.*, 19 December 1956.
116 *Ibid.*, 31 December 1956.
117 *Ibid.*, 4 January 1957.
118 This was no mere affectation. When summertime began, on 14 April, he wrote: 'I was glad because it's the first step to winter', and another entry, on 1 June, reads: 'Only 3 weeks off the longest day, which I always welcome because winter is coming.' Reith's liking for the dark months of the year was a rooted preference.
119 Diary, 13 January 1957.
120 *Ibid.*, 27 January 1957.
121 *Ibid.*, 29 January 1957.
122 Letter dated 17 April 1957.
123 Diary, 6 August 1957.
124 *Ibid.*, 20 August 1957.
125 *Ibid.*, 24 November 1957.
126 *Ibid.*, 5 December 1957.
127 *Ibid.*, 7 December 1957.
128 *Ibid.*, 10 December 1957.
129 *Ibid.*, 23 December 1957.
130 *Ibid.*, 25 December 1957.
131 *Ibid.*, 27 December 1957.
132 *Ibid.*, 30 January 1958.
133 *Ibid.*, 2 February 1958.
134 *Ibid.*, 23 September 1958.
135 *Ibid.*, 2 October 1958.
136 *Ibid.*, 5 October 1958.
137 *Ibid.*, 13 October 1958.
138 *Ibid.*, 24 October 1958.
139 *Ibid.*, 30 November 1958.

140 *Ibid.*, 5 March 1959.
141 *Ibid.*, 26 March 1959.

CHAPTER 17
1 Diary, 10 December 1958.
2 Conversation with Sir Ian Jacob, Woodbridge, Suffolk, September 1990.
3 Diary, 26 September 1958.
4 Letter dated 1 December 1958.
5 Diary, 20 July 1959. On 13 July, Reith had written in his diary: 'A week today I'll be 70. I imagined there would have been some suggestion of a biggish lunch party.'
6 *Ibid.*, 27 July 1959.
7 *Ibid.*, 30 August 1959. Reith had not himself been teetotal for some time.
8 *Observer*, 7 June 1959.
9 *The Economist*, 8 August 1959.
10 Diary, 28 June 1959.
11 Conversation with Janet Adam Smith, London, September 1990. Andrew Boyle also had this story from Miss Adam Smith, but mistakenly places it five years later, on the eve of Reith's seventy-fifth birthday.
12 Diary, 30 July 1959.
13 *Investors' Chronicle News Letter*, 26 August 1959.
14 British Oxygen was at the time rather grandly housed in Bridgewater House, just beside St James's Palace. Reith's office had been the Earl of Ellesmere's bedroom, and his secretary sat next door in the dressing room.
15 Diary, 11 October 1959.
16 *Ibid.*, 13 October 1959.
17 *Ibid.*, 14 October 1959.
18 *Glasgow Herald*, 17 October 1959.
19 Diary, 9 November 1959.
20 *Punch*, 18 November 1959.
21 Diary, 10 December 1959. In spite of his bitterness, he took a touching interest in Marista's work for the Church Extension Committee, which was in debt to the tune of several hundred thousand pounds. He had recently written to the BBC's Scottish Controller asking whether the Committee might be featured in *The Week's Good Cause*, the space

set aside each Sunday for charitable appeals. (Letter to Andrew Stewart dated 9 November 1959.)
22 Diary, 6 December 1959.
23 Letter dated 31 December 1959.
24 Diary, 17 February 1960.
25 *Ibid.*, 10 May 1960. Donald Hodson was the Controller of the Overseas Service.
26 Conversation with Leonard Miall, Taplow, Buckinghamshire, March 1992.
27 *Sunday Times*, 11 October 1953.
28 This and other quotations later in the chapter are drawn from a conversation with Dawn Mackay (now Mrs Charles Hargreaves) in London, June 1992.
29 Conversation with Harman Grisewood, Eye, Suffolk, September 1990. Dawn Mackay recollected a conversation with Reith when it came out that all her godparents were dead. 'And have you *no* godparents?' he exclaimed. 'Then I shall appoint myself your godfather.' (Conversation with Mrs Charles Hargreaves, London, June 1992.)
30 *Glasgow Herald*, 23 June 1960.
31 Diary, 29 May 1960.
32 *Ibid.*, 25 January 1960.
33 *Ibid.*, 7 May 1960.
34 *Ibid.*, 30 May 1960.
35 *Ibid.*, 5 June 1960.
36 Conversation with Marista Leishman, Edinburgh, March 1990.
37 Diary, 30 November 1958.
38 Conversation with Rev. Murray Leishman, Edinburgh, March 1990.
39 Diary, 11 August 1960.
40 Letter dated 29 September 1960.
41 Letter dated 5 October 1960.
42 Conversation with Andrew Stewart, Glasgow, August 1990.
43 Diary, 28 October 1960.
44 *Ibid.*, 18 November 1960. Reith had been a customer of H. Huntsman and Sons in Savile Row since 1941. Colin Hammick, who used to fit Reith in the fifties and sixties, was still with the firm as a director more than thirty years later and remembered

Reith's talking about the wedding. Reith's card, preserved in the Huntsman records, shows that he had a new pair of striped cashmere trousers made for the occasion. (Conversation with Colin Hammick, London, February 1992.)

45 Conversation with Harman Grisewood, Eye, Suffolk, September 1990.

46 Letter dated 22 November 1960.

47 Diary, 3 December 1960.

48 *Ibid.*, 25 December 1960.

49 *Ibid.*, 27 December 1960.

50 Scrapbook, February 1961.

51 These pages draw on two lengthy conversations with Barbara Hickman in 1991 and 1992.

52 Barbara Hickman recalled that Muriel's memory was no longer very good. She was in the habit of writing notes to herself and leaving them in various places around the flat; what particularly infuriated Reith was her subsequent inability to find them.

53 'The Hick' was never asked to buy whisky for him, for instance. That sometimes fell to Phillips, the chauffeur, and sometimes he did it himself.

54 *The Times*, 15 May 1961.

55 These included Andrew Boyle, who published his biography a year after Reith's death without having had access to the diaries, and the present author.

56 Letter dated 10 August 1961.

57 Diary, 8 August 1961. The diaries were never sold in his lifetime. Christopher favoured burning them, but Marista thought differently. They eventually disposed of them to the BBC some years after his death for a little over £11,000.

58 *Ibid.*, 22 February 1961. Thirty years later, Dawn Mackay thought it highly unlikely that her mother had said anything of the sort.

59 Letter dated 11 May 1961 from M. C. Berry. The policy would have provided £1000 plus bonuses payable at the age of fifty or at previous death for an annual premium of £58-15s.-10d.

60 Diary, 8 June 1961. The author was the BBC's Staff Training Organiser at the time and was present at Reith's first two Uplands appearances.

61 *Ibid.*, 5 May 1960. This conversation took place over lunch at the Hyde Park Hotel. 'Now you're talking,' Welensky had replied. The Earl of Dalhousie was only halfway through a five-year term, however, and the appointment was in any event not in Welensky's gift. It was highly unlikely, after their dealings with Reith over the CDC, that the government would have thought much of the idea.

62 *Ibid.*, 21 February 1961.

63 Transcript of oral evidence, 7 April 1961.

64 Richard Hoggart, *An Imagined Life*, Chatto & Windus, London, 1992.

65 Letter dated 12 June 1961.

66 Diary, 25 April and 12 May 1961. Lusty told the story in his introduction to *Wearing Spurs*, which Hutchinson published. The cartoon went for £70. The Sotheby's director who was bidding for Reith dropped out at £65.

67 *Ibid.*, 9 August 1961.

68 *Ibid.*, 8 November 1961.

69 *The Times*, 15 December 1961.

70 Diary, 15 December 1961.

71 *Ibid.*, 4 September 1961.

72 *Ibid.*, 29 November 1960. (Dawn Mackay said that nobody much liked it; it was far too big and 'would have been better suited to a cathedral'.)

73 *Ibid.*, 27 September 1961.

74 *Ibid.*, 19 October 1961.

75 *Ibid.*, 24 November 1961. 'Shooglie – shaky, unsteady, tottery, insecure.' *The Concise Scots Dictionary*, editor-in-chief Mairi Robinson, Aberdeen University Press, 1985.

76 *Ibid.*, 28 November 1961.

77 *Sunday Express*, 19 March 1962.

78 Diary, 3 March 1962.

79 *Ibid.*, 5 May 1961.

80 *Ibid.*, 4 June 1962.

81 *Rhodesia Herald*, 30 April 1962.

82 Diary, 28 April 1962.

83 'Dear Sir,' he had written, 'This is to

let you know, in accordance with House of Lords practice, that if I speak on May 9th as at present scheduled, you may be considerably mentioned . . .' (Letter dated 17 April 1962.)

84 *The Times*, 10 May 1962.

85 Letter dated 10 May 1962.

86 Diary, 8 June 1962.

87 Arkell, who had been at Christ Church, had recently been involved in finding a new bursar for his old college, and passed on to Reith the names of some of the unsuccessful candidates. (Conversation with John Arkell, Henley-on-Thames, November 1991.)

88 Diary, 19 and 20 June 1962.

89 *Ibid.*, 23 June 1962.

90 *Ibid.*, 17 August 1962.

91 Letter dated 29 July 1962. fforde was reminding Reith of the famous Pauline passage quoted in the Latin inscription in the lobby of Broadcasting House (see page 420, n.55).

92 Diary, 12 August 1962.

93 Letter dated 7 October 1962.

94 Letter dated 12 December 1962.

95 Diary, 28 December 1962.

96 *Ibid.*, 24 January 1963. It wasn't. Both still hang there thirty years later.

97 *Ibid.*, 18 April 1963. Nearer the time he allowed himself to be persuaded.

98 *Ibid.*, 10 May 1963.

99 Letter dated 25 April 1963.

100 Letter dated 9 July 1963.

101 Diary, 18 August 1963.

102 *Ibid.*, 22 August 1963.

103 *Ibid.*, 7 September 1963.

104 *Ibid.*, 27 September 1963.

105 Letter dated 20 October 1963 from Leslie Durbin, MVO, 62 Rochester Place, NW1.

106 Diary, 30 October 1963.

107 Letter dated 29 November 1963.

108 Diary, 1 January 1964. Hugh Greene had been knighted in the New Year Honours List.

109 *Ibid.*, 10 January 1964.

110 Letter dated 18 May 1964.

111 fforde suffered from heart trouble. In an earlier letter to him, Reith had written: 'If I had heart trouble, I would do whatever I was specifically told not to do; and moreover do it with vehemence . . .' (Letter dated 25 April 1964.)

112 Letter dated 15 March 1964.

113 Diary, 14 July 1964.

114 *Ibid.*, 22 September 1964.

115 *Ibid.*, 19 March 1964.

116 *Ibid.*, 14 October 1964.

117 Letter dated 12 November 1964.

118 Letter dated 1 May 1964.

119 *Oldham Evening Chronicle*, 13 May 1964.

120 Letter dated 19 May 1964.

121 Diary, 6 July 1964.

122 *Ibid.*, 9 October 1964.

123 Letter dated 27 August 1964.

124 Letter dated 27 August 1964.

125 Letter dated 17 December 1964.

126 Diary, 14 May 1964.

127 *Ibid.*, 4 December 1964. Murray had been called to the Barony Church in Glasgow. When Muriel and Reith went to inspect it, the church officer's wife told them that the new Minister had married 'a daughter of the BBC'.

128 *Ibid.*, 27 January 1965. He did, however, paste the formal invitation into his scrapbook: 'The Earl Marshal has it in Command from the Queen to invite the Rt. Hon The Lord Reith and Lady Reith to be present at the Cathedral Church of St Paul in London on the occasion of the State Funeral shortly to be held there . . .' Reith wrote in pencil at the bottom, 'Declined (vehemently) by telephone when rung up.'

129 House of Lords *Hansard*, vol. 262, col 1001, 20 January 1965.

130 Letter dated 11 February 1965.

131 Diary, 12 February 1965.

132 Letter dated 22 February 1965.

133 Diary, 29 March 1965. The Leishmans had already decided on Martha Katharine. The child had been born on Muriel's birthday, and Reith was indignant that it had not been named after her. He thought Martha 'hideous', and assumed that it must be the name of Marista's mother-in-law. He was mistaken.

134 *Ibid.*, 22 July 1965.

135 *Sunday Express*, 23 May 1965.

136 Diary, 23 August 1965. Miss Mackay did eventually marry Major Hargreaves and they ran a school for foreign students together, first in Surrey and then in Scotland. The Heathfield governors found it difficult to decide whether the school's charter allowed for the headmistress to be married; a more substantial problem was that the Major had been married before.

137 The cottage was on Loch Linnhe, not far from Ballachulish. Reith paid for it by disposing of 950 Phoenix five-shilling shares. He got £6 $\frac{19}{32}$ a share. The transaction was reported at a board meeting on 22 September. (Sun Alliance Archives.)

138 Conversation with Christopher Reith, Methven, Perthshire, June 1992.

139 Diary, 14 October 1965.

140 Ibid., 10 July 1965.

141 Letter dated 21 September 1965.

142 Letter dated 6 October 1965.

143 Memorandum dated 27 July 1966.

144 Memorandum dated 14 March 1968.

145 Minutes of News and Current Affairs Meeting, 15 March 1968.

146 Ibid., 22 March 1968.

147 Ibid., 22 January 1971.

148 Ibid., 5 February 1971.

149 The papers mentioned here are all to be found at the BBC Written Archives Centre at Caversham, file BBC WAC R78 B687–3, Obituaries: Individual Cases.

150 Diary, 27 October 1965.

151 Ibid., 29 October 1965.

152 Ibid., 18 November 1965.

153 Ibid., 28 November 1965.

154 The Scotsman, 25 November 1965.

155 Letter dated 26 November 1965.

CHAPTER 18

1 The Public Corporation in Great Britain, Oxford University Press, 1938.

2 Letter dated 26 February 1966.

3 Letter dated 11 March 1966.

4 Diary, 15 March 1966.

5 Ibid., 17 March 1966.

6 Ibid., 16 August 1966.

7 Ibid., 20 March 1966.

8 Ibid., 10 April 1966.

9 Ibid., 11 April 1966.

10 Ibid., 16 May 1966.

11 Ibid., 4 June 1966.

12 Reith illustrated his diary entry with a small sketch of the line the car took.

13 Diary, 5 June 1966.

14 Ibid., 21 June 1966.

15 Western Mail, 24 June 1966.

16 Diary, 6 July 1966.

17 Ibid., 11 August 1966.

18 Observer, 4 September 1966.

19 Daily Telegraph, 9 September 1966.

20 Diary, 28 October 1966.

21 Ibid., 30 October 1966.

22 Ibid., 9 January 1967.

23 Ibid., 23 January 1967.

24 Ibid., 9 March 1967.

25 Ibid., 16 April 1967. The fact was that Christopher was plagued by deafness, and found such occasions a trial. His hearing had been impaired during his National Service; he was standing too close to a naval gun when it went off.

26 Conversation with Mrs Charles Hargreaves, London, June 1992.

27 Letter from Miss Stanley to author dated 26 February 1993.

28 Diary, 14 December 1966.

29 Ibid., 18 April 1967.

30 Conversation with Andrew Stewart, Glasgow, August 1990.

31 Diary, 5 July 1967.

32 Boyle, op. cit., p. 350.

33 Diary, 28 June 1967.

34 As John Maclay, Muirshiel had been Secretary of State for Scotland under Harold Macmillan.

35 Diary, 9 April 1968.

36 Letter dated 20 February 1969. McKinsey's were the first in a long line of management consultants called in from the 1960s on to advise the BBC on questions of organisation and efficiency.

37 Diary, 26 August 1967.

38 Ibid., 12 May 1967.

39 Talking to Eddington, who had been Professor of Astronomy at Cambridge, would not have been easy, as he had died in 1944. The 'Eddington Principle' was elaborated

in his posthumous book *Fundamental Theory* (Cambridge University Press, 1946). It attempted to relate phenomena on the atomic scale to those on the cosmological scale, and was greeted with some scepticism by most leading theoretical physicists of the day, who found the arguments advanced incomprehensible. Eddington believed that the whole system of nature was built round a number of the order 10^{78}, which he called the *cosmical number*. Professor Robert Rankin told the author that Reith was all for introducing the subject into his address as Lord High Commissioner, but that he had dissuaded him. (Letter from Professor Rankin, 9 September 1992.)

40 Diary, 29 June 1967. His lunches with Haley were coming to an end. He heard in September that he was going off to Chicago to be Editor-in-Chief of the new edition of the *Encyclopedia Britannica*. 'What a wonderful thing to happen at 66,' Reith wrote. 'I envy him enormously. My one friend in high places disappears, and I shall get nothing from *The Times* in life or death as he would have continued to give me.' (Diary, 26 September 1967.)

41 *Ibid.*, 29 July 1967.

42 *Ibid.*, 19 September 1967.

43 *Ibid.*, 14 October 1967.

44 *Ibid.*, 27 October 1967.

45 *Ibid.*, 6 November 1967.

46 Letter dated 7 December 1967.

47 Letter dated 27 January 1968.

48 Letter dated 16 April 1968. Cock added: 'I expect you guessed the name of my Cabinet friend – a man I knew soon after he came down from Oxford – brilliant and with great political flair. Yet he came a cropper and great was the fall thereof. Although a bit unscrupulous (like all successful politicians) I don't think he deserved his fate which was to die in almost complete obscurity.' The minister who best meets Cock's description is Leslie Hore-Belisha.

49 Diary, 21 March 1968.

50 *Ibid.*, 22 March 1968.

51 *Ibid.*, 3 May 1968.

52 Reith knew that his audience would be as familiar with the violent narrative of the Second Book of Kings as he was. Elisha was at Dothan, on the main caravan route from Damascus to Egypt, when the Syrians encompassed the town and were smitten with blindness in answer to the prophet's prayer. A good deal of revolutionary activity was, as it happened, already taking place around the world in that summer of 1968, mostly on university campuses. There were quite a lot of horses in evidence, too, but they belonged in the main to riot police.

53 Castle Dangerous, made famous by Scott's novel of the same name, was built in the thirteenth century or earlier, but later destroyed. Only the tower now remains of the rebuilt castle. It stands on the estate of the Home family.

54 Diary, 22 May 1968.

55 Isaiah, 62:10.

56 Diary, 12 August 1968. Lady Elliot, the widow of Walter Elliot, his old companion from Glasgow OTC days, was standing for the Conservatives, and George Macleod for Labour.

57 *Ibid.*, 21 October 1968.

58 Christopher remembered it as a brown paper folder, with 'Matters re my demise' written on it in blue crayon, full of drawings and crossings-out.

59 Diary, 18 August 1968.

60 *Ibid.*, 5 September 1968.

61 *Ibid.*, 3 February 1969.

62 *Ibid.*, 28 February 1969.

63 *Ibid.*, 24 February 1969.

64 *Ibid.*, 18 March 1969.

65 *Ibid.*, 21 March 1969.

66 *Ibid.*, 18 April 1969.

67 *Ibid.*, 2 May 1969.

68 The author had this story from Aidan Thomson, at that time Assistant Head of Scottish Programmes.

69 Conversation in London, July 1990.

Christopher's diplomatic recollection of his father's behaviour on the day was that it was 'a lot better than I thought it would have been.'

70 Letter dated 11 June 1969.
71 Diary, 27 August 1969.
72 *Ibid.*, 2 September 1969.
73 *Ibid.*, 28 September 1969. It is from this period that the various letters mentioned on pp. 14–15 *supra* date.
74 *Ibid.*, 1 February 1970.
75 *Ibid.*, 20 February 1970.
76 *Ibid.*, 25 February 1970.
77 *Ibid.*, 21 May 1970.
78 *Ibid.*, 23 June 1970.
79 *Ibid.*, early 1971. He noted that it cost £64.
80 *Ibid.*, 21 February 1971.
81 *Ibid.*, March 1971. The article, 'Sir Basil Liddell Hart: The Captain who taught Generals', appeared in the January 1971 issue of *International Affairs*. Reith described Ronald Lewin as a General, but he had been only a wartime soldier. A publisher and a military historian, he had also been head of the Home Service at the BBC – and had twice produced the Reith Lectures.
82 Letter dated 20 June 1971. Reith had been one of Alick Buchanan-Smith's sponsors when he was made a life peer in 1963 and took his seat as Lord Balerno. He took his title from the village just outside Edinburgh where he farmed, and he had kept a kindly eye on Reith after the latter's return to Edinburgh.
83 Stuart, *op. cit.*, p. 70.
84 *The Times*, 17 June 1971.

Index

Abdul Rahman Putra, Tunku, 328, 332
Aberdeen, 2, 109, 114
Acheson, Dean, 296
Adam, Kenneth, 391
Adam Smith, Alick, *see* Buchanan-Smith
Adam Smith, Sir George and Lady, 109
Adam Smith, Janet, 190–1, 205, 338
Adam Smith, Margaret, 205
Adams, Mary, 340
Adeane, Sir Michael, 369
Addison, Christopher, 1st Viscount, 284
Air Ministry, 245–6
Airways Corporation Bill, 247
Alba, Duke of, 215
Alexander, A.V. (*later* 1st Earl Alexander of
  Hillsborough), 272
Alexander Gibb, 261
Alexandra Palace, 209
All Wave, 223–4
Allen, Walter, 298
Amery, Leo, 252, 254
Anderson, Sir John (*later* 1st Viscount
  Waverley), 257, 265, 267–71, 275, 278,
  281, 283
Anderson, Major P.F., 117, 120, 125
Anderson, Thomas, 402
Anne, Princess, 342
Anstey, F., 17
Architects' Journal, The, 261
Architectural Review, 199
Ariel, 192
Arkell, John, 362, 366, 399
Armentières, 33–6
Ashbridge, Noel (*later* Sir Noel), 211
Asquith, Herbert Henry (*later* 1st Earl of
  Oxford and Asquith), 133
Astor, J.J., 124, 217
Astor, Nancy, Viscountess, 178
Atatürk, Kemal, 115
Athenaeum, 156, 172
Atkinson, C.F., 148–9
Atterbury (VP Pennsylvania Railroad), 76–7
Attlee, Clement (*later* 1st Earl Attlee):
  Ullswater Committee/Report, 215, 216,
  221; Reith's opinion, 216, 279; wartime
  Coalition 256–7; Chamberlain's funeral,
  260; DCOM assistance, 272; PM 284,

290, 293, 301; Reith's appeals for work,
  284, 293, 301
Auden, W.H., 190
Australia, 279–80
Azikiwe, Nnamdi, 329

Baird, John Logie, 184, 208–9
Baldwin, Lucy, 144, 152, 220
Baldwin, Stanley (*later* 1st Earl Baldwin of
  Bewdley): Coalition collapse, 115;
  election broadcasts, 133, 173–4;
  relationship with Reith, 133, 164, 176,
  177, 204, 252; Daventry transmitter
  opening, 137; General Strike, 141–6;
  BBC dinner, 152; *Listener* debate, 169;
  Reith drafts speeches for, 174, 177, 220,
  231; Davidson's funeral, 183; broadcast
  on death of King, 220–1; abdication
  crisis, 229
Balfour, Arthur James, 1st Earl of Balfour,
  157
Balfour of Burleigh, George Bruce, 11th
  Baron, 265, 267, 278
Banks, Sir Donald, 215, 246–7
Banks (friend of Charlie Bowser), 59, 61
Barker, Ernest (*later* Sir Ernest), 207
Barlow, Sir Alan, 263
Barnes, George (*later* Sir George), 293,
  314, 324
Barrie, Sir Charles, 251
Baschet, Marcel, 206
Battin, Dr and Mrs, 66
BBC (British Broadcasting
  Company/Corporation): Reith joins, 114,
  116–18; origins, 119–20; Children's
  Hour, 121; licence fee, 122–3, 129, 135,
  147; Crawford Committee, 137–40, 147;
  Board, 138, 170, 176; monopoly, 140,
  309–11, 324, 361; General Strike
  coverage 141–8; Corporation, 147, 151;
  Charter, 147, 151, 165, 169, 178, 212,
  214; sports coverage, 157, 230; Empire
  Service, 158–9, 209–10; ban on
  controversial material lifted, 165; first
  television play, 184–5; number of
  licences, 185; drama, 186; light
  entertainment, 186; news broadcasting,

BBC – *cont'd*.
186, 217; staff, 189–90, 202–3, 230, 238;
responsibilities of Governors, 196–7;
Broadcasting House, 198, 199–200;
tenth anniversary, 205–6; television
service, 208–9, 230; Ullswater
Committee/Report, 215–16, 219–20,
221–2, 226–7; Variety, 218; Lambert
mongoose case, 225–8; Stamp Report,
227–8; staff association vote, 227–8;
Remembrance Day coverage, 230;
Coronation coverage, 230; Spithead
review coverage, 231; foreign language
broadcasting, 236; Second World War,
252; 21st anniversary celebrations, 289;
Reith lectures, 291; Silver Jubilee, 291,
292; Beveridge Committee on
Broadcasting, 301, 304, 336, 362; Third
Programme anniversary, 304–5; White
Paper on commercial television, 309–11;
commercial television proposals, 317;
Pilkington committee, 348, 355, 356–7,
362, 363; management training courses,
355–6; fortieth anniversary, 364; *Juke Box
Jury*, 368; Reith obituary plans, 376–7
BBC Amateur Dramatic Society, 224
BBC National Lectures, 191
BBC Sound Archives, 200
BBC Staff Operatic and Dramatic Society,
139
BBC Symphony Orchestra, 185, 402
BBC Year Books, 185–6, 210
Beadle, Gerald, 209, 237, 343, 348
Beardmore, Sir William (*later* 1st Baron
Invernairn), 96, 100
Beardmore, William, & Company, 95,
96–101, 108, 111
Beaver, Hugh (*later* Sir Hugh), 261
Beaverbrook, Max Aitken, 1st Baron:
campaigns against BBC, 123, 202;
relationship with Reith, 123, 135, 260;
press coverage of Reith, 202, 203–4;
wartime government, 254–5, 257–9, 281;
Reith's opinion, 263; prose style, 308; in
West Indies, 321; Reith diaries, 354
Beeching, Richard (*later* Baron), 357
Beerbohm, Max, 357
Beharrell, Sir George, 238, 239, 244
Bell, George K.A., 124, 135, 153, 320
Benn, Sir Ernest, 236
Betts, Gladys, 13
Betts, John Valentine, 8, 13
Bevan, Aneurin, 240
Beveridge, William Henry Beveridge, 1st
Baron, 301, 304
Beveridge Committee on Broadcasting, 301,
304, 336, 362

Bevin, Ernest, 284
Binyon, Basil, 138
Birkenhead, Frederick Edwin Smith, 1st
Earl of, 115, 125, 142
Birley, Oswald (*later* Sir Oswald), 206
Birmingham Post, 174
Blair, Alistair, 387, 395
Blake, William, 145, 175
Blanesburgh, Robert Younger, Baron, 138
Bonham-Carter, Lady Violet, 282
Boult, Adrian (*later* Sir Adrian), 185, 193,
402
Bowden, Herbert (*later* Baron Aylestone),
373
Bowser, David Charles (Charlie, DCB):
Reith's passionate friendship, 18, 19–21;
background, 19; Reith family attitude, 19,
104, 109–10, 212; Reith edits
relationship from records, 21, 134–5,
162, 179, 197, 389; moves to London,
20, 21; relationship with Reith, 21–7, 32,
34–5, 36–7, 41–2, 48, 52–4, 57, 58–62,
65, 68, 73–4, 78, 80–1, 83–5, 306;
relationship with Muriel, 85–9, 91–2, 96,
99, 103, 162; Reith's father's death,
92–3; Reith arranges Ministry of
Munitions job, 97; Reith suggests OBE,
98; Reith arranges Beardmores job, 99;
Reith arranges meeting with Maysie,
100–1; engagement to Maysie, 102–8;
Reith's wedding, 103; wedding, 108–9;
breaks off friendship with Reith, 109–11;
Bowser family attitude to friendship, 113;
letters after end of friendship, 117, 126,
131, 162, 197, 219, 233–4, 319; Reith's
continuing thoughts of, 125, 153, 264,
270, 282, 302, 328, 352; mother's death,
126; married life, 130; chilly meetings
with Reith, 158, 251, 386; Reith returns
photographs, 162, 197; Argaty House
home-coming, 177; County Council
work, 198; Dunblane Cathedral, 198,
302, 386; correspondence with Reith's
mother, 212–13, 234; Reith's mother's
death, 219; son's education, 233–4;
farm-hunting for Christopher, 319; new
house, 392
Bowser, Maysie (née Henderson), 101–9,
112, 155, 177, 212, 319, 392
Bowser family, 19–20, 22–3, 34, 59–60,
61–2, 113, 126
Boyle, Andrew, 238, 281
Bracken, Brendan (*later* 1st Viscount
Bracken), 254, 267
Bridgeman, Caroline Beatrix, Lady, 221, 225
Bridgeman, William Clive, 1st Viscount,
115, 206, 216

Bridges, Sir Edward, 288, 302
Bridges, Robert (*later* 1st Baron), 164, 191
Briggs, Asa (*later* Baron): on Reith's
  writings, 123, 134; on General Strike
  coverage, 146; on DG-Board
  relationships, 156; on Reith's departure
  from BBC, 238; meeting with Reith,
  335–6; suggestions for diaries, 354–5;
  shows material to Reith, 365; on
  Crawford Committee, 380
British Airways 245
British Broadcasting Company, *see* BBC
British Expeditionary Force, 254–5
British Film Institute, 225
British Gazette, 141, 147
British Overseas Airways Corporation
  (BOAC), 247, 270–1
British Oxygen Company, 335, 339, 350–1,
  352–4, 365–7, 381
British Thomson-Houston, 120
Broadcast Over Britain, 133–4, 138, 188
Broadcasting House, 198, 199–200
Brookmans Park, 184
Browett, Sir Leonard, 256
Brown, F.J., 125
Brown, Neil, 371
Browne, Sir James Crichton, 164
Bryant, Sir Francis Morgan, 181
Bryce, James, 1st Viscount, 95
Buccleuch, Mary, Duchess of, 390
Buchan, John (*later* 1st Baron Tweedsmuir),
  204
Buchanan, Sir George, 95
Buchanan, Dr Robert, 2
Buchanan-Smith, Sir Alick (*formerly* Adam
  Smith, *later* Lord Balerno), 402
Buchman, Frank, 357
Bull, Sir William, 114, 115–16, 138
Bulwer-Lytton, Edward, 17
Bunyan, John, 314
Burger, Die, 211
Burgess, Guy, 279
Burnett, Frances Hodgson, 192
Burnham, Harry Lawson Webster Lawson,
  1st Viscount, 124, 138, 183
Burns, Robert, 1, 67, 164–5, 386
Burrows, Arthur S., 117, 158
Business Science Association of
  Philadelphia, 67–8
Butler, R.A. (*later* Baron Butler of Saffron
  Walden), 252, 260, 375
Byng, Julian Hedworth George, 1st
  Viscount Byng of Vimy, 172–3

Cable and Wireless, 220, 274, 278–9, 281
Cable and Wireless Bill, 283
Cadogan, Sir Alexander, 312, 324, 336

Caird, 141
Camrose, William Ewert Berry, 1st
  Viscount, 240, 246
Canada, 280–1, 291
Caradon, Hugh Foot, Baron, 374–5
Carlyle, Thomas, 2, 43, 97, 238, 298
Carnegie Church Peace Union, 69
Carpendale, Charles (*later* Sir Charles):
  joins BBC, 125–6; King's wireless set,
  130; relationship with Reith, 131, 150,
  153, 157, 176, 180, 245, 320, 392;
  amateur acting, 139, 168; reads news
  bulletins, 141; presentation to Reith, 152;
  complains about Mrs Snowden, 158;
  skiing holiday, 163; Reith-Clarendon
  ructions, 178–9, 181; staff association
  statement, 202; knighthood, 206; Deputy
  Director-General, 208; television plans,
  209; retirement, 230, 236, 239, 393;
  Casino party, 241; eightieth birthday,
  318, 320; death, 394
Chalmers, Thomas, 177, 267, 327, 390
Chamberlain, Annie, 238
Chamberlain, Sir Austen, 115, 116
Chamberlain, Neville, 174, 231, 237–40,
  245, 249, 250–3, 260
Chaplin, Charlie, 194
Chappell's, 158
Charles, Prince, 342
Cherwell, Frederick Alexander Lindemann,
  1st Viscount, 259
Chesterton, G.K., 17
Children's Hour, 121
Cholmondeley, George Cholmondeley, 5th
  Marquess of, 370
Christian Science Monitor, 196
Christie (ATS officer), 263–4
Churchill, Clementine, 145, 311
Churchill, Randolph, 311
Churchill, Winston (*later* Sir Winston):
  Reith's first sight of, 36; Coalition
  election plans, 115; loses seat, 116;
  General Strike, 142–3, 144–5, 311;
  relationship with Reith, 144–5, 157,
  251–2, 258, 285, 311, 322, 401; Budget
  broadcast, 165; *The World Crisis*, 180;
  abdication crisis, 229; Chamberlain's War
  Cabinet, 251–2; wartime leadership,
  254–60, 262–3, 267–72; Reith's opinion,
  263, 267, 270, 275, 281–2, 298; sacks
  Reith, 264–6, 285; 1945 election, 284;
  The Gathering Storm, 295; 1951 election,
  304; death, 372
Clarendon, George Herbert Hyde Villiers,
  6th Earl: Chairman, 147, 151, 154–5;
  PMG meetings, 148, 152; Reith's
  opinion, 148, 152, 155, 204; Reith's

Clarendon, George Herbert Hyde Villiers –
cont'd.
  knighthood, 153; relationship with Reith
  as DG, 155–7, 160–1, 163, 176–81, 196;
  Eckersley affair, 172; Governor-General
  appointment, 181, 182
Clark, Sir Beresford, 341
Clark, Kenneth (later Baron), 253
Clynes, J.R., 95–6, 100
Coatbridge, 98–100, 103, 105, 108–9
Cochrane, C.B., 164
Cock, Gerald, 208, 209, 393
Cockburn, Margaret, 398
Cohn-Bendit, Daniel, 395
Colefax, Sybil, Lady, 357
Collins, 294
Collins, Norman, 324, 349
Colonial Development Corporation (CDC),
  302–9, 315–17, 320–5, 328–9, 331–4,
  335, 337–8
Colonial Office, 303, 324–6, 328
Columbia Broadcasting System, 196
Commonwealth Communications Council
  (CCC), 278, 284, 293, 296
Commonwealth Telecommunications
  Board, 296
Conservative Party, 115, 140, 173, 203, 238,
  265
Cooper, Sir Alfred Duff (later 1st Viscount
  Norwich), 254, 255
Corey (US Steel), 66
Cotara, Molly, 325, 332, 333–4, 339, 350
Coughtrie, Tom, 338
Coward, Noël, 192
Crawford, David Lindsay, 27th Earl,
  137–8, 147, 148, 313
Crawford Committee/Report, 138–40, 147,
  151, 158, 188, 380
Creedy, Sir Herbert, 207
Cripps, Sir Stafford, 221, 226, 302
Crocombe, Leonard, 127
Croft (Adjutant), 37–40, 43, 45–50
Cromer, Rowland Thomas Baring, 2nd
  Earl, 241
Cromwell, Oliver, 52–3, 209, 254
Curran, Charles (later Sir Charles), 377,
  399
Curtin, John, 279

Daily Express, 123, 159, 202–3, 258, 312
Daily Herald, 187
Daily Mail, 164, 224, 230
Daily News, 164
Daily Telegraph, 222, 251, 298, 315
Dalton, Hugh, 283, 284, 300
Dante Alighieri, 282
Daventry, 136–7, 209–10

Davidson, J.C.C. (later 1st Viscount), 140,
  141–4, 148–9, 173, 320
Davidson, Randall Thomas, Archbishop of
  Canterbury, 124–5, 143, 167, 183
Dawnay, Alan, 207–8, 217, 222
Dawson, Geoffrey, 135, 204, 207
Dawson of Penn, Bertrand, 1st Viscount,
  220, 221
De L'Isle, Sidney William Philip, 1st
  Viscount, 395
Desta, Prince Alexander, 386
Dickens, Charles, 2, 134, 298
Dill, Sir John, 216, 256, 263
Dillon, Francis, 371
Dinwiddie, Melville, 319, 327
Directorate of Combined Operations
  Material, 271–3
Disraeli, Benjamin, 1st Earl of Beaconsfield,
  136
Dodds, Kathleen, 358–9
Douglas, Colonel (CO), 42, 45–9, 61–2
Douro, Marchioness of, 203
Dunardoch, Dunblane, 99–100, 104, 127,
  130, 133
Duncan, Sir Andrew, 283
Dunn, Mr and Mrs, 101, 106, 109, 111,
  113
Dunstan, Eric, 175

Eckersley, Peter: Chief Engineer
  appointment, 121; description of
  Carpendale, 126; relationship with Reith,
  134; General Strike experiences, 146;
  Empire broadcasting, 159; divorce and
  departure from BBC, 171–3, 176;
  television, 208
Eckersley, Roger, 161
Economist, The, 337
Eddington, Arthur, 391
Eddystone Works, Philadelphia, 63–5
Eden, Anthony (later 1st Earl of Avon), 257,
  322
Edward, Prince of Wales (later Edward VIII,
  then Duke of Windsor), 35, 139, 221,
  228–9, 371
Eliot, T.S., 191
Elizabeth II, Queen, 313, 390–1, 396, 398
Elizabeth, Queen Mother, 387, 393
Elliot, Sir John, 385
Ellis, Dr William T., 69, 70–1
Emerson, Ralph Waldo, 162
Ervine, St John, 159–60
Eton College, 166, 207, 263, 274, 289
Evening Standard, 315, 363

Faber, Geoffrey (later Sir Geoffrey), 289
Face to Face, 348–9

Farquharson, David, 198
Fellowship of Reconciliation, 72
fforde, Sir Arthur, 336, 348, 356, 363, 365–6, 369
Fichte, Johann Gottlieb, 397
Financial News, 169
Fisher, Geoffrey Francis, Archbishop of Canterbury, 319–20, 322
Fisher, H.A.L., 230
Fisher, May, 27
Fisher, Sir Warren, 233, 237–41, 246
Fleming, Archibald, 117, 166
Foster, Lord, 140
Franckenstein, Baron Georg, 215
Franco, Francisco, 230
Frankau, Gilbert, 194
Franks, Oliver Shewell Franks, Baron, 362
Fraser, Ian (*later* Sir Ian, *then* Baron Fraser of Lonsdale), 138, 140, 229–30
Freeman, John, 348–9, 351
French, Sir John (*later* Earl French of Ypres), 55
Freud, Sigmund, 112
Friend, Mrs, 249
Froude, James Anthony, 235

Gainford, Joseph Albert Pease, 1st Baron: BBC (Company) chairman, 125; relationship with Reith, 125, 260; Reith's opinion, 138; Crawford Committee/Report, 138, 140; General Strike, 143; BBC (Corporation) Vice-Chairman, 151; Mrs Snowden-Reith clash, 155, 161; Clarendon-Reith clash, 179; suggested for Chairman, 182; Whitley's Chairmanship, 184; leaves Board, 206
Gaitskell, Hugh, 302, 357
Gangulee, Nagendra Nath, 139
Garbett, Cyril Foster, 208
Gawsden (artist), 94
General Electric, 120
General Strike, 141–8, 174
George V, King, 35, 130, 132, 145, 206, 210, 213, 220–1
George VI, King, 229–31, 237, 313
Gibbon, Lewis Grassic, 1
Gibbs, Sir Humphrey, 360
Gibbs, Molly, Lady, 360
Gielgud, Val, 168
Gill, Eric, 199–200
Gillard, Frank, 376
Gladstone, William Ewart, 132, 136, 386
Glasgow, 2–3, 6, 98, 136
Glasgow Academy, 4, 6, 343, 351
Glasgow and South Western Railway, 21–2
Glasgow Herald, 251, 298, 309, 343

Glasgow Technical College, 11, 17
Glasgow University, 374–5, 385–6
Goebbels, Joseph, 252
Goldwater, Barry, 370
Gordon, Lincoln, 380
Gort, John Standish Surtees Prendergast Vereker, 6th Viscount, 250
Graham, William, 138
Graves, Cecil (*later* Sir Cecil), 201, 233, 241–2, 245–6, 327
Gray, John, 138
Greene, Hugh Carleton (*later* Sir Hugh): Director-General, 336, 365; relationship with Reith, 340–1, 342, 368; Reith's opinion, 342, 373, 391; Uplands croquet, 356; resignation called for, 373; successor, 377, 399
Greenfield, Julian, 356
Greenwood, Arthur, 256
Gresham's School, Holt, 7–8, 10, 36, 46, 112, 114, 160, 398
Gretna works, 59–61
Grey of Fallodon, Edward Grey, 1st Viscount, 144–5, 205
Gribbel, John, 67, 73
Grigg, Gertrude, Lady, 274
Grigg, Sir James, 207, 274
Grisewood, Freddie, 189–90
Grisewood, Harman, 189–90, 231, 342, 348, 372–3
Gulland, J.W., 23
Guthrie, Tyrone, 186
Gwyer, Sir Maurice, 227

Haddow, Sir Douglas, 393
Hadow, Sir Henry, 138
Haig, Douglas, 1st Earl, 314
Haley, Sir William: Director-General, 289; relationship with Reith, 289–93, 300–1, 304–5, 307–8, 347, 363, 367, 369, 381, 391; illness, 300; Third Programme, 304–5; *Times* editorship, 309; successor, 311–12; Foyle's lunch, 385
Halifax, Edward Frederick Lindley Wood, 1st Earl of, 238, 250, 260, 308
Hamilton, Mary Agnes, 206, 212, 217, 221, 233, 238–9, 266
Hamilton, Patrick, 177
Hamilton, Sir William, 17
Hankey, Sir Maurice (*later* 1st Baron), 204, 216–17, 222
Hanmer, Dora, 14, 34, 41
Harley, Connie, 27, 399
Harley, George, 13, 27, 58
Harrias House, Beaconsfield, 183, 193, 198, 202, 204, 263, 290, 306, 318–20
Harris, Harold, 354

Hart, Basil Liddell, 401
Harty, Sir Hamilton, 185
Hastings, Sir Patrick, 227
Hay, Ian, 168, 224, 235
Heath, Edward (*later* Sir Edward), 374
Hemel Hempstead, 288, 293, 298, 300
Henderson, Arthur, 96
Henderson, Maysie, *see* Bowser
Henry, Mrs Bayard, 78
Herriot, Edouard, 215
Hertzog, James Barry Munnik, 210
Hibberd, Stuart, 220
Hickman, Barbara ('The Hick'):
  background, 350; Reith's secretary,
  350–1; relationship with Reith, 350–1,
  353–4, 365–6; on Dawn Mackay
  relationship, 351, 388; absence, 362;
  pirate radio letter, 370; Churchill lying in
  state, 372
Hill, Erskine, 265
Hill of Luton, Charles, Baron, 391
Hitler, Adolf, 202, 245, 259, 282, 381
Hoare, Sir Samuel (*later* 1st Viscount
  Templewood), 246
Hobart, A.W., 203
Hodder & Stoughton, 294–5
Hodder-Williams, Sir E., 133
Hodgkin, Edward, 298
Hodson, Donald, 341
Hoggart, Richard, 357
Holt, Colonel, 276
Home, Alexander Douglas-Home, 14th
  Earl, 331
Hoover, Herbert, 71, 195
Hore-Belisha, Leslie, 237, 239, 250
Horne, Kenneth, 302
Howson, G.W.S. (headmaster at
  Gresham's), 7–8, 46, 239
Hudson, W.H., 171
Huggins, Sir Godfrey, *see* Malvern
Hume, Sir Nutcombe, 333–4, 337
Humphery, G.E. Woods, 60, 232, 237,
  239–40, 244
Hutchinson's, 289, 357, 379, 381
Huxley, Aldous, 224

Iliffe, Edward Mauger Iliffe, 1st Baron, 216
Imperial Airways, 232, 237–9, 244–9, 263,
  275
India, 95, 251, 280, 367
India Act (1935), 201
India Office, 158, 209
Inman, Philip Albert Inman, 1st Baron, 289,
  290
Inskip, Sir Thomas (*later* 1st Viscount
  Caldecote), 223
Institution of Electrical Engineers, 120

Iona Community, 323, 337
Iremonger, F.A., 124, 208, 233
Isaacs, Godfrey, 129–30, 134

Jacob, Sir Ian, 312–13, 314, 317–18, 335,
  365
James, Robert Leoline, 358, 359, 360
Jardine Matheson, 101
Jeffries, Stanton, 125
Joffre, Joseph-Jacques-Césaire, 55
John Lane, 139
Johnston, Tom, 298
Joynson-Hicks, Sir William (*later* 1st
  Viscount Brentford), 123–4, 142
Juke Box Jury, 368

Kant, Immanuel, 310, 386
Kaunda, Kenneth, 325
KDKA, 119
Kekewich, Piers, 269–71
Kellaway, F.G., 120, 134
Kelly, Sir Gerald, 381
Kennedy, Joseph, 231
Kennedy, Major, 31, 32
Kenworthy, Joseph Montague (*later* 10th
  Baron Strabolgi), 95
Kenya, 280
Kerr, Donald, 6
Kerr, Mirita, 6
Kilroy (lift attendant), 241
Kipling, Caroline Starr Balestier, 217
Kipling, Rudyard, 138, 217
Kirkpatrick, Ivone (*later* Sir Ivone), 253
Knight, Dr, 136
Knox, John, 362, 390
Koussevitsky, Serge, 217
Kyrle, John, 3

Labour Party, 95–6, 135, 140, 145–6, 165,
  173, 207, 221, 358
Lamb, Helen, 302
Lambert, Richard S., 126, 169, 171,
  189–90, 199, 225–8
Lane, Margaret, 224
Lang, Cosmo Gordon, Archbishop of
  Canterbury, 179, 206, 207, 220
Lansing, Robert, 72
Laski, Harold, 187, 188–9
Lauder, Sir Harry, 139
Law, Andrew Bonar, 115, 116
Lawrence, D.H., 259
Lawrence, T.E., 207
Laws, Jeannette, *see* McCabe
Laws, Jimmy, 68, 73–4
Lehmann, John, 190
Lees-Smith, H.B., 182, 221, 228
Leishman, Mark, 372

Leishman, Murray: Reith's loathing, 323, 344–7, 350, 364, 381–2, 387; relationship with Marista, 323, 326, 330, 337; engagement and marriage, 344–7, 349–50; children, 364, 366, 371; Reith's memorial service, 402

Leishman, Susannah, 373

Lennox-Boyd, Alan (*later* 1st Viscount Boyd of Merton), 303, 324–6, 331

Lever, Sir Hardman, 244

Levita, Sir Cecil, 225–8

Levita, Florence, Lady, 225

Lewin, Ronald, 401

Lewis, C.A., 224–5

Lewis, C. Day, 190

Liberal Party, 95, 115–16, 136, 140, 144, 174

Linklater, Eric, 385

Listener, The, 169–71, 185, 190–1, 225–6

Livingstone, David, 312, 325

Lloyd, Selwyn (*later* Baron Selwyn-Lloyd), 336

Lloyd George, David (*later* 1st Earl Lloyd-George of Dwyfor), 59, 115, 116, 174, 194–5, 260

Logue, Lionel, 230

London, Midland and Scottish Railway (LMS), 180, 227

London School of Economics, 231

Longfellow, Henry Wadsworth, 300

Longford, Francis Pakenham, 7th Earl, 381

Lorimer, Sir Robert, 322

Lothian, Philip Henry Kerr, 11th Marquess, 260

Loudon, Jack, 13, 95, 105, 106, 233

Lovell, Sir Bernard, 391

Lusty, Robert (*later* Sir Robert), 357, 378

Lutyens, Sir Edwin, 246

Lyttelton, Oliver (*later* 1st Viscount Chandos), 315

McAllister, Gilbert, 287

Macaulay, Thomas Babington, 17, 129

McCabe, Jeannette (née Laws): Reith's admiration for, 73–4, 76, letters, 73–4, 77–8, 154, 317; marriage, 195; meets Reith again, 195–6; friendship with Reiths, 247, 249, 255, 328

McCabe, Tom, 247, 255, 328

McCarthy (secretary), 68, 77

MacDonald, Malcolm, 281

MacDonald, Ramsay: broadcasts, 133, 165, 174; Mrs Snowden's position, 151, 155; Reith's knighthood, 153; relationship with Reith, 173–4, 177, 182, 204, 211, 219; 1929 election, 174; appointment of BBC Chairman, 182; Davidson's funeral, 183

Macdonald of Gwaenysgor, Gordon Macdonald, 1st Baron, 314

Mackay, Dawn (*later* Mrs Charles Hargreaves): meeting with Reith, 297–8; letter to Reith, 339–40; career, 340, 342; relationship with Reith, 341–4, 346–7, 348, 375, 388; Reith's obsession with, 350–5, 365, 378, 388; description of, 351; Heathfield headship, 358, 359–60, 362, 373; marriage plans, 373–4; Reith's editing of relationship, 388–9

Mackay, George, 340

Mackay, Janet, 346, 347, 351, 355, 374

Mackay family, 297–8, 339–40, 346–7, 349–50, 353, 358

MacKenzie, George, 21

Mackinnon, Lady, 229

McKinstry, Archibald, 132, 138

Maclean, Donald, 279

Macleod, George (Sir George, *later* Baron Macleod of Fuinary): Iona Community, 296, 337; support for Marista and Murray, 326, 344, 346, 347; Leishman wedding, 349; Glasgow Rectorship, 395–6; Reith memorial service, 402

Macleod, Iain, 374–5

Macmillan, Harold (*later* 1st Earl of Stockton), 363

Macmillan, Hugh Pattison, Lord, of Aberfeldy, 248, 250

MacPherson, Ian (*later* 1st Baron Strathcarron), 138

Macpherson, Sir John, 326

MacQueen, May, 14, 15, 339

Maerz, Barbara, 382–4, 385, 399

Maerz family, 382–4, 385

Makepeace (Albert Dock chief engineer), 25

Mallon, J.J., 229

Malvern, Godfrey Huggins, 1st Viscount, 321, 325

Manchester Guardian, 208, 308, 309

Manchester Luncheon Club, 159

Manchester University, 205

Marconi, Guglielmo, Marchese, 217

Marconi Company, 119, 120, 121, 129, 134, 157, 206

Marconi House, 118, 121

Margaret, Princess, 321, 341

Margesson, Henry, 258

Marr, Willie, 6

Masefield, John, 194

Massey, Vincent, 291, 317

Master Printers' Federation, 169

Masterman, J.C. (*later* Sir John), 207, 293

Matheson, Hilda, 153

Matheson, Rev, 37

Maugham, Somerset, 157
Mauzé, Jean, 376
Melba, Dame Nellie, 124
Melchior, Lauritz, 121
Merriman, Percy, 206
Metropolitan-Vickers, 120
Meynell, Charles, 268
Miall, Leonard, 341
Millais, John Everett, 3
Milligan, Dr, 136, 215
Millis, C.H.G., 232
Milne-Watson, Sir David, 90, 156
Milton, John, 97, 310
Ministry of Information, 245, 250–4
Ministry of Munitions 59–61, 63, 90, 97
Ministry of Transport, 254–8
Ministry of Works, 258–66, 277
Mitchell-Thomson, Sir William, *see* Selsdon
Mitcheson, G.G. (*later* Sir George), 199
Moberly, Sir Walter, 205
Moffat, James, 398
Moir, E.W., 23–4, 59, 63, 65
Moir, Helen, 235
Moir, Mrs, 59
Monckton, Walter (*later* 1st Viscount
   Monckton of Brenchley), 253, 254
Montgomery, Bernard Law (*later* 1st
   Viscount Montgomery of Alamein), 244
Moral Rearmament Movement (MRA),
   223, 295–6, 357
Moran, Charles, 1st Baron, 311
Morley, John, 2
Morning Advertiser, 269
Morning Post, 175, 203
Morris, Ann, 397
Morrison, Herbert, 252, 256, 293, 303–4
Morrison, W.S. (*later* 1st Viscount
   Dunrossil), 207
Moseley, Sydney, 185
Mosley, Sir Oswald, 194, 201
Mountbatten, Lord Louis (*later* 1st Earl
   Mountbatten of Burma), 255, 290
Much Binding in the Marsh, 302
Muggeridge, Malcolm, 298, 385, 392–3
Muirhead, Kitty, 29–30, 32
Muirshiel, Jack Muirshiel, 1st Viscount, 391
Murdoch, Richard, 302
Murray, Cissie, 15, 83–4, 339
Murray, May, 339
Murray, W.E. Gladstone, 135, 148–9, 152,
   181, 208–9, 225–6
Mussolini, Benito, 217, 282

Nairne, Sir John Gordon, 151, 179, 182
Nash, E.M. (Betty): Reith's knighthood,
   153; Reith's office, 158;
   Clarendon-Snowden-Reith clashes, 163,

179, 181; advises Reith to leave BBC,
   163, 167; Churchill meeting, 165; *Listener*
   row, 168, 170; influence on Reith,
   175–6; description of Reith, 192; design
   advice, 198; BBC tenth anniversary
   dance, 205; Reith's mother's death, 218;
   successor, 235
National Film Finance Corporation, 295,
   298
New College, Edinburgh, 327, 337
New Statesman, 169, 240, 287, 298
New Towns Committee, 284, 286–7
New Zealand, 280
Newnes, George, Ltd, 127, 130
News Chronicle, 203, 252
Newspaper Proprietors' Association, 122,
   124, 169
Nigeria, 328–9
1922 Committee, 203
Niven and Haddin, 61
Nixon, Richard M., 396
Nkrumah, Kwame, 328
Noble, Sir William, 114, 116, 119, 136
Norman, Montagu, 235, 236, 238–9, 245,
   248, 252
Norman, Ronald C., 206, 212, 225–7, 233,
   236, 238–42
Normanbrook, Norman Brook, 1st Baron,
   369, 372, 376, 380, 391
North British Locomotive Company, 10, 17,
   23, 338–9
Northcliffe, Alfred Harmsworth, 1st
   Viscount, 82
Noyes, Alfred, 137

Obert, Julia, 32
Observer, The, 307, 311–12, 317, 337
Odhams, Muriel, *see* Reith
Odhams family, 86–8, 89, 94, 96, 99, 100,
   105, 107, 150, 168
Odhams Press, 262
Ogilvie, F.W. (*later* Sir Frederick), 241, 264
Oldham Evening Chronicle, 370
Osborn, F.J., 288
Oxford University, 205, 293–4, 296, 298

Paley, Bill, 371
Pall Mall Gazette, 122
Papen, Franz von, 62
Pares, Sir Bernard, 247
Parker, Herbert, 130
Pavlova, Anna, 97
Payne, Jack, 140
Pearson, Clive 245
Pearson, Ernest, 60
Pearson, S. & Son, 23–4, 26, 43, 53,
   59–61, 63, 81

Pease, H.M., 138
Pennsylvania Scotch-Irish Society, 71
People, The, 209
Peppercorn (Albert Dock sub-agent), 28
Percy, Lord Eustace, 207
Perth, John David Drummond, 17th Earl, 331
Phillips (chauffeur), 353, 360
Phoenix Assurance Company, 315, 322, 335, 395
Pickles, Wilfred, 298
Pickthorne, Kenneth, 207
Picture Post, 268
Pierce, Sergeant, 45
Pilkington, Sir Harry (*later* Baron), 355, 356
Pilkington Committee/Report, 348, 355, 356–7, 362, 363
Plater (chief commissionaire), 241
Portal, Charles Frederick Algernon, 1st Viscount, 277
Position of the BBC in War, 217
Post Office, 119, 122–4, 147–8, 209
Postmaster-General, 122, 123–4, 135, 147–8, 151–2
Presbyterian Social Union, 70
Press and Censorship Bureau, 252, 253
Promenade Concerts, 158
Publishers Association, 169
Punch, 199, 203, 240, 340
Pusey, Edward Bouverie, 2

Radcliffe, Sir Cyril (*later* 1st Viscount), 233, 253
Radhakrishnan, Sarvepalli, 367
Radio Communication, 120
Radio Luxembourg, 188
Radio Normandie, 188
Radio Society of Great Britain, 124
Radio Times, 122, 127, 130, 146, 169, 205, 292, 366
Radiolympia Exhibition, 209
Raeside, Maggie, 3–4, 154
Railway Review, 269
Ramsey, Arthur Michael, Archbishop of Canterbury, 379, 394
Raverat, Gwen, 190
Rayleigh, John William Strutt, 3rd Baron, 138
Read, Sir Herbert, 190
Reading, Lady, 223
Reith, Adah Mary (née Weston, mother): family background, 2; marriage, 2–3; children, 3; relationship with son, 3, 23, 94–5, 109, 111, 149–50, 177, 212, 215–16, 302; son's letters, 35, 39, 73, 75, 104, 117, 149–50; son home on leave, 41–2, 52–4; son wounded, 57; son's visit,

59–60; son's engagement, 87–8; husband's illness and death, 89–90, 93–5; John-Jean tug-of-war, 94–5, 109, 127, 137, 219; visits son, 97–8; will, 98, 219; daughter Beta's death, 106; Charlie's wedding, 109; attitude to Charlie, 111, 212; meets politicians, 144, 177, 219; death, 218–19
Reith, Archie (brother), 5, 7, 89, 93, 219, 364
Reith, Beta (sister), 5, 16, 27, 54, 75, 106
Reith, Christopher John (son): memoirs dedication, 18; birth, 165; christening, 166–7; schools, 166, 232, 233–4, 235, 263, 274; family holidays, 224–5, 297; relationship with father, 225, 233, 235, 274, 320, 330, 337, 362, 387, 392; national service 289, 293; Oxford, 293–4, 296, 298; Henley, 296; farming, 319, 322, 328, 330, 371, 403; climbing holiday, 338; sister's wedding, 347, 349–50; property search, 374, 396; invitation to Holyrood, 387; engagement, 397; wedding, 398; father's death, 403; renounces title, 403
Reith, Cissie (sister-in-law), 364
Reith, Douglas (brother): career, 5, 13, 93; relationship with brother, 13, 104, 109–10, 121, 132, 149; brother's leave, 41, 53; tutoring Charlie, 60; father's death, 93–4; brother's wedding, 103–4; Charlie's birthday party, 106; illness, 151; death, 168
Reith, Ernest (brother), 5, 7, 15–16, 75, 83, 214–15, 279
Reith, George (father): son's admiration, 2, 16, 239; career, 2–3, 16, 68; marriage, 2–3; relationship with son, 4, 17, 21, 24, 83, 239, 302; son's career, 10, 23–4, 43–4, 400; hopes for daughter-in-law, 14; accident, 17; son's leave, 40–2, 54; letter to son's Colonel, 47; son's gifts, 54, 62; son's visit, 59–60; illness and death, 68, 82, 89–90, 93–5
Reith, Jean (sister): temperament, 5, 83, 89–90; relationship with brother, 5, 83, 127, 137, 337; relationship with mother, 94–5, 109, 127, 212, 215; Charlie's wedding, 109; nephew's christening, 167; mother's death, 218–19
Reith, John Charles Walsham, 1st Baron Reith of Stonehaven: birth, 1; family, 2–3, 5; childhood, 3–4; education, 4, 6–8, 10–11, 17, 43–4; apprenticeship, 11, 16–17; OTC, 12; Territorials, 12–13, 28; World War I, 26–30, 31–62; Transport Officer, 28–45, 315; transfer

Reith, John Charles Walsham – *cont'd.*
  to Royal Engineers, 45, 48, 53, 54; Battle
  of Loos, 55–8; wounded, 56–9; Ministry
  of Munitions, 59–79; Gretna works,
  59–61; in America, 63–79; honorary
  MSc, 75; return to Britain, 78, 80;
  Channel barrage, 81; engagement, 89;
  looking for work, 89–90, 95–6;
  Beardmore general managership,
  96–111; wedding and honeymoon,
  103–4; looking for work again, 111–12;
  British Broadcasting Company, 114,
  116–18, 119–243; knighthood, 153, 154,
  156; visit to Germany, 192–3; visits to
  America, 195–6, 247–9; academic
  honours, 205, 215, 244; attitude to
  television, 208–9; South African visit,
  210–11; CBE, 211–12; mother's death,
  218–19; Lambert mongoose case, 226–8;
  GCVO, 231; motor accident, 232; leaves
  BBC, 236–43; Imperial Airways, 244–9,
  263, 275; attitude to war 245–6, 264,
  274; Ministry of Information 250–4; MP
  for Southampton 251–2; Ministry of
  Transport, 254–8; maiden speech in
  Commons, 257–8; peerage, 258–9;
  Ministry of Works, 258–66; Coastal
  Forces, 268–71; Lords speeches, 269,
  309–10, 361–2; Directorate of
  Combined Operations Material, 271–3;
  Cable and Wireless, 274, 278–9;
  Commander of the Bath, 276–7; CCC,
  278, 284, 293, 296; world tour, 278–81;
  Commonwealth communications
  conference, 281–3; New Towns
  Committee, 284, 286–8; Hemel
  Hempstead chairmanship, 288, 293, 298,
  300; renewal of contact with BBC,
  289–93; television set, 290; National
  Film Finance Corporation, 295, 298;
  Commonwealth Telecommunications
  Board, 296; Colonial Development
  Corporation (CDC), 302–9, 315–17,
  320–5, 328–9, 331–4, 335, 337–8;
  commercial television debate 309–10;
  African visits, 312, 316, 325, 328–9,
  360–1; directorships, 315–16, 322, 335;
  Lambeth Palace tenancy, 319–20, 322;
  West Indies tour, 320–1; daughter's
  engagement and marriage, 330–1,
  344–7, 349–50; Far East tour, 331–3;
  North British Locomotive Company,
  338–9; State Building Society, 346; *Face
  to Face* television appearance, 348–9; ruby
  wedding, 355; BBC training courses,
  356; Heathfield headship involvement,
  358–60; grandfather, 360, 366, 373;

  Asian tour, 366–7; Glasgow University
  Rectorship, 374–5, 385–6, 389, 392;
  German holiday, 382–4; Advertising
  Report, 384; Lord High
  Commissionership, 387, 390, 393–5;
  'Lord Reith Looks Back' television
  programmes, 392; Order of the Thistle,
  396, 398; son's engagement and
  marriage, 397, 398; eightieth birthday,
  399; death, funeral and memorial service,
  402–3
  BELIEFS: religion, 32, 38–9, 44, 49, 52,
  91, 112, 114, 166, 179–80, 187–8, 223,
  232, 234, 256, 295–6, 320, 323–4, 357;
  teetotallism, 36, 39, 51, 236, 337; politics,
  95–6, 114, 115–16, 200–2, 217, 223,
  231, 245, 269, 282, 284–5, 290, 358, 370
  HEALTH: wartime, 39–40, 49, 51–2;
  war-wound, 56–9; Psychological Clinic,
  105–6; noises in ear, 106, 136; Muriel's
  concern, 107–8, 111; lumbago, 124–5;
  heart trouble, 214–15, 386, 394; ulcer,
  217–18; weight loss, 273; use of
  benzedrine, 292; check-up, 335;
  electric-shock treatment, 359;
  appendicitis, 366; old age, 375, 386–7,
  399, 402
  MONEY: attitude to money, 48, 53, 62,
  247; salary at BBC, 116, 132, 140, 196;
  finances, 263, 273, 274, 275, 279, 284,
  302, 307, 315, 335
  PERSONALITY: self-opinion, 8, 180, 196,
  245, 255, 264, 275, 400; ambitions, 8, 10,
  95, 204, 223, 224, 266, 286; descriptions
  by others, 14–15, 187–92, 197, 238–9,
  266, 307, 403–4; attitude to authority,
  46–7, 238–9; amateur dramatics, 139,
  168, 224; management style, 156, 171,
  256; literary tastes, 190–2, 300; mental
  state, 182, 221, 255, 267–8, 270, 272–3,
  286, 339, 345, 350–4, 359, 375–6, 381,
  386–7, 391–2, 400–1; sense of humour,
  221; sensitivity to slights, 246;
  self-assessment 275; tact and diplomacy,
  281, 285, 296
  RELATIONSHIPS: with parents, *see* Reith,
  Adah and George; with brothers and
  sisters, *see* Reith, Douglas and Jean;
  romantic interests as a young man,
  13–15, 18, 83–4; sexuality 15, 91–2, 110,
  113, 351, 352; passionate friendship with
  Charlie Bowser, *see* Bowser; courtship of
  Muriel, 84–8; engagement to Muriel,
  89–94, 96–9; relationship with Muriel
  after marriage, 113, 248, 263–4, 268,
  270, 274, 297–8, 302, 305, 307, 313–14,
  320, 325, 327, 352, 381, 385, 387, 390,

401; flirtations and relationships with women, 112–13, 193, 235, 263, 274, 281, 286, 297–8, 325, 341–4, 378, 382–4; friendships, 176; fatherhood, *see* Reith, Christopher and Marista; family holidays, 224–5, 247, 296–8, 301, 317, 338; dogs, 225, 273; relationships in public life, *see particularly* Churchill, Clarendon, Haley, Snowden, Whitley
WRITING: diaries, 15, 175, 193–4, 197, 354, 363, 385, 388–9, 391–2, 396; memoirs, 18; correspondence, 75; *Broadcast Over Britain*, 133–4, 138, 188; prose style, 134, 294–5, 298; *Wearing Spurs*, 233, 378, 381, 385; *Into the Wind*, 289–90, 291–2, 294–5, 298–9, 314, 380
Reith, Marista Muriel (daughter, *later* Mrs Murray Leishman): memoirs dedication, 18; birth, 198; family holidays, 224–5, 297; car accident, 232; health, 234, 326; American visit, 247, 249; relationship with father, 286, 302, 313, 323, 326, 330–1, 336–7, 340, 344–7, 360, 364, 371–2, 381–2, 387–8; education, 286, 289, 294, 305–6, 316, 322, 327–8, 330, 337; African tour, 312; Lambeth Palace flat, 319; Student Christian Movement (SCM), 323, 326; relationship with Murray Leishman, 323, 326, 330–1, 337, 344–7; engagement, 330–1, 344–7; Church of Scotland work, 337, 346; wedding, 347; meeting with Barbara Hickman, 351; children, 360, 364, 366; Extra Lady in Waiting, 387–8; description of mother, 403
Reith, Muriel (wife, née Odhams): Reith first meets, 81–3; first fiancé, 84–5, 150; Reith's courtship, 84–8; relationship with Charlie Bowser, 86–9, 91–2, 96, 105; engagement to Reith, 88–94, 96–9; relationship with Reith, 87–9, 91–2, 97, 99–100, 104, 107–8, 112–13, 127, 180, 193, 220, 233–4, 235, 248, 263–4, 267, 268, 270, 274, 276, 286, 287–8, 297, 302, 305, 307, 313–14, 320, 325, 327, 352, 381, 385, 387, 390, 401; wedding and honeymoon, 102–4; married life, 104–13, 116, 117, 149, 314, 352; social life, 124–5, 133, 135, 152, 157, 241, 313, 362, 372; holidays, 131, 137, 150, 158, 323, 338; husband's knighthood, 153; pregnancy, 162; childbirth, 165, 198; motherhood, 165–7, 224–5, 233–4, 274; moving house, 183; American visits, 195–6, 247–9; burglary, 198; mother-in-law's death, 218; family holidays, 224–5; abdication broadcast,

229; coronation seats, 230; motor accident, 232; husband's peerage, 258–9; wartime life, 264; health, 305, 307, 371, 401; African visit, 316; Lambeth Palace flat, 319; househunting, 322, 396; Marista's engagement and marriage, 330–1, 349; ruby wedding, 355; German holiday, 382–4; husband's High Commissionership 390; husband's illness, 394; son's wedding, 398; last years, 403
Reith, Robert (brother), 5, 7, 61, 83, 93–4, 98, 157, 366
Remington Arms Company, 64–5, 74
Rendall, Montague, 151, 161, 163, 199–200, 206
Rendell, William, 317
Rhodes, Cecil, 202
Rhodesia Herald, 361
Rhodesian Iron and Steel Commission (RISCOM), 325–6, 328
Rice, Sir Cecil Spring, 69–70
Riddell, George Allardice Riddell, 1st Baron, 169–70
Roberton, Ivor, 301
Roberts, Frederick Sleigh Roberts, 1st Earl, 35
Robertson, Sir William, 124
Rockefeller, John D., Jnr, 66
Röhm, Ernst, 202
Roosevelt, Franklin Delano, 260, 262–3, 282
Rothermere, Harold Sydney Harmsworth, 1st Viscount, 202
Rowntree, Seebohm, 167, 188
Roxburgh, J.A., 90
Royal Academy, 246
Royal Company of Archers, 232, 390
Royal Institute of British Architects, 261
Royal Institution, 200
Royden, Sir Thomas, 138
Runciman, Leslie, 246, 248, 249
Ruskin, John, 2
Russell, Constance, 76
Russell, Helen, 76
Rutherford, Sir Ernest (*later* Baron), 127

St Andrew's Society of Philadelphia, 66–7
St Andrews University, 305–6, 313
St Omer, 31–2
Samuel, Sir Herbert (*later* 1st Viscount), 140
Sankey, John, 1st Viscount, 182
Sarnoff, David, 128, 208
Sassoon, Sir Philip, 194
Savoy Hill (No. 2), 120, 130, 141, 157, 165, 167, 175, 178, 186, 199
Scannell, Paddy, 146

Scotsman, The, 288, 379
Scott, Hugh Lenox, 74
Scott, Michael, 313
Selborne, Roundell Cecil Palmer, 3rd Earl (*earlier* Viscount Wolmer), 147, 259, 266
Selfridge, Gordon, 122, 175
Selsdon, William Mitchell-Thomson, 1st Baron, 135, 147, 151, 215, 216
Selsdon Committee, 209
Shaw, George Bernard, 73, 191, 378
Shields, F.I. (Isobel), 120–1, 153, 163
Shinwell, Emmanuel (*later* Baron), 155, 258
Sieveking, Lance, 185
Silkin, Lewis, 284, 286–8
Simon, Sir John (*later* 1st Viscount), 229
Simon of Wythenshawe, Ernest Darwin Simon, 1st Baron, 290, 291, 312
Simonds, Gavin Turnbull Simonds, 1st Viscount, 310
Simpson, Wallis (*later* Duchess of Windsor), 221, 229
Singer, Miss D., 317–18
Smellie, W.A. (Bill), 345, 349
Smith, W.C., 121
Smuts, Jan Christian, 210, 280, 291
Smyth-Piggott, Major, 63–4
Snagge, John, 371, 384
Snow, C.P., 1st Baron, 372
Snowden, Ethel (*later* Viscountess): appointment as Governor, 151, 155; Reith's opinion, 154; opinion of Reith, 155; clashes with Reith, 154–7, 160–1, 162–3, 178, 182–4, 199, 202; Carpendale's complaints, 158; Eckersley affair, 172; friendlier relations with Reith, 185, 204; staff association suggestion, 202; leaves Board, 206
Snowden, Philip (*later* 1st Viscount), 174, 204
Society for Psychical Research, 225
Somerville, Mary, 190, 299, 303, 349
South Africa, 210–11, 280
Southwood, Julius, 262
Spectator, The, 259, 287, 298
Spengler, Oswald, 150
Stamfordham, Arthur John Bigge, 1st Baron, 163, 182
Stamp, Sir Josiah, 180–1, 227–8
Stanhope, James Richard Stanhope, 7th Earl, 217
Stanley, Jo: senior secretary, 235; drafts Reith's farewell message, 241; Droitwich visit, 242; leaves BBC, 245; Churchill's letter, 267; BOAC message, 270; work on memoirs, 290; Marista's wedding, 349; revision of diaries, 388–9; Muriel confides in, 401

Stanley, Oliver, 250
State Building Society, 346, 371
Stevenson, Adlai, 348
Stevenson, Frances (*later* Countess Lloyd-George), 120
Stewart, Andrew, 347, 389, 392
Stewart, Betty, 76, 78
Stewart, Sir Findlater, 227
Stobart, J.C., 190
Stocks, Mary, 362
Stonehaven, Kincardineshire, 1, 15
Stopes, Marie, 217
Strand Magazine, The, 194
Struthers, Lieutenant, 45, 47
Stuart, Charles, 238, 251, 261, 318, 336, 400, 403–4
Stuart, James (*later* 1st Viscount Stuart of Findhorn), 265
Student Christian Movement (SCM), 323, 326
Sturridge, Dr, 359, 396, 401
Sunday Express, 295, 319, 359, 373
Sunday Times, 240
Swarthmore, 195–6
Sykes, Sir Frederick, 124, 125
Sykes Committee/Report, 124, 125, 128–9, 130, 148

Tagore, Rabindranath, 139
Talbot, Dame Meriel, 138
Tallents, Sir Stephen, 226, 239
Taylor, A.J.P., 140
Taylor, Miss L., 203
Thomas, Dylan, 191
Thomas, Sir Godfrey, 228–9
Thompson, Colonel, 82, 84–6
Times, The, 135, 185, 204, 223–4, 230, 240, 298, 304–5, 308, 309, 311, 322, 345, 346, 358, 361–2, 370, 374, 402, 404
Tower, Sir Francis Thomas Butler, 276
Trefgarne, George Morgan Trefgarne, 1st Baron, 303, 315
Trevelyan, Charles, 124, 129
Tryon, Major George Clement, 217
Tube Investments, 315, 322, 335
TUC (Trades Union Congress), 140, 145, 147
Tudhope (batman), 39, 46, 47, 49
Tudsbery, Marmaduke, 342–3
Tuttle, John Ellery, 69, 78, 157, 196
Twining, Helen Mary, Lady, 312
2LO, 120, 121, 184, 206
Tyndall, John, 17, 177

Ullswater, James William Lowther, 1st Viscount, 215